Y0-BVQ-891

Novell NetWare 4:
The Complete Reference

Novell NetWare 4:
The Complete Reference

Tom Sheldon

Osborne **McGraw-Hill**

Berkeley New York St. Louis San Francisco
Auckland Bogotá Hamburg London Madrid
Mexico City Milan Montreal New Delhi Panama City
Paris São Paulo Singapore Sydney
Tokyo Toronto

Osborne **McGraw-Hill**
2600 Tenth Street
Berkeley, California 94710
U.S.A.

For information on software, translations, or book distributors outside of the
U.S.A., please write to Osborne **McGraw-Hill** at the above address.

Novell NetWare 4: The Complete Reference

4567890 DOC 998765

ISBN 0-07-881909-1

Acquisitions Editor	**Copy Editor**	**Computer Designer**
Scott Rogers	Laura Sackerman	J. E. Christgau
Associate Editor	**Proofreader**	**Illustrator**
Kristin D. Beeman	Nathan Arizona	Susie C. Kim
Project Editor	**Indexer**	**Cover Design**
Madhu Prasher	Tom Sheldon	Bay Graphics Design, Inc.
		Mason Fong
Technical Editor		
Robert Scarola		

This book is printed on acid-free paper.

Contents

13 ||||||||||||||||||||||||

14 ||||||||||||||||||||||||

Part IV
NetWare Installation

15 ||||||||||||||||||||||||

16 ||||||||||||||||||||||||

35 ||||||||||||||||||||||||||

Acknowledgments

This book is dedicated to aspiring Certified NetWare Engineers and Certified NetWare Instructors.

This book is also dedicated to all the people who helped make it possible. In particular, Scott Rogers at Osborne McGraw-Hill for his excellent editorial support, the French Roast, and the pressure that kept me going. Also, Robert Scarola, who took time out of his busy schedule to ensure the accuracy of this material, and Chris Germann of Novell (formerly of *LAN Times* magazine), who assisted in the completion of some of this material and provided technical support during the beta program.

Thanks to Kristin Beeman for pulling strings, polishing text, and pushing cookies. Thanks also to Madhu Prasher, the project editor, and to Laura Sackerman and Judith Brown for copyediting. Susie Kim did a great job on the art. Honorable mentions also go to Jeff Pepper and Frances Stack for their long term support and commitment.

The staff at Novell also deserve mention for their assistance, including Rose Kearsley, Jennifer Wahlquest, Kathy Peterson, Tom Oldroyd, David Hacking, and of course Ray Norda.

Thanks to Held Investments in San Luis Obispo, California, and ComputerLand in Santa Barbara and San Luis Obispo, California, who helped with "live" networks, equipment, and general technical expertise. In particular, thanks to Lloyd Balkin of ComputerLand, San Luis Obispo, for lending a hand. Also thanks to Gordon and Julia Held for their friendship and support—we've been in this business a long time now.

Last but not least I thank all my friends and family who helped or were close at hand, including Alexandra, John, Susie, April, Anna, George, Sandy, Bob, Martha, Christopher, Jim, Beth, Ryan, Dan, Dario, Cindy, Carl, Sandi (and her cats).

Introduction

Novell NetWare 4: The Complete Reference is, above all, a reference. That is the original intent of the Osborne McGraw-Hill Complete Reference series. While some of the material here is also available in the NetWare manuals, you'll find this text more portable, easier to access, and full of tips and techniques. The most essential information about networks and NetWare is included for a diverse audience that includes:

- Network administrators
- Department-level network supervisors
- Managers of departments that use networks
- Certified NetWare Engineers (CNEs)
- Certified NetWare Instructors (CNIs)
- Hardware and software technicians
- Support personnel
- Users of the network

New NetWare users will learn the basics of networking and NetWare. If you are studying to become CNEs or CNIs, or just brushing up to maintain CNE/CNI status, you'll find this book an excellent resource that provides a good conceptual overview. Keep in mind, however, that the Novell CNE/CNI class material provides the best information for testing purposes.

This book is designed to guide you through the tasks of managing and using a NetWare network. It ties together concepts, techniques, tips, commands, utilities, and many other diverse topics to help you quickly set up equipment, install and configure software, overcome problems, and generally manage the network. You'll find many cross references in the book that direct you to related information and topics. You'll also find a larger-than-normal index that helps you quickly locate and cross-reference topics.

The book begins with a basic overview of computer networking, and each subsequent chapter builds upon concepts you've learned. Each chapter also provides a self-contained discussion about particular topics that you can open and refer to at any time. After the basics, you'll learn about Novell's networking strategy, NetWare's architecture, and the new features in NetWare v.4, including NetWare Directory Services (NDS). Chapter topics then advance into more technical discussions of network communications, hardware, operating systems, and other information you'll need to know when planning and purchasing a network. Next, you'll learn how to install network equipment and NetWare. The remainder of the book is then devoted to the NetWare operating system. You learn about NetWare commands, utilities, and techniques for managing, monitoring, and using the network.

THE
COMPLETE

REFERENCE

PART **ONE**

Overview

CHAPTER 1

Networking Concepts

When IBM announced the Personal Computer in 1981, *personal* was an appropriate adjective to use in the name. It appealed to people who wanted their own computer to run their own applications and manage their own personal files instead of using minicomputers and mainframes that were strictly controlled by an information systems department. Soon, personal computer users started connecting their systems together into networks so they could share files and resources such as printers. But a funny thing happened. By around 1985, networks became so big and complex that control returned to the information systems department. Networks today are not simple, easily managed devices. They require security, monitoring, and management. In addition, networks often extend beyond the local office into the metropolitan or global environment, and they require experts who can handle the challenge of telephone, microwave, or satellite communications.

This chapter introduces the concepts and terminology of networking. If you're new to networks, you'll learn the basics. If you already have a network and need to expand it, this chapter covers those topics as well.

 NOTE: From here on, NetWare version 4 is often referred to as simply NetWare, except where comparisons are made to previous versions.

Networks Defined

The simplest network connects two computers for sharing files and printers. A much more complex network links all the computers of a worldwide company. A simple switchbox is all you need to share printers, but when you want to efficiently share files and run network applications, you need network interface cards (NICs) and cable to connect systems. While various serial and parallel port interconnection schemes are available, these inexpensive systems don't provide the speed and integrity required for a secure, high-performance network operating system that supports many users and resources. Figure 1-1 illustrates the basic components of a typical high-performance network system.

Once network connections are made, you install the network operating system (NOS). There are two basic types of NOSs: *peer-to-peer* and *dedicated-server*.

- *Peer-to-peer* This is an operating system that allows users to share the resources on their computers and to access shared resources on other computers. Microsoft Windows for Workgroups and Novell Lite are peer-to-peer operating systems. In this scheme, you can share a directory or a printer on your computer so other users can access it, and they can do the same on their computers. Peer-to-peer implies that all systems have the same status on the network. No system is a "slave" to another.

- *Dedicated-server* In a dedicated-server operating system, such as Novell NetWare, one or more computers are set aside as file servers and are not used for anything else. Users access shared directories and resources on the dedicated file servers, but not on each others' systems. This improves security and doesn't rob from the performance of individual computers.

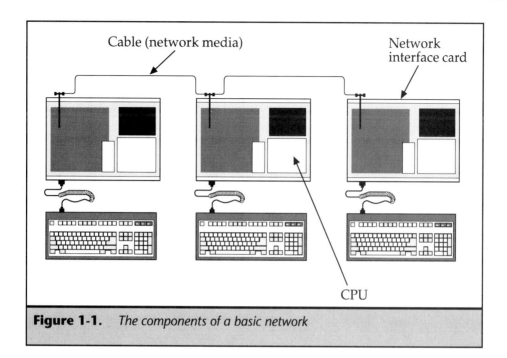

Figure 1-1. *The components of a basic network*

To understand the importance of network operating systems, it's useful to compare them to centralized processing systems such as minicomputers and mainframes. In a network, each computer accesses programs and files from a central server, but runs those programs in its own memory and with its own processor. A minicomputer or mainframe system has centralized processing; it handles the processing tasks of the terminals attached to it. These terminals are often called *dumb terminals* because they have no processor or memory of their own. Networks are *distributed processing systems* because each computer does its own processing. The file server is not overloaded with the processing tasks of individual workstations and can optimize file and network services such as file storage and retrieval, management tasks, monitoring user access, printer sharing, and security.

NOTE: A distributed processing system is sometimes called a client-server *system because it uses the full computing power of a front-end client and a back-end server. The client runs at a workstation. The server runs on the network server and provides data management and multiuser functions.*

Minicomputers and mainframes were not made obsolete by the introduction of networks, however. Instead, they are playing a different role in the computing needs of business. As shown in Figure 1-2, these large systems can be attached to a network and accessed as peripheral devices by any user who needs their specialized features. This arrangement can use a company's resources more efficiently. The network in Figure 1-2 is an *enterprise network* because it allows all of a company's computer resources, including Apple Macintosh systems, OS/2-based systems, UNIX-based systems, and other workstations to attach to the same network. The network is a plug-in *platform* that supports a variety of systems.

Components of a Network

A computer network consists of both hardware and software. The hardware includes network interface cards and the cable that ties them together, and the software includes the drivers (code used to handle peripheral devices) and the network operating system that manages the network. Each component is listed

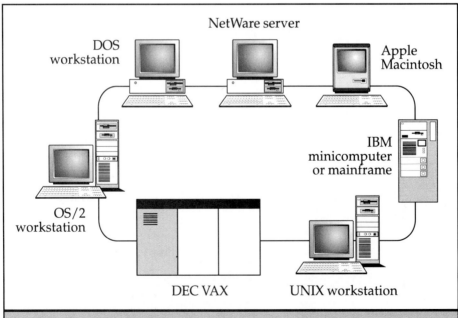

Figure 1-2.   *Computer networks can be used as modular platforms for the interconnection of many types of systems*

and described here and illustrated in Figure 1-3.

■ Server

■ Workstations

■ Network interface cards (NICs)

■ Cabling system

■ Shared resources and peripherals

SERVER The server runs the network operating system and offers network services to users at their individual workstations. These services include file storage, user management, security, network commands and options for users, system manager commands, and much more.

WORKSTATIONS When a computer is attached to a network, it becomes a node on the network and is referred to as a *workstation* or *client.* Workstations can be DOS-based personal computers, Apple Macintosh systems, UNIX-based systems, systems running OS/2, and diskless workstations.

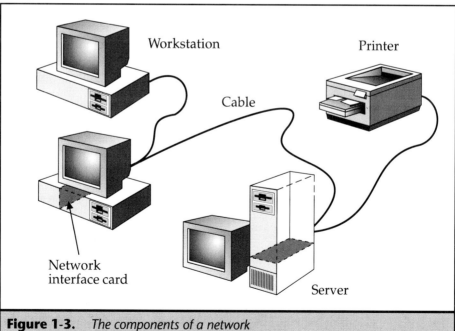

Figure 1-3. *The components of a network*

NETWORK INTERFACE CARDS (NICS)   Each computer attached to a network requires a network interface card (NIC) that supports a specific networking scheme such as Ethernet, ArcNet, or Token Ring. The network cable attaches to the back of the NIC. Radio and infrared cableless networks are also available.

CABLING SYSTEM   The network cabling system is the media used to connect the server and the workstations together. In the case of wireless networks that use radio or infrared technology, cable is not required.

SHARED RESOURCES AND PERIPHERALS   Shared resources and peripherals include the storage devices attached to the server, optical disk drives, printers, plotters, and other equipment that can be used by anyone on the network.

How Network Connections Are Made

To connect a network, you need network interface cards and cable (unless you're going wireless). There are several different types of interface cards and cabling schemes.

Network Interface Cards (NICs)

Network interface cards are available from a variety of manufacturers. You can choose from several different types; your choice will depend on how you want to configure and wire your network. The three most popular types of network interface cards are ArcNet, Ethernet, and Token Ring. The differences among these network types has to do with the method and speed of communications, and price.

In the old days of network computing (two or three years ago), cabling was more standardized than it is now. ArcNet and Ethernet cards used coaxial cable and Token Ring cards used shielded twisted-pair cable. Today, you can purchase network cards that support a range of media, which makes network planning and configuration much easier. You now base your decisions on cost, cabling distance, and topology.

You can think of a network's topology as a map of its cable layout. *Topology* defines how you run the cable to individual workstations and plays an important part in the decision you make about cable. As illustrated in Figure 1-4, a network can have a linear, ring, or star topology. When you consider the topology of your network, think about which method will be best for wiring your building.

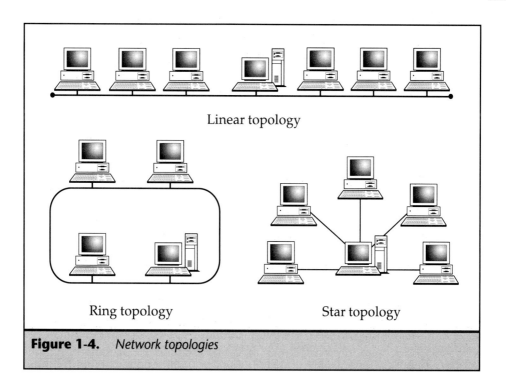

Figure 1-4. *Network topologies*

Cable

Coaxial cable was one of the first cable types used for networks, but twisted-pair cable has been gaining in popularity. Fiber-optic cable is often used when speed is important, but advances in NIC design have produced cards that allow higher than normal transfer rates over twisted-pair and coaxial cable. Fiber-optic cable is still the best choice when high data-transfer rates are required, but as you'll learn in Chapter 7, there are a number of decisions you must make to choose the best cable or cable systems for your network.

Network Architecture

The architecture of a network is defined by its topology and the cable access method and communications protocols it uses. Before any workstation can access the cable, it must establish communication sessions with other nodes on the network. *Cable access methods* describe how a workstation gains access to the cable so as to avoid using it when it is in use by another workstation. *Protocols* are the rules that govern how packets of information are transferred from one workstation to another.

Topology

As mentioned previously, the topology of a network is its cable layout. The most important consideration when choosing a cable system is its cost, but you also need to consider its throughput and integrity. *Throughput* is a measure of the actual data-transfer rate of the cable once you add the overhead introduced by communications, error checking, and other management functions. Throughput depends on the network type.

Cable Access Method

The cable access method describes how a workstation gains access to the cable system. When the network interface card gains access to the cable, it begins sending packets of information, often called *frames* (or *cells* when discussing some telephone communications methods), to other nodes. Every workstation on the Local Area Network (LAN) must use the same access method.

Linear cable systems such as Ethernet use a carrier sensing method in which a workstation checks the cable to see if it is in use before transmitting. A transmission is like a radio broadcast across the entire cable: every node hears it and then determines whether the transmission is meant for it. If not, the node rejects the broadcast. If two nodes broadcast at the same time, a collision occurs and both back off, wait for a random amount of time, and try again. Performance degrades when network traffic is heavy because of these collisions and retransmissions.

Ring networks, or networks that behave like a ring, normally use the token passing method. In a token passing system, a station only transmits when it has possession of a token. Think of a *token* as a temporary ticket or pass to use the network. When a station is ready to transmit, it must wait for an available token and then take possession of the token. This prevents two machines from using the cable simultaneously.

Communications Protocols

Communications protocols are the rules and procedures used on a network to communicate among nodes that have access to the cable system. Protocols govern two different levels of communications. High-level rules define how applications communicate, and low-level rules define how signals are transmitted over a cable. Communications protocols can be compared to diplomatic protocols, in which the activities of each corps member are governed by rules at his or her level. When network protocols are defined and published, vendors can easily design and manufacture network products that work on multivendor systems.

The Range of Networks

Networks come in a range of sizes. Your network can start small, and then grow with your organization. The range of networks is illustrated in Figure 1-5.

LOCAL AREA NETWORK (LAN)   A Local Area Network (LAN) is a small network (3 to 50 nodes) usually located within a single building or group of buildings belonging to an organization.

INTERCONNECTED NETWORK (INTERNETWORK)   An internetwork is formed when two or more LAN segments are connected to form a

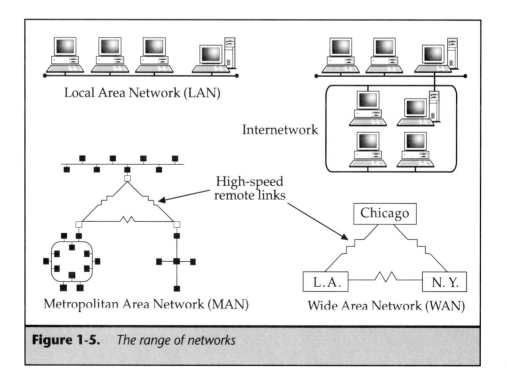

Figure 1-5.   *The range of networks*

company-wide system. This is often the case in departmentalized companies in which each department has its own LAN, and then these LANs are connected together. Large networks are often split into several smaller segments to optimize performance and management. A router is used to join two or more similar or dissimilar LANs. Novell NetWare provides internal routing. That means you can join a Token Ring segment to an Ethernet segment by simply installing a network interface card for each segment in the NetWare file server or in a dedicated router system.

ENTERPRISE NETWORK　An enterprise network (illustrated in Figure 1-2) is similar to an internetwork, but an enterprise network ties together all the computer systems within an organization, no matter which operating systems they use. An enterprise network may link minicomputers, mainframes, Sun workstations (UNIX-based), Apple computers, OS/2-based workstations, Microsoft LAN Manager-based servers, Microsoft NT-based workstations, Novell NetWare-based servers, and other computing resources into a single, interconnected system.

METROPOLITAN AREA NETWORK (MAN) AND WIDE AREA NETWORK (WAN)　A Metropolitan Area Network (MAN) or Wide Area Network (WAN) typically provides connections to distant networks and resources. MANs are usually high-speed fiber-optic networks that connect LAN segments within a specific area, such as a campus, industrial park, or city. A MAN uses special high-speed backbone cables (typically fiber) that connect servers directly. Alternatively, intercity microwave connections are available. Microwave dishes are mounted on top of buildings and pointed at each other to establish an internetwork link. A MAN consists of cabling and communications equipment that is usually owned and installed by the network owner.

　　WANs provide country-wide or global connections via telephone lines and satellites. Large corporations that have regional or worldwide offices use WANs to interconnect networks. Circuits are leased from long distance carriers to provide dedicated, full-time connections among systems. These connections are much slower than LAN connections, but the amount of traffic is typically lower than a normal LAN segment. A typical LAN transmits at 10 Mb/sec, and a typical WAN connection transmits at 1 Mb/sec. Fortunately, this is changing with the introduction of new fiber-optic national and global communications networks that provide more bandwidth and faster transfer rates.

Interoperability

Interoperability defines how hardware and software from different vendors work together. As your network grows, it is important to ensure that all the components you add are compatible. If all the equipment you purchase is from one vendor, interoperability is usually a simple matter; however, if you buy on a budget, as most companies do, be aware of the interoperability issues.

The term *Open Systems* refers to products that are designed to work together by following accepted standards, such as the Open Systems Interconnection (OSI) model put forth by the International Organization for Standardization. The OSI model consists of seven layers that describe how systems connect and communicate with one another. Most vendors create products that loosely comply with the standard, meaning that some layers are implemented as defined by OSI but others are not.

The FAX machine is an example of working interoperability. FAX machines almost never fail to establish connections with one another because all FAX machines comply with the Group 3 FAX standard. Computer operating systems and network hardware have not matured so well. There are differences in protocols and file management techniques that must be overcome. This topic is covered in more detail in Part Two of this book.

Why Establish a Computer Network?

Why establish a computer network? This may seem like a dumb question when so many organizations either have one or plan to install one, but it's not. Installing a computer network can offer many advantages to your business. This section discusses these advantages.

PROGRAM AND FILE SHARING   Networkable versions of many popular software packages are available at considerable cost savings when compared to buying individually licensed copies. The program and its data files are stored on the file server for access by any network user. Users can save files in personal directories or save them in public directories where they can be read or edited by other network users.

NETWORK RESOURCE SHARING   Network resources include printers, plotters, and storage devices. In a dedicated server system such as Novell NetWare, these resources are normally attached to a file server and shared by all users. Alternatively, some servers can be dedicated to printing (print servers) or communications (comm and fax servers).

DATABASE SHARING   A database program is an ideal application for a network. A network feature called *record-locking* lets multiple users simultaneously access a file without corrupting the data. Record-locking ensures that no two users edit the same record at the same time.

ECONOMICAL EXPANSION OF THE PC BASE   Networks provide an economical way to expand the number of computers in an organization. You can attach inexpensive diskless workstations to a network that use the server's hard drive for booting and storage.

ABILITY TO USE NETWORK SOFTWARE   A class of software called *groupware* is designed specifically for networks. It lets users interact and coordinate their activities.

ABILITY TO USE ELECTRONIC MAIL   Electronic mail lets users easily communicate with one another. Messages are dropped in "mailboxes" for the recipients to read at a convenient time.

CREATION OF WORK GROUPS   Groups are important in networks. They can consist of users who work in a department or who are assigned to a special project. With NetWare, you can assign users to groups, and then give each group access to special directories and resources not accessible by other users. This saves you the trouble of assigning that access to each individual user. It's also easier to address messages and electronic mail to groups of users. Network workgroups facilitate new "flat" corporate structures in which people from diverse and remote departments belong to special group projects.

CENTRALIZED MANAGEMENT   Because NetWare uses dedicated servers, you can group these servers in one location, along with the shared resources attached to them, for easier management. Hardware upgrades, software backups, system maintenance, and system protection are much easier to handle when these devices are in one location.

SECURITY   Security starts with the login procedure to ensure that a user accesses the network using his or her own user account. This account is tailored to give the user access only to authorized areas of the server and internetwork. Login restrictions can force a user to log in at one specific station and only during a specific time frame.

ACCESS TO MORE THAN ONE OPERATING SYSTEM   NetWare provides connections for many different operating systems, including DOS, OS/2, UNIX, AppleTalk, and others. Users of these systems can store and access files on the NetWare server.

ENHANCEMENT OF THE CORPORATE STRUCTURE   Networks can change the structure of an organization and the way it is managed. Users who work in a specific department and for a specific manager no longer need to be in the same physical area. Their offices can be located in areas where their expertise is most needed. The network ties them to their department managers and peers. This arrangement is useful for special projects in which individuals from different departments, such as research, production, and marketing, need to work closely with each other.

Network Operating System Features

Early network operating systems provided simple file services and some security features. But user demands have increased, and modern network operating systems offer a wide range of services. The following sections cover these features.

NETWORK ADAPTERS AND CABLES A network operating system must support many types and brands of network interface cards. Novell NetWare includes drivers to support the most popular cards and makes other drivers available as needed.

GLOBAL NAMING A global naming system provides a way for users to view and access resources and other users anywhere on the network without the need to know exactly where those resources are. Users simply browse and choose from a list.

FILE AND DIRECTORY SERVICES On a network, users gain access to programs and files on a central file server. Because users place private files on this shared server, security and integrity of data is important. Directory access must be controlled to prevent unauthorized users from viewing or changing files.

SYSTEM FAULT TOLERANCE A *fault-tolerant system* provides a way to ensure network survivability if components fail. With NetWare's System Fault Tolerance (SFT) feature, the server's hard drive can be mirrored by a second hard drive, thus providing continuous real-time backup. The mirrored drive can be on the same controller or attached to a second controller (called *duplexing*) that further ensures hardware integrity. Duplexing of an entire server is provided with SFT Level III, which is available as a second product.

DISK CACHING Disk caching improves hard disk performance by using some system memory as a holding area for blocks of data from disk that may need to be accessed again. Accessing the information in memory is much faster than getting it from the hard drive.

TRANSACTION TRACKING SYSTEM (TTS)   A transaction is a change in a record or set of records in a database file. A NetWare feature called *transaction tracking* is used to protect database files from corruption should a workstation or server fail, for example during a power outage. If a complete transaction is not finished, the TTS system backs out any changes made during the transaction and restores the database to its former state.

LOGIN SECURITY   Novell NetWare provides a sophisticated and reliable password and security system that can lock or limit user access to the server, its directories, and its files. Users can be prevented from logging into workstations other than those to which they are assigned. Time restrictions can be placed on a user's session so that, for example, no user can log in after 5:00.

BRIDGE AND ROUTER SUPPORT   Bridges and routers allow networks to interconnect with other networks. NetWare provides internal routing, which means that you can connect two networks simply by installing a network interface card for each network in the server. External routing is also available as an optional product to relieve the NetWare server of routing functions.

GATEWAYS   Gateways allow systems with different protocols to interconnect. For example, a gateway allows a NetWare network to interconnect with an IBM mainframe system. Users on the network can then access the IBM system through the gateway.

SPECIAL SERVERS   A network operating system should allow for special servers, such as those dedicated to handling a database or printing. There is also a new breed of superservers that provide special fault-tolerant disk arrays, multiple processors, and vast memories. Most manufacturers of these systems support Novell NetWare.

SOFTWARE MANAGEMENT TOOLS   Software management tools are essential as networks grow in size. It may be impossible to track the activities and performance of MANs and WANs without them. One solution is to centralize managers and then give them tools to manage servers and workstations remotely. NetWare does this with remote console capabilities and remote management features.

CHAPTER 2

Novell Networks

Novell has been a major influence in the growth of the microcomputer industry. It developed Z-80-based microcomputers in the 1970s and created its first networking products in the early 1980s. Novell's main product during the emerging years of the personal computer was a file-sharing device based on the Motorola 68000 processor. In 1983, when IBM announced the IBM Personal Computer XT, which has a hard disk, Novell quickly responded with a product that converted the hard disk system into a file-sharing system. A star-configured cabling system known as S-Net was used to attach workstations.

A few years later, Novell introduced NetWare/86, which provided file server capabilities. The new server operating system not only let users share files, it provided access to those files through a security system and helped manage other features of the network. As NetWare grew in popularity, its designers improved its hardware independence. Novell stopped pushing its own LAN hardware and began providing support for products from many vendors. This was one of the most important strategies in the advancement of NetWare as an industry standard. In 1986, a new version of NetWare called Advanced NetWare provided even more support for LAN hardware by bridging different network types within the file server or an external workstation. For example, you could install both an Ethernet and Token Ring card in the server.

Advanced NetWare 286 was developed to take advantage of Intel 80286-based systems. It provided multitasking capabilities long before products like OS/2 and Microsoft Windows existed. In addition, it ran in the protected mode of the 80286, which allowed it to provide advanced features not available when running only under DOS, and it did not have the 640KB memory constraints of DOS. Many users were getting better performance when accessing files on NetWare servers than when accessing files on their local hard drive! Up to four different types of network interface cards could be installed in an Advanced NetWare 286 server.

Eventually, Novell began splitting its product line. At the low end, it offered NetWare ELS (Entry Level System), which supported a small number of users. At the high end, it introduced NetWare SFT (System Fault Tolerance). NetWare SFT provided protection from disk failures by mirroring, or duplexing, the disk system. In this arrangement, two disks record the same information, and if one fails, the other can be put into use. Novell also began offering file storage support for Apple Macintosh computers on the NetWare server.

In 1989, Novell announced NetWare 386 v.3.0, an operating system that was completely rewritten to take advantage of features built into the Intel 80386 processor. NetWare 386 is a full 32-bit operating system that was designed for large networks with massive data handling needs. It also provided enhanced security, performance, and flexibility. (Operating system changes were much easier.) In June of 1990, Novell shipped version 3.1 of the operating system, which provided enhanced performance, reliability, and system administration. Then in 1991, Novell announced NetWare v.3.11, which supports DOS, Macintosh, Windows, OS/2, and UNIX file and print services.

The current Novell operating system product line includes NetWare Lite, a DOS-based peer-to-peer operating system; an 80286-based operating system called NetWare v.2.2; NetWare 386 v.3.11; and NetWare v.4. The stratification of these products is described next for those who are working in a mixed operating system environment.

NETWARE LITE   NetWare Lite is designed for 2 to 25 users who need to share resources on one another's systems in a peer-to-peer arrangement, but who don't need or want to dedicate a system as a full-time server.

NETWARE V.2.2   NetWare v.2.2 is suited for small to medium-size businesses and for workgroups within large companies. The server can be dedicated to increase performance or nondedicated to reduce costs. Up to 100 users are supported, and the product supports internetworking.

NETWARE V.3.11   NetWare v.3.11 is especially suited for large companies that need to network hundreds of users on a single server. It was designed for enterprise computing so that an organization can integrate various types of computer resources, such as minicomputers, mainframes, LAN Manager servers, OS/2 systems, UNIX systems, and Macintosh systems, into one computing platform. When compared to NetWare v.4, NetWare v.3.11 does not provide as much support for internetworking and Wide Area Networking. It also does not include NetWare Directory Services (NDS).

NETWARE V.4   NetWare v.4 improves on the features of NetWare v.3.11 by supporting Wide Area Networking. Its most important feature is NetWare Directory Services (NDS), which enables network administrators to organize users and network resources such as servers and printers the way people naturally access them. Each user and resource, which is called an *object* in the NDS system, is tracked in a network-wide database. Administrators who need to manage the system and users who need to access resources or contact other users can quickly find objects in the NDS system, no matter where they are located in the internetwork. The database is constantly updated throughout the network so that it holds the latest information about objects. NDS makes global networks under Novell NetWare a reality by simplifying setup, tracking, and management.

The remainder of this chapter discusses the features of NetWare v.4, and to some extent, NetWare v.3.11. These are the operating systems that most medium to large businesses will install or update to in the 1990s.

The Novell Product Strategy

Novell is a major force in the network industry, so we can assume their strategies for network operating systems and platform design are good indicators of the direction the whole network industry will take. Surveys and estimates indicate that Novell NetWare is used at approximately 60 percent of existing network sites. The remaining 40 percent is divided among Banyan Vines, Microsoft LAN Manager, and IBM and other network products.

Novell has adopted a network operating system strategy that focuses on the *enterprise network*, which encompasses all the computing resources of an organization. The network itself can be thought of as a platform to which you attach any type of computer system. Computers can share information with other computers, even those that run different operating systems, while maintaining the kind of performance, security, and reliability traditionally found in larger, centralized systems, at a much lower cost.

Enterprise networking is an evolutionary step beyond workgroup computing, which was concerned with integrating desktop computers into networks. Enterprise networking is both local and wide area in scope. It integrates all the systems within an organization, whether they are mainframes, minicomputers, DOS-based computers, Apple Macintoshes, UNIX workstations, or other systems. The goal is to provide network computing services to any user on the network. An interconnected network provides the communications platform, and Novell NetWare is the software component that helps you bind it all together using components supplied with NetWare or available as optional products.

The driving force behind Novell's enterprise networking strategy is a plan to make NetWare as open as possible to integration with other systems and other vendors' products.

Novell Integrated Computing Architecture

Novell's strategy for distributing network services on network computing platforms is called Novell Integrated Computing Architecture (NICA). NICA provides the network services listed in Table 2-1 to allow products and applications from different vendors to integrate with the network. These products are listed on the right in Table 2-1. The goal is to spur the integration of other architectures such as IBM's Systems Application Architecture (SAA), Hewlett-Packard's NewWave Office, and DEC's Network Application Support (NAS). NICA enhances these architectures by allowing applications designed for them to run in the distributed environment of the network computing platform. Any investment in existing applications is preserved.

The integration possible with NICA is based on a client-server architecture that divides an application into two parts. The client process runs on workstations and provides users with an interface to the application. The server process runs on the server and provides computer-intensive processing when necessary. NetWare is the core of NICA; it implements the client-server model and is designed to integrate and enhance the network's resources.

Services	Products
File and print	DOS, Macintosh, OS/2, and UNIX native file and print access
Database	Integrated record manager and SQL, and third-party SQL
Communications	SPX/IPX, SNA, TCP/IP, AppleTalk, OSI, T1, X.25, and asynchronous
Messaging	MHS, X.400, SMTP, and SNADS/DISSOS
Client operating system	DOS, Windows, OS/2, UNIX, and Macintosh
Application server OS	OS/2, UNIX, MVS, VM, VMS, and DOS
Data integrity	Disk mirroring and server mirroring
Security	User, administrator, data, resource encryption, and workstation auditing
Network management	Workgroup, administrator, enterprise, and NetView
Connection	Built-in SPX/IPX and TCP/IP router
Multivendor platform	Thousands of servers, adapters, disks, and backup systems
Application program interface	NetWare, NetBIOS, CPI-C, Named Pipes, and Berkeley Sockets

Table 2-1. *Novell Integrated Computing Architecture (NICA)*

NetWare Architecture and Protocol Support

The NetWare operating system resides in the server and provides services for workstations. The relationship between the server and workstations is illustrated in Figure 2-1.

The core functions provided by the NetWare server are file system management, memory management, and the scheduling of processing tasks. (See the text titled "The NetWare Core Protocol (NCP)" for more information about these functions.) Network services are applications that can run in the server. These applications are usually client-server based. The client portion of these applications runs in workstations and the server portion runs at the server. This improves performance and lets the server handle intensive computing tasks.

The network support software links the network hardware and cabling system to the operating system. This software uses specific drivers to support the types of network cards installed in the server and in workstations. Communications protocols send requests and receive replies across the network.

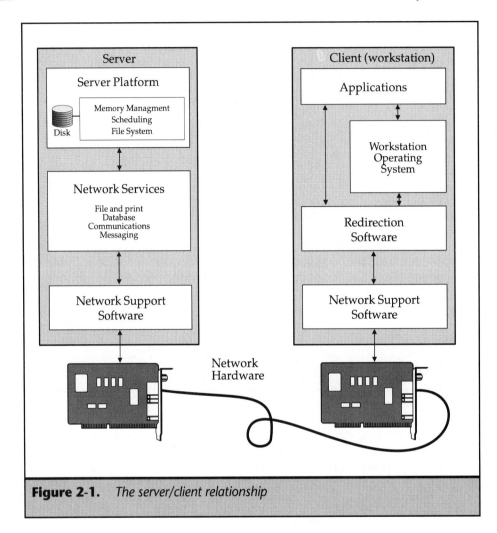

Figure 2-1. *The server/client relationship*

The redirection software determines whether commands from the application or the user should be sent to the local workstation operating system or to the network operating system. Likewise, messages from the server are redirected to the workstation operating system or the application running in the workstation.

NetWare v.4 Features

NetWare v.4 is a 32-bit network operating system that runs on Intel 80386 and above processors. While its architecture is similar to NetWare v.3.11, version 4 adds support for Wide Area Networking, primarily by adding NetWare Directory Services.

The NetWare Core Protocol (NCP)

The NetWare Core Protocol (NCP) defines the services that are available to users of Novell NetWare networks. These services fall into the following categories:

- File access (opening and closing files; reading and writing data to and from files)
- File locking
- Security
- Tracking of resource allocation
- Event notification
- NetWare Directory Services and synchronization with other servers
- Connection and communication
- Print services and queue management
- Network management

The NCP is transparent to both users and stand-alone workstation applications. For example, a user can request a file from the network server, which appears as a local drive. A redirector function in the workstation determines whether the file request is for a local drive or for the network drive, and then routes it appropriately. In this respect, the redirection software in the workstation works with the NCP to provide services to users.

You can expand the core services by installing NetWare Loadable Modules (NLMs) at the server. NLMs can provide network management and diagnostics, database services, communications services, backup services, store-and-forward message (electronic mail) delivery, and additional print services. Some NLMs are supplied with NetWare; you can obtain others from Novell, or from third-party vendors.

The NetWare Architecture

NetWare v.4 is a full 32-bit operating system that uses a single address space with no segmentation (a problem with DOS systems). This allows programs to operate more efficiently. It can handle thousands of interrupts and process thousands of client requests per second.

NetWare v.4 is modular and expandable. Changes, upgrades, and additions to the network are possible. You can load a NetWare Loadable Module (NLM) at the server to provide services like the following:

■ Support for operating systems other than DOS

■ Communication services

■ Database services

■ Messaging services

■ Archive and backup services

■ Network management services

These modules are added to the operating system as shown in Figure 2-2. You can load or unload any module at any time from the server console without bringing down the server. Each module uses additional memory, so you need to make sure the server has enough memory to handle the NLMs you plan to load. Because the modules are located in the server along with the operating system, they are tightly coupled with the operating system and have instant access to services.

NetWare is an ideal platform for server applications. It solves connectivity problems by handling multiple protocols and standards concurrently at the media level, the transport level, the service protocol level, and at the file system level, as shown in Figure 2-3. These levels are discussed further in Chapter 6.

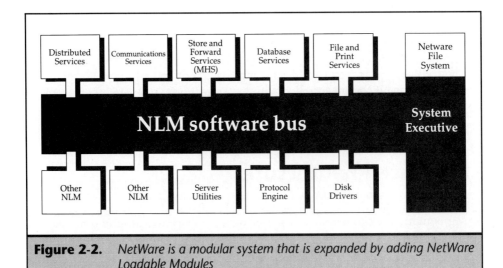

Figure 2-2.   *NetWare is a modular system that is expanded by adding NetWare Loadable Modules*

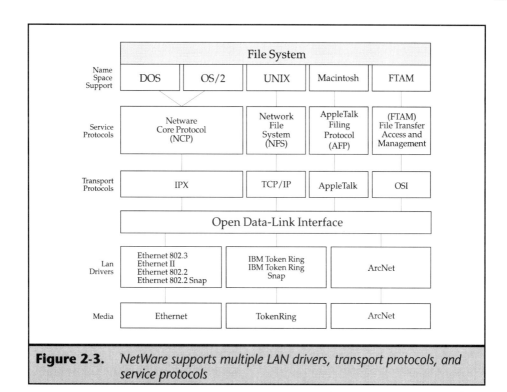

Figure 2-3.   *NetWare supports multiple LAN drivers, transport protocols, and service protocols*

Protocol Independence

One of the most important features of NetWare is its support for other operating systems. You can attach workstations that run DOS, Windows, OS/2, and UNIX. DOS, Windows, and OS/2 workstation support is bundled with NetWare, as are several management utilities that use the Windows interface. The NetWare OS/2 workstation software supplied with NetWare provides the support OS/2 workstations need to communicate with a NetWare server. NetWare allows OS/2 extended attributes and long filenames, and lets OS/2 server-based applications run on the network. Support for the Apple Macintosh, UNIX-based NFS, and OSI FTAM (File Transfer Access and Management) must be added to a NetWare network as optional products.

NetWare uses a protocol-independent structure known as the Open Data-Link Interface (ODI), which provides simultaneous support for different protocols on the network. The protocol engine that provides multiprotocol support at the server is shown as the bottom layer in Figure 2-3. Note that a variety of interface cards are allowed. The drivers of these cards attach themselves to the Open Data-Link Interface layer. Packets are directed to the appropriate protocol stack above the ODI layer, such as IPX, TCP/IP, or

AppleTalk. Near the top, service protocols provide file and system support for the various operating systems that you can install on a NetWare server.

A similar scheme is used at workstations to allow users to connect to networks that use different communications protocols, such as UNIX-based TCP/IP. You'll need Novell's LAN WorkPlace for DOS product to provide TCP/IP support for DOS and Windows workstations. In addition, Novell's LAN WorkPlace for Macintosh provides Apple Macintosh users with transparent access to a broad range of hosts, servers, and workgroups on a NetWare LAN, such as VAX minicomputers, IBM mainframes, and UNIX workstations.

If you need to connect workstations to NetWare LANs as well as to other types of networks, such as Microsoft LAN Manager, IBM LAN Server, and 3Com 3+Share networks, you can install the ODINSUP (Open Data-Link Interface network driver interface specification support) driver provided in the NetWare package. ODINSUP allows the coexistence of the ODI network driver interface and the Network Driver Interface Specification (NDIS), which is typically used by Microsoft products such as LAN Manager and Microsoft NT.

Name Space Support

The NetWare file system provides support for the file naming conventions of different operating systems through *name space* support, which is loaded at the server console. Name space support allows files with different name lengths, legal characters, and case sensitivity to be stored on the NetWare server. Name space support for the Macintosh is a module you load at the server.

Performance Features

One of the reasons NetWare is so popular is its performance. Novell long ago moved away from a network operating system that ran under DOS, and designed NetWare to access directly the advanced features of the server's CPU. NetWare 386 was the first 32-bit network operating system in the desktop computer arena. The kernel of the NetWare operating system is both multitasking and multithreaded, which means that it provides multiuser capabilities at the server and high performance during times when there are heavy loads on the system. Other performance improvements are discussed in the next sections.

Dynamic Configuration

NetWare dynamically configures itself to match current usage conditions on the network. The following features are dynamically configured:

- Memory usage

- Directory caching

- Number of volume directory entries

- Size of the open file table

- Routing buffers

- Turbo FAT indexing

- Service processes

- Active TTS (transaction tracking system) transactions

You can alter the limits and maximum values so that NetWare is not constrained. You can also adjust how quickly the operating system configures itself, and you can set the maximum amount of resources that are used.

Memory Management

NetWare supports up to 4GB (gigabytes) of RAM in the server, but with current technology, the maximum amount of memory a server will support is 256MB.

Memory management in NetWare v.4 is designed to have increased efficiency. NetWare v.3.11 allocated memory for different uses into five or more *pools*. This caused some applications to run out of memory because, when a process was done using the memory, the management routines did not reallocate it for other uses. NetWare v.4 manages memory as only one pool, and it is more effective at allocating memory from one operation to another.

The File System

The Universal File System in NetWare provides many performance-enhancing features:

- *Elevator seeking* This feature of the disk system prioritizes incoming read requests based on how they can best be accessed by the read head of the disk drive, given its current location. The operation of elevator seeking is analogous to that of a building elevator. A building elevator doesn't make random up and down trips among floors; it stops at floors on the way up or down to pick up passengers who need a ride. Elevator seeking minimizes disk head movement, thus improving access time and reducing hardware degradation.

- *File caching*   File caching minimizes the number of times the disk must be accessed. The files that are most often read are retained in the cache buffer, where they can be accessed if needed. This eliminates the need to go to disk for the information. Files in the cache are prioritized so that the least used files are flushed from the cache to make room for new files.

- *Background writes*   Disk writes are handled separately from disk reads in NetWare. This separation allows the operating system to write data to disk during moments when disk requests from users have slowed. Background writes give users who need to read data from the drive the highest priority, which improves performance from their point of view.

- *Overlapped seeks*   This NetWare feature is available if two or more hard disks are present and each is connected to its own controller (disk channel). NetWare accesses all the controllers simultaneously. If two disks are attached to one controller, only one of those disks is accessible at a time.

- *Turbo FAT*   This feature is also known as the Index file allocation table. The turbo FAT indexes the file allocation tables of files over 2MB so that the locations of their segments are immediately available to the operating system without the need to read the FAT.

- *File compression*   NetWare v.4 can increase disk space up to 63 percent with its file compression feature. NetWare manages the compression in the background. Administrators and users can flag files to indicate that they should be compressed after use or that they should never be compressed.

- *Block suballocation*   This feature maximizes disk space. If there are any partially used disk blocks (usually a block is 8KB in size), NetWare divides them into 512 byte suballocation blocks for the storage of small files or fragments of files.

Files up to 4GB in size are allowed, and the file system supports more than 2 million directories and files per volume and 100,000 open files. Volumes can span multiple disk drives, and the size of the volumes can be increased dynamically by adding new drives.

NetWare's salvageable file system allows recovery of deleted files. You can set a minimum amount of time that a deleted file must be kept recoverable, and you can mark files for immediate purging. You can also keep all deleted files until the volume runs out of disk space; then the oldest deleted files are removed to free space for new files. Trustee rights to files are preserved after a file has been recovered, and rights can be set to control who can salvage files. Deleted files are preserved even if a directory is deleted.

Data Protection Features

The NetWare network operating system contains several features that ensure the security and reliability of data. Security features protect data from unauthorized users and from virus attacks. NetWare supports hardware reliability features that provide redundancy to ensure that data is written correctly and is available should part of the system fail.

Security

The security features of NetWare are critical for large corporate-wide network environments. The NetWare file system and the DOS file system are quite different; a user cannot access the NetWare file system by starting the server with a DOS disk. Of course, this doesn't prevent people from stealing or destroying a disk; you still need to keep a backup to protect yourself against such disasters.

Security is provided at several levels:

- *Login/password security*   Users type the LOGIN command to gain access to the file system. They enter their user name and then a password. No access is allowed without the password. After they are logged in, users can access computers in an internetwork based on the access rights that have been assigned to them by the network administrator.

- *Account restrictions*   Under NetWare, each user has an account that is managed by the network administrator. Restrictions can be applied to accounts to control when users can log in, the workstations they can log in at, and when their accounts expire. It's also possible to force users to change their passwords on a regular basis and to require a unique password that is not similar to one recently used.

- *Object and file security*   The network administrator grants users *trustee rights* to objects, directories, and files. These rights determine exactly how the users can access the resources of the system. For example, a user who has been granted read-only rights to a file can look at the file but can't change it.

- *Internetwork security*   NetWare Directory Services tracks all objects on an internetwork, including user objects and their access rights. Network administrators use NDS to create and manage user accounts, track network resources, and assign user access to network resources. Users log in once to gain access to all the network resources granted to them through the NDS system.

In addition to implementing these user security features, NetWare performs behind-the-scenes security checks. It encrypts all passwords at the server and encrypts user passwords on the cable as they are transferred to the server. This last feature prevents electronic eavesdroppers from obtaining a password by tapping the cable and then accessing the system as a normal user.

Reliability Features

The NetWare network operating system provides several important features that ensure the survivability and quick recovery of data on the server:

- *Read-after-write verification*   This feature reads every write to the disk at the time it is written to verify that it is correct. If an error occurs, the data is rewritten while it is still in the cache. An error can indicate a bad sector, which can be marked as unusable by the Hot Fix feature described shortly.

- *Duplicate directories*   NetWare duplicates the root directory structure to provide a backup in case the main directory structure is corrupted.

- *Duplicate FAT*   A duplicate of the file allocation table is maintained as a backup. If the original is lost, the disk remains accessible through the duplicate.

- *Hot Fix*   This feature detects and corrects disk defects as the system runs. Data in defective sectors is moved elsewhere on the disk, and the sectors are marked as unusable.

- *System Fault Tolerance (SFT)*   This feature allows you to provide redundancy for hardware in the system. You can install two disks and then mirror the contents of the main disk on the secondary disk, as shown in Figure 2-4. Should the main disk fail, the secondary disk takes over. The disk controller can also be duplicated, or duplexed, to further protect from hardware failure, as shown in Figure 2-5. SFT Level III (available optionally) takes redundancy a step further by duplexing entire servers. If the primary server goes down, the secondary server takes over without an interruption.

- *Transaction tracking system (TTS)*   The transaction tracking system protects data files from incomplete writes. This can occur when a user is editing records in a database and the server goes down. When the server is restarted, it backs out the incomplete transactions so that the files are the way they were before the transaction began. Transactions must be either wholly completed or wholly abandoned under this system.

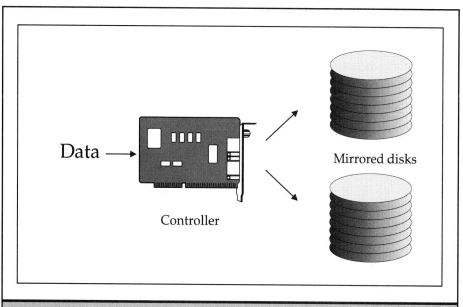

Figure 2-4. *Disk mirroring*

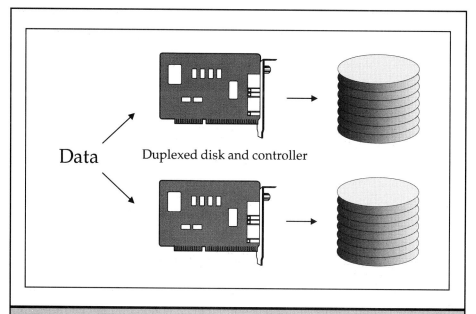

Figure 2-5. *Disk duplexing*

■ *UPS monitoring* NetWare monitors the status of an uninterruptible power supply (UPS) to determine if the server is running on backup power. A NetWare-compatible UPS is capable of providing this signal to NetWare. If a power failure occurs, NetWare warns users (who must be out of the blackout area or on their own UPS) and then begins to save any open information (cache data) and safely shut down the system.

Other Features

NetWare v.4 contains many additional features, some of which are covered in more detail in later chapters. The following sections describe some of these features.

Built-in Internetwork Routing

NetWare provides built-in internetwork routing services that allow you to interconnect as many network segments (Token Ring, Ethernet, ArcNet, and so on) as the server will hold network cards. The connected networks appear as one network to users. Creating a router is as simple as installing multiple interface cards in a NetWare server and then selecting drivers for those cards during setup or during post-setup maintenance. You can also install routing services in an external system to remove the additional workload from the server and improve its performance.

Communications Services

Novell sells a complete line of communications support packages called NetWare Communication Services that run in NetWare v.3.11 and 4 servers. These products provide LAN-to-host, LAN-to-LAN, and remote-to-LAN connectivity. NetWare Communication Services focuses on the LAN-to-host and network management requirements of organizations with large SNA (System Network Architecture) networks. The products include NetWare for SAA; NetWare 3270 LAN Workstation packages for DOS, the Macintosh, and Windows; and NetWare Communication Services Manager, a Windows-based management program.

Print Services

NetWare v.4 includes a print services package that lets you share up to 256 printers over the network. A print server manages print queues and the way that users access the printers. This print server can be installed in the NetWare file server or as a dedicated task on a workstation. You can attach printers to the print server or to any workstation in the network. Users access printers that are being shared through the print server.

Distributed Directory Services

Distributed directory services for NetWare are implemented as NetWare Directory Services (NDS). NDS is based on the International Organization for Standardization X.500 standard. The service keeps track of all network users, servers, and resources on an internetwork. This information is kept in a database. Administrators and users can access the database to locate users and resources, without regard for their location.

NDS was designed with large internetworks in mind. It provides centralized management of the entire network directory with a common naming service. The directory database of users and resources is updated at regular intervals. The service provides gateways to other directory services, including Apple Name Binding Protocol, Sun Microsystems' Yellow Pages (NFS support), and the TCP/IP Domain Name Service.

Backup Services

Backups in NetWare are handled by the SBACKUP utility, which is supplied with NetWare v.4 and works with a large number of third-party backup devices. It conforms to Novell's Storage Management System (SMS) as discussed in Chapter 30.

Management

NetWare provides several utilities for monitoring the status of a network, and Novell sells management software packages that provide enhanced features. These are described in the following sections.

NetWare Administrator

NetWare includes the NetWare Administrator, which is a Windows-based application used to manage NetWare Directory Services objects, such as users, network resources, disk directories, and files. Figure 2-6 shows a NetWare Administrator screen. A text-based version of NetWare Administrator called NETADMIN is also supplied with NetWare v.4, but it does not provide support for managing directories and files. NetWare Administrator can be used instead of several command-line utilities. It is easier to use and provides more functionality. NetWare Administrator requires an 80386 or higher system and workstations that run Microsoft Windows.

Note the directory tree in Figure 2-6. At the top is an organization's name. Branching from that are its eastern division (DivEast) and its western division (DivWest). The DivEast branch is collapsed so that you can't see users or resources in it, but the DivWest branch is expanded. You could click on any user or resource object under DivWest and then choose Details from the Object menu to make changes to the properties of that object. For example, you could select the AColgan object and then change its login restrictions or rights to the file system.

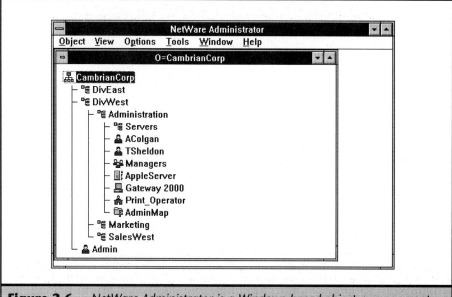

Figure 2-6.   *NetWare Administrator is a Windows-based object management program for NetWare*

Administrators use NetWare Administrator primarily to create user objects (accounts) and manage how users access the network, its resources, and its files. A browse feature lets you quickly locate similar objects. For example, you could list all users that live within a certain ZIP code area or that have rights to a certain server volume. Once you locate and select an object, you can use NetWare Administrator to change security rights, properties, and other aspects of the object. You can use NetWare Administrator to:

- Create additional objects, such as user and printer objects

- Change the login restrictions of users

- Change users' access to resources

- Change users' access to directories and files

- Change the trustees of objects. (A trustee is a user who can use a given object)

- Grant other users supervisory rights to objects on the network

- Specify groups of users and create login profiles for those users

- Create and edit system-wide and individual user login scripts

- Arrange and organize the structure of the NetWare Directory Services tree and its partitions

MONITOR

MONITOR is a NetWare Loadable Module that runs at the file server console or at a remote station if the Remote Management Facility (discussed next) is running. MONITOR lets you perform the following tasks from the console:

- Set password access for the NetWare console

- View the utilization of the server

- View the cache memory status

- View workstation connections

- See files opened by users

- Clear connections

- View the status of disk drives

- View the status of volumes

- Set verify levels for disk writes

- Activate and deactivate volumes and hard drives

- List the current LAN drivers

- List the currently loaded modules

- View the file lock status

- View memory usage

Remote Management

NetWare is bundled with the NetWare Remote Management Facility (RMF), which allows network administrators to install and upgrade NetWare, configure network services, and maintain NetWare from a remote workstation.

SERVMAN

SERVMAN is a new utility included with NetWare v.4. It runs at the console and lets supervisors view and change the server configuration.

Those familiar with previous versions of NetWare are familiar with the SET command, which is used to make changes to the operating system. SERVMAN automates the use of this command by displaying help information for each set option and by displaying recommended settings. If a setting is changed, SERVMAN automatically updates the server startup files.

Requirements for Running NetWare

The following list defines the hardware you need to install and run NetWare:

- An 80386 or higher system. Both the SX and DX versions of these processors are supported. Chapter 12 discusses network servers and so-called "superservers" for use with NetWare.

- A minimum of 5MB of memory, but 16MB is recommended as a starting point, because of the low price of memory and the benefits it offers to server performance. Servers on large networks might require more than

32MB of memory, depending on the software modules installed on the server and the number of users who will access it.

- A hard drive with a minimum of 30MB of storage. You need 5MB for a DOS partition and 25MB for the NetWare disk partition. If you're running NetWare for OS/2, you need a hard drive with a minimum of 120MB of storage. To provide fault tolerance, you need duplicate drives and controllers or even duplicate servers if SFT Level III is used.

- One or more network cards. Although one network card can support an entire network, performance improves when you split a LAN into segments.

- Network cabling. The type of cabling depends on the type of network card used. Refer to Chapter 7 for more details.

- To ensure job security, purchase an adequate power backup system and take measures to secure the hardware from theft, destruction, and other loss, as described in Chapter 13.

Additional information to help you evaluate and purchase equipment for your network is available in Part Three of this book.

CHAPTER 3

NetWare Directory Services, Hierarchy, and Security

This chapter describes the NetWare environment from the viewpoint of administrators and users. The first time NetWare v.4 is installed, an administrative account called ADMIN is created. ADMIN has unrestricted rights to the entire network, and the network administrator uses it to create the initial NetWare Directory Services tree structure. After that, the network administrator expands the directory services tree by adding organizational units, user accounts (called user objects), and resource objects, all of which are described in this chapter. On a large network, the network administrator might delegate supervisor-level tasks to others who create new user accounts and define security and access rights within a specific branch of the directory tree. A branch typically defines a department or division within a company.

This chapter presents an overview of the NetWare Directory Services system, the hierarchy of users, and security on the network. In Part Four of this book, you'll learn how to plan the basic directory structure required to install NetWare. In Part Five, you'll learn how to expand that structure by adding user and resource objects after NetWare is installed.

NetWare Directory Services (NDS)

NetWare Directory Services (NDS) is an implementation of distributed directory services as defined by the International Organization for Standards (ISO) X.500 specification. The service keeps track of all network users, servers, and resources, even on large internetworks. This information is kept in a global database that network administrators and users access when they need to manage or use services on the network.

NDS treats all network users and resources as *objects*. Ordinarily people might be offended if they were treated as objects, but a user object is simply the account of a network user and is analogous to a bank account or library account. A user object holds information about a user, such as his or her name, address, computer node address, login script, and other vital administrative information. Resources such as servers, printers, and volumes are also represented as objects. These objects have properties that specify who can use and change them.

Objects are stored in the NetWare Directory Database (NDB) and organized in a hierarchical tree structure, as shown on the left in Figure 3-1. It's not necessary to organize the tree structure to resemble the physical location of users and resources in an organization. Instead, you can organize it to reflect the management organization of a company. For example, Figure 3-1 shows a directory services tree as it appears in the graphical NetWare Administrator utility, which runs under Windows on a network workstation. Although salespeople are grouped under an organization called Sales in the directory services tree, they are physically at remote locations, as shown on the right. This example depicts a Wide Area Network, but the same organization can be used if the salespeople are at workstations located in different parts of a building.

Grouping users and resources together in the directory services tree can simplify network management. For example, if an organizational object called Sales contains a user object, and the Sales object is granted access rights to files on a particular volume, the user object inherits those access rights.

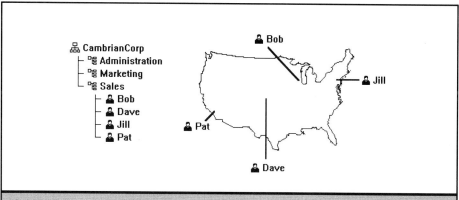

Figure 3-1. *With NDS, users at remote sites can be viewed and addressed as a group, without regard for their physical locations*

However, a network administrator or supervisor can block those access rights if they are not appropriate for the user.

The Directory Tree

The directory tree is made up of NDS named objects that represent the organization of the network. A named object can belong to one of four categories. Figure 3-2 shows a sample directory tree. The meanings of the abbreviations are listed here:

C = Country Name
O = Organization Name
OU = Organizational Unit Name
CN = Common Name

The picture of the directory tree shown in Figure 3-2 is taken from the display you would see when running the Windows-based NetWare Administrator utility. This utility shows the tree in graphical form and lets you expand and collapse parts of the tree. Country, Organization, and Organizational Unit objects can contain other objects. For example, in Figure 3-2, the Sales branch is expanded to show user and resource objects within it, and the Administration and Marketing

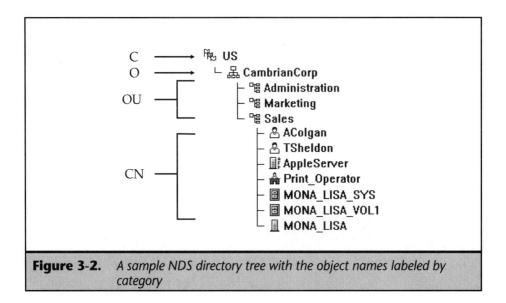

Figure 3-2.   *A sample NDS directory tree with the object names labeled by category*

branches are collapsed. The ability to view branches of the directory tree in this way makes it easy to locate and manage objects.

The Object-Naming Format

In NetWare, references to objects are made by their directory tree names. The name specifies exactly where an object is in the directory structure, similar to a house address that specifies a street, city, and country. The default name sequence is shown here using the *type name*:

    Common Name.Organizational Unit.Organization.Country

The type names are often abbreviated as follows:

    CN. OU. O. C

The complete name for the user AColgan in Figure 3-2 is as follows:

    CN=AColgan. OU=Sales. O=CambrianCorp. C=US

However, you can eliminate the type names and abbreviations in some cases, as shown below:

AColgan.Sales.CambrianCorp.US

Partial names can sometimes be used. If your current vantage point in the system is Sales.CambrianCorp.US, you can refer to Bob in Figure 3-2 simply as Bob.

Users and Resources as Objects

In NetWare Directory Services, objects are used to track and locate users and resources on the network. Remember that resources are network servers, printers, and other devices, and that objects merely hold information about a user or resource. This information forms the *properties* of the object. For example, a user object holds the login script for a network user. If the network administrator or supervisor needs to change a user's login script, he or she starts the NetWare Administrator or NETADMIN utility, selects the user object, and changes the login script. Several other examples of object management are described here:

- In addition to the account information for a network user, a user object can include information that is not essential for network operation. After creating a user object with the NetWare Administrator or NETADMIN utility, you can define properties such as the computers the user can log into, and when; the rights the user has to other objects on the network, such as printers and volumes; and the user's telephone or fax number.

- Administrators and supervisors can simplify the task of granting access rights to users by granting those rights to the objects that contain user objects. For example, if all users in an organization need read and write access rights to a directory called BBS, you could grant the access rights to the organizational object that contains the users. In Figure 3-2, if you granted these rights to the CambrianCorp organizational object, the rights would be inherited by the organizational unit objects Administration, Marketing, and Sales, as well as the objects they contain, unless the rights are specifically blocked at any level.

- A computer workstation on the network can be represented by an object. This is usually done for documentation purposes. For example, you could use computer objects to track the locations, serial numbers, node addresses, and users of the computers on your network.

As this last item illustrates, the NDS system can be used to document the network as well as to organize it and grant users access to it. For example, you can use the name and address property information of user objects to address mailings or electronic mail. Every property of an object can have its own attributes, which means that you can prevent users from changing or even viewing individual properties. For example, you can prevent other users from viewing the home addresses and telephone numbers of users to ensure their privacy. However, you could grant these property rights to the personnel or payroll department so they can do company newsletter or paycheck mailings.

An important aspect of objects is that other users can be granted access to view and change their properties. In this way, you can relieve yourself of the monumental task of managing all the objects on a network. Supervisors are typically assigned to manage each branch of the directory services tree.

Types of Objects

An object can be a *container* object that holds other objects, or it can be a *leaf* object that is contained within a container object. A leaf object cannot contain objects of its own, and is therefore sometimes referred to as a terminal object. Leaf objects represent physical entities such as users, printers, and servers.

TIP: The NDS tree is analogous to the directory structure used in the DOS filing system. Container objects are like DOS directories, which can hold files and other directories. Leaf objects are like files, which cannot contain directories or other files.

Figure 3-3 illustrates a typical organizational chart. In this case, it is the organizational structure of the tree shown in Figure 3-2.

Container Objects

Three objects are classified as containers: the *country* container, the *organization* container, and the *organizational unit* container.

THE COUNTRY CONTAINER   The country container is the organizational unit that specifies which country an object is located in. It can hold information about one or more organizations. The name of the country object must be two

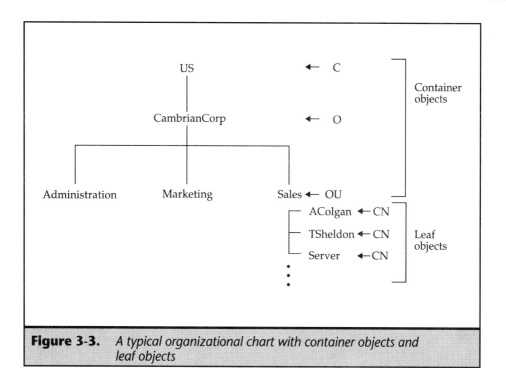

Figure 3-3.   *A typical organizational chart with container objects and leaf objects*

characters long, such as US for the United States. A directory tree with a country container is shown in Figure 3-4.

TIP: The country container is optional. In fact, it is not recommended that you use it, because it adds complexity when naming and searching for objects, as discussed later. You should use organization containers (discussed next) to organize international divisions of your company.

THE ORGANIZATION CONTAINER   There is usually one organization container and it is given the name of your company. If the country container is not used, the organization container is the start of the directory tree. In Figure 3-1, CambrianCorp is the name of the organization and forms the start of the directory tree. Even if your company has different divisions around the world, the organization container is the preferred container for these divisions, rather than the country container. For example, XYZ Corporation might have divisions in the United States, England, and Korea. The best tree structure would start with three organization containers, called XYZ-US, XYZ-England, and

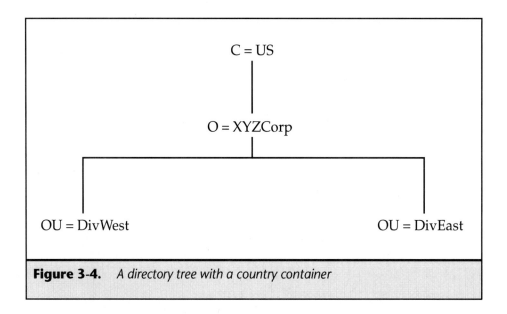

Figure 3-4.   *A directory tree with a country container*

XYZ-Korea, as shown in Figure 3-5. Note that the root is part of every tree and is created when NetWare is installed.

NOTE: When you install a NetWare v.4 server, you must specify its organization container. If all servers belong to the same organization container, you specify the organization's name when installing the first server and then use the same name when installing subsequent servers. To create different organization containers, you specify a new name when installing the first server in that division or create the container later.

THE ORGANIZATIONAL UNIT CONTAINER   Organizational unit containers are the departments or divisions within an organization container. Figure 3-6 shows the expansion of the XYZ company's U.S. division. Note that the U.S. offices are located in Los Angeles and New York City. This division is handled by the first level of organizational unit containers. Within the Los Angeles division is a second level of organizational unit containers for the departments within the Los Angeles office.

Leaf Objects

Once the container structure of an organization's directory tree is established, you can add objects that represent users and resources. The various kinds of

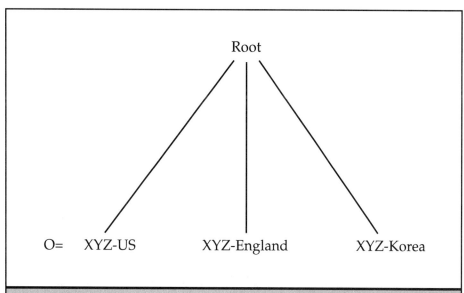

Figure 3-5.   *The organization container is the best place for the company name, so this tree structure is best for international companies*

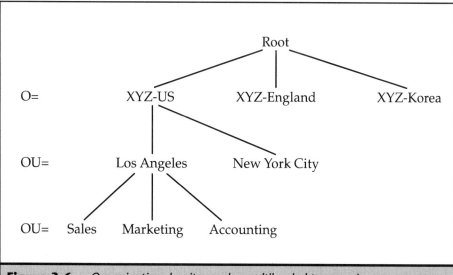

Figure 3-6.   *Organizational units can be multileveled to organize a company geographically and by department*

objects you can add are discussed in the following sections. Figure 3-7 illustrates how they appear as icons when running the Windows-based NetWare Administrator utility. Each icon is described below.

THE ALIAS OBJECT   An alias object points to an object elsewhere in the directory tree. You create an alias for an object in one branch of the directory tree that you often need to refer to in another branch of the directory tree. The alias object is discussed further in the next section.

THE AFP SERVER OBJECT   An AFP server is an Apple file server running the AppleTalk Filing Protocol.

THE BINDERY OBJECT   A bindery is an object that was upgraded from a version of NetWare that used server-specific binderies. Any object that was not identified during the upgrade is given the bindery object classification.

NOTE: In NetWare v.4, NDS replaces the bindery that was used in previous versions of NetWare. The bindery is a database that keeps track of users, groups, and workgroups on a single NetWare server, whereas NDS tracks an entire network of servers. NetWare v.4 has a bindery emulator that provides compatibility with previous versions of NetWare that use the bindery.

THE COMPUTER OBJECT   A computer object holds information about a workstation on the network, such as its serial number, node address, users, and location or department.

THE DIRECTORY MAP OBJECT   A directory map object specifies the locations of applications and simplifies the mapping of directories for a large number of

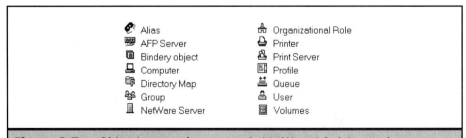

Figure 3-7.   *Object icons as they appear in NetWare Administrator's Directory tree*

users. Directory maps are used in login scripts to map directories for users. If the location of an application changes, you change the directory map rather than changing each user's login script.

THE GROUP OBJECT   The group object is used to group users into mail groups, project groups, management groups, or other types of groups you might need for your organization. Groups simplify the assignment of directory and file rights and make it easy to add new users to the network. For example, you might create a group that works on a special project, and then assign the group access rights to directories and create a specific login script. If new users need to work on the project, you simply add them to the group. The new users then gain all the rights of the group.

THE NETWARE SERVER OBJECT   The NetWare server object represents a NetWare server on the network.

THE ORGANIZATIONAL ROLE OBJECT   An organizational role is an object with specific rights that is assigned to a person such as an administrator, project leader, or temporary employee. If a different person takes over the job, a new person can be made a trustee of the object and thus inherit its rights.

THE PRINTER OBJECT   A printer object represents a printer that is attached to a print server or workstation and shared on the network.

THE PRINT SERVER OBJECT   A print server object represents a network print server. It can be part of the NetWare server or a stand-alone print server.

THE PROFILE OBJECT   A profile is a special login script that is shared by more than one user. The profile script is executed after the script of the user's container, but before the user's login script. Profile scripts make it easy to set up a network environment for a group of users who don't belong to the same containers (departments).

THE QUEUE OBJECT   A queue object represents a queue, which holds print jobs that are directed to one or more printers. Users send print jobs to queues.

THE USER OBJECT   A user object holds information about a user on the network.

THE VOLUME OBJECT   A volume object represents a physical volume on the hard drive of a file server. It also holds statistics about the volume. The name you assign to a volume object does not need to be the same as the hard disk volume name.

Alias Objects

An alias object provides a link between users in one organizational unit and an object they want to use in another organizational unit. For example, let's say that Bob in the Sales department of the New York City office wants to access the server in the Sales department of the Los Angeles office. The network administrator creates an alias object for the Los Angeles server within Bob's organizational unit, as shown in Figure 3-8. When the network administrator views the NDS tree by using an application such as NetWare Administrator, the Los Angeles server object appears as an alias object in the New York City organization. By using alias objects, administrators can get a better handle on exactly how resources are distributed and used. As you can see, this kind of map doesn't necessarily describe the location of resources, only how they are used.

NOTE: An alias is not required to access a remote object. You can search for an object or specify its full directory pathname instead. An alias simply makes it easier to access objects used on a regular basis.

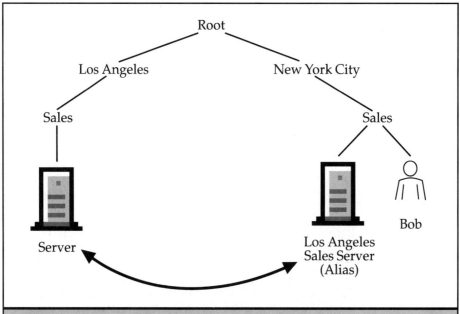

Figure 3-8.   *An alias object gives users in one organizational unit easy access to resources in another organizational unit*

Administrators can use aliases to pool objects that are scattered throughout an organization. Printers, modems, and fax machines at various locations can be grouped on the network so they are easier to select, without regard for their locations. Users can choose an object that is not in use, one that provides the best service, or one that is close to their physical location.

TIP: Aliasing helps network administrators manage the network by organizing remote physical resources into logical groups.

Properties of Objects

Each object has properties, the most important being its name. You specify the properties of an object when you create the object, and you can change them at any time by using the NetWare Administrator or NETADMIN utility. An example of the NetWare Administrator window used to change the properties of a user object is shown in Figure 3-9. You click the buttons on the right to view different property fields, such as login restrictions and rights to the file system. You can then change information about the selected properties. The network administrator can change any property field for any object. Other users can be restricted from changing or even viewing these fields.

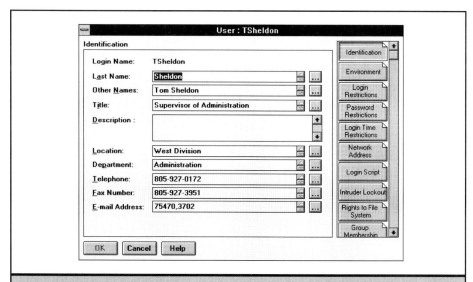

Figure 3-9. *The NetWare Administrator window used to change the properties of a user object*

Some of the property fields for a user object that you would see when working with the NetWare Administrator are listed here:

- The user's name, address, phone number, and fax number
- Account information, such as the balance amount
- Login restrictions, such as the allowed time, the allowed workstations, and password requirements
- The default server of the user
- The groups the user belongs to
- The user's print job configuration and printer controls
- The profile object used by the user
- The user's identification number

In contrast, some of the properties of a physical object such as a server are

- The organizational unit name assigned to the server
- A description of the server, which is used for reference only
- The location of the server, which is used for reference only
- The network address of the server
- The trustees of the server, which is basically a list of users who can change the properties of the server object
- A list of server operators
- Status information about the server's operation

The network administrator can make any user a trustee of an object and set which of the object's properties that trustee can view and change. As mentioned earlier, department managers are usually granted rights to create and manage objects.

NDS Partition Management

NDS uses a distributed database called NetWare Directory Database (NDB) to track objects. On multiserver networks, the database resides on a network of servers, not just on one server, to ensure its survival in the event a server crashes. This is accomplished by segmenting the database into partitions and storing each partition on an appropriate server on the network. You can copy or replicate partitions to other servers to provide backups and increase performance. The Partition Management utility is used to create, remove, join, divide, synchronize, and rebuild partitions. Partitions normally correspond to container objects in the NDS directory tree. (See Appendix C.)

Time Synchronization

In order for partitions to operate concurrently, time synchronization is used. NDS uses time of day stamps to establish an order of events and ensure that updates to partitions by administrators are handled correctly and in order.

Organizing Your NDS Directory

The initial organization of the NDS directory is performed during NetWare installation. You can specify the organization container the server belongs to as well as up to three levels of organizational unit containers. A typical directory tree after installation of the first NetWare v.4 server is shown here:

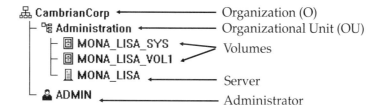

This structure assumes the following:

- CambrianCorp was specified as the organization.

- A branching organizational unit called Administration was created.

- The server was named MONA_LISA.

- Two volumes (SYS and VOL1) were created on the server disk storage system.

The ADMIN user is automatically created.

You can create organizational unit objects for additional departments after installing NetWare by using NetWare Administrator or NETADMIN. However, if other departments have their own servers, you can create organizational unit objects for those departments when installing the servers. You would specify the same organization and then specify a different department name in the organizational unit field of the install screen.

You'll learn more about planning and organizing your directory tree and the network environment in Chapter 15.

Administrators and Supervisors

In previous versions of NetWare, the supervisor was responsible for installing or overseeing the installation of NetWare on servers and had the highest level of access on a specific server. Under NetWare v.4, a network administrator oversees the entire internetwork, at least initially. The administrator can create supervisor-type users who manage partitions in the directory tree that relate to divisions or departments in a company. A supervisor in NetWare v.4 manages the server and users in a department. The administrator can also rely on supervisors to install additional servers on the network.

The administrator has supervisor rights to the root of the directory services tree, and thus has the highest level of access. The administrator can perform any task related to creating, changing, and deleting objects. The administrator can also change the rights and attributes of any object on the internetwork. The user who installs the first NetWare server in a directory tree specifies the ADMIN password, and thus has administrative powers.

Large internetworks require skilled users who can administer partitions of the network at remote locations or manage the server equipment within their own departments. These supervisors are designated by management, and they are given supervisor access rights by the network administrator. The tasks of an administrator are many. Some are listed here, but keep in mind that many of these tasks should be delegated to users at specific locations in the network.

- Install the server

- Create the initial administrator password

- Change the administrator password periodically for security reasons

- Administer the NDS directory

- Administer the security of servers and of the entire internetwork

- Create directory structures for programs and data within volume objects

- Install applications

- Create, manage, and delete user and resource objects

- Assign passwords to users or require them to periodically change their passwords

- Designate users as managers with special rights to manage other users

- Monitor the performance and integrity of the network

- Recommend new equipment or manage the expansion of the network when it becomes overloaded

- Ensure that data is properly protected with backup procedures and System Fault Tolerance (SFT) features, as well as by physically securing servers

Technically, the system administrator is the user who logs in with the ADMIN user name. This name and the password associated with it can be changed at any time by the administrator. This person should also have a normal login account that is used to access the network for nonadministrative tasks. Administrator-level access should not be taken lightly. If the administrator's workstation is left unattended, an intruder could walk up to it and gain unrestricted access to the entire internetwork.

The system administrator's password is the master key to the system. It should be written down and placed in a locked safe or given to a trusted person of authority for safekeeping. Another suggestion is to create a two- or three-word password and then give a portion of the password to two or three people in the company. This "fail-safe" approach ensures that others can gain administrative access to the server should something happen to the administrator. To gain access, they must do so together.

Users and Groups

Below the system administrator is a hierarchy of managers and users who have different levels of access to the network. Access to the internetwork is made with a single login, and access to resources on the network is controlled by the rights users have to objects, directories, and files.

Users

Users can gain access to the network as soon as the network administrator or a supervisor has created a user object for them with the NetWare Administrator or

NETADMIN utility. The user object holds the user's name and password. User names can be up to 47 characters long, but a naming format that combines a user's first initial and last name (TSHELDON, for example) is recommended. After a user object is created, the administrator or supervisor grants the user rights to the file system. If the user is to have management responsibilities, the administrator or supervisor might grant the user object rights as well.

You can assign a home directory to a user when you create his or her user object. Users typically have full access rights in this home directory so that they can create subdirectories and files as necessary. Novell recommends setting aside a separate volume for home directories on large networks. A home directory usually has the same name as its user and branches from a root-level directory called USERS. The following path specifies the user directory TSHELDON, which branches from the USER directory on the SYS volume of the MONA_LISA server:

    MONA_LISA\SYS:USERS\TSHELDON

User Restrictions

There are a number of restrictions that supervisors can place on a user's account. Restrictions are assigned in the NetWare Administrator or NETADMIN utility individually by user object, or by creating default settings that are used when any new user object is created.

ACCOUNT BALANCE RESTRICTIONS   You can restrict a user's access to the system and its resources by specifying a credit limit. A credit limit is a balance in an account that depletes as time and resources are used. Once depleted, the user can't log into the system until given more credit. See Chapter 31 for details.

EXPIRATION RESTRICTIONS   You can set an expiration date and time for a user account. The account is closed at the time specified. You might use this restriction for temporary employees.

PASSWORD RESTRICTIONS   The administrator or a supervisor can specify the length and uniqueness of login passwords. You can force users to change their passwords at regular intervals and to use passwords that they haven't used recently.

DISK SPACE RESTRICTIONS   Disk space restrictions prevent users from using too much of the server's disk space by loading unnecessary programs or files.

CONNECTION RESTRICTIONS   Connection restrictions can limit the number of stations a user can log into simultaneously.

TIME RESTRICTIONS   Time restrictions specify the hours, in half-hour blocks, that users can log into the system.

STATION RESTRICTIONS   Station restrictions prevent a user from logging in at any station other than the specified workstation. This prevents users from logging in at unsupervised workstations where their activities cannot be monitored.

Groups

Groups are collections of user objects. They make network management and electronic mail and message delivery easier. It is much easier for supervisors to assign login restrictions, trustee rights, and other properties to groups than it is to assign them to users on an individual basis. Group objects have names and can include users from many varied organizational units. For example, you could create a group that consists of managers at several remote sites and then use the group to address electronic mail to those managers.

When a new user object is added to a group, it acquires the rights set for the group. Therefore, it is best to create groups for users, projects, and management purposes early on and then simply add users to the groups as necessary.

Access Rights and Security

Access rights and security are vital in a network operating system. When security is managed correctly, corruption and loss of data by unauthorized users is prevented and privacy of data is maintained. The login restrictions discussed earlier are the first line of defense against unauthorized users. Access rights prevent logged-in users from snooping around in the file system and gaining access to sensitive files, such as those in payroll. Access rights also control who can use the various resources in the network.

When a user is granted access to a file, directory, or object, the user is a *trustee* of that file, directory, or object. NetWare access rights are grouped as shown in the following list:

- Object rights control who has access to system resource objects.

- Property rights control who can view and change the properties of objects.

- SMS rights control who has access to objects within the Storage Management System (SMS) applications.

- Directory rights control who has access to the directories in disk volumes and the files within them.

■ File rights provide control on a file-by-file basis over who has access to files within directories.

NOTE: *A complete list of rights can be found in Tables 21-1 through 21-4 in Chapter 21.*

Keep in mind the following information with regard to making users trustees of objects, directories, or files in the NetWare operating system:

■ You grant a user access rights to an object by selecting or specifying the object and then making the user a trustee of it. You do not select the user and then make the object a trustee of the user.

■ Users can grant access rights to directories and files if they have the Access Control right for the directories or files.

■ To grant object or property access rights, a user must have the Write right to the Access Control List (ACL) of the object. The ACL is like the trustee list for files and directories.

The Inherited Rights Filter

The Inherited Rights Filter (IRF) controls which rights users can inherit from parent directories and container objects. You can use the IRF to remove some or all of the rights a user inherited from the parent directory or object.

In the case of directories and subdirectories, if a user has certain rights in the parent directory, he or she also has those rights in the subdirectory. However, an IRF can be applied at the subdirectory level by the supervisor or directory owner to restrict the user's access in that subdirectory.

Effective Rights

A user's effective rights to a directory, file, or object are calculated based on the following parameters. By default, no rights are granted except in their personal directory and public directory.

■ The user's trustee assignments to the directory, file, or object

■ The user's trustee assignments to the parent directory or container object

- The user's trustee assignments in either of the previously listed parameters for groups that the user belongs to

- Security equivalents of the user

- The Inherited Rights Filter for the directory, file, or object

The File System

The NetWare file system consists of volumes that represent divisions of the disk storage system. Volumes are objects in the NDS directory, and they are at the highest (root) level in the NetWare disk directory structure. A NetWare server can support up to 64 volumes. The first volume is always called SYS and holds the directory structure shown in Figure 3-10.

- *SYSTEM* holds the NetWare commands and files used by the system administrator or a supervisor.

- *PUBLIC* holds NetWare files that are accessible by all NetWare users.

- *LOGIN* is the directory users access when they need to log into the system. This directory is mapped to the first available network drive letter.

- *MAIL* is a remnant of previous NetWare versions. It has been retained in NetWare v.4 for some applications that require it.

Volumes are mounted when the NetWare server is booted. The SYS volume is mounted automatically; other volumes are mounted by using commands in the

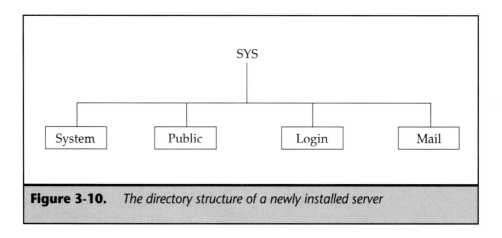

Figure 3-10.   *The directory structure of a newly installed server*

server startup file AUTOEXEC.NCF. You can also mount or dismount volumes by using the MOUNT or DISMOUNT commands at the NetWare server console. It is beneficial to leave unused or little used volumes unmounted because each volume uses anywhere from .5MB to 2MB of memory, depending on the size and type of volume (DOS name space, UNIX name space, or Macintosh name space).

You can expand volumes by adding hard disks to the system and using the NetWare Install utility to integrate the disks with existing volumes, in some cases without downing the server. Volumes are divided physically into segments that can span one or more hard disks. A volume can have up to 32 volume segments that span different disks, but each disk can hold only 8 volume segments. Spreading volume segments to different disks improves performance because it allows volume segments to be read or written simultaneously. The down side is that if one of the disks goes down, the entire volume will not mount. It is recommended that you always mirror segmented volumes.

NetWare Directories

You refer to directories on NetWare volumes in the same way you refer to DOS directories: by using paths. You add the volume name to a path to refer to another volume, and you add the server name to refer to servers. For example, the full name of the SYSTEM directory on the SYS volume is SYS:SYSTEM. If this directory had a subdirectory called UTILS, its full name would be SYS:SYSTEM\UTILS. You don't need to specify the volume name if you are already working on the volume. If this directory is on a server called ACCTG, you would refer to it as ACCTG\SYS:SYSTEM\UTILS.

The NetWare MAP command helps simplify the NetWare directory naming scheme by letting you refer to directories with drive letters. MAP is similar to the DOS SUBST command. For example, you could map the directory SYS:PUBLIC\APPS\LOTUS\DATA to the drive letter *R*. Then when you needed to switch to the directory, you would simply type **R:** and press ENTER. MAP is also used to create search paths to executable files, similar to the way the DOS PATH command is used. In most cases, MAP commands are inserted in the login scripts that execute when users log in. In this way, all the paths and drives they need to access are mapped for them.

NOTE: Before a user can access a directory, he or she must have access rights to the directory.

You add new directories with the NetWare Filer utility or with the DOS MD (make directory) command. You can also use the DOS CD (change directory) and RD (remove directory) commands with NetWare.

It is recommended that you separate application files from data files by creating a directory tree or volume for applications and another for data files. This prevents overwrites and helps you more easily manage rights. It also makes backup easier by separating the process of backing up data files from the backup of application files. Consider that data files are continually changed, whereas application files usually stay the same. If the two types of files are separated, you can, for example, perform daily backups on data and weekly backups on application files to save time and expense.

Users often need space on the hard drive for their personal files and programs. Most NetWare supervisors create home directories for users that branch from a parent directory called SYS:HOME or SYS:USERS. (Note that the parent directory doesn't need to be on the SYS volume.)

Printing Under NetWare

Users don't always have the type or quality of printer they need to print documents. Networks allow printer sharing so that expensive laser printers can be made available to everyone. These printers can be attached to the file server, a special print server, or individual users' workstations (and shared). Print server software manages the printers on the network. Users send print jobs to print queues, and the print server distributes those jobs to the appropriate printers.

Print queues hold print jobs sent to printers by network users. If several printers are assigned to one queue, the first available printer takes the job. Alternatively, several queues might be assigned to one printer. Each of these queues could have a different set of users or printing priorities assigned to it. Queues have names and descriptions, so users can select queues based on the types of service they provide. For example, a user who needs to print a job on the laser printer in the next office would choose that queue. Alternatively, a manager could print documents on printers at several remote locations (over wide area connections) by sending print jobs to the queues for those printers.

To install NetWare printing services, you install print server support in a NetWare file server. You can also dedicate a workstation as a print server by installing PSERVER.EXE on that workstation. After installing the print server, you create the queues to which users send print jobs. You then assign printers to those queues. The print server tracks all the queues and printers that have been assigned to network printing. To make a workstation printer available to other users on the network, you run the RPRINTER.EXE utility at that workstation.

NetWare v.4 supports access to printers on other print servers of an internetwork, as well as AppleTalk printers and UNIX printers.

CHAPTER 4

T his chapter presents an overview of the new features in NetWare v.4 and of the commands available for administrators, supervisors, and users. New features are covered first.

Commands and New Features in NetWare v.4

New Features in NetWare v.4

This section is beneficial for those who are familiar with NetWare 386. It presents a listing of the new features in NetWare v.4 and a comparison of old and new commands.

NetWare Directory Services (NDS)

NetWare Directory Services (NDS) is covered extensively in Chapter 3. NDS provides important new features that simplify internetwork management. NDS organizes local and remote users and resources into a hierarchical tree structure, which makes them easy to manage.

NetWare's management utilities and procedures have changed extensively because of NDS. Although user, group, trustee, and rights concepts are similar to those in previous versions of NetWare, the methods for implementing them are somewhat different. Users of previous NetWare versions should review the commands and procedures described later in this chapter to familiarize themselves with the changes.

The Windows-based NetWare Administrator is a graphical utility supplied with NetWare that network administrators can use to create and manage user and resource objects. A text-based version of NetWare Administrator called NETADMIN is available for those who don't have a Windows or OS/2 workstation.

Memory Allocation and Protection

NetWare v.4, unlike previous versions of NetWare, has one memory allocation pool. Memory is allocated among resources to optimize performance and ensure that memory is available to other NetWare Loadable Modules (NLMs) when a running NLM closes. In previous versions of NetWare, program modules could run out of memory, because memory was not always released back to the operating system.

Memory resources are structured in NetWare v.4 to ensure that different processes running on the server do not use the same memory. A number of 4KB memory pages are assigned to domains. NLMs are then loaded into the domains. Segments are created within domains for code and data, and a descriptor is assigned to each domain to protect the NLM running in it.

The operating system must also be protected from errant NLMs that might write to memory they do not own and consequently crash the server. To protect the operating system, privilege levels (also called protection rings) are used. There are four privilege levels, labeled 0 through 3, and the NetWare operating system runs in levels 0 and 3. If you suspect that an NLM is buggy and might crash the system, you can run it in level 3, which is a level that provides protection for the operating system. If an NLM tests successfully after a period of testing, you can move it to level 0.

International Support

NetWare v.4 provides support for languages other than English. English is the default language, but you can change the language for the server and for NetWare Loadable Modules. Support files for languages are stored in subdirectories that branch from the SYS:\SYSTEM\NLS directory or SYS:\PUBLIC\NLS directory. To specify the language that the server will use, you create a file called SERVER.MSG that contains an appropriate language-specifying command. This file is stored in the DOS directory you use to start the server and where SERVER.EXE is stored. To specify the language that NLMs use, you type the LANGUAGE console command at the server. After the language is specified, utilities started by users load using that language.

Security Features

NetWare v.4 provides enhanced security features. NetWare Directory Services allows users to log in once at any server on the network and have access to services over the entire network, based on their rights.

The Authentication feature verifies that users are authorized to use the network. It works in conjunction with the Access Control List, which contains information about objects. Users are not aware of authentication; it works in the background. Authentication assigns a unique identification to each user for each login session. The identification, not the user's password, is used to authenticate each of the user's network requests. Security is enhanced because the user's password is never transmitted across the network where it could be monitored. If the authentication data is monitored, intruders cannot use it to log in themselves, because it is not related to the login password.

Authentication guarantees that a user's password never goes beyond the login process. It is immediately converted to a different code that identifies the user and the station they are logged into during the user's current session.

Authentication also guarantees that messages are from the correct user at his or her workstation in the current session and not corrupted, counterfeited, or tampered with. The only way an intruder could access the objects and resources assigned to a user is to club the user over the head.

Optical Disk Jukebox and Tape Storage Support

NetWare v.4's High Capacity Storage System (HCSS) provides the ability to integrate libraries of optical disks or tapes into the NetWare filing system. Optical disk jukeboxes use autochanger techniques to mount and dismount optical disks, based on user needs. Users see files on jukeboxes as they see any other network files. When a user requests a file that is stored on an optical disk, the file is moved from the optical disk to faster hard disk storage. Files that are no longer needed are moved back to optical storage.

Moving files from the hard disk to an optical disk is known as *migration*. Moving the files back to the hard disk is called *de-migration*. Migrated files retain their original path names so that users can access them without knowing they are from the jukebox. When a user requests a migrated file, that file is de-migrated to the faster file server disk. Administrators and supervisors can mark specific files as migratable. After a period of nonuse, files marked as migratable are moved to optical or tape storage to free up space on the hard disk volume.

The HCSS is designed for archiving seldom used files. It is useful in image processing applications, which store graphics images of invoices, legal documents, contracts, and other documents online for quick referral, as discussed next.

Imaging System Support

Imaging systems are used to manage paper documents such as credit card applications, legal and insurance documents, bids, proposals, contracts, and other documents by allowing those documents to be imaged and stored on special archive storage systems such as optical disks. Imaging systems are the digital equivalents of microfilm storage-and-retrieval systems. Novell is working with Eastman Kodak in the development of imaging services for NetWare. In addition, Lotus and Kodak are working on an image-enabled version of Lotus' Notes information management software.

High-speed networks provide an ideal platform for imaging systems because they make imaged documents available to a large number of users. Workstations increasingly have high-resolution displays and sufficient memory to handle imaged documents.

Consider the benefits of archiving invoice images on an optical disk jukebox. If a customer wants to see a record of past purchases, the invoices are retrieved from the archive and printed on a local printer. In a paper system, old documents are retrieved from the back-office filing system or, in some cases, requested from an off-site storage area. Optical disks store large amounts of data for quick online retrieval at a relatively low price. With WAN links, users at remote offices can retrieve document images that would normally not be available to them.

Imaging services are installed at the NetWare server as a NetWare Loadable Module. These services provide for the compression, storage, and manipulation of imaged documents, as well as the transmission of those documents over the network.

New Graphical Utilities

In NetWare v.4 new Windows- or OS/2-based text utilities can be used instead of command-line utilities. A complete list of alternative commands is discussed later in this chapter in "NetWare v.3.11 Command and Feature Comparison." The Windows-based NetWare Administrator, for example, offers a new way to manage the network, its users, and its objects. NetWare Administrator does the work of almost all the command-line utilities, so if you run Windows (or OS/2), you can take advantage of its consolidated features. Refer to Chapter 3 for a discussion of the NetWare Administrator.

Changes in the File System

The NetWare file system has changed slightly. Its new features are listed in the following sections.

Block Suballocation

In previous versions of NetWare, a full block was used to store a file even if the file was much smaller than the configured block size. Block suballocation allows the last part of several files to share a disk block, thus increasing the amount of information that can be stored on a disk. Suballocation units are 512 bytes in size. Leftover fragments from other files can share these blocks.

File Compression

File compression lets you store more data on the file server hard disk by compressing the data. The compression ratio in a volume is approximately 63 percent. You can enable file compression during NetWare installation, or you can run the INSTALL utility at any time. Compression is handled in the background and has little impact on system performance. Before compressing a file, the operating system determines whether any disk sectors will be saved by doing so. Some files do not compress well. The original file is maintained on the server until a second file is successfully compressed to ensure that the file is not corrupted should the server go down.

New File and Directory Attributes

Several new file and directory attributes have been added to support the High Capacity Storage System. In addition, the old Write Audit and Read Audit attributes have been removed. The new attributes are listed here:

Letter	Attribute	Description
C	Can't Compress	A status attribute that indicates that a file cannot be compressed due to lack of disk space. Not used for directories
C	Compressed	A status attribute that indicates that a file has been compressed. Not used for directories
Dc	Don't Compress	Prevents the compression of a file. When applied to a directory, prevents the compression of all files in the directory
Dm	Don't Migrate	Prevents a file from being migrated to a secondary storage device such as an optical disk jukebox. When applied to a directory, prevents all files in the directory from being migrated
Im	Immediate Compress	When applied to a file, the file is compressed as soon as possible. When applied to a directory, the files in the directory are compressed as soon as possible
M	Migrated	A status attribute that indicates that a file has been migrated to a secondary storage device such as an optical disk jukebox

NetWare v.3.11 Command and Feature Comparison

This section discusses some of the specific changes made to NetWare v.3.11 commands and utilites in NetWare v.4.

The utilities in Table 4-1 have been removed because their functions are no longer necessary or are now handled by the NetWare Administrator or NETADMIN utility.

Table 4-2 lists the groups of NetWare v.3.11 utilities that have been consolidated into NetWare v.4 utilities. The NetWare v.3.11 utilities are listed on the left, and the updated NetWare v.4 utilities are listed on the right.

Table 4-3 lists the NetWare v.3.11 utilities that are no longer available and the new utilities that replace them.

The following paragraphs describe the new commands in NetWare v.4. Commands that are executed at the file server console are noted as such.

ABORT REMIRROR   A server console command. It disables the mirroring of a logical partition on server hard drives.

AUDITCON   A workstation auditing utility for examining network transactions to ensure that network records are accurate and secure.

ACONSOLE	ALLOW	ATOTAL	ATTACH
BINDFIX	BINDREST	CASTOFF	CASTON
CHKDIR	CHKVOL	DOSGEN	DSPACE
ECONFIG	EMSNETx	ENDCAP	FCONSOLE
FLAGDIR	GRANT	HELP	IPX
JUMPERS	LISTDIR	MAKEUSER	MENU
NBACKUP	PAUDIT	PURGE	REMOVE
REVOKE	ROUTE	SALVAGE	SECURITY
SESSION	SLIST	SMODE	SYSCON
TLIST	UPGRADE	USERDEF	USERLIST
VOLINFO	WSGEN	XMSNETx	

Table 4-1.   *Commands That Have Been Removed from or Replaced in NetWare v.4*

NetWare v.3.11 Utilities	NetWare v.4 Utility
ALLOW, GRANT, REMOVE, REVOKE, RIGHTS, TLIST	RIGHTS
CASTON, CASTOFF, SEND	SEND
ATTACH, MAP	MAP
CHKDIR, CHKVOL, VOLINFO	VOLINFO
NDIR, LISTDIR	NDIR
FLAG, FLAGDIR, SMODE	FLAG
FILER, SALVAGE, PURGE	FILER
SLIST, USERLIST	LIST
NVER, WHOAMI	WHOAMI

Table 4-2.   *Consolidated NetWare v.3.11 Utilities*

NetWare v.3.11 Utility	NetWare v.4 Replacement Utility
FCONSOLE	MONITOR.NLM
SYSCON	NETADMIN
NETCON	Replacement not necessary
BINDFIX	Replacement not necessary
BINDREST	Replacement not necessary
SESSION	USERTOOLS
NWSETUP	NETADMIN
DSPACE	Object Manager

Table 4-3.   *Replaced NetWare v.3.11 Utilities*

CX   Used to view or change the current context within the NDS tree.

DOMAIN   A server console command. It creates a protected operating system domain for running modules in ring number 1, 2, or 3.

DSREPAIR   A server console command. It fixes problems in the NDS information database.

LANGUAGE   A server console command. It specifies the language standard that subsequently loaded NLMs will use.

LIST DEVICE   A server console command. It displays device information about the server.

MAGAZINE   A server console command. It is used to confirm that magazine requests from the server have or have not been satisfied.

MEDIA   A server console command. It is used to confirm that media requests from the server have or have not been satisfied.

NETADMIN   A text-based menu utility for managing objects, properties, and rights.

NLIST   Displays information about users and groups, volumes and servers, and print queues.

NMENU   The new menu system in NetWare v.4. Replaces MENU in previous versions of NetWare.

NSWNUT   A server console command. It is an NLM Utility User Interface that provides library routines and functions for some NLMs.

PARTMGR   The Partition Manager used to create and manage partitions in the NDS tree structure.

REMIRROR PARTITION   A server console command. It mirrors a partition that was disabled by using ABORT REMIRROR.

RPL (Remote Program Load)   A server console command. It installs the RPL protocol stack, which enables remote booting of PC diskless workstations.

SCAN FOR NEW DEVICES   A server console command. It displays a list of disk hardware that has been added since the server was booted.

SERVMAN   A server console command. It is a menu utility used to view and configure NetWare operating system parameters such as the SPX/IPX configuration. You can also view adapter, device, disk, volume, and server information.

Printing Utility Updates

Like NetWare v.3.11, NetWare v.4 uses the PSERVER.NLM (server-based) and PSERVER.EXE (workstation-based) utilities to establish print servers. However, PSERVER has been enhanced for use with NetWare Directory Services. The changes are listed here:

- Printers can easily be selected as objects.
- If a primary printer fails, print jobs are redirected to a secondary printer.
- Third-party configuration files are supported.
- You can configure queue polling time.
- Macintosh and NFS (Network File System) users can access printers.
- Up to 256 printers can be accessed, compared to 16 in NetWare v.3.11.

Backup Utility Updates

The NBACKUP.EXE utility in NetWare v.3.11 is replaced and the SBACKUP.NLM utility is upgraded in NetWare v.4. SBACKUP.NLM takes advantage of NetWare Directory Services and now handles backup requests anywhere on the network.
The Storage Management (SMS) system supports the following name spaces:

MS-DOS
FTAM
Macintosh
NFS
OS/2

SMS supports 1/4-inch, 4mm tape media (Digital Data Storage certified tapes only) and 8mm tape media. Multimedia devices such as stackers and magazines are not supported as backup devices. The network adminstrator can designate backup supervisors, who in turn can designate backup operators, to assist in backup operations.

Bindery Support

NetWare v.4 no longer uses a server-specific bindery as did previous versions of NetWare. However, NetWare v.4 is compatible with bindery-based versions of NetWare, such as NetWare v.3.11. The NetWare Directory Services system provides bindery emulation. The differences between bindery-based versions of NetWare and NetWare v.4, which is NDS-based, are described here:

- *Users* A NetWare bindery-based system creates an account on each server, whereas the NetWare v.4 NDS system creates a global account used over the entire network. Under a bindery system, users must log in at each server to access its resources. Under NDS, users log in once to access resources anywhere on the network where they have been granted rights.

- *Groups* As with users, groups are created server by server in a bindery-based system, but are global under NDS.

- *Login* On a bindery system, users must log into each server. Under NDS, users log in once to access the entire network.

- *Printing* On a bindery system, printers are difficult to access. Under NDS, printers anywhere on the network can be selected from a graphical list.

- *Volumes* On a bindery system, users access volumes only on servers they are logged into. Under NDS, users access volumes as objects anywhere on the network.

NOTE: During an upgrade from NetWare v.3.11 to NetWare v.4, bindery objects are converted to objects in the NDS tree. You can change their status after the upgrade.

Upgrading to NetWare v.4

If you are upgrading from a previous version of NetWare to NetWare v.4, there are a few things you need to consider. If you are upgrading from NetWare v.2.1*x*, you'll need to upgrade to NetWare v.3.11 and then perform an upgrade to

NetWare v.4. If NetWare v.2.1x is running on an 80286 server, you'll need to upgrade the server to an 80386 or better machine. NetWare v.4 comes with an UPGRADE floppy disk that contains a special version of SERVER.EXE to handle the upgrade task.

Keep in mind that you might need to obtain new drivers from the manufacturer for the hard disk and LAN cards in the server you are upgrading. Many drivers written for previous versions of NetWare don't work with NetWare v.4; however, NetWare v.4 does come with a large set of drivers to support the most popular LAN and disk adapters.

NetWare v.4 Text Utilities

This section lists the text utilities you can execute at the command prompt in NetWare v.4. The utilities are grouped according to what they do or how you would use them.

Administrative Utilities

The NetWare v.4 administrative utilities are described in the following paragraphs.

AUDITCON   New in v.4. This utility is used by the system auditor to audit the NDS directory tree system. An auditor examines network transactions to ensure that network records are accurate and secure.

NETADMIN   New in v.4. This command is used to manage objects, properties, and rights. It is a menu utility that makes it easy for administrators and supervisors to manage the NetWare Directory Services and users.

NLIST   New in v.4. It displays information about users and groups, volumes and servers, and print queues. You can use NLIST, for example, to list users based on their properties, such as their names and groups. You can also list information about servers, volumes, printers, queues, and other NDS objects.

NVER   This command displays version information about the network and its attached servers.

RCONSOLE   This command allows you to access the NetWare server console from the workstation where the command is executed. Use REMOTE.NLM to install support for a remote console at the server.

SET TTS   This command sets logical and physical record locks for applications. A record lock prevents simultaneous access to the same record in a shared file.

SYSTIME   This command synchronizes a workstation's time with that of the default server or with a specified server.

WSUPDATE   This command searches for outdated shell, utility, and application files on network workstations and updates them.

File Management Utilities

The NetWare v.4 file management utilities are discussed in the next paragraphs.

FILER   This is a text-based utility for managing files and directories. At the Filer main menu, you can choose to do one of the following:

- Modify, add, delete, or view files

- Change the current directory or server

- Modify, add, delete, or view directories and subdirectories

- Modify the rights for files and directories. These rights are listed in Chapter 3, in Tables 3-1 and 3-2

- Modify file attributes, which are listed in Table 3-5

- Modify or view volume information

- Retrieve deleted, unpurged files or permanently remove files

FLAG   This command allows you to view and modify file and directory owners or file attributes. You can also view the search mode of executable files. On the command line, you can apply file attributes to directories or files. (File attributes are listed in Table 3-5.)

NCOPY   You use this command to copy files or directories from one location to another.

NDIR   This command displays information about files, directories, and volumes. NDIR can show file creation and modification dates, inherited and effective rights filters, file attributes, and other information. You can also use it to search for files and sort listings.

RENDIR   You use this command to rename directories.

NetWare Directory Services Management Utilities

The following paragraphs cover the NetWare Directory Services management utilities.

CX   New in v.4. It allows you to view or change the current context. Some tasks require that you specify your location in the NDS tree. The CX command is like the DOS CD (change directory) command in that you use it to move up or down the NDS tree structure, or to view the current context.

PARTMGR   New in v.4. This is the Partition Management utility. You use it to create and manage partitions in the NDS tree structure. A menu appears that lets you split or merge a partition, or add, delete, and modify replicas.

NETWARE ADMINISTRATOR   This is the Windows- or OS/2-based network administration program used to manage NetWare Directory Services. It also provides directory and file management features.

NETADMIN   This is the text-based version of NetWare Administrator. It does not provide file management features. Use FILER for file management.

Printing Utilities

The following paragraphs discuss the NetWare v.4 printing utilities.

NPRINT   You use the NPRINT command to print a file to a network printer. You can also use it to print screen displays and save data to network files.

PSC   This command is an alternative to PCONSOLE for controlling print servers and network printers. It is command-line-based and can be used more quickly than the PCONSOLE command.

PSETUP   You use this text utility to set up a print server, printer, and print queue.

RPRINTER.EXE   You use this utility to share a workstation-attached printer on the network.

PRINTCON   This command defines print job configuration by using the printers defined with PRINTDEF.

PRINTDEF   You use this command to define a printer and specify its special control codes.

CAPTURE   You use this command to print to a network printer from an application that doesn't support network printing. The command is usually placed in the login script to enable the printing commands whenever a user logs in.

PCONSOLE   You use this command to set up print servers and to control and view information about network printing.

User and Session Utilities

The NetWare v.4 user and session utilities are covered in the following paragraphs.

LOGIN   Users type this command to log into the network.

LOGOUT   Users type this command to log out of the network.

MAP   You use this command to create or change drive mappings. A drive mapping lets you refer to a directory more easily by shortening its path name to a single drive letter. The MAP command is similar to the DOS SUBST command.

RIGHTS   You use this command to view or modify the rights that users and groups have to files, directories, and volumes.

SEND   You use this command to send messages or to set how your machine receives messages. You can receive all messages, only system messages, or no messages.

SETPASS   You use this command to change your password.

WHOAMI   This command displays information about your current connection to the network, such as your security equivalents, group memberships, effective rights, and users or groups supervised.

CHAPTER 5

T his chapter covers products that are available from Novell as add-ons for NetWare. A brief description is provided for each product. You'll find a more complete description, including specifications, hardware and software requirements, and compatibility listings, in the *NetWare Buyer's Guide.* Contact Novell at 1-800-NETWARE to order this guide.

Other Products and Add-ons

NOTE: Products and features listed in this chapter are subject to change. Call Novell at 1-800-NETWARE for more information.

Workstation and Interoperability Products

The following Novell software products connect workstations to NetWare file servers or support alternate operating systems.

DR DOS

Novell purchased Digital Research in 1991 and acquired its DR DOS operating system, which is a DOS-compatible workstation operating system. DR DOS version 6.0 offers many advanced features that give it an edge over Microsoft's MS-DOS version 5.0. No doubt, Microsoft and Novell will upgrade their products further and maintain a heated battle over workstation operating systems.

Some of DR DOS's features are listed here:

- Includes MemoryMAX, a utility that optimizes memory by allowing the operating system kernel and various utilities and drivers to load into upper memory. This frees conventional memory for DOS applications

- Includes SuperStor, a disk compression utility that can double the data capacity of a hard drive. Its operation is transparent to the user

- Includes DISKOPT, a disk defragmenting utility that optimizes the performance of a hard disk by gathering the sections of each fragmented file and storing them together, as contiguous files

- Includes TaskMAX, a task-switching utility that allows up to 20 applications to load simultaneously. The utility doesn't multitask applications, but it does allow the user to easily switch among them and perform cut and paste operations

- Includes the NetWare shells for convenience

- Includes password protection so that users can require a password to be entered when the workstation boots and for access to directories and files

DR DOS runs on any DOS-compatible PC. To get the most benefits from the MemoryMAX utility, an 80386 or better system with 1MB of memory is recommended.

LAN WorkPlace Products

The LAN WorkPlace products allow DOS, Windows, OS/2, and Macintosh users to directly access resources that require TCP/IP access, such as UNIX systems, Digital Equipment Corp. VASs and VAXs, and IBM mainframes. There are three LAN WorkPlace products:

- *LAN WorkPlace for DOS* Uses Open Data-Link Interface (ODI) technology to provide IPX/SPX and TCP/IP support on Ethernet, Token Ring, and ArcNet adapters.

- *LAN WorkPlace for OS/2* Provides OS/2 users with direct access to Apple Macintosh computers, UNIX systems, VAXs, IBM mainframes, and other systems. Multiple concurrent sessions are possible because of OS/2's multitasking capabilities. This product also allows simultaneous communications to NetWare servers.

- *LAN WorkPlace for Macintosh* Allows Apple Macintosh users to access resources on TCP/IP networks. LAN WorkPlace for Macintosh includes TCPort transport system software, HostAccess network communications utilities, and the NetStat desk accessory, which displays network statistics. Up to eight sessions can be active at once. It supports LocalTalk or EtherTalk connections to TCP/IP and NetWare networks.

With these products, NetWare users can use applications running on UNIX-based systems or other systems that use TCP/IP transport protocols. The TCP/IP-compatible host system can be on the same LAN segment as the user or on a different LAN segment that is connected with a multiprotocol router.

NetWare for Macintosh

NetWare for Macintosh allows Apple Macintosh computers to connect to the NetWare file server and become part of the network. NetWare for Macintosh is client-server software that provides NetWare file, print, routing, and administrative functions. Users can take advantage of the fault tolerance, resource accounting, enhanced security, and other features available on NetWare servers.

NOTE: A five-user version of NetWare for Macintosh is available to reduce costs for networks with only a few Macintosh users.

NetWare for Macintosh uses the AppleTalk Filing Protocol (AFP), which allows Macintosh applications to run on a NetWare server. It supports AppleTalk Phase I and Phase II internetwork routing, so users can send AppleTalk data packets on most types of networks, including LocalTalk, ArcNet, Ethernet, and Token Ring networks. NetWare for Macintosh includes the following features:

- Files appear as familiar icons

- Printers on Macintosh AppleTalk networks can be shared by all network users, or NetWare printers can be used by Macintosh users

- Supervisors can manage network resources from a Macintosh

NetWare Network Filing System (NFS)

NetWare Network Filing System (NFS) is a distributed file system for UNIX environments. NetWare NFS gives UNIX users access to the NetWare environment from their systems. NetWare NFS is installed on the NetWare server, making files, printers, and other network resources shareable by UNIX users. The TCP/IP communications transport protocols are required to support NetWare NFS. See Chapter 10 for more details.

NetWare FTAM

FTAM (File Transfer Access and Management) is the OSI communications standard for transferring files among different types of computer systems. NetWare FTAM allows a wide variety of OSI FTAM clients to access the NetWare file server and enables NetWare DOS workstation users to attach to OSI networks and communicate with FTAM hosts on the network. The package includes OSI FTAM *server* (responder) and *client* (initiator) software, and it is fully compliant with U.S. Government OSI Protocols (GOSIP). When used in conjunction with X.400 mail gateways, NetWare FTAM satisfies the basic profile and service requirements of GOSIP 1.0.

NetWare FTAM is a set of NLMs that run on the NetWare server. An FTAM executable program runs on the DOS NetWare FTAM client workstation, allowing DOS workstations to communicate with OSI FTAM hosts attached to the network. Alternatively, OSI FTAM workstations can send files to and receive files from the NetWare FTAM server's disk, and can send files to NetWare print queues.

Wide Area Network and Internetwork Products

Novell offers several Wide Area Network and internetwork products that give users transparent access to file servers, printers, and mail systems across different types of networks.

NetWare WAN Links

NetWare WAN Links expands NetWare's enterprise networking capabilities by enabling the routing of IPX, TCP/IP, AppleTalk, and OSI network traffic across X.25-based public networks or private networks that are based on leased lines. The product can be installed on a NetWare file server if the Wide Area Network traffic is light, or on a dedicated NetWare MultiProtocol Router system (see the next section) if the traffic is heavy.

NetWare WAN Links combines existing Novell products such as Link/64 and Link/T1, which provide 9600 bit/sec to 64 Kb/sec (kilobits per second) or 9600 bit/sec to 2.084 Mb/sec speeds, respectively, on DSU/CSU, PBX, T1 multiplexers, modems, and modem eliminators. WAN Links is covered further in Chapter 9 and Chapter 19.

NetWare MultiProtocol Router

NetWare MultiProtocol Router is a software product that converts an 80386 or better system into a multiprotocol router, thus relieving the NetWare file server of routing tasks. The router supports OSI, IPX, IP, Novell NetBIOS, and AppleTalk protocols so that users can connect Ethernet, Token Ring, LocalTalk, and ArcNet networks together and route traffic from NetWare workstations, Apple Macintoshes, UNIX systems, and OSI systems. Off-loading routing tasks from the NetWare file server can improve its performance. In addition, the router can provide services even if the file server or servers are not running. Refer to Chapter 9 and Chapter 19 for more information.

Communications Products

The products covered in this section are used to connect NetWare LAN users to remote systems, or to allow remote users to connect to the local LAN.

NetWare Asynchronous Communications Services (NACS) is an NLM that you load on the server. It allows up to 32 users to share a pool of modems, ports to minicomputers, or X.25 Wide Area Network services, as illustrated in Figure 5-1. NACS is accessed from anywhere on the network. On a 386 system, performance seriously degrades with over 6 sessions. It's possible to improve performance by

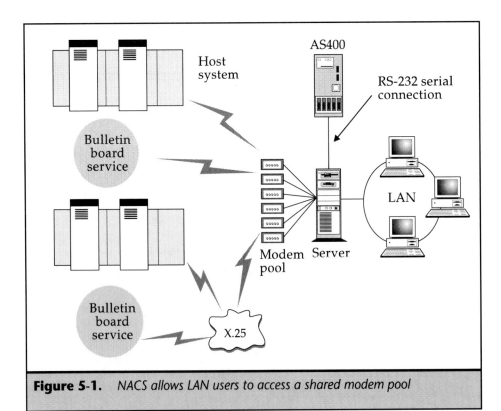

Figure 5-1.   *NACS allows LAN users to access a shared modem pool*

installing faster systems (Intel 80486-based) and specialized serial ports that can handle communications tasks with minimal assistance from the systems processor.

NetWare Access Server (NAS)

The NetWare Access Server (NAS) software enables up to 16 remote DOS, Macintosh, and ASCII workstations to dial into a NetWare LAN, as shown in Figure 5-2. Remote workstations appear to network users to be part of the LAN. NetWare Access Server must be installed on a computer with an 80386 or better microprocessor. It uses the virtual machine capabilities of these microprocessors to create up to 16 "remote connection PCs." The alternative to NAS is to use up to 16 separate PCs.

When a user connects to the Access Server, he or she is allocated one of the virtual machines within the file server. This machine performs all the processing required by the user. Only screen displays and keyboard commands are sent over the remote connection, which makes the connection operate more efficiently.

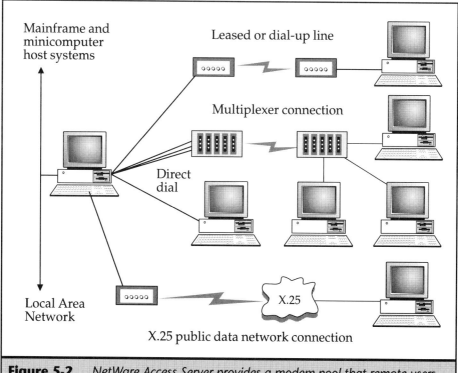

Figure 5-2. *NetWare Access Server provides a modem pool that remote users can dial in to and access the network*

IBM Connectivity Products

The following IBM host connectivity products are available for users on NetWare networks.

NetWare for SAA

NetWare for SAA gives NetWare workstations access to IBM mainframe and AS/400 host systems, as illustrated in Figure 5-3. The security, name services, and administration of NetWare are retained. Up to 506 display, printer, and APPC (Advanced Program-to-Program Communications) sessions are possible at once. Access to AS/400 applications is transparent to NetWare workstations.

NetWare for SAA is an NLM you install in the NetWare file server to provide gateway services to network users. It eliminates the need for a separate gateway to the IBM systems. Alternatively, the product can run in a dedicated

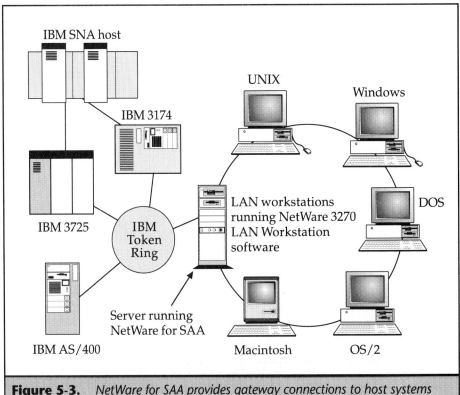

Figure 5-3.   *NetWare for SAA provides gateway connections to host systems*

communications server when the NetWare Runtime application is used. NetWare Runtime is bundled with NetWare for SAA. See Chapter 10 for more details.

Management Products

The following management products enable network administrators and supervisors to monitor the network and its performance, detect problems, and correct potential problems to avoid network downtime.

NetWare Hub Services

Hub cards are wiring centers that you install in the NetWare server to provide connections for NetWare LAN workstations. Typically, hub cards provide from 4 to 16 connection ports. A number of third-party vendors offer hub cards. NetWare Hub Services is used to monitor and manage network traffic on the hub ports. The Simple Network Management Protocol (SNMP) agent is provided so that remote management consoles can manage the hub.

Novell extended its Open Data-Link Interface (ODI) specification to include the Hub Management Interface (HMI) so that hub cards can communicate with the NetWare operating system. Hub cards provide a low-cost alternative to external concentrators because, with hub cards, the server itself is used as the chassis for the card.

NetWare Services Manager (Windows or OS/2 Versions)

NetWare Services Manager is a Windows- or OS/2-based network management application. The products are sold separately. It gives network administrators the tools they need to manage multivendor networks. Devices on the network are graphically displayed. Network problems are monitored and logged into a database, and supervisors are notified of them.

NetWare Services Manager accepts information from other third-party devices that monitor the network, integrating network management into one application. NetWare Services Manager is made up of two components:

- *Management workstation* This software runs under Microsoft Windows or OS/2 on a PC-compatible system.

- *Management agents* The agents reside on NetWare servers throughout the internetwork. They collect data for display on the management workstation. One agent comes with NetWare Services Manager, and additional agents can be purchased for other servers that need to be managed.

The graphical map on the management workstation lets users navigate through the network of IPX routers, client workstations, servers, and other objects. Multiple servers can be monitored from one location. Graphs and statistics are displayed for NetWare servers. Events are logged, and users are notified of priority events with alarms. The graphical display simplifies the management of network assets because all components of the network can be viewed and tracked. One of the biggest advantages that NetWare Services Manager provides is a reduction in downtime, because its continuous monitoring indicates problems in advance.

LANalyzer Network Analyzer

LANalyzer is an analysis and diagnostics tool for identifying and solving network problems. It is also useful for tuning network performance, as well as debugging protocols and applications. It includes a special adapter card and software that are installed in any network workstation that uses an 80286 or better processor. LANalyzer includes the Automated Troubleshooting System, which is a collection of tests designed to quickly troubleshoot network problems. LANalyzer kits are available for Ethernet and Token Ring networks. This product is covered further in Chapter 36.

LANtern Network Monitor

LANtern is a rack-mountable hardware device that helps network supervisors and service organizations centrally manage and maintain multivendor networks. It captures statistics and detects trends so that network performance and growth can be optimized. Network information is displayed on a central network management console.

The industry-standard SNMP (Simple Network Management Protocol) is used to communicate with the LANtern Services Manager software (discussed next), which runs on management workstations. LANtern can track all devices on an Ethernet network, regardless of the media used. Agents are not required in order to track devices.

LANtern can detect duplicate IP addresses, dead stations, cable failure, faulty transceivers or cabling, jabbering stations, or Ethernet topologies extended beyond the maximum workable length. Alerts appear at the remote console, based on alarm thresholds set by the administrator. LANtern allows network administrators to monitor the performance and growth of their networks. A smaller version of LANtern that monitors 32 stations on a single Ethernet segment is also available. It can be upgraded to the full LANtern.

THE
COMPLETE

REFERENCE

PART **TWO**

Network Connections

CHAPTER 6

Communi- cations Protocols

This chapter and the next few chapters discuss the computer hardware you need to connect networks at the local level (using network interface cards) and at the internetwork and wide-area level (using routers and various communications gear). It's impossible to discuss these interconnections without also discussing the underlying protocols, or rules of communications, used to get interconnected hardware talking.

A few years ago it looked as if most major computer and software manufacturers would conform to the International Organization for Standardization (ISO) specifications for Open Systems Interconnection (OSI). OSI defines how manufacturers can create products that work with other vendors' products without the need for special drivers or optional equipment. Its goal is "openness."

The only problem with implementing the ISO/OSI model was that many companies had already developed methods for interconnecting their hardware and software with other systems. Although vendors claimed future support for OSI standards, their own methods were often so entrenched that the move to OSI was slow or nonexistent. Novell and other networking companies expanded their own standards to provide support for other systems, and put openness on the back burner.

However, OSI standards do provide a useful way to compare internetworking and interoperability among vendors. In the OSI model, there are several layers of protocols in a *protocol stack*, each working at different levels in the hardware and software. You can examine what each layer in the stack does to see how systems communicate over LANs.

Protocol Stacks

The OSI model for interconnection, or protocol stack, is illustrated in Figure 6-1. A *protocol* is a defined way of communicating with another system. It specifies the

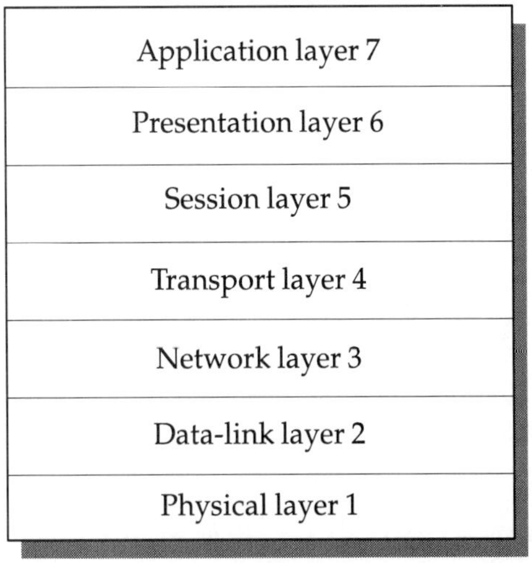

| Application layer 7 |
| Presentation layer 6 |
| Session layer 5 |
| Transport layer 4 |
| Network layer 3 |
| Data-link layer 2 |
| Physical layer 1 |

Figure 6-1. *The OSI protocol stack*

timing of signals and the structure of the communicated data. The lower layers in the protocol stack define the rules that vendors can follow to make their equipment interconnect with other vendors' equipment. The upper layers define how software interoperates. The higher you go in the stack, the more sophisticated the communications among software running on different systems becomes.

As previously mentioned, many vendors don't follow the OSI protocol stack exactly. They use other protocol stacks that closely resemble the OSI stack. (Refer ahead to Figure 6-4 for a comparison.) A product that uses one protocol stack cannot directly connect and interoperate with a product that uses another protocol stack. However, using various "repackaging" techniques and protocol conversions, it's possible to achieve certain levels of interoperability between them. Some of the major protocol stacks discussed in this chapter and later chapters are listed here:

- *OSI protocol stack*   The OSI protocol stack is defined by the International Organization for Standardization to promote worldwide interoperability. It is typically used as a standard to compare other protocol stacks.

- *NetWare SPX/IPX protocol*   The NetWare Sequenced Packet Exchange/Internetwork Packet Exchange (SPX/IPX) protocol is the native protocol used by Novell NetWare. It is derived from the Xerox Network Services (XNS) protocol stack.

- *TCP/IP protocol*   Transmission Control Protocol/Internet Protocol (TCP/IP) was one of the first network protocol stacks. It was originally implemented by the Department of Defense as a way to tie multivendor network products together. The IP portion provides one of the best definitions for internetwork connections available and is being used by many vendors as a way to interconnect products over local and wide areas.

- *AppleTalk protocols*   The AppleTalk protocols were defined by Apple Computer as a way to interconnect Apple Macintosh systems.

- *IBM/Microsoft protocols*   The IBM and Microsoft protocols for interconnectivity are often grouped because the two companies jointly developed products that use them, such as LAN Manager and OS/2.

Packets of Information

Before getting into a discussion of protocol stacks, it is important to understand how information is transferred across network media. Information is "packetized" into envelopes of data for transfer. Each envelope, often called a *packet* or *frame*, has an address and a description of the enclosed data. Each packet includes the following information:

- *Data, or the payload*   The information intended for transfer across the network, before any other information is added. The term *payload* is reminiscent of rocketry, and rocketry is an appropriate analogy to describe how data is "fired" from one location to another on the network.

- *Address*   The destination of the packet. There is an address for each network segment, which is only important on an internetwork that consists of multiple connected LANs. There are also a workstation address and an application address. The application address is required to identify which application in a workstation the packet belongs to.

- *Control codes*   Information describing the packet type and size. Control codes also include error checking codes and other information.

The OSI Protocol Stack

Each layer of the OSI protocol stack in Figure 6-1 has a specific purpose and defines a layer of communications among systems. When defining a network process, such as a file request from a server, you start at the top where the user makes the request. The request then passes down through the stack and is converted in each layer for transport over the network. Each layer adds its own tracking information to the packets, as shown in Figure 6-2. The flow of this data is illustrated in Figure 6-3.

The layers simply define the rules that applications, network drivers, and network hardware use to communicate over the network. Programmers work within the bounds of the rules to create various types of networking programs. Imagine that your company has defined a seven-step set of rules and procedures for managing the company. At the bottom are procedures that define what regular employees do. In the middle are rules and procedures for division or department managers. At the top are rules and procedures that the company president or CEO uses to oversee the entire company. As you move up the layers, rules become more sophisticated and encompassing.

Likewise, a protocol stack defines rules that programmers use to create network-aware applications. At the bottom are basic rules that define communications over hardware. A programmer working at this level designs drivers for network interface cards. In the middle are rules that define how networking hardware and software work together. Network software companies like Novell design application programming interfaces (APIs) that follow the rules of the middle layer. Programmers use APIs, which contain programming

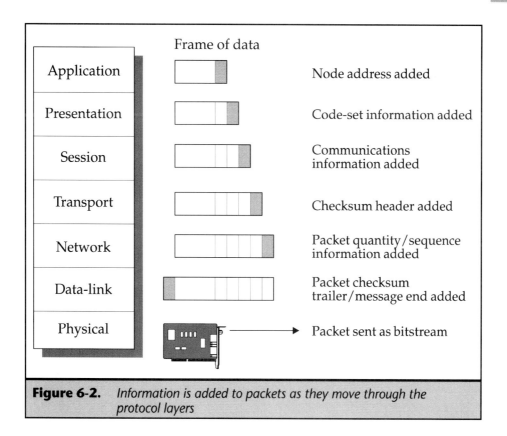

	Frame of data	
Application		Node address added
Presentation		Code-set information added
Session		Communications information added
Transport		Checksum header added
Network		Packet quantity/sequence information added
Data-link		Packet checksum trailer/message end added
Physical		Packet sent as bitstream

Figure 6-2. *Information is added to packets as they move through the protocol layers*

"hooks" and code modules, to simplify their programming tasks. At the top are network applications, like e-mail and groupware programs. They conform to higher-level networking protocols that define how applications on diverse network workstations communicate with one another.

The following sections describe network protocols. You must have the network hardware—the physical layer—in place before any of the other layers of communication can take place, so it is described first.

The Physical Layer

The physical layer defines the physical characteristics of the cable system. It encompasses all the networking methods available, including Token Ring, Ethernet, and ArcNet, which are discussed in Chapter 7. It also defines radio and

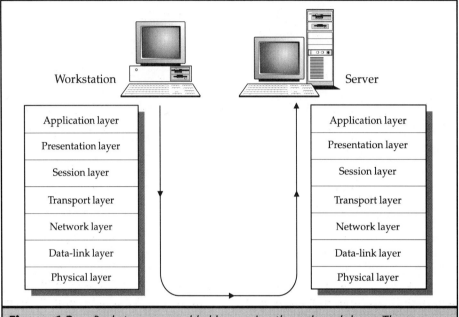

Figure 6-3.   *Packets are assembled by passing through each layer. They are then transported across the network and disassembled at the receiving station*

infrared communications, fiber-optics, and RS-232-C cable, which is used to connect modems to computers. The physical layer specifies the following:

■ Electrical and physical connections

■ How information that has been packetized (placed into envelopes or frames) is placed in a bit stream for transmission over the cable

■ How the network interface card gets access to that cable

NOTE: *The networking standards encompassed by the physical layer are defined by the Institute of Electrical and Electronics Engineers (IEEE), which is discussed in "Physical Layer Standards" later in this chapter.*

The Data-Link Layer

The data-link layer defines the rules for sending and receiving information across the physical connection between two systems; it assumes that the connection has already been established by the physical layer. The data-link layer controls a stream of packetized data. If the stream flows too quickly, the receiving station must indicate that it needs a pause to catch up. If a packet is corrupted or never received, the sending station must be told to send it again.

The data-link layer is divided into two sublayers. The MAC (Media Access Control) layer manages the transfer of packets to their destinations. The LLC (Logical Link Control) layer receives packets from upper layers and turns them over to the MAC layer.

The communications methods used depend on the type of network interface card in the network. A driver to control the card must be configured with the appropriate protocol stack to match the type of communications it will handle. Compatibility at this layer is not a problem as long as each system in a network uses the same type of network interface card.

The Network Layer

The network layer defines protocols for opening and maintaining a path on the network between systems. It is concerned with how data is moving. The network layer can look at the address of information to determine the best route for transferring it to the destination. This is important on internetworks that link many different LAN segments. If a packet is addressed to a workstation on the local network, it is sent directly there. If it's addressed to a network on another segment, the packet is sent to a routing device, which forwards it by using the best path through the routers. A packet may be sent through several routers before ending up at its destination. It's important to know the best route before sending the packet to avoid too many of these "hops."

When interconnecting networks, routing devices should be used to optimize packet delivery. Bridges are simpler devices that send packets without regard for the best route. Bridges operate at the data-link layer, and routers operate at the network layer. Novell NetWare IPX automatically provides network-layer routing services between two or more network cards that are installed in the server.

The Transport Layer

The transport layer provides the highest level of control in the process that actually moves data from one system to another. The transport layer provides quality service and accurate delivery by performing error detection and correction. The transport layer assigns packetized information a tracking number that is checked at the destination. If data is missing from the packet, the transport layer protocol at the receiving end arranges with the transport layer of the sending system to have packets re-sent. This layer ensures that all data is received and in the proper order. SPX (Sequenced Packet Exchange) is the NetWare protocol that works at the transport layer. A *virtual circuit*, which is something like a guaranteed phone connection, is established in this layer, between two systems. The two systems maintain communications of their own during the data transfer session.

The Session Layer

The session layer coordinates the exchange of information between systems. The layer gets its name from the communications session that it establishes and terminates. Coordination is required if one system is slower than another or if packet transfer is not orderly. The session layer adds information to the packet about which communications protocol to use and maintains the session until the transfer of information is complete.

The Presentation Layer

Protocols at the presentation layer are part of the operating system and application the user runs in a workstation. Information is formatted for display or printing in this layer. Codes within the data, such as tabs or special graphics sequences, are interpreted. Data encryption and the handling of other character sets is also handled in this layer.

The Application Layer

The network operating system and its applications make themselves available to users at the application layer. Users issue commands to request network services, and these commands are packetized and sent over the network through the lower protocol layers.

The Flow of Information

Figure 6-3 shows how data flows through the protocol stack and over the media from one system to another. Data starts at the application and presentation layers, where a user works with a network application, such as an electronic mail package or a distributed database. Requests for services are passed through the presentation layer to the session layer, which begins the process of packetizing the information and opening a communications session between the two systems. Once the session is established, each layer on one system basically communicates with the equivalent layer on the other system.

Routines at the transport layer prepare the packet for accurate transmission by adding information that helps in error detection and correction. This layer provides an interface between the application-level software and the networking hardware. One of several transport layer protocols, such as SPX or TCP (Transmission Control Protocol), may be selected at this point if the packet is going to a non-NetWare system. The transport layer adds tracking numbers and other information to the packet and sends it to the network layer.

Routines at the network layer plan the best route to the destination and add routing information to the packet. An internetwork protocol such as IPX or IP (Internet Protocol, the internetwork protocol for TCP) may be selected. The network layer sends the packet to the data-link layer, where it is prepared for transport across the network media. This layer also establishes a method for managing the stream of data across the connection.

Finally the packets are ready for transfer across the network. The network interface card gains access to the cable by using its built-in media access method—CSMA/CD (Carrier Sense Multiple Access/Collision Detection), token passing, or another method—and sends the packet as a bit stream across the cable. At the remote system, the process is reversed. This happens hundreds or thousands of times per second, depending on the number of packets it takes to send a request for service, a block of information, or a complete file.

Interconnectivity and Interoperability

Interconnectivity and *interoperability* are buzz words that refer to the art of getting multivendor hardware and applications to work together on a network. If your company uses only personal computers, you can create a network by simply adding a file server and the NetWare operating system, and then connecting them all together with network interface cards and cable. However, in a large corporation, several scenarios are likely:

■ Separate LANs, possibly using different media types, are already installed in different departments.

■ Users want to connect to a host mainframe system from their workstations.

■ A variety of systems are in use, including DOS-based systems, Macintoshes, Sun workstations, minicomputers, and mainframes.

Interoperability comes into play when you need to share files among computers with dissimilar operating systems, or manage those dissimilar systems from a central console. It's more than simply connecting hardware together on an internetwork. You must also provide the protocols that let the systems communicate with one another over the network cable. The native NetWare communications protocol is SPX/IPX. It is compared with OSI and other popular protocol stacks in Figure 6-4.

NOTE: TCP/IP has become extremely important in the internetworking of NetWare and in Novell's enterprise networking strategy. TCP/IP is more suited to internetworking than NetWare's native IPX protocol, so it's often used when you begin connecting networks together.

OSI	NetWare		UNIX				Apple				LAN Manager	
Application	Netware Core Protocol		Network Filing System (NFS)				Apple Share				Server message blocks	
Presentation							Apple Talk Filing Protocol (AFP)					
Session	Named Pipes	NetBIOS	SNMP	FTP	SMTP	Telnet	ASP	ADSP	ZIP	PAP	NetBIOS	Named Pipes
Transport	SPX		TCP				ATP	NBP	AEP	RTMP	NetBEUI	
Network	IPX		IP				Datagram Delivery Protocol (DDP)					
Data-link	LAN drivers		LAN drivers				LAN drivers				LAN drivers	
	ODI	NDIS	Media Access Control				Local-Talk	Ether-Talk	Token-Talk		NDIS	
Physical	Physical		Physical				Physical				Physical	

Figure 6-4. *A comparison of protocols*

Networks using different protocols cannot directly communicate. For example, it is not possible for an application running on a system that uses SPX/IPX to directly communicate with a system that uses TCP/IP.

However, *gateways* convert protocols at each layer so that workstation users can access the operating system features of a host system that uses a different protocol. The Novell NetWare for SAA and Novell 3270 LAN Workstation products provide gateways for DOS systems and Macintoshes into IBM host systems.

Multiprotocol routing gives NetWare Servers the ability to route (exchange) network traffic between dissimilar systems, as illustrated in Figure 6-5. Novell NetWare supports multiprotocol routing by using NetWare Loadable Modules (discussed shortly). If a user on a workstation needs to access the NetWare server, he or she uses an application that supports SPX/IPX. To access the UNIX workstation, he or she uses an application that supports TCP/IP. The NetWare server routes the TCP/IP packets to the UNIX system. Essentially it says, "These packets aren't for me, but I'll pass them on to the UNIX system."

Another scheme, often called *tunneling*, allows IPX (NetWare) packets to be transferred over a TCP/IP network by encapsulating the IPX packets in TCP/IP packets. Think of the IPX packets hitching a ride on the TCP/IP packets to get to an IPX network on the other side of the TCP/IP network, as shown in Figure 6-6.

Figure 6-7 shows how multiple protocols are handled at the workstation. The Open Data-Link Interface (ODI) handles two different protocol stacks simultaneously, sending both packet types through the same network interface card and over the network media. At the server, both protocols are recognized and routed

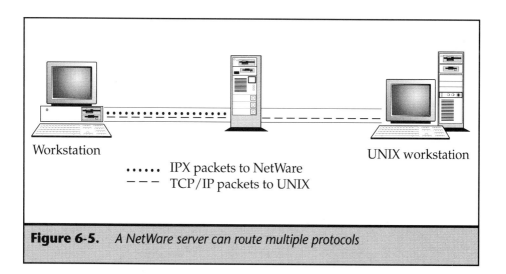

Workstation   UNIX workstation

•••••• IPX packets to NetWare
– – – TCP/IP packets to UNIX

Figure 6-5.   *A NetWare server can route multiple protocols*

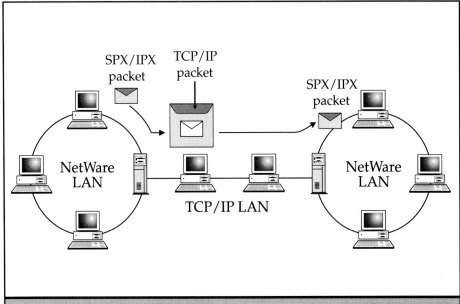

Figure 6-6.   *Tunneling encapsulates a packet in another packet for transport across*

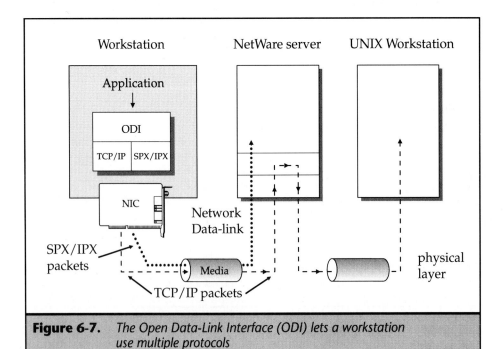

Figure 6-7.   *The Open Data-Link Interface (ODI) lets a workstation use multiple protocols*

if necessary. The following products allow workstations to support dual protocol stacks (SPX/IPX and TCP/IP).

LAN WorkPlace for DOS lets DOS and Windows users access systems that use TCP/IP. Users can make direct connections to TCP/IP systems or use the NetWare server to route packets to the TCP/IP systems.

LAN WorkPlace for Macintosh gives Macintosh users access to TCP/IP networks and resources, such as UNIX, VAX, and IBM host systems over NetWare networks.

LAN WorkPlace for OS/2 gives OS/2 users access to Apple Macintosh computers, UNIX systems, VAXs, and IBM mainframes over NetWare networks.

Novell provides the following operating system support products that let users of non-NetWare operating systems use the resources of a NetWare server:

NetWare for Macintosh implements the AppleTalk Filing Protocol standard so that Macintosh users can share files with NetWare network users and access printers on the NetWare network.

NetWare NFS runs the UNIX Network Filing System on a NetWare file server so that UNIX users can access files and printers on the NetWare network. Volumes on the NetWare server appear as they would on a UNIX system.

NetWare FTAM allows a wide variety of OSI FTAM (File Transfer Access and Management) clients to access the NetWare file system. It also enables DOS workstation users to attach to OSI networks and communicate with FTAM hosts. NetWare FTAM provides only simple file copying, renaming, and deleting features.

To make sense of the many different protocols and how you might implement them on your network, it is useful to categorize them as outlined here:

- Physical protocols cover the physical connection of similar hardware and the data-link layer protocols used by that hardware.

- Networking and internetworking protocols define the interconnection of similar and dissimilar equipment through bridging and routing.

- Application protocols define interoperability between operating systems and applications.

Physical Layer Standards

The Institute of Electrical and Electronics Engineers (IEEE) has developed a set of standards for defining the way network interface cards transfer data over the media they use. These protocols are accepted by ISO and work at the physical and data-link layers of the OSI reference model.

The IEEE 802 body is a group of committees that have the goal of ensuring that network interface products work together. Products that fall under these standards include network interface cards, bridges, routers, and other components used to create twisted-pair and coaxial cable networks. Also included are Wide Area Networks that use common carriers, such as the phone system.

The 802 committees are

802.1	Internetworking
802.2	Logical Link Control (LLC)
802.3	CSMA/CD LAN (Ethernet)
802.4	Token-bus LAN (similar to but not the same as ArcNet)
802.5	Token Ring LAN
802.6	Metropolitan Area Network

The 802.1 standard defines the relationship between the IEEE standards and the ISO Open Systems Interconnection model. The 802.2 through 802.5 standards allow computers and devices from many different vendors to locally connect by using twisted-pair cable, coaxial cable, and other media types. The 802.6 standard defines high-speed fiber-optic backbone networks. These networks are covered in Chapter 7.

Networking and Internetworking Protocols

The networking and internetworking protocol level involves the network and transport layers; it defines the bridging of similar networks and routing between similar and dissimilar networks. Interconnections between dissimilar topologies occur at this level, but interoperability does not occur. At this level, it is possible to *filter* packets on one LAN in an internetwork so that they don't needlessly hop to another LAN.

Networking and internetworking protocols encompass the network and transport layers of the OSI protocol stack, as you can see in Figure 6-4. Note the positioning of SPX/IPX in the NetWare stack and TCP/IP in the UNIX stack. Any discussion of connecting similar or dissimilar networks covers protocols in these layers. The various types of network connections possible—using repeaters, bridges, and routers—are covered next and illustrated in Figure 6-8.

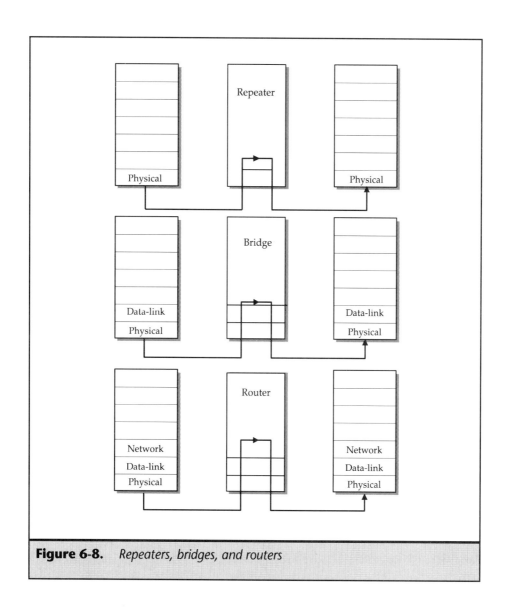

Figure 6-8. *Repeaters, bridges, and routers*

Repeaters

A repeater amplifies a signal on a network cable so that the physical length of the cable and network can be extended. It does not require software and is usually a stand-alone device that does not add overhead to the transmission of data. Once connected, a repeater passes data transparently and without delay.

Bridges

A bridge is a data-link layer device that interconnects two networks that have the same topology or different topologies. You can create a bridge in a NetWare server simply by adding two network cards to it. For example, by adding Ethernet and Token Ring cards to the server, users on each network segment can communicate.

A bridge uses the Media Access Control (MAC) layer, which is the lower half of the data-link layer. This layer contains the address of the destination workstation. Because the bridge sees all the workstations on all the interconnected LANs, it simply forwards the packet to the correct workstation. Traffic between LANs is not filtered as is done on a router, so there may be some performance loss in high volume situations.

Routers

A router operates one step up in the protocol ladder from a bridge. Routers interconnect network segments through the network layer. Instructions for routing packets are contained within the network layer of IPX. A Novell NetWare server automatically routes packets between two or more installed network interface cards. A router differs from a bridge because a router is capable of reading both the workstation address and the LAN address in a packet. Because of this, routers can filter packets and route them to a workstation using the best possible path.

Consider that a large internetwork may contain many LAN segments. Some are interconnected at the server, and others are interconnected at distant sites, as shown in Figure 6-9. Note that LAN D has a redundant connection to the server because it is connected through both LAN B and LAN C. If one connection should fail, the other handles all the routing.

A multiprotocol router is another important device. In the previous paragraphs, it is assumed that the packets are native NetWare IPX packets. NetWare routers know the format of the packets and how to read addresses. Now assume that the network passes both IPX and TCP/IP packets. A

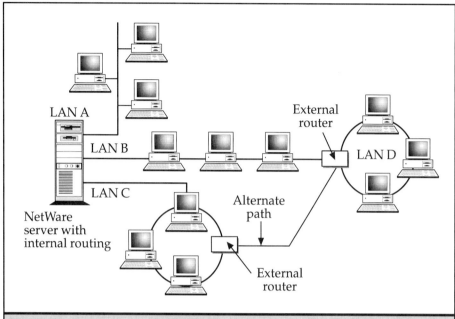

Figure 6-9. *A path to a LAN segment may have several routes. An intelligent router picks the best path*

multiprotocol router must know how to read the address in both types of packets and forward the packets to the correct LAN segments.

Chapter 8 discusses the NetWare MultiProtocol Router software, which you can use to establish a router outside of the NetWare server. This is an important consideration on internetworks with high traffic loads, because performing routing tasks can reduce a file server's performance and ability to handle the file services for which it was intended.

Application Protocols

Interoperability is defined in the upper layers of the protocol stack. You might have a database application in which the server portion runs on a network server, and client portions run on DOS, OS/2, Macintosh, and UNIX systems.

Other interoperable applications include electronic mail packages. They allows users on a variety of systems (DOS, Macintosh, UNIX, and so on) to exchange mail files. The software translates any difference in the packaged electronic mail information between systems.

Communications Methods for NetWare

This section covers how traditional DOS-based workstations establish communications with NetWare servers by using SPX/IPX. It also covers TCP/IP support, AppleTalk, and others.

The NetWare Shell

You establish a connection between a DOS workstation and the NetWare file server by first loading the DOS Requester software. This software automatically loads the SPX/IPX protocol stack, and through ODI support lets you load additional protocols or network interface cards. It determines whether the commands you issue are for the local operating system or for NetWare. If the commands are for NetWare, it directs them across the network. If they are for DOS, it keeps the commands local.

The IPX protocol is based on the Xerox Network System (XNS). XNS, like the OSI protocol stack, defines communications layers from the hardware up to the application layer. Novell used part of this stack (specifically, the Internetwork Data Protocol) to create IPX.

IPX is a routing protocol, and IPX packets contain both network addresses and a workstation address. This information is placed in the packet as header data. A packet sent by a workstation has three possible destinations:

■ A workstation on the same network segment

■ A workstation or server on another network segment

■ The server that performs routing

All packets are examined by the server to determine their destinations. If a packet has an address on the same network, the packet is simply sent to the appropriate workstation. If the packet is addressed to the server, it is sent to the server operating system. If the packet is addressed to another network segment, it is repackaged for that network and sent there, as illustrated in Figure 6-10.

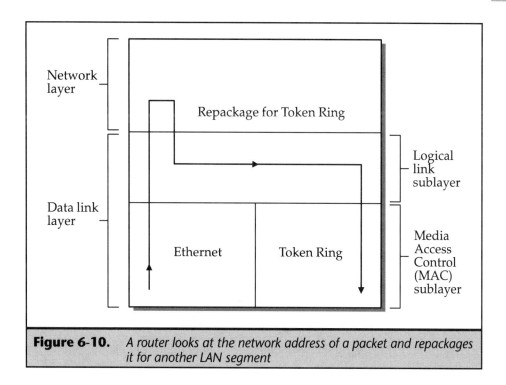

Figure 6-10. *A router looks at the network address of a packet and repackages it for another LAN segment*

IPX is used by various applications and processes on the network, as listed next. As a NetWare administrator implementing internetwork communications, you'll need to have some knowledge of these processes.

NetWare Core Protocol (NCP) NCP provides the basic services of the NetWare operating system to workstations. These include file access, printing, and maintenance services that are communicated by using IPX.

Sequenced Packet Exchange (SPX) SPX is an enhanced version of IPX. It is a programming interface used by third-party software developers to create applications that require guaranteed packet exchange between programs. "Guaranteed" simply implies that the receipt of packets is acknowledged by the destination system. It ensures that data is not lost or duplicated but requires more overhead.

IPX Sockets   Applications have *socket* addresses, just like workstations have their own addresses, so that incoming packets can be directed to them. When an application communicates with another application over the network, it does so by determining the address, or socket, of that application. The socket becomes part of a packet's address, along with the network number and workstation address.

Service Advertisement Protocol (SAP)   File servers, print servers, and other types of servers broadcast SAP messages to make workstations aware of their presence and the services they offer.

Routing Information Protocol (RIP)   A router uses RIP to maintain routing tables that contain information about other networks connected to the internetwork. Entries in the routing tables determine which network should be used to forward packets to workstations or, if necessary, to the next router. The number of hops is also listed, which is an indication of how many networks the packet must go through before it reaches its destination network.

TCP/IP Support in NetWare

As mentioned previously, NetWare provides support for the industry standard Transmission Control Protocol/Internet Protocol (TCP/IP). You install it as a NetWare Loadable Module in the server. The goal of TCP/IP development was to create a set of protocols that provided interconnectivity among a variety of independent host systems. In 1983, TCP/IP protocols became the official protocol suite for the Department of Defense Internet. This internet evolved to connect computers all over the country and in Europe that were involved in scientific research and government projects.

Workstations running TCP/IP (provided by the LAN WorkPlace products) can communicate directly with Sun workstations, VAXs, Macintoshes, minicomputers, and mainframes connected to the network cable. A NetWare server running TCP/IP can route these packets if necessary, depending on the location of the TCP/IP systems. You can look back to Figure 6-5 to see again how the NetWare server passes TCP/IP packets and serves as a link between workstation and host.

TCP/IP consists of the TCP transport protocol and the IP network protocol. TCP and IP are compared to the OSI model in Figure 6-4. IP holds the destination address for packets and interfaces with the TCP layer. TCP provides guaranteed connections similar to SPX. The TCP/IP upper layers consist of the protocols listed next which are important to workstations accessing a TCP/IP system.

- *Network Filing System (NFS)*   A filing system for UNIX hosts that is shareable and distributed. It was originally developed by Sun Microsystems.

- *Simple Network Management Protocol (SNMP)*   A network management protocol that collects information about the network and reports it to administrators.

- *File Transfer Protocol (FTP)*   Enables file transfers between workstations and a UNIX host or Novell NetWare NFS.

- *Simple Mail Transfer Protocol (SMTP)*   A simple protocol that enables electronic messaging.

- *Telnet*   DEC VT100 and VT330 terminal emulation.

Both TCP/IP and IPX are dominant protocols in the networking world. Both have advantages, but TCP/IP stands out as a protocol for implementing internetworks. With IPX, synchronized routing tables must be maintained by using the Routing Information Protocol (RIP). Entire tables must be transmitted across the network, which can drastically slow performance on a Wide Area Network that uses telephone lines or public data networks. TCP/IP doesn't have these routing capabilities—which has been to its advantage. Instead, specialized routers with advanced features were created by third parties to meet routing demands for TCP/IP.

TCP/IP is simple to implement on a NetWare network. You use NetWare's INSTALL program to load modules as described below. These are discussed in later chapters that cover NetWare installation.

- *TCPIP.NLM*   Provides the TCP/IP protocol services

- *SNMP.NLM*   Provides support for the SNMP functions. If it is not already loaded, TCPIP.NLM automatically loads it

- *SNMPLOG.NLM*   Enables the SNMP event logger to capture SNMP event information

- *TCPCON.NLM*   A console NLM that provides centralized management of TCP/IP protocol statistics. It can be used to update router tables, to enable IP forwarding, and to view statistics on any system that supports the SNMP Management Information Base (MIB)

AppleTalk Support in NetWare

The AppleTalk protocol is built into every Macintosh. Building a network with Macintosh systems is as easy as connecting the systems together with AppleTalk cable. The base system (AppleTalk Phase I) allows up to 254 systems to share files and printers, whereas AppleTalk Phase II supports up to 16 million nodes. AppleTalk is relatively easy to implement on other systems because it matches the OSI protocol well and allows the substitution of protocols at different layers, to integrate with other systems.

AppleTalk itself has a transfer rate of 230 Kb/sec (kilobits per second). AppleTalk cables and connectors are simple to install, and telephone cables and connectors can be substituted. If AppleTalk doesn't provide adequate speed, two other networking schemes, EtherTalk and TokenTalk, are available, but these require optional boards. The connection of these physical transports is done in the data-link layer of the OSI model.

Below is a list of transport and session layer protocols associated with AppleTalk:

- *DDP (Datagram Delivery Protocol)* Prepares data packets (called Datagrams) for transmission over the network. Like most packets, Datagrams contain the network address and data formatting. Software vendors can use AppleTalk Transaction Protocol (ATP) in the transport layer to increase the reliability of transmission

- *ATP (AppleTalk Transaction Protocol)* Provides guaranteed packet transmission and delivery

- *ASP (AppleTalk Session Protocol)* An extension of ATP, it sets up and manages a communication session

- *ADSP (AppleTalk Data Stream Protocol)* Provides a way to open a virtual "data pipe" between devices that have a connected session so that information can be read from and written to devices

- *AEP (AppleTalk Echo Protocol)* Sends and receives data packets between nodes

- *NBP (Name Binding Protocol)* Allows administrators to name devices based on the device address

- *ZIP (Zone Information Protocol)* Internetworks are divided into groups called zones. ZIP provides the NBP with the zone number for a device

- *RTMP (Routing Table Maintenance Protocol)* Used to update routers' tables, which define paths between two points

■ *PAP (Printer Access Protocol)*   Prepares a path to a printer, based on the information available from the NBP

Above the transport and session layer connections are the AppleTalk services, such as AppleTalk Filing Protocol, which allows file and application sharing. Also included in this layer is the PostScript language for network printing.

ODI and NDIS Network Interface Support

The traditional NetWare IPX communication method is ideal for networks that support only DOS and OS/2 workstations. IPX is a fast and efficient packet delivery system for local area networks. However, IPX is used only by Novell, which makes interoperability with other types of networks difficult. TCP/IP can provide multivendor and wide area networking. Although TCP/IP is getting the most attention in the move to interoperability, other standards also exist, such as AppleTalk and, of course, the OSI protocols. Because of this, Novell developed the Open Data-Link Interface (ODI), which allows multiple protocol stacks to exist within a server or workstation. In addition, it recently added support for the Network Driver Interface Specification (NDIS), an interface for network interface cards that was developed by Microsoft. NDIS is required to connect to dissimilar networks such as Microsoft's LAN Manager, 3Com's 3+Share, and IBM's LAN Server network. NDIS and ODI can coexist on a workstation so that users can still access NetWare networks.

NOTE: ODI support is installed automatically when running the NetWare 4 workstation support software.

The purpose of ODI and NDIS is to standardize the interface between drivers and interface cards. In this way, separate drivers are not required for each type of protocol you want to run on the card. ODI and NDIS are covered in the following sections.

The Open Data-Link Interface

The Open Data-Link Interface (ODI) is illustrated in Figure 6-11. It provides an interface among network interface cards and multiple protocols. When network

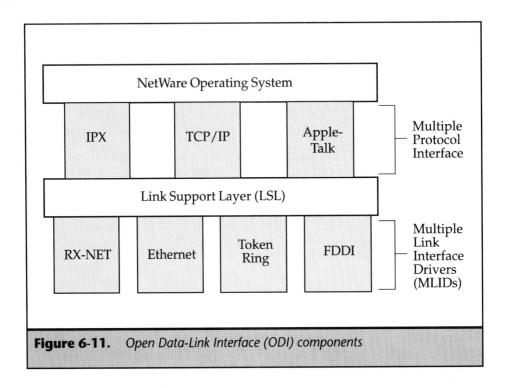

Figure 6-11.   *Open Data-Link Interface (ODI) components*

interface card drivers are written to the ODI specification, they can use one or more protocols, such as AppleTalk and TCP/IP.

ODI provides the following benefits to those who need to interconnect with non-NetWare systems:

- A single network card interfaces with different protocol stacks.

- A logical network board is created that processes packets from different systems. Those packets can be sent on the same network cabling system attached to a single network card.

- The workstation can use a different protocol stack without being rebooted.

- ODI allows NetWare servers and workstations to communicate with a variety of other systems, including mainframes that use different protocol stacks.

ODI standardizes the development of network interface card drivers; vendors no longer need to worry about writing their drivers to fit a specific protocol stack. Instead, drivers are written to attach to the Link Support Layer

(LSL). LSL is like a switchboard that ensures packets are directed to the proper protocol stack.

You can see the component layers of ODI in Figure 6-11. At the bottom are the interfaces for different types of network interface cards. At the top are the protocols that interface with the NetWare operating system. In between is the Link Support Layer, which directs traffic between the components.

MULTIPLE LINK INTERFACE (MLI)   The Multiple Link Interface (MLI) layer is an interface where device drivers for the network interface card are attached. The device drivers are written by vendors of network interface cards to match the Novell specification of the Link Support Layer. Drivers are referred to as Multiple Link Interface Drivers (MLIDs).

LINK SUPPORT LAYER (LSL)   The LSL provides a link for drivers at the bottom and protocols at the top. It acts as a switching board, directing network traffic from MLIDs to the proper protocol, and vice versa.

MULTIPLE PROTOCOL INTERFACE (MPI)   The Multiple Protocol Interface (MPI) provides an interface for the connection of protocol stacks, such as IPX, TCP/IP, and AppleTalk. Other protocol stacks such as OSI and SNA will be available in the future.

When a packet arrives at a network interface card, it is processed by the card's MLID and passed to the LSL. The LSL determines which protocol stack the packet should go to and hands it to the protocol. The packet passes up through the protocol stack in the normal way, where it is handled by higher-level protocols.

NDIS Support

The Microsoft Network Device Interface Specification (NDIS) was designed to give network users access to a variety of protocols by detaching those protocols from network interface cards. In the design, protocols don't need to know anything about the interface card. There is no card-specific interface, only a common interface for protocols, as shown in Figure 6-12. To use an NDIS card, you install the card and its driver, load all the protocols you want to use, and bind them with a command called NETBIND.

To provide support for NDIS along with ODI, Novell developed the Open Data-Link Interface Network driver interface specification support, or ODINSUP (SUP is derived from "support"). It allows coexistence of the two network driver interfaces and the connection of dissimilar networks from a workstation. NDIS protocol stacks can also communicate between the ODI LSL and MLID layers so that both protocol stacks can exist in the same system.

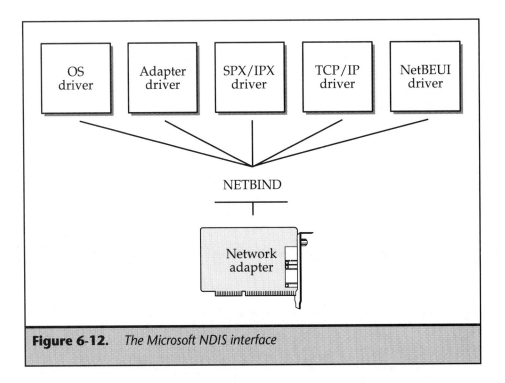

Figure 6-12.   *The Microsoft NDIS interface*

After loading ODINSUP in a workstation, a user can log onto a 3Com 3+Share network, a Microsoft LAN Manager network, or an IBM LAN Server network, in addition to being able to log onto the NetWare network. The same network interface card is used to gain access.

NetBIOS and Named Pipes

NetBIOS is an application program interface (API) that is used to create LAN applications for the IBM LAN Server, Microsoft LAN Manager, and OS/2 environments. Named Pipes is a similar but more advanced protocol that works with OS/2. NetBIOS and Named Pipes exist in the LAN environment as the protocols on which various applications are built. However, vendors of such applications are beginning to port them to the SPX/IPX environment, where they can run as NetWare Loadable Modules on a NetWare server. You need to be concerned with NetBIOS and Named Pipes in the NetWare environment only if you have applications that require them.

CHAPTER 7

A network is a modular and adaptable communication system that can be customized to meet many different site requirements. Its modularity makes it easy to add new components or move existing ones, and its adaptability makes changes and upgrades easy.

Network Interface Methods and Topologies

123

The types of networks discussed in this chapter are Ethernet, Token Ring, and ArcNet. The traditional methods of wiring these networks are described in the following list:

- Ethernet networks use a linear bus topology, a CSMA/CD (Carrier Sense Multiple Access with Collision Detection) access method, and thin or thick coaxial cable or twisted-pair cable.

- Token Ring networks combine star and ring topologies and use a token-passing access method and shielded or unshielded twisted-pair cable.

- ArcNet networks use a star or bus topology, a token-passing access method, and coaxial cable.

NOTE: Networks like Ethernet, Token Ring, and ArcNet are a combination of hardware and software that have specific topologies, access methods, and design criteria. Referring to them can be confusing. For example, you could say the "Ethernet network" or the "Ethernet topology," or even the "Ethernet standard," but for simplicity, it is common to just say "Ethernet."

Network Connection Overview

Network hardware consists of network interface cards and cables. Network software consists of drivers or built-in routines that control the access method to the cable and the protocols used to handle communications.

Network Interface Cards

Network interface cards are available to fit AT-class systems with 8-bit or 16-bit Industry Standard Architecture (ISA) bus slots. The 16-bit cards give better performance at a higher price. Cards are also available for Micro Channel Architecture (MCA) systems such as the IBM PS/2 line and for Extended Industry Standard Architecture (EISA) bus systems such as the Compaq DESKPRO 486 and Compaq SYSTEMPRO.

Use high-performance EISA-based or MCA-based computers and network interface cards for servers whenever possible. The server must be high performance to handle traffic and management for the entire network. You can use less expensive, low-performance cards in workstations that don't generate a lot of network traffic, such as word processing systems. However, high-performance graphics or engineering workstations need high-performance interface cards to maintain high throughput to the server. It's best not to scrimp on those systems.

Figure 7-1 illustrates Token Ring network interface cards and Multistation Access Units (MAUs). Note the MAUs in the background. These are wiring hubs that distribute the wiring of the ring-based LAN in a star topology, as discussed later in this chapter. Also note that the MAU at the top uses convenient telephone-type RJ-45 connectors.

NOTE: Chapter 12 includes a discussion of high-performance servers and server equipment.

Network Interface Card Functions

Network interface cards handle the communications among computers on the network, as defined by the protocol stack and media access rules used by the card. Some manufacturers build cards that fit the basic specifications of the network type (Ethernet, Token Ring, or ArcNet). Although these cards are inexpensive, they offer

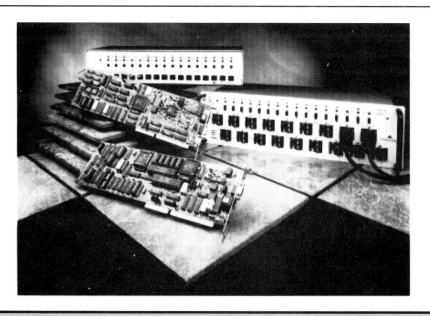

Figure 7-1. *Network interface cards and wiring centers (courtesy of Thomas-Conrad Corporation)*

no special features that might improve performance. Cards that do boost performance usually include special features such as bus mastering, large buffers, or on-board processors, as discussed later.

To prepare for data transmission, a *handshaking* process takes place between two stations. This handshaking establishes communication parameters, such as the transmission speed, packet size, timeout parameters, and buffer size. Handshaking is especially important when two cards involved in a communication session have slightly different hardware designs or specifications. Once the communication parameters are established, transmission of data packets begins. Data is converted in two ways before it is placed on the cable for transmission. First, a parallel-to-serial conversion transforms data for transport as electrical signals (a bit stream) over a cable. Second, data is often encoded and compressed to improve transmission speed.

Differences in hardware design among interface cards on a network can slow performance. For example, a network card with a 16-bit interface typically sends data to an 8-bit card faster than the 8-bit card can process it. To alleviate this problem, vendors place *memory buffers* on 8-bit cards to hold incoming data. This lets cards complete their data transmissions much faster. The top part of Figure 7-2 shows a bottleneck caused by an 8-bit card. In the bottom part of Figure 7-2, the 8-bit card processes the packets it has received in its buffer and does not continue to hold the attention of the network. The 16-bit card has completed its transmission, and the network is free for other uses.

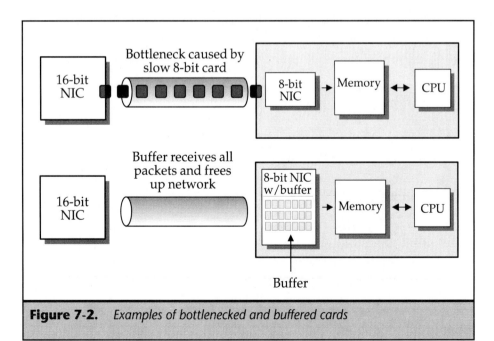

Figure 7-2.   *Examples of bottlenecked and buffered cards*

Performance bottlenecks are also introduced when moving information from the network interface card buffers to memory. There are four methods of doing this, some of which are more efficient than others. The price you pay for a card depends on the quality of its data handling features.

DIRECT MEMORY ACCESS (DMA)   When the direct memory access (DMA) method is used, a DMA controller on the PC takes control of the bus and transfers data from the network interface card's buffer directly into a designated memory location on the PC. This reduces some of the work of the CPU and increases its performance. While data is being transferred, the CPU can do some other task, but it cannot access memory.

SHARED ADAPTER MEMORY   With the shared adapter memory technique, cards have their own memory that the system processor can access directly. The memory is mapped to addresses in the upper memory blocks of a DOS system (above 640KB). In other words, the processor thinks the memory on the card is part of its system memory and accesses it accordingly. This can lead to problems if you are not careful to ensure that the memory area allocated to the network interface card is not used by another card or process (a driver or application, for example).

NOTE: When you set up a shared-memory card, you set switches on the card or set its startup commands to specify the memory area the card will use. The adapter's manual refers to these as base memory addresses. The shared memory starts at the base memory address and extends the length of the shared memory, which may be 8KB, 16KB, or 32KB. You need to ensure that no other card or process uses this memory. If so, you must change the base memory address of the network interface card or the adapter that it conflicts with.

SHARED SYSTEM MEMORY   The shared system memory technique uses a shared block of memory (usually 8KB to 32KB in size) in the system (not on the card) that is controlled by a special processor on the network interface card. The NIC places information in a shared memory area where the system processor can access it directly. As with the shared adapter memory technique, you must ensure that the shared memory area is not used by another card or process.

BUS MASTERING   With the bus mastering technique, a network adapter can transfer information directly to system memory without interrupting the system processor. Cards that use this method provide a form of enhanced DMA by assuming control of the system bus. Bus mastering is possible only on MCA and EISA machines because of their advanced bus designs. Although cards that use the bus mastering technique can increase performance by 20 to 70 percent, they are too expensive for common workstations, but they are highly recommended for servers.

Network Interface Card Drivers

Almost all network interface cards come with a disk that contains driver files used to install the card in a system and make it recognizable to NetWare. In addition, Novell ships drivers for the most popular cards with NetWare. Driver files are used to configure a card for use in a NetWare workstation or server. While the actual routines for encoding data and placing it on the cable are usually built onto the card itself, a driver defines how data moves on the card and how it interfaces with protocols (NDIS or ODI). Some vendor's cards emulate cards that have become industry standards, such as the Novell NE1000 (8-bit) and NE2000 (16-bit) Ethernet cards. You can use the Novell drivers with these cards, or you can use a compatible driver that offers better performance.

Global Addressing

Global addressing ensures that every network interface card has a unique identifying node address. Token Ring and Ethernet card addresses are hard-wired on the card. ArcNet addresses are switch-selectable by the end-user.

The IEEE (Institute of Electrical and Electronics Engineers) committee is in charge of assigning addresses to Token Ring and Ethernet cards. Each manufacturer is given a unique code and a block of addresses. When installing a card, it is a good idea to determine the card address and write it down for future reference. You can also use a diagnostics utility supplied with the card to determine its address after you've installed the card in a system. You might also find the address on a label attached to the card.

Remote-Boot PROMs

PROM stands for programmable read-only memory. Most network cards come with a socket for a remote-boot PROM. You use remote-boot PROMs on diskless workstations that can't boot on their own but instead boot from the network server. A diskless workstation is less expensive than a system with floppy disk and hard disk drives. It is also more secure because users can't download valuable data to floppy disk or upload viruses and other unauthorized software.

Topology

When choosing a particular type of network, its topology is an important consideration. As mentioned previously, the major network topologies are linear bus, star, and ring, but there are combinations of these. For example, ArcNet networks are configurable as both linear bus and star topologies; Token Ring networks physically look like a star, but logically their packets travel in a ring. Ethernet network transmissions are *broadcast* over a linear bus so that all stations see the signal at the same time.

If all your workstations are in a row—such as in a classroom or down a hallway in an office building, for example—a linear topology such as thin coaxial Ethernet is easy to install. You simply daisy-chain one machine to the next, running the cable up into the ceiling to the next office. If workstations are in clusters at various locations, as shown in Figure 7-3, a star topology such as Token Ring, ArcNet, or twisted-pair Ethernet (10BASE-T) is useful. Long cables attach distant clusters.

A true physical ring topology is rarely used today. Instead, logical rings are configured into a network topology as part of its transport and access method scheme. A ring describes the logical path a packet takes as it moves from one station to the next, eventually making a complete circle. In Token Ring networks, cables branch from a central hub called a MAU (Multistation Access Unit). The MAU has an internal ring that connects all the stations attached to it, and serves

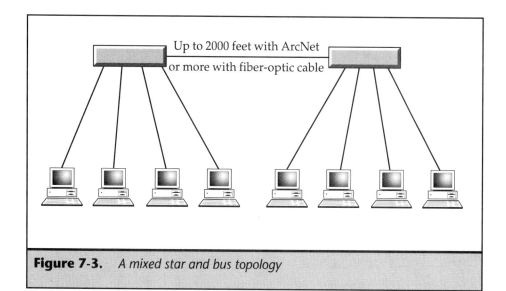

Figure 7-3. *A mixed star and bus topology*

as a sort of bypass switch in case one of the workstation cables is cut or disconnected. When a workstation cable is attached to the MAU, it simply forms an extension of the ring: cable signals travel out to the workstation and then back to the internal ring.

10BASE-T is a star-configured Ethernet topology that uses twisted-pair cable. Cables to workstations branch from a central concentrator box. Its concentrators serve to distribute the cable from a central location, but the cable access method is still CSMA/CD.

Star topologies provide protection from cable breaks. The whole LAN segment won't go down if a cable to a workstation is cut. It is also easy to diagnose connection problems since each workstation has its own cable segment that is connected to the hub. You simply locate the break in the wire run that goes to the inoperative workstation. The remainder of the network continues to operate normally.

There are some downsides to the star topology. First, you'll need a lot of cable to make those runs to each station. Second, wiring hubs tend to be expensive. Third, the wiring hub or hubs can become a conglomeration of cables that is hard to manage. However, most star topologies use inexpensive twisted-pair cable. In some cases, you can even use existing telephone twisted-pair cable. In addition, it's beneficial to have all wiring leads located in one place for diagnostics and testing purposes. Ethernet concentrators and Token Ring MAUs tend to be relatively expensive compared to ArcNet hubs. New concentrator and hub designs that include testing and diagnostics features are even more expensive.

Problems in linear topologies such as Ethernet (10BASE-2 coaxial cable) are harder to diagnose. If the cable is cut, broken, or disconnected, all workstations go down until you locate and repair the break. Testing devices such as time domain reflectometers (TDRs) are available to help you find problems (or potential problems) with Ethernet cable. They tell you how far a break is located from a certain point.

Table 7-1 lists the various forms of network topologies and the maximum length of segments in each.

Cabling

Cable type is another important consideration when installing a network. In the end, cable cost is often the most important deciding factor. That's why networks using unshielded twisted-pair cable are growing in popularity. They are easy to install, offer high transfer rates, and the cable is cheap.

Of course, you can avoid the cable decision altogether by using new wireless technologies that connect workstations by using radio or infrared signals. In fact,

Network Topology	Maximum Segment Length
Thick Ethernet (10BASE-5)	500 meters (1640 feet)
Thin Ethernet (10BASE-2)	185 meters (607 feet)
Twisted-pair Ethernet (10BASE-T)	100 meters (330 feet)
Fiber-optic cable	2 kilometers (6562 feet)
Twisted-pair Token Ring	100 meters (330 feet) from MAU
Coaxial ArcNet (star)	609 meters (2000 feet)
Coaxial ArcNet (bus)	305 meters (1000 feet)
Twisted-pair ArcNet (star)	122 meters (400 feet)
Twisted-pair ArcNet (bus)	122 meters (400 feet)

Table 7-1.   *Cable Lengths for Various Network Topologies*

wireless technology is becoming the predominant method for connecting portable computers to a network.

When you choose a type of cable, be sure to consider the importance of cable shielding and security. Shielding protects coaxial copper cable from interference, making coaxial cable more reliable, but also more expensive, than twisted-pair cable. Fiber-optic cable is secure because it doesn't emanate a signal that can be monitored, and it and does not require any shielding, but it is the most expensive. Twisted-pair cable is inexpensive and provides some protection from interference, but the distance allowed between connections is short. However, twisted-pair cable has become popular in recent years because of advancements in transmission techniques that have boosted its transfer speed to match Ethernet. Ethernet 10BASE-T is a good choice for Local Area Networks, but it requires relatively expensive concentrator boxes. A comparison of cable features is presented in Table 7-2.

Coaxial Cable Features

Coaxial cable has the following characteristics:

- It is affected by outside interference and must be shielded to reduce the interference.

Variable	Twisted-Pair	Coaxial	Fiber-Optic
Cost	Low	Moderate	High
Throughput	Moderate	High	Extra high
Length	100s of feet	1000s of feet	Miles
Interference	Some	Low	None
Reliability	High	High	Extra high

Table 7-2.   *A Comparison of Cable Features*

- It acts as an antenna as distance increases, picking up noise and interference from motors, radio transmitters, and other sources of electric power. This can distort the signals it carries.

- It has problems with grounding.

- It emits signals that can be monitored by intruders.

- It costs from $0.20 to $0.30 a foot in rolls of 1000 feet (for ThinNet RG-58A/U coaxial cable used in Ethernet 10BASE-2 or RG-62A/U coaxial cable used with ArcNet). Firesafe plenum cable costs about $0.50 a foot.

NOTE: Building and fire codes may require that plenum firesafe cable be used if the wire is strung through ceilings that serve as air ducts. Plenum cable does not give off poisonous gas in a fire.

Fiber-Optic Cable Features

Fiber-optic cable is the most expensive network cable, but recent competition among cable vendors has reduced its price. It has the following characteristics:

- It is commonly used in combination with other cable types as a backbone connection between servers and LAN segments.

- It has a greater potential segment length and faster transmission rates than other types of cable.

- It does not emit signals, so it can be used in high-security areas.

- It is not affected by outside electrical noise.

■ Cable taps can be detected by adjusting the amount of light through the cable. If a tap is made, the cable will fail because the system is not "tuned" for the addition of the tap.

■ It costs about $1.25 to $1.50 per foot in 1000-foot rolls. Firesafe plenum cable costs about $1.80 per foot.

Twisted-Pair Cable Features

Twisted-pair cable is the fastest growing choice for cable among network installers. It is already in place in some buildings in the form of existing telephone wires, but you must ensure that the wire is the correct type. Twisted-pair cable has the following characteristics:

■ It is the most economical wiring system.

■ It may be possible to use existing telephone twisted-pair lines.

■ It has length limitations, but these can be corrected by using coaxial or fiber-optic backbones to connect distant segments.

■ It is susceptible to some outside interference.

■ Type 3 Token Ring unshielded cable costs about $0.08 to $0.10 per foot. Type 3 firesafe plenum cable costs about $0.20 to $0.25 per foot. Telephone twisted-pair cable used in Ethernet 10BASE-T costs about $0.09 to $0.18 per foot.

Other Factors to Consider

Ease of installation is an important consideration in your cable decision. Of course, using wireless LANs or existing telephone cable makes that decision easy. But if you need to install cable, there are several factors that will affect your decision. These factors are covered briefly here and in more detail in Chapter 14.

 NOTE: Each network cabling scheme calls for a specific type of cable. Usually, only that type of cable can be used on the LAN segment. However, there is some flexibility, as you'll learn later in the chapter.

The distance to each workstation in your network affects the type of cable you will choose and the quantity of cable you need. Local wiring code restrictions may make twisted-pair cable preferable to coaxial cable. The signals on a LAN cable produce harmonic radiation that may interfere with external equipment. It can also be monitored by anyone involved in espionage. Coaxial cable reduces this radiation and meets government regulations by providing an outer conductor that acts as a shield. The twists in twisted-pair cable do the same thing.

As previously mentioned, twisted-pair cable is relatively inexpensive and is often already in place. But you should carefully evaluate such cable before using it. Your telephone wiring closet is the source of this cable. A punchdown block in the closet (illustrated in Figure 7-4) is the connection point for leads that extend to telephone faceplates or computer connections. You attach a cable from the network concentrator box at one of these leads to extend the network connection over the twisted-pair cable to the workstation.

NOTE: The cable running to the workstation must contain extra unused pairs.

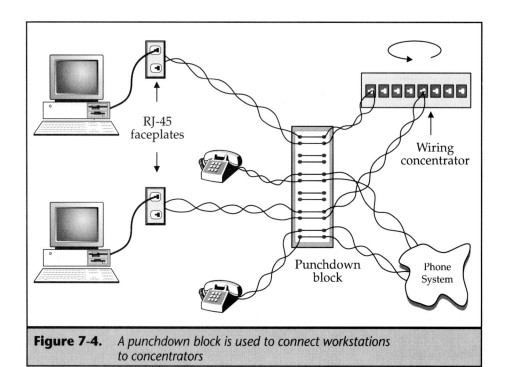

Figure 7-4.   *A punchdown block is used to connect workstations to concentrators*

Telephone cable acceptable for network use must have two twists per foot of 24-gauge or 26-gauge wire. A typical building might have bundles of wire with up to 300 wire pairs. All wiring is color coded and follows a recognized standard for use. A flat, gray wire called "silver satin" is not acceptable, nor is the four-conductor untwisted wire found in residences. In addition, wiring on a Public Branch Exchange (PBX) that is more than seven years old cannot be used. The cable in the wiring closet should be 24-gauge to 26-gauge solid copper wiring. The gauge should be imprinted on the cable itself, or you might see a UL code such as CM, CMR, and CMP. If you're not sure what gauge the wire is, call an electrical contractor or the phone company.

Even if the cable is the right type, it can cause problems if it has been strung over fluorescent lights or power leads in ceilings and walls. This type of interference is not a problem with voice transmission, but can seriously affect data transmissions. Once again, an electrical contractor can evaluate the integrity of any existing cable in your building. However, keep in mind that contractors often tend toward rewiring your building, not only because they want the work, but because they have reservations about ensuring the integrity of any existing cable.

NOTE: If you need to order twisted-pair cable, specify IBM Type 3 or Commercial Premises wire with a nominal impedance of 100 to 105 ohms and two to three twists per foot.

Some organizations that require continuous, uninterrupted LAN service, such as hospitals, financial institutions, and the military, create redundant cabling schemes. In this arrangement, a primary and a secondary cable are installed. The cables usually follow different paths through a building. Both can operate simultaneously to improve performance, and either can provide a path for network traffic should the other go down. Cable redundancy requires routers that can sort out network traffic and keep packets off of LANs where they don't belong. Routers also help packets find the best path through the network to their destination.

Wiring Hubs

The telephone wiring closet can provide a place where different types of cabling schemes come together. Cable management systems from various vendors use wiring hubs that often have their own processor and adapter bus to accommodate a range of networking options. A typical wiring hub might accommodate cards for connecting Ethernet star configurations (10BASE-T),

Token Ring stars, and fiber-optic segments, in addition to providing bridging, routing, and remote communications. Wiring hubs are discussed in Chapter 8.

Cable Access Method

Network interface cards use a specific access method to put data on a cable for transmission or take it off. The way packets are transferred to the cable affects transmission speed. Carrier sensing methods, which Ethernet cards use, broadcast messages so that every station hears the signal and either receives or rejects it. In token-passing methods, like Token Ring and ArcNet cards use, a workstation must have possession of a token before beginning transmission.

Carrier sensing is fast (Ethernet is rated at 10 Mb/sec, or megabits per second), but collisions that bog down the network can occur during heavy traffic. A collision occurs when two stations attempt access to the cable at the same time. They both back off for a random time and then try again. This adds even more traffic to the network. Token-passing methods avoid these types of cable contentions.

The Institute of Electrical and Electronics Engineers (IEEE) has developed a set of standards that have also been adopted by the International Organization for Standardization (ISO) as part of the OSI standard. Any discussion of cable access methods must include the standards defined by this organization. The IEEE 802 committees for LANs are

802.2	Logical Link Control (LLC)
802.3	CSMA/CD LAN (Ethernet)
802.4	Token Bus LAN (not ArcNet)
802.5	Token Ring LAN (IBM Token Ring)
802.6	Metropolitan Area Networks

These standards are used to define the physical and data-link layers of the OSI reference model, as shown in Figure 7-5 (refer to Chapter 6 for details). The data-link layer is divided into the Logical Link Control (LLC) and media access control sublayers.

The Logical Link Control layer provides a single standard interface between upper protocol layers and the lower-level Media Access Control (MAC) layer. The LLC layer is like a switchboard that organizes how data flows between lower and upper layers. Notice that the MAC layer consists of the other 802.*x* specifications, which can be seen as modular in design.

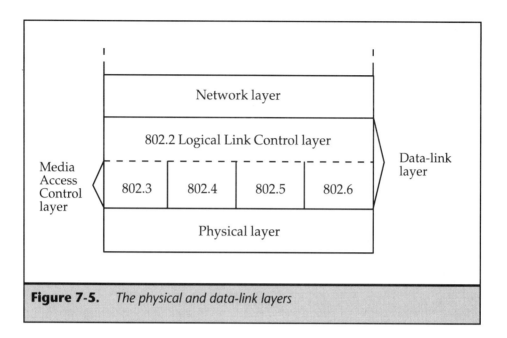

Figure 7-5. *The physical and data-link layers*

Ethernet and IEEE 802.3

The Ethernet networking system was originally created by Xerox, but it was jointly developed as a standard in 1980 by Digital Equipment Corporation, Intel, and Xerox. This standard became known as DIX Ethernet in reference to the developers' names. Ethernet has 10 Mb/sec throughput and uses a carrier-sensing (CSMA/CD) access method. IEEE 802.3 defines a similar, but slightly different, standard that uses a different frame format. (The *frame* is the structure and encoding of the packet.) Because the 802.3 standard is the default for NetWare and is more commonly used, it is discussed in this section. NetWare does provide a way to use the DIX Ethernet standard if necessary.

The adaptations of the IEEE 802.3 standard all have transmission speeds of 10 Mb/sec with the exception of 1BASE-5, which transmits at 1 Mb/sec but has long twisted-pair segments. Because 10BASE-5, 10BASE-2, and 10BASE-T are the most popular topologies, only they are discussed in this section, but all of the topologies are mentioned in the following list. Note that the first number in the name refers to the speed in Mb/sec, and the last number refers to the meters per segment (multiplied by 100). *BASE* stands for baseband and *BROAD* stands for broadband.

NOTE: Look for emerging "Fast Ethernet" products that bring 100-Mb/sec speeds to Ethernet LANs and compete with fiber-optic products.

10BASE-5   Coaxial cable with maximum segment lengths of 500 meters; uses baseband transmission methods

10BASE-2   Coaxial cable (RG-58A/U) with maximum segment lengths of 185 meters; uses baseband transmission methods

10BASE-T   Twisted-pair cable with maximum segment lengths of 100 meters

1BASE-5   Twisted-pair cable with maximum segment lengths of 500 meters and transmission speeds of up to 1 Mb/sec

10BROAD-36   Coaxial cable (RG-59/U CATV type) with maximum segment lengths of 3600 meters; uses broadband transmission methods

10BASE-F   Fiber-optic cable segments with transmission at 10 Mb/sec

The topology of 802.3 Ethernet networks is a linear bus with a CSMA/CD access method. Workstations are connected in a daisy-chain fashion by using segments of cable. The segments form a single large cable system known as the trunk cable. You can configure the twisted-pair version (10BASE-T) as a star in which the cable to each station branches from a central wiring concentrator.

CSMA/CD

CSMA/CD is an acronym for Carrier Sense Multiple Access with Collision Detection. Ethernet cards send packets, or datagrams, out on the network by accessing the cable when it is not in use by another system. That accounts for the Carrier Sense Multiple Access portion of the name.

Collision Detection refers to the method used to resolve simultaneous accesses to the cable. When a cable is not in use, two stations may attempt to access it at the same time. If both start transmitting data, a collision occurs, which corrupts the data. With the CSMA/CD protocol, a detection mechanism senses the collision, and both workstations back off for a random period of time and then try retransmitting the packets. The method works well unless the network traffic is high; more collisions and retransmissions occur, causing a loss of performance. To avoid excess collisions, you can divide a network into two or more segments by installing additional interface cards in the NetWare server, thus creating an internal router.

Thick Coaxial Ethernet (10BASE-5)

10BASE-5 Ethernet is often referred to as standard Ethernet because it was the original Ethernet implementation. Figure 7-6 illustrates a thick coaxial Ethernet cabling scheme. Each station on a thick Ethernet trunk is attached by using a transceiver and transceiver cable. The transceiver is not the same as the BNC T-connector used on thin Ethernet. It is a small box that provides electrical isolation of the workstation from the cable. A "heartbeat" test in the transceiver is used to determine if the station is connected properly.

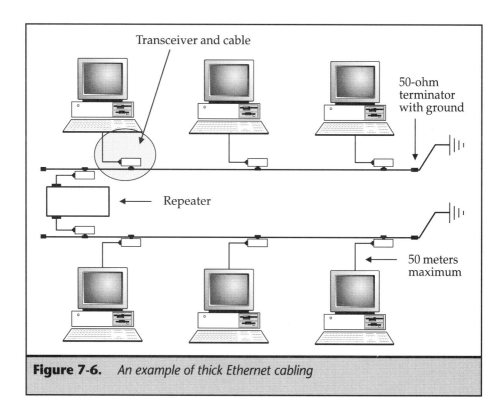

Figure 7-6. *An example of thick Ethernet cabling*

NOTE: 10BASE-5 is falling into disuse as a networking system. It is mentioned here because there are a large number of existing installations you may need to expand or adapt.

The components of a thick Ethernet network are described next.

NETWORK INTERFACE BOARD   Most Ethernet network interface boards support either thick or thin Ethernet cabling. The board should have a female DIX-type connector for the attachment of the thick Ethernet transceiver cable. If the interface card is for the server, install the best card available. If the card is for a workstation, you can scrimp a little, especially if the workstation only accesses the network occasionally. You'll need a remote-boot PROM if the card is for a diskless workstation.

REPEATER   A repeater is an optional device used to join two Ethernet trunks and to strengthen the signals between them. A repeater attaches to a transceiver on each cable trunk with a transceiver cable. Repeaters are discussed in Chapter 8.

TRANSCEIVER   A transceiver is a junction box on the thick Ethernet cable that workstations attach to. It has three connectors: two are the thick Ethernet in/out connectors, and the third is used to attach the workstation to the transceiver by using a transceiver cable. Transceivers attach to the network cable trunk in one of two ways. A clamping method pierces the cable, eliminating the need to cut the cable and mount connectors. Alternatively, a BNC version of the transceiver has a T-connector to which cable ends attach. You must cut the cable and attach connectors to it by using special tools.

TRANSCEIVER CABLE   A transceiver cable usually comes with a transceiver unit. A male and a female DIX-type connector are mounted on either end of the cable, along with transceiver connectors and slide locks to lock the cable to the network interface board. The transceiver cable is usually more flexible than the trunk cable.

THICK ETHERNET TRUNK CABLE   The cabling used for thick Ethernet is a 50-ohm 0.4-inch-diameter coaxial cable, which is stiffer than the transceiver cable. Thick Ethernet cable is available from many vendors in bulk or in precut lengths. A coaxial cable stripping and crimping tool is required to mount connectors. Note that cable is available as firesafe plenum cable, nonplenum interior cable, underground rated cable, and aerial rated cable.

N-SERIES MALE CONNECTORS   N-series male connectors are installed on both ends of the cable when T-connector-type transceivers are used. Preassembled cables have the connectors already mounted.

N-SERIES BARREL CONNECTORS   N-series barrel connectors are used to join two cable segments.

N-SERIES TERMINATORS   Each cable segment must be terminated at both ends with a 50-ohm N-series terminator. For each cable segment you need one terminator with a ground wire attached and one without a ground wire.
Specifications and limitations of the 10BASE-5 standard are listed here:

- The maximum trunk segment length is 500 meters (1640 feet).

- Transceivers are connected to the trunk segment.

- The maximum workstation-to-transceiver distance is 50 meters (164 feet).

- The minimum distance to the next transceiver is 2.5 meters (8 feet).

- Up to five trunk segments may be joined using four repeaters. Workstations are allowed on only three of the segments. The others are used for distance.

- The maximum trunk length of joined segments is 2460 meters (8200 feet).

- You can have a maximum of 100 workstations on one trunk. Repeaters count as workstations.

- A 50-ohm terminator must be placed at the end of each trunk segment, and one end of each segment must be grounded. Do *not* ground a segment at both ends.

Thin Coaxial Ethernet (10BASE-2)

Thin coaxial Ethernet cable is physically easier to handle than thick Ethernet and does not require transceivers at the stations. The cable is also cheaper, but the maximum trunk length is less. Figure 7-7 illustrates a thin Ethernet network, and Figure 7-8 illustrates the components of the wiring system.
The components of a 10BASE-2 network are discussed in the next sections.

NETWORK INTERFACE BOARD   Most Ethernet boards support either thick or thin Ethernet cabling. The board should have a BNC-type connector attached to the back and might also have a thick Ethernet connector. The trunk cable attaches

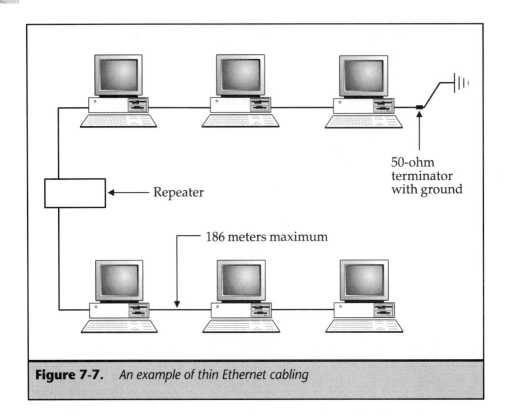

50-ohm
terminator
with ground

Repeater

186 meters maximum

Figure 7-7. *An example of thin Ethernet cabling*

to a BNC T-connector, which is then attached to a male BNC connector on the back of the board. You must use a remote-boot PROM if the card is installed in a diskless workstation.

REPEATER   A repeater is an optional device used to join two Ethernet trunks and to strengthen the signals between them. Repeaters are covered in Chapter 8.

THIN ETHERNET CABLE   The cabling used for thin Ethernet is a 50-ohm 0.2-inch-diameter RG-58 A/U or RG-58 C/U coaxial cable. Thin Ethernet cable is available from many vendors who have precut standard lengths ready to ship. Bulk cable can also be purchased, but BNC connectors must be mounted on the ends of the cables. Note that cable is available as firesafe plenum cable, nonplenum interior cable, underground rated cable, and aerial rated cable.

BNC CABLE CONNECTORS   BNC connectors must be attached to the ends of all cable segments. BNC cable connector kits include a center pin, a housing, and a clamp-down sleeve. A coaxial cable stripping and crimping tool is required to mount connectors. It can be purchased at electronics stores.

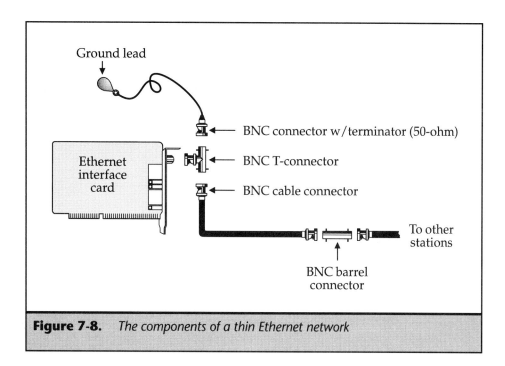

Figure 7-8. *The components of a thin Ethernet network*

BNC T-CONNECTORS   A T-connector is attached to the BNC connector on the back of the Ethernet interface card. The T-connector provides two cable connections for signal-in and signal-out. You will need a T-connector for each workstation, even if it is the last station in the trunk, in which case the BNC terminator is attached to the open end of the T-connector.

BNC BARREL CONNECTORS   BNC barrel connectors are used to join two cable segments together.

BNC TERMINATORS   Each cable segment must be terminated at both ends with a 50-ohm BNC terminator. For each cable segment you need one terminator with a ground and one without.

You must abide by the following rules and limitations when wiring Ethernet networks with RG-58 A/U or RG-58 C/U coaxial cable (ThinNet):

■ The maximum trunk segment length is 186 meters (607 feet).

■ T-connectors are used to connect the cable to the network interface card.

■ Up to five trunk segments may be joined using four repeaters. Workstations are allowed on only three of the segments. The others are used for distance.

- The maximum network trunk length is 910 meters (3035 feet).

- You can have a maximum of 30 nodes on one trunk. Repeaters, bridges, routers, and servers count as nodes. The total number of nodes on all segments cannot exceed 1024.

- A terminator must be placed at each end of a trunk segment, and one end must be grounded.

Combined Thick and Thin Cable

It is possible to combine thick and thin Ethernet cabling systems. For example, you might use thick Ethernet to connect two thin Ethernet segments that are far apart (beyond the reach of thin Ethernet cables). Note that a repeater can also be used to extend an Ethernet network. The maximum number of trunk segments is five.

Combination thick and thin cable segments can be created using a BNC to N-series adapter, which is available with an N-series female or N-series male adapter at one end. Combination thick and thin segments are usually between 607 and 1640 feet long. The following equation is used to find the maximum amount of thin cable that can be used in one combination trunk segment:

$$\frac{1.640 \text{ feet} - L}{3.28} = t$$

L is the length of the trunk segment you want to build, and t is the maximum length of thin cable you can use.

Twisted-Pair Ethernet 10BASE-T

10BASE-T offers most of the advantages of Ethernet without the need to use expensive coaxial cable. In addition, a star, or distributed, topology allows for clusters of workstations in departments or other areas.

Part of the 10BASE-T specification makes it compatible with other IEEE 802.3 standards, so the transition from one media to another is easy. You can retain existing Ethernet cards when converting from coaxial to twisted-pair cable. In addition, you can add twisted-pair trunks to existing trunks by using repeaters that support coaxial, fiber-optic, and twisted-pair Ethernet trunks. Many vendors make such products available as part of their Ethernet product line.

The 10BASE-T specification includes a cable testing feature called *link integrity testing*. With this feature, the system constantly tests the twisted-pair wiring for open wires and shorts. Monitoring is done from a central point.

A basic 10BASE-T network is shown in Figure 7-9. Workstations are attached to a central hub, or concentrator, that acts as a repeater. When a signal from a workstation arrives, the hub broadcasts it on all output lines. You can attach hubs to other hubs in a hierarchical configuration. Workstations are attached with an unshielded twisted-pair cable that cannot exceed 100 meters (328 feet). Cables connect to a transceiver near the workstation, and the transceiver is then connected to the workstation with a 15-wire cable that is up to 50 meters (164 feet) long.

A 10BASE-T connection using existing telephone wiring and a punchdown block is shown in Figure 7-10. In this example, a coaxial or fiber optic backbone connects the wiring centers or closets of different departments within a building. A 10BASE-T concentrator is connected to this backbone in the wiring closet. A 50-pin telephone jumper cable then connects the concentrator to a telephone punchdown block. Two pairs of existing unused twisted-pair wires are used to establish a connection between the punchdown block and the telephone faceplate near the workstation. At the workstation, a cable is strung from the faceplate to a transceiver, which then connects to the workstation. Most 10BASE-T cards today have a built-in transceiver, and the RJ-45 cable plugs directly into them.

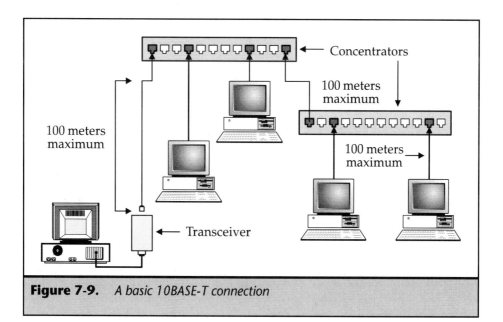

Figure 7-9.   *A basic 10BASE-T connection*

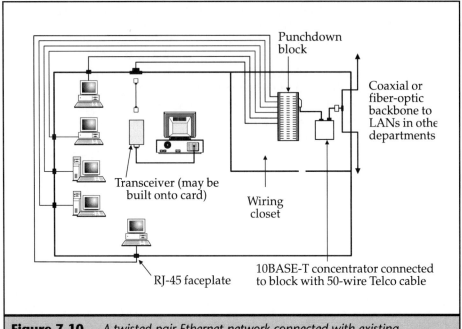

Figure 7-10.   *A twisted-pair Ethernet network connected with existing telephone wire*

NOTE: Don't count on being able to use existing telephone wire. It may not be the right grade or properly installed. If you're not sure, contact an electrical contractor. In most cases, you'll need to pull additional wire anyway to connect systems that are not near existing wire leads.

The components described in the following sections are typically part of a 10BASE-T network. Keep in mind that a system doesn't always require all of these components.

NETWORK INTERFACE CARD   An Ethernet card with a DIX-type 15-pin connector or 10BASE-T RJ-45 connector is required. Add a remote-boot PROM if you install the card in a diskless workstation.

NOTE: Several vendors make 10BASE-T "hub" cards for the server. The cards have an "octopus" cable that you attach the workstation to.

HUB   The hub (also called a concentrator) often has up to 12 ports; some have 10 or 11. A port for attachment to coaxial or fiber-optic backbones is usually attached to the box.

TWISTED-PAIR CABLE   10BASE-T uses twisted-pair cable with RJ-45 connectors that can be up to 100 meters long. You can purchase bulk cable and connectors to make custom cables. Be sure to purchase an RJ crimp tool.

TRANSCEIVER   The transceiver has an RJ-45 connector on one side and a DB-15 connector on the other. Alternatively, most cards today have a built-in transceiver.

TRANSCEIVER CABLE   The transceiver cable attaches the transceiver to the back of the network interface card.

PUNCHDOWN BLOCK CONNECTOR CABLE   If existing telephone cable is to be used, a 50-pin Telco cable that connects the concentrator directly to a telephone punchdown block simplifies the installation. Check with the concentrator vendor.

WALL PLATE   A wall plate is a connector with an RJ plug. If a phone connection is also required, dual plates can be purchased.
   The 10BASE-T specifications are listed here:

- Unshielded twisted-pair (20 to 24 AWG UTP) wire is used.

- RJ-45 connectors are generally used. Pins 1 and 2 are used to transmit and pins 3 and 6 are used to receive. Each pair is crossed over so that the transmitter at one end connects to a receiver at another.

- A transceiver and a 15-pin transceiver cable may be attached to each workstation. Some cards have built-in transceivers.

- The distance from a transceiver to a hub cannot exceed 100 meters (328 feet).

- A hub can typically connect 12 workstations.

- Up to 12 hubs can be attached to a central hub to expand the number of network stations.

- Hubs can be attached to coaxial or fiber-optic backbones to become part of larger Ethernet networks.

- Up to 1023 stations are possible on a network without using bridges.

ArcNet

ArcNet is a baseband, token-passing network system that offers flexible star and bus topologies at a low price. Transmission speeds are 2.5 Mb/sec. ArcNet uses a token bus access method, but ArcNet itself is not an IEEE standard. ArcNet was developed by Datapoint around 1970 and has been licensed to other companies. In 1981, Standard Microsystems Corporation (SMC) developed the first single-chip LAN controller based on the ArcNet token-passing protocol. In 1986, a new chip set supporting bus topology was introduced. Most industry standards, including those used by Novell, are based on the new chip set technology.

A typical ArcNet configuration is shown in Figure 7-11. Although ArcNet is generally considered to have a slow throughput, it does support cable lengths of up to 2000 feet when using active hubs. It is suitable for office environments that use text-based applications and where users don't access the file server often. Newer versions of ArcNet support fiber-optic and twisted-pair cable. Because its flexible wiring scheme allows long trunks, and because you can have star configurations on the same LAN, ArcNet is a good choice when speed is not a factor but price is.

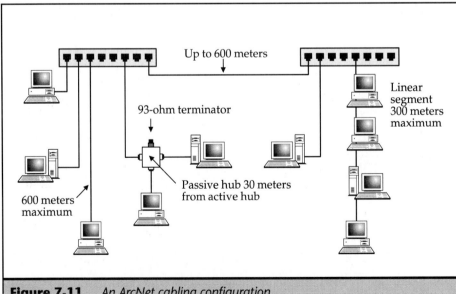

Figure 7-11.   *An ArcNet cabling configuration*

Several vendors recently announced ArcNetplus, a 20 Mb/sec version of ArcNet that is compatible with 2.5 Mb/sec ArcNet. Both versions can be on the same LAN. ArcNetplus supports larger packet sizes and eight times as many stations.

The components that are typically part of a standard ArcNet network are described in the next sections.

NETWORK INTERFACE BOARD   ArcNet boards are available from many vendors, including Standard Microsystems Corporation, Thomas-Conrad, and Puredata. Standard coaxial boards should have a BNC connector attached to the back. When ArcNet is configured as a linear bus, T-connectors are used on the cards, and jumpers must be set to specify the configuration. If the card is installed in a diskless workstation, a remote-boot PROM must be used.

ACTIVE HUB   The active hub is a network relay that conditions and amplifies the signal strength. Workstations can be a maximum of 2000 feet from active hubs. Most active hubs have eight ports to which workstations, passive hubs, or additional active hubs can be attached. It is not necessary to terminate unused ports on an active hub.

PASSIVE HUB   A passive hub is a four-port connector with BNC jacks that is used as a wiring center and simple signal splitter. Workstations cannot be further than 100 feet from a passive hub. Each unused port on a passive hub must be terminated.

ARCNET CABLING   The cabling used for ArcNet networks is a 93-ohm RG-62/U coaxial cable. BNC connectors are used to attach cable segments to active hubs, passive hubs, and network interface cards. ArcNet cable is available from many vendors who have precut standard lengths ready to ship. Bulk cable can also be purchased, along with BNC connectors that must be mounted on the cable ends. A coaxial cable stripping and crimping tool is required to mount connectors. Note that cable is available as firesafe plenum cable, nonplenum interior cable, underground rated cable, and aerial rated cable.

BNC COAXIAL CONNECTORS   Connectors can be purchased to mount on the ends of specially cut bulk cable. The BNC coaxial connector kits include a center pin, a housing, and a clamp-down sleeve.

BNC T-CONNECTORS   A T-connector is attached to the BNC connector on the back of an ArcNet interface card when it is used in a bus topology. The T-connector provides two cable connections for signal-in and signal-out. You will need a T-connector for each workstation, plus two for each repeater being used.

BNC TERMINATORS   A 93-ohm BNC terminating cap must be placed on all passive hub ports that are not in use.

The following rules and limitations apply to ArcNet networks:

■ Most active hubs have eight nodes. Workstations on active hubs can extend as far as 600 meters (2000 feet) from the hub.

■ You can connect active hubs to form a hierarchical configuration. The maximum distance between two active hubs is 600 meters (2000 feet).

■ Up to three workstations can be grouped around a four-port passive hub. One connection leads back to an active hub or file server. Each workstation cannot be farther than 30.5 meters (100 feet) from the hub.

■ Passive hubs cannot be connected to other passive hubs. They can attach to active hubs at a maximum distance of 30.5 meters (100 feet).

■ You must terminate unused nodes on passive hubs with 93-ohm terminator caps.

■ The maximum distance between stations at opposite ends of a multisegment network is 20,000 feet.

■ When stations are wired in a bus configuration, the maximum trunk length of the bus segment is 305 meters (1000 feet).

■ The maximum number of stations is 255.

Each station in an ArcNet network is assigned an address from 1 to 255. It is important to write this station number on the outside faceplace of each card as well as in a log book, in case you want to add more stations. The lowest numbered station broadcasts a permission token to each workstation, which grants them permission to access the cable. Other stations then access the cable based on their address numbers.

Token Ring

Token Ring is an IBM network implementation based on the IEEE 802.5 standard. It is a token-passing ring network that can be configured in a star topology. Up to eight workstations radiate from a central hub, called a Multistation Access Unit (MAU), which contains a logical ring wiring configuration, as shown in Figure 7-12. If a network card fails, the MAU immediately bypasses the station to maintain the ring of the network. Note that unconnected stations are bypassed.

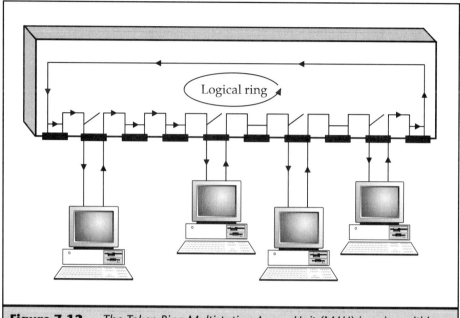

Figure 7-12. *The Token Ring Multistation Access Unit (MAU) is a ring within a box with bypass switching*

However, if a network interface card fails, a bypass is not possible, and the LAN is disrupted. Several non-IBM vendors make products that reduce this problem, but they require connection to a power source and are more expensive because they have management alerting capabilities.

You can install additional MAUs to the network, as shown in Figure 7-13. A ring-in and ring-out receptacle is provided on each MAU for connection to other MAUs. The ring formation is maintained when MAUs are connected in this way. In addition, a fault tolerance feature maintains the ring if one of the cables becomes disconnected, as shown in Figure 7-14. Signals simply reroute in the opposite direction to create a loop-back formation. Repeaters are also available to extend the distance of a Token Ring network. Figure 7-15 shows how a Token Ring network might be configured in a large office or multistory building. The main ring connects all the MAUs in a circular formation.

IBM Token Ring cards are available in a 4 Mb/sec version and a 16 Mb/sec version. The faster version has an increased frame length that requires fewer transmissions for the same amount of data. Token Ring networks that follow the IEEE 802.5 standard and use connection methods that expand on the IBM design are now available from several manufacturers. Unshielded twisted-pair cable and MAUs with 16 ports are common. In addition, two- and four-port hubs are

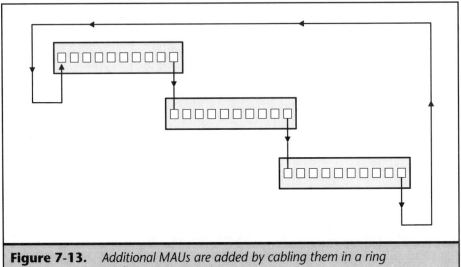

Figure 7-13.   *Additional MAUs are added by cabling them in a ring configuration*

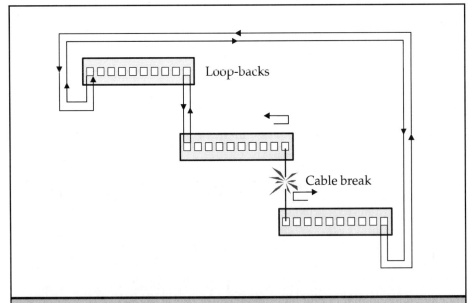

Figure 7-14.   *If a cable between MAUs is cut, a loop-back ring is formed that uses a redundant set of wires in the cable*

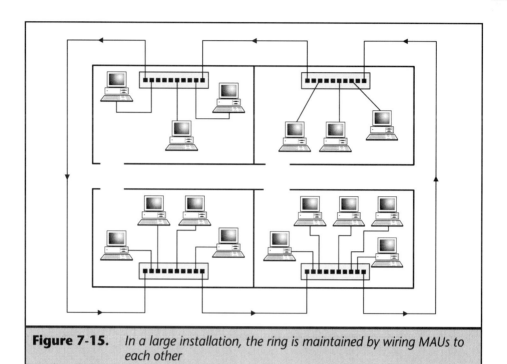

Figure 7-15. *In a large installation, the ring is maintained by wiring MAUs to each other*

available from some vendors. These hubs branch from an eight-port MAU and provide for the connection of two or more workstations in a cluster. Non-IBM vendors also make sophisticated MAU devices that contain many additional port connections as well as fault detection and management features. Token Ring connections are also available on minicomputer and mainframe systems.

IBM Token Ring specifications allow for the following cable types:

Type 1 A shielded cable containing two twisted-pair 22 AWG wires

Type 2 A voice/data shielded cable containing two twisted-pair 22 AWG wires for data with four twisted pairs of 26 AWG wires added outside the shield for voice

Type 3 Contains four solid, unshielded twisted-pair 22 or 24 AWG cables. A media filter is required for use with Token Ring networks. It cannot be used with 16 Mb/sec Token Ring cards

Type 4 Not specified

Type 5 Fiber-optic (100/140 micron) cable (two strands)

Type 6 Flexible, shielded twisted-pair patch cables of 26 AWG wire. Distance is limited to two-thirds that of Type 1. (See "Patch Panel" later in this chapter for cable distances.) A patch cable connects a PC to another device or a wall plug

Type 7 Not Specified

Type 8 Shielded twisted-pair 26 AWG cable for use under carpets. Distance limits are half of Type 1

Type 9 Shielded twisted-pair 26 AWG plenum firesafe cable. Distance is limited to two-thirds that of Type 1

Although Type 1 shielded cable is the most commonly used cable, Type 3 is becoming more popular. Type 3 cannot be used with 16 Mb/sec Token Ring cards, but a specification to implement it is in the works. The components of a standard Token Ring network that uses Type 1 cable are described in the following sections.

TOKEN RING ADAPTERS   Token Ring cards are available in a 4Mb/sec model and a 16 Mb/sec model. If a 16 Mb/sec card is used on a 4 Mb/sec network, it must be operated at 4 Mb/sec. To use both cards, place them on separate segments by installing a card for each speed in the NetWare server. If a Token Ring card is to be used in a diskless workstation, order a remote-boot PROM.

MULTISTATION ACCESS UNITS   A Multistation Access Unit (MAU) connects up to eight workstations by using network adapter cables. Up to 12 MAU devices can be connected. Each IBM MAU is shipped with a setup aid, which is a small device that tests the ports of the MAU. Many non-IBM MAUs have built-in testing devices and up to 16 ports.

TOKEN RING ADAPTER CABLE   The IBM Token Ring adapter cable has a nine-pin connector on one end to attach to the network interface card. On the other end, it has a special Type A data connector that plugs into the MAU. Adapter cables are usually only eight feet in length, but patch cables are available to extend them in increments of up to 150 feet.

PATCH CABLES   Patch cables extend the distance of a workstation from an MAU device, or they cable two or more MAU devices together. They should be

Type 6 cable of any length up to 150 feet. When used, they halve the potential workstation-to-MAU distance.

CONNECTORS   Type 1 cable uses IBM cabling system Type A data connectors, which are hermaphroditic. You can directly connect one Type A connector to another by flipping one over.

MEDIA FILTER   When Type 3 telephone twisted-pair cable is used, a media filter is required at the workstation. It converts cable connectors and reduces line noise.

PATCH PANEL   A patch panel is useful for organizing cable between the MAU and a telephone punchdown block, as shown in Figure 7-16. A standard telephone connector is used to connect the patch panel to the punchdown block. Another method is to wire the MAU directly to the punchdown block.

The maximum number of stations on one ring is 260 for shielded cable and 72 for unshielded telephone twisted-pair cable. The maximum distance from a workstation to an MAU when you use Type 1 cable is 101 meters (330 feet). This assumes that the cable is one continuous segment. If cable segments are joined by using patch cable, the maximum workstation-to-MAU distance is 45 meters (150 feet).

If multiple MAUs are used, they should be stacked together and cabled locally. Calculating the maximum distance of a Token Ring network can be complicated because of its ring nature. The total length of the LAN may vary as each station logs in. For example, if a station connected to an MAU with an

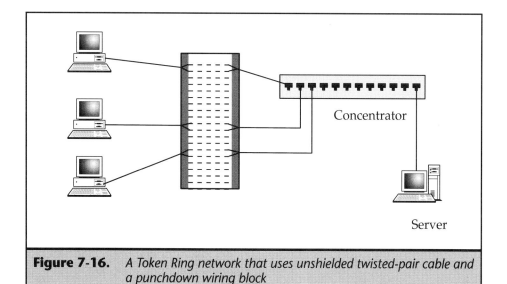

Concentrator

Server

Figure 7-16.   *A Token Ring network that uses unshielded twisted-pair cable and a punchdown wiring block*

8-foot patch cable logs in, 16 feet is added to the total ring distance because of the loop-back of the cable.

Anyone who intends to cable IBM Token Ring networks over large areas should refer to IBM publications on the subject. These are available from IBM dealers. If other vendors are used, refer to their specification sheets or catalogs. Black Box, Andrews, Star-Tek, and Nevada-Western are vendors of non-IBM Token Ring products who have excellent catalogs and planning guides.

Telephone Twisted-Pair Equipment

Token Ring equipment that uses Type 3 telephone twisted-pair cable is available from many vendors. Stations can be directly wired to the MAU units with RJ-45 connectors and cable, or you can use the existing telephone cable if it conforms to the specifications discussed earlier in this chapter. Patch panels provide an in-between connection from the MAUs to the telephone punchdown block. Existing telephone wire provides the connections to workstations, where a media filter adapter is needed to convert from a Type 3 cable connector to a DB-9 connector that attaches to the Token Ring network adapter card. The media filter adapter also reduces noise that may be picked up by the Type 3 cable.

Hubs

You've already seen how hubs, concentrators, and Multistation Access Units (on Token Ring networks) centralize the wiring of a network and create a star topology. Vendors have taken the hub concept even further by creating hub adapter cards and wiring centers, and then adding important management tools to assist network administrators with network monitoring. Management features include the ability to detect problem connections or gather statistical information about network traffic. This information is collected in a Management Information Base (MIB) where it can be accessed by a computer that is running an SNMP (Simple Network Management Protocol) management application.

Hub Adapter

A hub adapter is basically a concentrator box reduced to an interface card that you place in the server. An "octopus" cable that has plug-in ports for workstations extends from the card. Alternatively, a 50-pin Telco connector joins the card to a patch panel in a wiring closet. You can place several hub adapters in a single server and then tie them together by using wiring straps, thus creating a bridge between the ports on the card.

Hub Management Interface (HMI)

Novell's Hub Management Interface standardizes the way server-resident hub cards are implemented and managed. It consists of a set of five extensions to NetWare Open Data-Link Interface (ODI). NetWare Hub Services consists of a set of NLMs that allow hub cards to integrate into a NetWare server.

Management applications that are SNMP compatible can gather and make sense of the statistics provided by hub adapter cards. Administrators can determine whether a server or network is overloaded. HUBCON is an NLM that allows managers to control NHS from a DOS-based console.

Wiring Centers

A wiring center is a separate chassis with its own power supply and plug-in ports for a number of hub adapters. The manufacturers of wiring centers usually manufacture a number of boards for Token Ring networks, Ethernet networks, and fiber-optic backbones. Bridge and router cards are also available for internetworking all the components in the chassis.

The modules designed for wiring centers are not plug-compatible with the bus inside a desktop computer. They are usually about the size of this book. Wiring centers can be quite elaborate, as discussed in Chapter 8. Some wiring centers include high-speed interface buses to keep traffic between modules running as fast as possible. RISC processors and other speed enhancement techniques are used. Redundant power supplies are also common.

Laptop Connections

Laptop computers give users the freedom to take their computers on the road. But when users return to the office, they need a way to plug into the LAN. Most laptops are too small to have adapter interfaces, so to connect to a LAN, users can do one of the following:

■ Purchase a docking station that has adapter slots and then install a network adapter card

■ Purchase an external LAN adapter

■ Connect to the LAN by using a telephone link

■ Buy a new laptop with a built-in LAN adapter

This last choice is rather impractical, but it is an option, especially if someone else doesn't mind inheriting the old unit. The third option is practical for laptop users on the road. For the most part, the second approach is the most practical. A LAN adapter is a small device, about the size of 50 rolled up $10 bills (and that's approximately how much money you'll part with if you buy one).

NOTE: PCMCIA (Personal Computer Memory Card International Association) compatible network adapter cards are becoming popular. These are small credit-card-sized cards that slip into an expansion memory slot on a portable computer. Many new laptops include PCMCIA slots.

External LAN adapters connect to the parallel port of a laptop. Most are compatible with existing LAN card standards, so you can use drivers that are included with Novell NetWare. Vendors such as Xircom Inc. (Calabasas, California), D-Link Systems (Irvine, California), and IQ Technologies (Bothell, Washington) make Token Ring, ArcNet, and Ethernet cards with coaxial or twisted-pair connectors.

Wireless LANs

If you don't like the idea of wiring your building, or if you think workstations will need to be moved on a regular basis, you should consider wireless LAN technology. You won't need to worry about broken cables or people tripping over cables. There are several other advantages. You'll save the wire and labor costs of having cable installed, and you won't have to deal with permits to wire a building, which are required in some areas.

Wireless LAN equipment consists of transmitters and receivers, usually mounted above a workstation. The transmitter unit connects to a standard Ethernet cable system and broadcasts the signals to workstations around it.

There are three techniques for wireless data transmission: narrow-band (or single-frequency) radio, spread spectrum radio, and infrared light. There is not enough space here to discuss the physics of these techniques. However, you should be aware of the following benefits and drawbacks to each technique:

- *Infrared light* This method offers a wide bandwidth that lets it transmit at extremely high rates. It is also not regulated by the government, so there are no restrictions on transmissions. However, infrared light transmissions operate by line of sight. Infrared light transmissions are also susceptible to strong light sources, so systems that produce stronger beams are often necessary. Mirrors can be used to bend infrared light if necessary. Because of the number of obstructions within a typical office building, infrared transmission is probably best used as a link or backbone between buildings.

- *Narrow-band radio* This technique is similar to a broadcast from a radio station. You tune in to a "tight" frequency band on both the transmitter and receiver. The signal can penetrate walls and is spread over a wide area, so focusing is not required. However, narrow-band radio transmissions have problems with radio reflections (ghosting) and are regulated by the FCC. They must be precisely tuned to prevent interference from other frequencies. Motorola uses the narrow-band radio transmission technique in its Altair series. The company received licenses for frequencies in the 19-GHz range, which they allocate to customers based on geographic region. Motorola handles all the FCC licensing for their products.

- *Spread spectrum radio* This technique broadcasts signals over a wide range of frequencies, avoiding problems inherent in narrow-band communications. A code is used to spread the signal, and the receiving station uses the same code to retrieve it. In this way, a spread spectrum signal can operate at any range of frequencies, even if other spread spectrum signals are in the same range. Spread spectrum radio does not interfere with conventional radio because its energy levels are too weak.

If you're interested in wireless LANs, contact Motorola (1-800-233-0877) about their narrow-band products, contact NCR (1-800-544-3333) about their spread spectrum products, or contact BIC Communications (1-800-4-ISOLAN) about their infrared products.

CHAPTER 8

T his chapter describes how to expand a network by using repeaters, bridges, routers, wiring hubs, and other internetworking devices and methods. Because an understanding of protocols and network communications is necessary to understand the concepts in this chapter, familiarize yourself with the material covered in Chapter 6.

Internet-working

When workgroups or departmental networks (called LAN segments from this point on) are connected together, users throughout an entire company can share files, resources, and electronic mail. If all the networks within a company use the same network topology and access method (for example, Ethernet), the job of interconnecting the LAN segments will be relatively easy. Your needs might require sophisticated bridges, routers, wiring concentrators, switching boxes, or other gear as covered in this chapter.

The following topics are discussed

- Expanding the number of stations

- Expanding the distance of a network

- Maintaining network throughput, or performance, as a network expands

- Building internetworks with bridges and routers

- Building gateways to minicomputers, mainframes, and systems that use other operating systems

Internetworking Methods

Figure 8-1 illustrates how each internetworking product relates to the Open Systems Interconnection (OSI) reference model. The tasks these products perform on the network relate to the layers they are compatible with in the protocol stack. The higher a device is in the protocol stack, the more expensive and complex it is.

REPEATERS   Repeaters work at the physical layer. They send packets from a primary network trunk to an extended network trunk. They do not interact with higher-level protocols.

BRIDGES   Bridges interconnect two or more networks and pass packets among them. Different network types are supported.

ROUTERS   Routers are similar to bridges, but they look deeper into a packet's address and get involved in routing it to its destination.

BROUTERS   Brouters are combinations of bridges and routers. Some Brouters allow multiple connections, some of which are bridged and some of which are routed. Brouters tend to have proprietary routing schemes that enhance performance but make them incompatible with routers.

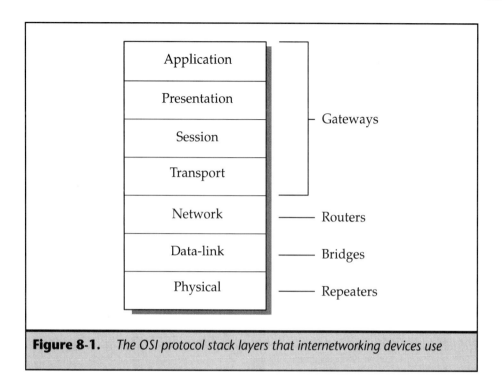

Figure 8-1. *The OSI protocol stack layers that internetworking devices use*

GATEWAYS   Gateways work at the highest levels of the protocol stack to allow systems and networks that use incompatible protocols to interconnect.

The range of interconnected networks can vary. For example, you could interconnect the LAN in sales, on the first floor, with the LAN in accounting, on the second floor with a bridge. To connect to the LAN segment in the manufacturing area at an off-site location, you could attach a router and use a direct-link fiber-optic connection or the telephone system. A router helps keep unnecessary traffic off the remote link. This type of link could also interconnect LAN segments in different states or countries. The following sections discuss the internetworking products in detail, starting with repeaters.

Repeaters

As electrical signals are transmitted on a cable, they tend to degenerate in proportion to the length of the cable. This is called *attenuation*. A repeater is a simple add-on device that boosts a cable's signal so that you can extend the length of the network. A repeater does not normally change a signal in any way except to boost it for retransmission on the extended cable segment. Some repeaters also filter noise. A repeater is basically a "dumb" device with the following characteristics:

- A repeater regenerates network signals so that they can travel further.

- Repeaters are primarily used in linear cable systems such as Ethernet.

- Repeaters operate at the lowest level of a protocol stack: the physical level. Higher-level protocols are not used.

- Both segments connected by a repeater must use the same media access method.

- Repeaters are normally used within a single building.

- Segments connected by a repeater become part of the same network and have the same network address.

- Every node on a network segment has its own address. Nodes on extended segments cannot have the same addresses as nodes on existing segments because they become part of the same network segment.

Repeaters normally operate at the same transmission speed as the networks they connect. The transmission speed of a repeater is in the range of 15,000 packets per second (pps) for a typical Ethernet network. Repeaters range in price from $1500 to $3000.

NOTE: Extending a LAN and adding more workstations increases congestion on the LAN. A general rule is to not exceed 50 workstations per LAN segment. If congestion is high, consider splitting the LAN into two or more segments by using a bridge. Think of repeaters as connections to distant workstations, rather than as a way to add more workstations.

Bridges

A bridge adds a level of intelligence to a network connection. It joins two similar or dissimilar LAN segments. You can think of a bridge as a mail sorter that looks at the addresses of packets and places them on the appropriate network segments. You can create a bridge in a NetWare server by installing two or more network interface cards. Each LAN segment can be of a different network type

(Ethernet, Token Ring, ArcNet, fiber-optic, and so on). NetWare's built-in bridge and router functions distribute network traffic among the LAN segments.

You can create a bridge to split a large network into two or more smaller networks. This improves performance by reducing traffic, because packets for individual workstations don't need to travel over the entire network, as shown in Figure 8-2. A bridge is also used to join two dissimilar LAN types, such as Ethernet and Token Ring, as shown in Figure 8-3.

Bridges work at the data-link layer. Any device that conforms to the Media Access Control (MAC) layer specifications can bridge with other MAC layer devices. Recall that the MAC layer is a sublayer of the data-link layer. The MAC layer is modular; a network interface card driver attaches its access control routines to the layer, as shown in Figure 8-4. The upper Logical Link Control (LLC) layer then serves as a switchboard and bridge between the modules in the MAC layer. Packets flow between networks by passing through the LLC layer. This extra processing introduces some latency in the bandwidth of the network as compared to not bridging or using a repeater. However, advances in bridge design have minimized this performance problem.

You can bridge devices that use different protocols, but the data-link layer doesn't know anything about the best path to a destination; there is no way to forward packets to a LAN segment that will get them to their destination in the quickest or most efficient way. That is the job of a router. Bridges do provide filtering, however. Filtering prevents packets for a local LAN segment from crossing a bridge and traveling on segments where they have no business. This helps reduce internetwork traffic and boosts performance. Without filtering, packets are sent everywhere on a network.

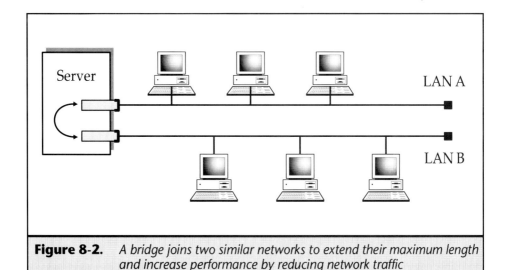

Figure 8-2. *A bridge joins two similar networks to extend their maximum length and increase performance by reducing network traffic*

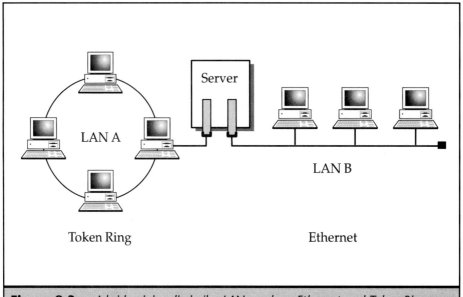

Figure 8-3.   *A bridge joins dissimilar LANs such as Ethernet and Token Ring*

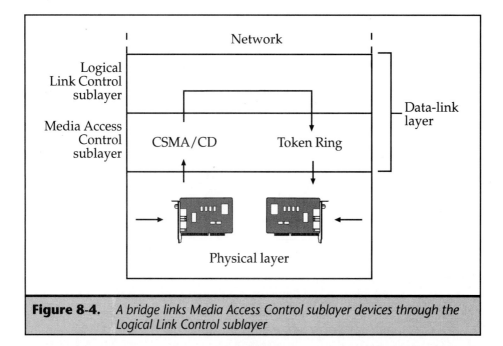

Figure 8-4.   *A bridge links Media Access Control sublayer devices through the Logical Link Control sublayer*

You install bridges for the following reasons:

■ To extend an existing network when the maximum distance has been reached

■ To remove traffic bottlenecks caused by too many workstations attached to a single LAN segment. This puts a smaller number of users on each LAN and increases performance

■ To connect different types of networks together, such as Token Ring and Ethernet networks

Each LAN segment connected by a bridge has a distinct network address. The network address can be thought of as a street, and each workstation can be thought of as a house on that street. The address of a LAN segment is assigned during network installation. It is used to route packets between segments. In addition, a network may have more than one server, so NetWare assigns each server a special IPX internal number to distinguish it from other servers.

Types of Bridges

The NetWare server isn't the only bridge available. A number of vendors make external bridging devices that connect one or more LAN segments, as shown in Figure 8-5. Many bridging functions are now performed by routers, which offer additional features and routing functions. Prices of routers have come down in the last few years, making them a better choice for interconnecting LANs. However, if all you'll ever need is bridging, there is no point in spending extra money. Several types of bridging devices are described in the next paragraphs.

Learning Bridges

Learning, or adaptive bridges "learn" the addresses of other stations on the LAN, making it unnecessary for the bridge installer or manager to create a table of these addresses in the bridge. Workstations constantly broadcast their identification signals, and the bridge builds tables from these addresses. Most bridges now on the market are learning bridges.

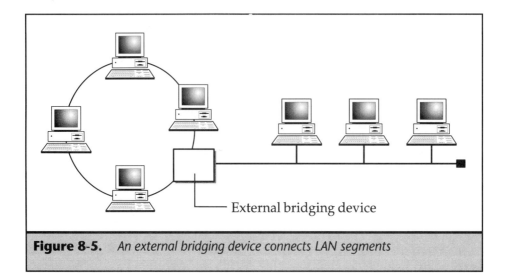

Figure 8-5. *An external bridging device connects LAN segments*

Spanning Tree Bridges

When a bridge connection is critical, it might be necessary to create fault-tolerant redundant bridges. If one bridge goes down, the other assumes the traffic load. However, when two links exist, there is the possibility that traffic will travel across one and loop back over the other, creating a circular traffic pattern that could continue endlessly. Spanning tree bridges detect and break circular traffic patterns by disabling certain links. The IEEE 801.2-D spanning tree protocol (STP) inhibits loops in redundant bridges by maintaining the secondary bridge as a backup. If the first bridge should go down, the secondary bridge takes over.

Load Balancing Bridges

The load balancing bridge is the most efficient form of bridge. It uses a spanning tree-type algorithm, and it uses a dual link to transfer packets, thus improving internetwork performance.

Bridge Forwarding and Filtering Functions

A bridge in a NetWare server (which is more appropriately a router) reads the destination address of a packet and determines whether the packet belongs to one of its workstations or should be sent to another LAN segment. The bridge filters all packets and forwards those not meant for its workstations. Novell often calls its bridges routers because they provide routing functions, which are described later in this chapter.

Filtering helps avoid bottlenecks on bridges by keeping local traffic off the internetwork. Since network and node addresses are the only information available to bridges, this is the only filtering they can perform. You should use routers if advanced filtering and "best-path" forwarding of packets through a complex internetwork route is required. Because routers work at the network layer, they have access to more information about the packet and its destination and can use this information to improve packet delivery. For example, a router to an IBM host system will filter out non-IBM packets.

Source Routing

IBM Token Ring networks use a special source routing routine that tells the bridge not only where packets should go but how to get there. In source routing, the packets themselves hold the forwarding information. The bridge does not maintain forwarding tables; it sends packets to LAN segments based on the packet address information.

Bridges that do source routing use a *discovery* method to determine the route a packet should take to a device. Note that although this sounds like routing, the source routing bridge is simply a forwarding device that knows the addresses of other bridges. Best-path routing information is contained within the packet.

A workstation that needs to send a message to a workstation or server on another LAN segment sends an *explorer* packet over the entire network. If there are multiple bridges on the network, multiple copies of the packet appear at the destination because each bridge sends its own copy of the explorer packet to the destination. The destination workstation receives all these copies and determines the best route through the internetwork based on information stored in the packets about the paths they took. It then communicates this best-path information back to the sending station, which stores it for future use and places it in packets that it sends to the destination.

Bridging Products

There are too many vendors who make bridging products to mention here, and many are converting their bridging products to routers. If you are in the market for bridges, it is useful to know some of their specifications, such as their packet transfer rates. For more information, refer to various industry journals and magazines. There you will find the latest information on these fast changing computer products.

Routers

Routers are critical to large internetworks and Wide Area Networks that use remote communications links. Routers keep traffic flowing efficiently over defined paths in a complex internetwork like that shown in Figure 8-6. If leased lines with low throughput are used, it is important to filter out packets that should not cross the line. In addition, large internetworks that span the globe might contain multiple and redundant remote connections. It then becomes important to find the best path from a source to a destination. That's where routers come into play. They are capable of looking at information in the network layer to determine best-path information. Many routing products provide support for various communications methods, such as T1 and X.25.

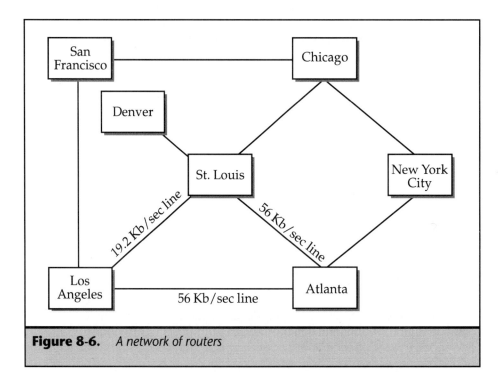

Figure 8-6.   *A network of routers*

Here are a few reasons why you would use routers instead of bridges:

■ Routers provide advanced packet filtering.

■ Routers are necessary when there are multiple protocols on an internetwork and specific protocol packets must be confined to a certain area.

■ Routers provide intelligent routing, which improves performance. An intelligent router knows the layout of a network and can easily find the best path for a packet.

■ Because routers perform advanced filtering, they are important when slow but expensive remote communications lines are used.

How Routers Work

A router examines network-layer routing information in packets and routes the packets to the appropriate network segment. If the router is in a server, it forwards packets destined for that server to its upper-layer protocols. A router processes only packets that are addressed to it, which includes packets that are addressed to other routers that it is attached to. Routers send packets via the best route to the destination. They maintain tables of adjacent routers and LANs on the network. When a router receives a packet, it looks at these tables to see if it can send the packet directly to the destination. If not, it determines the location of a router that can forward the packet to its destination.

NOTE: Some protocols, such as NetBIOS, are not routable because they don't include network address information in their packets. However, NetBIOS packets can be encapsulated into IPX or TCP/IP packets for transfer across internetworks. Likewise, IPX packets can be encapsulated into TCP/IP packets for transfer across TCP/IP network segments.

The forwarding process does reduce throughput, and if a NetWare server is handling the routing it can reduce its performance. If this occurs, you can move routing to an external system by installing the Novell MultiProtocol Router, which is discussed later in this chapter. Many third-party routers use advanced processing to minimize the overhead of packet processing.

Routers are either protocol specific or they can handle multiple protocols. A protocol-specific router can handle only one type of packet, such as IPX. This is the default mode when you install multiple network cards in a NetWare server to provide routing. A multiprotocol router can handle different protocols, such as

SPX/IPX and TCP/IP. A NetWare router becomes a multiprotocol router when you install NetWare Loadable Modules (NLMs) that provide support for other protocols. For example, you can install TCP/IP support at the server in addition to the default SPX/IPX packets.

Routers allow a network to be segmented into logical networks. These logical networks are easier to manage. Each LAN segment has its own specific LAN number, and each workstation on that segment has its own address. This is the information contained in the network layer that routers access. Segmenting prevents *broadcast storms*. Broadcast storms occur when nodes are connected improperly and the network becomes saturated with broadcast messages looking for a destination. Filtering and best-path methods used when segmenting help reduce the effect.

Choosing the Best Path

An internetwork is usually built with fault tolerance in mind. Several paths are created among routers to provide a backup path in case one or more should fail. Some of these paths may use high-speed networks such as the Fiber Distributed Data Interface (FDDI) in the campus or metropolitan area or direct digital lines (T1) for Wide Area Networks. Routers can send data over the best of these paths, depending on which is the least costly to use, the fastest, or the most direct. Best paths are often determined by the number of hops a packet must take through the router network to get to its destination. A best path might also be a path that goes around congested LAN segments, which is determined based on line speed. For example, high-priority packets can be sent over a 56 Kb/sec digital communications link, and low-priority packets can be sent over a 19.2 Kb/sec telecommunications link. The network administrator can decide what the best paths are on a network, or in some cases, have the routers choose the best path.

A network of routers is shown in Figure 8-6. If Los Angeles wants to send a message to St. Louis, the router can use the 19.2 Kb/sec direct-connect line or the 56 Kb/sec lines that go to Atlanta and then to St. Louis. In another situation, if New York City wants to send a message to Los Angeles, the router can choose the route through Chicago and San Francisco, or it can go through Atlanta. The router might base these decisions on the amount of congestion at Chicago or Atlanta or on the "hop count." The New York City to Los Angeles connection makes two hops if it goes through Atlanta and three hops if it goes through Chicago and San Francisco. Of course, if the New York City to Los Angeles traffic is regularly heavy, it would probably be best to install a direct connection.

Note the redundant links in Figure 8-6. If the Chicago to San Francisco line went down, messages from New York City to Los Angeles could be routed through Atlanta or through Chicago and St. Louis. Also note that Denver is isolated and would lose LAN connections if its line went down. Filtering and best-path selection become extremely important in a multiple-path network like this. Traffic on the New York City LAN segment that is meant for New York City workstations must be kept local, and internetwork traffic must find the most efficient paths to keep costs down.

Routing Protocols

Routing protocols define a method whereby routers can communicate with one another and share information about the network. The protocols run in the routers and build routing tables based on an exchange of routing information with other routers. Over time, the routing tables in each routing device should contain roughly the same routing information.

Routing tables contain information about the number of hops it will take to get to another router. They also provide information about downed routers, alternative routes, and throughput information that might assist in the routing of packets. There are several ways to obtain routing information, as described next.

Distance vector protocol methods A router using a distance vector protocol method periodically broadcasts its routing tables across the entire network. This network-wide broadcasting does not have much of an impact on small networks, but it can significantly impact the bandwidth of large networks. Distance vector methods find the best route to a destination based on the number of router hops to that destination, which, as you've seen in Figure 8-6, is not always the best or least costly path. The Routing Information Protocol (RIP) method used by SPX/IPX does not allow for more than 16 hops. Link-state protocol methods offer a better solution.

Link-state protocol methods A link-state protocol method is more suited for a large internetwork. Routing table information is sent only when there is a change in the information. It is not broadcast on a regular basis as with distance vector methods. With link-state protocols, you can set the best path by creating multiple paths or by specifying the route with the best speed, the highest capacity, or the highest reliability.

Some common routing protocols are listed here:

■ *RIP (Routing Information Protocol)* RIP was originally developed for the Xerox Network System (XNS) and is now used by SPX/IPX and TCP/IP. RIP is a distance vector protocol and is inefficient for Wide Area Networks.

- *NLSP (NetWare Link Service Protocol)*   NLSP is a protocol designed by Novell to replace the RIP protocol used by SPX/IPX. It improves packet transmission between users on different LAN segments. Each router knows the topology of the network, and broadcasting of routing tables is reduced.

- *OSPF (Open Shortest Path First)*   OSPF is a link-state protocol that is part of the TCP/IP protocol suite. OSPF routes according to traffic, line costs, priority, and congestion.

- *OSI IS-IS (Open Systems Interconnection Intermediate System to Intermediate System)*   OSI IS-IS is a link-state protocol that has many of the same features as OSPF but is designed for greater interoperability between OSI-compliant systems.

- *Apple RTMP (Routing Table Maintenance Protocol)*   RTMP is an Apple protocol that finds the best path between AppleTalk zones. Broadcasts occur every 10 seconds.

Router Specifications

If your network is small or in a single building, you can often get by with bridges. This assumes the number of interconnected networks does not create a complicated path from one end to the other. Large networks that consist of many different LAN segments connected by a number of different links (FDDI, modems, or digital lines) require routers to segment traffic and keep the internetwork bandwidth from being saturated by non-internetwork packets. Routers also offer management capabilities that bridges don't have, and in the case of hubs and wiring centers, can be placed in one central location. Multiprotocol routers, such as the Novell MultiProtocol Router (MPR), can handle multiple protocols. (Wiring centers and the Novell MultiProtocol Router are discussed later in this chapter.)

When evaluating and buying routers, make sure all the routers in your internetwork use the same routing methods and handle the same protocols. Some routers use data compression techniques to increase the throughput of packets. To avoid problems, always try to use the same routers in all locations. Although routing methods are generally standardized, a mismatch will inhibit or prevent proper communication between LAN segments.

Fault tolerance features, such as redundant power supplies and "live" module replacement, are now offered on high-end systems. Router setup is often difficult because features such as multiple protocols, redundant paths, performance, and security must be programmed into the device. A good installation program can ease this burden. Novell's MPR simplifies setup somewhat by supplying default parameters for packet size, timers, and other features that are tuned to NetWare networks.

Routers are available in several price ranges. At the high end are complete wiring hubs that integrate all network ports, bridges, and routers in one unit at one location. Prices for these units start at about $20,000. They typically include 16 ports with optional support for wide area connections, such as FDDI and T1. At the middle of the price range are units priced from $10,000 to $20,000. These units usually have fewer ports, but they do offer centralized wiring schemes and management. At the low end are stand-alone router units that you place at various locations on your internetwork to connect LAN segments together. These units are priced under $10,000.

Routers can be categorized as local or remote routers. A local router has connections for LAN equipment, such as Token Ring, Ethernet, and FDDI segments. A remote router has MAN and WAN connections that provide FDDI ports for connection to campus-wide networks, or it has X.25, T1, satellite, microwave, and other ports for long distance connections. Long distance connections are defined as telephone circuits that require modems or digital T1 lines that you can lease from the phone company or other providers or as satellite and microwave links. Long distance connections are covered in Chapter 9.

Looking at Speed

It's interesting to look at speed figures to get an idea of just how fast bridges and routers are. The number of packets per second (pps) forwarded is the usual gauge for bridge and router speed. Ethernet (10 Mb/sec, or megabits per second) forwards about 14,880 pps on its own cable if all the packets are 64 bytes. A bridge attached to Ethernet typically filters 14,000 pps and forwards 10,000. Routers commonly forward from 8000 to 15,000 packets per second. The store-and-forward latency of bridges and routers decreases throughput somewhat. Novell's MPR forwards packets at 3000 to 4000 per second.

The packet-per-second throughput of bridges and routers does not need to be higher than the capabilities of the LANs they are attached to. Also keep in mind that traffic across the bridge is less than local traffic. Although bursts from high-performance systems can saturate even the normal Ethernet wire bandwidth, the contention mechanism of the Ethernet cable access method adds enough overhead at high volumes to keep the traffic low at the bridge or router. A bridge or router that can process 5000 64-byte packets per second is usually adequate once you figure in this overhead. Token Ring networks have a similar saturation point. The wire itself constrains bandwidth more than a bridge does. Forwarding of Token Ring packets is handled adequately by bridges and routers that transfer from 2000 to 3000 packets per second. Note that high forwarding rates are less important for WAN connections because the WAN itself usually runs on a media type forwarding rate with much slower throughput than a LAN. Compare 1 Mb/sec for WANs to 10 Mb/sec for Ethernet LANs.

NetWare Routing

NetWare has its own bridging and routing capabilities that support multiple protocols. NetWare v. 3.11 was the first NetWare version to support SPX/IPX, TCP/IP, and AppleTalk routing. The architecture that allows multiprotocol routing in a NetWare server is Novell's Open Data-Link Interface (ODI). It provides two important features. First, it allows a single network interface card to use more than one protocol stack. Users can send SPX/IPX packets through the card to the NetWare operating system and route TCP/IP packets through the server to another system. Second, it's easy for card manufacturers to make their cards compatible with MPR. They simply write an ODI-compatible driver, which lets the card use any protocol stack supported by NetWare.

The ODI architecture in the server is modular. It consists of the protocol stacks, the Link Support Layer (LSL), and the Multiple Link Interface Driver (MLID). The protocol stacks and the MLID are modular. You install them by using commands at the NetWare console or the INSTALL utility. The LSL is the all-important link between the network cards and the protocol stacks. It provides a common interface that both plug into, and it serves as a switching device to direct the packets to the right protocol stack so that they can be processed by the server or sent on to their destinations. In other words, if the protocol stack that receives the packet determines that it is not for the current server, it sends the packet back to the LSL for forwarding to the MLID and the appropriate network.

The SPX/IPX protocol is built into NetWare. TCP/IP protocol support is included with NetWare, but it is installed as an option. Loading TCP/IP protocol support is menu driven in NetWare v.4.

Running the NetWare file server as a routing device is fine for small networks. However, each protocol stack takes up memory and some of the server's processing time. You can use the Novell MultiProtocol Router NLM product, which is discussed next, to move routing from the file server to a separate platform.

The Novell MultiProtocol Router

The Novell MultiProtocol Router is a set of NetWare Loadable Modules that can be installed in a NetWare file server or in a separate system. It comes with a limited version of NetWare called NetWare Runtime so that you can run the router in a system other than the NetWare file server. The software can route SPX/IPX, TCP/IP, AppleTalk, and Novell NetBIOS packets over Ethernet, Token Ring, ArcNet, and AppleTalk LAN segments. It also supports wide area connections through X.25, 64 Kb/sec (kilobit per second), or T1 lines. For SPX/IPX users, the NetWare Link Service Protocol (NLSP) is a link-state routing protocol that replaces the Routing Information Protocol (RIP) of SPX/IPX. For TCP/IP users, the Open Shortest Path First (OSPF) protocol is used. Both provide faster data transmissions between LAN segments.

MPR requires an 80386 or better computer system. It is bundled with NetWare Hub Services, a monitoring and management system for integrating hubs into NetWare platforms. With NetWare Hub Services, you can build router and hub connection systems. The multiprotocol router also includes WAN links for wide area network routing, as discussed in Chapters 9 and 19.

Backbones

A backbone is a cable that connects two or more LAN segments and provides a high-speed data pathway among them. Whereas a bridge is formed by placing two or more network cards in a server, internetworks are formed by connecting multiple servers or LAN segments, often to a backbone cable. Backbone cables are typically high-transmission media such as fiber-optic cable. Alternatively, wiring hubs, which are discussed later in this chapter, provide a way to create backbones that connect multiple LAN segments within a single box and are often referred to as "collapsed backbones."

A server-based backbone is illustrated in Figure 8-7. Each server contains two or more network cards. One of the cards connects the server to the backbone and provides the connection to the other LAN segments that are attached to the backbone. The other cards in the server attach to local segments. Server-based backbones provide alternatives to routers if your internetwork consists of only a few LAN segments.

A router-based backbone is shown in Figure 8-8. The router is the connection point to the backbone cable, which might be a dual-ring fiber-optic cable that follows the FDDI specification. Bridges or routers provide the transitions between LAN segments and the fiber-optic backbone. The configuration in Figure 8-8 illustrates some interesting connections. On the left, a router

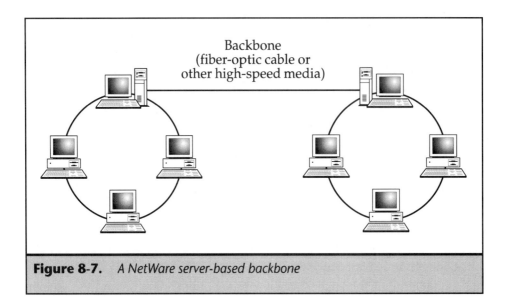

Figure 8-7. *A NetWare server-based backbone*

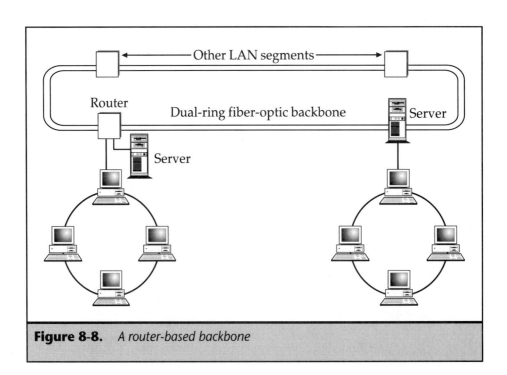

Figure 8-8. *A router-based backbone*

distributes backbone fiber-optic connections to a server and a LAN segment. On the right, a server is connected directly to the fiber-optic backbone so that it has a direct 100 Mb/sec connection to the line. This increases performance, especially if the server is a "superserver" system that can more than adequately handle the traffic on the backbone. The dual-fiber ring provides redundancy; if the line is cut, a loopback is formed to keep traffic flowing.

Figure 8-9 illustrates another way to use a backbone. In this case, the LAN segment on each floor of an office building is connected to a backbone that runs through the conduit from one floor to the next. In this example, the servers are connected to the backbone.

NOTE: Unlike copper-based cable, fiber-optic cable does not conduct electrical signals, and therefore it can be used to prevent grounding loops when connecting LAN segments connected to different power sources. Grounding loops can cause electrical disturbances and failure in delicate electronic equipment. This is discussed in more detail in Chapter 13.

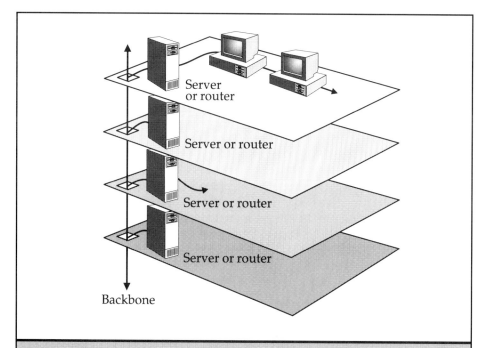

Figure 8-9.   *A backbone connection for a multistory office building*

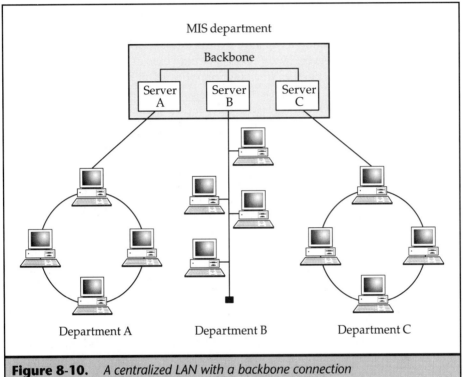

Figure 8-10.   *A centralized LAN with a backbone connection*

Backbones for Centralized Management

For management purposes, you can group servers in one location by using a backbone. For example, you could move the servers from each department in a company to a central location, as shown in Figure 8-10. From this location, network managers can more easily monitor and service the internetwork. Network cabling is run from the servers to each department. You can use fiber-optic cable as the backbone cable, or you can use wiring hubs, as discussed in the next section. Either give excellent performance for server-to-server and LAN-to-LAN interconnection.

Some of the advantages of centralizing your servers and network management are listed here:

■ Servers are centrally located to improve monitoring and maintenance.

■ Security is enhanced because the server area can be locked and fireproofed.

■ Servers are not locked into individual departments where maintenance personnel may have trouble accessing them during off-hours.

■ Performance is easier to monitor and improve when servers are centrally located.

■ Backups and other services can be performed in one area by trained personnel.

■ Backup power requirements and electrical filtering can be optimized for the server area.

■ It is simpler to make connections to campus-wide or Metropolitan Area Network backbone connections.

Backbone Bandwidth

Although a backbone might offer ten times the data transfer rate of a LAN segment, that bandwidth is shared by every workstation that uses the backbone. For example, if two workstations communicate over a 100 Mb/sec fiber-optic backbone, there is the potential to transfer data at 100 Mb/sec. If an additional two stations use the backbone, the potential bandwidth available to each station is halved. Each session uses some of the bandwidth, so the more traffic on the backbone, the more its performance degrades. This is covered later in this chapter in "FDDI and ATM."

Wiring Hubs

Wiring hubs are control centers that are used to manage and monitor the network wiring for a building, a campus-wide area, or an entire company. Often referred to as *structured wiring centers*, wiring hubs are similar to backbone networks, except that the backbone is the backplane or bus of a concentrator chassis.

These devices became popular in the desktop networking environment with the growth of star-configured 10BASE-T. Users were expanding their networks by buying additional 10-port or 12-port concentrator boxes and linking them together with connection cables. Why not build a single box with expansion slots, and then put the 10 or 12 RJ-45 connectors on an expansion card that you can plug into the chassis? The expansion bus in the concentrator module became the backbone (backplane) of the network. Users could then add expansion cards to the concentrator as they needed them. The shared bus provides connections between modules, and the cost of housing individual concentrators is removed. Vendors started improving the bus by boosting its transfer rate.

Figure 8-11 illustrates a typical concentrator, and Figure 8-12 shows one of the modules that mounts in the concentrator box. (Both photographs are courtesy of DAVID Systems Incorporated.) This concentrator accommodates 12 expansion slots for 10BASE-T, Token Ring (RJ-45), and FDDI modules. A WAN server module is also available to provide wide area links. Asynchronous connections run at 19.2 Kb/sec and synchronous connections run at T1/E1 speeds. Public Data Network X.25 interfaces are also supported.

Wiring hubs are platforms for the interconnection of many types of network communications modules. They are similar to a computer system in that they contain a power supply and a plug-in expansion bus, but they are also quite different. For example, the plug-in expansion bus is usually proprietary and extremely fast. Wellfleet Communications has a symmetric multiprocessing modular system that links a processor module to a link module. This pair, and others like it, connect to a set of four 256 Mb/sec buses that handle internetwork traffic. The unit supports major LAN, WAN, and FDDI interfaces. Depending on the number of modules installed, performance ranges from 100,000 pps to 500,000 pps.

Wiring hubs are central connection and management points for your network. They provide management facilities that you can control from a

Figure 8-11.   *A DAVID Systems Incorporated ExpressBus concentrator (courtesy of DAVID Systems Inc.)*

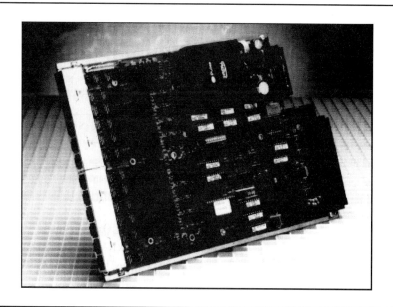

Figure 8-12. *A DAVID Systems Incorporated ExpressBus plug-in module (courtesy of DAVID Systems Inc.)*

workstation, usually with Windows graphics-based applications that show maps of the entire network and let you zoom in on individual segments to view statistics or auditing information. Management consoles are sometimes attached to an RS-232 port on the concentrator, which gives you the ability to manage the hub from a remote location by using a modem connection. Most concentrators are also manageable from a workstation on the network itself.

SNMP (Simple Network Management Protocol) is the most common management environment protocol. Novell recently announced the NetWare Management System (NMS), which lets managers control all NMS-compliant devices from a single management console. SNMP is a generally accepted standard that provides a common communications protocol among different vendors' products. It provides methods for recording information about devices in a management information base (MIB). This information might contain packet throughput values or error values. MIBs are common for devices that conform to SNMP; therefore, SNMP management utilities can collect the MIB information from any vendor's device and present it to the system administrator at the management console. However, SNMP is somewhat limited in functionality. It gained its current prominence mainly because it was an available standard that many vendors were already using. Other management techniques are emerging, and vendors are adding their own proprietary improvements to SNMP.

Wiring Hub Features

Wiring hubs use proprietary designs, so each vendor's product is different. If you're in the market for a wiring hub, you need to read the advertisements and literature from vendors and the product evaluations in industry journals. Products are changing constantly, and vendors are creating modular, expanding systems that give you room for future growth. Several hub features are described here:

- *Power redundancy*   Some units have a backup power supply that either shares the power load with the main power supply or kicks in when it fails.

- *Hot swap modules*   This feature lets you change a module without downing the entire unit.

- *Management*   As described earlier, management features usually include remote management capabilities and SNMP support.

- *Easy reconfiguration*   When workstations or users are moved among workgroups, it should be easy to reconfigure the station into the new arrangement. This can be done with software on some systems.

Some hubs use Ethernet or FDDI as the backplane instead of proprietary methods. There is potential for performance loss with Ethernet or FDDI methods because the bandwidth of the buses deteriorates as more workstations use the buses. Proprietary bus systems use hardware and software methods to boost performance, such as the use of RISC processors.

FDDI and ATM

Two data transfer technologies are used as backbones in the emerging high-speed internetwork environment. There is an increasing need for bandwidth. Engineering and scientific workstations are common on LANs and internetworks. They demand bandwidth when transferring large graphics files and when connecting to host systems. Client-server computer applications that distribute processing to various computers on a network also add to the need for better network bandwidth. FDDI and ATM are possible solutions. They are discussed in the following sections.

FDDI

The Fiber Distributed Data Interface is a fiber-optic cable standard developed by the American National Standards Institute (ANSI) X3T9.5 committee. It operates at 100 Mb/sec and uses a dual-ring topology. FDDI is being implemented as a backbone in the campus-wide and corporate environments. The dual counter-rotating rings offer redundancy. If a link fails in the ring, the ring reconfigures itself, as shown on the right in Figure 8-13, so it can continue passing network traffic until the break is fixed.

FDDI is an excellent medium for building backbones, as shown in Figure 8-8. LAN segments attach to the backbone, along with minicomputers, mainframes, and other systems. Currently, FDDI provides the fastest backbone available, although ATM is gaining ground. Small networks that consist of a few LAN segments will probably benefit more from a normal Ethernet backbone or one of the new 100Mbs systems. Large networks with many LAN segments and heavy traffic caused by high-performance workstations, graphics file transfers, or other internetwork traffic will benefit from FDDI. FDDI is a shareable medium, which means that its bandwidth goes down as more stations use it to establish internetwork connections.

NOTE: If you use a copper-wire-based backbone, be sure to protect against ground loopbacks, as discussed in Chapter 13.

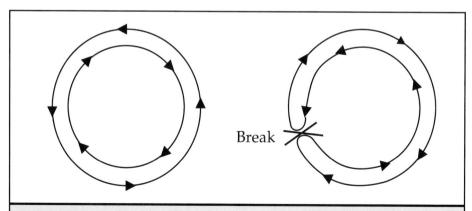

Break

Figure 8-13.   *FDDI reconfigures itself as a single ring when a link fails*

Some advantages of fiber-optic cable are listed here:

- Fiber-optic cable is immune to electromagnetic interference, making it ideal in areas where interference normally causes problems.

- Fiber-optic cable does not suffer from problems inherent in copper cable that causes data errors and the need to retransmit packets. Adding more modes does not reduce bandwidth as fast as occurs on Ethernet.

- Fiber-optic cable is secure. It does not emit a signal outside the cable that intruders can monitor.

- Fiber-optic networks can reach miles with few repeaters, and fiber-optic cable can replace other transmission methods, such as microwave and telecommunications links.

FDDI uses a token-passing access method. A token frame is passed around the network from station to station. If a station needs to transmit, it acquires the token. Stations act as repeaters by transmitting frames that they receive to the next station. Multiple frames can exist on the network if a station relinquishes the token while its frames are in transit. Other stations can be transmitting in such a case. Two stations can enter into a dialog and transmit data while other stations transmit the token in the normal way. Both rings can be used to transmit data in a counter-rotating way. A management mechanism called station management (SMT) enables system administrators to manage and monitor FDDI networks, isolate faulty nodes, and route traffic.

The maximum number of stations on one network is 500. There is single-mode and multi-mode fiber-optic cable. Single-mode cable passes one frequency of light, and multi-mode cable passes several frequencies of light. FDDI networks can span areas of approximately 200 kilometers (120 miles). The maximum distance between stations is 2 kilometers when using multi-mode cable and 60 kilometers when using single-mode cable. In reality, when using single-mode cable, most routers support a maximum distance of about half that, depending on the type of laser used in the device.

FDDI can be costly, with adapters in the $1000 range and cable costing about $1.50 per foot (compared to about $0.30 for Ethernet cable). FDDI concentrators can cost as much as $5,000. FDDI is also hard to install and maintain. A new standard called CDDI (Copper Distributed Data Interface) allows for the use of copper wire at the same speeds as FDDI. Copper wire is easier to install and is cheaper, making the CDDI standard more feasible.

ATM

ATM (Asynchronous Transfer Mode) is a broadband packet-switched data communications technology that is designed to combine the characteristics of dependable-delay time-division multiplexers (TDMs) and a variable-delay Local Area Network. So what does that mean? The terms are defined here:

- A broadband network is one in which signals travel as radio-frequency signals over separate channels. Data, voice, and video are supported simultaneously over multiple transmission channels.

- Packet switching is the ability to deliver small units of information (packets) on ATM channels. A message is divided into packets of 48 bytes each (called *cells* in ATM), and a 5-byte header is appended to create a cell size of 53 bytes. The packets are placed on an ATM channel, and they are usually mixed with other packets (multiplexed). At the receiving end, the packets are reassembled.

- Time-division multiplexing is a way to combine separate signals into a single high-speed transmission. With ATM, cells from many sources are placed on the media. They may be mixed together, but each has a specific destination address. In time-division multiplexing, signals arrive in order at regular time intervals. In other words, all cells are the same size, both in bytes and in time.

- Variable-delay is typical in LANs because each network method might use a different packet size. ATM simply splits large packets to fit within its cell size and sends them across the data channel; they are reassembled on the other side.

ATM provides a way to simultaneously send packetized information from many sources across a high-speed line, where it is reassembled and handed to each destination system. The most interesting thing about ATM is that it applies to a whole range of data communications, from the data bus of a wiring hub to an international data communications system. ATM cannot be overlooked as a potential standard for integrating all computer and communications systems. Vendors are marketing wiring hubs with ATM backplanes and ATM connections to Wide Area Networks.

ATM combines multiplexing and packet switching into a universal method of transferring data. LAN, voice, and video transfers are supported. Cells (ATM packets) are processed quickly because they are small. There is little delay in switching the packets. This is important for voice and video transfers, which are time sensitive.

ATM is a transport protocol that operates roughly at the MAC sublayer in the data-link layer of the protocol stack. Because of this, it can work above many physical-layer topologies. ATM does not rely on any particular protocol. It can map any kind of packet into its 53-byte cell and transport it over a backbone or a WAN.

ATM is defining the future of Wide Area Network communications. It will remove the barrier between LANs and WANs. That barrier is the drop in throughput associated with data transfers over public networks. LAN-to-WAN bridges or routers convert LAN data to WAN data, and introduce delays in doing so. ATM can use SONET (Synchronous Optical Network) as its physical medium for wide area networking. SONET is a fiber-optic cable standard that telephone companies are implementing in the public telephone and communications network.

ATM transfer rates are scaleable, depending on the capacity of the physical layer. With ATM, there is no standard that locks the transmission rate as there is with FDDI (100 Mb/sec). The small cell size does not require special processing, which is required with FDDI. ATM cells are easy to build, whereas FDDI requires protocol conversions that cause delays. ATM can be used now on existing T1 lines, subrate T1 lines, and T3 lines, as discussed in Chapter 9. A conversion is required to do the same for FDDI. ATM uses independent paths to network users when it is implemented on a LAN. FDDI is a shared medium; the more users accessing the cable, the more the bandwidth is reduced.

ADC/Fibermux is one company selling high-speed ATM backbone hubs. Called ATMosphere, this hub provides port-level LAN switching, increased network control, and the transportation of voice and video data. The Fibermux-designed ATM Backplane Matrix is capable of aggregate intrahub throughput of 9.6 gigabits per second, and the interhub backbone carries data at up to 400 megabits per second. ATMosphere is based on the Fibermux 14-slot CrossbowPlus multi-LAN hub chassis. The ATM Backplane Matrix gives each I/O module two independent data paths of 200 Mb/sec each for module-to-module or module-to-backplane communications. One interesting aspect of ATMosphere is that any user on a network can be grouped into a LAN segment, even if the chassis that user is connected to is across a wide area link.

The physical layer for the ATMosphere product is FibreChannel, an ANSI physical-layer standard. This layer features two 200 Mb/sec backbones that can run redundantly or combined to provide 400 Mb/sec throughput. SONET is also supported.

ATM desktop connections are just emerging. Hubs that provide about a dozen 100 Mb/sec ATM connections to workstations are under development by several vendors, including IBM and Hewlett-Packard. Users of scientific workstations and those who handle images and modeling are likely candidates for this type of equipment.

CHAPTER 9

Y ou can expand Local Area Networks (LANS) into Metropolitan Area Networks (MANs) and Wide Area Networks (WANs) by using remote connections or high-speed fiber-optic backbones. A remote connection can link two or more LANs on opposite sides of the street or on opposite sides of the globe. The methods you use to make these connections depend on the following.

Wide Area Net- working

- Your transmission speed requirements

- The distance of the link

- The amount of internetwork traffic

- The network traffic patterns

- Your budget

As the demand for MAN and WAN links increases, phone companies and other carriers are developing newer and faster methods for linking computer systems. Dial-up links, and even courier service methods of transporting data, are giving way to affordable dedicated links. However, there are still some hurdles in making the transition from LANs to WANs. LANs are optimized for data transmission, whereas WANs are not. Throughput drops when you use a WAN because LAN data must be formatted for transport over WAN links.

Wide Area Networks are effective only if they operate at a reasonable speed. Although fiber-optic connections can provide speeds from 10 Mb/sec to more than 100 Mb/sec, they are currently limited to campus and metropolitan areas. Phone lines and high-speed data links provide long-distance connections, but their transmission speeds are limited. A reasonable LAN-to-LAN connection requires a communications bandwidth in the 56 Kb/sec to 1.544 Mb/sec range. Anything below this range is suitable only for single users or occasional connections. Table 9-1 provides a comparison of network transmission speeds, as a point of reference.

Network Type	Speed	Use
ArcNet	2.5 Mb/sec	Local Area Networks
Token Ring	–4 or 16 Mb/sec	Local Area Networks
Thin Ethernet	10 Mb/sec	Local Area Networks
Thick Ethernet	10 Mb/sec	Extended LANs
Dial-up line	2400-19,200 bits/sec	Single-user remote connections
Packet-switching	Less than 64 Kb/sec	Low- to medium-use WAN links
Fractional T-1	64 Kb/sec	WANs and redundant links
T-1	1.544 Mb/sec	High-use WAN links
T-3	44.184 Mb/sec	High-use WAN links
Fiber-optic	10-100 Mb/sec	High-use MAN connections

NOTE: Worldwide fiber-optic networks with transmission speeds in the 50 to 256 Mb/sec range are under development.

Table 9-1. *A Comparison of Network Transmission Speeds*

Types of Remote Links

The current telephone network in the United States uses a combination of all-digital lines and analog lines. The phone company in your area is probably connected to phone companies in other areas with digital lines. However, typical home and office telephone lines use copper voice-grade wire similar to that used at the turn of the century. The goal of the phone companies is to convert to all-digital lines, as defined by the ISDN (Integrated Services Digital Network), which is discussed later in this chapter. This system will rely on a combination of copper and fiber-optic cables. Until then, modems will connect computers over voice-grade lines. Modem communications is rather limited, so you'll need to acquire special digital lines from a phone company or other carrier to establish high-performance MANs and WANs. In some metropolitan areas, high-speed fiber-optic cable is installed by companies who then lease the lines to others.

You use routers to make connections to MANs and WANs and to ensure that local traffic stays local and does not cross the remote connections for cost and performance reasons. Data traveling across WAN connections is susceptible to monitoring by eavesdroppers. Routers can encrypt data for WAN transport and can ensure that data for local workstations stays within the local network boundary.

There are several types of wide area connections, which are described in the following list:

■ *Dial-up phone lines* are the same phone lines used for voice communications. You'll need a modem on both ends of the connection to convert digital signals to analog signals and back again. Although dial-up phone lines are relatively slow, they provide an inexpensive way to transfer files and electronic messages that are not time critical. They can also provide links to a LAN for occasional users who use remote control software from their homes or hotels.

NOTE: Modem technology has improved greatly in the last few years. When modems at both ends of a connection use the same encoding and compression techniques, transmission speeds can reach 38.4 Kb/sec, almost half the speed of a direct digital line. At this speed, most users cannot tell that they are connected by a telephone line.

■ *Leased lines* are permanently connected lines that provide full-time connections between LAN segments. The lines can be digital.

NOTE: Voice communications is sampled and converted to digital data for transmission on modern phone lines. Therefore, it is commonly referred to as "voice data."

- *Public Data Network (PDN)* services are provided by companies such as CompuServe and Tymenet which make their packet-switching networks available for your wide area connections.

- *Microwave connections* provide across-town data links, and *satellite connections* provide global data links. You can purchase microwave systems and install them yourself. In addition, wireless LANs that use infrared or radio technology can provide simple and relatively inexpensive methods for bridging buildings in a campus or industrial park setting.

- *Campus backbones* provide a connection point for LAN segments within a building in a campus or industrial park setting.

Packets and Circuits

The way data, voice communications, and video information is sent from one point to another depends on the type of service you use. Network and telephone services can be categorized as connection oriented or connectionless.

Connection-oriented services provide a dedicated connection between two systems that need to communicate, similar to the connection you make when calling a friend. The connection is a physical link that is set up at a telephone switching center before voice or data communication starts. Connection-oriented links are called *circuits* and are illustrated in Figure 9-1. Dial-up and leased lines are connection-oriented services.

Connectionless services are often called datagram services. Information such as data and digitized voice information are placed as payloads in packets, given an address, and sent out over a web of interconnected links. The address in the packet determines the best path for the packet to take through the communications network. To users or systems at either end, it appears that a dedicated circuit exists, but in fact, it is a virtual circuit. A *virtual circuit* exists when data packets or cells travel across many paths in a network (which is called packet switching) to reach their destination, taking advantage of best-path methods to optimize throughput. A virtual circuit is conceptual rather than physical. Public Data Networks (PDNs) are connectionless services. Figure 9-2 illustrates a virtual circuit. As you can see in Figure 9-2, a packet-switching network is often referred to as a *cloud*. This term refers to the complex web of interconnections and switching equipment. It is explained in more detail later in the chapter.

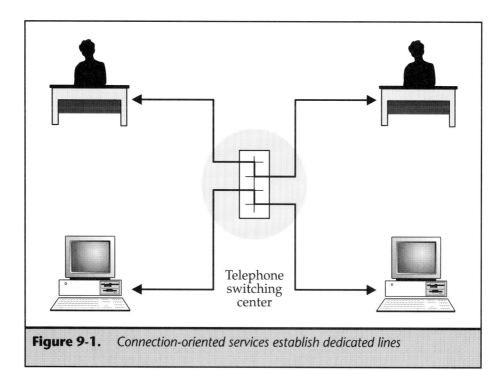

Figure 9-1.   *Connection-oriented services establish dedicated lines*

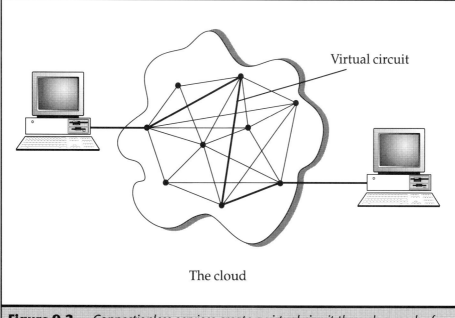

Figure 9-2.   *Connectionless services create a virtual circuit through a mesh of connections*

Multiplexing is a technique for transmitting a number of signals simultaneously over a single line or channel. With multiplexing, it's not necessary to run thousands of wires between switching centers for each potential communication connection. Multiplexing, as illustrated in Figure 9-3, mixes many signals on a cable, which forms a *logical* dedicated line. Each signal is separated by time, space, or frequency. The device used to mix the signals is known as a multiplexer.

Connection-oriented services require that a dedicated circuit be set up before data transmission can begin. Connectionless services do not require that circuits be established ahead of time, and so they are easier to use. Both services have their advantages, depending on the type and amount of information you need to send. Connectionless services are more expensive if they are continuously maintained, but continuous maintenance is essential for wide area networking services that are more complex than file transfers, such as real-time client-server computing applications. As discussed later in this chapter, client-server applications are a driving force behind the move to better and faster transmission rates on Wide Area Networks.

The 1990s will see a conglomeration of different services based on fiber-optic cable and packet-switching techniques, such as ATM. The next few sections cover existing communications services, followed by a discussion of emerging high-speed services.

Remote Workstations

A remote workstation commonly connects to a LAN via dial-up or dedicated voice-grade telephone lines. The link can connect a single user at a remote workstation to a LAN, or it can connect LANs to other LANs, for occasional use. Data communications over normal dial-up lines is recommended if your

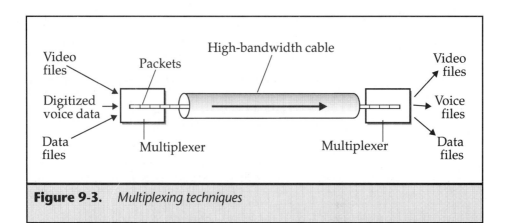

Figure 9-3.   *Multiplexing techniques*

internetwork traffic is less than a few hours a day. For example, your e-mail system could dial out during evening hours to send messages to, and collect messages from, remote sites. Dial-up lines are also useful for occasional file transfers. In this case, you only pay for the service you use, and no special equipment is required except for modems. Today, modems achieve extremely high transfer rates by using various encoding and compression methods, so dial-up lines should not be overlooked. If a dial-up line is used more than a few hours a day, you should consider leasing a line, which may have a lower monthly rate.

Remote control software improves performance over dial-up lines. A user sitting at a remote site can dial into a LAN and use a dedicated PC on the LAN as if he or she were sitting at that PC. Only screen and keyboard information travels across the remote modem-connected link. All processing is done at the LAN system and, most importantly, data remains in that system rather than crossing the phone line, which would bog down the connection. Basically, the remote computer acts as a dumb terminal connected to the computer that is connected to the LAN.

Campus-Wide Links

A *campus* is defined as an area in which LANs are interconnected by using *backbone* coaxial or fiber-optic cable and in which a phone company or other carrier is not necessarily involved. University campuses, industrial parks, and medical centers are examples of campuses. Because a campus is normally privately owned, there are few restrictions on cable runs. For example, in-house staff could run fiber-optic cabling between buildings in an underground conduit without obtaining special permits. Local codes and environmental restrictions must be followed, of course.

Currently, many campus-wide areas are connected with fiber-optic cable that follows the FDDI (Fiber Distributed Data Interface) standard.

Metropolitan Area Links

A Metropolitan Area Network might interconnect LANs that are in buildings across the street from each other or that are on opposite sides of town. Because it is difficult or impossible for a company to install private cable in public areas, a phone company or other carrier with established lines should be involved in the installation. These carriers may use fiber-optic, microwave, or satellite techniques for transmission.

Metropolitan Area Networks are defined by the IEEE 802.6 committee, which specifies a dual bus topology called the Distributed Queue Dual Bus (DQDB), rather than the ring topology of FDDI. It also specifies a different protocol scheme at the MAC layer. The dual bus transmits in opposite directions and provides full duplex communications between two nodes. A range of speeds and media are supported, including a digital signal level 3 (DS-3) rate of 45 Mb/sec and an optical-fiber rate of 155 Mb/sec.

Microwave Transmission

Microwave transmission provides a unique communications system in metropolitan areas. Companies can purchase and install their own equipment, or they can lease the equipment and services of outside organizations. The only requirement is that each remote site be within line-of-sight distance (about 5 miles). A microwave dish is installed on each building, typically on the roof or in a window. The dishes are pointed at each other and adjusted until the optimum signal strength is achieved between the two.

Motorola Microwave is a typical source for equipment and installation services. The hardware is priced under $10,000, and data throughput is 1.544 Mb/sec.

Leased-Line Services

When you need intercity network connections, and the throughput of dial-up telephone lines can't handle the traffic, you'll need to move to leased digital lines. T1 is the most common method used by the phone companies to provide digital service. T1 lines are multiplexed on a single cable by the phone company, which gives the phone company a way to provide a number of channels to a number of users on the same cable. Signals are separated by time, space, or frequency. Leased lines are made available by long-distance carriers such as AT&T Company, MCI Telecommunications Corporation, and Sprint, who ferociously compete for your business, as you probably know.

To set up a leased line, you can contact your local telephone company, or you can contact an interexchange carrier that competes outside local areas to provide connections between those areas. AT&T competes for these services with MCI and the others, but AT&T is regulated by the FCC. Its competitors aren't regulated, but they provide services at a price that is competitive (within a few cents, just like the ads say). You can also contact communications consultants who will guide you through the process of establishing a line and deal with the local and interexchange carriers for you. There is a range of services offered to organizations that need wide area networking capabilities.

Leased digital lines are classified as one of two types:

- *DS-0 (or fractional T1)* is a 64 Kb/sec line that provides one voice channel. Analog voice is sampled 8000 times per second to convert it to digital information. Because this line is the building block of T1 lines, it is often called fractional T1.

- *DS-1 (or T1)* is a 1.544 Mb/sec digital line that consists of 24 multiplexed DS-0 channels; it is commonly called T1 in the United States. Note that DS-1 service in Mexico and Great Britain refers to 2.048 Kb/sec line consisting of 30 DS-0 channels.

T1 Digital Lines

T1 is basically a conditioned line that runs over two twisted copper wires. A *conditioned* line is one that contains signal regenerators and noise filters. It can provide quality digital service for continuous LAN-to-LAN connections over wide areas. T1 services establish and maintain dedicated lines between two points, unlike packet-switching networks, which can form a mesh of LANs over Public Data Networks.

T1 is commonly used to build private voice and data networks. Its bandwidth of 1.544 Mb/sec can be divided into 24 64-Kb/sec channels, each carrying one voice or data transmission. Fractional T1 allows customers to buy T1 service in 64 Kb/sec channels at an affordable price. You can easily add channels to expand your service, because the phone company has already installed a full T1 line, and it doesn't charge for additional channels until you begin using them. However, you should weigh the cost of buying individual channels against the cost of buying a full T1 line. Prices are based on transmission speeds, distance, and other factors that the carrier determines when configuring and pricing the line. A T1 multiplexer divides a 1.544 Mb/sec T1 line into multiple 64 Kb/sec lines. T1 multiplexers are available from a number of vendors and usually have ports for combining voice and data lines.

The cost of T1 service is easily justified if the amount of traffic on an internetwork is high. T1 is usually priced per mile plus a monthly service charge. Prices range from about $3,000 a month for short distances to over $20,000 a month for a connection across the continental United States. A typical use for T1 is real-time access to a company's database by outlying offices. T1 is also justified when considering the cost and productivity of employees who need to access information on remote systems.

Redundant Lines

If the data crossing your WAN is critical, you should consider adding a backup line, usually from a different carrier to ensure that LAN links are not lost if the primary line goes down. Get an assurance from the phone company that the backup line does not follow the same physical route as the primary line. Lines usually go down because of local events such as storms or earthquakes. Satellite links make excellent backup lines for networks. You are usually charged only for the time you actually use the service, and the connections are not susceptible to natural disasters that terminate surface lines. Satellite hijacking has not yet become popular.

With T1, the local telephone company serves as a hub for each network within a certain geographic area. Networks at different company sites within the area serviced by the phone company (usually a metropolitan area) are connected to the hub provided by the phone company. The area serviced by a phone company is known as its local access and transport area, or LATA. It is possible to connect to other LATAs using links established by various long-haul carriers. You will then need to involve the local phone company, the remote phone company, and the long-haul carrier in your connection scheme.

A T1 connection starts with two twisted wire pairs at the customer site. These wires lead to the conditioned lines established by the phone company. To connect a LAN to a T1 line, you need the following equipment, which is illustrated in Figure 9-4.

- *CSU (Channel Service Unit)*   The CSU is the first point of contact for the T1 wires. It diagnoses and prepares the signals on the line for the LAN, and it keeps the line alive if there are problems with the LAN connection equipment.

- *DSU (Data Service Unit)*   The DSU connects to the CSU. It converts LAN signals to T1 signals.

- *Multiplexer*   A multiplexer is optional. It provides a way to send voice signals, multiplexed with data, over the digitized line.

- *Bridge or router*   The bridge or router provides the connection point between your LAN and the T1 line.

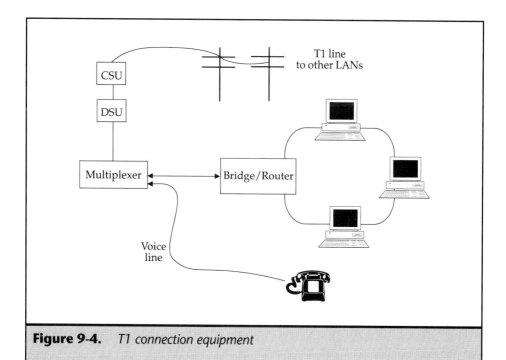

Figure 9-4. *T1 connection equipment*

Other Leased Services

There are a number of other leased digital services you can purchase from the phone companies. These include T-3 high-speed digital lines and satellite communications links.

T-3 HIGH-SPEED DIGITAL LINES   T3 is similar to T1, but it provides more services. T3 has a bandwidth of 44.184 Mb/sec, which can be divided into 28 T1 channels. A bandwidth management device can allocate the bandwidth to various networking devices, such as an Ethernet bridge, a PBX (Public Branch Exchange), an existing T1 multiplexer, and even an FDDI LAN.

SATELLITE COMMUNICATIONS LINKS   Several companies offer satellite communications links. These links can provide data rates at T1 speeds of 1.544 Mb/sec. Companies that offer this service are AT&T Tridom, Comsat General Corporation, and GTE Spacenet Corporation. Satellite connections are useful backup connections because you're usually charged (besides a flat fee) only for the time you actually use the connection. Satellite antennaes can be mounted on the roof of a building or in a parking lot. Interestingly, the larger the antenna, the faster the transfer speed you'll get out of the system. For T1 rates, you'll need an antenna that is about 4 meters in diameter. Monthly charges are usually under $1,000.

NOTE: The delay caused by satellite transmission may be intolerable for users who want immediate response from their WAN connections. Satellite links are most appropriate for data transfers and electronic mail, which are not time sensitive.

Packet Switching

Packet-switching networks were developed by the U.S. government in the 1970s to provide reliable digital communications over analog phones lines. Packet switching is a message-delivery technique that places data in small packets and transfers it from source to destination through one or more intermediate nodes, as shown in Figure 9-5. Packets can take different paths through the nodes of the packet-switching network to reach their destination, depending on congestion. The multiple packets of a message may each take different routes; they are reassembled at the destination. Traffic routing is also important to achieve the best path and fastest delivery.

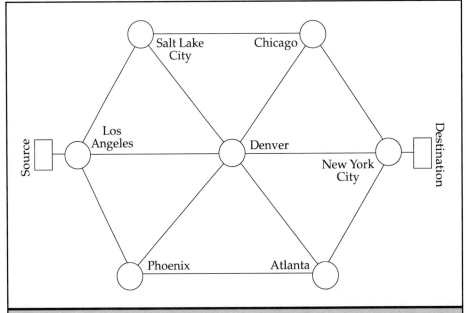

Figure 9-5. *A packet-switching network*

Packet switching provides a way to share a set of communications lines with other users, for the transport of data packets. Packet-switching networks are provided by Public Data Network (PDN) companies such as AT&T Company, Tymenet, Telnet, CompuServe, GE, Sprint, and Infonet Services. Some PDN companies offer international service. Note that local telephone companies offer their own packet-switching services that you can use if you need to connect LANs within a metropolitan area.

The connections you establish with these carriers are virtual connections. As discussed earlier, a virtual connection appears to users to be a dedicated connection between two systems. In reality, your transmissions are packetized and placed on a high-speed line with other packets going in the same direction, much like cars getting on a freeway. At the other end, the packets for your transmission are separated from packets that belong to other users, reassembled, and handed to the destination. Leasing packet-switching lines is fairly inexpensive because you share the costs of the high-speed lines with other users.

A packet-switching network is often referred to as a cloud. As shown in Figure 9-2, the network usually has many nodes that provide alternate or backup paths. The cloud is a complex web of interconnections and switching equipment. You can't always be sure which path through the cloud your data will take from one session to the next, nor do you care, as long as the data reaches its destination.

There are two packet delivery methods. X.25 is an older standard that is still very much in use. It provides high levels of error checking. The newer *frame relay* method takes advantage of today's more reliable digital telephone systems. It reduces the amount of error checking, which increases throughput.

X.25

X.25 is an international standard for sending packets over public data networks. It supports medium to high data-rate links for occasional or continuous use. A typical application would be store-and-forward electronic mail systems that dial out once or twice a day, or a user running an application that is not time critical from a remote LAN. The service is affordable because many users share the cost of the X.25 transmission lines. X.25 is popular for international networking because it has been an established standard in Europe and other areas for a long time.

X.25 is defined by the CCITT (Comité Consultatif Internationale de Télégraphie et Téléphonie) X.25 protocol, which describes how data is packaged and delivered over an X.25 network. A bridge or router with X.25 support is used to connect a LAN to the X.25 network. Access to the network is through leased lines or dial-up lines. Leased lines are usually synchronous, which improves throughput, and they have transfer ratings of 19.2, 56, and 64 Kb/sec. Dial-up lines use asynchronous communications methods requiring modems that have their own error correction circuitry. Transfer rates are dependent on the speed of the modem used.

NOTE: Asynchronous communication is a character-based transmission method that separates data by using start and stop bits. Synchronous communication is a block-oriented method that eliminates the need to transmit start and stop bits. Instead, it uses timing methods to separate data.

Frame Relay

Frame relay is an innovation that emerged from the ISDN specification. Frame relay streamlines and improves the performance of packet switching by removing the network-layer processing associated with X.25. Multiplexing and switching of logical connections takes place in the data-link layer.

Frame relay is becoming prominent in public and private networks. It reduces some of the overhead of X.25 by assuming that modern lines are more reliable and introduce less distortion. To improve performance, frame relay eliminates the need for intermediate nodes to acknowledge receipt of data frames, as is required in X.25. For example, in X.25, if data moves from the source through two or more intermediate nodes, each of those nodes must acknowledge receipt to the node that sent it the packet. When the packet finally reaches its destination, the destination sends acknowledgment to the source. This last step is the only acknowledgment required in frame relay. The state tables used in X.25 at each intermediate node to deal with management, flow control, and error checking are not necessary with frame relay. As a result, frame relay provides more throughput with fewer delays.

Sprint, CompuServe, Tymenet, Williams Telecommunications, and other carriers offer frame relay services. You realize the advantages of frame relay when connecting LANs over Wide Area Networks.

Future Trends

The current national and international phone systems are incapable of handling the multimegabit data transfer requirements of the future. It's worthwhile to look at some of the technologies and services that will support future global data, voice, and video networks. The amount of data traffic on networks will increase as the power and speed of computing systems improve. The data network might become as prevalent and transparent as the voice network.

The contender at the transport layer is Synchronous Optical Network (SONET). It defines a multiplexing standard for fiber-optic cable transmission. SONET data rates range from 51 Mb/sec to 2488 Mb/sec.

ATM (Asynchronous Transfer Mode) carries data on SONET networks. It multiplexes cells (packets) of data from many sources on the physical network (SONET). ATM provides virtual communications paths through the SONET network. A connection-oriented virtual circuit between two points can reach speeds from 45 Mb/sec to 622 Mb/sec. As discussed in Chapter 8, ATM switching is useful at the LAN level in wiring hubs. Is is also useful as a switching technology for international and global telecommunications networks.

Above ATM is Broadband Integrated Services Digital Network (BISDN). ATM is the engine for BISDN. BISDN is a successor to ISDN, which defined how to provide circuit-switching communications to the home, but was not completely implemented. BISDN uses ATM technology and the SONET physical network to deliver data transfer speeds from 155 Mb/sec to 622 Mb/sec.

Switched Multimegabit Data Service (SMDS) is a communications service developed by Bellcore, which is the research division of the Bell operating companies. SMDS is designed for public and private data networks and will move switching away from the local telephone switching office. It is currently being established as a national system. It provides a packet-oriented network with operating speeds of 1.5 Mb/sec and 45 Mb/sec, with a later implementation of 155 Mb/sec.

SMDS defines network-to-network communications schemes, but it is more limited than BISDN because it transports only data files, not voice and video files. SMDS is a connectionless technology, unlike ATM, which is connection oriented. SMDS does work with ATM cells and switching techniques. For example, an ATM switch can have an SMDS interface. SMDS services might help alleviate some potential problems with ATM; ATM, its standards, and its flow-control issues are still under development. Most likely, switch vendors such as AT&T will develop some proprietary techniques, which could create interoperability problems. Because SMDS is compatible with ATM, it could provide interoperability between two versions of ATM.

ISDN

The Integrated Services Digital Network (ISDN) standard has the goal of linking every home and business with high-speed digital data services by using phone lines, which will finally eliminate the analog phone line. When and if the standard takes hold, the telephone system will become completely digital, which means you won't need modems to interconnect computers by using phone lines. Personal computer users will benefit the most from ISDN. It will provide connections to data services, data bases, and international networks at reasonably fast transfer rates. Currently, ISDN is available only in certain areas. But more areas are converting to ISDN. The conversion needs to take place in the analog lines that run from your home or business to the phone company. Most telephone companies have already established digital connections to other telephone areas. At the home front, your house will probably need to be rewired, and you'll need a special adapter in your PC to match the voltage levels of the ISDN line. A realistic rate for the transfer of personal computer data over ISDN lines is about 150 Kb/sec.

SONET

Synchronous Optical Network (SONET) is an international set of standards that define synchronous fiber-optic data transmission at rates from 51.8 Mb/sec to 2.5 Gb/sec. SONET's maximum bandwidth is the equivalent of 48 T3 lines. SONET is an underlying transport network, much like Ethernet and Token Ring define transport mechanisms for LANs. It supports ATM, ISDN, FDDI, DQDB, and SMDS.

SONET's connections are defined as Optical Carrier (OC) data rates. OCs are like building blocks that accommodate T3 and E3 signals. A 45 Mb/sec T3 signal can be asynchronously multiplexed into a SONET optical transmission. OC-1 is a 51.2 Mb/sec channel, and OC-48 is a 2.5 Gb/sec channel. There are OC-3, OC-9, OC-12, OC-18, OC-24, and OC-36 subdivisions between these channels. The OCs are optical signals, so electrical signals must be converted in the device that connects a communications device to the optical fiber.

SONET's physical layer defines bit movement across the physical medium. It converts electrical signals to optical signals, handles frame transport and error management, synchronizes and multiplexes the path layer, and ensures reliable transport of data.

Making WAN Connections

You connect a LAN segment to a WAN connection by using bridges and routers. You need the services of a bridge or router to make sure the internetwork connections don't get bogged down with unnecessary traffic.

Routers are important if you maintain multiple connections to multiple remote LANs by using T1 or X.25 methods. Redundant lines are often installed to provide fault tolerance. The router ensures that packets use the best path to get to the remote site, bypassing congested areas or using the path that is the least costly. You can prioritize data to ensure that time-sensitive data gets the fastest lines and other data takes the slow lines. Managing the flow of data through your WAN connections ensures that costs remain low and service remains high.

Several methods and associated products for making wide area connections are described in the following sections. The discussion starts with simple remote workstation connections and moves up to LAN-to-LAN connections.

Remote Workstation Connections

A remote workstation is a single PC at a remote site that dials into a LAN by using an asynchronous communications method. The workstation might be used by an employee working at home, a manager at a remote site, or a field representative who needs to check the company database.

For connections made by using voice-grade phone lines, a modem must be used on both sides of the connection to convert digital signals for analog transmission and then convert the analog signals back to digital signals. Because the speed of such transmissions is limited, voice-grade lines are recommended only for occasional use to establish remote workstation-to-LAN connections or low-traffic LAN-to-LAN connections.

Two methods for establishing remote workstation sessions are described next.

REMOTE EXECUTION   With the remote execution method, all processing takes place at the remote workstation. All programs and data files the user needs must be transferred over the communications lines for processing in the user workstation unless the files are copied to the workstation in advance. This method is not recommended if large amounts of information are transferred over the lines. It is useful for connections by a user who occasionally uploads or downloads a file.

LOCAL EXECUTION   The local execution method connects a dedicated workstation on the LAN to a remote workstation. All processing takes place at the dedicated workstation; screen displays are echoed at the remote workstation, and the user can enter keyboard commands. This method is very efficient because only keyboard and screen information is transferred over the remote connection. However, a computer must be set up on the LAN to run the remote user's communications session.

The following sections describe products for establishing remote workstations that use the local execution method. PC AnyWare is designed for single-user use and is similar to third- party products such as Norton-Lambert Close-Up/LAN and LAN Assist Plus from Fresh Technologies.

PC AnyWare

PC AnyWare is a remote-connection software package that provides satisfactory performance for users who need to gain remote access to a LAN. It has the following features and benefits:

- Users at remote workstations operate as if they were sitting at a workstation attached to the LAN.

- Users can access database files in real time, with little delay in response.

- File and database access are performed at LAN speeds because all processing is handled by the local network workstation. Only keystrokes and screen displays are sent from the local PC to the remote workstation.

- Because this method does not perform any processing at the remote workstation, a dumb terminal can be used as the remote workstation.

A PC AnyWare connection is illustrated in Figure 9-6. It requires the following components:

- A dedicated computer on the network that runs ANYWHERE.COM. This station cannot be used for other tasks while a user is connected

- A remote workstation that runs ATERM.COM (a terminal program)

NetWare Access Server Software

Novell's NetWare Access Server (NAS) provides a dedicated communications server that runs up to 15 PC AnyWare sessions. The software runs only on 80386 or better systems, and an 80486 is recommended if you plan to run more than 5

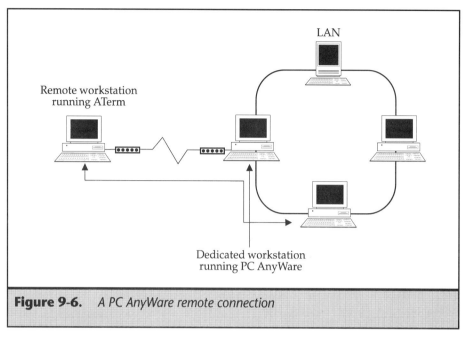

Remote workstation
running ATerm

LAN

Dedicated workstation
running PC AnyWare

Figure 9-6. *A PC AnyWare remote connection*

simultaneous sessions. The software takes advantage of the 80386's ability to divide its processing time into 15 virtual 640KB PCs that run under a multiuser version of Quarterdeck System's DesqView product. This provides 15 virtual computers for multiuser remote access. The Microdyne Wide Area Network Interface Module Plus (WNIM+) (described below) can be installed in the NetWare access server to provide four modem ports, and you can install up to four of these boards. Similar boards are available from other non-Novell sources. Figure 9-7 illustrates a NetWare Access Server configuration that uses two WNIM+ boards.

The Microdyne WNIM+ is a four-port asynchronous communications adapter board. Each board has four individual asynchronous ports that can communicate at speeds of up to 19.2 Kb/sec. You attach modems to these ports. The WNIM+ has an on-board processor that frees the server's processor of communications I/O tasks. Other vendors that make similar boards are Newport Systems, Hayes, and Digiboard.

Remote workstations dial directly into the NetWare Access Server by using asynchronous modems. The ATerm software that runs in the remote workstations is included. Each remote workstation dials into a dedicated session on the communications server. These sessions can each be configured for 640KB of memory, depending on the memory available in the NAS system and the number of simultaneous sessions. Each session requires a separate modem and phone line connection, but four modems may be adequate if user connections are intermittent.

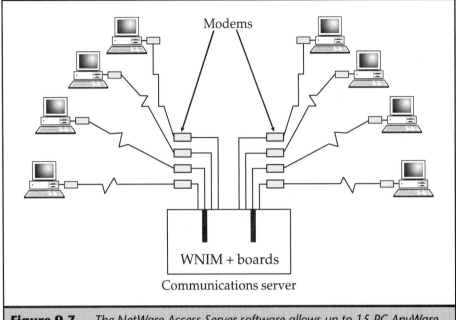

Modems

WNIM + boards

Communications server

Figure 9-7. *The NetWare Access Server software allows up to 15 PC AnyWare sessions to take place within a dedicated 80386 communications server*

The NetWare Access Server provides the same features as PC AnyWare in a single system that supports up to 15 users. Local network stations are not tied up performing tasks for remote users. The software provides a dial-back security feature that calls users back to verify the phone numbers of the locations they are calling from. This ensures that an unauthorized user at another location is not attempting to dial in.

NetWare Asynchronous Communications Services (NACS)

The Novell NetWare Asynchronous Communications Services (NACS) software is a NetWare Loadable Module that enables up to 32 users to access a shared modem pool, minicomputer ports, and X.25 services. The network cable provides users with a connection to modems attached to the NACS server. You'll need a modem and a connection port for each user who needs a simultaneous connection. For example, the Microdyne WNIM+ provides four modem ports. Each user needs to run an asynchronous terminal emulation package from their workstation, such as ASCOM/IV, Crosstalk, or Smartcom Exec.

Novell NetWare WAN Links

NetWare WAN Links v.2.0 is a software package designed to provide transparent and reliable WAN connectivity in multiprotocol networks. It is part of a series of LAN/WAN internetworking software products that Novell is offering. The current package integrates Novell's Link/PPP (Point-to-Point Protocol) and Link/X.25, and it replaces separately sold products known as Link/64, Link/T1, and Link/X.25.

NetWare WAN Links operates over a variety of transmission media, including X.25 and synchronous point-to-point communication lines. It offers the following features and functions:

- NetWare WAN Links can run on a NetWare file server, a NetWare MultiProtocol Router, or a router/hum.

- WAN Links supports IPX, IP, AppleTalk, and OSI protocols over X.25 and Point-to-Point Protocol.

- The Link/X.25 implementation in the package enables routers to access Public Data Networks (PDNs). It provides transport for QLLC, Message Handling Service, and FTAM.

- The Link/PPP implementation in the package allows high-speed transmission of network data up to T1 (1.544 Mb/sec) and E1 (2.048 in Europe) speeds. Link/PPP is best when high-speed links are required for direct file access.

- Clock rates for Link/X.25 range from 1200 bits/sec to 64 Kb/sec, and from 1200 bits/sec to 2.048 Mb/sec for Link/PPP.

NetWare WAN Links requires a server system that runs NetWare or the NetWare MultiProtocol Router. LAN boards and communications boards must be installed in the server. The Microdyne WNIM+ or compatible communications board is suitable. Customer-premise equipment such as modems, DSU/CSUs, multiplexers, or data switches are also necessary. You also need to arrange for telephone services or leased lines. It is best to work closely with a telecommunications service provider when installing any communications product.

While WAN Links can be installed in a NetWare file server to reduce costs, high demands for file services or WAN services can reduce performance. A Microdyne WNIM+ installed in the server can provide four communications ports with throughput of 3 Mb/sec. However, it may be necessary to configure WAN Links in a dedicated router for performance reasons.

CHAPTER 10

For most Novell network managers, connectivity means connecting workstations that use many different operating systems to the same network platform. The network is often viewed as a "data highway" that many different computers share. UNIX systems may use this cable to talk with other UNIX systems, or PCs and Macintoshes may use it to connect with a NetWare file server. The point is that the network itself is an open modular communications system. When you start talking about systems with dissimilar operating systems using this network to talk among themselves, you are talking about interoperability.

Host Connectivity and Inter- operability

Interoperability is defined at many different levels. Simple file sharing and electronic mail messaging are common, but client-server computing and other trends will see applications on different operating systems working transparently with each other. Some of the immediate advantages provided by connectivity and interoperability are listed here:

- **E-mail.** Electronic mail is typically a companywide activity that shouldn't be hindered by differences in operating systems. Applications like Lotus's cc:Mail run on several different platforms, such as PCs and Macintoshes, and provide the link between users of these systems. Lotus also makes mail gateways that handle the transfer of mail to UNIX or other systems. In fact, electronic mail is becoming a primary method for transferring information between unlike systems.

- **Client-server computing.** Client-server applications let users on diverse systems connect with a centralized database using an application that runs on their native operating system. In other words, Windows users and Macintosh users access the same database using Windows-based or Macintosh-based applications, respectively.

- **File sharing.** Applications available from some vendors provide information in a number of formats that users on diverse operating systems can access and use without reformatting the data. Also, users can access file servers with their native operating systems. Using appropriate software, a NetWare server can appear as AppleShare volumes to Macintosh users, and as Network Filing System (NFS) volumes to UNIX users.

Interoperability describes how diverse operating systems actually work together. This chapter explores methods of connecting network computers with mainframes, minicomputers, and workstations that use diverse operating systems.

Connecting to IBM Host Systems

Mainframe systems typically provide companywide services such as accounting and database applications. Access to these systems is usually via terminals or PCs running as terminals over asynchronous links. If a PC is attached, it runs an emulation program to make it act like a terminal, and it usually has a special interface card that attaches it to the host system. After you install a LAN, you gain new ways to attach these PCs to the host, as outlined here:

- Keep the existing terminal connections for PCs and also attach them to a LAN segment, as shown in Figure 10-1.

- Install a host gateway on the LAN that links the host system to the network. Workstations then access the host through the gateway, as shown in Figure 10-2.

- To connect IBM hosts to Token Ring LANs, add a Token Ring attachment to the host and then attach it directly to the network, as shown in Figure 10-3. This configuration requires that the host be equipped with a Token Ring Interface Coupler (TIC).

An advantage of installing a LAN in a mainframe environment is that you can connect new terminals for the mainframe through the LAN, which reduces the costs of connecting each workstation to the mainframe. This section looks at IBM hardware and describes Novell's NetWare for SAA product, which serves as a gateway to IBM hosts. When using this product, you must use the gateway and direct connect approach to connect PCs to the host.

Connecting a NetWare LAN to an IBM Host

This section primarily covers Novell's NetWare for SAA (Systems Application Architecture) product for connecting workstations on a LAN to an IBM SNA host

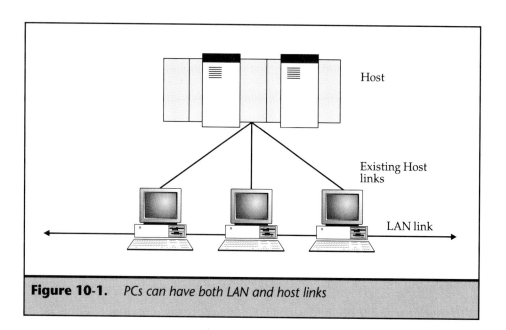

Figure 10-1.   *PCs can have both LAN and host links*

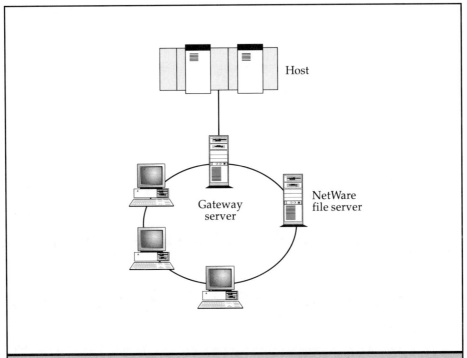

Figure 10-2. *A gateway allows all LAN workstations to access the host*

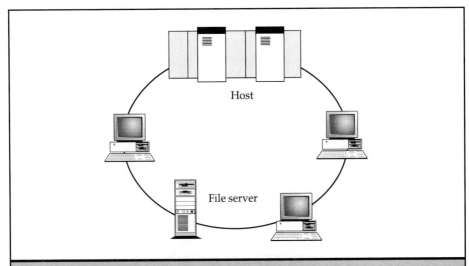

Figure 10-3. *A direct connection using Token Ring*

or an IBM AS/400 minicomputer. The connections to the host systems are made through a computer that serves as a *gateway*. The NetWare for SAA software can run as a NetWare Loadable Module on a NetWare file server, or it can run on a dedicated server. NetWare RunTime, the kernel-only version of NetWare, is supplied with the package so that you can run NetWare for SAA on a system other than the file server without buying another serialized version of NetWare. The Novell LAN-to-IBM host connectivity products are listed here:

■ *NetWare for SAA* provides a gateway into IBM host systems for up to 506 display, printer, and APPC sessions on multiple hosts simultaneously. It also provides access to AS/400 applications.

■ *NetWare Communication Services Manager* provides Windows-based management tools for network administrators.

■ *NetWare 3270 LAN Workstation for DOS* gives PCs access to multiple hosts.

■ *NetWare 3270 LAN Workstation for Macintosh* gives Apple Macintosh systems access to multiple hosts.

■ *NetWare 3270 LAN Workstation for Windows* gives DOS workstations running Microsoft Windows access to multiple hosts.

IBM Terminology

SAA (Systems Application Architecture)   A standard developed by IBM that defines the appearance and operation of applications on all IBM systems.

SNA (System Network Architecture)   The underlying architecture that defines the exchange and processing of data on IBM systems. It is similar to the OSI protocol stack, which is covered in Chapter 6, except that there is no physical or application layer.

APPC (Advanced Program-to-Program Communications)   A protocol developed by IBM that enables applications running on different computers to communicate and exchange data directly. There is no master-slave relationship between the systems, but rather a peer-to-peer relationship. Both systems are assumed to have intelligence of their own (that is, their own processor and memory).

3270 family   IBM's host system products are referred to as the 3270 family. They include a range of terminals and printers that use the same naming conventions (for example, the 3278 and 3279 terminals).

Cluster controllers IBM 3174 and 3274 cluster controllers are coaxial cable wiring centers for 3278 and 3279 terminals. They pass information from the terminals to the mainframe. One or more cluster controllers connect to front-end processors (FEPs).

FEP (front-end processor) The IBM 370, 3725, and 3745 are front-end processors that run the Network Control Program (NCP), which communicates with programs running in physical units (PUs). FEPs connect to IBM 3270 hosts.

SDLC (Synchronous Data Link Control) The data-link level protocol used on IBM SNA networks. It defines the format for information transmitted over the network.

Terminal A dumb workstation that connects to a cluster controller. Examples are the IBM 3278 and 3279 terminals. A terminal can also be a PC running emulation software that is connected to a cluster controller or a LAN connection.

Session Each connection from a terminal to the host is called a session. A 327x terminal can typically run five sessions at once, so a user can run five programs and switch among them with the press of a key. Programs run on the host, not at the terminal; however, programs written for the Advanced Program-to-Program Communications (APPC) interface can distribute processing between host and PC.

Physical units (PUs) The 3x74, 37x5, and 327x terminal products are referred to as physical units (PUs).

Logical units (LUs) Programs in PUs are referred to as logical units (LUs). An LU communicates with the NCP in the FEP.

Multiplexer The IBM 3299 multiplexer provides connections for eight coaxial-connected terminals on a single wire. It connects to the cluster controller. This product saves cable by connecting distant terminals over one wire. Note that each terminal connected over the wire still uses one or more sessions in the host.

AS/400 An IBM minicomputer system that is a descendant of earlier IBM System 36 products. It connects to 5250 terminals over dual coaxial cable called *twin-ax*.

NOTE: *A number of third-party products are available that give OS/2 and UNIX workstations access to the host through the NetWare for SAA gateway.*

Host connections are made through Novell/Memorex 9340 Enterprise Gateway, Token Ring, SDLC, and QLLC/X.25 links. A Token Ring connection is made to a 317x cluster controller, to a 37x5 front-end processor, or to integrated Token Ring controllers on 9370 and AS/400 systems. SDLC connections are made through synchronous modems to a 37xx front-end processor or an AS/400, at speeds up to 64 Kb/sec. The Token Ring method of connecting to IBM hosts can provide throughput at 16 Mb/sec. Long distance connections are made over an X.25 network to a host with a 37xx front-end processor running the Network Packet-Switching Interface (NPSI).

The Novell/Memorex 9340 Enterprise Gateway

Novell and Memorex Telex NV jointly produced the 9340 Enterprise Gateway to improve LAN-to-IBM host integration. The gateway hardware uses IBM's Micro Channel Architecture and is packaged with Novell's NetWare for SAA. The Micro Channel bus provides a high-speed interface between the server and the mainframe at up to 4.5 Mb/sec. No front-end processor is required. It is possible to transfer files directly from the mainframe's hard disk to the server's hard disk. This removes the bottleneck that occurs when executing file transfers across the LAN.

The gateway is similar to the IBM 3172 gateway, but it has the ability to support up to three network interface cards and route multiple protocols over those cards. Its list price is in the range of $25,000 to $50,000, depending on the configuration.

Before connecting the NetWare for SAA server to the host, the Virtual Telecommunications Access Method (VTAM) software on the host must be configured. This software controls the host network or controls the Network Control Program software running on the front-end processor, depending on which configuration is used. Similar information is also entered into the configuration utility on the NetWare for SAA server.

You should carefully evaluate the connection method used to give network users access to the host. The Token Ring Interface Coupler (TIC) that provides a Token Ring interface on a host is expensive and might not be available for older systems, or it might require an upgrade. You'll also need to work closely with the host administrators who must define each attached PC on the host.

AS/400 connections are made through a Token Ring interface. The NetWare for SAA server needs a Token Ring card to connect to an AS/400, but it can also contain cards that bridge other networks, such as Ethernet and ArcNet. If multiple AS/400s are attached to their own network, LAN users can access any of those AS/400 systems through the NetWare for SAA connection. Note that the NetWare 3270 LAN Workstation products give workstations access to AS/400 systems.

NetWare for SAA allows supervisors and administrators to manage a NetWare LAN by using the IBM NetView management system. It also allows commands to be sent to NetWare servers from the host. An optional Windows-based package called NetWare Communication Services Manager provides network management tools that run on LAN workstations. It allows managers to monitor faults and performance, as well as do configuration management for the system.

NetWare for SAA provides the following features:

■ Gives LAN users access to applications such as OfficeVision, NetView, DB2, CICS, TSO, and CMS

■ Supports IBM's APPC and LU6.2 distributed application environment

■ Supports up to two host connections, which can each have up to 254 host sessions

■ Allows up to 253 NetWare users to access AS/400 applications and folders from the NetWare LAN by using SPX/IPX protocols

■ Provides utilities for tracking the status of host sessions, performing diagnostics, auditing user access, and converting software

NetWare for SAA requires an 80386 or better system with 6MB of RAM for 16 sessions, 8MB of RAM for 64 sessions, or 12MB of RAM for the full 254 sessions. You'll need an adapter to connect to the network and an adapter to connect to the host system. The type of LAN adapter you'll need depends on your network. The host adapter can be an SDLC adapter such as the Novell NetWare for SAA Synchronous Adapter or a similar third-party product.

If you're connecting to a host via Token Ring, you'll need only one Token Ring card in the system, but Novell recommends two in heavy traffic situations. One card connects to the LAN and the other card connects to the host. The host connection can be made by using any of the following IBM products:

■ A 3174 Establishment Controller with the Token Ring Network Gateway feature

- A 3172 Interconnect Controller Token Ring LAN Gateway

- A 3701/25/45 front-end processor with a Token Ring Interface Coupler or Token Ring Adapter

- An IBM AS/400 with the IBM Token Ring Network Adapter

- The IBM Token Ring Network Subsystem

- A 937x or ES9000 with the IBM Token Ring Subsystem Controller option

Note that the Token Ring Adapter must be on the same ring as the host device or must be connected to the host ring via an IBM Token Ring Bridge. Check with your IBM dealer for more information about these connection products.

The NetWare Communication Services Manager

The NetWare Communication Services Manager is an optional product that helps supervisors or network administrators manage the NetWare for SAA product. Its features are listed here:

- Provides network management capabilities for configuring, monitoring, and maintaining communication services on the NetWare network

- Provides tools for fault, performance, and configuration management

- Allows centralized management of Novell communications products, including NetWare for SAA, throughout the corporate network, from a single console

- Provides a user-friendly, Microsoft Windows environment that is open to third-party development

- Includes trace and diagnostic facilities for fault isolation and resolution

- Allows collection of performance statistics for trend analysis

- Allows remote configuration of communications resources from anywhere on the internetwork

NetWare Communication Services Manager requires an 80286 or 80386 system with a color VGA monitor and a mouse, as well as Microsoft Windows.

TCP/IP and UNIX Connections

As many network administrators know, an increasing number of UNIX workstations are finding their way into organizations, in addition to UNIX minicomputer systems that may already exist. Many are engineering workstations or systems that run specific UNIX client-server applications. Sun Microsystems, NeXT, Digital Equipment, and Hewlett-Packard are just a few of the companies that make these UNIX systems. Of course, UNIX users want and need to be part of the network. Because Novell and other companies have seen an increased number of these machines in corporate environments, they have made it easier to connect them to the network. UNIX systems tend to be high-performance systems, so they are useful as servers. Novell has developed products that let NetWare users take advantage of their features.

Fortunately, Ethernet is the common network standard among UNIX systems, which makes it easy to connect them physically to NetWare LANs. TCP/IP (Transmission Control Protocol/Internet Protocol) is the protocol standard for connecting UNIX systems.

When UNIX systems and UNIX-based networks are connected to NetWare LANs, users on the interconnected networks can access resources as follows:

■ Workstations and UNIX systems can communicate over the network cable. In addition, a NetWare server can route TCP/IP requests to the UNIX (or other) system, as shown in Figure 10-4.

■ UNIX system users can connect to a NetWare server that is running the NetWare for NFS (Network Filing System) software, and they can access files. (See Figure 10-5.) The NetWare server appears as another drive to the UNIX users.

There are a number of ways to connect PC systems to UNIX resources on the network. The need to share electronic mail (e-mail) is often the primary reason for making the connections. Another reason is the desire to access UNIX database applications. Terminal emulation programs can be run on PCs to access applications and information (such as e-mail) on a UNIX server. In addition, PCs can run programs that package files and e-mail going to UNIX systems and unpackage files and e-mail coming from UNIX systems. There are a number of products that work under Microsoft Windows or other graphical user interfaces and provide connections to UNIX-based systems.

NetWare's Open Data-Link Interface (ODI) provides the multiprotocol support required to transport packets from PCs to UNIX systems. At the server, you install the TCP/IP protocol stack to route TCP/IP requests through a

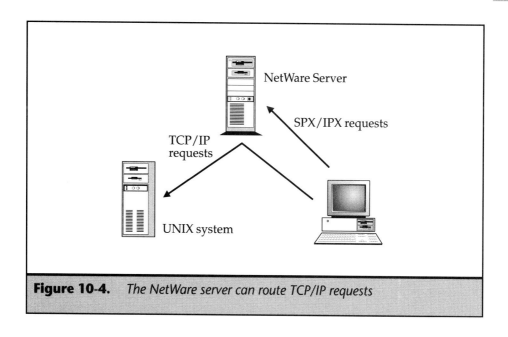

Figure 10-4.   *The NetWare server can route TCP/IP requests*

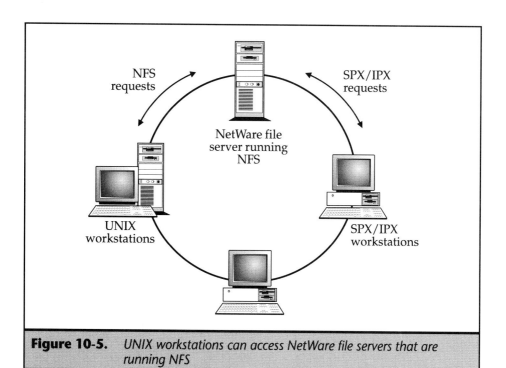

Figure 10-5.   *UNIX workstations can access NetWare file servers that are running NFS*

NetWare server. If the traffic becomes too heavy and bogs down the file server, you can install Novell's MultiProtocol Router software on a separate system.

At workstations, you load a TCP/IP driver along with the normal SPX/IPX driver. Each workstation can then use one network interface card to access either the NetWare server, through SPX/IPX, or the UNIX system, through TCP/IP. A PC does not have to be rebooted in order to access one or the other system. TCP/IP support is provided in Novell's optional LAN WorkPlace for DOS software.

UNIX Services

TCP/IP is an extremely useful and common internetworking protocol. It was developed by the Department of Defense as a way to connect many dissimilar systems. TCP/IP has several commands to facilitate file transfers and access between a system and a host that use the protocol. The utilities and upper-level protocols described in the next sections manipulate the data transferred by TCP/IP.

TELNET   Telnet is a remote terminal program that lets a user control a program on a host system. It typically emulates a terminal, such as the DEC VT-100. Vendors use Telnet as a base on which to design more sophisticated products.

FILE TRANSFER PROTOCOL (FTP)   File Transfer Protocol (FTP) provides for file transfers between UNIX computers and dissimilar systems. The commands can be used locally or over internetworks. Programs that are built on FTP let users list files that are in either system and copy files between systems. Users who log onto a host system usually access its file system from an application.

NETWORK FILING SYSTEM   Simply providing the protocols for communications with another system isn't enough. You need an application that can take advantage of the resources on the remote system. A file system such as NFS (Network Filing System) can provide these capabilities. NFS is a distributed file system developed by Sun Microsystems that is built upon TCP/IP. It lets users access files on remote systems as if the remote systems were part of their own system. No extra commands or procedures are required to list files, view their contents, create new files, or copy files to the local hard drive. The remote file system is "mapped" so that it appears as a local drive.

FLeX/IP

The Novell FLeX/IP product is a NetWare Loadable Module (NLM) that solves some of the basic file, print, and management problems in the NetWare UNIX environment. FLeX/IP contains three individual products, which are represented by the letters *F*, *L*, and *X*. *F* stands for FTP (File Transfer Protocol), which provides file transfer capabilities. *L* stands for Line Printer Daemon, which provides standard UNIX print utilities that make printer access more transparent between UNIX and NetWare systems. Without the *L* utilities, NetWare print sharing and UNIX print sharing tend to get in each other's way on an internetwork. *X* stands for X-Windows protocol support. When the protocols are installed, a network administrator can run the NetWare console on a UNIX system and manage the NetWare network from a remote location.

NetWare NFS

NetWare NFS is Novell's implementation of the Network Filing System that runs on the NetWare server. With NetWare NFS, users of UNIX systems can access the NetWare environment from their native operating system. UNIX users can use NetWare NFS to share files, printers, and other resources on the NetWare LAN.

NetWare NFS uses TCP/IP to establish connections to the UNIX users. Using the NetWare server as an NFS server has several benefits: One system can be used as the server for both NetWare and UNIX clients. This single system is easier to manage and to keep secure. In addition, UNIX users benefit from NetWare features, such as its high performance and fault tolerance.

NetWare NFS runs as an NLM on the NetWare server. It allows UNIX users to view the NetWare file system as an extension of their native NFS environment. They mount NetWare volumes by using standard UNIX/NFS commands. Several other NLMs are provided with NetWare NFS, and they are listed here:

- The UNIX name space NLM provides the NetWare file system with UNIX file attributes and naming conventions. File sharing is possible across all name spaces, including DOS, Macintosh, and OS/2.

- The LPD NLM enables UNIX clients and other TCP/IP clients to submit print jobs to NetWare print queues.

- The LPDGWY NLM enables NetWare clients to spool print jobs to printers attached to UNIX systems.

- The FTPD NLM allows any FTP client with valid NetWare access to connect to any NetWare server and initiate file transfers to and from any NetWare volume or directory.

- The XCONSOLE NLM provides an alternative NetWare management console so that UNIX supervisors can manage NetWare servers through X-Windows sessions.

- The Lock Manager NLM supports file and record locking in the NFS environment.

NetWare NFS runs on any 80386 or better system that is running NetWare v.3.11 or above. A minimum of 5MB of RAM is required. The TCPIP.NLM module must be loaded at the NetWare server to support the NFS system.

Univell UnixWare

Univell started as a partnership between Novell and UNIX System Laboratories, Inc., but Novell eventually purchased UNIX System Laboratories in late 1992. The company's mission is to position NetWare and UNIX as a standard interoperable computing platform. In this arrangement, NetWare links PC users and workgroups together, and UNIX adds a powerful application platform and interconnectivity solution to the NetWare desktop environment. UnixWare consists of two configurations: a client version and a server version. Both configurations are described next.

- *UnixWare Personal Edition* adds a UNIX desktop environment to the NetWare network. The Personal Edition implements UNIX System V Release 4.2 and Univell's NetWare UNIX client software in one integrated package. The software requires an Intel-based 80386 or better system and a minimum of 6MB of memory, but 8MB is recommended. It includes a graphical desktop manager that supports Motif and the Open Look interface.

- *UnixWare Application Server* is an application platform that integrates full NetWare SPX/IPX protocols with UNIX System V Release 4.2. UnixWare Application Server enables DOS, UNIX, and other PC operating system clients to take full advantage of UNIX-based client-server applications, while simultaneously maintaining access to NetWare services and LAN resources. The Application Server is designed as an engine for distributed database programs, transaction processing programs, and other multiuser and client-server applications. It can optionally serve as a traditional

TCP/IP network server and support NFS as well as the standard Internet utilities. In addition, it provides support for multiple X terminals for running the graphical desktop. An Intel 80386 or better system with 8MB of memory is required, but 12MB is recommended. A 120MB or larger hard drive is also recommended.

Add-ons for UnixWare Personal Edition and Application Server include support for NFS and TCP/IP. The current version uses SPX/IPX to more easily integrate into existing NetWare LANs.

The Univell UnixWare product line competes with Open Desktop from SCO and Solaris 2.0 from SunSoft. All of these products are UNIX-based operating systems for Intel processors, and they run hundreds of existing applications. The UnixWare products include the integration of NetWare features. UnixWare also competes with Microsoft NT and OS/2, which are non-UNIX products but designed as a multitasking client-server operating system that will compete against UNIX. However, Microsoft NT is a relatively new product without the range of applications that UNIX has.

Interoperability

Complete interoperability among major systems is a goal that might be met by the end of this decade, but for now, interoperability is limited. For example, it's possible for a Macintosh user to store files on a NetWare server, but it will be a long time before a PC can run a program written for a Macintosh. True interoperability would allow any system to access any other system and use its resources. Many of the OSI protocols define the interaction of different operating systems and the applications they support.

The importance of complete interoperability is questionable today, but complete interoperability has obvious advantages, which should be considered for future product planning. Currently, most users are perfectly happy with the systems they have and the applications that run on them. Novell NetWare's ability to store files from many systems gives system administrators a way to manage and protect data at a central location. This is often the main reason for allowing Macintosh and OS/2 users to store files on a NetWare server. But as applications become more sophisticated and require more processing power, interoperability among applications and systems will become an important consideration. Distributed processing and client-server computing are prime examples of tasks that would benefit from complete interoperability. If an application can split up a processing task and hand "pieces" of the task to available processors on the network, ideally that application should be able to use any system without regard for its hardware.

Interoperability will come in phases. Many of the rules for interoperability have not yet been written or even proposed. An organization of developers and users called the Open Systems Foundation (OSF) is developing a networking scheme called Distributed Computing Environment (DCE) that will provide a sophisticated distributed file system on enterprise networks. Its file system provides a common network environment to users, no matter which workstation or operating system they use, assuming the DCE scheme is used. DCE is primarily being developed on UNIX systems for now, but proprietary operating systems from Digital Equipment Corporation and IBM are in the plans. In the meantime, applications provide interoperability by using standards like the one discussed in the following sections.

The X.400 Message Handling System

The OSI X.400 standard defines an electronic system for exchanging messages among mail systems running on a wide variety of platforms. X.400 is an OSI model that is also accepted by the Comité Consultatif Internationale de Télégraphie et Téléphonie (CCITT). Its goal is to provide compatibility among multivendor products and interfaces as well as public and private message services.

Using the analogy of an envelope, X.400 electronic messaging provides a way to fill an envelope with any information and send it to another user or system. Since formats are the same among X.400 systems, users can send messages to a variety of X.400 applications on a companywide or global internetwork. Messages can include simple notes or data taken from an applications program such as a spreadsheet or word processor. An application can use X.400 in the background to transfer information to a central system. An X.25 public data network can be used to exchange messages.

The following modules make up the X.400 messaging system:

■ *The User Agent (UA)* prepares messages for routing to a destination by addressing them with information found in a lookup table. The table contains the names and addresses of other X.400 users. The directory might follow the X.500 specification for object addressing, which is discussed in the next section.

■ *Message Transfer Agents (MTAs)* accept messages from the UA and route them to other MTAs.

■ *The Message Store (MS)* is a storage area for messages that need to be distributed to other users. This store-and-forward feature allows messages to be sent at convenient times.

■ *The Directory System* contains a complete list of the names and addresses of other X.400 users. It usually follows the X.500 standard.

A number of companies provide X.400-compatible packages that run on Novell NetWare networks. The Novell Global Messaging System provides a gateway to Simple Mail Transfer Protocol (SMTP), a messaging standard in the UNIX environment, and System Network Architecture Distribution Service (SNADS), an IBM mainframe-based messaging system.

Global Naming

The X.500 global naming specification, which NetWare Directory Services conforms to, is another application-level protocol. It helps users locate other users and resources within large internetworks. Global naming is not easy to implement, especially across a multitude of systems. A global database of users and resources must be continuously updated and synchronized. The X.500 standard defines how the database is implemented and how systems access and update it.

A naming system is like a phone book or directory of services. Consider how confusing it would be to use a phone system without a phone book or to send a letter without knowing an address. In the X.500 global naming specification, you refer to resources by using a multipart name. This name first describes the resource's object type (user, printer, server, and so on). Thus, the first part of a name might be SERVER. The next part of the name describes the resource's location, so the name could be SERVER.ACCOUNTING. From there, additional name components could describe the company name and its location. You can refer to an object by typing out its name, but in most cases, you select from a list in an application that handles electronic mail or gives you access to objects on the network.

A global naming system places users and resources into domains that help administrators organize the system and help users quickly locate objects.

Management

A management system lets supervisors view and manage all the resources on a network, no matter which hardware or operating system they use. As internetworks expand, administrators need a way to manage remote resources without actually traveling to them. Management systems provide a way to collect information from a variety of systems at diverse locations and display the information on a central system, where managers can manipulate and interpret it. Novell provides management links to NetView, an IBM network management facility, through its NetWare for SAA product.

Simple Network Management Protocol (SNMP) is a standard for collecting network information that got its start on the Internet, a university and governmental internetwork that uses primarily TCP/IP. SNMP provides agents that collect information from network devices and send the information to a management information base (MIB). Applications that are SNMP compatible can use this information to report network status and other information to system administrators. Another management standard is the OSI Common Management Information Protocol (CMIP).

Although CMIP offers more functionality than SNMP, SNMP has raced ahead in terms of industry acceptance. Most hardware and management products advertise their SNMP compatibility. Decisions on which wiring hub or other hardware device to use are usually based on their SNMP compatibility.

Novell makes several network management products that are SNMP compatible. For example, the NetWare MultiProtocol Router, which is SNMP compatible, can be managed by using Novell's NetWare Services Manager for Windows or any other SNMP-based console, such as IBM's NetView or Sun Microsystems' Net Manager. The Novell LANtern product is an SNMP agent for Ethernet networks that reports to Novell's LANtern Services Manager software. The Novell NetWare Management System (NMS) is a management system that supports SNMP as well as MSAPI, which is a proprietary management protocol for managing NetWare services. The OS/2 version of this product supports only MSAPI, however, and does not support SNMP.

File System Interoperability

File transfer protocols, such as those discussed earlier for TCP/IP, provide low-level interoperability among different systems. For example, you can dial into a bulletin board service and download a file by using a transfer protocol like XMODEM. Even though the two systems might be entirely different, the file is sent, and error checking is done to ensure its integrity. At a higher level of interoperability, two dissimilar systems can share a common file system. So far this is possible only with the Network Filing System (NFS) developed by Sun Microsystems, as discussed earlier. The ability of Novell NetWare to store and share files from Apple Macintosh and OS/2 clients can also be considered a form of file system interoperability. In the future, many operating systems will interoperate and allow transparent file sharing and application execution.

Interoperable Applications

Applications software for networks can be divided into three categories: LAN-ignorant applications, LAN-aware applications, and LAN-intrinsic applications. *LAN-ignorant applications* are written for use on a single-user computer. Although they might run on a network, they do not contain the features that are required in a multiuser environment to protect files and data. These features are included in the second category of software, which is known as *LAN-aware applications*. LAN-aware packages contain file-locking and record-locking features that prevent more than one user from updating the same file or database record at the same time.

LAN-intrinsic applications distribute various processing tasks among the server and workstations. They are also called *client-server applications* or *front-end/back-end applications*. With a LAN-intrinsic application, the workstation is referred to as the client (or front end), and the server is the back-end processor. A LAN-intrinsic database program has separate program modules for the workstation and the server. The client portion is used to display menus and data and to accept commands executed by the user. Some commands are executed by the workstation's processor, such as a command to display new menus or list the data that is currently being worked on. Other commands are executed by the server, such as sorting or indexing commands that manipulate the entire database. In this way, the data that needs to be sorted stays where it is stored, rather than moving across the LAN to the workstation.

After a request is processed at the back end, the results are sent to the front end for display. Front-end processing activities include formatting the data and displaying it on the screen. Keeping the data at the back-end server has several important benefits:

- Network performance improves because there is less traffic on the network.

■ If the server is a high-performance machine, some processing activities are better executed there, where the processing and file system I/O can work together in a tight-knit arrangement.

■ Security is enhanced because the entire database is not transferred over the network, where it could be monitored.

In client-server relationships that involve database applications, the back-end server process is sometimes referred to as the database engine. Such engines operate in accordance with certain rules. For example, relational integrity rules ensure that information in the database cannot be changed unless a user has the rights to do so. Managers can also apply such rules globally to the entire database.

Distributed Versus Centralized Client-Server Applications

Keep in mind that client-server applications don't all work the same. Most current client-server database applications are really no different than centralized databases that perform all the processing; the workstations only display the data. This method wastes the processing power available at the workstations and increases the load at the server. This may remind some readers of a centralized minicomputer or mainframe system that uses dumb terminals. In fact, many current client-server databases were ported over from those environments and still retain their characteristics.

A true distributed client-server application places some of the processing in the workstations. Obviously this method is harder to implement. Novell's idea of a true client-server "model" is to distribute to the workstation processing that is not directly related to finding and manipulating data records. This processing includes managing an application's front end and the presentation of information. Basically the server farms out part of its workload. By doing this, client-server systems, considered as a whole, can approach the processing speeds of minicomputer and mainframe systems.

The idea of distributed processing can be taken a step further. Eventually applications that take advantage of the aggregate processing power of many different machines on a network will be common. Machines that sit idle during off hours will be given the mutual task of calculating extremely complex problems. They might also be used for everyday tasks. For example, if a user requests a report from a database, the database engine might find an idle processor on the network to do the job, thus freeing itself for other tasks.

SQL

SQL is an acronym for Structured Query Language. It is an English-like database language that was developed in the 1970s by IBM. Using SQL, queries can be made in the form of verbs to retrieve information from a database. The language has virtually become a worldwide standard and is available for almost every operating system, including UNIX, DOS, Macintosh OS, and OS/2. Any database application that supports SQL can exchange data with any other SQL-compatible database.

Almost every client-server database system is based on SQL. Many of these applications hide the SQL commands with easy-to-use interfaces. Almost any type of application—for example, electronic spreadsheets and accounting programs—can use SQL commands to access a database.

Novell makes SQL available as a NetWare Loadable Module. NetWare SQL allows many applications to share a common database, and it supports a variety of front ends, including Lotus 1-2-3 version 3 or above, Concentric R+R, Oracle, and WordTech Quicksilver/SQL. NetWare's integrity and security features enhance the reliability of the database. NetWare SQL can be used by developers to write applications, or it can be used in conjunction with the interfaces previously described to access information.

Available Applications

The following provides a list of vendors who are selling or working on client-server applications for those who need more information:

> Advanced Data Servers, Boise, ID
> Gupta Technologies, Menlo Park, CA
> Informix Software, Menlo Park, CA
> Microsoft Corporation, Redmond, WA
> Novell, Provo, UT
> Odesta, North Brook, IL
> Oracle, Redwood Shores, CA
> Sybase, Berkeley, CA
> VIA Information Systems, Princeton, NJ
> XDB Systems, College Park, MD

Groupware

Groupware is a network software concept that defines applications used by a group of people. It is based on the assumption that because networks connect users, those users should be able to interact as well, to increase the productivity of the group as a whole. Electronic mail is a good example of groupware. Beyond that, groupware is a term used in many different places to define many different things. This section explores several groupware packages that can be run on NetWare networks.

A true groupware package allows users on many different systems to interact. For example, editing a file and then sending it to another user for review might not be groupware. On the other hand, a remote control program that allows a manager to tie into other users' workstations and help them through tough situations is an excellent example of interactive groupware. This type of arrangement is often used in training classes where workstations are connected to a network. Any changes the instructor makes on his or her workstation are echoed on the students' workstations.

Taking this a step further, network-wide meetings can be scheduled by a group of users in different parts of a building or organization. This "meeting" takes place over the network. All members remain seated at their workstations while the meeting coordinator establishes a connection among their workstations. When the connection is made, any activities on the main workstation are echoed to the other workstations. A simultaneous conference call can allow group members to talk together, or an onscreen dialog box can be used to type messages. Changes are made to onscreen documents in real time by a designated user, or if the package is really sophisticated, any user can make a change that is echoed to all other users' screens. This type of application is useful in engineering, architectural, and planning environments.

Another interesting groupware concept is interactive conferencing, which can best be described as an ongoing conference in which members hold onscreen conversations. Messages typed by users immediately appear on the screen. Members can respond to other members or simply watch as messages scroll by. Members can also sign in and sign out without disrupting the conference. CompuServe and other bulletin boards already provide this type of service on a worldwide basis to any type of machine. Members can join several different conferences at any time of the day or night, assuming other users are "in conference." One aspect of the service is that members can remain anonymous. An organization can establish its own conferencing facility over a network to allow employees to discuss projects, weekend parties, or company policies.

THE
COMPLETE

REFERENCE

PART THREE
Planning and Setup

CHAPTER 11

Network Planning

This chapter will help system designers and managers plan and purchase a network. Although no network has a final plan that is set in concrete, preparing an initial plan is essential. Technology and user needs change constantly, so the plan is bound to change. You should develop your initial plan in the most professional and responsible way possible, no matter what the size of your LAN.

It's common to hire outside organizations to help plan a network because they bring methodologies and experience to the planning stages. Furthermore, a systems analyst or consulting organization can work as an unbiased mediator with your users, managers, and system supervisors to determine hardware and software needs, budget requirements, policy implementation, and other factors concerned with the move to or growth of a network. Staff interviews typically identify problems and requirements. A few of the most likely are listed here:

- The current system, whether paper-based or computerized, is inefficient.

- There is insufficient storage capacity on existing systems.

- There is a need to run a multiuser program or centralized database that requires a LAN.

- Management wants to centralize backup of data.

- Users want to use printers and other hardware that is attached to other computers.

- Users need an easy way to communicate with one another, and an electronic mail system is the best solution.

Part of the planner's job is to develop technical specifications for the network that include server and other hardware requirements as well as software requirements. The plan must also include methods for implementation and a description of new procedures. In addition, training of new and existing personnel will be necessary.

As any professional systems analyst knows, it's important to work up a plan in stages and then present a report for each stage so that management can decide whether to go ahead with the next phase of the project, based on budgets and benefits. It is also important to document the planning stages every step of the way so that management can track the plan's progress and see how solutions are arrived at.

Eventually, a request for proposals (RFP) is developed and sent to vendors and retailers, who can then provide pricing and configuration information. A complete blueprint of the proposed system and an identification of its parts and their cost is developed. A cost-benefits report is produced for management, who then approve or reject the proposal. If approved, a detailed list of components is given to purchasing.

From that point on, installation and maintenance of the system can proceed as components and parts arrive. System testing begins, and equipment logs are produced to track components and to track problems with the equipment. Software is installed, and security measures are implemented. The system is brought on line, and users are trained.

The remainder of this book covers installation and post-installation activities for Novell NetWare and provides useful information for systems analysts or others in the process of planning and designing a network system.

Identifying LAN Needs

Anyone trying to identify the requirements of a LAN must become familiar with the current system, if any, and its limitations. The following sections provide a brief outline that you can use to assess your current environment and determine problems and solutions.

IDENTIFYING EXISTING EQUIPMENT   You should write down any information known about the current in-house systems, such as the types of computers, storage devices, backup systems, printers and plotters, and communications equipment. Don't forget to take into account computers and communications equipment at remote sites.

MAPPING THE POTENTIAL LAN ENVIRONMENT   Draw a map of the complete installation site and include the locations of the computers and peripheral devices you defined when you identified existing equipment. Locate wiring closets, existing cable runs, wire outlets, and existing cable tracks.

EVALUATING USAGE   If possible, try to determine the number of users who will access the network, and determine the server and disk requirements of those users. If a company has multiple departments, involve the department managers. Some of the questions that should be answered include: Will each department have its own network segments that are bridged to other segments? How much disk space will each department require on shared servers, or will each department have its own server? If each department has its own server, will the servers be managed by each department, or will all the department servers be managed at a central location by special network managers and technicians?

ESTABLISHING PROCEDURES   All businesses require procedures. Some are manual and some are automated. You must identify existing procedures and specify new procedures to implement for the network. Procedures have a cost and they require personnel to implement them, so they should be figured into any network plan. You should also identify the procedures that users must follow to access the network and use its resources.

LOCATING INTERDEPENDENCIES   Identify the interrelationship among users and departments in a company so that you can physically connect them over the LAN and give them access to information on other systems. For example, sales and accounts receivable are dependent on each other. Although this relationship is obvious, other relationships might not be. You might need to query users and department managers to identify exactly which data they use, where it is, and when they need it. You'll need this information when you set up the NetWare security system and file access rights.

DETERMINING COST RESPONSIBILITIES   Departments usually manage their own budgets, so they will need to determine how they will pay for the cost of shared data. The NetWare accounting systems provide tools for gathering information about resource usage. You can track how much time or how many resources users or departments access on a system, and charge the departments based on that usage. The difficult task is to determine these charge values in the planning stages so that you can establish how much each department must allocate in its budget for the network system. Also note that these values may not be measured in dollars. They may be accounting or trade-out values only.

Evaluating Hardware and Performance Needs

Network performance is affected by the number of users on the system and the type of work they do. It helps to closely evaluate who will access the network. A typical server these days has 16MB of memory and more than 300MB of storage. Prices have fallen so much that this type of system is typically found on desktops. It's not worth your time to evaluate whether you need 8MB or 16MB of memory because the difference in cost is as low as $250. The same holds true for disk storage. If you think you might need more than 300MB, it's best to calculate the cost for the larger hard drive into the budget. The difference between a 300MB and a 600MB hard drive is about $400.

If your server requirements are high, you should concentrate on evaluating the need for so-called "superserver" systems that include massive and redundant storage devices, high-speed buses, and multiple processors. Superservers are designed primarily to reduce bottlenecks. A *bottleneck* is a location or condition in the network environment that reduces access to resources. The speed at which a network handles peak traffic is referred to as its *throughput*. Throughput is affected by several factors, including the cabling system, the performance of the server, and the performance of the workstations. Bottlenecks at the server affect the throughput of the entire network, so it's important to purchase equipment that can handle your network loads and reduce bottlenecks.

If the cabling system, network interface cards, or server are inadequate, performance drops when many users simultaneously access the network. On the other hand, performance can drop when only one user accesses the LAN if that user overloads the server with intensive computing tasks or uses up the cable bandwidth by transferring large data files. Therefore, it's usually necessary to place high-performance users on their own LAN segments or even to add a second server for their exclusive use. Although it's next to impossible to evaluate network and server requirements until you actually have the system in place and users are accessing it, proper planning and evaluation can help you more accurately determine where the bottlenecks will be and work to reduce their impact on performance.

Consider the following methods for improving performance. Some are relatively inexpensive to implement.

- Make sure the server has adequate RAM. It is recommended that you start with 16MB.

- Use a high-capacity, high-performance hard drive.

- Select a server that uses a high-performance bus design, such as EISA or MCA, which are discussed in Chapter 12.

- Use a high-performance superserver. These are also discussed in Chapter 12.

- Install high-performance network interface cards in the server that use 16- or 32-bit interfaces, large buffers, and bus mastering.

- Use 10 Mb/sec Ethernet or 16 Mb/sec Token Ring boards and cable, or consider new proprietary technologies that boost network performance even higher.

- Use high-speed backbone cable systems and routers to connect LAN segments.

- If the LAN has more than 40 workstations, split the network into two LAN segments.

- Add a second file server to distribute the file server load.

The NetWare operating system uses memory extensively to increase its operating speed. Memory is used for file cache buffers, communications buffers, directory caching, and various other tasks. Novell provides a complicated formula for calculating the amount of memory you'll need, which is based on the number of users and the number of NLMs installed in the server. For simplicity, I recommend starting with 16MB of memory and expanding from there. Memory is inexpensive when compared to the cost of NetWare in the time users may need to wait for the server if its performance is slow.

Disk Storage

The hard disk storage system of a server is a major factor that contributes to the overall speed of a network. Only a few years ago, it was important to evaluate the type of drive and its performance. Today, most systems designed for server use contain hard drives that have extremely high performance ratings and large storage capacities.

Disk space is another requirement that is practically impossible to evaluate in advance. The server's disk must hold application files as well as data files. Users also often need disk storage space for their personal applications and data. If you use an electronic mail system, disk requirements can skyrocket as users get familiar with the system and take advantage of its capabilities. Hundreds or thousands of e-mail messages might linger on the disk for days or months unless you keep the system well managed.

As mentioned earlier, you should start out with a disk that meets your near-term needs and make sure you have the budget and hardware to accommodate future growth. NetWare v.4 uses compression techniques that can reduce an ASCII text file's size by as much as 50 percent. Consider that a bonus in disk space, but don't assume that all files will be compressed or will compress that much. Also keep in mind that NetWare v.4 supports data migration to optical disk or tape archive systems. This frees space in main storage by moving seldom used files to secondary storage. Migrated files are still available to users and retain their original filenames.

After you've determined the disk size and type you need, buy two: If you have the budget, you should implement the disk duplexing features offered by NetWare. If you compare the prices of disk drives today with the costs of downtime caused by failed drives, you'll see the benefits of disk duplexing. Also, if you plan to span NetWare volumes over multiple drives, disk duplexing is essential. There should be a law that requires it, like the seat belt law.

Backup Systems

Backing up the data on the servers is another essential requirement. If you centralize the servers, backups are often easier and more cost effective. For example, you could designate a manager to implement the same backup procedure for all the servers at a designated time. If servers are not centralized, you must rely on each department to back up its own systems, implement automatic backup systems, or run the backups over the network from a central location, which could affect performance.

Centralized backups can be a cost-effective option. For example, you could attach a dedicated high-performance, high-capacity backup system to the network backbone and provide backup services for a multitude of servers. Alternatively, you could use tape backup systems, optical disk backup systems, or real-time systems such as Novell SFT III (an optional product) or other systems that duplicate not only data, but hardware as well. Keep in mind that backup systems must be specifically designed to recognize the structure and attributes of the NetWare file system.

You can install third-party backup systems at the server or in network workstations. Backups usually take place during off-hours; however, some forms of backups can take place at any time of the day. Keep in mind that if users are logged in during a backup, files they have open will be excluded from the backup or will be backed up improperly. There are a number of automatic backup systems, some of which include automatic tape changers. Optical disk or removable magnetic disk backup systems are convenient because they offer quick access to backed up files when necessary.

Diskless Workstations

Diskless workstations are inexpensive computers without floppy disk drives or hard disk drives. They provide users with network access at a reasonable price and offer data security because users can't download data to floppy disks. You might consider using diskless workstations if your data is sensitive and you hire temporary employees.

When using diskless workstations, you'll need a network interface card that supports the use of a remote boot PROM. Most interface cards have this option, but it's a good idea to make sure. Remote boot PROMs cost about $50 and are added to cards as an option. The PROM allows the workstation to boot from a boot file located on the network server, which means that cards that use PROMs immediately connect with the network cable and server when you turn them on.

Cabling

It is important to fully understand the cable installation of a network. The managers and installers should be familiar with the way the cable is assembled and connected to network components such as repeaters, hubs, bridges, and routers. It is important to make a detailed map of the network topology, including the location of all accessories. Planning for growth is also important. Mark the locations where future stations might be added.

There are state and local codes that govern the types of cable that can be used in buildings. Cable that produces toxic gas when burned is prohibited in air ducts and ceiling areas that air moves through. You'll need to use fire-safe plenum cable there, or you can sometimes run non-plenum cable through metal conduit. These requirements affect the types of cable you choose, so it's best to consult with local cable installers before making any decisions. Although plenum cable meets code requirements, it is often cheaper to run less-expensive, non-plenum cable through conduit and still meet code requirements.

Drilling holes to run cable is prohibited or not practical at some sites. For example, you can't drill holes in asbestos ceilings because that would present a health threat.

You'll need to estimate not only the cost of cable but also the cost of installing it. When estimating cable costs, accurately measure the distances between workstations and include any extra length you'll need to get around obstructions. Also, try to map out where future workstations might be placed, and run wire to those locations if possible.

System Protection Equipment

Be sure to plan for the purchase of system protection equipment, such as an uninterruptible power supply (UPS), surge suppressors, and line filters. A UPS protects the server from blackouts or other power problems. A UPS allows the server to shut itself down properly, saving cache buffers, closing open files, and completing transactions. Although users in the vicinity of the server will lose power to their systems (unless they also have a UPS), remote users might not be affected by the blackout. Messages from the server inform those users that it is shutting down.

When buying a UPS, it is important to consider how long the UPS provides power to a server. A UPS must provide a method of alerting the server when it is operating under standby power. A cable from the UPS attaches to a UPS monitoring board or connection on the server. You might need to purchase this cable separately.

Identifying Application Requirements

This section discusses some of the things you should be aware of when evaluating the software that users will access on the server. You must determine where those applications will reside and who will use them. Large company databases might require a dedicated server that is not used for other storage or processing.

Make sure the software purchased for the network is either *network-aware* or designed specifically for network use. Typically, network-aware software monitors usage and prevents other users from starting the program when the number of licensed users has reached its limit. This doesn't sound like a benefit, but keep in mind that your company won't be sued for copyright infringement. Look for software that includes unlimited site licenses if you can't calculate the number of users who will need the software at one time.

A *network-ignorant* program doesn't provide adequate protection from file overwrites if several people access a file or database record at the same time. On a network, you need applications that provide file and record locking to protect against overwrites if two users edit and save the same file or database record simultaneously. Network-aware programs keep track of how data files are used and by whom, thus preventing data from being updated improperly.

Today, most programs sold for use on networks are network-aware, but you should always check to make sure. Also look at how licensing is implemented. Licenses are sometimes sold in increments—for example, five users at a time—and sometimes you buy a single site license. The latter is often more expensive in the short term but more economical over the long term if you expect growth.

CHAPTER 12

Choosing a Server

It was only a few years ago that costs conscious buyers had to spend a lot of time balancing equipment with their budget. Today, falling prices have made server buying decisions much easier. An 80386 or 80486 system for a small network (about 10 workstations) costs less than $2,000. Because prices are low, it doesn't make sense to skimp on quality when you buy a server. You can fully load the server with 16MB or more of memory and fast SCSI hard drives and still keep the price below $4,000. Of course, not all networks are small. Server vendors add special features to their servers to dramatically improve performance.

The remainder of this chapter covers file server features for small and large networks. Of the features described, the type of bus used by the system is usually the most important consideration when choosing a server. The bus is the "highway" used to transfer data among the components in the server and among the server, its network interface cards, and the workstations. This chapter classifies servers three ways:

- *Basic servers* are excellent for small LANs. They are relatively inexpensive, even when fully loaded with 16MB of RAM and a pair of fast hard drives (one for duplexing). These systems typically use the ISA bus. A basic server is a desktop system with a single network interface card to handle up to about 50 workstations at moderate performance.

- *Enhanced systems* have a number of features that improve performance, such as 32-bit EISA or MCA buses, special disk arrays that provide fault tolerance, and high-performance network interface cards.

- *Multiprocessor superservers* are typically proprietary systems that provide performance many times greater than that of typical server systems. A superserver uses a special bus that can run as fast as 250 MHz, compared to the 12 MHz ISA bus. Multiple microprocessors plug into the bus to share processing tasks or run individual applications. For example, one microprocessor could handle the network operating system while another handles a client-server database application. When you buy a superserver, you never need to buy another server; instead, you simply add another microprocessor to the superserver's bus.

Other factors to consider are memory requirements and the type of hard drives to use. This chapter explores these topics for those who are making a purchasing decision or people who are evaluating and recommending the purchase of equipment.

Throughput and Bottlenecks

Throughput and *bottlenecks* are terms used to describe how a server and a network perform when used. Picture the server as a sort of Grand Central Station, and network interface cards as tracks on which data moves in and out. Data moves from the cards to system memory, where it is processed by the CPU. A network's throughput is the speed at which it handles peak traffic. Throughput measures the combined performance of all components that transfer data. Bottlenecks are locations or conditions in the network environment that slow its throughput. Bottlenecks in the server occur at the locations shown in Figure 12-1.

Performance problems can occur outside the server as well as inside it. You might have the fastest server you need, but users still complain about how slow the network is. The problem might be their workstations, the network cabling system, or the fact that too many users are accessing the cable at the same time. After testing to eliminate problems, you may find it necessary to upgrade components. For example, you could upgrade workstations to 80386 or 80486 systems and install 16-bit network interface cards. You could also upgrade to a high-performance optical cable system.

To get the most performance from NetWare servers, eliminate any weak links in your network, as described in the following sections.

NOTE: For the purposes of this discussion, a small network has fewer than 50 workstations. A medium size network has from 50 to 200 workstations and internetworked segments. A large network has 200 or more users on internetwork and WAN links.

MICROPROCESSORS   The minimum system on which NetWare v. 4 runs is an Intel 80386 microprocessor; however, an 80486 or better system that runs at 33 MHz or faster is recommended for medium size networks. For large networks, multiple servers or superserver systems are recommended.

BUS DESIGN   The best way to enhance server performance is through improvements in bus design and the use of intelligent network adapters. An ISA bus system is good only for small networks. EISA and MCA systems are recommended for medium to large networks.

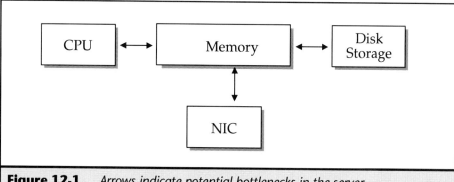

Figure 12-1.   *Arrows indicate potential bottlenecks in the server*

BUS MASTERING   In a bus mastering scheme, the CPU is relieved of some processing tasks by shifting the execution of those tasks to a coprocessor on another board. A network interface card with a bus mastering design writes data directly to memory, which leaves the system microprocessor free to handle operating system tasks.

CACHING   Bottlenecks occur when data is not shuffled in and out of memory quickly enough. Caches can reduce bottlenecks caused by exchanges between the CPU and memory and between disk storage and memory.

DISK INPUT/OUTPUT   One of the most important considerations when evaluating performance is the speed of disk input/output (I/O). You can reduce bottlenecks by using better disk channels and drives with low average access times.

NETWORK INTERFACE CARDS   Network interface cards with improved buffering techniques and bus mastering designs (EISA and MCA systems) improve performance. A card with a 16- or 32-bit interface bus is recommended. These specifications apply to the server and to any workstations that generate a lot of traffic.

WORKSTATIONS   A workstation can cause bottlenecks when it demands too much of the server's time, which results in large amounts of network traffic. As mentioned earlier, you can reduce bottlenecks by improving the network interface card in the workstation or by improving the microprocessor and bus size of the workstation. You can also split a network into multiple segments by adding a separate network interface card in the server for each segment.

THE NETWORK CABLING SYSTEM   Although this chapter is about servers, don't forget that the bottleneck might be the network cabling system and the type of cable access method it uses.

The Microprocessor

The microprocessor is the heart of any computer system. To run NetWare v. 4, a server based on the Intel 80386 or 80486 microprocessor is required. This section briefly describes the features of 80386 and 80486 systems as well as multiprocessing systems that use both chips. For reference, Table 12-1 lists the performance of some common microprocessors in MIPS (million instructions per second).

System	MIPS
Apple II (1979)	.04
IBM PC (1981)	.25
Apple Macintosh (1984)	.40
16 MHz 80386 systems	4
25 MHz 80386 systems	7
DEC Microvax	2 to 3
25 MHz 80486 systems	8 to 40
66 MHz 80486 systems	50

Table 12-1. *Performance of Common Microprocessor Chips in Million Instructions per Second*

NOTE: The Pentium chip, the successor to the Intel 80486, runs at 100 MIPS. In order to get the best performance from this chip, special bus architectures are needed. For example, Compaq has developed the TriFlex that takes advantage of the 64-bit-wide microprocessor bus. Software will also need to change in order to take advantage of the chip's features. Expect a Pentium-compatible upgrade of NetWare in the near future.

The Intel 80386

The Intel 80386 is the successor to the Intel 8088, 8086, and 80286 family of microprocessors. The 80386 has a full 32-bit I/O port that provides a connection point for high-speed 32-bit memory and peripheral expansion. On 32-bit MCA and EISA systems, the bus itself provides a full 32-bit path to the microprocessor.

The 80386 is significantly faster than its predecessors. Its other features include the following:

- Addresses 4096MB (4 gigabytes) of memory

- Has built-in features that make task switching simple and efficient, thus allowing several programs to run at once

- Can act like several 8086 microprocessors running simultaneously. The exact number of 8086 microprocessors depends on the amount of memory available. Each process gets its own protected block of memory

- Contains a memory management unit (MMU) that is capable of speeding access to memory

The Intel 80486

The Intel 80486 microprocessor is completely compatible with the 80386; therefore, software for the 80386 works on 80486 systems. However, the 80486 is a completely redesigned microprocessor that improves on the 80386's features and operational characteristics. Many functions are integrated onto the chip itself such as the Intel 80387 numeric coprocessor and the Intel 82385 memory cache controller.

The 80486 is fast; special techniques are used to keep it supplied with data for processing. It has an 8 KB cache on the chip itself to improve performance, and it includes four write buffers that help keep the external bus from becoming a bottleneck. Some 80486 systems come with external cache buffers to improve performance even further.

Multiprocessing Systems

Multiprocessing systems have two or more microprocessors and usually have specialized buses to improve performance. These superserver systems are designed to optimize throughput to each microprocessor, to disk storage, and to the network. Multiprocessing systems are available from NetFRAME Systems, Compaq, and other vendors and are discussed at the end of this chapter.

The Server Bus

A computer system's bus is the communications channel used to transfer data among I/O devices, memory, disk storage, and the CPU. The type of bus selected is extremely important to the performance and throughput of a server.

The ISA bus has been around for a number of years, but newer and faster microprocessors, storage devices, and I/O devices demand better performance from a system bus. In the late 1980s, IBM introduced its MCA bus. In addition, a consortium of microcomputer vendors including Compaq, AST, Hewlett-Packard, Epson, and Zenith developed the EISA bus. The MCA and EISA buses deliver increased performance over the older ISA bus, as shown in Table 12-2.

NOTE: *DMA stands for direct memory access.*

Bus	Bus Size	DMA Transfer	Bus Master Speed	Clock Rate
ISA	16-bit	Up to 1.5 Mb/sec	N/A	8 MHz
MCA	32-bit	Up to 5 Mb/sec	Up to 40 Mb/sec	10 MHz
EISA	32-bit	Up to 33 Mb/sec	Up to 32 Mb/sec	8 MHz

Table 12-2.   *A Comparison of Bus Performance*

The ISA Bus

The Personal Computer bus has been around since the introduction of the IBM PC. It was expanded from an 8-bit data path to a 16-bit data path in 1984 with the introduction of the IBM PC/AT. After that, it was popularly referred to as the Industry Standard Architecture (ISA) bus.

Each add-in adapter card on an ISA bus uses a different interrupt line to signal the CPU when it wants access to the bus. No two cards can share the same interrupt, and only 11 interrupts are available in the ISA bus. It is important to plan ahead when building a server with an ISA bus to avoid interrupt conflicts among cards. The ISA bus is a bottleneck in most LAN environments.

The exact timing information for the ISA bus was never published, so any attempts to increase the performance of the bus would make it incompatible with the thousands of boards that are designed for it.

The VESA and Intel PCI Standards

In 1992, to boost the performance of ISA systems, a consortium of more than 120 companies called VESA (Video Equipment Standards Association) developed a local bus standard called VL-Bus. It allows video cards and hard disk controllers (and it will eventually allow network interface cards) to connect directly to the system microprocessor bus, where they run at 33 MHz rather than 8 MHz. VL-Bus operates at the speed of the CPU. There can be no more than three VL-Bus slots per motherboard because the microprocessor can't drive more than this number without reducing its clock rate. There is currently some debate about the benefits of VL-Bus. You should base your buying decisions on test reports.

Although VL-Bus is considered by some a short-term solution to the ISA bottleneck, Intel is working on a new bus standard called PCI that is more compatible with Intel microprocessors. It puts less stress on the CPU and is designed more with the future in mind. At this writing, no VL-Bus or PCI products are available that benefit network traffic.

The EISA Bus

The EISA bus was designed by a consortium of industry manufacturers to offer support for existing ISA expansion boards as well as provide a platform for future growth. To support ISA cards, an 8 MHz clock rate is used, but the bus can provide direct memory access rates of up to 33 Mb/sec. An EISA bus has separate I/O and microprocessor buses, so the I/O bus can maintain a low clock rate to support ISA boards while the microprocessor bus runs at higher rates. EISA machines can provide high-speed disk I/O to multiple users.

The EISA bus is a full 32-bit bus, so its design accommodates more pins than the ISA bus can handle. The connector has a two-tier slot design that can accept both ISA and EISA cards. The top tier makes contact with ISA boards, and the lower tier makes contact with EISA boards. Although EISA buses can maintain the 8 MHz clock speed of the ISA for compatibility, they support a burst-mode data transfer method that transfers data at up to three times the speed of an ISA bus. Most servers designed for medium to large networks use the EISA bus.

The MCA Bus

The MCA bus was developed by IBM to help resolve the difficulties of combining fast microprocessors with the relatively slow ISA bus. Although MCA buses do not accept ISA-style boards, they provide a 32-bit interface that is faster than ISA and is a better match to 80386 and 80486 microprocessors.

The MCA bus has a single bus design that handles both memory and I/O transfers by using multiplexing, which allows several processes to share the bus simultaneously. Multiplexing splits the bus into several channels that can each handle different processes. This design is not as fast as multiple-bus systems, but in many cases it is adequate for medium size NetWare networks. If microprocessor-intensive applications are run at the server, a superserver might be a better choice because of its superior throughput and multiprocessor capabilities.

The MCA bus is protected by patents and licensing agreements that inhibit its growth as a standard. In addition, IBM has imposed some limitations in MCA to prevent it from competing with its minicomputer systems. Because of this, many vendors use EISA or have developed proprietary bus standards.

The Disk System

A common bottleneck on any server is the disk system. Some disk system considerations include the following:

■ Disk caching is important, and NetWare allocates all available memory to this task. In addition, NetWare improves the performance of the disk by using such techniques as elevator seeking and file allocation table caching.

■ A high-speed bus such as the MCA or EISA bus is important to move data quickly to and from other components in the server.

■ The construction of the drive determines how quickly data is read or written. As the capacity and number of disk surfaces in a drive increase, its access time improves.

■ Various encoding methods reduce the amount of space data uses on a disk and improves access to that data.

There are several standard disk interfaces, which are described in the following sections.

THE ST506 INTERFACE   The ST506 interface was one of the first disk drive interfaces used in personal computers. It was originally marketed by Seagate Technologies. The ST506 interface typically uses Modified Frequency Modulation (MFM) when writing data, and has a data transfer rate of 5 Mb/sec. If Run Length Limited (RLL) encoding is used, data storage and transfer rates increase. ST506 controllers were commonly used in 80286 and early 80386 systems, but they are decreasing in popularity because of their slow transfer rates. Systems that use these controllers are only suitable for the smallest NetWare v.4 networks.

THE ESDI INTERFACE   The Enhanced Small Device Interface (ESDI) is similar to the ST506 interface, but it provides 512 bytes per sector and 34 to 36 sectors per track. Its transfer rates are in the range of 10 to 15 Mb/sec. ESDI disk systems use high-capacity drives with storage capabilities greater than 100MB. Up to two ESDI drives can attach to an ESDI controller.

THE SCSI INTERFACE   The Small Computer System Interface (SCSI) differs radically from the ST506 interface and ESDI. It allows up to seven devices, such as hard drives, tape drives, and CD-ROM drives, to share the same SCSI host adapter, which takes up only one slot in the server. The card provides a shared bus that all peripherals use to pass data to and from the system. The bus is 8, 16, or even 32 bits wide and supports transfer rates that can exceed those of other standards. A new SCSI standard called SCSI-II provides even faster data throughput.

The SCSI *host adapter* provides bus services (a connection point) for intelligent devices. Intelligent devices, such as SCSI disk drives, optical disks, and backup systems contain their own control circuitry. In the ST506 and ESDI world, this control circuitry is built onto the controller card. The SCSI adapter monitors the data throughput and commands between the system and the SCSI devices. Each device handles only the requests assigned to it. Because the control circuitry is built into each SCSI device, configuration and compatibility issues are minimized. Theoretically, you can plug any SCSI device into any SCSI controller, but it's best to check compatibility and software drive requirements before doing so.

THE IDE INTERFACE   The Intelligent Drive Electronics (IDE) interface is a hybrid that combines features of the other interfaces and offers new features of its own. IDE devices were originally designed as low-cost alternatives to ESDI devices. However, like SCSI devices, IDE devices have their own control circuitry. They attach to an IDE adapter, which is inexpensive and is often built right onto the motherboard, saving a slot. Systems that have VL-Bus slots often include IDE controllers that fit in the VL-Bus for 32-bit access.

An IDE adapter supports only two devices. Because IDE is relatively inexpensive to implement, most of the low-priced systems on the market today use it. Don't think that because IDE costs less it is inferior to the other interface methods; when both price and performance are considered, IDE is probably superior. The IDE interface operates at around 4 Mb/sec, close to the SCSI rate. A typical IDE drive has an access rate of 16 ms (milliseconds). Some have built-in intelligent caches to improve performance.

NetWare Storage Options

Disk mirroring and disk duplexing provide protection against disk failures. Mirroring provides a way to back up one drive by continuously duplicating its contents on another. It requires that you buy one secondary backup drive for every primary drive. Data written to the primary drive is automatically written to the backup drive. Should the primary drive go down, the backup drive can take its place until a new drive is installed. Disk duplexing provides the same level of mirroring but adds a second controller. The first controller handles the primary drive, and the second controller handles the mirrored backup drive. In this way, should the first controller and drive go down, the second controller and drive can take over.

Novell NetWare provides commands and utilities for handling disk mirroring and duplexing. To configure a system for disk mirroring, you add a controller card and then attach drives to it. IDE and ESDI controllers support the attachment of only two drives per card, as shown in Figure 12-2. To expand this configuration, you'll need another controller, as shown in Figure 12-3, which illustrates a disk duplexing configuration in which the second controller handles the two drives that mirror the two primary drives.

SCSI controllers provide attachments for up to seven drives. This means that you could add two primary drives and two mirroring drives to one controller.

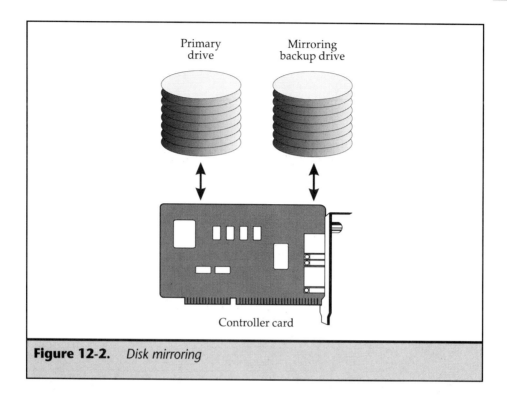

Primary
drive

Mirroring
backup drive

Controller card

Figure 12-2.   *Disk mirroring*

But this arrangement does not provide protection if the controller should fail, so it's recommended that you use two SCSI controllers: one to handle the primary drives and one to handle the mirroring drives.

Volume Spanning

Volumes are the primary unit of storage in the NetWare operating system. You can divide a single disk into two or more volumes, or you can span a volume over several disks. Spanning a volume over several disks provides some performance enhancements; it is possible with one controller and multiple drives or with several controllers and multiple drives.

NetWare lets you increase the size of a volume by simply adding another drive and making part of that drive available as a volume attachment. It is not necessary to reformat the original volume, because NetWare simply adds the new volume to it.

Although spanning can improve performance, it can also be risky unless precautions are taken. If one drive in a spanned volume should fail, NetWare cannot use the entire volume. Because of this, it is necessary to duplex drives that have spanned volumes.

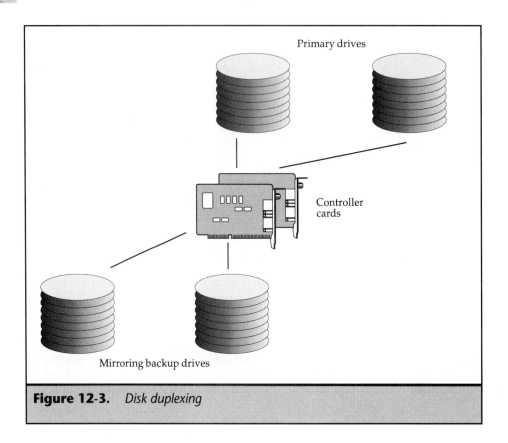

Primary drives

Controller cards

Mirroring backup drives

Figure 12-3.   *Disk duplexing*

Disk Arrays

A RAID (redundant arrays of inexpensive disks) is a set of drives that appears as a single drive. Data is written evenly across the drives by using a technique called *striping*. Striping divides data over two or more drives, as shown by the crude example in Figure 12-4. Data striping can occur at the bit level or on a sector level. A sector is a block of disk data. Striping improves throughput and provides a form of redundancy that protects against the failure of one disk in the array by encoding the scattered data to a backup drive known as the parity drive.

    The disk controller is a very important piece of hardware in a RAID system because it affects performance and fault tolerance. Several controllers are often used to protect against controller failure. SCSI adapters are used almost exclusively in RAID systems because of their improved read and write performance. After issuing a read or write command to one drive, a SCSI controller can disconnect from it and turn its attention to another drive. The drive continues the operation on its own.

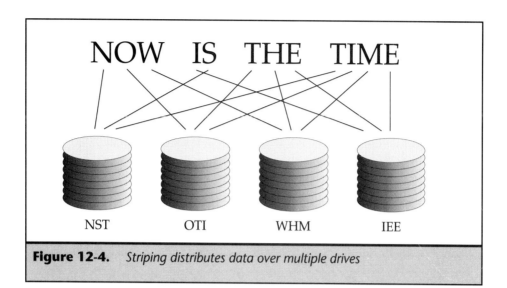

Figure 12-4. *Striping distributes data over multiple drives*

RAID provides redundancy (that is, mirroring and duplexing). The level of redundancy depends on the RAID level used, which is described later in this chapter. In a normal mirroring configuration like that used by the standard NetWare mirroring method, one backup drive is matched to one primary drive. In RAID level 3, one parity drive provides mirroring for two or more primary drives. A coding scheme is used to write information to the parity drive that represents the data written to the other drives. If one drive should fail, the parity code and the data on the remaining drives are used to come up with the missing portion of the data.

Buying a single parity drive is much cheaper than buying a backup mirroring drive for each primary drive. However, a single parity drive provides adequate protection only if one drive fails at a time. If two or more primary drives fail, the parity code drive won't contain enough information to rebuild the data. Only standard mirroring configurations that provide a backup drive for each primary drive can provide this type of protection. On the other hand, the chances of two drives failing at the same time are low, and if they failed within a few days of each other, you would probably have already restored the information on the first failed drive.

Many RAID systems allow *hot replacement* of disks, which means that disks can be replaced while the system is running. When a disk is replaced, the parity information is used to rebuild the data on the disk. Rebuilding occurs while the operating system continues handling other operations, so there is some loss of performance during the rebuilding operation.

There are several levels of RAID. When buying systems that use RAID, you need to check their levels against your system needs.

■ *RAID level 0*   Data is striped over several drives, but there is no redundant drive. Level 0 provides RAID performance without data protection.

■ *RAID level 1*   Data is striped to an array of drives and each drive is mirrored to a backup drive. In a four-drive array, two are used as primary drives and two are used as mirroring drives. This level provides the performance benefits of striping and the highest level of protection by mirroring all primary drives.

■ *RAID level 2*   This level is not normally implemented. It provides data striping at the bit level over all drives in the array. RAID level 3 is similar, but it is implemented more widely.

■ *RAID level 3*   Data is striped at the bit or byte level (your choice) to all drives in the array except one, which becomes the parity drive. In a four-drive array, data is striped to three drives and parity information is written to the fourth. This level provides good read performance but relatively slow write performance because the parity drive is written to with every write operation.

■ *RAID level 4*   This level is similar to RAID level 3, except that data is striped in disk sector units rather than as bits or bytes. Read times are improved because each drive can retrieve an entire disk sector.

■ *RAID level 5*   Data is written in disk sector units to all drives in the drive array. Error-correction codes are also written to all drives. This level provides quicker writes because the parity information is spread over all the drives rather than being written to a single parity drive as is the case in RAID level 3. Disk reads are improved because each drive can retrieve an entire disk block.

Most RAID systems designed for server use on the market today use either RAID level 4 or RAID level 5. The Compaq SYSTEMPRO, implement RAID level 4 but offer an upgraded software driver that implements RAID level 5, which offers better performance. Such disk arrays are expensive and you need to weigh their price against your need for continuous online data protection. You also need to weigh the price and performance of a RAID system against the standard disk mirroring and disk duplexing techniques that NetWare supports (or server duplexing provided by SFT Lever III). An additional consideration is that RAID systems are often proprietary, which ties you to the manufacturer for future support and service.

Superservers

Superservers provide speed, fault tolerance, and security for large networks. They are typically classified as systems that provide the following:

- Multiple microprocessors

- A high-performance bus, or multiple buses

- Tens of megabytes of error-correcting memory

- RAID disk arrays

- Advanced system architectures that reduce system bottlenecks

- Redundant features such as two power supplies

A superserver's multiple-processor architecture lets you add microprocessors within a single chassis rather than buying additional servers. There are two situations in which you should consider a superserver system:

- You have a client-server database or other computer-intensive application that needs to run at the server.

- There is a large traffic load on the network and the current server is incapable of handling the traffic.

The high-performance bus in a superserver can quickly move data among multiple network cards, disk controllers, and CPUs, as shown in Figure 12-5. Superservers typically use a proprietary high-speed bus or the EISA bus. Systems that use the EISA bus accept industry standard adapters and provide many times the throughput of ISA systems.

In desktop systems that use a single-bus structure such as ISA, a single process takes control of the bus to perform a task and then releases the bus for use by another process. Superservers with proprietary buses, such as those from NetFRAME Systems, do not use the bus as a locking device to prevent processes from conflicting. Instead, multiple independent buses can run at the same time, and the system can be expanded by adding more buses, so the bus does not need to be redesigned for each new generation of microprocessors or operating systems.

NetFRAME superservers use a high-bandwidth bus that can coexist with older buses such as the 16-bit ISA bus. Interprocess communications are performed in shared memory that all microprocessors have access to, and all microprocessors operate simultaneously to form a true parallel processing system. NetFRAME superservers are designed to take advantage of future

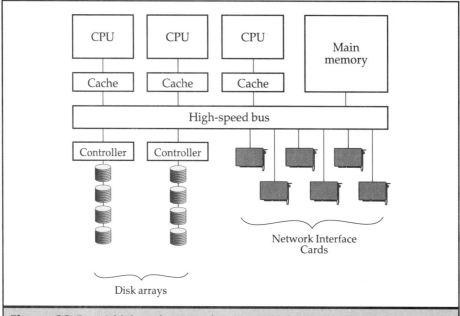

Figure 12-5.   *A high-performance bus is essential in a superserver system*

client-server applications by allowing multiple microprocessors to handle multiple server-based applications.

Because superservers typically use tens of megabytes of memory, the potential for errors increases. Some systems include ECC (error correction code) memory that can detect and correct memory errors. The NetFRAME system even checks memory errors on the system bus that occur when data is in transit between the CPU and memory. Some systems include dual power supplies with separate power cords for each.

Symmetrical and Asymmetrical Multiprocessor Systems

There are two types of multiprocessor system designs: symmetrical and asymmetrical. Each type has different features and benefits.

In symmetrical multiprocessor systems, system resources such as memory and disk I/O are shared by all the microprocessors in the system. The workload is distributed evenly to available microprocessors so that one doesn't sit idle while another is overworked with a specific task. The performance of symmetrical multiprocessor systems increases for all tasks as microprocessors are added. A drawback to symmetrical multiprocessing is that a single microprocessor cannot be set aside to handle a single task, such as the execution of a client-server database application. In addition, operating systems that take advantage of symmetrical multiprocessing systems are harder to design.

In asymmetrical multiprocessor systems, tasks and system resources are managed by different microprocessors. For example, one microprocessor handles I/O and another handles network operating system tasks. Asymmetrical multiprocessor systems do not balance workloads. A microprocessor handling one task can be overworked while another microprocessor sits idle. Symmetrical processing systems distribute the workload evenly.

Currently, NetWare will run on symmetrical multiprocessor systems, but it does not take advantage of their ability to share processing loads among microprocessors. (On the NetFRAME asymmetrical multiprocessing system, NetWare has been modified slightly so that network interface cards are handled by a separate microprocessor.) However, there are still a number of performance benefits when NetWare is run on a symmetrical superserver system. The primary focus of most vendors is to increase system throughput for multiple network users on multiple LAN segments. This strategy is similar to that used in wiring centers, as discussed in Chapter 8. A high-speed bus provides quick transfer of information among network segments. A high-speed server bus adds to this strategy by improving the performance of all server processes.

One thing to keep in mind, however, is that NetWare doesn't take full advantage of symmetrical multiprocessing products such as the Compaq SYSTEMPRO and the ALR Powerpro Array although future versions should provide it. Despite this, because the systems are designed from the ground up for high performance on medium to large scale networks, they always provide better performance than typical desktop systems. In addition, they provide for future growth.

Two systems are discussed in the next sections as a representative sampling of superservers. The Compaq SYSTEMPRO is an EISA-based system for medium to large networks. The NetFRAME superserver is an expandable asymmetrical processing system that easily scales up for use on large networks.

NetFRAME Systems Superservers

NetFRAME Systems, which is located in Sunnyvale, California, sells several high-performance servers the company refers to as "network mainframes." The systems use a 64-bit data bus that operates at 100 Mb/sec. All systems come with redundant network connections and cooling systems, as well as error correcting memory, duplexing capabilities, and RAID level 0 and 1. Prices are from $15,000 to $70,000. The systems use Intel and other types of processors.

Because the NetFRAME superservers are asymmetrical multiprocessing systems, they can use a separate microprocessor to handle the processing for a server-based application such as a client-server database. You expand the system by adding plug-in cards that double the I/O capability or the computing capacity of the system. This type of expandability is possible through NetFRAME's microprocessor clustering architecture, which allows microprocessors and I/O processes to communicate by using shared memory rather than conventional bus methods.

The Compaq SYSTEMPRO

The Compaq SYSTEMPRO is designed to take advantage of both 33 MHz 80386 microprocessors and 33 MHz 80486 microprocessors in a system that has the architectural design of a minicomputer. You can install any combination of these microprocessors. The base 386 microprocessor systems come with 4MB of memory, which is expandable to 256MB, and these systems are optimized with a 64KB cache memory design. The 80486 systems come with 8MB of memory, which is expandable to 256MB. The SYSTEMPRO uses Compaq's flex architecture with multiprocessing support (Flex/MP), which allows simultaneous processing I/O activity.

The EISA bus is used for I/O and the support of up to six 32-bit expansion cards. A second bus that can transfer data as quickly as 100 Mb/sec is used between the microprocessor and memory. Hard disk performance and reliability are enhanced with drive array technology that implements RAID level 1. The drive arrays can also be used to implement hardware-level system fault tolerance. Mirroring can be done by using hardware, thus separating it from the software. Hardware mirroring also allows more control in the case of failure.

The system memory is expandable to 256MB without using an EISA slot. A total of 11 expansion slots are available. Up to 11 storage devices can be mounted internally in the system for up to 1.68 gigabytes of storage. External storage devices can increase capacity to 4.28 gigabytes. The 80386 systems start at $11,000 and the 80486 systems start at $14,000.

CHAPTER 13

A s a network administrator, you must protect network data and equipment from theft, destruction, virus attacks, intruders, power surges, power outages, equipment failure, data corruption, and more. This chapter provides an overview of physical security and protection techniques.

Protecting Network Data and Equipment

Protecting the Network and its Data

The most important part of your network is the data in its storage devices. Everything else can be replaced. If someone walks off with your server or the server goes down, you can replace the hardware in a day, but you can't bring your network back up and running if you don't have proper backups of the data. In addition, if your company is like most, even a day of downtime is intolerable, and thousands or millions of dollars could be lost while a system is not operating. Duplicate servers running NetWare SFT Level III (an optional product that is discussed later in this chapter) might be necessary.

The following sections cover steps you can take to guard against costly equipment and data loss.

PROTECTING AGAINST THEFT You must protect the file server from theft, because it holds your company's valuable data. Although data backups are important, the server must be protected because it provides the primary means of getting at the data. Here are a few server security options:

- Bolt the server chassis to a table and lock the case to the chassis. This prevents removal of the hard drive, which could easily be carried out of the building.

- Lock the server in a protective case that contains an adequate cooling system to prevent the server from overheating.

- Lock the server and associated equipment in the wiring closet. Make sure the closet is adequately cooled.

- Create a data center that requires a keycard or fingerprint verification for access.

- Place the server in a central management facility that is staffed 24 hours a day.

- Ensure that your personnel are trustworthy, competent, and know the security procedures.

You can justify the costs of elaborate security facilities for your network equipment by figuring in other materials and information that need to be secured, such as paper records and telecommunications equipment.

PROTECTING AGAINST FIRE AND NATURAL DISASTERS Protecting valuable equipment and data against fire is a prime concern. Consider placing equipment in a vault or room that has internal or external fire protection. Many organizations already have banks of fireproof filing cabinets in rooms with sprinkler systems or halon gas systems to reduce fire loss.

Protect equipment from natural disasters such as earthquakes and floods. You might need to reinforce or elevate the server area and develop plans so that users can access server data in case there is a disaster. For example, gas-powered generators can supply power to servers and workstations that must be accessed after a disaster that cuts off electricity.

CENTRALIZING MANAGEMENT   Move network resources such as servers, wiring centers, concentrators, routers, and even printers to central management areas.

PROTECTING AGAINST POWER LOSS AND POWER PROBLEMS   Don't consider the power supplied to servers and other equipment dependable. Refer to the "Power Problems and Solutions" section later in this chapter for more details.

USING FAULT TOLERANCE TECHNIQUES   NetWare supports fault tolerance techniques such as disk mirroring and disk duplexing for quick recovery from disk failures. The highest level of fault tolerance is offered by Novell's NetWare SFT Level III. It mirrors whole servers in the same way that disk mirroring duplicates disk data.

KEEPING ADEQUATE BACKUPS   Ensure that data is properly backed up. Implement a backup plan that rotates backup to offsite storage. Backups can be classified as follows:

- Backups used to restore an entire server in case of a disaster

- Backups used to restore blocks of data that have been corrupted or accidentally altered. For example, you might need to restore the accounting information from a previous day and reenter data because of data entry errors

- Backups that archive unused data to tape or optical disks. NetWare also provides data migration and de-migration as discussed in Appendix D.

- Backups that provide a way to recover single files that were accidentally deleted or copied over by users

- Backups of NetWare Directory Services database

See the "Backup Procedures" section later in this chapter for more information.

PREVENTING DATA TAPS   Prevent monitoring of data that traverses the network by using fiberoptic cable or encoding techniques. Refer to the discussion of "Packet Signature Security" in the NetWare manual under "Supervising the Network".

NOTE: NetWare v.4 includes a new security feature called NCP packet signature that protects the forgery of packets traversing the network communications system. Refer to the NetWare manual "Supervising the Network" for more information.

USING DISKLESS WORKSTATIONS   Use diskless workstations to prevent users from uploading or downloading data.

PROTECTING AGAINST VIRUSES   Computer viruses are everywhere and have the potential to infiltrate your network whenever a user logs in. This is especially true for users who work on a LAN remotely from their home systems or take laptop computers on the road. Bulletin boards, public domain utility disks, and demonstration disks can carry viruses. It is essential that you have and use virus detection software.

Viruses are sometimes even found in the software that comes in shrink-wrapped packages. You should install all new software and updates on a test system and check for viruses before installing the software for use on the network server. You should also use appropriate file and directory rights to ensure that users can't alter executable files in program directories. An antivirus utility from Fifth Generation Systems called Untouchable Network NLM can protect NetWare servers against known and unknown viruses. It uses a special identification process that can detect even viruses that change when executed (so-called self-mutating viruses). The Untouchable Network NLM marks all known executable files and creates a record for future use. It then creates a special protected disk partition for itself and its database. Finally, it scans for and detects viruses on a regular basis by looking for changes in executable files. You can contact Fifth Generation Systems at 504-291-7221.

PROTECTING AGAINST INTRUDERS   Intruders can use various methods to gain access to a network. You can prevent intruders from accessing a local LAN by ensuring that users log off. You can force users to log in at only specific stations and at only one station at a time. You can also add time restrictions to prevent access before or after normal working hours. If an intruder gains access to the system with a supervisor-level password they can create another supervisor-level account, and then erase their tracks by altering the system log. The NetWare auditing features (Chapter 32) can reveal potential security breaches.

Unauthorized access by users at remote workstations poses another threat, but a call-back system can provide a level of security against these intruders. When a user dials in from a remote station, the system hangs up the call and calls the user back to ensure that he or she is at the expected location. However, this call-back feature cannot be used to protect a remote LAN or system that has a full-time connection. In that case, an intruder could find a way to set up an account that appears legitimate to your system. You should take steps to prevent intruders from discovering passwords or back-door methods of entering your network.

ADMINISTERING ACCESS RIGHTS   Directory and file access rights are one of the most important tools NetWare administrators and supervisors have to protect data against malicious or accidental loss or corruption by users. Users should never be given more rights than they need in program and data directories. Read and File Scan rights are adequate in program directories. Anything more opens program files to corruption and virus attack. Administering access to data directories is a little more complicated. Some users need to only look at files, such as databases; they need only Read rights in the directory or perhaps Read rights to only the database file within the directory. Users who need to update database files or other files need Read, Write, and File Scan rights. Use caution when granting other rights, such as Erase, Create, Modify, and in particular, Supervisor and Access Control rights.

TRAINING USERS   Train users to properly log in and log out of the network and to protect their passwords. If they need to leave their computers unattended, make sure they log out or know how to activate a password-protected screen saver that locks the computer (but maintains login) while they are gone. Screen savers also provide a way to run unattended tasks without possibility of disturbance. You can set options in user accounts that force users to change their passwords at a predetermined interval and prevent them from reusing recent passwords or require passwords that haven't been used before.

One of the most common causes of data loss on a network is accidental erasure or corruption by an untrained user. Use security rights to prevent users from issuing potentially destructive commands, or make sure they are properly trained in the use of the commands to avoid accidents. Although users typically have full access rights in their own personal directories, you might want to prevent users from installing any files or software on the server. This not only protects against virus infection, but prevents users from filling a disk with unnecessary files.

TRACKING USERS   Keep track of users. Have department administrators inform you of users who have left the company or changed roles so that you can remove or alter their user accounts appropriately. Audit trails created by the NetWare auditing system can help you track users who disrupt the network either accidentally or on purpose.

Data Backup and Protection Techniques

You can protect data by backing it up to magnetic tape or optical disks or by copying it to other disk drives. You can also use System Fault Tolerance features such as mirroring and duplexing (SFT Level II) or server duplexing (SFT Level III). Backup methods and SFT Level III are covered here.

Backup Procedures

Although NetWare provides a number of built-in data protection mechanisms, such as duplicate file directories and bad-block redirection, you must ensure that the data on a hard drive is backed up so that it is available even if the hard drive crashes. You must also ensure that the operating system configuration and environment, including user accounts and passwords, are backed up so that you don't need to reconfigure the entire network.

You should have a schedule of backups. There are several types of backups, all of which are important to your backup strategy:

- You need to back up the entire server, including its directory structure, operating system configuration, user accounts, and other setup information, on a regular basis or as often as it changes.

- You need to back up data files on a regular basis or as often as they change, which is usually daily.

- An incremental backup procedure provides for a complete backup of the entire system on a regular basis with incremental backups of new and changed files in between.

- A rotational backup system ensures that multiple backup sets exist at one time. You might want to store some of these sets off-site to protect against fire, but use caution when transferring data off-site—someone might steal your data.

- Run a restoration test to ensure that your backup and restore procedures work. You might want to set aside a spare server and then run the test using this server on a regular basis. Having a spare server is not a far-fetched idea. Remember, a downed network can cost your company thousands or millions of dollars, depending on how long it takes you to get the system back up and running.

Chapter 30 discusses backups in more detail. You'll learn about the backup devices that are compatible with NetWare and how to schedule multiple backup sets to protect your data—and your job.

NetWare SFT Level III

NetWare SFT Level III is an optional Novell software product that provides true fault tolerance. It ensures that mission-critical applications are continuously available to users. An SFT III configuration consists of two servers that are connected by a high-speed data link. One server mirrors the data of the other and is immediately available should that server go down. There is no loss of service to users. SFT III is a software-only solution that works with off-the-shelf server hardware.

SFT III protects against failures that occur in RAM, on disk, and in LAN adapters. Servers can be placed in geographically different areas to protect against local disasters or power problems (high-speed links are required, i.e. 100MB). In addition, because the servers are mirrored, routine service and upgrades can take place on one while the other continues operation. When the upgraded server is brought back online, its file system synchronizes with the other server.

To improve performance under SFT III, Novell recommends using dual-processor systems. One microprocessor performs all hardware-related I/O and mirroring synchronization, and the other microprocessor handles file services and runs other server applications. You'll also need compatible high-performance Mirrored Server Links (MSLs) in each server. MSLs are typically 100 Mb/sec Ethernet or fiber-optic links and are available from vendors such as Standard Microsystems and Thomas-Conrad.

For more information about SFT Level III, contact Novell at 1-800-NETWARE.

Power Problems and Solutions

A network that is protected against theft, data corruption, and data loss is still susceptible to uncontrolled electrical input that can damage equipment or shut it down completely. A server with reliable data is no good if you can't get to that data. Electrical power is rarely supplied as a smooth wave of steady energy. You can see this when lights flicker or when the TV goes haywire while you blend a milk shake. Electrical connections are polluted with surges and spikes (collectively called *noise*). You can think of these surges and spikes as shotgun blasts of energy. The way electronic equipment handles this transient energy is unpredictable. There are three likely scenarios:

- ■ *Data corruption*   Electrical disturbances can cause memory to change states or can disrupt the information in data packets traversing a wire. These glitches can alter a program in memory and cause it to fail. You might see general protection interrupt (GPI) errors and nonmaskable interrupt (NMI) errors. These errors, which are frequently mistaken for program bugs, are often caused by electrical noise.

- ■ *Equipment failure*   If transient energy is high, it will cause permanent damage to equipment. Small microprocessor circuitry is especially susceptible to this energy. Surge suppressors should be used to protect equipment, but if the energy is high enough, the surge suppressor can burn out. As discussed later, some surge suppressors do not provide the right kind of protection against surges.

- ■ *Slow death*   Equipment that is repeatedly subjected to low-energy surges will fail over time. The delicate circuits in a chip break down, and the equipment eventually fails for no apparent reason. Transients that cause this type of problem "sneak" through surge suppressors that are not designed to protect against them. After a period of abuse, the chips weaken and release the energy in unknown patterns throughout the chip, and the chip ultimately fails. I remember a hard drive that would become inaccessible after a few minutes of operation. I sprayed cooling Freon on its controller to reduce overheating and was able to recover important files before the controller failed completely.

As previously mentioned, the cause of these problems is often hard to determine. Equipment repair technicians can testify to the number of systems they diagnose as having no problems. As soon as the customer returns to the office, the problems reoccur. A savvy technician will often suspect that the problem stems from the power supplied to the equipment and will recommend the proper filtering and conditioning equipment. As discussed later in this chapter, improper grounding is also often a source of problems. In fact, surge suppressors are often the cause of grounding problems because it is in their design to route surges to ground. The surges then find their way back into the electrical system, where they can cause problems.

There are various tools available for checking a building's power system. For example, Ecos Electronics Corporation makes a device called Accu-Test II that you can use to check the quality of a building's electrical system wiring and grounding. Accu-Test II performs various tests to detect wiring problems. Ecos estimates that up to 90 percent of all equipment failures are the results of poor building wiring and inadequate electrical system grounding.

The electrical environment is noisy. Equipment such as air conditioners, elevators, refrigerators, and even laser printers cause transients when they are switched on and off. The electric company causes transients when it switches grids to balance the system. In fact, any device that uses electricity in a nonlinear way can cause transients that affect other devices. Common electrical line problems are listed here:

■ *Noise* Often referred to as surges, spikes, or transients. Noise problems, which are illustrated in Figure 13-1, cause slow or immediate damage to sensitive electronic equipment. Additional problems are caused by air conditioners, elevators, and other devices with electric motors. Most computer power supplies include built-in protection against low-level noise, but surge suppressors can protect against transients that are stronger than normal, such as those caused by lightning. In fact, cheap devices often block such surges by simply burning out and preventing any further flow of electricity.

■ *Sag* When the power drops below the required level, a sag or dropout occurs, usually because the circuit is overloaded. A sag might continue for a period of time if the building is incorrectly wired or the utility company is having a problem. A long sag can cause damage to power supplies.

■ *Swell* A swell is the opposite of a sag and can also cause damage to power supplies.

■ *Hum* Hum is high-order harmonics caused by neutral-to-ground connection problems. Such problems indicate a defect in one of the electrical wires to ground. Hum can cause transmission errors in data communications lines. As errors occur, the communications software must check and resend incorrect packets, which causes a decrease in throughput.

Grounding Problems

In 1991, Novell Research published a report called "Power and Grounding for Distributed Computing" by David Fencl and Larry Fish of ONEAC Corporation. In this report, Fencl and Fish pointed out many problems and misconceptions about established power grounding methods.

Buildings contain a low-resistance ground connection to the earth to protect people from electric shock. A good ground basically drains electrical charges into the earth. If equipment is not properly grounded and a person touches the equipment, a charge will pass through the person to the earth. Fencl and Fish point out that current grounding practices are incompatible with the

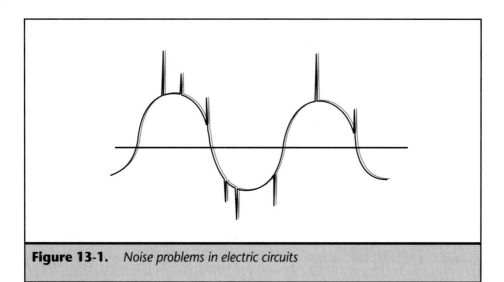

Figure 13-1.   *Noise problems in electric circuits*

requirements of digital electronics. Connecting electronic equipment to earth grounds can subject the equipment to noise that seeks the shortest path to ground. In modern buildings, the shortest path to the ground is often through electronic equipment like computers. Put simply, noise on the AC circuit can infiltrate sensitive electronics through the grounding circuit, not just through the hot lead.

Grounding problems are especially prevalent in a network environment because the cabling system can provide a path for *ground loops*. Consider that devices on networks are usually connected to different sources of power, which are grounded. When these networks are interconnected, the cable bridges the two grounded systems together, which causes the potential for energy on the circuit to seek equilibrium by flowing from ground to ground. In doing so, it flows through the computer systems attached to the cable and causes noise problems. To solve ground-loop problems, according to Fencl and Fish, equipment on one power source must be isolated from equipment on other power sources.

On a large network, the creation of a single-point ground is usually impossible to achieve. Interconnected networks form links between close or distant points, any one of which can produce electrical problems due to poor wiring. These separate power sources might be in separate buildings or in a multistory office building that has separate power transformers on every floor or every other floor. Each transformer has its own electrical characteristics and should not be connected to equipment connected to other transformers.

Solutions

One solution to the problems of ground loops, line noise, and surges is to connect the entire network to one central power source and ground. However, this is usually impractical and defeats the purpose of a network, which is to spread computing resources to users at outlying locations. The only practical solution is to provide power conditioning and a proper ground point at the location of each network component.

Figure 13-2 illustrates the Fencl and Fish method for connecting network equipment within a single building or power source area. Note that a power conditioner and an uninterruptible power supply are used at the server. The power conditioner provides dedicated transformer isolation, a clean source of power, and a solid reference ground. Similar devices should be attached to workstations if your budget allows. Note that surge suppression equipment is placed at the feed to the electrical panel. If the surge suppressors are placed on the branch circuits, they will divert surges to ground and back into the circuits of other systems through the ground connection.

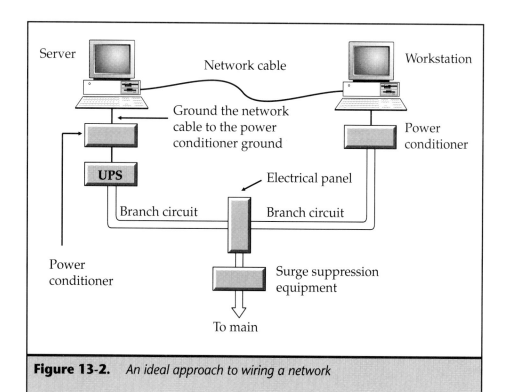

Figure 13-2.   *An ideal approach to wiring a network*

There are a few things to watch out for in this installation. You should not run electrical cables in parallel with power circuits or other sources of interference such as light fixtures and motors. If you do, electrical transients can enter the network through the cable systems. Some circuits improperly divert neutral to ground intentionally to solve noise problems. They produce a repeating, low-frequency waveform on the network cable that can corrupt data. If you have this problem, have an electrical contractor check the line.

NOTE: Ensure that a single LAN segment is connected to circuits that branch from a single power source and that no point in the segment shares a ground with other power sources. An electrical contractor can perform this service.

Figure 13-3 illustrates the Fencl and Fish method for connecting an internetwork. Nonconductive fiber-optic cable is used to eliminate ground loops between the networks, which are on different power supplies. The primary

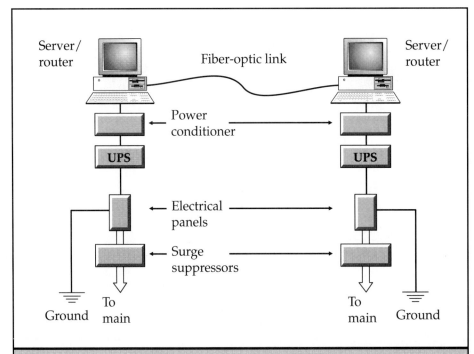

Figure 13-3. *Fiber-optic cable isolates each segment of an internetwork and prevents ground loops between the different power distribution and grounding systems*

reason for ensuring the separation of the power sources is that they will most likely have different ground potentials, which can cause problems in sensitive electrical equipment if they are linked together. In this figure, each LAN segment is a self-contained environment in which you can more easily control grounding and noise problems. Note that internetwork devices are connected to power conditioning equipment. If fiber-optic interconnections are not possible, supplemental transient protection should be installed with the cable.

Protection Devices

It is a good idea to buy uninterruptible power supplies and surge suppressors to protect your network equipment. These products are described in the next sections.

Uninterruptible Power Supplies

Your basic power and grounding system can be augmented by an uninterruptible power supply (UPS). A UPS provides electrical power to computers or other devices during a power outage. A UPS can be one of the following:

- A battery system

- A rotary UPS that uses the inertia of a large flywheel to carry the computer system through brief outages

- Internal combustion motors that run AC generators

UPS devices come in two forms: online and standby. A *standby* device kicks in only when the power goes down. It must therefore contain special circuitry that can switch to backup power in less than 5 milliseconds. An *online* device constantly provides the source of power to the computer. Because of this, it doesn't need to kick in. If the outside source of power dies, the batteries within the unit continue to supply the computer with power. Although online units are the best choice, they are more expensive than standby units. But because online units supply all the power to a computer, that power is always clean and smooth.

When purchasing a battery backup system, you need to know the following about the devices:

- The amount of time the UPS battery supplies power

- Whether the UPS provides a warning system to the server when the UPS is operating on standby power

■ Whether the UPS includes power conditioning features that can clip incoming transient noise

■ The life span of the battery and how it degrades over time

■ Whether the device warns you when the batteries can no longer provide backup power

■ Whether the batteries are replaceable

You also need to know the power requirements of the devices you'll hook to the UPS. For a server installation, this might include the CPU, the monitor, external routers, concentrator units, and wiring centers. You can find out the power requirements of these devices by looking at the backs of the equipment. Labels on the equipment list the power drawn by the unit in watts. Simply add the values of all the devices to come up with the requirements you'll need from the UPS.

ATTACHING A UPS TO THE FILE SERVER   A UPS attached to a file server requires an additional cable that alerts the file server when the UPS is running on standby power. The server will then proceed with shutdown procedures. One end of the monitor cable should have either a stereo phone plug (for plugging into the stand-alone UPS monitor board or the SS keycard in a non-PS/2 file server) or a 4-pin mouse plug (for plugging into the mouse port of an IBM PS/2 file server). The other end of the monitor cable should have the type of connector required by your particular UPS.

Some vendors have developed special power protection equipment. American Power Conversion's Smart-UPS series provides network managers with diagnostics information via a software control program called PowerChute. The software is installed on the server and communicates with the UPS over a cable. Managers can then track power quality, UPS operating temperature, line frequency, UPS output voltage, maximum and minimum line power, battery strength, line voltage, and UPS load. American Power Conversion can be reached in West Kingston, Rhode Island at 401-789-5735.

Surge Suppressors

The primary job of a surge suppressor is to protect systems against spikes. A UPS is required to protect against sags and power outages. Most power supplies in desktop systems can handle surges of up to 800 volts. You'll need a surge suppressor to protect against surges above these levels. Most off-the-shelf surge suppressors divert surges to the ground line, so you'll want to avoid them in most cases. Look for surge suppressors that use coils and electrolytic capacitors to absorb excess energy rather than diverting it to ground. Ground line diversion is used primarily to prevent the surge suppressor itself from burning out. Currently, most surge suppressors use this technique, but more products are becoming available that avoid it.

Spike protection ratings should be as high as 6,000 volts. Units are often equipped with EMI (electromagnetic interference) and RFI (radio-frequency interference) noise filtration circuitry. However, most desktop systems already include this type of filtering in their power supplies, so you should view ads that stress EMI/RFI noise filtration with skepticism.

Be leery of surge suppression devices that use transient voltage surge suppressor (TVSS) technology. They might protect against large transients, such as lightning bolts, but fail to recognize transients below a certain level that can still be destructive to electronic equipment. In addition, they pass transients to the ground, where they can find their way back into the equipment. The problem is exacerbated if networks have multiple ground connections.

Sources

A useful source of information about power problems and solutions is *Power and Grounding for Distributed Computing*, an application note from Novell Research. You can call Novell Research in Provo, Utah at 1-800-453-1267, extension 5380.

CHAPTER 14

Hardware Setup

This chapter discusses the setup of a number of network hardware components that you'll need to adjust before you install NetWare. The setup of workstations, cabling, routers, and wide area links can take place after NetWare is installed. From the server, you can run console utilities to view and change settings, but to run applications such as NetWare Administrator that manage objects and files, you'll need to log into a workstation. Chapter 18 covers workstation installation.

When you run the installation program on the next server, it then identifies any existing servers and helps you place the new server in the appropriate context of the NetWare Directory Services (NDS) tree.

If you are upgrading an existing network, you are ready to start upgrading the NetWare operating system on the existing servers. You can jump ahead to Chapter 15 to learn more about NetWare's installation procedure.

Preparing the Site

Your first step when installing a network is to set up the environment. For this step, it's helpful to know where your servers will be located and who will supervise and maintain them. Typically, existing networks consist of LAN cable segments within departments. Under NetWare v. 4, these departmental LANs are brought under the global management of NetWare Directory Services. However, those departmental LANs are still physically located in their respective departments, so you might want to retain the existing supervisors. The NDS system lets you grant supervisor trustee rights for a departmental branch of the directory tree.

On large LANs or WANs, delegate the responsibilities of supervising users and maintaining equipment to other users, such as department managers. Define who will manage and monitor the following:

- Servers and workstations within a department

- Servers managed for departments by network specialists

- The cabling system

- Internetwork equipment, such as routers and switchboxes, and their associated cabling

- Wide Area Networking equipment, such as routers that handle connections to public and private data networks

- Remote services at outlying locations to which a support person might need to travel

After the network is installed and operating, hardware must be monitored for potential points of failure, overuse (such as a nearly full storage system), throughput, and general loss of performance. Monitoring tools are included with NetWare and covered in Chapters 34 through 37.

Installing or upgrading a network can easily disrupt the normal activities of people at the sites. Make sure these people know who you and your staff are and what you are doing, especially if you need to crawl over and under desks to install cable or set up systems. It's best to develop a schedule of installation activities that you can present to department managers and employees. In addition, be sure to consider the department's needs. You won't win friends if your installation takes place when employees need to meet sales quotas, get the payroll out, or do month-end posting.

You can approach the installation in several ways. One method is to set up and test equipment in your service department before installing it on-site. For example, many workstations in a network use the same components and setup parameters. You could connect one of these systems to a server in your service department to test the configuration and connection. This isolates any major problems up front, such as incorrect drivers or configuration file settings. It also helps isolate on-site cabling problems if you already know that workstation-to-network configuration parameters work.

If the installation must be completed as quickly as possible, you'll probably need to assemble teams who can install servers and workstations at different sites simultaneously. If you're not in a hurry, it's a good idea to work with the servers for a while before putting them into actual use. This gives you a chance to create user and resource objects, set up directory structures, install applications, and create the login environment for each user. It also gives you a chance to make sure everything works before you commit the company's data to the new server.

The upgrade of existing systems can pose logistical problems. You might find yourself working late at night or on weekends so that users can begin using the new system when they return to work. The upgrade of an existing server to NetWare v. 4 requires proper backup of its data, so you'll need to have your backup systems in place before beginning the upgrade. You should also be prepared to restore everything as it was just in case the upgrade doesn't go as planned. Consider upgrading a server on Friday night or Saturday so that you have plenty of time to get things in order or restore the old system before Monday.

Setting up the Server

The installation of NetWare v. 4 begins at a server. As previously mentioned, you can install NetWare on the server without configuring the rest of the network or adding workstations. Although it's possible to install and configure network interface cards and secondary disk systems after installing the NetWare operating system, your task will be much easier if you install all the equipment in the server ahead of time. If you do, you can follow the NetWare installation program's routines for specifying equipment and selecting default settings. In addition, you won't need to install equipment after users have begun using the system.

Start by installing any additional memory in the server. These days, memory is usually installed and tested by the system vendor, but if you're upgrading an existing system, you'll need to add the memory yourself.

CAUTION: Be careful when installing more than 16MB of memory in AT systems that use the Industry Standard Architecture (ISA) bus. Corruption of the file server's memory might occur. Check with the system vendor or Novell for network compatibility.

After installing the basic components, run the computer setup utility, which is located either in the ROM of the system or on a separate floppy disk. To access ROM-based setup utilities, you typically press the ESC or DEL key while the computer is booting.

Avoiding Interrupt and I/O Port Conflicts

On ISA and EISA systems, you need to avoid conflicts among system interrupts (IRQs), I/O port addresses, and in some cases, base memory addresses, when installing network adapters and other cards in servers and workstations. You can change the settings of the switches or jumpers on interface cards to avoid conflicts with the settings already used by components in your system. Common settings are listed in Table 14-1 and described in the following sections.

INTERRUPTS   Think of an interrupt, or IRQ, as a request for service. When a component within the computer, such as a COM port or floppy disk controller, needs the attention of the CPU, it sends a request over its interrupt line. Each component has its own interrupt line, so when you install new adapters in the system, it's important to use an interrupt line that's not already in use. If you can't find an available interrupt, you might need to disable an unnecessary component, such as the second COM port or the second parallel port. (See Table 14-1.) When installing multiple adapters, make sure that none of the adapters use the same interrupt. Change interrupts on cards by moving jumpers or setting dip switches as directed in the manuals that come with the cards. When there is an interrupt conflict with the hard drive controller, the system usually fails to boot. Make a list of the interrupts used by your system, and then change the settings on your adapter cards to avoid conflicts.

I/O PORT ADDRESSES   An I/O port address is a memory location that network cards and other devices use to transfer information to the CPU. No two

	IRQ	I/O Port Address
System timer	0	
Keyboard	1	
Interrupt cascade	2	3C0 to 3CF
EGA/VGA video in color mode	2	3D0 to 3DF
COM1, COM3	4	3F0 to 3FF
COM2, COM4 (if used)	3	2F0 to 2FF
Floppy disk controller	6	3F0 to 3FF
Parallel port LPT1	7	3B0 to 3BF
Parallel port LPT2 (if used)	5	370 to 37F
System clock	8	
Math coprocessor	13	
Hard disk controller	14	320 to 32F
Game port		200 to 20F
Bus mouse		230 to 23F

Table 14-1.   *Common Interrupts and I/O Ports. IRQ 9, 10, 11, 12, and 15 Are Often Available for Use*

devices can share the same port address. Again, change port addresses by moving jumpers or setting dip switches on the boards.

BASE MEMORY ADDRESSES   Except for ArcNet cards, most network interface cards do not require a base memory address setting. This is the location in memory that a network card uses to transfer packets between itself and the CPU. The base memory address is the start of a block of memory that is usually 16KB or 32KB in length. No two devices can use the same block of memory. Also make sure that the 16KB or 32KB block of memory does not overlap memory used by another device. Typical starting addresses are in upper memory blocks (above the 640KB barrier on DOS machines) at C000, C800, D000, and D800.

You should install network cards and resolve conflicts before proceeding further, especially if you are installing multiple network cards in the server. If a computer doesn't boot, or behaves erratically, especially after installing interface boards, check the interrupt and I/O settings described previously. Here are some tips:

■ If a computer fails to boot, check for conflicts with a floppy disk or hard disk controller.

- If your system locks up when running a utility or peripheral device, there is probably an I/O port or base memory conflict.

- In some cases, an interrupt conflict between a network card and another device locks the system when you make the first network call, or results in slow or erratic performance. You might see numerous send and receive errors.

- If a mouse is attached to a system that uses a VGA monitor, the mouse might be using IRQ 2. Because a mouse is not necessary on a server, you could disable it and configure a network card for IRQ 2.

Installing Disk Controllers and Drives

The most serious problem in any network is the failure of a storage device. It is imperative that disk systems have some form of backup or redundancy. There are a number of disk configuration choices, including:

- Disk mirroring

- Disk duplexing

- RAID systems

- Server duplexing (NetWare SFT Level III)

This section covers the installation of mirrored and duplexed disk systems in servers. RAID drives are typically external subsystems that attach to a controller card installed in the server. The NetWare installation program usually sees the drive array as a single SCSI disk system, but some systems require that you go through the normal partitioning and mirroring steps during NetWare setup. Refer to the operator's manual for specific instructions on installing RAID systems.

Note that some disk controllers handle mirroring on their own and do so more efficiently than the mirroring provided by the NetWare operating system. You set up this mirroring when installing the disk controller. If enabled, do not install NetWare's software mirroring. Duplexing of drives attached to two controllers, on the other hand, is provided only at the software level, and you configure it while installing the NetWare operating system. Do not set up hardware mirroring if you plan to duplex drives.

NOTE: Duplexing, rather than mirroring, is highly recommended. Not only does it provide a higher level of fault tolerance, but it improves performance as well. Do not attempt to mirror IDE drives. NetWare does not properly handle mirrored IDE drives in the event of a crash. Duplex these drives.

During installation, you load a driver for each disk controller or SCSI host bus adapter (HBA) installed in the server, not for each drive attached to the controllers or adapters. Always try to load disk drivers in the same order every time you start the server so that disk device numbering (covered in a moment) remains the same. Each controller or HBA forms a disk channel. Hard disks used for mirroring must be of the same type and size. Chapter 15 provides a list of disk controller drivers that appears during NetWare installation. If the driver for your disk system is not listed, you can still load a driver from floppy disk during installation, but make sure you have the correct driver from the disk manufacturer before you begin. You don't want to find yourself with the wrong driver during an overnight server conversion.

There are a number of ways you can configure disk devices to achieve disk mirroring and duplexing. Each drive has a specific five-digit number that identifies it to the operating system. You use the device number to identify drives used for mirroring. The digits of the device number are shown in Figure 14-1 and defined as follows:

- The first two digits are assigned by the operating system when you select a driver for a disk controller. They identify which driver is used.

- The third digit is the number of the controller board or host adapter in the server, but not its channel number. The first driver you load becomes the first board in the numbering scheme, so make sure you always load drivers in the same order every time you start the server.

- The fourth digit represents the controller number. On SCSI systems, more than one controller can be attached to the host bus adapter.

- The fifth digit represents the actual disk attached to the controller.

You use the disk ID numbers when configuring (mirroring and duplexing) and maintaining the drives in the server. NetWare might display the number when a disk error occurs. For example, you might see an error similar to this:

```
Device #3 (20101)
```

This indicates an error on the third logical drive. The number in parentheses is the device number, and #3 is a logical number that relates to the order in which the disk drivers were loaded. This number can change if you change the load order, as can the third digit in the device number, so be careful when identifying drives.

ST-506 Controller Installation

Many old AT systems use ST-506 controllers. If you have one of these systems, you might want to use it as a NetWare v. 4 server. You can attach two drives to each controller and install two controllers in a server. Set both drives to the DS2 position (DS1 if drive numbering starts at 0), and then make sure both drives are terminated. Device numbering for duplexed ST-506 systems is shown in Figure 14-1.

ESDI Controller Installation

The ESDI interface is an improved ST-506 interface that usually supports two drives per controller, but the standard is written to support the daisy-chaining of up to eight drives. Set the jumpers on the first ESDI drive to select 0 and the jumpers on the second ESDI drive to select 1. Figure 14-1 illustrates device numbering for duplexed ESDI drives.

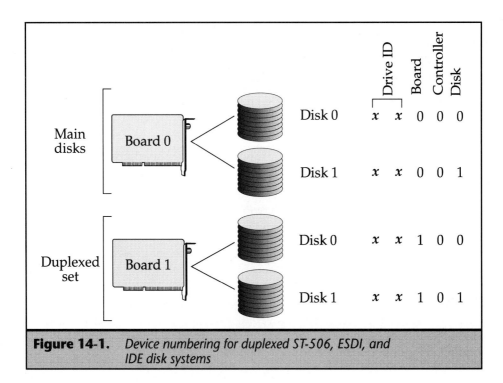

Figure 14-1.   *Device numbering for duplexed ST-506, ESDI, and IDE disk systems*

SCSI Controller Installation

The SCSI interface is perhaps the best choice for high-end servers. It consists of a host bus adapter to which multiple SCSI devices (such as disk drives, tape backup units, and CD-ROM drives) attach. Each device usually has an embedded controller mounted directly to it. However, some external subsystems have multiple devices attached to multiple controllers, which in turn attach to multiple host bus adapters. One HBA forms a channel, and NetWare can handle up to five host bus adapter channels. Up to four controllers can attach to each channel, and up to eight drives can attach to each controller, for a total of 32 drives. If you have large disk requirements, it's possible to run out of slots. If this is the case, consider a RAID system, which typically attaches to the server by using one controller.

SCSI drives are connected to the SCSI host adapter by using a 50-pin flat cable. Some external SCSI devices might connect by using a 25-pin D connector or a 50-pin Amphenol connector. Figure 14-2 illustrates the device numbering for embedded SCSI drives when two host adapters are mounted in a server that has an existing controller (ST-506, ESDI, or IDE). Note the significance of embedded controllers in the device numbering scheme. Because each disk attached to the host adapter boards is the first (and only) on its respective controller, each disk is numbered 0.

Figure 14-3 illustrates the device numbering for SCSI systems that use nonembedded controllers. In this case, each controller supports multiple drives, all of which are attached to a single host adapter.

IDE Controller Installation

The IDE interface is similar to SCSI in that each drive has its own embedded controller and attaches to a host adapter. Many IDE host adapters are mounted directly to the motherboard of a computer. Most IDE adapters support two drives; however, you cannot mirror these drives under NetWare. Duplexing is supported, but you must make sure the second IDE controller can be set at an interrupt and I/O address other than that of the first controller. Ultrastor and NCL are two manufacturers of such boards.

The IDE interface uses a single 40-pin cable, and if two drives are supported by the adapter, the cable might have two connectors. If the cable doesn't have dual connectors, check the manual to ensure that two drives are supported, and then replace the cable with a dual-drive cable. Jumper the boot drive as the master drive, and jumper the second drive as the slave drive. Figure 14-1 illustrates device numbering for duplexed IDE drives.

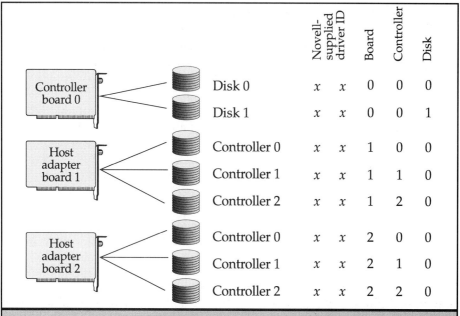

Figure 14-2.   *Device numbering for multiple SCSI host adapters with embedded controller drives attached*

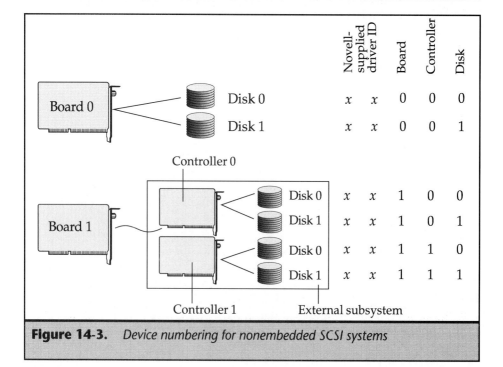

Figure 14-3.   *Device numbering for nonembedded SCSI systems*

NOTE: *Be sure to check the release notes that come with NetWare for information on IDE controller and driver compatibility. If the IDE.DSK driver does not work with your IDE drive, you might be able to use the ISADISK.DSK driver. Call Novell for more information on these drives.*

A Word About Partitions

Chapter 15 discusses methods for setting up disk partitions and volumes, but you should be aware of the way partitions are established on a duplexed system. (From here on, it will be assumed that you are duplexing rather than mirroring.) Figure 14-4 shows a system that has two controllers and has two drives attached to each controller. The first controller and its two drives form the primary data storage area. Note that a small DOS partition exists on the first drive. The second controller and its drives form the duplexing system. Each drive has its own partition numbers. The DOS partition is physical partition 0, and the remaining partitions are numbered from 1 to 4. However, NetWare assigns logical partition numbers to mirrored drives, so partitions 1 and 3 are viewed as logical partition 1 and physical partitions 2 and 4 are viewed as logical partition 2.

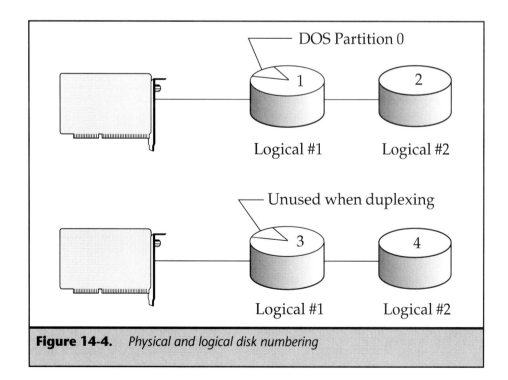

Figure 14-4.   *Physical and logical disk numbering*

These logical partition numbers are important when you are viewing information about mirrored disks. Logical mirrored partitions are listed as follows in the INSTALL and MONITOR server utilities:

```
Mirrored:               Logical Partition #1
Mirrored:               Logical Partition #2
```

However, the physical partitions that make up a mirrored set are listed as follows. Note the device number at the end of each line that identifies the driver, controller, and disk attached to the controller.

```
In Sync -               NetWare partition 1 on Device #0 (20000)
In Sync -               NetWare partition 3 on Device #1 (20100)
```

Installing the Network Interface Cards

The installation of network interface cards is relatively straightforward. Make sure the cards do not conflict with interrupts or I/O port addresses that are already in use by the system. If you are installing more than one network interface card, make sure the cards don't conflict with each other. You can install several different types of network interface cards in a server, to provide routing. You can also install a separate routing server by using Novell's NetWare MultiProtocol Router software, which is discussed later in this chapter.

You must document all the settings made on each board. You will need to know interrupts, I/O port settings, and other information when you are installing NetWare on the server. It's a good idea to tag each board on the back of the machine so that you can differentiate the boards after they are installed.

Hub Management Interface (HMI) boards provide a number of network ports per card and eliminate the need for external concentrator boxes. Workstations connect directly to the server by using twisted-pair wiring. Although hub cards are installed in the server, you can manage them by using software that runs either at the server or at a remote PC. If you are installing multiple hub cards, daisy-chain the cards together by using the cables supplied by the vendor and according to the instructions in the operator's manual.

Installing the UPS

The next step is to set up the uninterruptible power supply (UPS) and, if necessary, install the UPS monitor board in your server. The UPS monitor board is used to attach the signal cable between the server and the UPS. The UPS uses this cable to inform the server that the UPS is operating under standby power. Some UPS systems come with their own interface boards. Others connect to the server's COM port or use a standard stereo jack cable that attaches to an AT-compatible host bus adapter or a Novell Standalone UPS monitor board. If you have a Micro Channel server, the UPS can be attached to the mouse port and does not require a special board.

Ensure that the UPS has enough power to handle all the devices you're going to attach to it. Add up all the wattage ratings of the equipment you're going to attach, and make sure the total doesn't exceed what the UPS can provide.

Setting up Routing

NetWare provides internal routing, which means that you can install multiple network interface cards in a server. For example, you can install an Ethernet, a Token Ring, and an ArcNet card in the same server. NetWare handles the task of converting and forwarding packets that need to travel among these different networks. If workstations send packets that use protocols other than SPX/IPX, you'll need to install support for those protocols at the server. This is a simple matter of installing a NetWare Loadable Module (NLM).

The NetWare operating system can support an unlimited number of network interface cards. The number is limited only by the available slots in the server. As mentioned previously, segmenting a large LAN into smaller LANs, each of which is attached to its own interface card, can improve performance. However, it's impossible to install this many cards in a standard computer system unless it is a superserver. Installing even four cards can be a problem on ISA systems due to interrupt and I/O address problems.

To set up routing in a NetWare server, first install each network interface card, making sure to avoid interrupt and I/O port conflicts. Then, during the installation of the NetWare operating system, specify a driver and network number for each of the boards installed. As discussed in Chapter 15, no two network segments can share the same network number.

On large networks that have a lot of internetwork traffic and multiprotocol routing, it is beneficial to remove routing from the server. It makes sense to remove wide area communications and routing from the server in any case, because if the server were brought down for service, those functions would not be available so users could communicate with other systems on the network. That's where products such as Novell's NetWare MultiProtocol Router software come into play.

NetWare MultiProtocol Router

The NetWare MultiProtocol Router (abbreviated MPR in this book) is an optional software product that provides extensive internetworking services. MPR provides a connection point for LAN segments outside the NetWare file server, thus relieving the file server of routing tasks and improving its performance. These segments can support the SPX/IPX, AppleTalk, TCP/IP, and OSI protocols, as well as the most popular LAN media, such as Ethernet, Token Ring, ArcNet, Apple LocalTalk, and FDDI, as shown in Figure 14-5. An alternative installation method involves the creation of a backbone by using multiple MultiProtocol Router systems, as shown in Figure 14-6.

The MPR package also includes Novell's Wide Area Network (WAN) Links product so that you can connect over X.25 and synchronous point-to-point communications lines. The next section, "NetWare WAN Links," covers this product. Similar products are available from other vendors, but they are not covered here.

MPR is designed to run on 386 and 486 PCs that use many types of ODI-certified network interface boards. You'll need an 80386- or 80486-based PC with at least 8MB of RAM, 40MB of hard disk space, and one high-density floppy disk drive to load the software. Note that additional hard disk space is unnecessary because the system is dedicated to routing and has no need to store additional files.

For best performance, use an EISA or MCA system and appropriate high-performance network interface cards. Novell recommends the following cards, and many compatible cards are available from various vendors:

- Novell NE2000 (ISA) or compatible

- Novell NE3200 (32-bit EISA) or compatible

- Novell ME/2 (MCA) or compatible

- Novell NE/2-32 (32-bit MCA) or compatible

MPR also supports hub cards. The software includes NetWare Hub Services (NHS), which lets you manage NetWare-resident hubs from the servers where the hub cards are installed or from a remote workstation. The software lets you monitor ports and turn them on and off.

To set up a router, configure a system in the same way you would configure a NetWare file server. Install the network interface cards, making sure to avoid interrupt and I/O port conflicts. Also install one of Novell's Synchronous/+ boards if you plan to run WAN Links at the router.

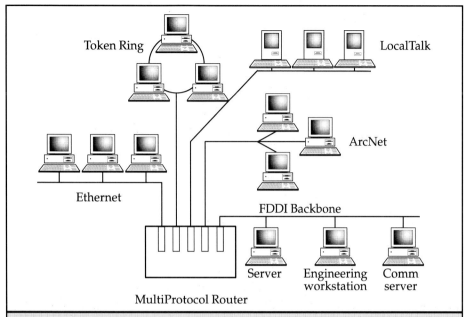

Figure 14-5.   *The NetWare MultiProtocol Router software provides routing outside the file server. It supports many protocols and LAN media*

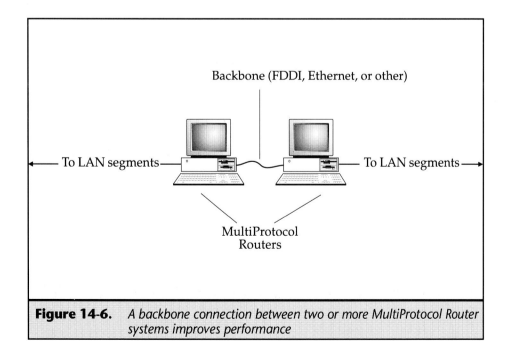

Figure 14-6.   *A backbone connection between two or more MultiProtocol Router systems improves performance*

NetWare WAN Links

Although NetWare WAN Links is included in the MultiProtocol Router software, it is also available as a separate product for those who want to establish WAN Links in a NetWare file server rather than in an external router. Because WAN speeds (supported by WAN Links) are generally slower than LAN speeds, file server performance is not compromised. Figure 14-7 illustrates a WAN Links connection.

NetWare WAN Links routes IPX, IP, and AppleTalk packets concurrently over wide area links on the same port. Ethernet, Token Ring, LocalTalk, ArcNet, and FDDI networks can use the leased lines or X.25 packet-switched networks made available by WAN Links.

WAN Links can use any of the Synchronous/+ adapters from Novell:

- Novell Synchronous/v.35 (2.048 Mb/sec)

- Novell Synchronous/RS-422/x.21 (2.048 Mb/sec)

- Novell Synchronous/RS-232 (19.2 Kb/sec)

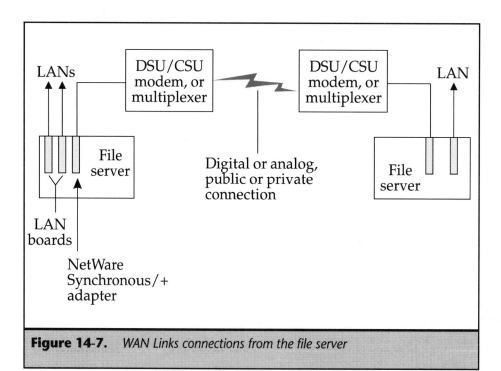

Figure 14-7. *WAN Links connections from the file server*

Each board has four ports, and you can install up to four boards in a file server or external multiprotocol router.

You'll need a Novell Synchronous/+ board, and a DSU/CSU (Data Service Unit/Channel Service Unit) synchronous modem, or a T1 multiplexer, at each end of the WAN connection. Select the card that matches the communications equipment you plan to use. Note that WAN Links will also work with private transmission facilities such as satellite, microwave, and optical fiber, assuming you have the correct DSU/CSU equipment.

On larger LANs, you can install WAN Links externally on a system that is running Novell's NetWare MultiProtocol Router, as shown on the left in Figure 14-8. The connection shown on the right in the figure is running WAN Links on a file server. Note that two links are made between the sites. The second provides redundancy should the first fail, and both are supported from the same Novell Synchronous/+ board (although you might want to duplex the boards as well). The high-speed boards can provide lower transfer rates if necessary out of one of the ports, so you could have a high-speed link and a low-speed backup link connected to the same board.

The Novell Synchronous/+ boards compete for interrupts, I/O ports, and base memory addresses along with other boards. You'll need to ensure that there

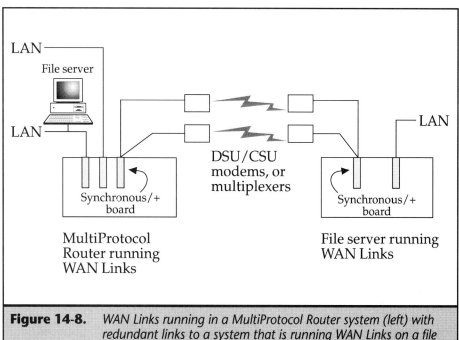

Figure 14-8.   *WAN Links running in a MultiProtocol Router system (left) with redundant links to a system that is running WAN Links on a file server (right)*

are no conflicts when configuring the boards, and be sure to record the settings. A Synchronous/+ adapter has one switch for changing the I/O port address. Interrupt and memory settings are configured by using a program called INETCFG. The three base memory options are A000, C000, or D000, and they span 64KB of upper memory. A000 is available only on ISA/EISA systems, and C000 is available only on MCA systems. If you are installing multiple Synchronous/+ adapters, configure all of the adapters to share the same memory range.

When you are ready to connect WAN Links to the public or private data network, contact a qualified installer or vendor.

Setting up Workstations

On new networks, the setup of workstations can proceed at any time. You can assign workstation setup to your staff while you or other supervisors install the servers. On ISA systems, avoid interrupt, I/O port, and memory conflicts when installing network interface cards on workstations. Mark down the settings of the cards on your network documentation sheets.

So you can better isolate problems that might occur later when connecting to the network, run the diagnostics software that comes with the network cards. You can also use this software to identify the node address that is electronically stamped on Ethernet and Token Ring cards. Write down any problems and their resolutions on workstation log sheets, along with the network node addresses.

Diskless Workstations

Diskless workstations have no drives of their own, so you can't boot DOS or other operating systems on them. For each diskless workstation, you'll need a network interface card that contains a boot PROM so that the workstation can boot by accessing the operating system files on the file server. A boot PROM causes the workstation to identify itself immediately to the server when the workstation is started. The server then sends it a designated startup file that contains the same information you would find on a bootable floppy disk, such as the DOS system files and the network connection software. This information is contained in a boot disk image file. Refer to the NetWare manuals for information on diskless workstation installation.

Installing and Testing Cable

You can install the cable at any time. In fact, most companies have third-party cable installers perform this operation either before or during the network installation, and for good reasons. Third party cable installers have the equipment, expertise, and in some cases, the necessary licenses to do so. (If your building contains asbestos, you will need to hire cable installers who have the appropriate licenses.) They are usually more capable of ensuring that a cable run is good and is free from interference before any network equipment is connected to it. They can also determine whether existing cable can be used and has proper continuity. In addition, you can always go back to them if connections are faulty.

Professional cable installers install cable so that it is out of sight and out of traffic areas, and most importantly, they make sure cable runs meet local specifications and avoid areas of possible signal interference. They can bid for a job, including the installation of wall mounts, conduits, and other cable accessories at competitive rates because they install cable all the time and have the equipment, parts, and expertise to do it right. Obviously, you should request bids from several installers and let them know they are competing.

If you plan to expand the cable system in the future, make sure you designate the locations of future runs and future workstations. A well-planned cabling system might cost more up front, but it will require less maintenance and retrofitting in the future.

If your network is small, you might want to do all the cabling yourself. Be careful to follow a plan and have the building blueprints available. Locate cable runs, risers, conduit, wiring closets, and existing equipment you want to attach to the network.

There are several cases in which you might need to call in professionals. Fiber-optic cable tends to be hard to install, and you might be better off relying on experienced installers. If you're using telephone twisted-pair cable, you should first have an expert determine whether it is suitable for network use. Tapping into punchdown blocks in the wiring closet might require experts and, in some cases, might be illegal without prior consent from the building owners or the telephone company.

Keep the following in mind if you plan to do the cabling yourself:

- Document and map the entire installation. Documentation for existing telephone wiring might be available from the original cable installer. Log all problems for future reference.

- Talk with people who have installed similar network cabling systems, such as members of your local NetWare user group.

- Check the local building codes for requirements in your area.

■ Get familiar with the ceilings and walls of your building to avoid surprises. You might find solid concrete walls or fire blocks in unexpected places. Look up under ceiling tiles when looking for places to run cables, and make sure to avoid electrical equipment such as air conditioners, power cables, and fluorescent lighting fixtures.

■ Avoid running cable in walkways and other traffic areas.

■ Make sure workstation attachment points are near a source of electric power.

■ Schedule the cable installation and allow enough time to do the job right.

■ Work during off-hours when you won't bother employees.

■ When attaching connectors to twisted-pair wire, make sure the wires are connected to the correct leads.

■ When using twisted-pair wire, check for continuity between the wiring closet and the workstation location. Testing tools can help with the job; they are discussed later in this chapter.

■ If using coaxial cable, avoid bending, creasing, pulling, or stretching it, which can introduce changes in the electrical characteristics of the wire and cause packet transmission errors.

■ Rubber balls and rocks can be a cable installer's best friends. Attach a string to a tennis ball and then throw it to a coworker in a crawl space so that you can drag a cable across the space. A string attached to a rock can be dropped down to a drill hole in a wall. Lightweight rods or poles are useful when you need to push wire through a cable housing.

■ Walkie-talkies are useful when you need to communicate with a coworker on the other side of a wall or floor.

■ Avoid running cable near fluorescent lights in drop ceilings. Plan on running extra cable so that you can avoid fixtures.

■ Avoid running cable next to other electric cable, if possible. Although shielding inhibits interference, there's no point in taking chances.

■ Prop up coaxial cable with fasteners, staples, or clamps, and avoid bending it too sharply. Don't stretch it when pulling it through conduit.

■ Make sure all cable runs are of the same type of cable and preferably from the same manufacturer. Cable might look similar but have different electrical characteristics. A single length of the wrong cable can cause transmission problems on an entire network segment.

■ Moisture can damage cable, so protect outside cable runs from the elements by using conduit or other casing materials.

■ Long cable runs are susceptible to interference. Metal cable tends to act like a giant antenna that picks up stray electric fields and interference from devices along its path. As cable length increases, its signal carrying capacity decreases. If monitoring and analysis programs report a large number of errors in the form of resent packets, this might point to interference problems on the cable.

■ Avoid grounding problems, as discussed in Chapter 13.

■ Cable problems are relatively easy to detect on star-configured networks. If one workstation doesn't establish network communications, check its network card or the cable that connects it. If several workstations attached to the concentrator don't work, check the concentrator.

■ Keep a look out for interesting and unique gadgets that can solve simple network problems and make your life easier. Contact the distributors listed here for free catalogs:

> Inmac, Santa Cruz, CA, 800-547-5444
> Specialized, Irving, TX, 800-527-5018
> Black Box, Pittsburg, PA, 412-746-5500

These catalogs are essential reading material for network managers and maintenance personnel.

Cable Testing Equipment

Cable problems are the most common source of failed network connections. There are a number of devices you can use to test cable runs. Some are quite affordable and should be part of any cable installer's toolkit. More expensive equipment can be rented, or you can rely on the services of consultants and professional cable installers.

If you have no equipment, you can rely on a process of elimination to test cable connections. This process is practical only on small networks or where you can isolate the problem to a single segment. First determine whether the problem is in the hardware or in the cable by connecting the server and a single workstation with a separate cable. If the workstation and server communicate, the problem is most likely in the cable system. Connect each workstation to the server, one at a time. If you use coaxial cable, make sure to terminate the T-connector on each station as you go. You must restart the server and workstation each time to establish a clean connection. If the network malfunctions during one of these tests, replace that cable segment or check the adapter at the workstation.

A simple voltage meter is a useful cable testing tool. You can use it to test the continuity of a cable. To test the continuity of bulk cable, set the meter to its ohm or resistance setting and touch the leads against each end of the center wire and then against each end of the ground. The meter should jump to the 0 setting each time. If a cable run is already installed, you can still check continuity. Attach a terminator to one end of the cable, and then at the other end, touch the ground with one lead and the center wire with the other. You should get a reading that matches the terminating resistor's value.

Cable Tracers

You *trace* a cable to determine its path in a wall or ceiling, or its source and destination. A cable tracer is useful if you need to determine the destination of one wire in a bundle of wires. A tone generator is attached to one end of the cable and an amplifier is then used to listen for the tone at the other end, which is typically a punchdown block. The amplifier indicates when it is near the wire that is producing the signal.

A popular product is the Microtest Tracer. With it, you can locate any coaxial, twisted-pair, or other type of wire hidden inside a floor, wall, or ceiling. The Tracer's sending unit is connected to the wire or cable, and then its pocket-size receiving unit is run over the areas where you suspect the wire runs. When the Tracer's receiving unit passes over the wire, an alarm sounds; the alarm grows stronger as you get closer to the wire.

Time Domain Reflectometers

A time domain reflectometer (TDR) determines the locations of breaks and shorts in cables. It sends a high-frequency pulse down the length of the cable and then measures the time it takes for the reflection of the signal to return. Reflections occur at shorts and breaks, and the time and amplitude of the reflection indicates the distance to the problem. In addition, the polarity indicates whether the problem is a short or an open connection. TDRs are now available for as little as $1000 from Black Box.

The Microtest Cable Scanner (approximately $1,500) is a stand-alone hand-held TDR. It has a 32-character display that reports fault problems in plain English, such as "Short at 306 ft." The Cable Scanner can print a hard copy to any serial printer and save test results in memory for later review. You can test Ethernet, ArcNet, and Token Ring networks that use coaxial or twisted-pair cable. The Cable Scanner also provides real-time monitoring of a LAN's activity to help determine when a bridge or repeater might need to be added, and you can attach the Cable Scanner to an oscilloscope to analyze waveforms. The Tracer product described earlier is included with the Cable Scanner.

Protocol Analyzers

Protocol analyzers are diagnostics tools that monitor and track the activity of networks. They can come in the form of software or a combination of software and hardware. Hardware protocol analyzers are self-contained units that you can take with you. Protocol analyzers run on a network workstation and typically perform the following tasks:

- Display information about the types of packets traversing the network so that you can determine the accuracy of transmission

- Query all nodes and perform point-to-point communication testing between any specified node and all other nodes on the internetwork

- Determine the entire internetwork configuration

- Analyze critical data from one or all nodes and report only unusual activity based on a user-defined set of thresholds

- Display performance data such as traffic volume and packets serviced

- Provide useful information about network efficiency, network performance, possible hardware errors, noise problems, and problems with application software

Protocol analysis products are available from Novell (LANalyzer) at 800-243-8526, Gateway Communications (EtherStat) at 800-367-6555, Triticom (LANdecoder) at 612-937-0772, and Intel (NetSight Analyst) at 800-538-3373. You'll find more information about protocol analysis in Chapter 36.

THE
COMPLETE

REFERENCE

PART **FOUR**

NetWare
Installation

CHAPTER 15

Preparing to Install NetWare

This chapter prepares you for the installation of NetWare and helps you gather the information you'll need during the installation process. The next chapter lists the menus you'll see as you install NetWare and helps you make decisions about which options to select in the menus. If you're unfamiliar with the installation process and how to specify disk partitions, volumes, LAN driver settings, and other information, this chapter is for you. If you're familiar with the installation of NetWare, refer to Chapter 16 for instructions on starting the INSTALL program.

There are two types of installations. You can install NetWare on a new server, or you can upgrade an existing NetWare v.2.1x or v.3.x server to NetWare v.4. Refer to the section "Upgrading Existing NetWare Servers" later in this chapter and to Appendix A for information about upgrading servers.

This chapter assumes that you have installed the server hardware and have the correct memory and disk configurations to begin the NetWare installation.

A NOTE ABOUT DOCUMENTATION   As you read through this chapter, create log sheets for your server and the options you'll need to set on it. You should have already identified most of the hardware settings, such as interrupts and I/O addresses, while setting up the hardware, as discussed in Chapter 14.

Installing New Servers

There are several methods you can use to install NetWare on a new server:

- *Install from floppy disk*   This is the method described in this chapter, so simply follow the instructions listed here.

- *Install from CD-ROM*   This method requires that you install a CD-ROM drive in the system that will be the server. If you have an existing network with a server that has a CD-ROM volume, switch to that volume. Type **INSTALL** to start the installation; then follow the remainder of the instructions in this chapter, beginning with creating a DOS partition.

- *Install from a network drive*   This method requires that the server be connected to a network initially as a workstation. First you copy all the NetWare v.4 disks to a directory on an existing NetWare server. Then you go to the new server and create a DOS partition, connect to the existing NetWare server, map a drive to the directory where you copied the files, and type **INSTALL**. From that point, you continue with the instructions in this chapter.

Booting DOS and Creating the DOS Partition on the Server

The first step when you install NetWare v.4 is to boot the new server by using the NetWare v.4 Install disk, and create a DOS partition. If a partition doesn't exist, NetWare INSTALL recommends a 5MB partition (if you boot with the INSTALL disk), but you can change its size if necessary. If a partition already exists, you can retain it. The DOS partition holds the NetWare server startup file SERVER.EXE and associated files. The partition should be small (about 5MB) so you can use the remainder of disk storage for the NetWare operating system, but it should be large enough to hold any future NetWare-related files you might need to place within it, in addition to the server startup files.

NOTE: If you already have a DOS partition on the drive and you want to retain it, boot the server, then place the NetWare v.4 Install disk in a floppy drive, switch to the drive, and type **INSTALL**.

The Install boot disk contains DR DOS 6.0, and that is the operating system used to create and format the DOS partition. If you want to create and format the DOS partition by using MS-DOS, start the server system by using your Microsoft MS-DOS boot disk. Next partition the disk by using FDISK, and create a DOS partition that is about 5MB in size. Format the DOS partition and copy any DOS files to it that you think you will need in the future. Then, to start the normal NetWare v.4 installation, switch to the floppy drive, insert the NetWare Install disk, and type **INSTALL**.

Naming the Server

Name your file server with a name that describes where the file server is or what it is used for. The name can be 2 to 47 characters long. It can include hyphens, underscores, numbers, and the letters *A* through *Z*.

TIP: Try to keep the server name short. You'll appreciate the short name when you need to type it in the future.

Assigning the IPX Internal Network Number

Each server must be assigned a unique IPX internal network number that identifies its server operating system. This number must be different from all other IPX numbers on an internetwork. Do not confuse the IPX internal network number with other numbers associated with LANs, such as the network address and node address.

■ *The network address* identifies LAN segments; there might be several LAN segments attached to one server.

■ *The node address* identifies workstation and server interface cards. Network cards usually have a unique address assigned at the factory that you can't change, but numbering standards ensure that no two cards have the same address.

During the installation, INSTALL recommends a unique internal IPX number. Be sure to write it down for future reference.

TIP: Because the IPX number is in hexadecimal notation, the letters A through F can be used in it, which allows some room for creativity. For example, you could assign the server in the graphical engineering department the IPX number CAD1.

On large networks, you should devise a numbering scheme that identifies the location of servers. For example, in a campus environment, you could devise a numbering scheme that identifies a building by a letter and the room where a server is located by a number. So the server numbers might be A101, A102, B101, B102, and so on.

Specifying Disk Drivers

During installation, you must specify the drivers that provide communications between your disk controller board and the NetWare server. If you install multiple boards, you still install a driver for each board. Here is a list of drivers that appears during the installation:

ADAPTAPE.DSK	TAPE DAI
AHA1540.DSK	ADAPTEC AHA-1540/1542 ASPI Manager and SCSI Disk Module
AHA1640.DSK	ADAPTEC AHA-1640 ASPI Manager and SCSI Disk Module
AHA1740.DSK	Adaptec AHA-1740/1744 ASPI Manager and SCSI Disk Module
ALWAYS.DSK	Always Technology IN-2000 Disk Driver

ASPITRAN.DSK	UltraStor NetWare 4 ASPI Administration Driver V1.00
BT40.DSK	BusLogic (ISA/EISA/MCA) NetWare 4 SCSI driver
BTASPI.DSK	BusLogic ASPI Support Manager v1.0
CDNASPI.DSK	Meridian Data NetWare CD-ROM Device Driver
DCB.DSK	ADIC SCSI DCB, Disk Driver v4.0 (ISA)
DCB3200.DSK	ADIC BusMASTER SCSI DCB, Disk Driver v4 (EISA, MCA, ISA)
DCBASPI.DSK	ADIC BusMASTER SCSI DCB, ASPI Driver v4
DCBASPI2.DSK	ADIC BusMASTER SCSI DCB, Alternative ASPI Driver v4
DSKSHARE.DSK	NetWare for OS/2 Disk-Sharing Device Driver
DTC80AS4.DSK	DTC3280 ASPI Manager for NetWare 4
DTC80HD4.DSK	DTC3280 Disk Driver
DTC90AS4.DSK	DTC3290 ASPI Manager for NetWare 4
DTC90HD4.DSK	DTC3292 Disk Driver
FUTD40.DSK	Future Domain Future/CAM Disk Driver
FUTXPT.DSK	Future Domain Future/CAM Transport Layer (XPT)
IDE.DSK	Novell IDE (AT-compatible) Driver
ISADISK.DSK	Novell ISADISK (AT-compatible) Driver
SCSINW4A.DSK	Quantum CAM Disk Driver
SCSINW4B.DSK	Quantum CAM Transport Layer (XPT)
SCSINW4C.DSK	Quantum TMC-1800 CAM SIM Module
SIM1800.DSK	Future Domain TMC-1800 Future/CAM SIM Module
SIM7000E.DSK	Future Domain TMC-7000EX Future/CAM SIM Module
SIM950.DSK	Future Domain TMC-950 Future/CAM SIM Module
TAPEDAI.DSK	Tape Driver
U14_40X.DSK	UltraStor U14F SCSI Host Adapter
U22_40X.DSK	UltraStor 22X EISA ESDI Controllers
U24_40X.DSK	UltraStor U24F SCSI Host Adapter

If you don't see a driver for your disk controller in this list, you can load a driver from a third-party disk during the installation. You simply press the INS key when asked to specify a driver. INSTALL asks you to place the disk in a floppy drive and then displays a list of any drivers on the disk.

Table 15-1 lists the drivers recommended for various controllers and server buses.

Possible settings for several of these drivers are described next. You choose these settings after selecting a driver during the installation process.

ISADISK.DSK   The ISADISK.DSK driver supports ST506 and ESDI controllers. Up to two of these controllers can be installed in a server. You load the driver once for each controller, making sure to specify different interrupt and I/O port values for each. Interrupt values are B, C, E, or F, which are the hexadecimal equivalents of 11, 12, 14, and 15. Port values are 170 and 1F0.

IDE.DSK   The IDE.DSK driver supports up to four IDE adapters. The supported interrupt values are A, B, C, E, and F, which are the hexadecimal equivalents of 10, 11, 12, 14, and 15. Supported port values are 170, 1F0, 168, and 1E8. You can also set a Scatter/Gather option that causes the driver to queue requests and send them out at one time. Although this option improves performance on systems that have large amounts of traffic, it can slow down servers that aren't busy.

Bus Type	Controller Type	Driver
ISA	ST506 or ESDI	ISADISK.DSK
ISA	IDS (ATA)	IDE.DSK
ISA	Novell SCSI	DCB.DSK
Micro Channel	ESDI	PS2ESDI.DSK
Micro Channel	MFM	PS2MFM.DSK
Micro Channel	IBM SCSI	PS2SCSI.DSK
EISA	ST506 OR ESDI	ISADISK.DSK
EISA	IDE (ATA)	IDE.DSK
EISA	EISA	Vendor disk

Table 15-1.   *Disk Driver Recommendations*

NOTE: You cannot mirror two drives on the same IDE controller, but you can duplex drives if you have two IDE controllers set to different interrupt and port values.

DCB.DSK   The DCB.DSK driver supports ADIC SCSI controller boards. Up to four boards can be installed, and the driver loads reentrantly to reduce memory requirements. You can specify port values of 320, 328, 340, 348, 380, and 388. Interrupt settings are not required with this board. Note that some older boards require you to program their EEPROMs by using the DISKSET utility. You can specify the use of EEPROM settings during the installation.

Partitioning the Drive

During the installation, you are given the choice of manually creating partitions or having INSTALL automatically create them. Choose the manual option in the following cases:

- To install mirroring or duplexing

- To install NetWare for OS/2

- To delete a partition or change its Hot Fix redirection area, which you might want to increase if you are using an older drive

If you select the automatic option, INSTALL uses all available disk space (not including the DOS partition) for the partitions. Extended DOS partitions are destroyed. A partition is created on each disk.

Each partition is assigned a unique device number and a logical number. The device number, as discussed in Chapter 14, identifies the physical disk and which controller it is attached to. The logical number identifies partitions based on the order the disk drivers were loaded. Error messages typically identify failed drives by their device numbers. The logical numbers are used to identify mirrored and duplexed drives. Refer to Chapter 14 for more details on disk numbering.

Each partition is assigned a Hot Fix redirection area that is two percent of the partition's space. By default, NetWare verifies all data it writes to disk to ensure that it matches the data in memory. If the verification fails, NetWare assumes the disk block is defective, stores the data in the redirection area, and marks the block as unusable. If you are using an older drive, you might want to increase the redirection area size, since the disk might be more susceptible to block failure than a newer drive and will need more space for redirection.

Establishing Disk Mirroring and Duplexing

Disk mirroring and duplexing provide redundancy in the disk storage system to protect against hardware failure. Mirrored drives are attached to the same controller, whereas duplexed drives are attached to separate controllers and provide a higher level of protection. This book assumes you are duplexing, rather than mirroring, since duplexing provides more protection and is easily cost justified. If you installed a RAID system or SFT Level III, you can ignore the mirroring and duplexing instructions.

To establish duplexing, install a controller for each drive or each set of drives, as covered in Chapter 14. Depending on the drive interface, you can attach multiple drives to each controller. Each disk is partitioned separately, but a partition can be combined with other partitions to form volumes, as discussed in the next section.

In each mirrored or duplexed set, there is a primary drive and a secondary drive. Typically, the partitions on the primary and secondary drives are the same size. NetWare makes adjustments to the partition sizes so that both partitions have the same disk space. For example, the primary disk usually includes a 5MB DOS partition. Assuming that the primary and secondary drives are the same model from the same vendor, 5MB of disk space on the secondary disk is not used because INSTALL adjusts its partition size to match that of the primary disk.

- *Two controllers with one drive each*   An example of this configuration is shown in Figure 15-1. If two controllers are installed with one drive attached to each, the first controller and its drive are the primary drive and appear as logical partition #1. This assumes that a DOS partition is logical partition #0 and that the disk contains no other partitions.

- *Two controllers with two drives each*   See Figure 15-2 for an example of this configuration. If two controllers are installed in the server and two drives are attached to each, the drives on the first controller are the primary drives and appear as logical partition #1 and logical partition #2, assuming a DOS partition is logical partition #0. The drives on the secondary controller appear as logical partition #3 and logical partition #4. You can mirror partition #3 to partition #1 and mirror partition #4 to partition #2. You can also reverse this order and mirror partition #3 to partition #2 and mirror partition #4 to partition #1. Just make sure each mirrored drive is on a separate controller.

REMEMBER: *The load order of the disk drivers determines the logical partition numbering. If you want a particular drive to be logical partition #1, load its driver first during the installation process.*

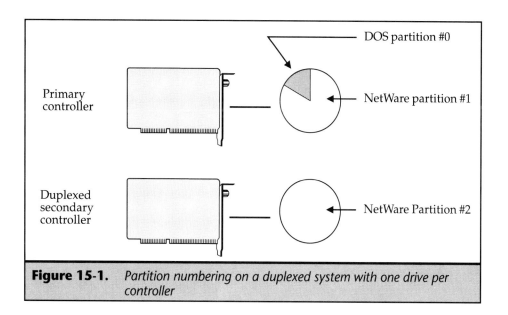

Figure 15-1. *Partition numbering on a duplexed system with one drive per controller*

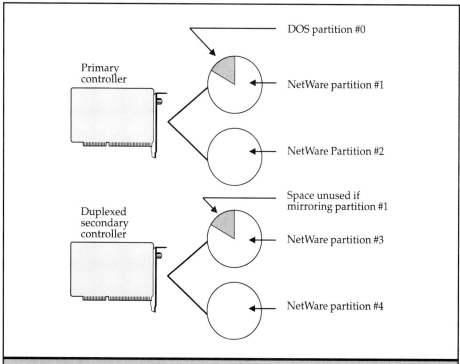

Figure 15-2. *Partition numbering on a duplexed system with two drives per controller*

Creating Volumes

Volumes are collections of directories, subdirectories, and files. NetWare allows more than one volume per server. The first volume on a server is called SYS and is automatically created in the free space of the first disk (logical partition #1, assuming that logical partition #0 is the DOS partition). The SYS volume is required on every server and must be at least 25MB in size. You cannot change its name; however, you can change its size.

INSTALL recommends using a disk's remaining free space for a volume. You can reduce this amount to make room for other volumes. Additional volumes are assigned default names of VOL1, VOL2, and so on, but you can rename them anything you want. For example, you could name volumes DATA, USER, and MAIL.

The SYS Volume

Novell recommends reserving SYS for the NetWare files and NetWare Loadable Modules. This offers several advantages:

- Having these files in one volume makes them easy to back up. At the same time, moving data files off the SYS volume and placing them into data-specific volumes helps organize your filing system and simplifies the backup of data.

- If the SYS volume is small, it takes less time to restore the drive (and the network attached to it) after a disk failure. You can quickly get the server back online and then begin the work of restoring the most important data.

- Security is improved. Except for the files in the PUBLIC directory, only supervisor-level users need object and directory/file access to the drive.

- If the SYS volume won't mount (possibly from virus corruption), even after trying to repair it by using utilities, you can recreate the SYS volume in the partition and reinstall NetWare without affecting data in other volumes.

Name Space Volumes

The OS/2 operating systems and the Macintosh store files differently than DOS, so if you need to store Macintosh or OS/2 files on your network, a special disk area called a *name space* must be set aside for them. It's a good idea to create a separate volume for each type of name space.

You must plan the locations of the name spaces in advance. Once you've created a name space on a volume, it cannot be removed without re-creating the volume or using a repair utility. Files in a name space use about twice as much disk space as DOS files. You can save disk space by creating name spaces on only volumes that need them. This also reduces the amount of RAM used by the name spaces, leaving more available for other processes.

Spanning Volumes

Volumes can range in size from small to large. Multiple small volumes can fit on a single disk partition. Large volumes can span several disk partitions, as shown here:

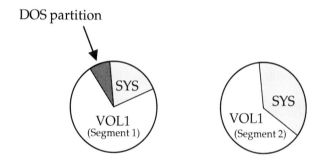

Note that part of SYS is on the NetWare partition of the first disk and part is on the second disk. Likewise, the VOL1 volume is divided over two disks. Spanning volumes in this way improves performance. It is also the only way to increase the size of a volume. To increase a volume, you add another drive and then create and attach the partition (or part of it) to the existing volume.

CAUTION: Always duplex drives that have spanned volumes. If a segment of the volume fails, the entire volume will not mount.

Because volumes can be spanned, it is relatively easy to specify volume sizes during the installation. Think of all your partitions as one large block of disk space, and then simply assign any amount of that disk space to any volume.

Volume Parameters

During the installation, you can change the parameters of any volume. The following menu appears:

```
╔══════════════════════════════════════════════╗
║            Volume Information                  ║
╠══════════════════════════════════════════════╣
║  Volume Name:            SYS                   ║
║  Volume Block Size:      8 KB Blocks           ║
║  Status:                 New, Not Mounted      ║
║  File Compression:       On                    ║
║  Block Suballocation:    On                    ║
║  Data Migration:         Off                   ║
╚══════════════════════════════════════════════╝
```

You scroll to each field and make changes, as described in the following sections. Have these configuration parameters ready when you run INSTALL.

VOLUME NAME   In the Volume Name field, you can specify a different name for the selected volume, unless it is the SYS volume. You might want to rename volumes according to the type of data stored on them or the name space they support.

VOLUME BLOCK SIZE   For the sake of efficiency, a file is not stored in a block of disk space that exactly matches its size. Instead, disks are divided into blocks that are typically 8KB in size, and files are stored in one or more of these blocks. If a file is smaller than the block size, it won't use all the space. The extra space will be unused (unless you use block suballocation, as discussed shortly). The block sizes available under NetWare are listed next. Note that the default block size depends on the volume size.

Volume Size	Block Size
0MB to 32MB	4KB
33MB to 150MB	8KB
151MB to 500MB	16KB
501MB to 2000MB	32KB
More than 2000MB	64KB

INSTALL sets a specific block size that depends on the size of the volume. Typically, you don't need to change the value. However, depending on the type of files you plan to store on the volume, you can increase or decrease the block size to improve performance. For example, assume you set aside one volume to store larger graphics files. It would make sense to set the block size on this volume to a large value that matches the size of a typical graphics file. Keep in mind, however, that large blocks require longer read and write times, which can affect performance. If a volume is used to store many small files, you might want to specify the smallest block size. Because the most efficient block size depends on the type of files stored on the volume, consider organizing volumes by file type.

STATUS   The Status option contains two fields, Mount and Dismount. Volumes must be mounted before users can access them. During the installation, you don't need to change this field, because INSTALL will mount the volume for you. Later, during maintenance, you can access this field to dismount a volume for service or to free up the RAM memory it uses if users don't need the volume.

FILE COMPRESSION   By default, the File Compression field is set on. This means that files that have not been accessed for a certain period of time are automatically compressed. When a compressed file is accessed, it must first be decompressed, but the time to do so is usually negligible. In most cases, you should specify file compression, but check with vendors to ensure that compression is compatible with their applications. You might need to store some applications on volumes that don't compress files.

BLOCK SUBALLOCATION   With the Block Suballocation field set on, the volume can store files in smaller increments than the value set in the Volume Block Size field. Block Suballocation conserves disk space. For example, if Block Suballocation is set off and the volume block size is 4KB, a 6.5KB file would require 8KB of disk space. With Block Suballocation set on, that file requires only 6.5KB of disk space. Any leftover parts of free blocks are used to store fragments from other files.

Using both file compression and block suballocation maximizes the disk space on a volume.

Data Migration

NetWare's data migration feature lets you migrate seldom used files to an alternate optical storage device, to free up space on the server's disk storage system. Set the Data Migration field on to enable the migration facility for the volume.

Loading LAN Drivers

After the disk drivers are installed, partitions and volumes are created, and the NetWare files are copied, you are ready to choose the drivers for the network interface cards in the server. INSTALL displays a list of common network interface cards. If you don't see your card listed, you can load a driver from floppy disk by pressing the INS key.

You must load a driver for each network card. INSTALL differentiates cards by their interrupt and I/O addresses. Have these values ready to enter in the LAN drive install menu during the installation.

The Ethernet frame types are listed next. These variations exist because of the different ways vendors have implemented the standard. Workstations must use the same standard that is used on the network or supported by the server.

- *Ethernet_802.2* The default standard for NetWare

- *Ethernet_802.3* An alternate Ethernet standard. Do not use it on a network that uses protocols other than IPX

- *Ethernet_II* Used to communicate with DEC minicomputers. Also used on TCP/IP or AppleTalk Phase I networks

- *Ethernet_SNAP* The IEEE 802.2 frame standard with an extension added to the header to support AppleTalk Phase II

NOTE: INSTALL binds the IPX protocol to the LAN driver for you. INSTALL gives you a chance to bind other protocols such as TCP/IP at the end of installation. See Chapter 19.

Specifying NetWare Directory Services Information

During the installation, you must specify time zone and time server information for the server. You must also specify the root name of your NetWare Directory Services (NDS) tree and the context of the server you are installing. The context is the organization container and organizational unit container where the server will reside. When installing additional NetWare v.4 servers, INSTALL looks at the network to locate the first server, and then recommends the context of that server for the server you are installing. Of course, if you want to specify a different context, you can do so. At this point in the installation you can also specify the network administrator.

Naming the NetWare Directory Services Tree Root

Every directory tree has a root name. The root name should not be confused with the first-level organization container, which typically contains your company name, or the country container. The root name is simply the name of the NDS tree. After you've named the tree, you rarely need to refer to the root name again.

A NetWare Directory Services tree contains its own database of objects, and the objects in one tree are not visible to objects in another tree. Data cannot be shared across different trees. Most companies will have only one tree, and thus you will specify only one tree root name. However, some organizations might require two separate and distinct directory trees. For example, a firm that manages networks for other companies might create a NetWare Directory Services tree for each of those companies.

During the installation of the first server, you are asked to name the root of the tree into which the server will be installed. This name can be simply ROOT or TREE_ROOT, or it could include your company name, such as XYZ_CO. Spaces are not allowed in tree names, but you can use an underscore instead. When installing additional NetWare v.4 servers on the same network, the root you specified on the first server is suggested.

Specifying the Time Zone

During the installation, you'll need to specify time zone information for the server. A screen appears on which you can select the time zone you are in. After selecting the time zone, a menu similar to the following appears. It contains all the information for your time zone.

```
Time server type:                                  Primary

Standard time zone abbreviation:                   PST
Standard time offset from UTC:                     8:00:00 AHEAD

Does your area have daylight savings time (DST):   YES
DST time zone abbreviation:                        PDT
DST offset from standard time:                     1:00:00 AHEAD
DST Start: First Sunday of April at    2:00:00 am
DST End:   Last Sunday in October at   2:00:00 am
```

STANDARD TIME ZONE ABBREVIATION   This field contains the abbreviation for the time zone you selected. The commonly used time zone abbreviations for the United States are listed here, but you can enter your own abbreviation if you prefer:

EST	Eastern Standard Time
CST	Central Standard Time
MST	Mountain Standard Time
PST	Pacific Standard Time

STANDARD TIME OFFSET FROM UTC   The UTC is the Universal Coordinated Time, which was formerly Greenwich Mean Time. The offset is the number of time zones you are away from UTC, and whether you are ahead or behind it. These are the settings for the United States:

EST	Offset of 5 and behind
CST	Offset of 6 and behind
MST	Offset of 7 and behind
PST	Offset of 8 and behind

DST TIME ZONE ABBREVIATION   If your time zone switches to daylight saving time and back to standard time during the year, the daylight saving time abbreviation for your time zone is in this field. If you don't specify an abbreviation, you won't be able to observe the time change. You can enter your own abbreviation or a commonly used abbreviation.

DST OFFSET FROM STANDARD TIME   This field holds the difference between standard time and daylight saving time. It is usually one hour ahead.

DST START   The date daylight saving time starts.

DST END   The date daylight saving time ends.

CURRENT DAYLIGHT TIME STATUS   This field specifies whether you are currently in the daylight saving time mode.

Specifying the Time Server Type

NetWare Directory Services must ensure that servers on an internetwork are time synchronized so that timestamps are accurate throughout the internetwork. Timestamps establish the order of events on the internetwork. Time synchronization is important because internal computer clocks can deviate from each other. It ensures that all systems know the correct time so that the updates to the same data from various parts of the internetwork are handled correctly.

There are four time server types:

- *Single reference server used on geographically close networks*   The sole source of time on the network. Any time changes are set on this server, and then others synchronize with it. A single reference server should not be used if a primary time server is used.

■ *Primary server used on geographically diverse networks* Synchronizes time with other primary time servers or a reference time server, and provides the correct time to secondary time servers. If there are multiple primary servers on a network, they "vote" on what the common network time should be.

■ *Reference server* A reference server gets its time from an external source (such as a radio clock) and is a contact to what the outside world says the time should be. A reference server does not use or change its internal time clock. A reference server helps primary time servers set a common time by using a "voting" procedure. Eventually all time servers are set to the time indicated by the reference server's outside time source.

■ *Secondary server* All other servers on the network can be secondary time servers. They merely get the time from single reference, primary, or reference time servers and do not participate in the establishment of a common time over the network.

During installation, specify the type of time server based on whether the internetwork covers large geographic areas. The main criterion is the cost of long-distance WAN links; secondary servers should get their time from a local primary or reference server rather than using a WAN link to access a distant time server.

Use multiple primary time servers on internetworks that span large geographic areas. This provides fault tolerance and redundant paths for secondary time servers: if one primary time server is offline, secondary servers can get the time from another primary time server. Place primary time servers in each geographically distant location so that other servers can access them without having to use expensive wide area links. Install one server as a reference time server and attach an external time source to this server. All other servers not participating in the establishment of a common time on the internetwork should be set up as secondary time servers.

Use single reference servers on small networks that are not connected by WAN links. If you set up a NetWare v.4 server as a single reference time server, do not install a primary server.

Specifying the Server Context

The next step in the installation is to specify the context of the server. As mentioned previously, INSTALL will suggest the same information you enter for the first NetWare v.4 server for any additional servers you install, but you don't need to use the suggestions. During the installation, the following menu appears to collect information about the server context:

```
╔══════════════════════════════════════════════════════════════╗
║            Directory Services Server Context                   ║
╠══════════════════════════════════════════════════════════════╣
║ Company or Organization:                                       ║
║ Level 1 (Sub)Organizational Unit (optional)                    ║
║ Level 2 (Sub)Organizational Unit (optional)                    ║
║ Level 3 (Sub)Organizational Unit (optional)                    ║
║                                                                ║
║ Server Context:                                                ║
║                                                                ║
║ Administrator Name:                                            ║
║ Password                                                       ║
╚══════════════════════════════════════════════════════════════╝
```

In the Company or Organization field, you enter your company name, such as XYZCorp. You use the next three lines to specify the level where the server will exist. You can specify one, two, or three levels. If the server's context should be at a level greater than 3, you can type the appropriate level on the Server Context line. This line displays the context as you specified it in the preceding lines.

Figure 15-3 shows the directory tree for an example company called Cambrian Corporation, which has three divisions: Administration, Marketing, and Sales. Let's assume that you are installing the first NetWare v.4 server in the Administration department. To create this context during installation, you would fill out the Directory Services Server Context menu as shown here:

```
╔══════════════════════════════════════════════════════════════╗
║            Directory Services Server Context                   ║
╠══════════════════════════════════════════════════════════════╣
║ Company or Organization: CambrianCorp                          ║
║ Level 1 (Sub)Organizational Unit (optional) Administration     ║
║ Level 2 (Sub)Organizational Unit (optional)                    ║
║ Level 3 (Sub)Organizational Unit (optional)                    ║
║                                                                ║
║ Server Context: OU.=Administration.O=CambrianCorp              ║
║                                                                ║
║ Administrator Name:                                            ║
║ Password                                                       ║
╚══════════════════════════════════════════════════════════════╝
```

The Server Context field is filled out automatically.

NOTE: If you want to specify a country, add it to the end of the Server Context field. For example, highlight the field and type .C=US to add the United States country code. Keep in mind that Novell does not recommend using country codes due to the inconvenience they add when specifying a context.

```
┌──────────────────────────────────────────────────────────────┐
│                                                                │
│                    🖧 CambrianCorp                              │
│                      ├ 🖳 Administration                        │
│                      ├ 🖳 Marketing                             │
│                      └ 🖳 Sales                                 │
│                                                                │
└──────────────────────────────────────────────────────────────┘
```

Figure 15-3.   *An example of a company organization with only level-1 departments*

Figure 15-4 illustrates what the directory tree looks like after the server is installed in the Administration object. Note that the server's name is MONA_LISA, and it has the volumes SYS and VOL1, which appear as objects contained by Administration.

As another example, assume your company has an east coast and a west coast division, as shown in Figure 15-5. Within each division are departments, such as Administration and Sales. Let's assume that you want to install the first server as an object of the Administration department, which itself will be an object of the western division (DivWest). You would fill out the Directory Services Server Context menu as follows:

Company or Organization: CambrianCorp
Level 1 (Sub)Organizational Unit (optional) DivWest
Level 2 (Sub)Organizational Unit (optional) Administration

If you then installed a server in the Sales department in the eastern division (DivEast), you would fill out the Directory Services Server Context menu for that server as follows:

Company or Organization: CambrianCorp
Level 1 (Sub)Organizational Unit (optional) DivEast
Level 2 (Sub)Organizational Unit (optional) Sales

The directory tree would then appear as shown in Figure 15-6, assuming you named the new server MARANTZ and added the volumes SYS and VOL1 to it.

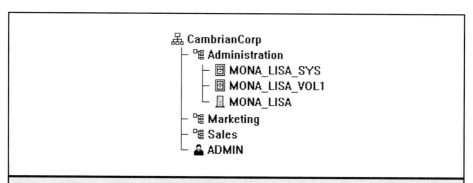

Figure 15-4.   *A directory tree after a server and volume have been installed*

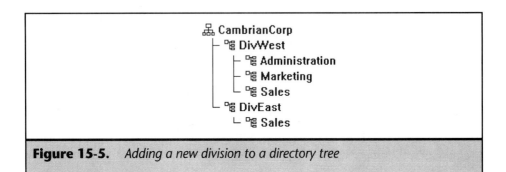

Figure 15-5.   *Adding a new division to a directory tree*

Specifying the Network Administrator

When installing the first server, you can specify the name and password of the administrative user. INSTALL recommends the name ADMIN. To change the name and password, simply type new values in the lower part of the Directory Services Server Context menu, which is shown earlier in the chapter. You can change this name at any time in the future by using the NetWare Administrator or NETADMIN utility.

Write down the context of the administrator (for example CN=ADMIN.O=CambrianCorp) for future reference. You'll need it to log in as the administrator and if you want to specify this user as the administrator for other servers.

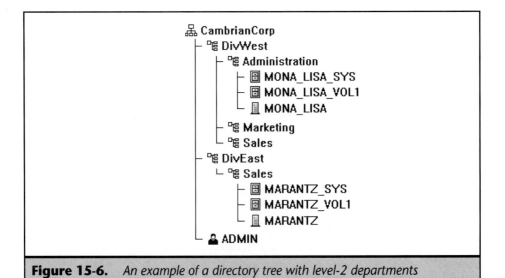

Figure 15-6.   *An example of a directory tree with level-2 departments*

Upgrading Existing NetWare Servers

Installing NetWare v.4 on a new server is relatively easy. You don't need to worry about protecting existing data and user accounts. However, upgrading from NetWare v.2.1x or v.3.x requires extra precautions to ensure that data is saved and users are migrated to the new servers. Novell has included several installation features that help you make a successful upgrade, as described in this section. The upgrade steps are listed in Appendix A.

NOTE: NetWare v.2.1x servers must be upgraded to NetWare v.3.x servers before you can upgrade them to NetWare v.4.

THE ACROSS-THE-WIRE UPGRADE METHOD   In this upgrade method, you install a NetWare v.4 server as described in this chapter and Chapter 16. You then attach it to the NetWare v.3.x network and transfer the files across the network cable. Bindery information (such as user account information and security rights) is translated and then copied to the NetWare v.4 server, where it is accessible through bindery emulation. You temporarily store the bindery information on the hard drive of the workstation where you work during the upgrade, so this workstation must have a hard disk of its own. The across-the-wire method retains the existing network environment and lets you quickly restore services should something go wrong.

THE SAME-SERVER UPGRADE METHOD   This method is used to install NetWare v.4 on the same server. The binderies on the server are copied to a local hard disk and then translated when restored after NetWare v.4 has been installed on the server. Data files must be backed up and then restored. This method does not provide the benefits of data migration, as the in-place method does. Also, if the upgrade doesn't go as planned while installing NetWare v.4, you might need to reinstall the previous version of NetWare on the server and restore the data to put your network back into operation until you can resolve the problem.

THE IN-PLACE UPGRADE METHOD   This method goes beyond the same-server method by analyzing and inventorying the system, analyzing and modifying the disk, and creating a NetWare v.3.11 bindery on a NetWare v.2.1x server, if necessary. This method also lets you migrate directories and files. If you have a NetWare v.2.1x server (it must be an 80386 or better system), use this method to update the server to NetWare v.3.11 and then upgrade the server to NetWare v.4. Although you still must ensure that you have adequate backups, the upgrade process does not move files off the server disk and then restore them. Instead, it creates a NetWare v.3.11 disk layout and then a NetWare v.4 disk layout, moving files around as necessary. Note that you can't use this method to upgrade a NetWare v.2.0a server. You must back up that data, install a new NetWare v.4 server, re-create the user environment, and restore the data.

What Happens During an Upgrade

During an upgrade, you choose one of two migration options: standard or custom. The standard option migrates all NetWare v.3.x bindery information to the NetWare v.4 server. The custom option lets you choose specific information to copy from the bindery and the file system. When you are upgrading to NetWare v.4, directories and files that were on several servers might be consolidated on one NetWare v.4 server. Note the following:

- Files that have names of existing files are not copied. Rename and copy the files after the migration.

- The system login script is stored as a property of the container object at the bindery context level. Only the login script of the first upgraded server is saved; others are discarded. The MEMBER_OF_GROUP and ATTACH commands are no longer valid in NetWare v.4 login scripts. You must edit the scripts to remove these commands.

- If more than one directory has the same name, the files in these directories are merged into one directory that has the same name on the new server. Change the directory names beforehand if you don't want to merge the files.

- Existing users are migrated. If users have more than one account under the same name, those accounts are merged.

- User accounts are changed as follows:

  - *User account manager*   Retains rights to supervise previously managed objects. Cannot create new objects

  - *Workgroup manager*   Has supervisor rights to user objects that were created before the upgrade

  - *Console operator*   Gets the Operator property of the server object

  - *Security equivalence*   Gets the Security Equivalence property of objects created before the upgrade

- Passwords are not migrated, but they can be generated randomly.

- NetWare 2.1x VAPs (Value Added Processes), core printing, and volume/disk restrictions are not upgraded.

Custom Migration Features

If you choose the custom option when migrating from a previous NetWare server (using the across-the-wire or in-place method), you can control how the following options are migrated:

■ *Data files*   All directories and data files, along with their attributes can be migrated. You cannot migrate data files if you use the same-server upgrade method. You can only back up the files and restore them to the new server.

■ *Trustee assignments*   All user and group rights can be migrated.

■ *Users*   All user accounts are migrated unless they already exist on the new server. Print job configurations, login scripts, and user restrictions (except volume/disk restrictions) are not migrated. The guest user becomes the user object CN=Guest.

■ *Groups*   All groups are migrated, including the group member list and trustee rights. Groups from multiple servers that have the same name are merged. Groups become directory services objects with the name CN=*GROUP NAME*. For example, the EVERYONE group becomes CN=EVERYONE.

■ *System defaults*   All system defaults related to account balances and restrictions are migrated, along with accounting charge methods.

■ *Printing*   All existing print operators, print queues, print users, and print servers are migrated.

NOTE: NetWare v.2.1x rights and attributes are translated to the NetWare v.4 format. The maximum rights mask is replaced by an inherited rights filter. There is no change in directory and file rights between NetWare v.3.x and NetWare v.4.

Preparing for an Across-the-Wire Upgrade

The across-the-wire migration method lets you upgrade from an existing server to a new server. You'll need to install NetWare v.4 on the new server, as described in this chapter and in Appendix A, and then attach the server to the same network as the existing NetWare server and run the upgrade from an attached workstation. The workstation must have at least 5MB of free disk space and a setting in its CONFIG.SYS file that reads FILES=20 (or greater).

You can choose the standard upgrade method, which migrates all information, including bindery information and data files, or you can choose the custom migration method, which lets you select the exact information you want to migrate.

The first step is to make sure all users except the supervisor are logged off the system and then back up the server for protection. It's a good idea to remove any unnecessary files and files that are incompatible with NetWare v.4, such as these NetWare v.2.1x or v.2.0a files:

LARCHIVE.EXE (2.1x)
LRESTORE.EXE (2.1x)
MACBACK.EXE (2.1x)
NARCHIVE.EXE (2.1x)
NRESTORE.EXE (2.1x)
Q.EXE (2.0a)
QUEUE.EXE (2.0a)
SPOOL.EXE (2.0a)
ENDSPOOL.EXE (2.0a)

The 14-character naming convention used in NetWare v.2.15 is no longer used. You'll need to change these files to the standard 8-character filename and 3-character extension format. Also note the following:

- Subdirectory depths cannot exceed 25 levels on the new server. Change your existing servers, if necessary, before proceeding.

- Make sure you have enough space on the new server to handle all the servers that might migrate to it.

- Update or replace applications or NLMs to work under NetWare v.4, if necessary. Check with the vendors ahead of time.

- Run BINDFIX on the existing server before upgrading to remove unused user accounts and mail directories.

Preparing for a Same-Server Upgrade

Preparation for a same-server upgrade is relatively simple. Because the existing server partition must be altered, you must make sure you have adequate backups of the system. You'll also need a workstation that has enough hard disk space to hold the bindery files. The steps involved in a same-server upgrade are listed here:

1. Back up the existing data.

2. Copy the bindery information to the workstation hard disk.

3. Install NetWare v.4 on the server as outlined in this chapter and Chapter 16.

4. Restore the data.

5. Translate and copy the bindery information from the workstation hard disk to the upgraded server.

Preparing for an In-Place Upgrade

If you are upgrading from NetWare v.2.1x, remember that NetWare v.4 requires an 80386 or better system with 8MB or more of memory. In addition, when you upgrade from NetWare v.2.1x to NetWare v.3.11, you'll need about 10 percent more disk space to accommodate the new files. You should also plan for a 5MB DOS disk partition.

- Data is vulnerable in this upgrade method, so make sure you have adequate backups.

- To start the upgrade, make sure you have the Upgrade disk that is included in the NetWare v.4 disk set.

- If this is a NetWare v.3.1x to NetWare v.4 upgrade, run SALVAGE if you need to restore any deleted files before beginning.

- All users except the supervisor must be logged out.

- Upgrade applications and NLMs to versions that operate under NetWare v.4, if necessary.

- If you are upgrading multiple servers, consolidate the different names users might have on those servers into one name. If two users have the same name, change one of the names so they won't be consolidated on the new server.

CHAPTER 16

Installing NetWare on a New Server

This chapter provides a step-by-step description of the process of installing NetWare v.4 on a new server. If you are upgrading a NetWare v.2.*x* or NetWare v.3.*x* server, refer to Appendix A. The instructions in this chapter are intended only as a guide to help you make the correct decision at each step of the installation. You should have all the server hardware installed, as discussed in Chapter 14, and you should have all the prerequisite information at hand, as discussed in Chapter 15.

Installation Options

There are several methods you can use to install NetWare:

■ Install from floppy disk   This method is described in this chapter. You start the server by using the Install disk supplied with NetWare v.4 and then follow the instructions in this chapter, starting with step 1.

■ Install from CD-ROM   To use this installation method, you must have installed a CD-ROM drive or have access to one over a previously installed network. Switch to the CD-ROM drive and type INSTALL to start the server and installation process. Then follow the instructions in this chapter, beginning with step 2.

■ Install from a network drive   This method requires that the server be connected to a network as a workstation. First you copy all the NetWare v.4 disks to a directory on an existing NetWare server. Then you go to the new server and create a DOS partition, as discussed in step 2 in this chapter. After the DOS partition is created, you connect to the existing NetWare server, map a drive to the directory where you copied the files, and type INSTALL. Then you continue with the instructions in this chapter, starting with step 3.

Installing NetWare

Follow the steps described in the remainder of this chapter to install NetWare on a new server. In the second step, you'll need to partition the server's hard disk, so if it contains existing information, back up that information for future use.

A WORD ABOUT THE INSTALLATION MENUS   During the installation, you make selections from menus. Use the up arrow and down arrow keys to select an option, and then press ENTER to execute that option. In some cases, the menus can get confusing because you press ESC to select an option, but this is usually because you are backing out of a "chain" of menus to a starting menu. Press F1 to get help, or press ALT-F10 to exit back to DOS. If you get confused, look at the bottom of the screen for a list of available keystrokes.

Step 1: Boot the Server

Place the NetWare Install disk in the new server's floppy drive and restart the system. The installation program starts immediately, and you see the following screen:

If you are upgrading an existing server, refer to Appendix A. Otherwise, select the Install new NetWare v4.0 option.

If you want to create an MS-DOS partition instead of a DR DOS partition, follow these steps:

1. Start the system by using your Microsoft MS-DOS boot disk.

2. Create and format the partition.

3. Place the NetWare Install disk in the floppy drive.

4. Switch to the floppy drive and type **INSTALL**. Skip over step 2, and proceed with step 3.

Step 2: Create a DOS Partition

After choosing to go ahead and install NetWare v.4 on a new server, you see a screen similar to the following:

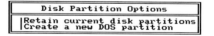

The free space on your disk is listed at the top. If you already have a DOS partition set up, you'll see its starting and ending cylinders and its size listed. To retain the partition, choose the first option.

To create a new partition, choose the second option. Another menu appears that gives you the option of going ahead with the partitioning, or exiting to DOS so that you can save any files you might have forgotten to save. Partitioning destroys any files on the disk. Choose the Create a new DOS partition option to proceed with the partitioning. NetWare INSTALL recommends a 5MB partition.

You can select the recommended partition size or make the partition larger, but you can't make it smaller.

As soon as the partition is created, you must reboot the system. Remove the Install disk from the drive and select the reboot option. After the system reboots, the INSTALL program asks if you want to format the drive. Choose Yes, and then continue with the next step.

Step 3: Name the Server

The next menu asks you for your server name, as shown here:

```
                    Enter Server Name:
Server name:
```

Type the name you selected for your server, and press ENTER to continue.

Step 4: Specify the IPX Internal Network Number

On the next menu, a default IPX number appears, as shown in this example:

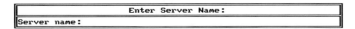

```
     Enter IPX Internal Network Number:
Internal network number: 2B33ABA3
```

Make sure this number doesn't conflict with the IPX number of any other server on the network. If it doesn't, press ENTER to accept this number. If you prefer to use a different IPX number, type it in. Refer to Chapter 15 for more information about IPX numbers.

Step 5: Specify the Server Boot File Directory

On the next menu that appears, you specify the location where the server boot files should be copied. INSTALL recommends a directory called SERVER.40 on the C drive. You can change this directory name and drive, if necessary. Press ENTER to continue.

At this point, INSTALL begins copying files to the directory you specified. You'll be asked to insert various disks, so follow the screen prompts. When the copying is done, a menu appears that asks if you want AUTOEXEC.BAT to load

SERVER.EXE. Choose Yes if you want the NetWare server to start every time you boot the system. Choose No if you prefer to start the server yourself. If you choose No, you'll need to execute the SERVER.EXE file in the SERVER.40 directory when you want to start the server.

After choosing an option, the SERVER.EXE file is executed, and the server loads NetWare v.4. If there are any problems starting NetWare, your hardware configuration is incorrect. Check the specifications listed in Chapter 15. If everything is fine, you are prompted to insert the NetWare disks in sequence as the installation proceeds.

Step 6: Select and Load a Disk Driver

Now you're ready to specify the disk driver or drivers that the server will use. If you have multiple controllers in the system, you select a driver for each. Then you specify the interrupt and address for each controller card. A menu similar to the following appears:

```
IDE.DSK          Novell IDE (ATA Compatible) Driver
ISADISK.DSK      Novell ISADISK (AT Compatible) Driver
SCSINW4A.DSK     Novell ISADISK (AT Compatible) Driver
SCSINW4B.DSK     Novell ISADISK (AT Compatible) Driver
SCSINW4C.DSK     Novell ISADISK (AT Compatible) Driver

Use this driver with ESDI, MFM, and ST-506      Loaded drivers
drives that have adapter boards using the
standard AT disk interface. The ISADISK
driver can use controllers at both the
primary and the secondary addresses.
```

You select a driver in the top box by pressing the up arrow and down arrow keys. As you highlight a driver, installation information about that driver appears in the help window below. To scroll the help window, press the PGUP and PGDN keys. To the right of the help menu is a box that lists drivers as they are installed.

NOTE: To load a driver from floppy disk, press the INS *key and then follow the instructions on the menu.*

Highlight a driver and press ENTER. A parameters menu appears so that you can specify the interrupt, the port number, and other values for the driver. Make sure these values are different from those of any other drivers you install.

After loading the driver, you can choose to load another driver like the one you just loaded. Specify a driver for a different type of controller card, or choose to continue with the installation. Choose the first two options to install more drivers, or choose the last option.

If you want to change a driver you already loaded, press the F2 key. The highlight jumps to the Loaded drivers box so that you can select the driver to change. Press DEL to unload the driver, and then press F2 again to jump back and load another driver.

NOTE: If you get a message that there are no accessible disk drives, or that a drive is inaccessible, you've loaded an incorrect driver for the controller. Repeat the above procedure, and select the correct driver. Note that the ISADISK driver might be necessary for some IDE adapters.

Step 7: Create the NetWare Partitions

After loading the drivers for the disk controllers, you must create NetWare partitions. The following screen appears:

```
╔═══════════════════════════════╗
║ Create NetWare disk partitions ║
╠═══════════════════════════════╣
║|Automatically                  ║
║|Manually                       ║
╚═══════════════════════════════╝
```

- ■ If you choose Automatically, INSTALL creates a partition that spans the entire disk space. Continue with step 8 in this chapter.

- ■ Choose Manually to create mirrored or duplexed drives, to install a NetWare for OS/2 server, or to specify partitioning parameters yourself.

NOTE: The following discussion assumes that you are installing a disk duplexing system with two controllers. If not, you will not see the mirroring and duplexing options on the menus. Go to step 7A and then to step 8.

When you select Manually, the following menu appears, along with a partition table that shows the starting and ending cylinders for the DOS partition:

```
╔═══════════════════════════════════════╗
║ Disk Partitions and Mirroring Options  ║
╠═══════════════════════════════════════╣
║|Create, delete, and modify disk partition ║
║|Mirror and unmirror disk partition sets   ║
╚═══════════════════════════════════════╝
```

Step 7A: Partition the Disk

Choose the first option to create the NetWare partitions. You'll see a list of available disk drives appear if your server has more than one installed. Choose the first drive from the list, and then choose Create NetWare disk partition. A menu similar to the following appears:

```
┌────────────────────────────────────────────────────┐
│            Disk Partition Information               │
├────────────────────────────────────────────────────┤
│ Partition Type: NetWare Partition                   │
│ Partition Size:  2272   Cylinders,    204.0 MB      │
│ Hot Fix Information:                                 │
│    Data Area:          51208 Blocks,  200.0 MB      │
│    Redirection Area: 1048  Blocks,      2.0 %       │
└────────────────────────────────────────────────────┘
```

On this screen, you can change the partition size and the Hot Fix redirection area. Typically, you increase the Hot Fix redirection area size only for old disks, which will need more space for bad block redirection. Use the down arrow key to access the Redirection Area field, and then increase the percentage amount.

NOTE: *If this is the first disk, part of its space is allocated to the DOS partition.*

When done, press the ESC key to jump back to the previous menu. Answer Yes to create the partition, and then repeat step 7A to partition any additional disks. Go to step 7B to mirror the disks.

Step 7B: Specify Mirroring and Duplexing

To mirror or duplex disks, follow the same procedure. If disks are connected to the same controller, you can mirror the disks. If disks are connected to different controllers, you can duplex the disks. From the Disk Partitions and Mirroring Options menu, choose Mirror and unmirror disk partition sets. Assume for this example that your disk and partition arrangement is like that described in Chapter 15 in which two drives are each attached to two disk controllers. You'll see a menu similar to the following that lists each partition:

```
┌────────────────────────────────────────────┐
║           Available Disk Partition          ║
╠────────────────────────────────────────────╣
║ Not Mirrored:  Logical Partition #1         ║
║ Not Mirrored:  Logical Partition #2         ║
║ Not Mirrored:  Logical Partition #3         ║
║ Not Mirrored:  Logical Partition #4         ║
└────────────────────────────────────────────┘
```

The DOS partition is not listed and cannot be mirrored.

Assume partition #1 and #2 are connected to the first controller, and partition #3 and #4 are connected to the second controller (as is usually the case in this arrangement). You'll mirror #3 to #1, and #4 to #2. Highlight Partition #1 and press ENTER. You see a screen similar to the following, which indicates that Partition #1 is in sync (with itself) but not mirrored:

```
┌────────────────────────────────────────────────────────┐
│              Mirrored NetWare Partitions               │
├────────────────────────────────────────────────────────┤
│ │In Sync -    NetWare partition 1 on Device #0 (21000)  │
└────────────────────────────────────────────────────────┘
```

Now press INS to see the partition list again so that you can choose a secondary mirroring partition. Only partitions that are the same size or larger than the first partition appear in this list.

Highlight a partition on a different controller and press ENTER. If the secondary partition is larger than the primary partition, you'll see a warning message. Press ESC to go ahead and mirror the partition. The extra space on the mirrored disk is not usable.

INSTALL begins synchronizing the two partitions. When it is done, you can mirror other partition by pressing the INS key and repeating step 7B. Press F10 to save the configuration and continue with the next step.

Step 8: Create Volumes

By default, INSTALL assigns all the disk space on the first drive to the SYS volume. A SYS volume must exist on each server. Additional volumes are given the names VOL1, VOL2, and so on by default, but you can change these names if you wish. The minimum size of the SYS volume is 25MB, but it is recommended that you make it at least twice this size to leave room for future add-ons and upgrades. You'll see a list of proposed volumes similar to that shown here:

```
┌────────────────────────────────────────────────────────┐
│ Volume Name            Size (MB)                       │
├────────────────────────────────────────────────────────┤
│ │SYS                   195 (new system volume)         │
│ │VOL1                  200 (new volume)                │
└────────────────────────────────────────────────────────┘
```

To alter a volume size, highlight the volume and press the F3 key; then follow the instructions on the menu. You need to alter a volume's size if you want to split disk space into several small volumes. If you reduce a proposed volume's size, free space is opened up that you then assign to a new volume. Highlight the free space and press ENTER to assign it a name and make it a new volume.

To change the name, block size, and other parameters of a volume, highlight the volume and press ENTER. A screen appears, as shown next, and you can change any item by using the information you collected in Chapter 15.

```
╔══════════════════════════════════════╗
║          Volume Information          ║
╟──────────────────────────────────────╢
║ Volume Name:              SYS        ║
║ Volume Block Size:        8 KB Blocks ║
║ Status:                   New, Not Mounted ║
║ File Compression:         On         ║
║ Block Suballocation:      On         ║
║ Data Migration:           Off        ║
╚══════════════════════════════════════╝
```

After you've created your volumes, press F10 to continue with the installation. You are asked if you want to save the volume changes. Answer Yes to continue with the next installation step, or No to redefine the volumes.

Step 9: Copy NetWare Files

The next screen to appear gives you a chance to specify the NetWare files you want to install. An *X* appears in the box before each file group. To deselect any group of files, highlight the group name and press ENTER. For a description of the file groups, press F1, which activates the help system.

Press F10 to continue with the installation and load the files you selected. INSTALL will ask for each disk in turn.

Step 10: Load the LAN Drivers

After files are copied from the last disk, you are ready to specify one or more LAN drivers. The Load LAN Driver screen appears, which has a menu similar to the following:

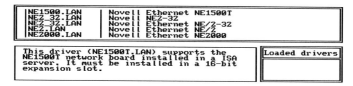

Scan through the list by pressing the up arrow and down arrow keys to locate the driver or drivers for the LAN cards in your system.

NOTE: If you don't see a driver listed for your card, press the INS key and then insert a disk that contains a vendor-supplied driver into the floppy drive.

Highlight a driver, and press ENTER to select it. INSTALL copies the driver files from floppy disk and displays a menu similar to the following:

```
          Driver NE2000 parameters
            Version 3.20 (921009)
    Interrupt number: 3
    Port value:       300
    Node Address:
    Frame types:      (select from list)
    Retries:          5
```

For each driver you select, enter the settings you configured for each card, and specify other information according to the worksheets you created in Chapter 15.

After making changes, press F10 to continue. INSTALL binds IPX to the drivers and displays their network numbers and node addresses. Write down these addresses for future use, and press ENTER to continue. If you're installing Ethernet cards, a screen appears for each frame type you select.

If you have multiple network cards installed in the server, you must load a LAN driver for each card and specify the interrupt, I/O port, and other settings for each card. On the Select an action menu, choose to install another LAN driver or continue with the installation. Once you've loaded all the drivers, continue with the next step.

NOTE: To bind other protocols in addition to IPX to a network card, finish the installation, and then refer to Chapter 17.

Step 11: Specify the Directory Services Root

The options you specify in this step depend on whether this is the first NetWare v.4 server on the network. If your network is connected to an existing NetWare v.4 server, you see the root name of its directory tree. Press ENTER to accept it or INS to start a new NetWare Directory Services tree.

NOTE: It is unlikely that you will need more than one tree unless your company has two or more completely separate divisions.

If another NetWare v.4 server cannot be found, the following menu appears:

```
Is this the first v4.00 server on this internetwork?
Yes (This is the first Directory server)
No  (Recheck the nearest server)
No  (Check a specific network and node address)
```

Choose Yes if this is the first server. If a first server has already been installed, make sure it is running and the network connections are good, and then choose one of the No options.

Step 12: Set Time Synchronization

Next, you see the time zone selection menu. Scroll through the list and select your time zone area, and then press ENTER. Then a menu similar to the following appears that displays information about the time zone you selected:

```
Time server type:                                       Primary
Standard time zone abbreviation:                        PST
Standard time offset from UTC:                          8:00:00 AHEAD

Does your area have daylight savings time (DST):        YES
DST time zone abbreviation:                             PDT
DST offset from standard time:                          1:00:00 AHEAD
DST Start: First Sunday of April at     2:00:00 am
DST End:   Last Sunday in October at    2:00:00 am
```

If any of the information is incorrect, change it on this form. You might need to change the Time server type field. If this is the first server, it can be either a primary server or a single reference server. Refer to the worksheets you developed in Chapter 15 for the information you need to fill out on this menu. When the menu is complete, press F10 to continue the installation.

NOTE: If you install other servers after the first NetWare v.4 server, the Time server type field for those servers shows Secondary. *This is appropriate because the first server is the primary time server.*

Step 13: Specifying the Server Context

NOTE: If you are installing a secondary server (not the first NetWare v.4 server), refer to Step 13A.

Next, you see the following menu for specifying the server's context:

```
            Directory Services Server Context
Company or Organization:
Level 1 (Sub)Organizational Unit (optional):
Level 2 (Sub)Organizational Unit (optional):
Level 3 (Sub)Organizational Unit (optional):

Server Context:

Administrator Name:
Password
```

Refer to your worksheet and the section "Specifying the Server Context" in Chapter 15 for information on filling out this menu. Example directory trees and methods for specifying them on this menu are given there.

■ If you need to specify more than three levels of organizational units, type them into the Server Context field, separating each with a period.

■ If you want to enter a country code, type it at the end of the Server Context field. For example, you could type .C=US to specify the country code for the United States. However, Novell doesn't recommend using country codes because they add some complications when typing name contexts.

Step 13A: Specifying a Secondary Server Context

If you are installing a secondary server (not the first NetWare v.4 server), the following menu appears so that you can specify an administrator for this server:

```
Administrator Name: CN=Admin.O=
Password
```

■ If you are the ADMIN user for the first server and you want to be the administrator for this server, type the top-level organization name you specified on the first server. Just start typing in the field to change it.

■ If you want to grant another user supervisor rights to this server, specify his or her full name context. In the example shown next, the user AColgan, who belongs to the Administration department of the western division of Cambrian Corporation, is named supervisor. Note that this user object must have already been created.

```
                    Enter the Administrator Name:
>CN=AColgan.OU=Administration.OU=DivWest.O=CambrianCorp
```

The next screen to appear recommends the context of the first NetWare server, but you can change any field. In the following example, the Sales department in the eastern division office of the Cambrian Corporation is specified as the location for the server. Note that the full context is listed at the bottom. If you need to specify more than three levels, add them directly to the Server Context field.

```
                 Directory Services Server Context
Company or Organization:                      CambrianCorp
Level 1 (Sub)Organizational Unit (optional):  DivEast
Level 2 (Sub)Organizational Unit (optional):  Sales
Level 3 (Sub)Organizational Unit (optional):
Server Context: OU=Sales.OU=DivEast.O=CambrianCorp
```

NOTE: If the branch you specify for the server context does not already exist, it is added to the NetWare Directory Services tree.

Step 14: Edit the Startup Files

The next to the last step before exiting the NetWare installation is to verify the NetWare startup files. The parameters you specified during NetWare setup, such as the disk and LAN driver types, directory tree context, and other information, are saved in these files as commands that execute whenever you start the server. You can add more commands to these files, if you like.

NOTE: You can add or change commands in the NetWare startup files now, or at any time. Refer to Chapter 17 for instructions.

The New STARTUP.NCF menu appears. Unless you have specific commands you need to enter in this file now, press F10 to save it. A third party product you have installed might provide directions for entering commands in the file, for example.

Next, the New AUTOEXEC.NCF File menu appears. Press F10 to save it, unless you have specific instructions to add commands to it. Chapter 17 discusses changes you can make following the installation.

Step 15: Other Installation Options

You can install additional (optional) products at this time. The following menu appears:

Note that you can exit INSTALL at this time and reenter it again at a later time to select any of the options on this menu.

- ■ Select the first item to create a floppy disk that contains registration information, which you can send to Novell.

- ■ Choose the second option if you've upgraded from a NetWare v.3.1*x* server and you have printer support on the server to upgrade.

- Choose the third item to install support for other languages. You'll need disks that contain different language support files to complete this step. Contact Novell to obtain disks for other languages.

- Choose the last item to add support for other protocols, specifically TCP/IP, on the server. This is covered in Chapter 18.

NOTE: *To install a product that is not listed, press the* INS *key and then insert the first disk for that product in the disk drive.*

Step 16: You're Done—Now You Can Exit

You have completed the NetWare installation. You can now refer to Chapter 17 for information about customizing the server. There are a number of startup commands you might need to add that customize or alter the settings of the server. If you want to make the changes now, move on to Chapter 17, otherwise proceed as instructed below.

Press ENTER to exit the INSTALL program. You see the server console screen, which displays the name of your server as a prompt. There are a number of actions you can perform at the console, including the following:

- Type LOAD MONITOR to view information about the server, such as disk and LAN driver information, processor utilization, and memory utilization.

- On the MONITOR screen, choose Memory Utilization. If the Percent Free field indicates less than 20%, you should add more memory. On a new server this is unlikely to be the case, but it's a good idea to check this field periodically as users access the server and loadable modules are installed.

If you changed any commands or added any commands to the startup files, you should reboot the server as follows:

1. At the console prompt, type **DOWN**. This closes all binderies, directory services, and volumes.

2. Type **EXIT** to return to the DOS prompt. You might need to place the INSTALL disk back in its drive to fully exit.

3. To restart the server, make sure you are in the SERVER.40 directory (or the directory where you loaded the server files) and type **SERVER**.

CHAPTER 17

T his chapter covers mandatory and optional tasks you perform after installing the NetWare v.4 operating system on the server. Many of the tasks described here involve loading additional modules, such as support for uninterruptible power supplies, other name spaces, and protocols besides IPX. You don't need to be at a work-station to perform these tasks. The next chapter describes how to set up workstations so you can log into the network as the ADMIN user.

Post-Installation Procedures

Methods for Starting the Server

The SERVER.EXE file on the DOS partition starts the NetWare v.4 server. This file is located in a directory called SERVER.40, or a name you specified during installation. It runs automatically if you instructed INSTALL to add it to the AUTOEXEC.BAT file during the installation. If not, you'll need to switch to the directory and type **SERVER**.

SERVER executes the STARTUP.NCF that is stored in the same directory on the DOS partition where SERVER.EXE is stored. SERVER also executes AUTOEXEC.NCF, which is in the SYS:SYSTEM directory on the NetWare partition. These files contain commands to load the disk drivers and LAN drivers you specified during the installation. In this chapter, you'll see how to add commands and startup parameters to those files.

The SERVER command has several startup parameters, described here, that you can use to test or troubleshoot the server. You add these parameters to the SERVER command line if necessary.

-S Use this option, followed by a filename, when you want to load an alternate STARTUP.NCF file. Include a path if the file is in a directory other than the current boot directory. For example, to execute commands in a file called ALTSTART.NCF instead of STARTUP.NCF, you would type the following:

```
SERVER -S ALTSTART.NCF
```

-NA Using this option prevents the commands in AUTOEXEC.NCF from executing. Use this option to prevent a driver you want to replace from loading.

-NS Using this option prevents both the STARTUP.NCF and AUTOEXEC.NCF files from executing. As with the -NA option, use this option to change the way the server boots.

-C Use this option to change the block size of the cache buffers. You must specify the new size. Increasing the buffer size can improve performance. For example, to specify a buffer size of 8KB, start NetWare with the following command:

```
SERVER -C 8
```

The Server Console

The server console displays the name of the server and a flashing cursor. As with the DOS prompt, you issue commands to the operating system from it. The console is not the same as a workstation connection, however. At a workstation, you can access programs that run in the DOS, OS/2, or other operating system environments. At the NetWare console, you can only issue NetWare console commands that set server parameters and options, or load NetWare Loadable Modules.

NOTE: *Press* ALT-ESC *to switch among loaded modules and the console command prompt.*

NetWare Loadable Modules

NetWare Loadable Modules (NLMs) are executable programs that run at the server and provide services to network users. You load NLMs by typing the LOAD command followed by the name of the module. NetWare includes a number of NLMs for monitoring and maintaining the network, including SERVMAN (Server Manager) and MONITOR, discussed later in this chapter. NLMs are also available from third parties. For example, you might purchase a client-server database program in which the server portion is an NLM. In this way, the database runs directly on the server and takes full advantage of NetWare's efficient file handling mechanisms.

The LOAD command is used extensively at the server console to load NLMs. You simply type LOAD followed by the name of the NLM. Once the NLM is loaded, you can load other modules or execute other commands at the console prompt. Some NLMs display menus or other screens that hide the console prompt. Simply press ALT-ESC to return to the prompt. Alternatively, you can quit the module and return to the prompt. The UNLOAD command is used to remove an NLM from memory.

To avoid the need to type a search path every time you load the NLM, specify a search path as follows, replacing *servername* and *path* with the path to the directory where the NLM is stored:

SEARCH ADD *servername:path*

If the NLM uses a message file of a different language than English, set up the language before loading the NLM with the LANGUAGE command, as shown here:

LANGUAGE *xx*

Replace *xx* with one of the following numbers, depending on the language support you need:

Number	Language
0	Canadian French
1	Chinese
2	Danish
3	Dutch
4	English
5	Finnish
6	French
7	German
8	Italian
9	Japanese
10	Korean
11	Norwegian
12	Portuguese
13	Russian
14	Spanish
15	Swedish

You can also change the keyboard type used at the console from the U.S. English default. Type **LOAD KEYB** and then pick a different keyboard type from the list that appears.

Providing Operating System Protection

Some NetWare Loadable Modules may be unsafe to run in the so-called "Operating System (OS) Domain." This is the core of the operating system where modules can run most efficiently. However, a faulty NLM running in the OS Domain can corrupt memory. If you are running a new NLM and you suspect that it could be faulty, you can run and test it for a period of time in the OS Protected Domain where it will not corrupt memory.

NOTE: Not all NLMs are capable of running in the OS Protected Domain. Check with the vendor for more information.

To load an NLM in the OS Protected Domain, type the following commands at the server:

```
LOAD DOMAIN
DOMAIN=OS_PROTECTED
```

Now you are ready to load the NLM that needs testing. Type the following command, replacing *nlm-name* with the name of the NLM you want to run:

LOAD *nlm-name*

To restore the normal OS Domain so you can load other NLMs that you know are not faulty, type the following command:

```
DOMAIN=OS
```

You can check the status of NLMs and the domains they are running in by typing **DOMAIN**. You'll see a list of NLMs running in the OS Domain and a list of NLMs running in the OS Protected Domain. To move an NLM from the OS Protected Domain to the OS Domain, you must first unload it with the UNLOAD command, then follow the procedures above to load it in the OS Domain.

Name Space Support

You can store files from other operating systems on the NetWare server in special areas called *alternate name spaces*. For example, you can store Macintosh files on the NetWare server. Macintosh files are unlike DOS files in that they have two parts—a data fork and a resource fork. The *data fork* holds all the data for the file, and the *resource fork* holds other information about the file, such as its attributes.

To support Macintosh files on a NetWare server, you first need to load the MAC.NAM name space support module at the server where the files will be stored, then add the name space to a volume on that server using the ADD NAME SPACE command. It's a good idea to place name space support on volumes other than SYS:, and it is best if you can dedicate a volume to the name space. Name spaces have different memory and disk requirements, so it's best to isolate them if possible.

NetWare also provides name space support for OS/2 and UNIX files, which use different file-naming conventions than DOS files.

NOTE: Each name space support you load increases the size of the directory tables. The tables may grow so large that the server does not have enough memory to load the volume. You'll need to increase server memory or move the name space to another server.

To load name space support for Macintosh files, execute the following command at the server console:

```
LOAD MAC
```

To load name space support for OS/2, execute the following command at the server console:

```
LOAD OS2
```

NOTE: If you purchased the optional NetWare for NFS and NetWare for FTAM, refer to Chapter 19 for installation instructions.

After loading the name space module with the LOAD command, you need to add the name space to a volume. This is done with the ADD NAME SPACE command. You specify the name space to add and the name of the volume you want to add it to, using the following form:

ADD NAME SPACE *name* TO *volume*

Here, *name* is the name of the name space and *volume* is the name of the volume you want to add the name space to. You can list currently loaded name spaces by typing ADD NAME SPACE by itself.

The following command adds Macintosh name space support to the VOL1 volume:

```
ADD NAME SPACE MAC TO VOL1
```

To add OS/2 name space support to a volume called OS2VOL, you would type the following command:

```
ADD NAME SPACE OS2 TO OS2VOL
```

NOTE: *You may need more memory to support name space volumes.*

Installing CD-ROM Support

Novell's intention is to support CD-ROM drives in the server with the CDROM.NLM module, although support for some drives will not be available in the initial release of the product. While the information in this section is pending, it should provide enough information for you to load a CD-ROM when the support becomes available. The CD-ROM becomes a read-only volume that users can access like any other volume. To load CD-ROM support, type the following:

```
LOAD CDROM
```

Next, load the CD-ROM device driver as instructed in the CD-ROM manual.

Once the CD-ROM support is loaded, you can issue the following commands to check the status of the drives. Note that a CD-ROM drive is the *device*, and the disk within the drive is the *media.*

GETTING HELP   Display help information about CD-ROM drives.

CD HELP

LIST DEVICES   The following command displays a list of CD-ROM devices, including their device numbers, device names, media volume name, if any, and status (mounted or unmounted).

CD DEVICE LIST

LIST AVAILABLE MEDIA   The following command is similar to CD DEVICE LIST, but it doesn't display information if the CD-ROM device does not have media present. Thus the list is shorter.

CD VOLUME LIST

MOUNT CD-ROM MEDIA   The following command mounts the CD-ROM volume indicated by either typing its device number or device name. To decrease the amount of time it takes to mount new media, specify the /r parameter, which prevents the system from rebuilding index files for the media.

CD MOUNT *devicenumber/volumename* /r

DISMOUNT CD-ROM MEDIA   Dismounting a volume frees its resources for use by other server processes. The following command dismounts the CD-ROM volume you indicate. Type either the device number or device name, which you can get by executing CD DEVICE LIST or CD VOLUME LIST.

CD DISMOUNT *devicenumber/volumename*

LIST CD-ROM DIRECTORY   The following command lists the directory of the CD-ROM you specify. Type either the device number or volume name.

CD DIR *devicenumber/volumename*

CHANGE THE MEDIA   The following command lets you change the disk in a CD-ROM device. It dismounts the existing disk and prompts you to insert the new media, which it mounts.

CD CHANGE *devicenumber/volumename*

Installing Uninterruptible Power Supply (UPS) Support

A UPS provides backup power to the server, usually long enough for users to log out of the system, for files to close properly, and for disk caches to write to disk. However, the server must "know" that the UPS is supplying it with backup power. Typically, a cable connection between the UPS and the server provides the signal the server needs to begin its shutdown procedure. UPS.NLM provides the software that allows the server to monitor the UPS's signals.

Many older UPSs connect to Novell DCB boards or mouse ports. The UPS.NLM module supplied with NetWare supports the following connections:

DCB	Disk controller board
EDCB	Enhanced disk controller board
STANDALONE	Novell stand-alone UPS card
KEYCARD	Novell keycard with UPS connection
MOUSE	Mouse port
Other	Vendor's interface card

Newer models provide more elaborate features and their own server interface cards. If you are installing a UPS that comes with its own interface card, use the Other option listed in the preceding table. Some UPSs may come with their own NLMs, which you should copy to the SYS:SYSTEM directory on the server; then follow the instructions in the UPS manual.

To install a UPS, execute the LOAD UPS command as shown here (the command is typed on one line):

LOAD UPS TYPE=*name* PORT=*number* DISCHARGE=*number*
RECHARGE=*number*

Replace the parameters with values as follows:

TYPE=*name*   Replace *name* with the name of the interface board that has a UPS connection, as listed in the preceding table.

PORT=*number*   Replace *number* with the port address of the interface card. Possible values are

DCB: 286, 28E, 326, 32E, 346, 34E
EDCB: 320, 328, 380, 388
STANDALONE: 231, 240
KEYCARD: 230, 238
MOUSE: Not required
Other: See vendor documentation

DISCHARGE=*number*   This is the amount of time it takes the UPS to discharge normally. It specifies how long the server can operate on battery power before it must shut down. Replace *number* with the number of minutes the UPS is rated for backup, based on the UPS's manual.

RECHARGE=*number*   Replace *number* with the number of minutes it takes to recharge a depleted battery.

After UPS.NLM has been loaded, you can change its discharge and recharge times by executing the UPS TIME command at the server console, as shown next. The values for the settings are the same as for those just described.

UPS TIME DISCHARGE=*number* RECHARGE=*number*

To view the status of the UPS, type the following command:

```
UPS STATUS
```

You'll see a menu similar to the following illustration. It indicates whether the server is running on commercial power or battery power; the remaining time if the battery is being discharged; the status of the battery (recharged, low, or being recharged); the recharge time; and the amount of time before shutdown if the server is running on battery power.

```
             UPS Status for Server Mona_Lisa
          Power being used: Battery
   Discharge time requested: 25 min.      Remaining: 10 min.
            Battery status: low
    Recharge time requested: 200 min.     Remaining: 0 min.
Current network power status: Server going down in 5 minutes

NOTICE: If your battery is over 6 months old, you may need to
        lower the discharge time.  (Consult the UPS
        documentation for details.)
```

Console Security Measures

Once you've set all the server parameters and loaded modules, you can use the options discussed in the following sections to set security at the console and prevent others from changing the settings. Of course, to provide maximum security, you should also physically lock the server in a special room or cabinet to prevent theft, or to prevent someone from turning it off.

Securing the Console

Type the following command at the server console prompt to secure the console:

```
SECURE CONSOLE
```

When this command is issued, the following security measures are put into effect. Note that this command does not fully lock the console—you can still load and unload NLMs. The option discussed in the next section fully locks the console.

- NLMs will only load if they are located on the SYS:SYSTEM directory of the server. This prevents intruders from loading NLMs that might cause damage to the server or access secure information. If SECURE CONSOLE is not executed, intruders could load NLMs from a diskette, from a volume on the server they have access to, or even from a workstation floppy drive if they are running the RCONSOLE program.

- Access to the operating system debugger, which intruders could use to look at data on the server, is prevented. (You can bet that only hard-core intruders will be doing this.)

- Integrity of the accounting system is protected by ensuring that intruders can't change the date and time. It also ensures that users can't change the date and time to bypass their login time restrictions. Only users with console operator rights can change the date and time.

- DOS is removed from memory, and the memory is made available to NetWare processes.

By removing DOS from the server memory, an intruder can't return to DOS and load a program that could access the server's secure data. If DOWN is typed at the server console, the server reboots since DOS is not in memory. To make this effective, you must also set a power-on password for the server to prevent the intruder from loading DOS from diskette.

Locking the Console

To establish password-only access to the console and fully protect it from intruders, follow the procedure described next to lock the console, and also execute the SECURE CONSOLE command just discussed.

1. Type **LOAD MONITOR**.

2. Choose "Lock File Server Console."

3. Type in a password and then retype the password to verify it.

NOTE: *The password can be different every time you lock the console. Make sure you lock the console before anyone else does to prevent yourself from being locked out.*

Shutting Down the Server

You may need to shut down the server for maintenance or hardware expansion. Doing so is a two-step process. Never simply turn the server off without following these two steps.

   1. Type **DOWN**.

   The DOWN command properly closes the filing systems and most importantly, saves data in cache memory to disk. The directory and file allocation tables are also properly updated. Note that the file system of a server that has been shut down is no longer available for network use, but the file server is still available as a network node and can handle network traffic. From the server console, you can issue console commands. To exit to DOS, do the following:

   2. Type **EXIT**.

   This command shuts down all network communications at the server and displays the DOS prompt.

The INSTALL Utility

You can reenter the INSTALL program to make changes to the NetWare operating system after you have installed it on the server. For example, you could modify the size of volumes or change their names. You can also expand a volume by adding a drive, then INSTALL to partition it and add it to an existing volume.

   To take a look at INSTALL's maintenance features, type the following at the server console:

```
LOAD INSTALL
```

In a moment, the INSTALL menu appears.

```
┌────────────────────────────────────────┐
│ Select an Installation Method          │
├────────────────────────────────────────┤
│ Install a new v4.00 server             │
│ Upgrade a v3.1x or v4.0 server         │
│ Maintenance/Selective Install          │
└────────────────────────────────────────┘
```

Choose the last option, "Maintenance/Selective Install," on this menu to display the Installation Options menu shown next. From here you can make changes to volumes and other server features.

```
┌─────────────────────────────────────────────────────────────────┐
│                    Installation Options                         │
├─────────────────────────────────────────────────────────────────┤
│ Disk Driver Options  (Configure/Load/Unload Disk Drivers)      │
│ LAN Driver Options   (Configure/Load/Unload LAN Drivers)       │
│ Disk Options         (Configure/Mirror/Test Disk Partitions)   │
│ Volume Options       (Configure/Mount/Dismount Volumes)        │
│ Copy Files Option    (Install NetWare System Files)            │
│ Directory Options    (Install NetWare Directory Services)      │
│ NCF File Options     (Create/Edit Server Startup Files)        │
│ Product Options      (Install/Reconfigure Products)            │
└─────────────────────────────────────────────────────────────────┘
```

DISK DRIVER OPTIONS   Select this option to load a new disk driver after installing a new disk controller, or to change the configuration of an already installed disk driver.

LAN DRIVER OPTIONS   Select this option to load a new LAN driver after installing a new LAN card, or to change the configuration of an already installed LAN driver.

DISK OPTIONS   Select this option to do any of the following:

- Create a new partition on a disk you've just added to the system
- Change the partitioning of an existing disk
- Change the Hot Fix redirection area of an existing disk
- Delete a partition
- Mirror and unmirror partitions
- Test the surface of a disk

VOLUME OPTIONS   You can use this option to change the volume configuration of existing partitions (doing so destroys data on those volumes), or to allocate the space on a new disk partition to existing or new volumes.

COPY FILES OPTION   Use this option to install or reinstall the NetWare system files.

DIRECTORY OPTIONS   Use this option only when necessary to reinstall the NetWare directory services.

NCF FILE OPTIONS   Choose this option to manually create or edit the NetWare startup files AUTOEXEC.NCF and STARTUP.NCF.

PRODUCT OPTIONS   Choose this option to install additional products on the server, such as non-U.S. language support, NetWare for Macintosh, NetWare for NFS, NetWare for SAA, and other protocols.

NOTE: Select "Product Options" to install TCP/IP support at the server as outlined in Chapter 19.

The SERVMAN Server Management Utility

SERVMAN, along with the MONITOR NLM, is your window on the performance and reliability of the server. While some of the information MONITOR displays tends to be technical, it provides information that can help you locate the source of server, disk, and LAN problems. A further description of the utilities can be found in Chapters 33 through 36.

SERVMAN displays information about the server configuration and features. You can also use SERVMAN to change SET options that alter the server's environment. To load SERVMAN, type the following at the server console:

```
LOAD SERVMAN
```

In a moment, you'll see two menus. The top menu (called GENERAL INFORMATION) displays statistics about the server, including the following useful information.

Processor Utilization   The percentage of the server's CPU that is in use is displayed. This number changes as users log in or out and work with applications or files. This value should remain below 80 percent; otherwise you may need to upgrade the processor or move some processes, applications, or heavy users to another server.

Server Up Time   The amount of time the server has been up is significant. NetWare adjusts its settings over time to match the load placed on it by workstations and internal processes. The longer the server is up, the more likely the settings will match those required for everyday use. If a server has been up only a few hours or days, operating information displayed in SERVMAN and MONITOR is not likely to be representative of your system's normal requirements.

Processor Speed   This is the speed rating of the processor in your system. It is determined by the CPU clock speed (25 MHz, 33 MHz, 66 MHz, and so on); the CPU type (80386, 80486, Pentium, and so on); and the number of memory wait states. For comparison, a 16 MHz 80386 processor is rated at 120 while a 33 MHz 80486 processor may have a rating of 260. Unusually low values may indicate that the processor has been set at a slower clock speed. Check the front panel or run diagnostics for the system to make sure it is running at its fastest clock speed.

The Available Options menu provides a list of options you can view or change. The *Console Set Commands* option is discussed here.

```
╔══════════════════════════════╗
║      Available Options        ║
╠══════════════════════════════╣
║ Console Set Commands          ║
║ IPX/SPX Configuration         ║
║ Storage Information           ║
║ Volume Information            ║
║ Network Information           ║
║ Exit Server Manager           ║
╚══════════════════════════════╝
```

Console Set Commands   Selecting this option displays another menu (shown in the following illustration), which lets you change operating system parameters for the items listed.

```
╔══════════════════════════════╗
║          Categories           ║
╠══════════════════════════════╣
║ 1.  Communications            ║
║ 2.  Memory                    ║
║ 3.  File Caching              ║
║ 4.  Directory Caching         ║
║ 5.  File System               ║
║ 6.  Locks                     ║
║ 7.  Transaction Tracking      ║
║ 8.  Disk                      ║
║ 9.  Time                      ║
║ 10.NCP                        ║
║ 11.Miscellaneous              ║
╚══════════════════════════════╝
```

SERVMAN simply provides a quick way to browse the commands and automatically insert them in the startup files. Some commands take effect only after restarting the server; others can be set on or off during the current session for testing and benchmarking purposes. If you make changes to console SET commands from within SERVMAN, you are asked if you want to save those changes to the AUTOEXEC.NCF or STARTUP.NCF file if the commands are normally placed in those files. The following menu appears:

```
╔══════════════════════════════════════════╗
║             Update Options               ║
╠══════════════════════════════════════════╣
║ Update AUTOEXEC.NCF & STARTUP.NCF now     ║
║ Update TIMESYNC.CFG now                   ║
║ Copy all set parameters to file           ║
║ Exit to main menu                         ║
╚══════════════════════════════════════════╝
```

Altering Server Set Parameters

As mentioned previously, you can use the SERVMAN utility to view and change the operating parameters of the server. You can also view the current settings by typing **SET** at the server console prompt and then choosing the type of settings you want to see.

NOTE: NetWare uses default settings that should be adequate in most cases. You may need to change settings depending on your hardware configuration or the NLMs you are running at the server. The settings discussed in the following sections are not mandatory. You can set them at a later date, after the server has had time to run under the load of users and NLMs.

Warnings and Alerts

Some of the settings simply turn on warning messages to alert you of conditions on the server. For example, a warning message might indicate that a network adapter is failing. You can then view its status in MONITOR. If multiple cards exist, be sure to check the statistics for each card.

It's a good idea to occasionally check the error log since it contains a list of error messages that have scrolled off the screen. You might want to make this a daily or weekly procedure. A text file called SYS$LOG.ERR is created in the server's SYSTEM directory. You can view this file with the server's EDIT utility by typing the following at the console (or from a remote console):

```
LOAD EDIT
```

Type in the name of the error log file to view its contents.

Communications Settings

The Communications settings from the Categories menu let you control the size and quantity of the communications buffers in order to improve server performance (by increasing the values), to correct problems, or to free memory for other uses. Refer to Chapter 36 for more details.

Memory Settings

Memory settings let you adjust the way memory is used in the server. Refer to Chapter 34 for more details.

File Caching Settings

The file caching system is one of the most important features of NetWare. It ensures that files are available on a timely basis by keeping the most used information in memory. Most of the default file cache settings are adequate, but you can change some settings by accessing these options. Refer to Chapter 35 for more details.

Directory Caching Settings

Directory caching ensures that files are easily located by keeping the directory tables in memory. Note that directory caching and file caching must be balanced. If you provide too many directory caches, memory is taken away from file caches, and vice versa. You can check memory and cache statistics with MONITOR (covered later in the chapter) and then make changes to the settings in the Directory Caching menu option. Refer to Chapter 35 for more details.

File System Settings

Use the options on the File System menu to set warnings for low volumes, to control what happens to purged files, and to set file compression parameters. Refer to Chapter 35 for more details.

Locks Settings

Applications may fail to run because they cannot open enough files or because there are not enough record locks. If this is the case, try doubling the four settings in the Locks menu. In some cases, you may need to reduce their values below the default settings. For example, a workstation may continuously request too many resources from the server.

Transaction Tracking Settings

The Transaction Tracking System (TTS) protects database files that might otherwise be corrupted if a server crashes during an incomplete transaction. The incomplete transaction is completely backed out and must be reentered. When you reboot the server after a crash, the TTS will ask if you want to back out the transactions. You can set "Auto TTS Backout Flag" to on if you want the backouts to occur automatically when the server starts. Some supervisors prefer to monitor the backout process themselves, and so leave "Auto TTS Backout Flag" off. However, you can store the information in a log file called TTS$LOG.ERR (in the SYS:SYSTEM directory) by setting "TTS Abort Dump Flag" to on.

NOTE: Check with database vendors to make sure their products support TTS.

Disk Settings

The most important setting on the Disk menu is "Enable Disk Read After Write Verify." When on (the default), data written to disk is checked to make sure it was written correctly. Setting this feature off exposes your data to possible corruption, but almost doubles disk write speed. You can safely set this feature off if your disk controller verifies on its own, as most SCSI drives do. Refer to Chapter 35 for more details.

Time Settings

The settings on the Time menu are for the time synchronization system, which ensures that all servers on a NetWare Directory Services tree use the same time to record events. The file TIMESYNC.CFG holds commands that set the time system parameters when the server boots. Time commands do not belong in the AUTOEXEC.NCF or STARTUP.NCF file.

NCP Settings

Settings on this menu control NetWare Core Protocols (NCP). An important option in this category is "SET NCP Packet Signature Option." It sets the level at which a packet signature option protects against packet forgery. Refer to the NetWare manuals for more details.

Miscellaneous Settings

There are a number of miscellaneous settings, some of which enable the display of warning messages. Scan through the options under the menu, watching the help menus as you go.

- Set "Display Disk Device Alerts" on to display activity messages about disk drives, such as when they have been added, activated, deactivated, or shut down. Such messages can help you isolate disk problems.

- Set "Display Lost Interrupt Alerts" on to display a message whenever a driver or board makes a request for service that is dropped. These alerts indicate problems with a driver or board. Follow the steps in the previous section, "Warnings and Alerts," for detecting which board is causing the alerts.

- Set "Display Spurious Interrupt Alerts" on to display alerts whenever one board creates an interrupt that is defined for another device. A board that creates these messages typically must be replaced.

MONITOR Utility

MONITOR is a utility you can use to view the activities and status of the server. While some of the information it displays is technical and designed for programmers who are developing NLMs, it provides useful information that can help you isolate bottlenecks in your network and resolve other problems. To start MONITOR, type the following:

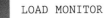 LOAD MONITOR

In a moment, you'll see a display and menu similar to the following illustration, which shows statistics about the server and an Available Options menu.

```
                    Information For Server MONA_LISA
 Server Up Time: 28 Days  6 Hours 48 Minutes   7 Seconds
 Utilization:                        23    Packet Receive Buffers:   20
 Original Cache Buffers:          1,516    Directory Cache Buffers:  32
 Total Cache Buffers:               928    Service Processes:        18
 Dirty Cache Buffers:                 5    Connections in Use:       14
 Current Disk Requests:               2    Open Files:               22

                       Available Options
                    Connection Information
                    Disk Information
                    LAN/WAN Information
                    System Module Information
                    Lock File Server Console
                    File Open / Lock Activity
                    Cache Utilization
                    Processor Utilization
```

Some of the information displayed at the top is similar to what you see when running SERVMAN, such as the server name and the amount of time it has been operating. "Utilization" is an indication of the amount of time the processor is busy. The cache information indicates the number of buffers available, with "Dirty Cache Buffers" indicating buffers that need to be written to disk. The remaining information indicates current settings for the functions listed. Several things you can check on a regular basis are described next as examples. Refer to Chapter 33 for more details.

Checking Server Memory

All the memory in a NetWare server that is not used by NLMs and other processes is used to cache the disk storage system. A large cache improves performance because information can be obtained from memory rather than the disk. As NLMs are loaded at the server, the amount of memory available for the cache is reduced. You can check whether a reduced cache is affecting performance by checking the cache hits value, as described below.

1. Load Monitor.

2. Choose "Cache Utilization" from the Available Options menu.

3. Note the "Long Term Cache Hits" value.

A *cache hit* occurs when information is found in the cache and does not have to be read from disk. The cache hits value must be evaluated over time. A new server without any attached workstations will show a high percentage, but you should write this value in a log for future reference. As you add NLMs and users begin to access the server, continue to monitor the cache hits. It should remain at about 90 percent. If it drops below 90 percent, add more RAM to the server or add other servers to take up some of the load.

Checking Utilization

After you've loaded NLMs and set other features at the server, you should make sure the server can handle the new processing loads adequately. Start by loading MONITOR with the following command:

```
LOAD MONITOR
```

On the upper window of the MONITOR menu, note the "Utilization" percentage. If it is equal to or greater than 80 percent, one of the loaded modules or other processes may be monopolizing the system.

To investigate further, you can view the utilization of each process. Choose "Processor Utilization" from the Available Options menu, then press F3 to view a list of loaded processes and the percentage load that they put on the system.

If you locate a module that seems to monopolize the system, you can unload it. However, if the module is necessary, you might need to move it or other modules to another server on the network, or upgrade the existing server with a more powerful processor.

Remote Console

Console commands only execute at the server, but you can still issue those commands from a remote workstation by using the remote console loadable module (REMOTE.NLM) and the workstation RCONSOLE.EXE command.

Instructions for configuring the remote console are presented in Chapter 33.

Other Console Commands

Console commands that display useful information about the new server are listed here. This is only a small sampling of the commands available at the server.

CONFIG   The CONFIG command quickly displays a useful list of information about the server and its network communications system, such as the loaded LAN drivers and their communications protocols.

Display Networks   This command lists all the networks that are known on the network.

Display Servers   This command lists all servers that are known on the network.

Memory   This command displays the memory installed in the server that the NetWare operating system can address.

Mirror Status   This command displays a list of mirrored logical partitions and their current status.

Modules   The Modules command displays a list of currently loaded modules, including their version number and creation date.

Protocol   The Protocol command lists the protocols currently registered on the server. It is used to register additional protocols.

Volumes   The Volumes command displays volume information, including the name spaces loaded on them.

CHAPTER 18

T his chapter covers the installation of the workstation software supplied with NetW for DOS, Windows 3.1, and OS/2 workstations. The installation is simple and menu driven. You run an install program from a diskette in the floppy drive that configures the workstation, then reboot the workstation and let users log in.

Installing Work-stations

If NetWare Is on CD-ROM

If you have purchased NetWare on CD-ROM, you will need to extract the workstation software and place it on disk in order to install workstations. Follow the steps given here, which assume the CD-ROM drive is installed and you can access its files.

1. Format four high-density disks for DOS or three for OS/2. Label the disk according to the following table. This is important because the workstation installation program asks for disks by these names.

Disk	DOS Label	OS/2 Label
1	WSDOS_1	WSOS2_1
2	WSWIN_1	WSOS2_2
3	WSDRV_1	WSDRV_1
4	WSDRV_2	

2. Switch to one of the following directories on the CD-ROM:

   CLIENT\DOSWIN   To create DOS and Windows workstation diskettes

   CLIENT\OS2   To create OS/2 workstation diskettes

   NOTE: *If you are installing a language other than English, use the command SET NWLANGUAGE=**language,** replacing language with a name. You'll find a subdirectory with this language name branching from one of the directories listed in step 2. Make sure this SET command is entered in each workstation's CONFIG.SYS file.*

3. Now enter the MAKEDISK *drive* command, where *drive* is the letter of the drive where the diskettes are located. Be sure to insert the diskettes according to the labels you created.

The NetWare DOS Requester

The NetWare DOS Requester is a set of modules that replace the NETX.COM utility in previous versions of NetWare. The DOS Requester intercepts requests for NetWare service and sends them to a module called IPXODI, which adds header information and packages data for delivery over the network.

DOS Requester Modules

After the workstation software is installed, you load it by running a batch file called STARTNET.BAT (normally located in the NWCLIENT directory). The batch file executes the following commands:

```
LSL
NE2000.COM (or other LAN driver)
IPXODI
VLM
```

LSL (Link Support Layer)

The LSL is a software driver that directs traffic between multiple communications protocols and a network interface card driver that supports Novell's Open Data-Link Interface (ODI) specification, as shown in Figure 18-1. Think of the LSL as an intermediary or switchboard operator that receives packets and directs them to the correct protocol stack, or sends packets from different protocols out over the same network card.

There are several possible LSL configurations. The LSL can act as an intermediary between the following:

■ A single network card running a single protocol stack

■ A single network card and multiple protocol stacks

■ Multiple interface cards and a single protocol stack

■ Multiple interface cards and multiple protocols stacks

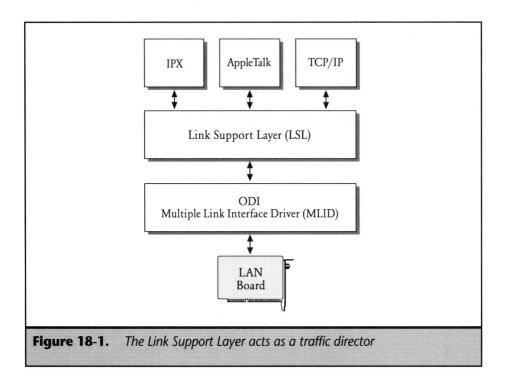

Figure 18-1. *The Link Support Layer acts as a traffic director*

LAN Driver

The LAN driver listed in the STARTNET.BAT file depends on the network interface card selected during the installation of the workstation software. The LAN driver provides hardware-specific information about the network card installed in the system. Drivers written to the ODI Multiple Link Interface Driver (MLID) specification are not directly linked to a communications protocol stack. The MLID simply handles media access information and lets the LSL do all the protocol-specific handling.

IPXODI

As shown in Figure 18-1, the LSL driver sits between the IPX protocol stack and the network interface card driver. IPXODI is the driver that loads an IPX protocol stack and attaches it to the LSL layer. IPXODI is the only protocol that is automatically installed at the server. Other stacks must be optionally installed. You need to purchase the Novell LAN WorkPlace products (DOS, Macintosh, or OS/2) to provide ODI compatible TCP/IP protocol stacks for workstations.

VLM (Virtual Loadable Module)

VLM is an executable (EXE) file that loads the DOS Requester software. The DOS Requester has the all-important job of determining whether requests for service by the workstation should go to DOS or go out over the network to a server. VLM.EXE is only the tip of the iceberg, however. It loads the following modules, which you can see if you list the contents of the NWCLIENT directory:

CONN.VLM   The connection manager that lets a workstation connect with one or more servers simultaneously. It tracks network services and storage devices available to users on the network.

IPXNCP.VLM   This is the IPX packet handling module.

AUTO.VLM   This module provides reconnection services.

TRAN.VLM   This module directs information to the correct transport protocol, such as IPX or TCP/IP.

NDS.VLM   This module provides access to NetWare v.4 Directory Services.

BIND.VLM   This module provides access to bindery-based (pre-NetWare v.4) services.

NWP.VLM   This is a multiplexer module that directs information to either NetWare v.4 Directory Services, bindery-based (pre-NetWare v.4) services, or Personal NetWare, depending on which is in use. The multiplexer allows any or all of these to be mixed.

RSA.VLM   This module provides RSA (Rivest, Shamir, and Adleman) encryption and authentication capabilities.

FIO.VLM   This is the file input/output module. Control of cached or non-cached read/writes, burst mode-based read/writes, and Large Internet Packet read/writes are handled by this module.

GENERAL.VLM   This is a module that provides functionality to the other modules listed here.

REDIR.VLM   This module provides the actual DOS redirection services.

PRINT.VLM   This module provides print redirection from the workstation to printers attached to the network.

NETX.VLM   This is an optional module that provides backward compatibility to previous versions of the NetWare shell. Some applications need the functions available in the previous shell.

Installing the NetWare DOS Requester

The NetWare DOS Requester provides Open Data-Link Interface services so workstations can use several protocols to communicate with a variety of systems. ODI also allows the use of multiple frame types, such as Ethernet 802.2, 802.3, Ethernet II, and Ethernet SNAP.

To install the software, you run the INSTALL utility located on the NetWare Workstation for DOS disk (WSDOS_1), then make some optional changes to a configuration file called NET.CFG.

NOTE: The NET.CFG file discussed in Appendix B holds parameters that control the settings of those modules.

Here are some things you should know before beginning:

- By default, the software is installed in the directory C:\NWCLIENT, but you can specify another directory if necessary.

- You can choose to install support for Windows during the installation. Changes are made to the WIN.INI, SYSTEM.INI, and PROGMAN.INI (Program Manager) initialization files.

- The installation program will add a network startup command to the AUTOEXEC.BAT file, but you can prevent this and instead add the command to a separate batch file, such as NET.BAT.

- Be sure you know the type of network interface card installed in the workstation and its settings. Settings you may need to provide are

  Interrupt (IRQ)
  Frame type for Ethernet and Token Ring cards
  I/O port address
  Memory address range, if used
  Direct memory access (DMA) channel
  Slot number on MCA and EISA systems

- After installation, you can modify the NET.CFG file, which contains startup parameters for connecting with the network. There are a number of options for customizing the startup, which you can set in this file. In addition, if you need to change the hardware or software configuration, you can do that in this file. Options for the NET.CFG file are covered in Appendix B.

■ If workstations have similar hardware and software configurations, you can copy the NET.CFG file from one workstation to another once you make changes to it.

■ You might want to optimize the memory in your workstation before starting by loading utilities into high memory. Refer to your DOS manual for more details.

The INSTALL Utility

Once you've prepared the workstation by installing the network interface card, and once you know all the settings information you'll need, you are ready to run the installation routine. Insert the WSDOS_1 disk in a floppy drive, and type the following:

```
A:INSTALL
```

In a moment, the installation screen pictured in Figure 18-2 appears. Each setting you need to supply is listed by steps on the screen and described here:

1. Press ENTER in the "Step 1" field to change the directory where the client files are installed.

2. Press Y in the "Step 2" field to update the AUTOEXEC.BAT and CONFIG.SYS files with the commands listed. If you don't want to make network connections when the workstation boots, press N in this field and create an alternate startup file, as discussed in the next section, "Creating a Startup File." You'll need to add the LASTDRIVE=Z option to the CONFIG.SYS file on your own if you choose No.

3. Press Y in the "Step 3" field if you want to install Windows network software, then specify the directory where the Windows files are located.

4. Press ENTER in the "Step 4" field to select from a list of network drivers. You're asked to insert the driver disk. Scan through the list and press ENTER when the correct network card is highlighted. If you don't see a listing for the card, choose an option that it may be compatible with. For example, many Ethernet cards will work with the Novell Ethernet drivers. When you press ENTER, you are asked to supply interrupts, I/O ports, and other information. Press ESC after filling out the form.

5. Press ENTER here to start the installation, or scroll back up to change other options. Insert diskettes as requested.

6. After software installation, reboot the computer.

If the startup commands were placed in the AUTOEXEC.BAT file, the network connection is made and you are asked to log in. To log in as the ADMIN user, switch to the first network drive and use the following command, replacing *organization* with the name you specified for your organization container.

LOGIN .ADMIN.*organization*

Creating a Startup File

If you choose not to install the NetWare startup commands in your AUTOEXEC.BAT file, you can create a batch file that connects with the network, switches to the first network drive, and logs in with your login name. For example:

```
NWCLIENT\STARTNET
F:
LOGIN .ADMIN.CAMBRIANCORP
```

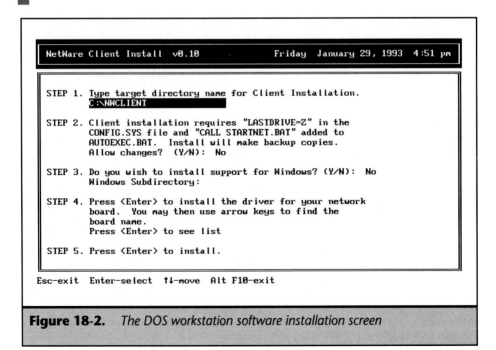

```
NetWare Client Install  v0.10                Friday  January 29, 1993  4:51 pm

    STEP 1. Type target directory name for Client Installation.
            C:\NWCLIENT

    STEP 2. Client installation requires "LASTDRIVE=Z" in the
            CONFIG.SYS file and "CALL STARTNET.BAT" added to
            AUTOEXEC.BAT.  Install will make backup copies.
            Allow changes?  (Y/N):  No

    STEP 3. Do you wish to install support for Windows? (Y/N):  No
            Windows Subdirectory:

    STEP 4. Press <Enter> to install the driver for your network
            board.  You may then use arrow keys to find the
            board name.
            Press <Enter> to see list

    STEP 5. Press <Enter> to install.

  Esc-exit  Enter-select  ↑↓-move  Alt F10-exit
```

Figure 18-2. *The DOS workstation software installation screen*

These commands assume the startup files are in the NWCLIENT directory, that the first network drive is drive F, and that the login name is ADMIN. Create a similar file for each user. You can avoid typing the context in the LOGIN command by specifying a context with the NAME CONTEXT option in the NET.CFG file.

Diskless Workstation Setup

If your network has diskless workstations, you can boot those workstations with a version of DOS that is stored in a special Remote Boot disk image file on the server. This file holds the image of a DOS boot disk. Network adapters in diskless workstations must have special boot PROMs that run a routine to automatically connect with a server and boot using the Remote Boot disk images.

Several image files can exist, each with a different boot configuration. For example, one image file might start DOS v.3, while another might start DOS v.5. You determine which image file a workstation accesses based on the workstation node address burned into its network adapter board.

The entire procedure for installing diskless workstations is straightforward and described in detail in the *NetWare Workstation for DOS and Windows* manual. Refer to the section in the manual, "Booting DOS Workstations from the Network," for more information.

The NET.CFG File

The NET.CFG configuration file contains settings used by the DOS Requester and other utilities when they load. Changes to NET.CFG are optional, and in most cases, you won't need to make changes. However, placing commands in the file can help you customize the environment of the workstation and overcome problems with software and hardware.

Refer to Appendix B and the *NetWare Workstation for DOS and Windows* manual for more information about the NET.CFG file.

Other Options and Utilities

The workstation software for NetWare 4 automatically supports packet burst mode and Large Internet Packet (LIP) exchange. In previous versions of NetWare, these were optionally installed.

Packet Burst Mode

Packet burst improves network communications by letting clients and servers transmit multiple packets of information without the need to reply to each packet. If for some reason you can't use packet burst (perhaps on the recommendation of a software vendor), you can disable it by adding the following line to the NET.CFG file. (Packet burst mode is also covered in Chapter 36.)

```
PB BUFFERS=0
```

Large Internet Packet Exchange

With the presence of a router, previous versions of NetWare automatically set packet size to 576 bytes. This ensured that packets could cross the router, since NetWare could not be sure what the router could handle. Large Internet Packet exchange in NetWare 4 lets clients and servers negotiate an appropriate packet size without the server specifying the 576-byte limit if a router is present. However, you must be aware of the packet size handling capability of the routers on your network. If any router cannot handle packets larger than 576 bytes, add the following option to the NET.CFG file to set LIP off:

```
LARGE INTERNET PACKETS = OFF
```

Task Switching Support (TBMI2.COM)

This utility allocates buffers used to virtualize IPX/SPX requests so you can run the MS-DOS v.5 DOSSHELL program or the Novell DR DOS v.6 TaskMAX utility to take advantage of task switching. If you are not running these task-switching applications, you do not need to load TBMI2.

Copy the TBMI2.COM utility on the Workstation for Windows diskette to the NWCLIENT directory. Execute the file by typing its name, then run the task-switching software. If you are not sure you need this utility, you can load it anyway, since it takes up little memory. After a while, you can check to see if applications are using TBMI2 by typing the following:

```
TBMI2 /D
```

If the Far Call Usage field is 0, the application is not using TBMI2, and you can run the application without it. If an application is using TBMI2, you can recover the memory it uses after running the application by typing the following command, which unloads TBMI2:

```
TBMI2 /U
```

Named Pipes Support (DOSNP.EXE)

This DOSNP.EXE utility extends DOS by giving it the capability to use remote Named Pipes. An OS/2 Named Pipes server must be present. Copy the utility from the NetWare Workstation WSDOS_1 diskette to the NWCLIENT directory and then execute it directly, or place a command in the AUTOEXEC.BAT file to execute it. You can get information about the command by typing

```
DOSNP /i
```

You can unload it by typing

```
DOSNP /u
```

Token Ring Networks Support (ROUTE.COM)

The ROUTE.COM utility loads the IBM Token Ring Source Routing Driver that enables communications across IBM Token Ring network bridges. The routing driver works with any DOS ODI protocol stack and must be run on all workstations that need to communicate across the bridge.

To install the driver, copy it to the NWCLIENT directory if it is not already there, then add a command to load it into the STARTNET.BAT file. Insert the command just before the IPXODI command, but after commands that load the interface driver and Link Support Layer. However, if the workstation is diskless and you are using remote boot, load ROUTE.COM before the Token Ring LAN driver. The ROUTE.COM startup command can take the following form:

ROUTE *options*

Here, *options* is one of the following options. Note that some of these options are used after ROUTE has already been loaded to change the configuration or unload the driver. Refer to the *Novell NetWare Workstation for DOS and Windows* manual for detailed information.

/U   Unload the routing driver from memory.

BOARD=*number*   Replace *number* with a board number for the Token Ring card in the workstation if more than one LAN driver is being loaded and the board number determines the load order.

> *NOTE: Load ROUTE.COM for each logical board number (frame type) enabled by the Token Ring LAN driver.*

CLEAR   Specify this option to clear the Source Routing table and force a dynamic rebuild.

DEF   Prevents frames with unknown destinations from crossing a Single Route IBM bridge.

GBR   If used, General Broadcast frames are sent as All Routes Broadcast frames.

MBR   If used, all Multicast Broadcast frames are sent as All Routes Broadcast frames.

NODES=*number*   Replace *number* with the number of table entries in the Source Routing table.

REMOVE=*number*   Replace number with a node address you want to remove from the workstation's Source Routing table.

Enhancing Security

NetWare 4 provides the NCP packet signature option as a way of preventing packets from being forged by a knowledgeable client who could then gain access with higher privileges. NCP packet signature security is optional because it affects performance. However, if you install it, there is little chance that an intruder can forge packets.

    The security option is installed by adding the SIGNATURE LEVEL option to the NET.CFG file. There are several levels of security, each offering improved security, but also slowing performance. For more information on these options, refer to the *NetWare Workstation for DOS and Windows* manual.

Using ODI and NDIS Drivers Concurrently

IBM, Microsoft, and other network vendors have committed to the Network Driver Interface Specification (NDIS). NDIS is used with Microsoft LAN Manager, Microsoft NT, Microsoft Windows for Workgroups, IBM LAN Server, and 3Com 3+Share. Novell developed ODINSUP.COM to allow NDIS protocol stacks to work with ODI.

Basically, the ODINSUP program interconnects dissimilar networks. It lets the NDIS protocol stack communicate through the ODI Link Support Layer (LSL) to the ODI-compatible network interface card driver. ODINSUP eliminates the need to reboot the workstation when you want to switch from the ODI to NDIS networking schemes, or vice versa.

As pictured in Figure 18-3, ODINSUP sits on top of the LSL like another protocol stack. It can then accept packets from the LSL, which it passes on to the NDIS protocol stack. The reverse is true if packets need to be transferred out over the network.

To use ODINSUP, make sure it is located in the NWCLIENT directory or another suitable directory, then use the following steps to install it. Note that the following presents a general outline for installing ODINSUP. These procedures may change as new products are announced for NetWare 4. Refer to the NetWare manuals for more information.

1. Remove any existing NDIS MAC drivers from the CONFIG.SYS file. For example, you might remove a line like the following:

   DEVICE=C:*path*\\ELINKII.DOS

2. Copy the ODINSUP.COM file from the WSDOS_1 disk to the NWCLIENT directory or the directory where your NET.CFG file is located.

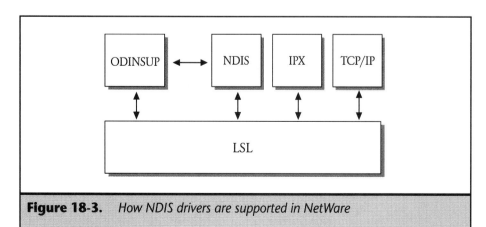

Figure 18-3.   *How NDIS drivers are supported in NetWare*

3. Add the NDIS Protocol Manager command to the CONFIG.SYS file if it doesn't already exist. Use the following command, replacing *path* with the directory path to the command:

   DEVICE=C:*path*\PROTMAN.DOC /I:*path*

4. Change the STARTNET.BAT file in your NWCLIENT directory as follows:

   a. Add the ODINSUP command after the command that loads the Novell ODI LSL and the ODI LAN drivers.

   b. Add the NETBIND command after loading ODINSUP. Note that NETBIND is a command usually located in the directory where the NDIS drivers are located. Specify a path to this directory if necessary.

   c. After the NETBIND command, include the NET START command to load the LAN Requester software for NDIS. Other commands may be necessary after the NET START command, such as CALL INITFSI.BAT, to initialize a full-screen interface, and NETBIOS, to install support for the NetBIOS protocol.

   d. Following these commands are the normal commands found in the STARTNET.BAT file, such as IPXODI and VLM.

5. Now make changes to the NET.CFG file that enable the Ethernet and/or Token Ring frame types and bind the ODINSUP protocol to a particular ODI driver. The Link Driver section for Ethernet NE2000 (for example) might look like the following. Other options will also exist in this section.

   ```
   LINK DRIVER NE2000
        frame ethernet_802.3
        frame ethernet_802.2
        frame ethernet_ii
        frame ethernet_snap
   PROTOCOL ODINSUP
        bind ne2000
   ```

6. Finally, you must make changes to the PROTOCOL.INI file, which is located in the directory where the LAN Manager or other software drivers are located. In this file, remove the NDIS MAC driver completely and replace it with a BINDINGS command similar to the one that follows. Replace NE2000 with the name of the network driver you are using.

   ```
   BINDINGS=NE2000
   ```

If this procedure seems complex, don't give up. Running ODI and NDIS drivers together is not a simple task, but it is workable if you know all the parameters. You should refer to the *NetWare Workstation for DOS and Windows* manual for other details, and also check with Novell's technical support for the latest information on getting these drivers to work together.

Windows on the Network

If users have Windows installed on their local workstation's hard drive, the DOS Requester loads drivers and options so network resources can be accessed from inside Windows. Several alternate options for using Windows are described in this section. They are mainly designed to ease the burden of network administrators and supervisors who need to install Windows for users and manage how users access the network through Windows.

The procedures outlined here copy all of the Windows files to a shared directory on the network. Users or supervisors can then install Windows on workstations by accessing the Windows setup routines and files on the shared network directory instead of installing Windows from diskettes at the workstation. Supervisors need to "expand" the Windows files from the Windows source diskettes to the shared directory. Alternatively, users can simply execute Windows directly from the files in the shared network directory.

The three possible installation scenarios, pictured in Figure 18-4, are as follows:

- *Method 1*   Users install Windows completely on their workstations by accessing the setup routines and files in the shared Windows directory on the server. Windows then runs from users' local hard drives.

- *Method 2*   In this method, only the files that are different for each user's installation are copied to the user's workstation. All other files remain on the network in a directory where they are shared by other users. Windows loads from the network, but reads and writes the custom configuration files for each user on the user's workstation.

- *Method 3*   Users start Windows completely from the network. Their custom configuration files are stored in their personal directories, and shared Windows files are kept in a shared directory used by all other Windows users.

The first method is best, but workstations must have enough hard disk space to hold the Windows files. A drawback to this method is that each individual

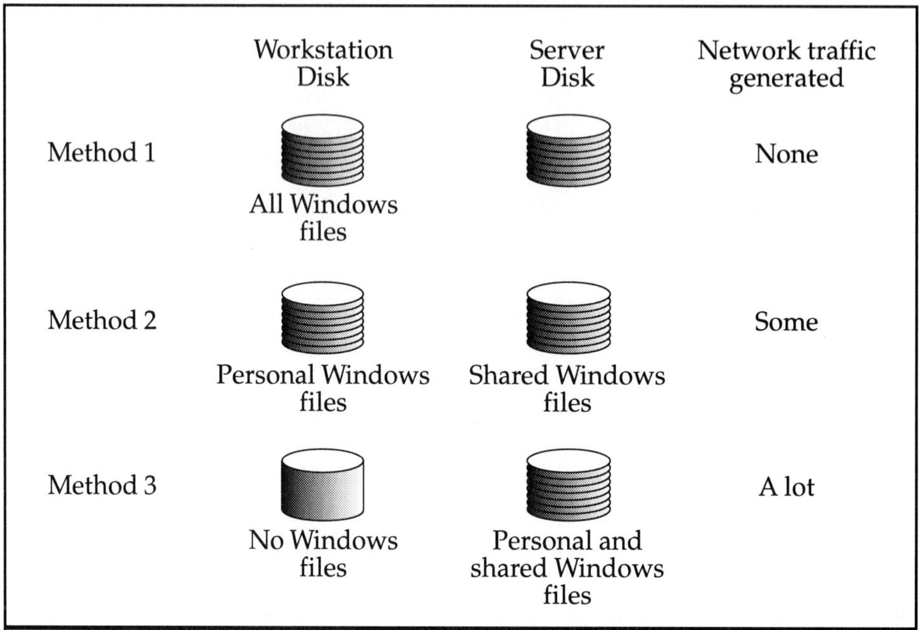

	Workstation Disk	Server Disk	Network traffic generated
Method 1	All Windows files		None
Method 2	Personal Windows files	Shared Windows files	Some
Method 3	No Windows files	Personal and shared Windows files	A lot

Figure 18-4. *The three methods of Windows installation and the network traffic Windows generates once installed*

user is responsible for updating the Windows files and applications on his or her own system. When Windows is installed on the server, network administrators can control and perform these tasks. The second method saves disk space on local workstations since only a few Windows files are located there, such as the INI files. However, network traffic increases since users now access the shared Windows files from the network. Upgrades are performed at the server, making management easy in the second method. The third method is the easiest to manage from a network administrator's point of view, but it produces the most network traffic. The personal directory of each user contains the Windows INI files and other Windows files, while the shared directory contains the remaining Windows files shared by all users. The third method must be used to run Windows on diskless workstations.

When the second and third methods are used, the following files are copied to the users' workstations or to their personal directories:

HIMEM.SYS	Extended memory manager
EMM386.SYS	Expanded memory manager
SMARTDRV.SYS	Disk cache manager

RAMDRIVE.SYS	RAM drive utility
WIN.COM	Windows startup file
*.INI	System and application initialization files
*.GRP	Program Manager group files
_DEFAULT.PIF	The default PIF file

The other Windows files stay in the shared directory where they are accessed by all Windows users. These files should be marked as shareable and read-only, and Windows users should have rights in the directory.

The Swap File

The location of Windows swap files is an important consideration when using windows on a network. The *virtual memory* feature of Windows 3.1 can make a computer appear to have more memory than is physically installed. Part of virtual memory is a high-speed swap area on a hard disk. Thus, a system equipped with little memory can run memory-intensive graphics and CAD applications. The swap area on the disk is a special hidden file that is either temporary or permanent. If a *permanent* area is created, it always resides at the same location on disk and is optimized to speed disk transfers. However, its disk space is not available for other use. A *temporary* swap file is created in available disk space every time Windows starts. While a temporary swap file is less efficient than a permanent one, disk space is not permanently allocated to it.

You should always locate swap files on a local hard drive, rather than the server, unless the workstation is diskless. Transfer of swap data across the network drastically reduces performance of the virtual memory feature and increases traffic on the network.

Copying Windows Files to the Server

To set up Windows for use on a network, you first copy the entire set of Windows disks to a shared directory on a network volume. The files in this directory are then used to create executable copies of Windows on users' workstations, or to start Windows directly from the network drive. Follow the steps here to copy the files:

1. Insert the Windows 3.1 disk #1 in a floppy drive and switch to that drive.

2. Type **SETUP /A**. You are prompted for the name of the network drive where SETUP should copy the files. The setup procedure prompts for each disk, expands the files, and copies them to the directory.

3. After the files have been copied, use the FLAG command to mark them as shareable so multiple users can access them at once. The following command assumes you are in the directory where the files are located:

```
FLAG *.* S
```

Workstation Setup

The commands described in this section are executed at the user's workstation to install a working copy of Windows from the files copied to the server in the previous section. If you are the supervisor, read through the remainder of this section before letting users run the setup procedure. There are many setup options and variables. For example, you can specify exactly which hardware configuration gets installed at a workstation, or customize the Windows environment for individual workstations by including or excluding icons and groups in the Program Manager.

NOTE: Users must have the correct access right in the shared Windows directory and in their personal directories to run SETUP or Windows from the network.

Full Workstation Installation from the Server

The full installation method simply installs all the necessary files on the user's local workstation from the files copied to the server in the previous section. It is no different than the normal setup from diskette, except that no disk handling is required after the Windows files are copied to the server from the original diskettes. Here are the steps:

1. Go to the workstation, or inform the user of this procedure.

2. Log into the network and switch to the Windows directory on the server where you previously expanded the Windows files.

3. Type **SETUP**, then specify the local drive as the destination for the Windows files, and follow the normal Windows installation steps.

Shared Installation

The shared installation method copies only the personal Windows files to a user's local hard drive or to his or her personal directory on the server. The remaining Windows files are accessed in the shared Windows directory. To set up a shared copy of Windows, follow these steps:

1. Go to the workstation or inform the user of this procedure.

2. Log into the network, then switch to the shared Windows directory on the server.

3. Type **SETUP /N** to start the shared Windows setup program.

4. When prompted for the directory for personal files, indicate a directory on the local hard drive, or the user's personal directory on the server.

The setup program copies only the relevant files to the user's directory, then modifies the AUTOEXEC.BAT and CONFIG.SYS files on the workstation.

Automatic Installation

During the setup process, decisions must be made about video hardware and network connections. To ensure that users make the correct decisions if they install Windows themselves, use the automatic setup routine described here.

During automatic setup, an information file is read that contains the exact specifications for a particular setup. You can create several files, each with its own setup specifications. Windows comes with a template file called SETUP.SHH that is located in your shared Windows directory. You copy this file for each different type of setup you need, then modify it for a particular setup. For example, to make a copy of the file for use on workstations with VGA monitors, you would type the following, then change the new file.

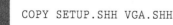

```
COPY SETUP.SHH VGA.SHH
```

The command for automatic Windows setup using the VGA.SHH file as an example is as follows. You can give this command to users of VGA workstations so they can set up Windows themselves.

```
SETUP /H:VGA.SHH
```

To install Windows using the shared directory method, include the /N parameter as shown here:

```
SETUP /H:VGA.SHH /N
```

NOTE: Users must have Open and Read rights in the shared Windows directory.

To create a new SHH file for a particular configuration, copy the SETUP.SHH file, make necessary changes to it, then save the file. The SHH file, like INI files, contains headers between square brackets. Refer to SETUP.SHH and the Windows manual for details on the options you can place under the headings. The SETUP.SHH file contains its own instructions; open it with Windows Write or another text editor, but be sure to save it as a text file without any formatting codes.

Other Setup Options

A number of other installation settings can be specified for a Windows setup, as described in the following list. The specific options are too extensive to cover here, but you can refer to *Windows 3.1: The Complete Reference,* by Tom Sheldon (Berkeley, CA: Osborne/McGraw-Hill, 1992) for more information.

- Add groups to Program Manager during setup.

- Add applications to any Program Manager group during setup.

- Include additional files in the setup process, such as special drivers, TSRs, PIF files, or special INI files for applications.

- Set up third-party device drivers during setup.

- Set Program Manager features. You can disable Run, Exit Windows, Save Settings on Exit, and set restrictions on what users can modify in Program Manager. You can disable the File menu, if necessary.

General Windows Guidelines

Every large network will surely have users who want or need Windows. The strategy may be to use Windows throughout. The network administrator must decide whether users run Windows from their local workstations or over the network. The main issue is network traffic versus network management as mentioned previously. Here are some important points to consider when setting up Windows for network users:

■ Create a special Windows user group, then assign that group access to the shared Windows directory.

■ Use commands in the system login script that execute if a user is a member of the Windows user group. The "IF MEMBER OF" login script command executes commands if users are members of the Windows group.

■ When creating the search path mappings for users in the login script, insert the MAP command for users' personal Windows directories before the MAP command for the shared Windows directory. This order is important because both directories contain files with the same name. Those in the users' personal directories are customized for their configuration. Those directories must be searched first to ensure execution of the correct files.

■ Minimize the number of drive mappings for users. Each map appears as an icon in File Manager that soon clutters the screen. Consider branching application directories from a single directory, such as APPS, then map a drive to APPS. Give users rights to APPS and its subdirectories. In File Manager, they'll see all the branching subdirectories of APPS as folders.

■ MAP ROOT is important when running NetWare. If you don't use it, all drive icons in File Manager point to the root directory. If you MAP ROOT users' personal directories, they can't see parent directories, only subdirectories. This keeps them from "exploring" other directories and from inadvertently changing their mappings. MAP ROOT also speeds searching. File Manager starts its searches at the root; MAP ROOT shortens that search by specifying only one branch of the directory tree. An example of the correct form for the MAP command is

```
MAP ROOT F:=SYS:USERS\ASHLEY
```

■ On NetWare networks, add the following SHOW DOTS line to the NET.CFG file. It makes the parent directory [..] visible when listing subdirectories. If not used, the parent directory icon is not visible, and users will have trouble getting back to the directory in File Manager.

```
SHOW DOTS = ON
```

Also include the following option to increase file handles from the default of 40 to approximately 60, making sure the value matches the value of FILES= in the CONFIG.SYS file.

```
FILE HANDLES = 60
```

■ Make sure users always have the same drive mappings to the directories they use. If a mapping is changed, program icons in the Program Manager that access network drives may not work.

■ A Windows application may not run properly if it requires a larger buffer than Windows normally provides for transferring data over the network. You can increase the NetHeapSize setting in the SYSTEM.INI file [standard] or [386Enh] sections from the default value of 4KB to 16KB or more.

■ If you enable the AllVMsExclusive= setting in the SYSTEM.INI file, all non-Windows applications are forced to run in exclusive full-screen mode, which avoids some network-related problems.

■ Windows keeps 14 handles open by default. If users are having problems running a shared copy of Windows from a server, increase the value of CachedFileHandles in the SYSTEM.INI file. However, doing so may slow Windows down.

OS/2 Workstations

To connect an OS/2 workstation to a NetWare network, you must load the NetWare Requester for OS/2 software. Locate the WSOS2_1 diskette and follow these steps to install the software:

1. Start OS/2 and open a window to the OS/2 command prompt. Double-click either the OS/2 Full Screen icon or the OS/2 Window icon.

2. When the OS/2 command prompt appears, insert the NetWare Workstation for OS/2 diskette and type the following, which assumes the disk is in drive A:

```
A:INSTALL
```

3. In a moment, the OS/2 Installation Utility window appears. Choose "Requester on workstation" from the Installation menu.

You can complete the installation by following the onscreen prompts and accessing help if necessary. The following takes place during the installation:

- A directory called NETWARE is created, and the Requester files are copied into it.

- A group icon called Novell is created on the OS/2 desktop. The group contains an icon to run the installation program, a NetWare Workstation Tools utility, and the RPRINTER remote printing utility.

- The CONFIG.SYS file is altered.

After the installation, you must close the OS/2 session, then reboot the computer to initialize network support.

Changes in the CONFIG.SYS File

The NetWare Requester installation program makes changes similar to the following in the CONFIG.SYS file. You can view these changes by listing the file, which resides in the root directory.

- Adds the NETWARE directory to the LIBPATH=, SET PATH=, and SET DPATH= statements.

- Adds the following set of commands at the end of the file. Some of the commands will be different on each workstation, depending on the type of network card installed.

```
REM --- NetWare Requester statements BEGIN ---
SET NWLANGUAGE=ENGLISH
DEVICE=C:\NETWARE\LSL.SYS
RUN=C:\NETWARE\DDAEMON.EXE
DEVICE=C:\NETWARE\NE2000.SYS
DEVICE=C:\NETWARE\IPX.SYS
DEVICE=C:\NETWARE\SPX.SYS
RUN=C:\NETWARE\SPDAEMON.EXE
rem DEVICE=C:\NETWARE\NMPIPE.SYS
rem DEVICE=C:\NETWARE\NPSERVER.SYS
```

```
rem RUN=C:\NETWARE\NPDAEMON.EXE
DEVICE=C:\NETWARE\NWREQ.SYS
IFS=C:\NETWARE\NWIFS.IFS
RUN=C:\NETWARE\NWDAEMON.EXE
DEVICE=C:\NETWARE\NETBIOS.SYS
RUN=C:\NETWARE\NBDAEMON.EXE
DEVICE=C:\NETWARE\VIPX.SYS
DEVICE=C:\NETWARE\VSHELL.SYS PRIVATE
REM --- NetWare Requester statements END ---
```

CAUTION: If you modify the CONFIG.SYS file, do not remove the REM statements before or after the NetWare Requester commands. The installation program uses these remarks to locate the NetWare section if you run it to change the configuration.

The NET.CFG File

The NET.CFG configuration file contains settings used by the OS/2 Requester and other utilities when they load. Changes to NET.CFG are optional, and in most cases, you won't need to make changes. However, placing commands in the file can help you customize the environment of the workstation and overcome problems with software and hardware.

The NET.CFG file is a standard ASCII text file that you can change with most editors. However, it is best to change it with the Installation utility in the NetWare group. To change the file, do the following:

1. Open the Novell group and double-click the Install icon.

2. Choose "This workstation" from the Configuration menu.

3. The default location for the NET.CFG file appears. The default is the root directory. Click Edit to choose that file.

4. You then see a window with NET.CFG options listed on the right. Click on any option to view its description.

5. To add an option to the NET.CFG file, type it on the right after reviewing its options and requirements in the Help window.

6. To save your changes, click the Save button, then click the Cancel button to exit the window.

NetWare Session Customization

By default, all DOS, Windows, and OS/2 sessions that you run with OS/2 provide global login support. That means they share a single login to the NetWare server. All drive mappings and printer port captures are the same whether the user switches to the DOS session, Windows, or back to an OS/2 session. If users can have only one connection to the server at a time, this global setting is best.

A *customized private login session* can be created that doesn't share the settings of other sessions. You can create a customized session if you need to log in twice, or log in as two different users. Administrators or supervisors might need to log in as two users for testing purposes, or some users might need more than one session for accounting reasons. When the accounting system is enabled, the time and resources used in each session are tracked and accounted for. Users who need to access the network in several different ways and keep track of each session separately can use private login sessions.

To customize NetWare sessions for the Win-OS2 and DOS startup icons, follow these steps:

1. Click the icon to customize with the right mouse button, then click the arrow button on the Open option. Choose Settings from the pop-up menu.

2. The "book" that appears has tabs on the right. Click Session.

3. Click on DOS settings and make the changes to the settings described in the following list. After making the changes, click the Save button.

    NETWARE_RESOURCES Choose GLOBAL or PRIVATE in the Value field, depending on the type of session you want to create.

    DOS_LASTDRIVE Make sure Z is in the Value, if not, type it.

    DOS_FILES If this is a private session, set the value to 214. Do not set this value for global sessions.

    VIPX_ENABLED Set this property to on for both global and private sessions.

    DOS_DEVICE Click this property, then use the following command in the Value field for both global and private sessions, if you want to use the NetWare capture command from the session. Replace *drive* with the boot drive letter.

    drive:\OS2\MDOS\LPTDD.SYS

4. Add optional parameters. The following parameters are available

Private DOS Session If you are configuring a private DOS session, click the Program tab on the side of the Settings book. In the Optional Parameters field, type the following command to load the NETX.EXE program, then close the Settings window.

```
/K C:\NETWARE\NETX.EXE
```

WIN-OS2 Session If you are editing the settings of a WIN-OS2 session icon, click the Program tab on the side of the Settings book. In the Optional Parameters field, type the following command to load task-switching support, then close the Settings window.

```
/K C:\OS2\MDOS\WINOS2\SYSTEM\TBMI2.COM
```

5. If you want to boot a DOS session from a version of DOS other than the one built into OS/2, add the following lines to the CONFIG.SYS file on the DOS diskette or partition that boots the session. *Path* in all cases is the drive and directory where the NetWare Requester files are located, usually C:\NETWARE.

DEVICE=*path*\DOSVIPX.SYS
DEVICE=*path*\DOSVSHLL.SYS
FILES=214   (only required for private sessions)
LASTDRIVE=Z

Drive Mappings in OS/2

In OS/2, mapped drives appear as if they branch from the root of the volume. If you map a drive in an OS/2 session, then switch to a global DOS session, you will see the mapped drives as root drives. On the other hand, if you map a drive in a global DOS session, it will appear as a normal drive in the OS/2 session. OS/2 does not require search drive mappings, so if you create a search drive map in a global DOS session, it does not appear when you switch to an OS/2 session. That search drive will also not appear in other DOS sessions.

CHAPTER 19

This chapter provides an overview of the installation procedures for non-IPX protocols, in particular, TCP/IP. They provide a general overview of the information you will need to prepare for the installation, along with an explanation of some of the parameters you'll need to set.

Installing Internet-working Support

Installing TCP/IP Support on a Server

You can install TCP/IP support using the INSTALL utility at the server. During the server installation, you have the option of installing the communications protocols. You can also install them at any time after the installation by loading INSTALL. Both methods display the same menus and options. If you are just finishing the server installation and were referred here from Chapter 16, you see the Internetworking Configuration menu. You can skip to the next section for an explanation of the procedures.

To install TCP/IP support on an already installed server, type the following:

    LOAD INSTALL

When the Installation Options menu appears, choose Other Options, then choose Configure Communication Protocols. The following menu appears:

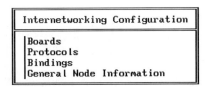

```
┌─────────────────────────────────────┐
│ Internetworking Configuration        │
├─────────────────────────────────────┤
│ Boards                               │
│ Protocols                            │
│ Bindings                             │
│ General Node Information             │
└─────────────────────────────────────┘
```

The Internetworking Configuration menu is a series of menus and submenus you use to configure communications protocols besides IPX. This discussion covers TCP/IP. The settings you make while using the menus are automatically saved into the server's configuration and take effect when the server is rebooted. The menu procedures described here supersede the need to use the LOAD and BIND commands at the console prompt to install the protocols.

The items on the menu are in the order you should follow to install the protocols. Each menu option is described in the sections that follow.

Board Configuration

Select the Boards option on the Internetworking Configuration menu to configure the boards installed in the system. This list will initially be blank because you are configuring boards for use with multiple protocols. To list the actual boards already installed in your system during the installation of NetWare, press the INS key.

A list of drivers already located in the SYS:SYSTEM directory of the server is listed in the Available Drivers menu. If you don't see the board you want to configure in this list, exit this utility and return to the Installation Options menu. Choose LAN Driver Options to copy and load a new LAN driver. The LAN driver's name will then appear in the list when you return to the board configuration menu.

If you see the board you want to configure, highlight it and press ENTER. You then see the Board Configuration menu, where you can change the name and other settings for the board. Refer to the help options or the LAN driver installation section in Chapters 15 and 16 for more information on setting interrupts, I/O base addresses, and other settings.

NOTE: You must configure one logical board for each frame type that will be routed across the associated physical card. One physical board can be configured as multiple logical boards, each with a different frame type and board name.

Press ESC to exit the Board Configuration menu. The new driver will appear in the Configured Boards menu, and you can press ENTER to change its configuration (if necessary), press INS to add another board, or press ESC to return to the Internetworking Configuration menu.

Protocol Configuration

When you select Protocols from the Internetworking Configuration menu, you see a list of supported protocols (IPX and TCP/IP).

Choose the TCP/IP protocol in the list and press ENTER. The Expert TCP/IP Configuration Options field is highlighted. Press ENTER to display the following menu:

```
┌─────────────────────────────────────────────────────┐
│          Expert TCP/IP Configuration Options          │
├─────────────────────────────────────────────────────┤
│  IP Packet Forwarding:      Forward IP Packets ("Router:"│
│  RIP Routing Protocol:      Enabled                   │
│                                                       │
│  Static Routing Configuration: Disabled               │
│  Static Routing Tables:     (Select For List)         │
│                                                       │
│  SNMP Manager Table:        (Select For List)         │
└─────────────────────────────────────────────────────┘
```

Use this menu to set the following options. IP addressing is covered later under "About IP Addresses."

IP Packet Forwarding The default for this setting is Forward IP Packets, which is appropriate for a server since it acts as a router.

RIP Routing Protocol The default for this option is Enabled, which is appropriate for the server. RIP provides the means by which the server exchanges information with other routers on the network. If you disable this option, a static routing protocol is used for this server. Static routing allows you to build a set of routes that RIP can find, and you can add them to the internetwork's routing database. Static routes are rarely required.

Static Routing Configuration The default for this option is Disabled. Select this option and enable it only if you need static routing. When enabled, the static routing information database is automatically loaded during system initialization.

Static Routing Tables Select this option only if you need to create a static routing table. Press ENTER, then press INS to display the Static Route menu. Specify the following information on the menu:

Route to Network or Host Set this option to Host or Network, depending on whether the database entry will route to a specific host, or any host on a given network.

IP Address of Network or Host Type the IP address of the network or host where the data should be routed. Enter the network portion only of network addresses, without trailing zeros.

Next Hop Router on this Route Type the address of the closest router on the same network.

Metric for this Route This value is the number of hops that data must go through to reach its destination. Routes with lower metric values are chosen first. The value can be from 1 to 16.

Type of Route Specify either active or passive. Active routes are continually updated by RIP to indicate their current status. Passive routes are permanent entries that are entered only by IP during initialization.

SNMP Manager Table In this field, enter the address of the SNMP (Simple Network Management Protocol) management workstation that will receive any SNMP traps from this router.

After changing the TCP/IP configuration, the status of the protocol is Enabled on the Protocols Supported menu. Press ESC to return to the main Internetworking Configuration menu so you can bind the protocol to a network card.

Binding TCP/IP to the LAN Card

Once you've configured TCP/IP options for the server, you are ready to bind the protocol to one of the board configurations you created earlier. Select the Bindings option on the Internetworking Configuration menu and press ENTER. A list of current protocol/network board bindings appears, if there are any at all.

1. Press the INS key to create a new binding.

2. Select the TCP/IP protocol and press ENTER.

3. On the next menu, choose one of the network cards you configured.

The menu titled "Binding TCP/IP to an Interface" appears. Fill out this menu as described in the following list of options. Refer to "About IP Addresses" for information about assigning addresses in the fields.

Local IP Address of Interface   Type the IP address assigned to this network interface.

Subnetwork Mask of Connected Networks   Enter the subnetwork mask, which must match the mask used by other nodes on the network. The mask must set every bit of the network portion of the address to 1 and every bit of the host number to 0.

Permanent WAN Call Destination   Type the name of the WAN Call Destination used for a permanent connection. This field is not available when connecting to a LAN.

Expert Configuration Options   If you highlight the Expert Configuration Options field, you are presented with the following options:

Default Router   The address of the router where packets without specific routes are sent. RIP normally supplies this information, so no value is required in the field. Be careful not to configure two routers that specify each other as default routers.

About IP Addresses

The Internet Protocol address (IP address) for a node is a logical address that is independent of the physical address assigned to a network interface board by its vendor. The IP address is also independent of the network configuration. IP addresses have the same form, no matter what network type is used. This form is a 4-byte (32-bit) numeric value that identifies both a network and a local host or node on the network. Each IP address must be unique and consist of four decimal numbers separated by dots—123.45.6.78, for example.

As mentioned, IP addresses are not dependent on any type of network. That means packets can traverse network types. On each network type, the TCP/IP protocol maps the IP address to a physical node address for delivery. Packets contain the sender's IP address so a receiving station can reply if necessary. The IP address identifies the network and the node on the network where the sender is located.

One way to set IP addresses is to join the DARPA Internet community, which will assign your network a registered Internet address. Contact the DDN Network Information Center, which is part of SRI International in Menlo Park, California.

If you don't care to officially register your network, you can choose an arbitrary number that follows the IP addressing scheme (four decimal numbers separated by periods).

The 4-byte IP address is divided into a network portion that identifies the network and a host portion that identifies the computer (node). The network portion must be the same for every node on the network, while the host portion must be unique for every node on the network. There are several different schemes for mapping these numbers:

- In Class A addressing schemes, the first byte is the network address, and the last three bytes are the node address. This allows 126 networks with 16 million nodes per network.

- In Class B addressing schemes, the first two bytes are the network address, and the last two bytes are the node address. This allows 16,000 networks and 65,000 nodes.

- In Class C addressing schemes, the first three bytes are the network address, and the last byte is the node address, which allows 2 million networks with 254 nodes each.

Some addresses are reserved, and the highest order bit in each address requires a special identifier number. Refer to the TCP/IP manual that comes with NetWare or your NetWare MultiProtocol Router for more information.

It is possible to split a single network into a number of subnetworks. To outside remote networks, your network still appears as a single network with a single network address. You split a network so you can use multiple media types, or to reduce congestion by reducing the number of workstations on a network. When subnetworks exist, the IP address consists of a network address, a subnetwork address, and the host address. The host address portion of the IP address is split to include the subnetwork address and the host address.

Default Broadcast Address   The address the router will use to broadcast on the network.

Multicast Override IP Address   The IP address to which IP should direct IP multicast packets; this overrides IP's standard multicast handling.

Originate Default Route   Sets whether the router announces itself as a default router using RIP.

Cost of Interface   A number from 1 to 16 that can discourage the use of this interface, with 16 indicating the highest discouragement.

Use "Poison Reverse"   The default for this option is Disabled, which reduces network traffic but can introduce some instability.

General Node Information

Select the General Node Information option from the Internetworking Configuration menu to specify general information about the SNMP (Simple Network Management Protocol) or the configuration itself. You can specify information about the hardware, physical location, and person to contact in case of problems. This information is generally used to troubleshoot the connections.

Installing TCP/IP Support at Workstations

The Novell LAN WorkPlace products are used to connect DOS, OS/2, and Macintosh workstations to TCP/IP networks. The three products are called LAN WorkPlace for DOS, LAN WorkPlace for OS/2, and LAN WorkPlace for Macintosh. All products provide the TCP/IP protocol suite, along with a collection of other features.

During the installation process, you specify many of the same parameters you specified during the installation of TCP/IP on the server. The IP address for each workstation must be unique, but follow the addressing scheme of the networks you have installed. For more information about IP addressing, refer to the previous sections, or the installation manuals.

THE
COMPLETE

REFERENCE

PART **FIVE**

Managing and Using the Network

CHAPTER 20

Post Setup Activities

This chapter covers the procedures you follow to log into a NetWare v.4 server. If you are not the ADMIN user, it is assumed that the network administrator has already created a user object for you and given you a password so you can log in. You'll learn the steps required to log in, and then you'll explore the NetWare environment, including disk directory structures, NetWare Directory Services (NDS) contexts, drive mapping, and login scripts.

This chapter is written for all users who need to log into a server, but some of the material is most appropriate for administrators and supervisors. Keep in mind that this chapter discusses the general environment

413

of a new NetWare server. If your server was upgraded from a previous version of NetWare, directory structures will already be in place, but in most cases they will closely resemble the descriptions given here.

The network administrator (ADMIN user) is the first person to log into the network. He or she creates organizational unit containers that represent divisions or departments in the company. The network administrator then creates supervisor-level user objects within those containers and grants them Supervisor rights to the division or department branch.

Although branch supervisors can have unlimited rights within their branch, they can't access objects outside the branch (up the directory tree) unless the network administrator or another higher-level administrator grants them specific rights to do so. The right to even see other parts of the tree might be revoked, so the structure you see may not resemble some of the examples presented here. For example, INSTALL creates a SYSTEM and a PUBLIC directory in the root directory of the SYS volume. If you are a branch supervisor, your branch might not have access rights to these directories. In fact, you might not have access rights to any of the SYS volume, but only to other volumes. Keep this in mind as you read through this chapter.

NOTE: *Typically, all network users have Read and File Scan rights to the PUBLIC directory so that they can run NetWare utilities.*

Logging Into the System

Before you can log into the system, you must run the workstation utilities that establish a communications link to the network. Commands to make this connection are normally inserted in your AUTOEXEC.BAT file when the workstation software is installed. If this has been done, you're ready to log in. You might see a message that your system is attached to a server. Note that *attached* doesn't mean you are logged in, only that the communications link is established.

At the DOS prompt, switch to the first network drive, which is usually the drive letter that follows the letter of your last local drive. For example, if your system has local hard drives, RAM drives, or CD-ROMs, and the last of these devices is H, the first network drive is I. Switch to this drive so that you can execute the LOGIN command, and then jump to the next section. Note that the minimum letter for the NetWare drive is F. If your last local drive is C or D, the first NetWare drive is still F.

Customizing the Network Connection Procedures

On DOS workstations, the following command is usually inserted in your AUTOEXEC.BAT file:

```
@CALL C:\NWCLIENT\STARTNET
```

This command executes STARTNET.BAT in the directory where the NetWare workstation files have been stored. (In this example, they are stored in the NWCLIENT directory.) You can add the following commands to your AUTOEXEC.BAT file, if they aren't already there. The first command switches to the network drive and the second command executes the LOGIN command. Replace *loginname* with your login name and context, if necessary.

```
F:
LOGIN loginname
```

If you don't want to make the network connection every time your system starts, remove these commands from your AUTOEXEC.BAT file, create a new batch file called NET.BAT (or something similar), and add the commands to it.

Directory Services Naming

Before you can log into the network, you must be in the proper context, or at least know how to change your context. The LOGIN command discussed in the next section can be frustrating if you don't know a little about the Directory Services tree, your current context in that tree, and how to change it. If you attempt to log in in the wrong context, you'll get error messages such as "user does not exist in this context." At that point, you would issue a CX (Change Context) command to view your current context, then another CX command to switch to the correct context and log in. You can specify a default context in the NET.CFG file.

The CX command is your key to viewing your current tree context and changing it. The basic CX command is covered here. For details about other options available with the command, refer to "The CX Command" later in this chapter. If your attempt to log in failed, type **CX** by itself on the command line. Your current context appears. You can then type the following to move up one level and try logging in again.

```
CX .
```

The LOGIN command will search down the directory tree, but not back up, so login problems can usually be fixed by moving up the directory tree. If you need to move up more than one container level, type two or more periods in the CX command, as shown here:

```
CX ..
```

When using the CX command to move around in the Directory Services tree, you really need to know how to specify context names. That is covered here. You can use the CX command to move around in a directory tree in the same way you use the DOS CD command to move around in a file system directory structure.

First, every user has a user object that is located in a particular context of the directory tree. For example, assume that user AColgan belongs to the Administration department, which belongs to the western division (DivWest) of CambrianCorp. Therefore, the context of AColgan's object is as follows:

CN=AColgan.OU=Administration.OU=DivWest.O=CambrianCorp

This name forms a unique path constructed from *partial names.* Partial names are the names of Organization (O) and Organizational Unit (OU) containers, and the Common Names (CN) of the object. Each partial name is separated by a period and, in the preceding example, explicitly defined with a *type* abbreviation (CN, OU, or O). You can eliminate the type abbreviations to save some typing, as shown here:

AColgan.Administration.DivWest.CambrianCorp

This is an *implied* or *typeless* naming context, because you are assuming that the operating system will recognize that AColgan is a CN (Common Name) and CambrianCorp is an O (Organization). However, the operating system may not always recognize the context you are referring to if you don't use a type abbreviation, as discussed shortly.

The path formed by the sequence of partial names defines exactly where an object is from the root of the directory tree, much like a DOS filename path identifies exactly where the file is. However, note that NetWare Directory Services names are reversed in order from filename paths. This full path is referred to as the *distinguished name* or *complete name* of the object.

Since AColgan belongs to the Administration department and uses resources in that department like printers and servers, the network supervisor can ensure that AColgan's context (when first logging in) is always in the Administration container by placing a "Name Context=" statement in the NET.CFG file at AColgan's workstation. The line in the file would appear as follows. The context must be between quotation marks and must include the type specifiers (OU and O).

NAME CONTEXT="OU=Administration.OU=DivWest.O=CambrianCorp"

If AColgan's context is Administration.DivWest.CambrianCorp and she wants to refer to a printer called HPLASER in that same context, she does not need to specify the full distinguishing name of the object. Instead, she can simply refer to it as CN=HPLASER, or simply HPLASER.

Specifying Partial Names

Now we get to an important concept regarding how the operating system infers contexts from the names you type. Note the following:

- The most significant partial name is always interpreted as the Organization (O)

- The least significant partial name is always interpreted as the Common Name (CN)

- All partial names between O and CN are considered Organizational Units (OU)

So in the following name, AColgan is interpreted as the CN, CambrianCorp is interpreted as O, and the partial names between are interpreted as OU.

AColgan.Administration.DivWest.CambrianCorp

Consider the significance of this if you forgot to specify "CambrianCorp" at the end of the context. The operating system would infer that DivWest is the Organization container.

NOTE: Earlier, in the Name Context statement mentioned for the NET.CFG file, it is important to specify a name type (OU and O) so that the operating system knows exactly what Administration is.

The Period Qualifier

If you use typeless context names with the CX command to move around in the directory tree, you sometimes need to use special qualifiers that help the operating system place you in a new context. The qualifier is the period. If a type abbreviation or qualifier is not specified, the context you specify is added to the current context. For example, assume your current context is as follows:

Current Context: O=CambrianCorp

You type the following command to switch context:

```
CX ADMINISTRATION.DIVWEST
```

Your new context is as shown here:

OU=Administration.OU=DivWest.OU=DivwestO=CambrianCorp

The context you specify is simply added to the current context because no qualifiers or type abbreviations were specified in the CX command. An error can occur if you duplicate any part of the name context. For example, assume your current context is as follows:

Current Context: OU=DivWest.O=CambrianCorp

You type the following command in an attempt to switch to the Administration context:

```
CX ADMINISTRATION.DIVWEST
```

When the context you specify is added to your current context, the partial name DivWest is repeated as shown next. The operating system can't interpret this and returns an error message.

OU=Administration.OU=DivWest.OU=DivWestO=CambrianCorp.

TRAILING QUALIFIER   A period can be used at the trailing end of a qualifier to control how the name context you type will be added to the current context. For each period added to the trailing end, a partial name is removed. If two periods are added, then two partial names are removed. If more periods are used than there are partial names, an error occurs.

For example, assume your current context is as follows:

Current Context: OU=DivWest.O=CambrianCorp

You want to switch to the context:

"OU=Sales.OU=DivEast.O=CambrianCorp."

To make this switch, you type the following:

```
CX SALES.DIVEAST.
```

The period at the end removes DivWest from the previous context and adds the context you specify to O=CambrianCorp to place you in the following context:

OU=Sales.OU=DivEast.O=CambrianCorp

PRECEDING QUALIFIERS   When a period precedes a context specification, the current context is ignored. In other words, the context specified is not added to the current context. The operating system assumes you are specifying a new context and uses the following basic rule to build the new context.

■ The most significant partial name is assumed to be the Organization (O).

Therefore, when using the preceding period qualifier, always make sure the most significant partial name is the Organizational Unit (OU). So, assuming the tree has the following path:

"OU=Administration.OU=DivWest.O=CambrianCorp"

You could type the following to switch from any context to the "OU=DivWest.O=CambrianCorp" context.

```
CX .DIVWEST.CAMBRIANCORP
```

An error would occur if you typed the following:

```
CX .ACOLGAN.DIVWEST.CAMBRIANCORP
```

The operating system would assume the Common Name AColgan is an Organizational Unit. Likewise, the following would also return an error because the operating system would assume DIVWEST is the Organization (O).

```
CX .ACOLGAN.ADMINISTRATION.DIVWEST
```

The LOGIN Command

Logging in is as simple as typing **LOGIN** on the command line. If you don't enter your context and user name, messages appear that ask you for them. You are then asked for your password.

The LOGIN command has the following form:

LOGIN *server* / *context* / *options*

where *server* is the name of the server you want to log into, *context* is your user name and any required context, and *options* are any of the options listed here:

Option	Description
/NoScript or /NS	Prevents the login script from running and does not log you out of any servers you might currently be logged into
/Script or /S <*pathname*>	Replace *pathname* with the name of a special login script file to run when you log in
/SWAP	Lets you run external commands from the login script
/PR=*name*	Replace *name* with the name of a profile object to run with the login script. A profile object contains a login script that is assigned to only specific users, who might not belong to any one container in the NDS tree
/TR	Use this option to log into another directory tree. Most organizations have only one directory tree that encompasses the entire company, so this option is rarely used
/B	Specify this option for a bindery login

It is important to specify the server when you log in if you want to make sure you log into the same server every time. The directories and files on that server are then conveniently available, but keep in mind that the MAP command can make any directory on any server you have access to appear as a drive letter. For example, you could switch from a directory on the current server to a directory on another server simply by typing a different drive letter.

NOTE: To always log into the same server, specify the PREFERRED SERVER option in the NET.CFG file.

If you use LOGIN to access a server, you are logged out of all other servers unless you use the /NS option. For example, to log into a new server without logging out of existing servers, type a command similar to this, replacing MARANTZ with the name of your server:

```
LOGIN MARANTZ/AJONES /NS
```

The next example illustrates how to specify a profile object called MANAGERS when logging in. Note that the context is specified.

```
LOGIN AJONES /PR=MANAGERS.ADMINISTRATION.CAMBRIANCORP
```

What to Do if You Can't Log In

If you can't log into the server, it's possible that one of the following problems exists or that one of the following login restrictions is in place:

- You are specifying the wrong context. Refer to the previous section for more information on determining the current context.

- You are already logged in at another workstation and aren't allowed to log in from more than one workstation at a time.

- You can log in only during a certain time of the day.

- You can log in only at a specific workstation.

Changing Your Password

After you've logged in, you can change your login password at any time by using the SETPASS command. Supervisors can change passwords for other users. The command takes the following form:

SETPASS *username* /SE=*servername*

where *username* is the name of the user whose login password you want to change and *servername* is the name of a pre-v.4 NetWare server. To change your own password, just type **SETPASS**.

Messages appear that ask you to enter your old password and the new password. You are then asked to type your new password again to verify it.

The WHOAMI Command

The WHOAMI command provides useful information about your current session. Type the following to display the name of the current tree and the context of your user name:

```
WHOAMI
```

To display information about servers, type the following:

```
WHOAMI /B
```

To continuously scroll long screens of text, specify the /C option, and to get help with the command, specify the /? option.

Logging Out

It is essential that users log out (or enable a password-protected screen saver) whenever they leave their workstations. If a logged-in machine is left unattended, intruders could access files and possibly do damage in areas they wouldn't normally be able to access.

To log out of the network, simply type the LOGOUT command. This logs you out of all servers on the network. If you want to logout of specific servers, type the server names after the command. For example, to log out of the MARANTZ server, type the following:

```
LOGOUT MARANTZ
```

The CX Command

As mentioned, you use the CX command to browse in the NetWare Directory Services tree and determine your current context or the context of other objects. For example, you might want to refer to a server or volume in the directory tree. The CX command helps you determine the name of that server or volume and its context.

The command takes the following form:

CX *newcontext options*

where *newcontext* is replaced by the context you want to switch to and *options* is one or more of the options listed here:

Option	Description
/CONT	Lists containers at the current context or at a specified context
/R	Makes your current context the root of the directory tree
/T	Lists all containers below your current location
/A	Specify this option with either the /CONT or /T option to list all objects at or below the current context
/C	Lists the display continuously
/?	Displays help instructions

You can type CX by itself to see what your current context is. Use the options to display information about the directory tree and objects in it. For example, typing **CX /CONT** would display a list of container objects at your current context, similar to the following:

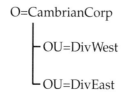

If you specify the /T option, you'll get a list of the container objects below the current context, similar to that shown here:

```
[Root]
  └ O=CambrianCorp
       ├ OU=DivWest
       │    ├ OU=Administration
       │    │    └ OU=Servers
       │    ├ OU=Marketing
       │    ├ OU=SalesWest
       │    └ OU=SERVICE
       └ OU=DivEast
            └ OU=Sales
```

Assume your current context is [Root], as shown in the previous illustration. You could type the following command to make the SERVICE organizational unit your context:

```
CX SERVICE.ADMINISTRATION.DIVWEST.CAMBRIANCORP
```

From this level, you could move back up the tree and make the container CambrianCorp your current context by typing the following:

```
CX ...
```

Each period represents a level in the tree. To switch from one complete context to another, type a period in front of the context. For example, to switch from LEVEL1.BRANCH1 to LEVEL1.BRANCH2, you would type

```
CX .LEVEL1.BRANCH2
```

The NLIST Command

After you have established your context in the directory tree, you can use the NLIST command to list objects and obtain information about them. NLIST is covered more thoroughly in Chapter 22, but it is mentioned here because it does provide information you can use when you first log in. NLIST does the following:

- Displays information about objects and their properties
- Displays information about users, groups, volumes, servers, and print queues
- Lets you search for objects by their properties

You can get a complete description of the NLIST options, including examples, by typing the following command:

```
NLIST /? ALL
```

The NetWare Filing System

The NetWare filing system consists of servers that have one or more volumes. The first volume on each server is always called SYS. The default names for additional volumes are VOL1, VOL2, and so on, but you can give them custom names, such as OS2VOL, MACVOL, USERS, or EMAIL, that describe what is stored on the volume and who might use it. Each volume has its own directory structure.

The name context that you use to refer to files is illustrated in Figure 20-1. If you need to refer to a file on a server other than your default server, you type the full context of the filename. The server name is followed by a backslash, and the volume name is followed by a colon. A slash separates directory and subdirectory names, as it does in DOS. However, in NetWare, you can use either a forward or backward slash.

For example, to refer to a file called BUDGET.XLS in the BUDGDOCS directory on the APPS volume of the ACCTG server, you would use the following context:

```
ACCTG/APPS:BUDGDOCS/BUDGET.XLS
```

The slash after the server name and the colon after the volume name are important. NetWare uses them to determine exactly what you are referring to. If you used a backslash instead of the colon in the previous example, NetWare would interpret APPS as the starting directory and BUDGDOCS as a subdirectory within it.

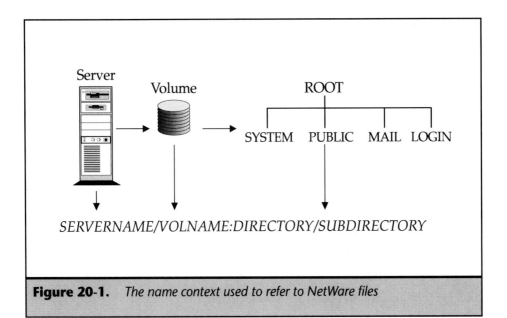

Figure 20-1. *The name context used to refer to NetWare files*

NetWare Volumes

The volume is the highest level in the NetWare filing system. A volume has a root directory and branching subdirectories. As mentioned, the first NetWare volume on a server is called SYS, and it contains the NetWare system and public files, unless they have been moved.

Other volumes are accessible by mapping their names to a drive letter by using the MAP command, as discussed later in this chapter. NetWare allows up to 64 volumes per server. For example, you could map the BUDGDOCS directory on the APPS volume to drive letter R, and then switch to the volume and directory by typing the drive specification **R:**. For users to list or work with the files in a directory, they must have rights to that directory.

NetWare Directories

The NetWare directory system is similar to the DOS directory system. Each volume has one root directory. Directories can branch from the root, and subdirectories can branch from these directories. The NetWare installation program creates the directory structure of the SYS volume, which is shown in Figure 20-2 and described in the following paragraphs.

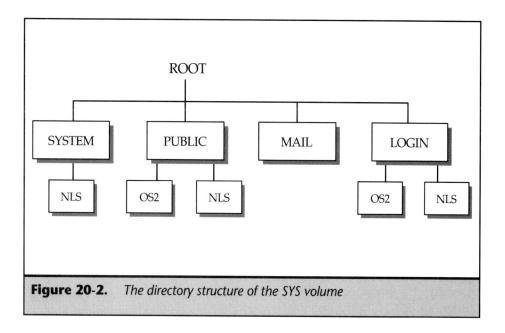

Figure 20-2.   *The directory structure of the SYS volume*

NOTE: The OS2 subdirectories in Figure 20-2 hold login files and workstation utilities for OS/2 workstations. The NLS subdirectories hold NetWare language system files (which are English by default).

SYS:SYSTEM   The SYSTEM directory holds NetWare executable files and other modules that are normally accessed only by supervisors.

SYS:PUBLIC   The PUBLIC directory holds the NetWare utilities that are typically accessed by all users.

NOTE: Users are automatically granted Read and File Scan rights to the PUBLIC directory of a SYS volume that is at their context level. For example, in Figure 20-3, AKING has Read and File Scan rights to the PUBLIC directory of the MONA_LISA_SYS volume because both AKING and MONA_LISA_SYS belong to the Administration container. A default login script automatically maps a search path to this directory.

SYS:LOGIN   The LOGIN directory contains the LOGIN commands and other files required to log users into the system. It is mapped to the first network drive at workstations before logging in.

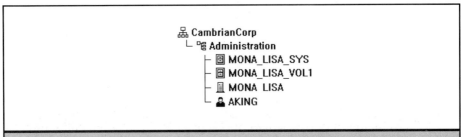

Figure 20-3. *Objects within the same container have similar rights*

SYS:MAIL   The MAIL directory is a remnant of previous NetWare versions. NetWare used to create a subdirectory in MAIL for each user and store their login scripts in these subdirectories. Login scripts are now stored as part of user objects in the NetWare Directory Services system. However, MAIL is retained for applications that require it.

Organizing Directories

The directory structure on your volumes should be optimized to improve performance and simplify its administration. A number of tips are listed in this section to help you with the organization, but the most important is to separate document files from program files to organize the directory structure in a way that makes backups easier. Program files don't need to be backed up every day since they typically do not change. Data files, however, usually require daily backup. Storing data files in the same directory as the programs used to create them would force you to back up all the files, which could take a considerably longer time and require more backup media. Of course, on large networks, backups should occur automatically at night on a regular basis with no user intervention required.

Remember that rights flow down, so if you grant users Read and File Scan rights to a directory called APPS (for applications), they will be able to run any program in APPS or its subdirectories. Figure 20-4 illustrates a directory structure that separates programs from data and makes the assignment of rights easier. The APPS directory holds subdirectories where applications are stored. You can back up this branch every week. The DOCS directory holds subdirectories where document files are stored. You back up this branch every day.

To let users run programs in the LOTUS and WORD directories, grant them Read and File Scan rights in the APPS directory. Since rights flow down, they can run the programs in the subdirectories. To let a user run Lotus 1-2-3, but not

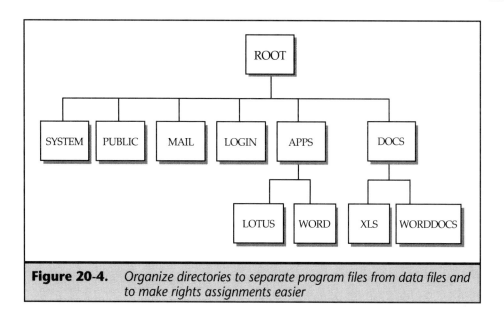

Figure 20-4.   *Organize directories to separate program files from data files and to make rights assignments easier*

Word, assign rights for that user only in the LOTUS directory. You would follow the same strategy to assign rights in the DOCS directory, except that you might grant some users read-only rights and grant other users the rights to create and edit files.

NOTE: Trustee rights assignments granted to a user in a directory override any rights inherited from directories higher up in the directory structure.

Figure 20-4 shows a rather simplified directory tree, but it illustrates the basic structure for program and data files. In reality, large corporations that have many servers and volumes will have many directory tree branches that look like this. Here are a few points to keep in mind when organizing directory structures:

■ Place name space support for other file types, such as UNIX, Macintosh, and OS/2 files, on separate volumes.

■ If you have hundreds of users, install a separate server to hold users' personal directories. This separates the users' personal traffic from the traffic that needs to access services on the main NetWare server.

■ Some files require auditing, as discussed in Chapter 32. Group these files together, if possible.

■ Files that need to be compressed should be organized into separate directories. Files targeted for migration should ideally have their own volume.

■ Applications use executable files that are prone to virus attack. Keep these files separate so that you can apply security features to them that prevent attacks. Never give casual users any rights in program directories except Read and File Scan.

User Directories

When you create a new user object, you can specify a directory where that user has full Supervisor access rights. Within that directory, the user can create subdirectories, store files, and load applications. The user can also grant other users access rights to the directory or its subdirectories if he or she wishes. User directories are optional. Disk space limitations might prohibit their use. If users have hard drives at their own workstations, consider letting them store some of their personal files on those drives, but make sure the users follow a strict backup procedure because the files won't be included in the central backup strategy provided for the network.

The best way to organize user directories if you decide to use them is to create a directory called USERS or HOME, and then attach all user directories to it. If your network has a lot of users in different departments, create directories such as SALES/USERS and ACCTG/USERS to further separate and organize the directories. If there are hundreds of users accessing files in their user directories, consider moving user directories to a separate volume or a separate server to improve performance.

DOS Directories

It is rare that a company will standardize on a single version of DOS. Some users might have DOS version 4.1 and others might have DOS version 5. If you want to keep a copy of DOS files on the server, you need to make sure that every version used throughout the company is available to users. For example, if users boot their workstation by using DOS 5, they will need access to DOS 5 files on the server.

Login scripts can contain commands that examine the type of DOS loaded at a user's workstation and then create a search path to a directory that holds the same version of DOS. The standard way of organizing DOS versions is to place them in subdirectories of the PUBLIC directory. In this way, users get Read and File Scan rights in the DOS directories through inheritance from PUBLIC.

For example, you can create subdirectories of the PUBLIC directory that are called MSDOS/4.1 and MSDOS/5.0. If the login script detects DOS 4.1 at a user's workstation, it creates a search drive mapping to SYS:PUBLIC/MSDOS/4.1.

Drive Mappings and the MAP Command

A drive mapping is a shorthand reference to a long directory name, and a search drive mapping is a search path to a directory that contains executable program files. You create drive mappings so that you can easily switch to or reference a directory by using a drive letter. The DOS SUBST command accomplishes the same thing. Search drive mappings let you execute programs in directories other than the one you are in, just like path statements in DOS.

The MAP command is used to create drive maps and search drive maps. Although you can execute it at the prompt during any NetWare session to create new mappings, those mappings are not saved for your next session. Therefore, MAP commands are more commonly placed in login scripts, as you'll see in Chapter 28. Occasionally, however, you'll need to execute a MAP command during a network session, so the basic features of the command are covered here.

To display your current drive mappings, simply type the MAP command by itself. You'll see a list of the mapped drive letters you can switch to, followed by a list of search drive maps. An example is shown here:

```
Drives A,B,C,D map to a local disk
Drive F: = MONA_LISA_SYS:USERS\JJONES
Drive G: = MONA_LISA_SYS:DOCS\XLS
Drive H: = MONA_LISA_SYS:DOCS\WORDDOCS
         -----      Search Drives      -----
S1:= Z:. MONA_LISA_SYS:PUBLIC
S2:= Y:. MONA_LISA_SYS:APPS\WORD
S3:= X:. MONA_LISA_SYS:APPS\LOTUS

S4:= C:\WINDOWS
S5:= C:\DOS
```

The first line lists the local drives. The second line indicates that the first network drive is F, which is mapped to the user's local directory. Drive G and drive H are mapped to document directories so that the user can easily switch to them by typing the drive letters. At the bottom are the search drive mappings.

Note that directories listed in your DOS path are translated into NetWare search drives and listed at the bottom.

New NetWare users are often confused by search drives. In DOS, a single path specifies all the directories that are searched for program files. However, NetWare's server, volume, and directory designation can't be specified in a DOS path because of the colon and backslash separators. So NetWare's designers created a separate feature that lets you assign a search path that includes server, volume, and directory names to a drive letter. Note that search drive mapping is not necessary or possible under OS/2 because the OS/2 PATH, LIBPATH, and DPATH commands support NetWare's naming schemes.

Search drive mappings are actually numbered in the order the operating system searches the directories, but you refer to each search map by using a drive letter. The first search drive is S1 and is also called Z. You can map up to 16 search drives by using letters. You start with Z and work backwards up to K.

NOTE: You can have only 26 drive mappings. Some of those drive mappings are assigned to the local directories specified in the DOS path.

Mapping Commands

This section illustrates a few MAP command examples. You can execute similar commands at your workstation. When you're done, simply log out and then log back in. The mappings you create at the console are not saved from one session to another.

NOTE: Do not remove the search drive mapping for the PUBLIC directory. You won't be able to execute NetWare public commands, including the LOGOUT command, unless you remap the search drive or switch to the PUBLIC directory.

You would type the following command to map the drive letter H to the SYS:PUBLIC directory. Note that this does not destroy the search drive mapping already in place.

```
MAP H:=SYS:PUBLIC
```

You can now switch to the PUBLIC directory and list its files by typing **H:**, pressing ENTER, typing **DIR**, and pressing ENTER.

This command maps drive letter I to the BUDGDOCS directory on the APPS volume of the ACCTG server:

```
MAP I:=ACCTG/APPS:BUDGDOCS
```

To create a search drive mapping, you need to specify a search drive number. The following command creates a search drive mapping with a path to the SYS:APPS\LOTUS directory so that you can run the program files in it:

```
MAP S4:=SYS:APPS\LOTUS
```

To insert a search drive mapping without replacing any existing mappings, including those used for your local DOS directories, use the INS (Insert) parameter, as shown here:

```
MAP INS S4:=SYS:APPS\LOTUS
```

To view MAP help information, type the following:

```
MAP /?
```

Drive mappings are covered in more detail in Chapter 26 and in Chapter 29, which covers login scripts.

Login Scripts

Login scripts are a vital feature in NetWare. They include commands that are executed when a user logs in, and they establish a working environment for users who need to access directories and run programs. The MAP command discussed previously is one of the primary commands placed in login scripts. Login scripts are created and edited by using the NetWare Administrator or NETADMIN utility. Login scripts are briefly discussed here to familiarize you with their importance and the way they establish a user's working session.

There are three types of login scripts:

■ *System login scripts* are part of a container object, such as an organization object or organizational unit object. The login scripts in a container execute for all users under that container. In Figure 20-5, a login script could be created in the CambrianCorp container that would run for all users inside the CambrianCorp container, but not for users in containers under CambrianCorp. A login script in DivWest would run only for users that belong to DivWest. Finally, a login script in the department container Administration would run only for users in the Administration department.

■ *Profile login scripts* execute for specific users, who might not be part of the same container object. For example, a login script that displays messages for the company bowling league might run for selected users in any department under DivWest or DivEast in Figure 20-5. Unlike system login scripts, container objects do not impose a boundary on who can be assigned a profile login script.

■ *Personal login scripts* can be created for every user, and users can change them if supervisors grant them access rights to do so. For example, users who create their own directory structures under the personal USER directory need to create drive mappings that let them switch among directories. They can add these drive mappings to their own login scripts.

Login scripts are covered in more detail in Chapter 29. You can refer there any time you are ready to start creating login scripts for users.

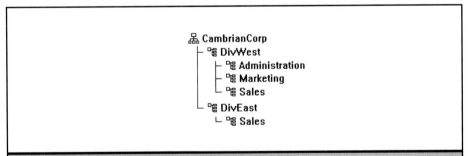

Figure 20-5.   *Login scripts created in a container object run for all users under that container*

Tasks Ahead for Administrators and Supervisors

In the next few chapters, you'll learn more about NetWare security and about object management. You'll also see how to create objects for users, groups, and supervisors. In addition, you'll see how to change the properties of these user objects, such as how to change their login or workstation restrictions, and you'll see how to grant users or groups access rights to objects, directories, and files.

CHAPTER 21

T he most prominent feature of the NetWare operating system is its security system. Password protection ensures that only authorized users log in, and you can use login restrictions to limit logins to specific times and specific workstations. After a user logs in, you can restrict the areas of the network he or she can access by using various trustee rights. There are two types of trustee rights, as described on the next page.

Network Hierarchy and Security

NOTE: Trustees *of an object, directory, or file are users who have been granted rights to access the object, directory, or file.*

■ *Directory and file rights*   These are the rights you grant to give users access to directories and files so they can use the data and programs stored in them. Access rights to a directory include access rights to all the files in that directory, but you can revoke rights for individual files if necessary. Users obtain rights to directories and files by being specifically granted those rights or by *inheriting* them because they have the rights in parent directories.

NOTE: *Rights that flow down from a container object to leaf objects, or from a directory to a subdirectory, are referred to as* inherited rights.

■ *Object and property rights*   All users and resources on the network are represented by objects. Supervisor-level users manage these objects by being granted rights to view and change object properties. *Object rights* determine who can create and change objects. *Property rights* determine who can view and change specific properties of those objects.

NetWare Directory Services provides a higher level of security than was provided by previous versions of NetWare. When you use the Windows-based NetWare Administrator, the process of managing objects and granting access rights is greatly simplified. Administrators can grant department managers rights to create and manage objects within the containers that represent their departments.

Planning is critical in NetWare v.4. With proper planning, you'll set up a NetWare Directory Services tree structure that corresponds to the structure and needs of your company and also simplifies the assignment of trustee rights. For example, containers provide a simple way to grant users access to a whole assortment of objects or to directories and files on volumes. If you make a user a trustee of a container, the user obtains the rights of the container such as rights to files and directories on volume objects.

NetWare Security Features

NetWare security starts with the login process. After a user is logged in, their rights on the network are determined by NDS. This section discusses access rights, how they are assigned, and how they affect access to the system.

Trustee Rights

Trustee rights give users the ability to access directories and files and to manage objects:

- A trustee of a NetWare Directory Services object can be given rights to view it in the NDS tree, delete it, rename it, and if it is a container, create other objects within it. A trustee can also be given the rights to view and change the properties of the object.

- A trustee of a directory can be given rights to view, change, delete, and create files within the directory. A trustee can also be given the rights to change the attributes, name, trustee assignments, and Inherited Rights Filter for the directory.

- If a user is granted the Supervisor right to an object, directory, or file, that user has unrestricted rights to the object, directory, or file.

NOTE: If a user is granted Supervisor rights to a container that holds a volume object, he or she has supervisor rights to all the directories on those volumes and servers. You can block object Supervisor rights, but not directory and file Supervisor rights, by using an Inherited Rights Filter.

Root Directory Rights in the File System

The file and directory rights for the root directory of each volume are recorded in each volume object. These are separate from the object and property rights that control access to the volume object. When a NetWare server and its volumes are installed, the user installing the server and its volumes is assigned as a trustee of the root directory with Supervisor file and directory rights. As in previous versions of NetWare, the Supervisor right to files and directories cannot be blocked by an Inherited Rights Filter.

The user who installed the server and volumes can make other trustee assignments to the directories and files by using the FILER or NetWare Administrator utility. If another trustee has been granted the Supervisor directory right to the root directory of the volume, the original installer trustee can be deleted.

NOTE: If a user object is created in a container without a volume, search drive mappings to the PUBLIC directory in the default login script will fail. You must make the user object a trustee of the PUBLIC directory on a volume in another container.

User Hierarchy

A NetWare network can contain users who have many different types of access and control. This section classifies those users and describes their functions on the network. Users fall into two general groups:

- *Supervisors* This group consists of administrators and supervisors who have the Supervisor right or who have a few limited object and property trustee rights to manage NetWare Directory Services objects.

- *Normal users* Users who need to access the file system but don't need to manage other users or resource objects belong to this group. These users are granted directory and file trustee rights.

Within these general groups there are many different types of users. These types of users are described next, starting with the ADMIN user, who is the first user to log into the sytem.

The Network Administrator

The NetWare installation program creates the network administrator (ADMIN) user object by default. The ADMIN user belongs to the root directory, and because rights flow down through the NDS directory tree, the ADMIN user has unlimited rights to all objects in the tree.

CAUTION: Use care when you are logged in as the ADMIN user. It's possible to remove your own Supervisor right to an object. If you do, and no other user has been assigned Supervisor rights to the object, access to it is cut off completely.

If you decide to remove the ADMIN user object, be sure you have created other user objects and assigned them the appropriate rights to manage branches of the directory tree.

Users

Everybody who logs into the system is a user and is represented by a user object in NetWare Directory Services. A user object holds the user's name, location, phone number, and other information, including login restrictions, account balances, and personal login scripts. When creating a new user object, you can specify a home directory where the user can store his or her personal programs and files. Users should have full access rights to this directory so that they can create subdirectories and files within it as needed.

After you create a user object, you can change its properties, some of which are listed here:

- Login restrictions

- Password restrictions

- Login time restrictions

- Login scripts

- Security equivalences

- Rights to the file system

- Group memberships

Changing properties for individual users can be tedious. Instead, you can create a *user template* in every container, which defines the properties you want to assign to any users added to the container. When you create a new user object, you can specify that you want to use the template values. Other ways to simplify the management of user objects are listed here:

- Make users members of groups, and then assign trustee rights to the groups.

- Assign files system rights to containers. Every user object that belongs to the container will then have these rights.

- Delegate management tasks to other users by granting them Supervisor rights to specific branches of the NetWare Directory Services tree or to the file system.

Supervisors

In the context of this book, a supervisor is a user who has the Supervisor right to a container object in the NetWare Directory Services tree. That means the user has unrestricted rights to that container and any container or leaf objects that branch from it, unless a higher-level supervisor has blocked some of these rights. A network might have many supervisors, each managing a particular branch of the directory tree. Branches typically represent departments within companies.

NOTE: *A supervisor doesn't necessarily need to have the Supervisor right. You can create "limited supervisors" with only specific rights.*

If you are the ADMIN user and you are just beginning to set up the directory tree structure, one of the first things to do is create the organizational unit objects for each division or department (if they weren't created as part of the server installation). Then you can create supervisor objects to manage the organizational units. If you grant the supervisors the Supervisor right, they can create and manage the directory tree structure within the organizational units.

For example, assume you've just installed the server Mona_Lisa in the Administration department and the server Marantz in the Sales department. NetWare creates the organizational unit containers Administration and Sales during the setup. You log in from a workstation and start NetWare Administrator. Then you create the user object ASmith in the Administration container and the user object AJones in the Sales container, as shown in Figure 21-1. You grant the user objects the Supervisor right in their respective containers, thus making them supervisors of that branch.

Supervisors can exist at branches in the NDS tree to manage the objects in that branch. For example, suppose that ASmith creates an organizational unit container called Personnel that branches from the Administration container, as shown in Figure 21-2. ASmith then creates a user object called TMalone to

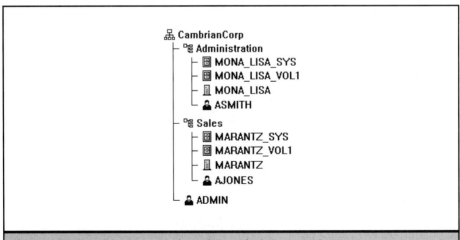

Figure 21-1. *Directory tree branches with their supervisors*

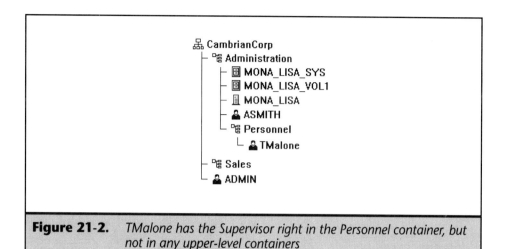

Figure 21-2.   *TMalone has the Supervisor right in the Personnel container, but not in any upper-level containers*

supervise the new container. After TMalone is granted the Supervisor right to the Personnel container, he can create new objects in that container or expand the directory tree by adding container objects that branch from Personnel.

> NOTE: *Keep in mind that TMalone's Supervisor right in the example encompasses only the Personnel container, not any upper-level containers.*

Operators

An operator is a user who has responsibility for a system resource such as a printer or a server. You grant the user limited rights to the resource object so that he or she can change the object's property fields if necessary. For example, a printer object has property fields that contain information about the location of the printer, its description, its queues, its notification list, and its configuration. The operator of a printer should have sufficient rights to change these fields if necessary.

As you have seen, operators are usually associated with some hardware device. They are usually on the list of users to notify or contact when there is a problem with the device. For example, if a printer runs out of paper or needs a form change, users of that printer can view the printer object's properties to see who is in charge of the printer. They can then either send an e-mail message to the user, or call the user on the phone.

Groups

Groups are collections of user objects. You create groups to simplify the task of managing large numbers of user objects. Rather than assigning directory and file access rights to individual users, one at a time, you include those users in a group and then assign the rights to the group. Each member of the group gets the rights that are assigned to the group. A user can be a member of more than one group. Here are some examples of ways you could use groups:

- You could create a word processing group and then grant the group rights to run a certain word processing program and store files in its data directories.

- You could create electronic mail groups such as Managers and Marketing, and then send e-mail to those groups rather than to each member of the group individually.

- Groups provide a convenient way to change or remove the rights of a large number of users. You can delete an entire group, and you can remove user objects from a group. Those user objects still exist, but they no longer have the rights of the group.

NOTE: A group is not a container object. It is simply a collection of user object names.

Looking at Rights

Let's take a closer look at rights. You've seen that network users need access rights to access resources on the network and to work with files in the filing system. Rights determine exactly how a user can access another object and how a user can access directories and files in the filing system. Tables 21-1, 21-2, 21-3, and 21-4 list the directory, file, object, and property rights.

NOTE: An object contains a list of its trustees, but a trustee does not hold a list of what objects it has rights to.

Right	Description
Supervisor	All rights to the directory, its files, and its subdirectories. The directory Supervisor right cannot be blocked by an Inherited Rights Filter. Users with this right can grant other users rights to the directory, its files, and its subdirectories
Read	The right to run programs in the directory and to open files in the directory and read their contents
Write	The right to open and change the contents of existing files in the directory
Create	The right to create new files and subdirectories in the directory
Erase	The right to delete the directory, its files, and its subdirectories
Modify	The right to change the attributes or names of the directory, its files, and its subdirectories, but not the right to change their contents
File Scan	The right to see the directory and its files by using the DIR and NDIR commands
Access Control	The right to change the trustee assignments and Inherited Rights Filter of the directory, its files, and its subdirectories

Table 21-1.   *Directory Rights*

How to Assign Rights to Files and Directories

To create trustee assignments for a directory, you first open the volume that contains the directory by double-clicking the volume object. A listing similar to that shown in Figure 21-3 appears.

Next you click the folder of the directory you want to work with by using the right mouse button, and choose Details. A Details dialog box similar to that shown in Figure 21-4 appears.

To add a trustee, you click the Add Trustee button and then select an object, such as a user or group, from the list. Note that the Managers group is highlighted in the figure and that its current access rights are indicated in the Access Rights box. You can change the rights at any time (assuming you have rights to do so) by changing the options in this dialog box.

NOTE: The details for this procedure are covered in Chapter 24.

Right	Description
Supervisor	All rights to the file. The file Supervisor right cannot be blocked with an Inherited Rights Filter. Users who have this right can grant other users any rights to the file and can change the file's Inherited Rights Filter
Read	The right to open and read the file
Create	The right to salvage the file after it has been deleted
Write	The right to open and write to an existing file
Erase	The right to erase the file
Modify	The right to change the attributes and name of the file, but not the right to change its contents
File Scan	The right to see the file by using the DIR and NDIR commands, including the directory structure from the file to the root directory
Access Control	The right to change the trustee assignments and Inherited Rights Filter of the file

Table 21-2.   *File Rights*

How to Assign Rights to Objects

There are two ways to assign trustee rights by using NetWare Administrator:

■ The easiest way is by using the drag and drop method. You click the object you want to make a trustee of another object, and then you drag and drop it onto the object you want to make it a trustee of. An Object Trustees dialog box appears, as shown in Figure 21-5, so that you can specify rights to the object.

■ The second method is to click the object itself by using the right mouse button and then choose Trustees of this Object from its pop-up menu. You then need to specify exactly which object you want to make a trustee of the current object.

Let's assume that you wanted to grant the Managers group mentioned previously trustee rights to the MONA_LISA_SYS volume shown in Figure 21-3.

Right	Description
Supervisor	All access privileges to the object, including access to all the object's properties. The object Supervisor right *can* be blocked by an Inherited Rights Filter, both for objects below where the Supervisor right is granted and for individual properties of an object
Browse	The right to see the object in the directory tree. The name of the object is returned when a search is made that matches the object
Create	The right to create a new object that is subordinate to the object in the directory tree. Rights are not defined for the new object. This right is available only for container objects, because noncontainer objects cannot have subordinates
Delete	The right to delete the object from the directory tree. Objects that have subordinates cannot be deleted unless the subordinates are deleted first
Rename	The right to change the name of the object, in effect changing the naming property. This changes what the object is called in complete names

Table 21-3. *Object Rights*

Note that volumes are objects, not directories. You drag and drop the Managers group icon onto the volume object, which opens the Object Trustees dialog box, as shown in Figure 21-5. From this dialog box, you choose the appropriate rights for the group and click OK.

If you use the second method for assigning trustee rights, the same dialog box shown in Figure 21-5 appears, but NetWare Administrator doesn't know which object you want to make a trustee of the object. You must click the Add Trustee button and then browse the directory tree to locate the object you want to make a trustee.

NOTE: Be careful when granting rights to volume objects. The volume object is the transition point between NetWare Directory Services objects and the file system. If you grant a user object Supervisor rights to a volume object, that object also has Supervisor rights to the root directory (and consequently all other directories) in the volume.

Right	Description
Supervisor	All rights to the property. The property Supervisor right *can* be blocked by an object's Inherited Rights Filter.
Compare	The right to compare any value to a value of the property. A compare operation can return True or False, but you cannot see the value of the property. The Read right includes the Compare right
Read	The right to read the values of the property. Compare is a subset of Read. If the Read right is given, compare operations are also allowed
Write	The right to add, change, or remove any values of the property. The Write right includes the Add Self and Managed rights
Add Self	A trustee with the Add Self right can add or remove himself or herself as a value of the property. The trustee cannot affect any other values of the property. This right is meaningful only for properties that contain object names as values, such as group membership lists and mailing lists. The Write right includes the Add Self right

Table 21-4.   *Property Rights*

Object Property Rights

Every object has a set of properties that define its name, location, department, and other information. These properties are displayed in fields on the Details dialog box of the object, as shown in Figure 21-6. You can double-click any object in NetWare Administrator to see its Details dialog box.

You can control which users can view and change these fields by specifying property rights in the Object Trustees dialog box. Note the Property Rights field in the Object Trustees dialog box shown in Figure 21-5. Currently, All Properties is selected. If you click Selected Properties in this dialog box, you can change the rights that selected objects have to individual properties of the current object. The properties listed in the box are the names of the fields you see when you work with the Details dialog box. For example, you could revoke the Read right to the Telephone field so that the trustee of the object cannot see the telephone number. Alternatively, you might give users in the Personnel department the Write right to the Telephone field so that they can change this field.

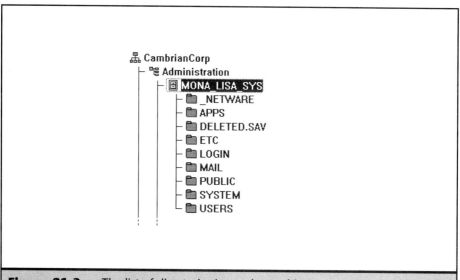

Figure 21-3. *The list of directories in a volume object*

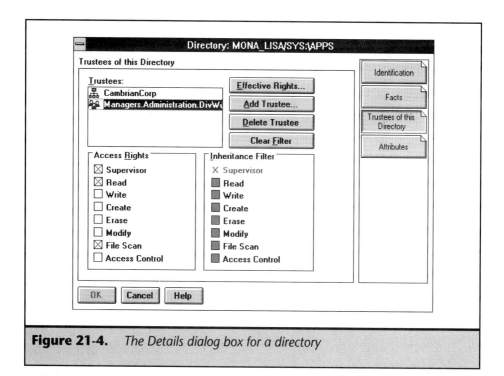

Figure 21-4. *The Details dialog box for a directory*

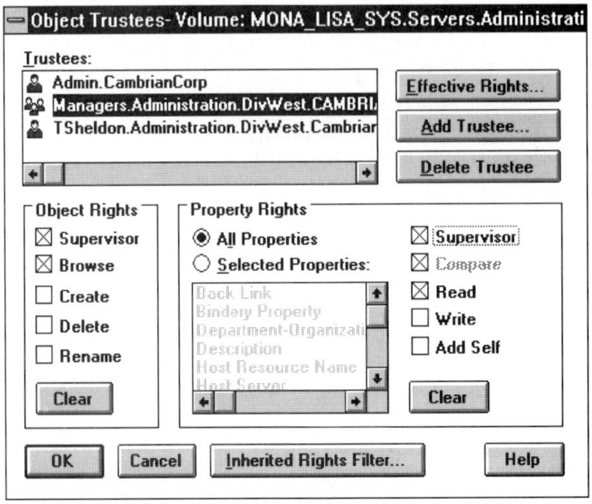

Figure 21-5. The Object Trustees dialog box is used to add trustees to an object and grant them rights

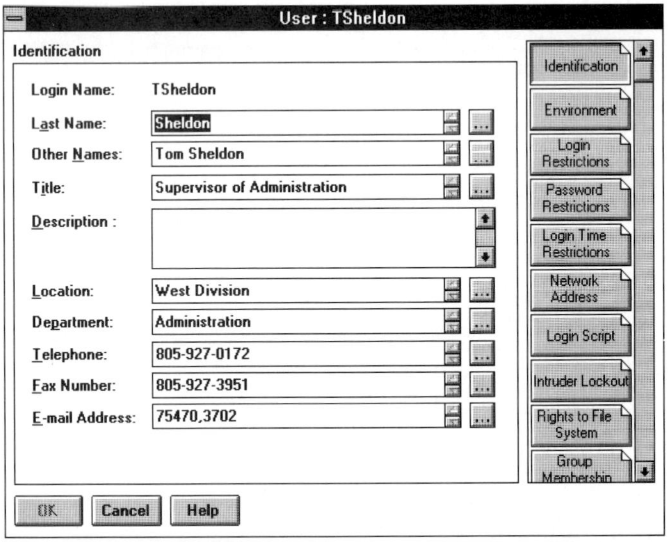

Figure 21-6. The Details dialog box for a user object. The Property Rights field on the Object Trustees dialog box (Figure 21-5) controls access to the fields in the Details dialog box

NOTE: By default, all users can view the properties of an object but cannot change them. Users can change the login script of their own user object, however.

The Details dialog box (see Figure 21-6) is a multipage dialog box. The buttons on the right open other pages that display different properties. This first page contains basic information about the object, in this case a user object. Note the names of the other pages of information, such as Login Restrictions and Login Script. Typically, other network users can view the Details dialog box for an object, but they can't change the fields unless you've granted them specific rights to do so. A supervisor normally has rights to view and change all the property values of the objects he or she supervises. To assist in updating information, you can add operator trustees who have limited rights to change fields such as Telephone, Fax Number, and E-mail Address. To grant those specific rights, you return to the Object Trustees dialog box. After adding an operator as a trustee of an object, you click Selected Properties and choose the properties to change. For example, you could pick Telephone from the list and then click Read and Write.

Inheritance

Perhaps the most important concept to grasp about the NetWare object and file security system is that rights flow down. This is easiest to understand by examining the file system. If a user has Read, Write, and Create rights to a directory, that user has those same rights to its subdirectories, unless the rights are specifically changed. The rights flow down the directory structure. When a supervisor *specifically changes* rights, it means that he or she blocks the rights from being inherited in the subdirectory for all users, for a group of users, or for a single user.

The same concept applies to objects. If a user has trustee rights to a container object, that user has the same rights to any container and leaf objects that belong to the container object. For example, if a container holds a printer object and a user is made a trustee of the container, the user has the same trustee rights to the printer. This flow of rights continues down through every container unless the rights are blocked.

In a similar fashion, a user belonging to a container gets all the trustee rights of that container. An example will help explain why you might want to make containers trustees. Assume that your company has a directory structure like that shown in Figure 21-7. User object ACrumb in the west coast (DivWest) sales office needs to access the DOCS directory on the SYS volume of the Marantz

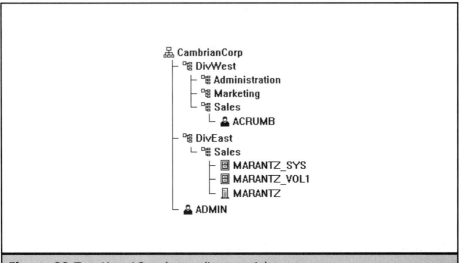

Figure 21-7. *How ACrumb gets directory rights*

server in the east coast (DivEast) sales office. To make ACrumb a trustee of the DOCS directory, you choose the directory and then create a trustee assignment. The trustee assignment could be any of the following:

■ Grant ACrumb trustee rights to the DOCS directory.

■ Grant the Sales container in the DivWest container trustee rights to the DOCS directory. Because the ACrumb object is a leaf of the Sales container, it gets the same rights by inheritance. Any other objects in the Sales container also get the trustee rights.

■ Grant the DivWest container trustee rights to the DOCS directory. Now every object belonging to DivWest is granted trustee rights.

■ Grant the CambrianCorp container trustee rights to the DOCS directory. Although impractical, you could make this container a trustee, which would grant every object in the directory tree trustee rights to the DOCS directory.

This demonstrates how rights flow down the tree structure. Starting at the bottom of the tree, only user object ACrumb is granted the rights. As you go up the directory tree and assign trustee rights to container objects at higher levels, the number of objects assigned the trustee rights increases. Assigning trustee rights to container objects can simplify your job, but you need to be careful. It might not be appropriate to grant some of the objects in the containers trustee rights. A better way to assign trustee rights is to add users to groups and then assign rights to the groups.

NOTE: If you create a new user object in the container object that contains the SYS volume, that user object has the ability to list files and run programs in the PUBLIC directory. This is because the container object holding the SYS volume automatically has Read and File scan directory rights to the PUBLIC directory.

Inherited Rights Filters

Now it's time to discuss how you can prevent inherited rights from getting out of control. An Inherited Rights Filter (IRF) is used to block the normal flow of rights down the directory tree. Basically, if a user has Read, Write, Create, and File Scan rights to a directory, the user also has those rights to the directory's subdirectories unless you block some or all of them by using an IRF (or make new trustee assignments in the subdirectories). For example, you could block the Write and Create rights to prevent users from creating and modifying files in a subdirectory.

NOTE: The most important point about IRFs is that they belong to a NetWare Directory Services object or a directory in the file system and that they apply to all users who access the object or directory.

An IRF changes the way inherited rights flow down through the directory structure or the NDS directory tree. You use an IRF when the rights that flow down are sufficient but need to be altered slightly. Note the following:

- If the IRF is on a container object, rights are blocked for the container object and everything within it. A container object IRF blocks rights for the container's leaf objects.

- Every object or directory can have its own IRF.

- An IRF or a new trustee assignment cannot block Supervisor rights to directories. The Supervisor directory right is inherited in all subdirectories and by all files. However, an IRF can block object Supervisor rights.

Effective Rights

The actual rights that a user has to a directory or object depend on the following, which combine to form the object's *effective rights*:

- The object's trustee assignments to the directory or file
- Inherited rights from parent directories
- Rights granted to groups that the user belongs to
- Security equivalences (discussed in the next section)

NOTE: Don't forget that users are also granted rights for the groups they belong to. These group rights might not immediately be obvious.

Let's look at an example to help explain how effective rights can change. Assume that a new directory called ACCTG is created and that the user object TBones is made a trustee of that directory object with Read, Write, Create, and File Scan rights. This is shown under *A* in Figure 21-8. Because rights flow down, TBones also has Read, Write, Create, and File Scan rights to the DATA subdirectory in ACCTG, as shown under B.

Now assume that TBones' supervisor creates a REPORTS subdirectory in DATA and applies an Inherited Rights Filter to it that blocks the Write and Create rights. TBones' effective rights to the REPORTS directory are now as shown under C. Finally, the supervisor creates a special data directory for TBones called TBONES, and makes TBones a trustee of the directory with Read, Write, Create, and File Scan rights, as shown under *D*. This specific trustee assignment overrides the Inherited Rights Filter.

REMEMBER: Specific trustee assignments override an Inherited Rights Filter, as shown by D in Figure 21-8.

Security Equivalences

You can make user objects *security equivalent* to other objects, which means they get all the login restrictions, station restrictions, and access rights of the objects they are security equivalent to. For example, if the user JArnold, a supervisor of a

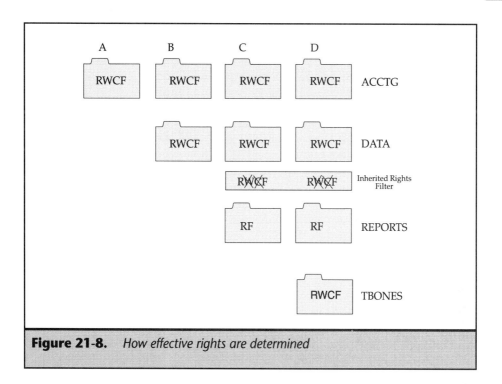

Figure 21-8.   *How effective rights are determined*

directory tree branch, is going on vacation, you could make another user object security equivalent to JArnold. That user then has Supervisor rights in the branch and can perform the same tasks as JArnold. The security equivalent user even has the same rights to JArnold's private directory, so you need to use this feature with caution. Security equivalences can simplify a manager's tasks, but use them sparingly and with caution, making sure you don't give users rights where they don't belong.

Security Equivalences is a button on the Details dialog box for user objects. A trustee of a user object can add other user objects to its security equivalences list. To do so, this trustee must have the Write property right to the Security Equivalences property of the object.

NOTE: Do not grant users the right to change their own security equivalence properties. They could add an object that has the Supervisor right and thus gain access to areas of the network they are not authorized to access. You can even go so far as to block the Write right on the Security Equivalences field by using an Inherited Rights Filter.

Special Objects and Templates

The following objects and templates can help you administer objects and rights in the NDS tree:

- ■ *Organizational role object* This object defines a position or role within an organization. Use an organizational role object to specify a position that people in the organization can fill, such as Team Leader or Vice President. In this way, if a new user takes over the role, you don't have to reassign rights to the new user. Instead, you simply make that user a member of the organizational role.

- ■ *Profile objects* You use a profile to create special login scripts for users in different branches of the directory tree. Normally, the organizational unit container a user belongs to has a login script that runs for every user in that container. Although users also have personal login scripts, you might want to create login scripts for users who are spread out over the network, not just within one container. For example, you could create a profile for a company bowling league that displays messages about upcoming events to all users who belong to the league, no matter which department (container) they belong to.

- ■ *User template* A user template simplifies the creation of new user objects by allowing you to assign them predefined property values and object/directory rights. You can create user templates in every container where you plan to add user objects. Then, when you create a new user object, you can choose to give it the property values and rights of the user template, or you can specify those values and rights individually.

- ■ *Alias object* An alias object points to an object in another container. For example, if users in one department print to a printer in another department, you might want to create an alias of that printer object in their branch of the directory tree. This simply makes it easier to refer to the object. Alias objects can also be useful to managers who are assigning trustee rights.

Security Rules in a Nutshell

This section provides a review of the NetWare Directory Services access rights and the NetWare filing system access rights.

■ Container objects can hold other container objects and leaf objects. Directories can contain subdirectories. Rights flow down through these structures unless the rights are blocked by a new set of trustee rights or by an Inherited Rights Filter.

■ When an Inherited Rights Filter changes the rights of a container or file system directory, the new set of rights flow down to everything below that point.

■ The Access Control right is required to change the trustee rights or IRF of a file or directory.

■ The Supervisor right grants a user unrestricted capabilities in file system directories and in objects.

■ It's possible to revoke all rights for all users (even ADMIN) to an object, so be careful. Never remove a user's Supervisor right to an object unless another user is granted the Supervisor right to the object. Doing so would cut off object management rights to the object.

■ Rights to the file system are granted separately from rights to NDS objects. You can grant directory trustee rights to a user without the need to make that user a trustee of the volume, server, or container object that holds the directory. However, users who have the Supervisor right to a volume have the Supervisor right to all directories on that volume.

■ Trustees of an object can change or delete the object and can create other objects within it, depending on the trustee rights they have been granted.

■ Objects hold property information about the entity they represent. Properties can be viewed and changed by other users, depending on the property rights they have for the object.

■ Object property rights can be all-inclusive or specific. If All Property rights is granted, the trustee has the specified rights for all properties for which Selected Property rights are not granted. If Selected Property rights are granted to one or more properties, those rights override the property rights granted by the All Property rights.

■ Selected Property rights in a container do not flow down to other objects. The reason for this is obvious—objects within other objects are usually not the same type of object and thus have different properties.

■ To change object rights and properties, the Write property right is needed.

■ In the NDS directory tree, the Supervisor right flows all the way down into volume objects so that the supervisor has the Supervisor right to directories and files.

- Inherited rights can be overridden by creating new trustee assignments at lower levels in the NDS directory tree or in a file system directory tree.

- Supervisor rights cannot be blocked in the file system, but they can be blocked in the NDS directory tree.

- A user with object trustee rights to a container object has those same rights to every object in that container, including other containers within the container. An Inherited Rights Filter can block these rights, however.

- Leaf objects in a container obtain any trustee assignments granted to that container. If a container is made a trustee of a directory, all leaf objects in that container are also trustees of the directory.

- To give a user immediate access to the network, grant him or her security equivalence to a user who has the access to the system the user needs. Keep in mind that this user can browse any directory that belongs to the user he or she is security equivalent to.

- Create user templates in containers and assign default rights and restrictions to the templates before creating users within the containers. All user objects created in the container then obtain the rights and property values of the user templates if you specify it.

CHAPTER 22

N etWare v.4 includes two Windows-based or OS/2-based utilities and two text-based (DOS) utilities that network supervisors can use to administer NetWare Directory Services objects, directories, and files.

The NetWare Administrator and NETADMIN Utilities

■ *NetWare Administrator for Windows* A utility that helps you manage the NDS tree. It displays the tree in graphical format and displays commands and options on pull-down menus.

■ *NetWare User for Windows or for OS/2* A utility that is similar to the text-based NETUSER utility. You use NetWare User to log into the network, map drives, send messages to other users, and change the settings of your current session. NetWare User is discussed in conjunction with the NETUSER utility in Chapter 26.

■ *NETADMIN* The text-based version of NetWare Administrator; you run it at the DOS command line. Use this utility to manage NetWare Directory Services when you are not at a Windows or OS/2 workstation. NETADMIN does not provide file management features. You must use FILER or NetWare Administrator to work with the filing system.

■ *FILER* A directory and file management tool for both supervisors and users. Supervisors can use FILER to grant directory and file rights to users, to manage files, and to view volume information. Regular users can also use the utility, but which of its features they can use depends on their access rights. FILER is discussed in Chapter 24.

There are several other DOS command-line utilities, which are covered in later chapters. The first part of this chapter covers the basic operation of NetWare Administrator. Managing your system with NetWare Administrator is covered in Chapter 23. The second part of this chapter discusses how to use NETADMIN.

Using Windows Management Tools

This section assumes you are familiar with the basic techniques used to operate Windows, including working with window features such as scroll bars, drop-down menus, buttons, and dialog boxes. If you're not familiar with Windows, refer to one of the following Osborne/McGraw-Hill publications:

■ *Windows 3.1 Made Easy*, by Tom Sheldon (ISBN 0-07-881725-0)

■ *Windows 3.1: The Complete Reference*, by Tom Sheldon (ISBN 0-07-881889-3)

Windows 3.1 Made Easy is written for beginning and intermediate Windows users. It discusses basic operating techniques and the use of the Windows accessories. *Windows 3.1: The Complete Reference* is written for intermediate to advanced users. It includes discussions on networking, startup file settings, and other advanced and technical information.

Creating Startup Icons

When you install the NetWare workstation software on a Windows workstation (and choose to install the Windows utilities), Windows creates a group called NetWare Tools in the Program Manager. This group initially contains a startup icon for the NetWare User utility, as shown in Figure 22-1. If you don't see the NetWare Tools group, instructions for creating it and adding icons to it are discussed in the next section. You can add a startup icon for NetWare Administrator and some of the text-based utilities, such as PCONSOLE and RCONSOLE, to the NetWare Tools group. When you start a text-based utility from Windows, it appears in a full-size DOS window. The advantage of running text-based utilities under Windows is that you can quickly switch among applications by pressing CTRL-ESC.

Setting up Windows Utilities

This section explains how to create a NetWare Tools group if it doesn't exist, and how to add NetWare program icons to it. Before starting Windows, make sure you log into the network. This discussion assumes that drive Z is mapped as a search drive to the NetWare PUBLIC directory. It also assumes you installed Windows support when you set up network files on the workstation, as discussed in Chapter 18.

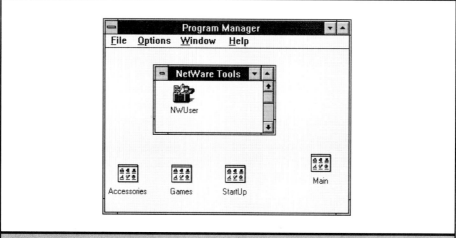

Figure 22-1.   *The NetWare Tools group with the NetWare User startup icon*

If the NetWare Tools group doesn't exist, start Windows and follow the steps listed next to create the group. If this group already exists and you want to create startup icons for NetWare User and NetWare Administrator, refer to the paragraph following this list.

1. Choose New from the File menu.

2. Click the Program Group button on the New Program Object dialog box, and then click OK.

3. In the Description field, type **NetWare Tools**, and then click OK.

The new group appears. Now you can create startup icons for NetWare User and NetWare Administrator by following the steps listed next. Follow the steps once for the NetWare User icon and then again for the NetWare Administrator icon, replacing the appropriate properties where instructed.

1. Click the NetWare Tools group to make sure it is selected.

2. Choose New from the File menu.

3. The Program Item field should be highlighted. Click OK.

4. When the Program Item Properties dialog box appears, type **NWUser** or **NWAdmin** in the Description field, depending on which icon you are creating.

5. Click the Browse button and use the dialog box to locate the executable file for the program. For NetWare User, locate NWUSER.EXE in your local Windows directory. For NetWare Administrator, locate NWADMIN.EXE in the PUBLIC directory on the NetWare server (in the drive list, choose the mapped drive letter of the PUBLIC directory).

6. Click the Change Icon button, and click OK to any messages that might appear. When the Change Icon dialog box appears, click the Browse button and use the techniques described in step 5 to locate the same files. Icons for Windows applications are located within their executable files.

7. The icon appears in the lower box and is already selected. Just click OK to return to the Program Item Properties dialog box, and then click OK again to create the startup icon.

8. A message appears that says the specified drive may not be available in a later session. This message is simply reminding you that Windows can't guarantee you'll always be connected to network drives and that if you're not, references to them won't work. Click Yes to complete the operation.

NOTE: The preceding procedure assumes NWADMIN.INI is located in your Windows directory. If it isn't, copy it from the SYS:PUBLIC directory on the server.

You can also run NetWare Administrator in OS/2 as a migrated Windows application. Follow the instructions in your OS/2 manual for migrating the NWADMIN.EXE file in the SYS:PUBLIC/OS2 directory on the server.

Running Text-Based Utilities from Windows

You can run NetWare's text-based utilities from Windows. Doing so makes it easy to switch among the utilities and other applications. Normally, DOS applications run in full-screen mode; to switch among applications, you press CTRL-ESC. However, you can run a DOS application in a resizable window, as shown in Figure 22-2, by highlighting the application's startup icon and then pressing ALT-ENTER. If you always want to run it in a window, you can specify the "windowed" option in a PIF file.

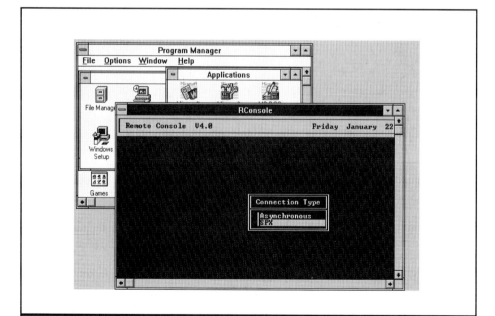

Figure 22-2.   *The DOS application RCONSOLE running in a resizable window*

NOTE: A DOS application running in a window does not obtain any of the Windows features associated with the graphical user interface. Running a text-based application in a window just makes it easier to switch among applications.

To create startup icons for DOS applications, you need a program information file (PIF) for each application. The NetWare workstation utilities includes a PIF called NWRCON.PIF in your Windows directory. This PIF contains startup parameters for the NetWare RCONSOLE utility. To start RCONSOLE from within Windows, you'll need to edit NWRCON.PIF by using the PIF Editor and specify the SYSTEM directory on your network drive where RCONSOLE.EXE is located. If you logged in as the network administrator, you should have a drive mapped to this directory. After NWRCON.PIF knows where the RCONSOLE.EXE program is, you can save it and create a startup icon for NWRCON.PIF in the Program Manager. Note that you create a startup icon for NWRCON.PIF, not for the RCONSOLE.EXE file. Follow these steps:

1. Start the PIF Editor, which is located in the Windows Main group.

2. Choose Open from the File menu, and then select NWRCON.PIF from the list. Click OK to open the PIF file for editing.

The settings in this file are designed to let you run text-based NetWare applications in resizable windows. Notice that the Windowed option is set in the Display Usage field. If you want to run the utility in full-screen mode instead, choose Full Screen. This might be necessary if your screen loses control when running the utility.

3. In the Program Filename field, type the drive letter and path to the RCONSOLE.EXE file in the NetWare SYSTEM directory. For example, if SYSTEM is mapped to drive F, type

```
F:\SYSTEM\RCONSOLE.EXE
```

4. Save the changes, and then follow the steps in the previous section to create a startup icon for NWRCON.PIF in the NetWare Tools group.

TIP: To run other NetWare utilities, make a copy of NWRCON.PIF, and then change the information in its Program Filename field to reflect the executable program name of the text-based utility you want to run on the NetWare server. Note that all NetWare utilities except RCONSOLE and ATOTAL are located in the PUBLIC directory.

Using NetWare Administrator

You use NetWare Administrator to manage objects, directories, and files. To start NetWare Administrator, double-click its icon in the Program Manager. A window similar to that shown in Figure 22-3 appears. In this example, the directory tree is displayed in the O=CambrianCorp document window. Your tree will look different, depending on how you installed your servers and if the directory tree has been modified.

Container objects form the branches of the directory tree. They can hold other containers or leaf objects. When you start NetWare Administrator, leaf objects in the directory tree are collapsed so that you see only the top organization container and its branching organizational unit containers. You can double-click these containers to expand or collapse the objects within them. In Figure 22-4, DivWest is expanded.

NOTE: Double-clicking a leaf object opens its Details dialog box, which shows all the properties for that object. To open the Details dialog box for a container object, click the object by using the right mouse button, and then choose Details.

The document window called O=CambrianCorp in Figure 22-3 is a *browser window.* You can open up nine browser windows at a time to view the directory

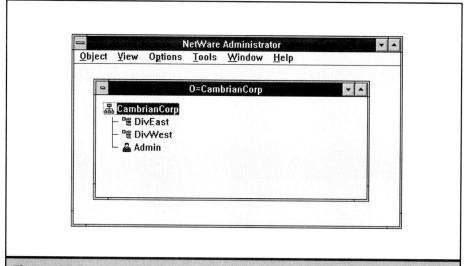

Figure 22-3. *NetWare Administrator showing the directory tree*

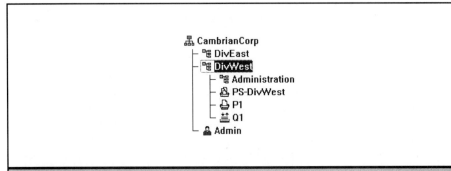

Figure 22-4.   *The directory tree with DivWest expanded*

tree. For example, you might open another window to view a specific branch of the tree, and still another to view all the printer objects and queues over the entire network. To open additional windows, choose Browse from the Tools menu. Then you can use filtering techniques to specify the types of objects you want to see in the window.

Types of Objects and Their Properties

The following list describes each type of container object and leaf object you can create and manage in NetWare Administrator. If you've just started to set up your directory tree, you will see only server and volume leaf objects in the containers where you installed your servers.

AFP Server   An Apple file server running the AppleTalk Filing Protocol.

Alias   Represents an object that is in another organizational unit container. An alias simplifies any references you need to make to that object. For example, if a supervisor in one branch of the tree has rights to access and manage a volume in another branch of the tree, create an alias for the volume in the branch where the supervisor's user object is located. When you use aliases, it's not necessary to specify long context names to refer to objects in other parts of the directory tree. The alias in the local branch points to the object instead.

Computer   Holds information about a workstation on the network, such as its serial number, node address, users, and location or department.

Directory Map Holds MAP commands to volumes and directories. You can reference these commands in a login script. If the location of an application changes, you simply change the directory map rather than changing each user's login script.

 Group Holds a list of users who belong to a group, such as Managers, Clerks, or Engineers. You can send mail to everyone in a group by sending mail to the group rather than to each user individually. Supervisors can assign trustee rights and other properties to groups; these rights and properties apply to each member of the group.

 NetWare Server Represents a NetWare server on the network.

 Organizational Role An object that has specific trustee rights. When you add user objects to the role, the user objects get all the rights of the role. An Organizational Role is similar to a group, except that the people occupying the role might change positions in the company and no longer need the rights of the role, even though they might still belong to the same groups, such as Managers, Clerks, or Bowling League. When users no longer need the rights of the role, you delete them from it.

 Organizational Unit A container object used to organize branches of the directory tree. It falls under organization objects or other organizational unit objects.

 Printer A printer that is attached to a print server, or a printer that is attached to a workstation and shared on the network.

 Print Server Represents a network print server located in the file server, or a stand-alone print server.

 Profile A special login script that is shared by more than one user. The profile script is executed after the script of the user's container but before the user's login script. Profile scripts make it easy to set up a network environment for a group of users.

Print Queue Holds print jobs that are directed to one or more printers. Users send print jobs to print queues.

 User The object that holds login account information for a network user.

 Volume Represents a physical volume on the hard disk of a file server. It records statistics about the volume. The user who installs a server automatically has Supervisor trustee rights to all volumes on that server.

Each object has a set of properties you can view by selecting the object and then choosing Details from the Object menu. Click any object on your window now. You'll see a Details dialog box similar to that shown in Figure 22-5. (This example dialog box displays the properties of a user object.) Although some properties might be common among objects, each object has a unique set of properties.

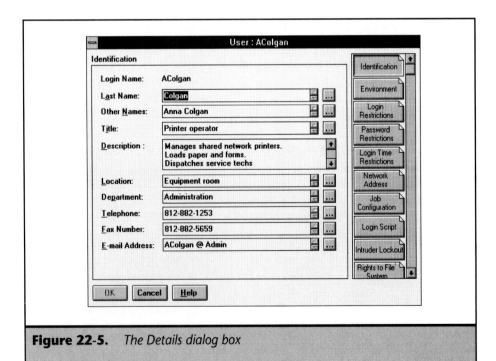

Figure 22-5. *The Details dialog box*

Each field in the Details dialog box holds a property of the object. You click the buttons on the right to view other *pages* of the dialog box, which hold other sets of properties. For example, if you click Password Restrictions, the dialog box displays the Password Restrictions page, as shown in Figure 22-6.

Users who have Supervisor rights can modify the fields in these pages to alter the properties of a user's account and apply restrictions to their access of the network.

TIP: If all user objects you create under a container object must have the same properties, you can create a user template to simplify the task. A user template holds default settings for new user objects.

Controlling Access to Properties

It's important to realize that supervisors can control who can change and who can view the information in the fields of the Details dialog box. By default, a user who doesn't have the Supervisor right can view the properties of his or her own

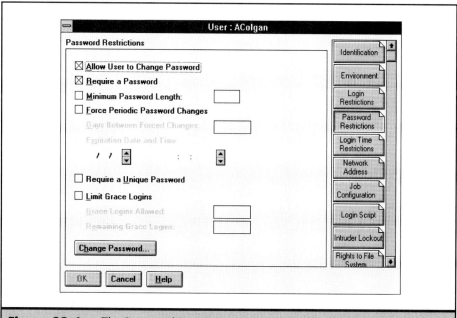

Figure 22-6. *The Password Restrictions page of the Details dialog box*

user object, but the user can change only the login script unless he or she is given rights to make other changes. Likewise, users can't change any of the properties of other user objects unless a supervisor gives them rights to do so.

Supervisors are not the only people who can use NetWare Administrator and NETADMIN. Users can run the programs to view the properties of their own user objects and those of any other objects; in some cases the users can change properties for those objects. Assume AColgan is assigned the task of updating the Telephone, Fax Number, and E-mail Address properties for each user object in her department. (You can see these fields in Figure 22-5.) To allow this, you grant her the Read and Write rights to those fields for every user object in the department.

NOTE: You can create an organizational role for certain tasks, then make a user a member of the role. Later, you can assign other users to that role.

Supervisors can grant a self-moderating right to users. This gives the users the right to add or remove themselves from certain groups, usually e-mail groups. In this way, users can decide on their own whether they want to receive the mail sent to the group. If they want to remove themselves from the list, they can open the group object and remove their name from it.

NOTE: Property rights are not inherited, so you'll need to assign them to each object individually. For example, granting AColgan the right to change the telephone numbers of a container object doesn't give her the right to change the telephone properties of its leaf objects. The properties of containers are quite different from leaf objects. Property rights are individually assigned for each object.

To assign property rights, you click the object that you want to make a trustee of another object, and then you drag it and drop it over the other object. Let's assume that you drop the user object AColgan over the user object DBoone. The Object Trustees dialog box opens, as shown in Figure 22-7. AColgan's name is highlighted in the Trustees box, and her current rights to this object appear in the lower fields.

The Object Rights field displays which rights AColgan has to the object itself (not the properties of the object). In Figure 22-7, AColgan has Browse rights to the object, which means she will see it listed when browsing the directory tree in NetWare Administrator and NETADMIN, or when using the NLIST or CX commands. She can't delete or rename the object.

Now look at the Property Rights field. The options here can be a little confusing at first because they display property rights two ways. If you click All Properties, you see the *default* rights a user has to the properties of an object

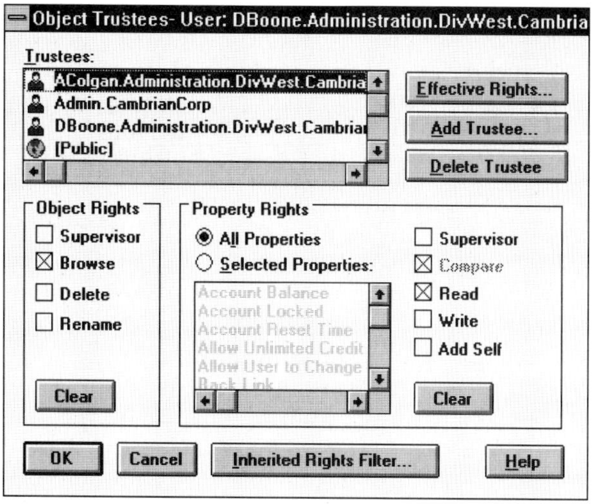

Figure 22-7. *The Object Trustees dialog box*

unless they are individually changed as discussed in the next paragraph. In this case, AColgan can read (view) the property fields. Note that Compare is marked but unavailable. That is because the Read right includes the Compare right.

When you click the Selected Properties button, you can change access rights to individual properties. Figure 22-8 illustrates this. Note that the options in the scroll box become available, whereas in Figure 22-7 they are unavailable. These options are the names of the fields in the Details dialog box pages, such as those shown in Figures 22-5 and 22-6.

In Figure 22-8, Telephone is highlighted and AColgan's property rights to Telephone have been changed to Read and Write. AColgan can now change the telephone number for DBoone. All the rest of the fields stay at their default settings unless you selectively change them.

NetWare Administrator Commands and Options

Most of the NetWare Administrator commands work on objects. Other commands control the view you have of the directory tree and the way NetWare Administrator operates. To work with an object, click it with the mouse. Some

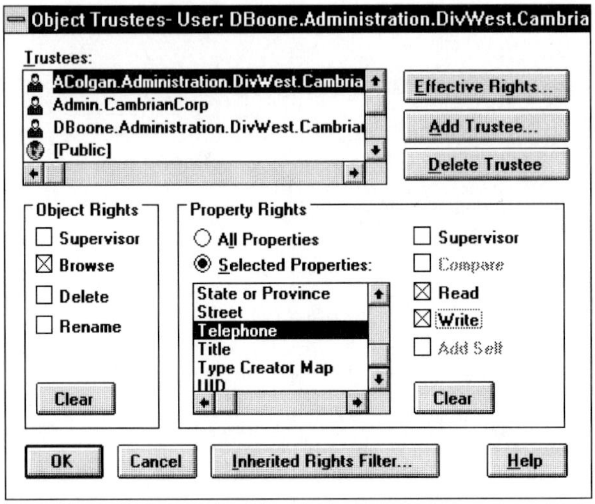

Figure 22-8.   *Changing AColgan's property rights to Telephone*

menu options might not be available, depending on the type of object you have selected. For example, the Salvage option is available only when a volume object is selected. Also, what you can do with an object depends on the access rights you have to that object.

NOTE: To display a description of what each menu option does, use the arrow keys to scan through the options rather than clicking them with the mouse.

A quick way to access commands for any object is to click the object with the *right mouse button*. You'll see a menu similar to that shown in Figure 22-9. The options available on the menu depend on the object selected.

The Object Menu

The Object menu contains commands for creating and modifying objects in the directory tree. You can also expand a volume object and work with its directories and files by using some of the options on the Object menu.

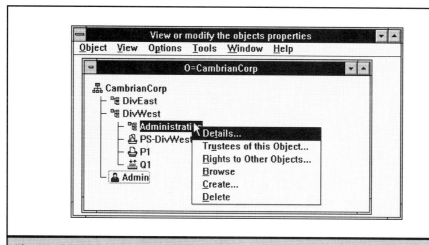

Figure 22-9. *Accessing commands for an object with the right mouse button*

■ *Create* Select this option to create a new object. This option is unavailable if a leaf object is selected. If selected, a list of objects appears, from which you select the type of object you want to create.

■ *Details* Select this option to display details about a selected object directory, or file. A Details dialog box similar to that shown in Figure 22-5 appears. You can also simply double-click an object to display the menu.

■ *Trustees of this Object* Select this option to see who has trustee rights to the object. You'll see a dialog box similar to that shown in Figures 22-7 and 22-8.

CAUTION: Viewing the trustees of an object gives you a list of only objects that have been specifically assigned trustee rights at the object's level. It does not show objects that have inherited rights from a higher level. Click the Effective Rights button and then specify the name of an object you suspect might have inherited rights to the object to see what those rights are. You can apply an Inherited Rights Filter to an object to block inherited rights.

■ *Rights to Other Objects* Select this option to see what rights a user has to other objects.

CAUTION: The complete set of property rights a user has to an object is not immediately apparent by looking at the Object Trustees dialog box. Click Selected Properties, and then use the arrow keys to scan down the list, noting the rights for individual properties.

- *Salvage* Choose this option to recover deleted files. It is available only if a volume object is selected or if you've expanded a volume and have a directory or file selected.

- *Move* Choose this option to move one or more objects, directories, or files.

- *Copy* Choose this option to copy one or more directories or files to another location in the file system.

- *Rename* Choose this option to rename a selected object, directory, or file.

- *Delete* Choose this option to delete the selected object, directory, or file.

- *User Template* Choose this option to create a user template. A Details dialog box like that shown in Figure 22-5 appears. Any changes you make to the properties of the template apply to all new user objects you create.

- *Search* Select this option to search for objects that have certain values. Located objects are displayed in a separate window. For example, you could search for all user objects that have the same job title. The search can start from any branch of the tree, so to search the company's entire directory tree, highlight the organization object at the top of the tree.

The View Menu

The options on the View menu become more important to you as your directory tree expands. As you add new branches (container objects) and leaf objects, you won't be able to see the entire tree at once. The View menu commands let you expand or collapse selected portions of the tree, or view only selected types of objects.

- *Show Hints* This option can be toggled on and off. When on, descriptions of menu options are displayed as you scroll through the menu options. Leave this on in most cases.

- *Set Context* This is a useful option that helps reduce screen clutter. Select it to specify exactly which branch of the tree you want to view. Any objects above the branch are not visible.

- *Include* Select this option to specify exactly which objects you want or don't want to see. For example, if you are working with users in a container, you can choose to display only user objects.

- *Expand* This option expands the selected container in the directory tree. Double-clicking the collapsed container is more efficient than choosing this menu item.

■ *Collapse*   This option collapses the selected container in the directory tree. Double-clicking the expanded container is more efficient than choosing this menu item.

The Options Menu

The Options menu contains two items. Choose the Confirmations option to select whether you want a warning message to be displayed when deleting files. Choose the Preferred Name Space option to set the way you want to view file and directory names. Files and directories in all volumes are displayed by using the selected name space.

The Tools Menu

The Tools menu has options for starting additional utilities or creating browse windows.

■ *Partition Manager*   Choose this option to manage partitions of the directory tree. Refer to Appendix C for details on partition management.

■ *Browse*   This option is available only if a container object is selected. It opens a window so that you can browse a branch of the tree separately.

■ *Remote Console*   This option starts the Novell Remote Console utility so that you can manage the server console from your workstation. Instructions for installing a Remote Console startup icon in the Windows Program Manager are given earlier in this chapter.

The Window Menu

Choose options from the Window menu to organize the document windows that are open in NetWare Administrator. If you used the Browse command to open several windows, choose Cascade or Tile to arrange them, or choose Close All to close all the windows at once. If you can't see a window, choose its name from the list at the bottom of the menu.

The Help Menu

Options on the Help menu provide useful information about the operation of NetWare Administrator, terminology, and error messages. Choose About NetWare Administrator to view its version number in case you need to call Novell technical support about a problem.

Creating and Modifying Objects

This section walks you through the creation of a user object to familiarize you with the procedure and to point out some features of NetWare Administrator. Detailed instructions for creating user objects are covered in Chapter 23. Follow along with these instructions on your computer to familiarize yourself with the process. You can remove the example user later.

1. Click the container object where you want to create the new user with the right mouse button. Choose Create from the pop-up menu that appears. The New Object dialog box then appears.

2. Click the user object icon, and then click the OK button.

The Create User dialog box appears, as shown in Figure 22-10. In the Login Name field, type **TBones**, for example. This is the name the user must type to log in. First initial, last name format is usually appropriate. In the Last Name field, type **Bones**, which is the user's last name. You can search on this name later, so when you create user objects, don't enter any uncommon abbreviations or first

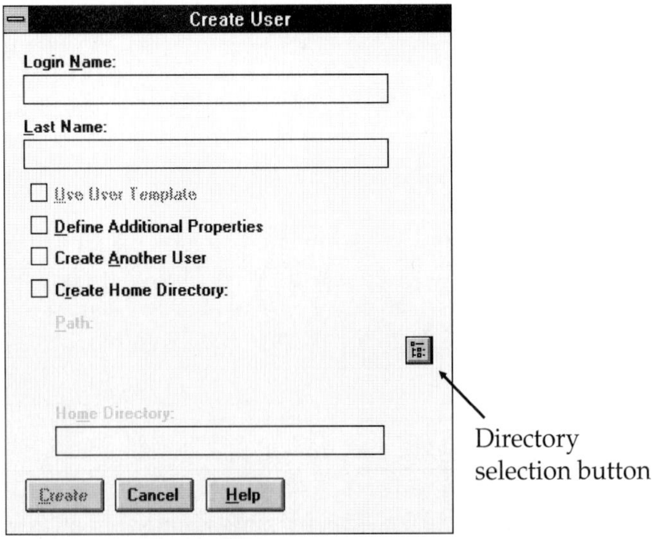

Figure 22-10.   *The Create User dialog box*

name initials in this field; just enter the last name exactly as it's spelled. If a user template existed in this user object's container object, you could choose to accept its default settings. User templates are covered in Chapter 23.

3. You can press TAB to jump to the next field. Press SPACEBAR to check the Define Additional Properties box so that you can fill out a few properties for this example and see how some of the dialog box features work. When you check this box, the Create Another User box becomes unavailable.

4. Tab to the Create Home Directory field, and press SPACEBAR to mark it. The Path field becomes available.

A home directory is created for the user at the location you specify. You should create a directory called USERS or HOME that users' home directories can branch from. Press CTRL-ESC to switch to the Program Manager, and then start File Manager and create the directory on an appropriate network volume. After the directory is created, you can specify it in the next step.

5. Click the directory selection button, which is labeled on Figure 22-10. The Select Object dialog box appears, which is shown in Figure 22-11.

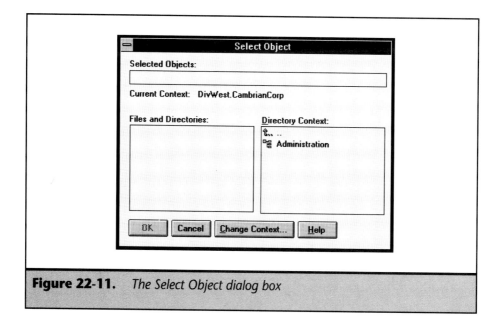

Figure 22-11. *The Select Object dialog box*

Remember this dialog box. You will frequently use NetWare Administrator's Select Object dialog box to change your context in the directory tree, select objects, and select directories in the filing system. Although you can type a context in the Selected Objects field, it's easier to select the context with the mouse.

6. Double-click objects in the Directory Context box to move up and down through the directory tree. When creating a home directory for a user, your objective is to locate the server volume that will hold the home directory. Double-click the container object that holds the volume, or click the up arrow icon to move up the tree and locate the volume in another branch. When the volume appears, double-click it to display a list of directories, as shown in Figure 22-12.

7. Assuming that the USERS or HOME directory branches from the root of the volume, click the directory on the left. Its name appears in the Selected Objects field, and you can click OK to return to the Create User dialog box. The directory name and context appear in the Path field of the Create User dialog box.

NOTE: You'll use these same "browse" techniques in other areas of NetWare Administrator, so don't forget them.

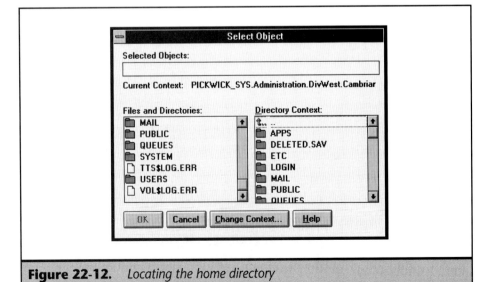

Figure 22-12.   *Locating the home directory*

8. The user's name appears in the Home Directory field. In this example, the directory name will be \USERS\TBONES. Click Create to save the changes.

NetWare Administrator creates the directory and then displays the Details dialog box for the new user, similar to that shown in Figure 22-13. The only field you need to fill out for now is Other Names. You type the user's full name in this field, or you type the name by using a name format that your company has decided to use. Remember, you can search on information in the fields, so consistency is important. You can fill out other information if appropriate. Most are obvious, but you can click on Help for more information.

Before closing this dialog box, notice its assortment of buttons. On the right are buttons you can click to view all the different properties you can specify for users. Click any of these buttons now to review the properties. Chapter 23 covers them in more detail.

Each field has a set of browser buttons that you can click to select information from lists. Initially, the lists are blank. When you type information in the fields, that information is added to the lists; any time you change the information in fields, the new information is added to the lists. You press the up arrow and down arrow keys to scroll the lists and view any information that has been typed

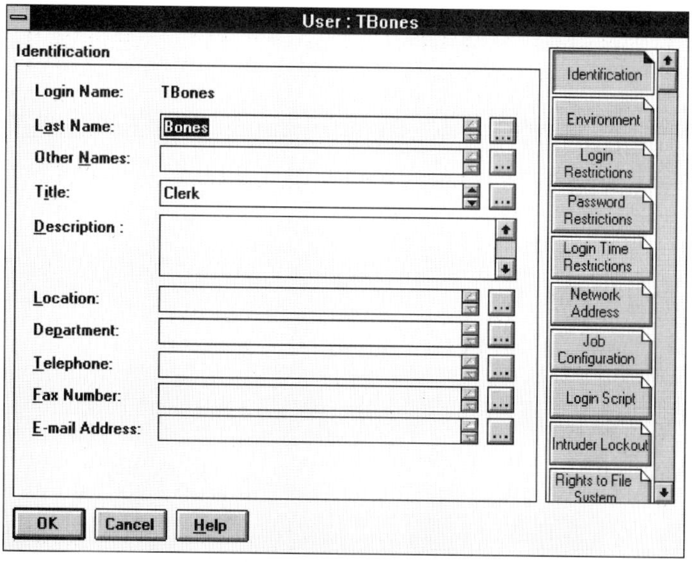

Figure 22-13.   *The Details dialog box for the user TBones*

in the fields. To add or delete any information in the fields, click the rightmost button on the field.

9. To finish creating the user object, click the OK button at the bottom of the dialog box.

NOTE: If you don't want the example user object you just created, select the object, then choose Delete from the Object menu.

Moving Objects

You can move any object in a container to a new container by holding down the CTRL key and dragging the object to the new container. If you can't see the destination container because there are too many objects in the window, try collapsing part of the directory tree, or choose Browse from the Tools menu to create another window. Place the two windows side by side, and then drag the icon from one to the other.

TIP: To display a list that shows only containers into which you can then drag and drop objects, open a new window by choosing Browse from the Tools menu, and then choose Include from the View menu. Click the Exclude All button, and click OK.

If the mouse techniques seem like too much trouble, just choose Move from the Object dialog box, and fill out the fields as appropriate. Be sure to select the icon you want to move before choosing the Move option.

About Trustee Rights

There are a number of places where you can view or change the trustee rights of an object, and view or change what objects an object is the trustee of. Follow these instructions to open dialog boxes that show this information:

■ To view the trustees of an object, click the object with the right mouse button and then choose Trustees of this Object. You'll see a dialog box similar to that shown in Figure 22-7. Any users or other objects that have been granted trustee rights to the object are listed in the Trustees field. Click one of these objects to view its rights in the lower fields.

■ To view the trustees of a directory or file, open the volume object where the directory or file exists, and then select it. Choose Details from the Object menu.

■ To view the rights a user or other object has to other objects, click the object with the right mouse button, and then choose Rights to Other Objects. A Search Context dialog box appears in which you can select the branch of the directory tree where you want to start the search. On large networks, don't start searching any higher than you have to, in order to minimize search time.

■ To view the rights a user or other object has to a directory or file, click the object with the right mouse button, and then click Details. When the Details dialog box appears, click the Rights to File System button.

As mentioned, you'll learn more about using these dialog boxes in Chapters 23 and 24. If you want information now, click the Help button on each dialog box.

Listing and Searching for Objects

One of the most useful features of NetWare Administrator is its search capabilities. You can search for user objects and resource objects that have specified properties. For example, you could search for all users that have a title of *Printer operator* or *Server operator*. NetWare Administrator displays the user objects it finds in a separate browse window. You can then select one of the objects and view or change its properties.

To start a search, first click the branch of the tree where you want to start the search. You would click the organization container to search the entire tree. Choose Search from the Object menu to display a dialog box like that shown in Figure 22-14.

The Start From field displays the context of the object you selected before choosing the Search option. Do the following to prepare a search:

1. To search all the containers that branch from this context, make sure the Search Entire Subtree field is marked.

2. In the Search For field, click the down arrow button to select from a list of objects, such as User, Server, Printer, and Computer. Click Help to get a description of some non-standard objects. Once you've selected an object,

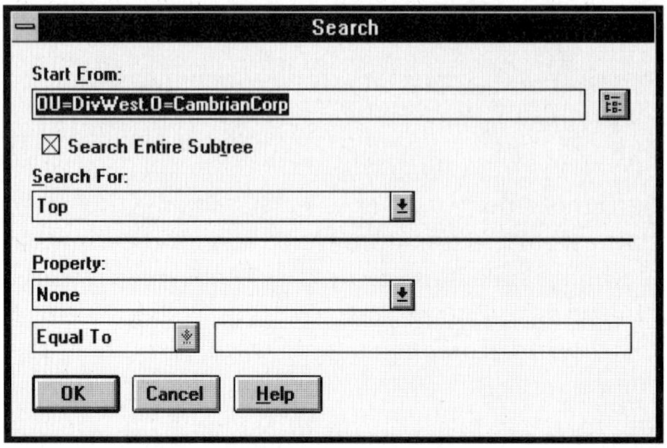

Figure 22-14. *The Search dialog box*

you can click OK to list all objects of that type, or you can further refine the search, as described in step 3.

3. Jump to the Property field by pressing TAB, and then press the up arrow and down arrow keys to view a list of properties. Choose a property, and then define the two lower fields. For example, you could select Title in the Property field, select Equal To in the field below it, and type *Print operator* in the lower-right field to display a list of users who have the Print operator title.

4. Click OK to start the search. When complete, a list of found objects appears. You can double-click any listed object to view or change its properties.

Using NETADMIN

This section assumes that you have familiarized yourself with NetWare Administrator and are now somewhat knowledgeable about object management techniques. NETADMIN is a text-based version of NetWare Administrator that does not include directory, file, and printer management capabilities. You can use it when you're at a non-Windows workstation and you need to manage objects. If you need to manage the file system from a non-Windows workstation, use

FILER, which is discussed in Chapter 24. If you need to manage printers, use the
PCONSOLE utility.

> NOTE: *Regular users can use NETADMIN to view information about objects
> and to change object properties if they have the rights to do so.*

To start the utility, type NETADMIN at the command-line prompt. In a moment,
the screen shown in Figure 22-15 appears. You have the following three choices:

■ *Manage objects*   Select this option to begin working with objects. Refer to
the next two options before selecting this option.

■ *Manage according to search pattern*   This option lets you specify exactly
which type of objects you want to work with, such as users, printers, or
servers. You can also specify a wildcard pattern for the name of the objects,
so if you've named computers IBM-STATION1, IBM-STATION2, and so
on, for example, you could list all IBM computers by specifying IBM*.

■ *Change context*   Choose this option to display only objects in specific
branches of the directory tree.

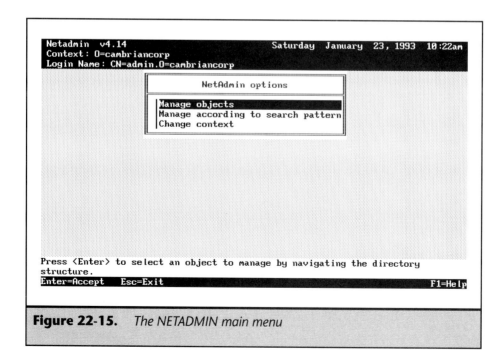

Figure 22-15.   *The NETADMIN main menu*

To begin using NETADMIN, you can choose Manage objects from the main menu. The other menu items are optional; you don't need to specify search patterns or contexts to work with objects. However, as your directory tree grows, you'll want to select these options so that you can reduce the amount of information displayed in the windows.

When you choose Manage objects, a screen similar to Figure 22-16 appears. In this example, two container objects are available: DivEast and DivWest. The type of object is displayed on the right, and the plus sign to the left of an object's name indicates that it is a container object and that it has objects within it.

You can change your context ("browse") in the directory tree by doing one of the following:

■ To view the contents of a container, highlight the container and press ENTER. You might see a list of other containers and need to choose one of those as well.

■ To move up the directory tree, highlight the double-dot (parent) item in the list and press ENTER.

■ Go back to the NETADMIN main menu and choose Change context, and then type the name of the new context, or press INS to select from a list.

NOTE: When you want to specify a new context starting from the root, start by typing a period; otherwise NETADMIN thinks you are specifying a path that branches from the current context.

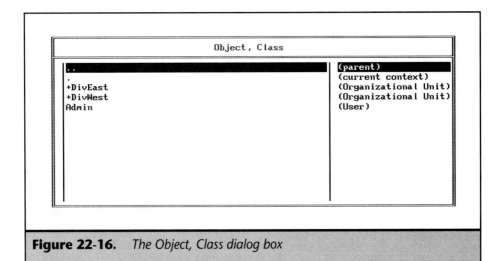

Figure 22-16.   *The Object, Class dialog box*

Working Inside Containers

As soon as you've located the container that holds the objects you want to work with, you'll see a menu similar to that shown in Figure 22-17. All objects in the container are displayed unless you specified a search pattern. (See "Specifying Search Patterns" later in this chapter for more information.)

NOTE: Press the INS *key to insert a new object into the current container.*

Use the arrow keys to highlight an object, and then do one of the following:

- Press ENTER or F10 to view or edit the object's properties and trustee assignments.

- Press F5 to mark the object. Use the mark option to mark a group of objects you want to delete or move to another context.

- Press DEL to delete an object or a group of marked objects.

- Press F10 and choose Move to move an object or a group of marked objects.

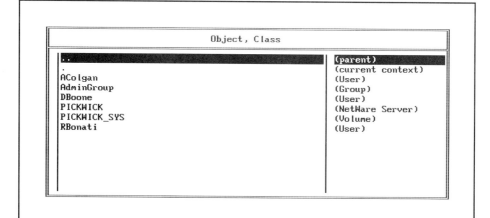

Figure 22-17.   *The Object, Class dialog box showing a menu of specified objects*

Adding New Objects

To add a new object, make sure you are at the context where you want to add the object, and then follow these steps:

1. Press INS to insert a new object. You'll see a list of possible objects from which to choose. Scan down the list, and press ENTER when you've selected an object type.

2. Type a name for the new object, and specify other information as necessary.

If the object is a user, use the first initial, last name format. If the object is a resource, use the naming conventions that your company has established. Keep in mind that naming conventions simplify searches later on.

3. After typing the name, press ENTER. Another menu might appear (depending on the object type) so that you can enter additional information.

After the object is created, it appears in the Object, Class dialog box. To change the object, select it and press ENTER or F10. Procedures for changing objects are covered next.

Working with Objects

To view and change the properties or trustees of an object, or to move objects, first highlight the object and press ENTER or F10. Use the F5 key to mark a group of objects if your intention is to move them to another context. A screen similar to Figure 22-18 appears.

From this menu, you can choose the first option to view or edit the object's properties, or you can choose one of the last two options to view or edit trustee rights.

CHANGING AN OBJECT'S PROPERTIES   Choose the "View or edit properties of this object" option from the menu. You will see a list of possible properties you can change, such as Identification, Environment, and Account Restrictions. Choose one of the items, and a properties dialog box opens. Figure 22-19 shows an example of the Identification information dialog box for a user object. Instructions for changing these fields can be found in Chapter 23 or by pressing F1 to display help.

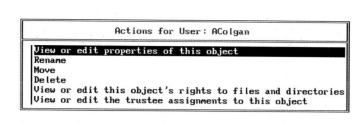

```
                    Actions for User: AColgan
   ┌──────────────────────────────────────────────────────────────┐
   │View or edit properties of this object                        │
   │Rename                                                         │
   │Move                                                           │
   │Delete                                                         │
   │View or edit this object's rights to files and directories    │
   │View or edit the trustee assignments to this object           │
   └──────────────────────────────────────────────────────────────┘
```

Figure 22-18.   *The menu that appears for viewing or changing the properties or trustees of an object*

RENAMING, MOVING, AND DELETING AN OBJECT   The functions of the Rename, Move, and Delete options are obvious. If you choose Rename, you can type in a new name for the object. If you choose Delete, the object is removed. To move an object, choose Move, and then specify the new context in the New Context field. If you don't know the context, press INS twice. A window appears that lets you work your way up or down the directory tree by choosing container or parent objects.

VIEWING AND EDITING FILE AND DIRECTORY RIGHTS   Select the "View or edit this object's rights to files and directories" option to view the directories and files to which the user has rights. You can specify four options:

NOTE: Press INS *on any field to choose from a list of options. Alternatively, you can type in the text of the field if you know it.*

```
                      Identification information
   ┌──────────────────────────────────────────────────────────────┐
   │Login Name:          AColgan                                   │
   │Last name:         ↓ Colgan                                    │
   │Other name:        ↓ Anna Colgan                              │
   │Title:             ↓ Printer operator                         │
   │Description:         Manages shared network pri ...            │
   │Telephone number:  ↓ 812-882-1253                            │
   │Fax telephone number: ↓ 812-882-5659                          │
   │E-mail address:    ↓ AColgan @ Admin                         │
   │Location:          ↓ Equipment room                           │
   │Department:        ↓ Administration                           │
   └──────────────────────────────────────────────────────────────┘
```

Figure 22-19.   *The Identification information dialog box for a user object*

- *Volume Object Name*   Specify the volume you want to search in this field.

- *Beginning Path*   In this field, specify the path of the volume where you want the search to begin. You can type a backslash to start at the root.

- *Directories/Files*   Press ENTER to choose either Directory, File, or Directory and File from a list.

- *Trustee Search Depth*   Press ENTER to choose either All subdirectories or Current directory only from a list.

Press F10 to start the search after all the fields are filled out. A list of current assignments appears if there are any. As soon as the Trustee assignments window appears, you can do either of the following:

- Select a listed item and press ENTER to change it.

- Press INS to add a new trustee assignment.

The procedure for adding a trustee assignment is listed next. The INS key is important because it opens lists of directories, files, or access rights from which you can choose.

1. At the Trustee Assignments list, press INS. Your screen will look similar to that shown in Figure 22-20. Choose whether you want to assign trustee rights to a directory or a file.

2. You must specify the name of the directory or file. Here you can press INS and browse through a list of available directories. Make a selection and press ENTER. When done, press ESC to add the selection. If you are adding a file, you are asked for a filename. Press INS to choose from a list, then make a selection.

3. Press ENTER to add the new directory name or filename to the Trustee assignments menu. It appears with the Read and File Scan attributes by default.

4. To change directory rights, highlight the directory you just added, and press ENTER. The Trustee rights granted menu appears. Now press INS to select additional rights. Your screen should look similar to that shown in Figure 22-21.

5. To add a single right, highlight the right, and press ENTER. To add multiple rights, highlight each right and mark it by pressing F5. Then press ENTER to add them to the list.

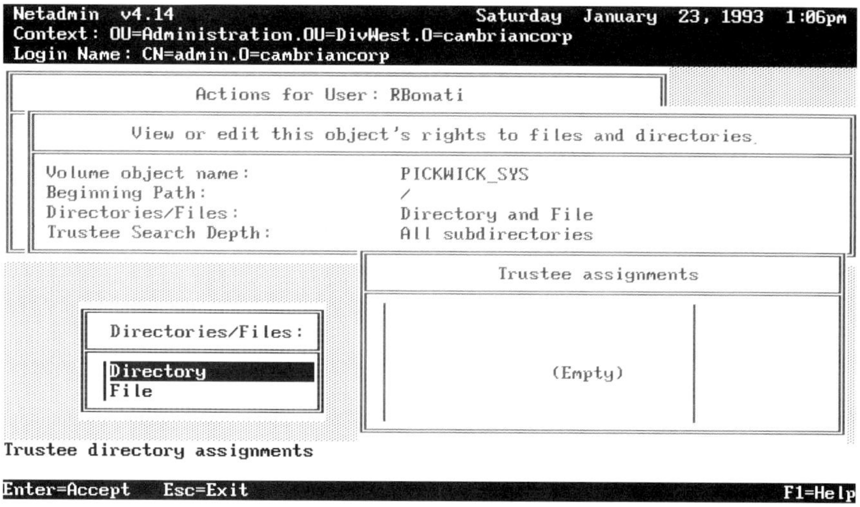

```
Netadmin  v4.14                        Saturday  January  23, 1993  1:06pm
Context: OU=Administration.OU=DivWest.O=cambriancorp
Login Name: CN=admin.O=cambriancorp
┌──────────────────────────────────────────────────────────────────┐
│              Actions for User: RBonati                           ║
│  ┌────────────────────────────────────────────────────────────┐  │
│  │    View or edit this object's rights to files and directories │
│  │                                                            │  │
│  │  Volume object name:          PICKWICK_SYS                 │  │
│  │  Beginning Path:              /                            │  │
│  │  Directories/Files:           Directory and File          │  │
│  │  Trustee Search Depth:        All subdirectories          │  │
│  └────────────────────────────────────────────────────────────┘  │
│                              ┌──────────────────────────────────┐ │
│                              │       Trustee assignments        │ │
│         ┌──────────────────┐ │ ┌──────────────────────────────┐ │ │
│         │ Directories/Files:│ │ │                              │ │ │
│         │ ┌──────────────┐  │ │ │                              │ │ │
│         │ │Directory     │  │ │ │         (Empty)              │ │ │
│         │ │File          │  │ │ │                              │ │ │
│         │ └──────────────┘  │ │ │                              │ │ │
│         └──────────────────┘ │ └──────────────────────────────┘ │ │
│  Trustee directory assignments                                   │
└──────────────────────────────────────────────────────────────────┘
Enter=Accept   Esc=Exit                                    F1=Help
```

Figure 22-20.   *Assigning trustee rights*

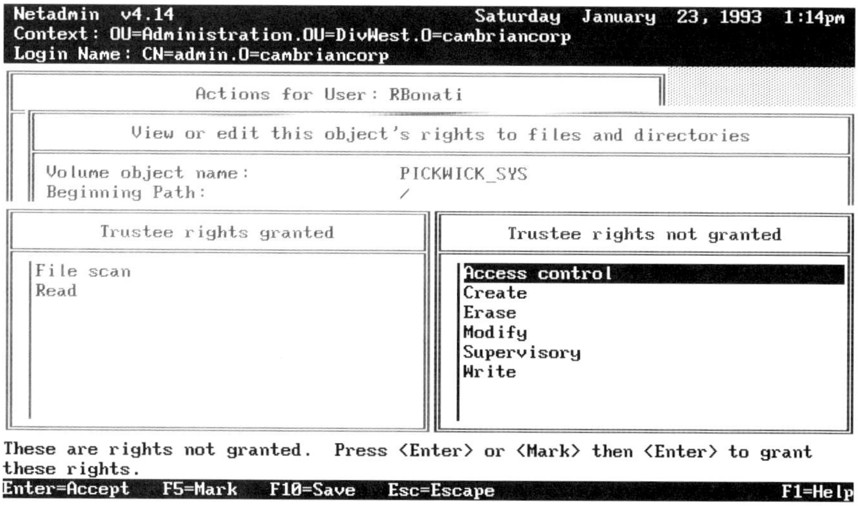

```
Netadmin  v4.14                        Saturday  January  23, 1993  1:14pm
Context: OU=Administration.OU=DivWest.O=cambriancorp
Login Name: CN=admin.O=cambriancorp
┌──────────────────────────────────────────────────────────────────┐
│              Actions for User: RBonati                           ║
│  ┌────────────────────────────────────────────────────────────┐  │
│  │    View or edit this object's rights to files and directories │
│  │  Volume object name:          PICKWICK_SYS                 │  │
│  │  Beginning Path:              /                            │  │
│  └────────────────────────────────────────────────────────────┘  │
│  ┌──────────────────────────┐  ┌──────────────────────────────┐  │
│  │  Trustee rights granted  │  │   Trustee rights not granted │  │
│  │ File scan                │  │ Access control               │  │
│  │ Read                     │  │ Create                       │  │
│  │                          │  │ Erase                        │  │
│  │                          │  │ Modify                       │  │
│  │                          │  │ Supervisory                  │  │
│  │                          │  │ Write                        │  │
│  └──────────────────────────┘  └──────────────────────────────┘  │
│  These are rights not granted.  Press <Enter> or <Mark> then <Enter> to grant │
│  these rights.                                                   │
└──────────────────────────────────────────────────────────────────┘
Enter=Accept   F5=Mark   F10=Save   Esc=Escape              F1=Help
```

Figure 22-21.   *Assigning additional rights*

You can continue adding more rights to directories or files by using the procedures described in this list. The methods you used to display lists of options and select from those options are commonly used in all NetWare text utilities. You use similar options when working with objects, as discussed next, or when working with utilities like NETUSER.

VIEWING AND EDITING OBJECT RIGHTS   To view or edit the trustee's and trustee rights of the selected object, choose the "View or edit the trustee assignments to this object" option from the menu shown in Figure 22-18. The menu shown in Figure 22-22 appears.

■ Choose the Inherited rights filters option to view or change the IRF at any container object level. Use the INS key method described in the previous section to add new IRFs.

■ Choose Trustees to view a list of trustees for the selected object. The list is organized by property. Press INS to add a new trustee, select the properties you want to assign to the trustee, then choose a new trustee. To delete a trustee, highlight the trustee and press DEL. To see a list of the rights a trustee has to a property, highlight it and press ENTER.

■ Choose the Effective rights option to view the current effective rights for the object. Remember that effective rights are a combination of the user's trustee rights to an object, the rights the user inherits, and the rights that are blocked by an IRF.

To add trustees and to insert rights for those trustees, press INS when asked to enter information, and then select from lists.

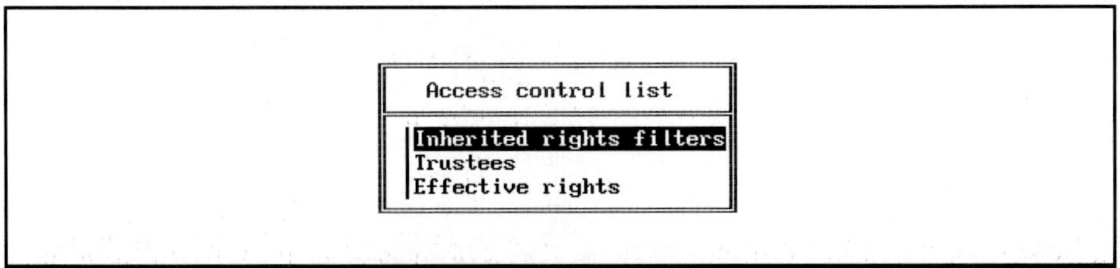

```
        ┌──────────────────────────┐
        │   Access control list    │
        ├──────────────────────────┤
        │ Inherited rights filters │
        │ Trustees                 │
        │ Effective rights         │
        └──────────────────────────┘
```

Figure 22-22.   *The Access control list*

Specifying Search Patterns

You can specify search patterns to list only selected objects or simply to reduce the number of items in directory tree listings. Choose the Manage according to search pattern option from the NETADMIN main menu to display the Search patterns dialog box, which is shown in Figure 22-23. You set the options on the menu as described in the following sections.

THE ENTER OBJECT NAME FIELD   In the Enter object name field, you can specify a wildcard parameter for the names of objects you want to see. The asterisk specifies that any characters can occupy its place. For example, to list objects with names that start with *T*, you would type T* in this field. If your company uses a manufacturer ID to name computers, you could list all IBM computers by specifying IBM*.

THE OBJECT CLASS FIELD   Select the type of object you want to list in the Object class field, or leave it blank to list all objects. Highlight the field, and then press ENTER. Press INS to choose from a list of objects. You can specify more than one type of object in the listing.

THE SHOW ALIAS CLASS OPTION   Set the Show alias class option to Yes if you want to see alias objects listed as *Alias object*, rather than as the objects they represent.

After you've filled out the fields, press F10 to save the changes and return to the main menu. Choose Manage Objects from the main menu to begin working with objects. You will see only those objects you have selected. Search options are not saved from one NETADMIN session to another.

```
                        Search patterns
  Enter object name :        *
  Object class:            ↓ /All classes/
  Show alias class (Y/N):    No
```

Figure 22-23.   *The Search patterns dialog box*

CHAPTER 23

Managing Objects

I n this chapter, you'll explore how to create and change user and resource objects. A procedural format is followed, so you can refer to this chapter at any time. Creating container objects is covered first, so you can start organizing your directory tree. Creating user templates in the container objects for users is covered next. You then learn how to create user and resource objects and how to control access rights.

All examples use the Windows-based NetWare Administrator. Log into the network as the ADMIN user if you are creating the initial directory tree and the supervisor objects for each department.

If you are a department manager, log in as the supervisor of that department. Start Windows and load NetWare Administrator.

You should arrange your view of objects before you begin working with NetWare Administrator, and any time you need to work with a special set of objects. Tips for changing or organizing your view are listed here:

- If you need to work within a specific branch and you want to remove the screen clutter caused by all the other branches, choose Set Context from the View menu and then specify the container you want to work with.

- To view only certain types of objects, choose Include from the View menu and then choose the type of objects you want to see. Click Exclude All to view only container objects.

- Choose Browse from the Tools menu to open additional browser windows (up to a total of nine), and then set the view for those windows as described in the preceding two points.

- Use the Search option on the Object menu to search for objects at any point in the directory tree and display them in a separate browser window. You can then work with any listed object without changing your context in other browse directions.

Creating Container Objects

Containers are branches of the directory tree that hold other containers or leaf objects. With the organization plan for your directory tree in hand, you can start creating the container objects that represent the divisions or departments in your company. Some containers will already exist; they are added when you install NetWare v.4 servers and specify the context of each server.

Locate the container that will hold the new container, and click it by using the right mouse button. Choose the Create option from the pop-up menu. The New Object dialog box appears, and you select the type of object you want to create. Choose Organizational Unit, and click the OK button. The Create Organizational Unit dialog box appears, as shown in Figure 23-1.

1. Type a name for this container in the Organizational Unit Name field. Keep it short if users will need to type the context of this container often.

2. Tab to the Define Additional Properties field and press the SPACEBAR.

NOTE: Mark the Create Another Organizational Unit option only when you want to create a set of containers at one time.

3. Mark the Define User Defaults field to create a user template in the container. If you don't mark the option, you can still create a template at a later time.

4. Click the Create button to create the container. A message box appears that asks if you want the container to inherit user template properties from the parent container object. Choose Yes if that container has properties you want to pass down to the user template of the new container.

The Details dialog box for the organizational unit now appears, as shown in Figure 23-2, so that you can edit the properties of the object.

Filling Out the Details Dialog Box

The following sections describe how to fill out the fields in the Details dialog box. The buttons on the right are used to access different pages of properties for the organizational unit object.

Create Organizational Unit

Organizational Unit <u>N</u>ame:

☐ <u>D</u>efine Additional Properties
☐ Create <u>A</u>nother Organizational Unit
☐ Define <u>U</u>ser Defaults

[Create] [Cancel] [<u>H</u>elp]

Figure 23-1.   *The Create Organizational Unit dialog box*

Organizational Unit : Sales

Identification

Name:	Sales
Other Names:	
Description :	
Location:	
Telephone:	
Fax Number:	
E-mail Address:	

Identification

Postal Address

Job Configuration

Print Forms

Print Devices

Rights to File System

See Also

Login Script

Intruder Limits

OK   Cancel   Help

Figure 23-2.   *The Details dialog box for an organizational unit*

NOTE: *Each of the buttons on the right side of this dialog box has a small fold-over tab at the upper right. When you change any field in a page of properties, this tab turns black to remind you that you've made changes to that page.*

Clicking the OK button saves information you have changed and closes the dialog box. Clicking Cancel closes the dialog box and discards any changes you've made, but a warning appears to confirm your action before this happens.

The Identification Page

The Identification page, which is shown in Figure 23-2, holds descriptive information about the organizational unit object. You can jump among fields by pressing the TAB key or by clicking the fields with the mouse. You can't change the Name field. All other fields are optional; you provide information for your own use, and you can search for objects based on the information in these fields.

In the Other Names field, you can type another name to describe this container, such as the full name of your division or department. Be sure to type a name that other users will recognize if they decide to search on this field. In the

Description field, you can type a short description of what the container represents, who manages it, or what it is meant to organize. In the Location field, type the physical location this container object represents. For example, in a campus environment, the location could be *North Hall*. In the remaining fields, supply the phone numbers and e-mail address of the person to contact for more information about this container.

The Postal Address Page

Click the Postal Address button to view the Postal Address page, which is shown in Figure 23-3. You use this page to provide address information about the object; you can search on this information later. You can also specify mailing label information that third-party programs can access to create mailings for your departments and users. Fill out the fields at the top of the page, and then click the Set Address button to add the information to the Mailing Label Information field.

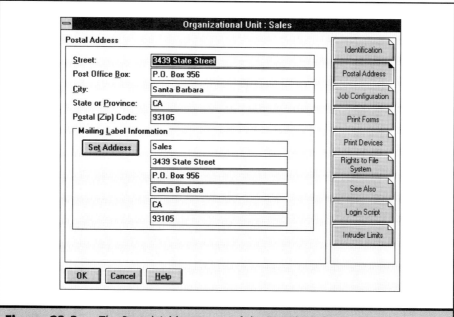

Figure 23-3.   *The Postal Address page of the Details dialog box for an organizational unit*

The Job Configuration Page

The Job Configuration page lets you create customized print job configurations that users in the container can select when printing to printer objects in the container. You create print job configurations to set up print jobs such as company mailings or mailing labels. Click the New button on the dialog box to see the options available for print job configurations. Refer to Chapter 27 for more information.

The Print Forms Page

The Print Forms page lets you specify one or more print forms. A print form sets up a printer for a specific paper size. The forms are used when printing to a printer object in the container. To add a print form, click the Create button and then specify a name and number for the form, along with the length and width of the paper. See Chapter 27 for more details.

The Print Devices Page

The Print Devices page can contain a list of printing device definitions (called printer definition files, or PDFs). For example, the device driver HP3.PDF is required when printing to a Hewlett-Packard LaserJet III printer. To add this driver to the list and make it available to all user objects in the container, click the Import button. See Chapter 27 for more details.

The Rights to File System Page

Click the Rights to File System button to display the Rights to File System page, as shown in Figure 23-4. From this page, you can make the container object a trustee of a volume or a directory within a volume. All user objects in the container will also be trustees unless you block the inheritance of the rights for specific user objects. The steps for filling out this form are listed here:

1. Click the Include button to display the Select Object dialog box. In the Directory Context field, you need to specify the location of the volume that contains the directories you want to view or assign rights to. If a volume is not visible, double-click a container to open its contents, or

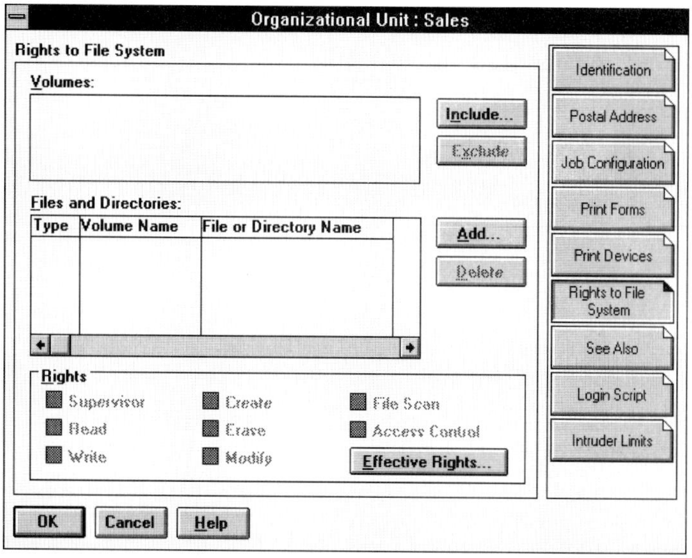

Figure 23-4. *The Rights to File System page of the Details dialog box for an organizational unit*

double-click the up-arrow icon to move up the directory tree and into another branch. This browsing technique is outlined in Chapter 22.

2. When you locate the volume, it appears in the Volumes list on the left. Click the volume. Its name appears in the Selected Objects field at the top. Click the OK button to accept the volume.

A volume name is now included in the Volumes field. If there are several volumes listed in this field, make sure the volume you want to work with is highlighted.

3. Click the Add button. Another Select Object dialog box appears. If you want to view or assign rights to the root directory of a volume, click the volume's name on the left in the Files and Directories field. To select a specific directory, double-click the volume's name on the right in the Directory Context field. You'll see a list of directories similar to that shown in Figure 23-5.

In Figure 23-5, note that the same list of directories appears on both the right and the left. To choose a directory and complete the operation, click a directory

Select Object

Selected Objects:

Current Context: PICKWICK_SYS.Administration.DivWest.Cambriar

Files and Directories: Directory Context:

APPS   ..
BACKOUT.TTS   APPS
DELETED.SAV   DELETED.SAV
ETC   ETC
LOGIN   LOGIN
MAIL   MAIL
PUBLIC   PUBLIC
QUEUES   QUEUES

OK   Cancel   Change Context...   Help

Figure 23-5.   *The Select Object dialog box with a list of directories in the Directory Context field*

name on the left. To open up subdirectories of any directory, double-click a directory folder on the right.

4. When the target folder finally appears in the listing on the left, click it and then click the OK button.

The selected directory now appears in the Files and Directories field, and the rights this object has to the directory are listed at the bottom in the Rights field.

5. To change the rights this container object has to the directory, click any box in the Rights field.

REMEMBER: All user objects within a container object will inherit the same rights.

6. To view the effective rights the container has to the directory, click the Effective Rights button. Recall that effective rights are a combination of trustee rights, inherited rights, and security equivalences. From the Effective Rights dialog box, you can click the directory tree button to select other directories and view their effective rights.

At this point, you can view other trustee rights by clicking the Include button or you can assign trustee rights by clicking the Add button. Click Include to locate directories and files on other volumes.

TIP: You can rearrange the columns in the Files and Directories field to make information easier to view. Point to one of the column headers; the mouse pointer turns into a pointing finger. Drag the header to the right or left over another header. The column assumes the new position.

The See Also Page

You use the See Also page to record information about the object or include the names of other objects related to it. Click the Add button to select from a list of objects to add to the See Also field. The contents of this field are purely informational and have no effect on the object.

The Login Script Page

The Login Script page for container objects is very important. The commands you place in a container's login script execute when any user within the container logs into the network. The commands do not execute for any other users. Login scripts are covered in Chapter 28.

NOTE: Before a container login script will run for a user, you must first make the user a trustee of the container. Drag and drop the user object (or group object) on the container.

The Intruder Limits Page

Intruder limits provide protection against unauthorized people trying to log into the system. An intruder might try several passwords to gain access. You can limit the number of incorrect logins on the Intruder Limits page. The limits you set apply to all user objects in the container.

To set intruder limits, click the Detect Intruder box. The other options become available. Set the limit for the number of incorrect logins in the Incorrect Login Attempts field. In the Days, Hours, and Minutes fields, specify how long you want to inhibit further login attempts before resetting to the normal login attempts setting.

You can lock the account after an intruder detection by clicking the Lock Account After Detection box. Specify how long you want the account locked in the Days, Hours, and Minutes field.

NOTE: The NAME CONTEXT option in NET.CFG sets the container that users log into.

Creating and Changing User Objects

To create a user object, you locate the container object in the directory tree where you want to add the user object, click the container object by using the right mouse button, and choose Create from the pop-up menu. The Details dialog box appears so that you can specify the properties of the user object. It is likely that everyone within a container will have some properties in common, so the process of creating a user template is discussed first. Then when you create new user objects, you will have the option of assigning them the properties of the user template.

The User Template

Because user objects have such a large number of properties, it doesn't make sense to configure the properties for each user object separately. Creating a user template makes the process of assigning properties to user objects much easier. A user template contains the properties of a regular user object; after you create the user template, it becomes an object itself.

NOTE: You don't need to create a user template if you had NetWare Administrator create one when you created the container object. Instead, open the container and double click the template.

To create a user template within a container object, click the container and then choose User Template from the Object menu. NetWare Administrator asks if you want the template to inherit properties from the upper-level container. Click Yes if objects in both levels share the same properties. If some properties are

different, you still might want to click Yes. It might take less time to edit these
fields than it would to type in all the information from scratch.

In a moment, the Details dialog box for the user template appears, as shown
in Figure 23-6. The properties that can be assigned are the same as for a user
object. Each page of the dialog box is discussed in the following sections.

> *NOTE: The following sections discuss creating a user template, but they also
> apply if you are creating a regular user object.*

The Identification Page

On the Identification page, all the fields except Last Name and Login Name are
optional and are informational only. The content of the fields does not affect the
access a user has to the network. However, it's highly recommended that you fill
out this information, especially when creating the user template. Leave *template*
in the Last Name field for the user template.

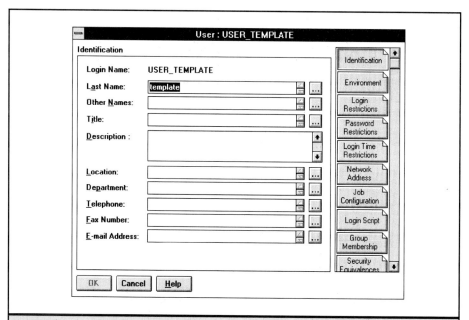

Figure 23-6. *The Details dialog box for the user template*

When you create a new user object, you must specify the Login Name and Last Name. You also specify whether you want to use the user template. Last Name is an important search field that administrators and users can search on to display information about other users. If you wanted to send e-mail to the user AColgan, for example, but you didn't know her e-mail address, you could search for *Colgan*. The Details dialog box for AColgan would appear.

On the user template, leave the Other Names field blank. This field normally holds the full name for the user. Fill out the remaining fields based on the information that is common to the user objects you will create by using this template.

The Environment Page

The Environment page is shown in Figure 23-7. Its property fields display additional information about user objects, such as:

- The language in which messages to the user are displayed

- The address of the network workstation where the user works

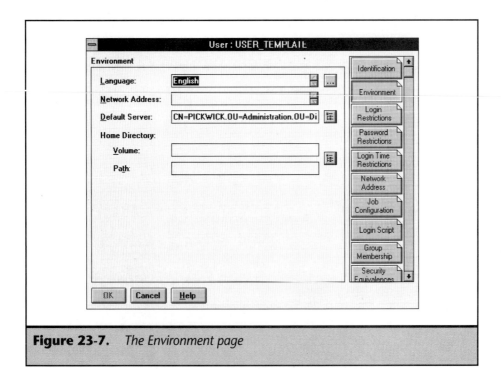

Figure 23-7. *The Environment page*

- The server to which the user's workstation is connected after login

- The user's home directory

The only fields you can specify on the template are Language and Default Server. The other fields will be specific to each user.

The Login Restrictions Page

You use the Login Restrictions page, which is shown in Figure 23-8, to set various login security features for users in the container. It is best to specify login restrictions on the user template rather than to set them individually for each user. The Account Disabled field is the one exception to this rule. There is little reason to check this on the user template unless you want user accounts to be disabled when they are first created. This might be useful if you are creating a new user workgroup that won't need to log in until the group is formed.

If the user objects you create in the container should exist for only a certain period of time, check the Account Has Expiration Date box and then specify the

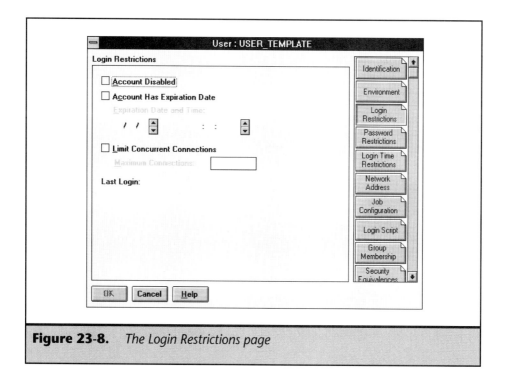

Figure 23-8.   *The Login Restrictions page*

range of time. Use this option when creating user objects for temporary employees or for an employee who is leaving the company.

To prevent users from logging in at more than one workstation simultaneously, click the Limit Concurrent Connections box and then type in the number of concurrent connections that the user can have. Set this value to 1 for maximum security.

The Password Restrictions Page

The Password Restrictions page is shown in Figure 23-9. Settings for all of these fields should be made on the user template to simplify management. Each field is explained here:

- *Allow User to Change Password* Check this box if you want to let users change their own passwords.

- *Require a Password* Check this box to require passwords for login. Doing so makes the remaining options available.

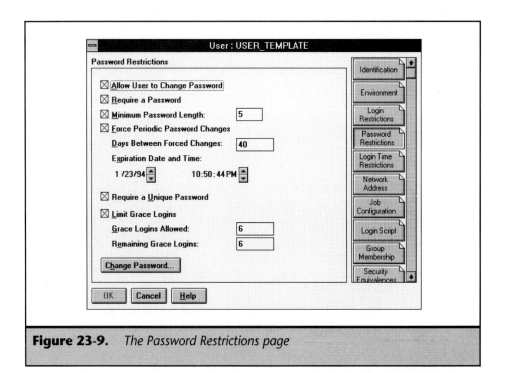

Figure 23-9.   *The Password Restrictions page*

■ *Minimum Password Length* If users are creating their own passwords, check this box to require their passwords to contain a minimum number of characters. This heightens security by ensuring more diverse passwords. Specify the length in the text box.

■ *Force Periodic Password Changes* If users are creating their own passwords, you can force them to change their passwords after a specific period of time. Check the box, and then fill out the fields below either with the number of days between changes or with the date when the current password must be changed.

■ *Require a Unique Password* When checked, NetWare remembers the eight previous passwords a user has created and does not let the user reuse one of these passwords.

■ *Limit Grace Logins* Check this box if you want users to be able to log in by using expired passwords for a specific number of logins. You specify how many times users will see a message telling them to change their password before they can't log in by using the password anymore.

The Login Time Restrictions Page

If you need to limit the time that users can log into the network, specify the time on the Login Time Restrictions page, as shown in Figure 23-10. Use the mouse to drag over the blocks of time that users can log in. As you move the mouse, the exact time of the block appears below it.

The Network Address Page

The Network Address page shows the network address through which the object can be accessed. You don't need to specify this information when creating user templates. If multiple protocols exist on the network, click the button of a protocol to see addresses for it.

The Job Configuration Page

The Job Configuration page lets you create customized print job configurations that the users in a container can select when printing to printer objects in the container. You create print job configurations to set up print jobs such as company mailings or mailing labels. Click the New button on the dialog box to

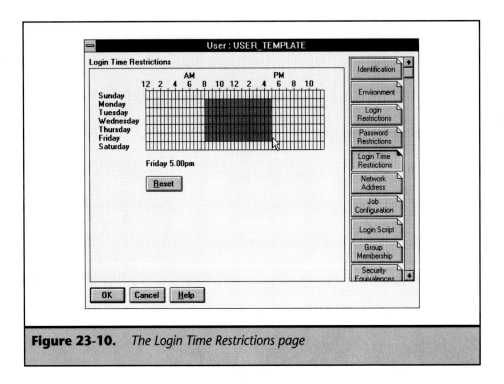

Figure 23-10. *The Login Time Restrictions page*

see the options available for print job configurations. Refer to Chapter 27 for more information.

The Login Script Page

You can create a personal login script for users on the Login Script page. If you are creating a user template, every user you create will get the same login script. The Login Script page includes the Default Profile field. In this field, you can specify a profile object as a login script. See the section "Profile Objects" later in this chapter for more information.

The Group Membership Page

On the Group Membership page, click the Add button and then choose a group that all the users you create by using the user template will belong to. If no groups have been created, there will be no groups to select.

The Security Equivalences Page

You use the Security Equivalences page to specify other users that a user is equivalent to. You should not specify security equivalences on a user template because security equivalence is usually only a temporary status for users who need to share rights. To grant multiple users trustee rights to objects, directories, and files, make them members of a group and then assign those rights to the group.

The Postal Address Page

Click the Postal Address button to view the Postal Address page, which is shown in Figure 23-3. You use this page to provide address information about a user object; you can search on this information later. You can also specify mailing label information that third-party programs can access to create mailings for your departments and users. You fill out the fields at the top of the form and then click the Set Address button to add the information to the Mailing Label Information field.

The Account Balance Page

The NetWare accounting system lets you specify credits that users deplete when they log in and access the network. These credits help control users in several ways. First, you can charge them for services rendered if they are students or nonemployees. You can also keep tabs on users who might be wasting the network's resources and time. You can give users a limited amount of credit and then review their operating procedures if they run out of credit too soon. Refer to Chapter 31 for more information.

The See Also Page

The See Also page contains an informational field that you can fill out on the user template if all user objects must have the same information. You could create a list of objects related to this object, or you could record information about the template.

Finishing Up

After you've modified all the necessary fields on the user template, click its OK button. The user template is added as an object to the container. If you ever need to change the template's properties, click the user template object by using the right mouse button, and choose Details from its pop-up menu.

Creating User Objects

Now that you've created the user template, you can begin creating user objects within the container. If you are the ADMIN user, it is assumed you are creating the first user object within one of the divisions or departments in the company, and that this user will be assigned Supervisor rights over the container and its branch of the company.

Follow these steps to create a user object:

1. Use the right mouse button to click the container object where you want to add the user object. Choose Create from the pop-up menu. The New Object dialog box appears, as shown in Figure 23-11. Objects you don't have rights to create are unavailable in this list.

2. Click the user object icon, and then click the OK button. The Create User dialog box appears, as shown in Figure 23-12. Fill it out as follows:

   ■ Type the login name for the user in the Login Name field.

   ■ Type the user's last name, exactly as it's spelled, in the Last Name field. Don't use an abbreviation.

   ■ Mark the Use User Template box to assign template properties to the new user object.

   ■ Mark the Define Additional Properties box if you want to define the properties for the user object immediately. This disables the Create Another User field.

   ■ If you didn't mark the Define Additional Properties box, you can mark the Create Another User box to create another user object after creating this user object.

   ■ Mark the Create Home Directory box if you want to specify a directory where the user can store personal files. Users become supervisors of their home directories.

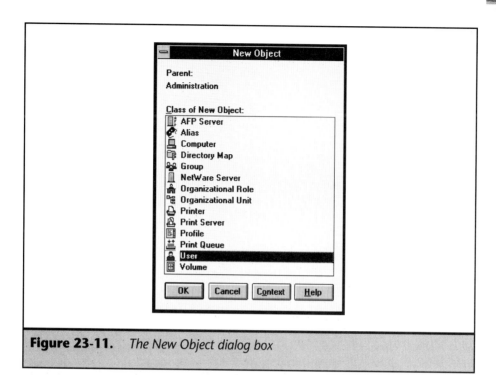

Figure 23-11. *The New Object dialog box*

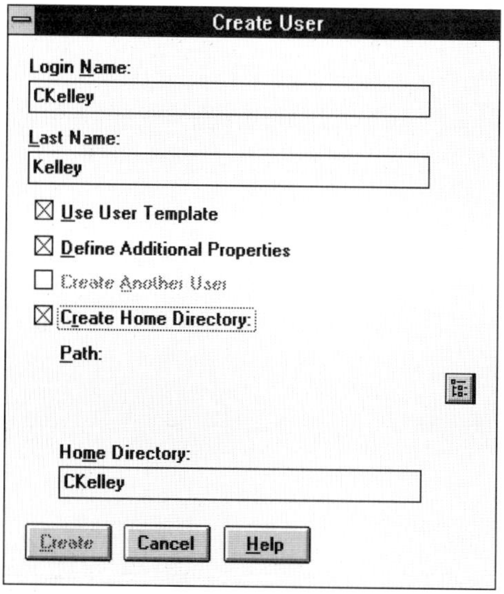

Figure 23-12. *The Create User dialog box*

3. To create a home directory, mark the Create Home Directory box, and then type a path for the home directory in the Path field. If the path you specify contains a directory that doesn't yet exist, you can switch to the Windows File Manager and create it now. Call it USER or HOME.

4. To select a home directory, click the directory selection button on the Create User dialog box.

    The Select Object dialog box appears, as shown in Figure 23-5, so that you can select a volume object; then you can select the USER or HOME directory.

5. Browse the dialog box as discussed previously to locate the directory. Click the directory on the left, then click OK.

6. Click Create to create this user object if the fields are set the way you want.

NetWare Administrator creates the new directory and then displays the Details dialog box for the new user object, similar to what you see in Figure 23-6. Some of the fields might be filled out if a user template exists and you checked the Use User Template box. Now you are ready to set other property options. Refer to the section "The User Template" earlier in this chapter for a discussion of the fields on each of the pages of the Details dialog box. They are the same as those on the template.

When you are done filling out the property fields, you can jump ahead to the section "Controlling Access Rights" to set rights for this user, if you like.

Creating Other Objects

The following sections describe how you create other objects in container objects of the directory tree. Some of these objects are covered in more detail in other chapters:

- Directory map objects are covered in Chapter 28.

- NetWare server and volume objects are created during installation, which is covered in Chapter 16. However, the objects hold useful information that you can view and change.

- You create print server, printer, and print queue objects by using PCONSOLE, as discussed in Chapter 27.

Group Objects

You create group objects so that you can quickly assign trustee rights to a group of people. Groups also simplify the task of sending e-mail to a large number of people.

To create a group, locate the container object in the directory tree where you want the group to exist. Typically, this is the same container that holds most of the group's potential members. Here are the steps for creating a group:

1. Click the container by using the right mouse button, and then choose Create from its pop-up menu.

2. Choose the group object on the New Object dialog box and click OK.

3. The Create Group dialog box appears, as shown in Figure 23-13. Fill out the dialog box as listed here:

   - In the Group Name field, type the name for this group.

   - Check Define Additional Properties if you want to define those properties immediately. Checking this box disables the Create Another Group box.

   - If you didn't check the Define Additional Properties box, you can check the Create Another Group box to create another group as soon as you've created this one.

4. Click the Create button to create the new group. In a moment, the Details dialog box appears. You fill out the fields on the Identification page in the same way you fill them out for container and user objects. Note the following:

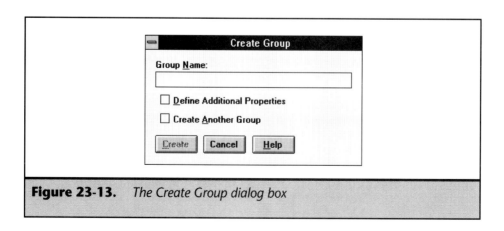

Figure 23-13.   *The Create Group dialog box*

■ Group objects have the Owner identification property, where you can specify the person who is responsible for the group.

■ Group objects have the Department identification property, where you can specify the department to which the group reports.

■ Group objects have the Organization identification property, where you can specify the organization to which the group belongs.

5. Click the Members button to add user objects as members of the group. A list of current members appears, and you can click the Add button to add members. A dialog box appears that you can use to move up and down the directory tree to find the users you want to include in the group.

6. Click Rights to File System to make this group a trustee of directories and files in the file system. Follow the procedures listed earlier in this chapter in the section "The Rights to File System Page."

7. Click the See Also button to supply additional information about the object, as discussed in the previous section.

When you are done specifying properties for the group, click the OK button. Refer to the section "Controlling Access Rights" later in this chapter for information about assigning trustee rights to the group.

Alias Objects

An alias object is an object that refers to another object. Only the name of the object to which the alias refers is stored in an alias object. You use alias objects when you need to refer to an object in another branch of the directory tree; creating an alias of that object in your current branch makes the object easier to access.

NOTE: You can't change the information in an alias object. Instead, you must delete the object and create it again with the new information.

As an example, assume you want to have a manager be responsible for all server objects. You create a container called Servers, and then you add to it an alias object for each of the servers located in different branches of the directory tree. Next, you give the manager Supervisor rights to the Servers container. Because of inheritance, this gives the manager Supervisor rights to all the servers that have aliases in the container. Now the manager can view server information and change the property fields of the servers. You could create similar arrangements for managers of communications equipment, printers, computers, groups, and other objects.

The steps for creating an alias object are outlined here:

1. Locate the container where you want to place the alias object. Click the container object by using the right mouse button, and choose Create from its pop-up menu.

2. Choose Alias from the New Object dialog box. The Create Alias dialog box appears.

3. In the Alias Name field, type a name for this alias.

You can be somewhat descriptive in the Alias Name field. You might want to include the name of a department or a code that identifies the location of the object the alias refers to. For example, names like "Admin's E-mail Server" or "Personnel's Server for Users" are helpful.

4. Click the search button to the right of the Aliased Object field to locate the object this alias will refer to.

The standard Select Object dialog box appears. You scan through the directory tree by clicking container objects or the up-arrow object in the Directory Context field.

5. When the object appears in the Objects field, select it and click the OK button to return to the Create Alias dialog box.

6. To create additional aliases, click the Create Another Alias box.

7. Click the Create button to create the alias.

The alias in the container now represents an object in another container. You can now view and change details about the object represented by the alias by clicking the alias with the right mouse button and choosing Details from the pop-up menu. The properties on the Details dialog box are exactly the same as if you had selected the actual object and viewed its properties.

Server, Volume, and Computer Objects

Server, volume, and computer objects represent physical devices on your network. All have interesting properties, which are described in the following sections.

The Server Object

A server object is created when you install a NetWare v.4 server. At that time, you specify which container will hold the server object. The Details dialog box displays useful information about the server, such as accounting information and network addresses, as described in the following list. Open the Details dialog box for a server on your network at this point to view its information.

- The *Identification page* lists the server's network address and version number.

- Note the *Accounting button* at the bottom. This is where you view and change charge rates for file services, such as disk block reads and writes, server connection time, and disk storage. If you click this button and the NetWare accounting features are not installed, you are asked if you want to install them. Refer to Chapter 31 for more information on NetWare accounting features.

- The *Error Log page* displays a list of errors that have occurred on this server. The file grows in size, so you might want to click the Clear Error Log button occasionally after viewing the log.

- The *Operators page* lets you record a list of operators who are in charge of this server. The information in the list is for reference only.

- On the *Supported Services page,* you can create a list of services provided by this server. The list is informational only.

- On the *Resources page,* you can create a list of resources available at this server, such as volumes and printers. The list is informational only.

- The *See Also page* and *User page* provide lists of other information and users who access this resource.

The Volume Object

Volume objects provide vital information about the file systems in your servers. The *Identification page* displays the name of the volume and the server on which it is located. The *Statistics page* displays information about the usage of the volume, as shown in Figure 23-14. In this box, you can view statistics about available disk space, deleted files, compressed files, and other information.

The *Dates and Times page* shows the date and time the volume was first created, the date the information was last updated, and archive information, such as the last time the volume was partially or completely backed up.

On the *User Space Limits page,* you can specify how much disk space is available to individual users. For example, you can limit temporary employees to 5MB of disk space. A list of user objects in the same container as the volume appears, including the user template. You click one of these names and then click the Modify button. For example, to limit the disk space available to the user template (and thus to all user objects created with the template), select the user template in the list and click the Modify button. The Volume Space Restriction dialog box appears, as shown in Figure 23-15. Click the Limited Volume Space box, and then specify the amount of disk space the object should be limited to.

The *Trustees of the Root Directory page*, which is shown in Figure 23-16, displays a list of users who have trustee rights to the root directory of this volume. You can add trustees to or delete trustees from the list. When you click one of the trustees, the rights that trustee has to the volume are listed in the

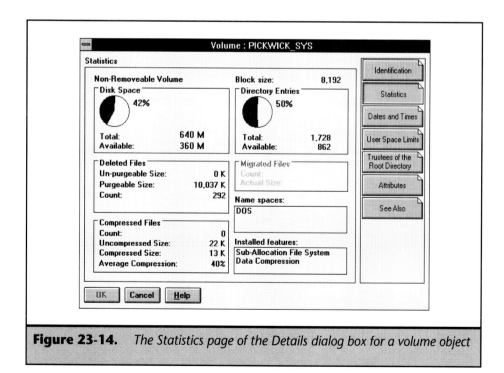

Figure 23-14. *The Statistics page of the Details dialog box for a volume object*

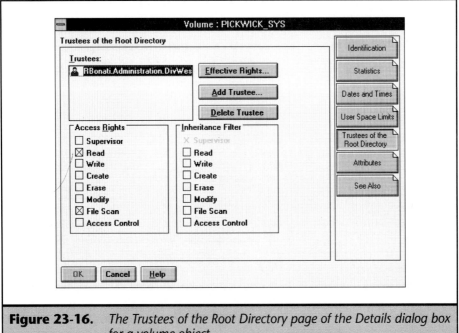

Figure 23-15.   *The Volume Space Restriction dialog box*

lower fields. You can change these rights by clicking the check boxes. Note the
following regarding trustee rights:

■ If a user has trustee rights to a higher object in the directory tree, such as
the container holding the volume, that user will have those same rights for

Figure 23-16.   *The Trustees of the Root Directory page of the Details dialog box
for a volume object*

the volume, by inheritance. Users who have inherited rights are not listed in the Trustees field of the dialog box. To view the rights a user has in the volume, click the Effective Rights button and then specify the user's object to view rights.

■ Inherited rights that users have from higher-level containers can be controlled for the volume by marking the check boxes in the Inheritance Filter field. If a right in the field is marked, users can inherit that right. If a right is not marked, the right is blocked and users can't inherit it.

■ Users who are specifically made trustees of a volume will have the same rights they are granted in the root of the volume in all subdirectories of the volume, unless the rights are changed by a new trustee assignment or blocked by an Inherited Rights Filter.

■ Trustee rights combine with inherited rights (and any security equivalences) to form the effective rights a user object has to the root or subdirectories of a volume.

■ The Supervisor right cannot be blocked by an Inherited Rights Filter in the file system.

To add new trustees to the root directory of the volume, click the Add Trustee button, and then use the Select Object dialog box to search for user objects in the directory tree. To delete a trustee of the root, highlight the user's name in the Trustees field and click the Delete Trustee button.

The *Attributes page* displays a list of directory attributes. Mark the box of any attribute you want to set for the directory. If you need an explanation of these attributes, click the Help button.

You use the *See Also page* to view or supply information about the volume. The contents of this field are informational only and do not affect the volume.

The Computer Object

The Computer object is designed to help you manage the workstations on your network. The main purpose of the object is for documentation, because the properties are informational only and do not affect the computer.

■ On the *Identification page,* type useful information about the computer, such as its serial number, location, and other descriptions.

■ On the *Operators page,* include a list of people who use this system.

- On the *Network Addresses page,* view and add network addresses for the workstation for each of the protocols listed, if they exist on the network. Click each protocol button to view its network addresses in the upper field.

- On the *See Also page,* include additional information about the computer or the resources attached to it, such as shared printers.

Print Server, Printer, and Print Queue Objects

You use the print server, printer, and print queue objects to track shared network printers. A print server is the core of the printer management system. It keeps track of printers on the network and manages queues, to which users send print jobs. Any number of print queues can be created. For example, you could create a print queue that holds and prints jobs after hours, or you could create a print queue with high priority that managers can use to supersede the print jobs of other users. Multiple printers can service a single queue, or several queues can send print jobs to a single printer. The printing system is described in detail in Chapter 27.

Profile Objects

A profile object contains a login script that executes for a set of users or groups who are not part of the same container object. The profile login script is optional and can be assigned to any user. You assign a profile login script to a user by specifying the name of the profile as part of the user object's property information. Specifically, you select the Login Script page of the user object's Details dialog box and type the profile name in the Default Profile field.

Click the Login Script button to create the login script for the profile, then refer to Chapter 28 for details on login scripts.

Organizational Role Objects

The organizational role object defines a position or role within your company. Use it as you would a group object to define special access rights to the system for users who don't necessarily fit into any group context. For example, you could create an organizational role called Update Clerk and then assign file system rights to the object in program directories that need occasional updating.

When a program needs updating, you make a user object a temporary trustee of the organizational role object so that the user has rights to modify files in the program directories.

The Details dialog box of the organizational role object includes the Identification page, Postal Address page, Rights to File System page, and See Also page, all of which are discussed earlier in this chapter.

Controlling Access Rights

Last, but not least, we discuss how to view and change access rights objects have to other objects or the filing system. There are several places where you can view and change this information, as discussed in the following list.

To view object rights, click any object by using the right mouse button, and choose one of the following options:

- *Trustees of this Object*   Displays a list of trustees for the current object. The Object Trustees dialog box appears, as shown in Figure 23-17.

- *Rights to Other Objects*   Displays a list of objects the selected object is a trustee of. The Object Trustees dialog box appears after you specify a context. See the next section for details about working with this dialog box.

Methods for viewing and changing directory and file rights are listed here:

- Double-click an object to open its Details dialog box. Open the Rights to File System page (see Figure 23-4), and then select the volumes, directories, and files you want to view or change rights to.

- Double-click a volume object to display its directories, and if necessary, double-click a directory to list subdirectories or files. Click a directory or file by using the right mouse button, and then choose Details from the list. Click Trustees of This Directory (or Trustees of This File) to view or change the trustee list. (See Figure 23-16.)

Assigning Trustee Rights

The easiest way to make an object a trustee of another object is to drag and drop the object onto the other object. The object you drag on top of another object

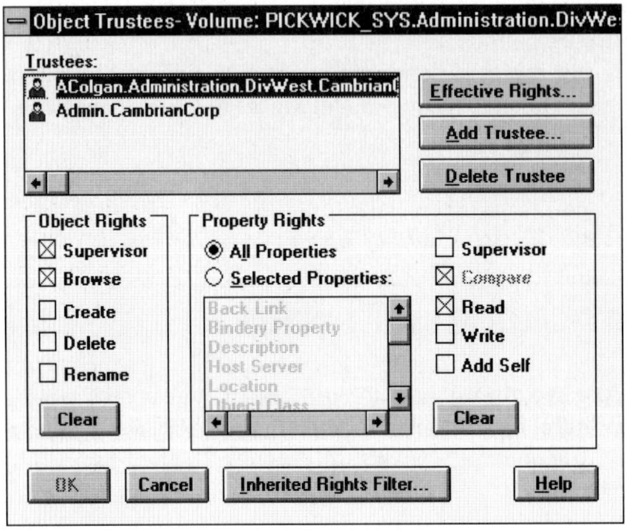

Figure 23-17. *The Object Trustees dialog box*

becomes the trustee of that object. The Object Trustees dialog box appears (see Figure 23-17) so that you can assign trustee rights to the object.

In Figure 23-17, you can see that AColgan (the highlighted user object in the Trustees field) has Supervisor object rights to the volume. Although it is not listed, she also has the Supervisor right for all the property rights listed on the right. You would see this if you clicked the Effective Rights button.

Don't always rely on the information in the rights fields. These are the trustee rights granted to the user, but the user might have additional rights through inheritance or group membership, so always click the Effective Rights button to view the true rights the user has to the object. The same holds true when viewing directory and file rights in the dialog boxes shown in Figures 23-4 and 23-16.

You might recall from Chapter 22 that the Property Rights field specifies which properties of an object trustees can view and change. For example, by default, a user who doesn't have the Supervisor right can view the properties of his or her own user object, but the only thing the user can change is the login script. Likewise, other users can't change any of the properties unless a supervisor gives them rights to do so.

By using NetWare Administrator or NETADMIN, users can view the properties of their own user objects and any other object; in some cases, they can change properties for those objects. If you don't want users to view a property of an object, you can revoke the Read right for just that property. Alternatively, if you want users to be able to change some of the properties for their own user objects, you can grant them Read and Write rights for those properties.

NOTE: Property rights are not inherited, so you'll need to assign them to each object individually.

The options in the Property Rights field display property rights two ways. If you click All Properties, you see the *default* rights the user has to all the properties of an object. However, you can click Selected Properties to change the rights for individual properties. Doing so keeps all other properties at their default (or custom) settings; only the selected right is changed.

When you click the Selected Properties button, the list of individual properties for the object becomes available. If you scroll through this list, you will notice that each name matches a field you see on the pages of the Details dialog box for the object. Select any property and then click one of the rights boxes on the right. To save the changes, click the OK button.

CHAPTER 24

This chapter covers the directory and file management features of the NetWare Administrator utility and the text-based FILER utility. Salvaging deleted files or purging them from volumes is covered at the end of the chapter in the section "Salvaging and Purging Files." You can use either NetWare Administrator or FILER to salvage and purge.

Administering the File System

Directory and File Management with NetWare Administrator

You can copy, move, and change the attributes of directories and files by using NetWare Administrator. Locate a volume object and then double-click it to display a list of its root-level directories, as shown in Figure 24-1. By double-clicking a directory, you can list its subdirectories and/or files. You can select any directory or file and choose the Move, Copy, Rename, or Delete option from the Object menu. If you select a volume object or directory, you can also choose the Salvage option, which is covered later in this chapter.

Choosing either Move or Copy from the menu displays the Move/Copy dialog box, as shown in Figure 24-2. In the Move/Copy dialog box, you can choose to move or copy the directory or file by selecting the appropriate option in the Operation field. Moving a directory or file removes it from its current location and places it in the destination location. Copying a directory or file makes a copy of it and places the copy in the destination location. Click the button to the right of the Destination field to specify where you want the directory or file moved or copied to. Click OK when you're done.

NOTE: The Move command provides a convenient method for reorganizing the directory structure. When you move a directory, all its subdirectories and files are moved with it to the new location.

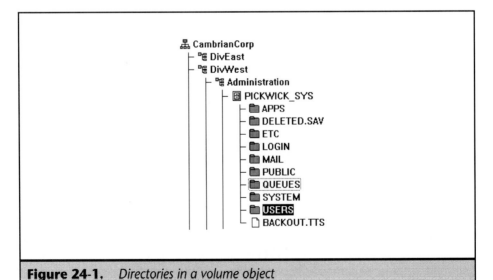

Figure 24-1.   *Directories in a volume object*

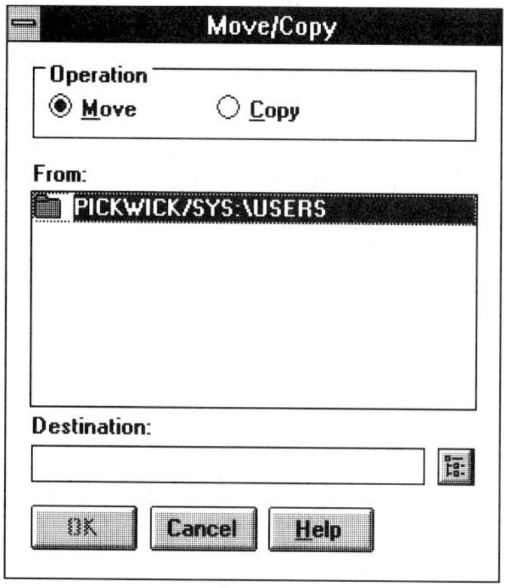

Figure 24-2. *The Move/Copy dialog box*

The Rename option lets you specify a new name for a directory or a file, and the Delete option lets you delete a directory or a file. If you accidentally delete a directory or a file, use the Salvage option to recover it, as discussed in the section "Salvaging and Purging Files" later in this chapter.

After you select a directory or file, you can view and change its trustee rights; if it is a directory, you can also view and change its inherited rights. Refer to Chapter 23 for more information on working with trustee rights in NetWare Administrator.

Directory and File Management with FILER

The primary purpose of FILER is to help you manage directories and files. You can use it in place of NetWare Administrator or commands you would execute at the DOS prompt. Type **FILER** at the command prompt to display the FILER Available options menu, as shown in Figure 24-3. Note the information at the top of the screen. It indicates your current context in NetWare Directory Services, the current volume, and the directory you are working on in that volume.

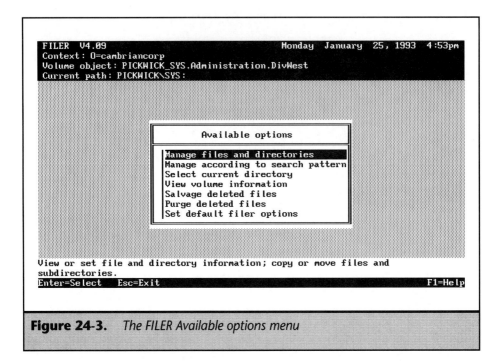

```
FILER  V4.09                        Monday  January  25, 1993  4:53pm
Context: O=cambriancorp
Volume object: PICKWICK_SYS.Administration.DivWest
Current path: PICKWICK\SYS:



                        ┌──────────────────────────────┐
                        │       Available options      │
                        ├──────────────────────────────┤
                        │ Manage files and directories │
                        │ Manage according to search pattern
                        │ Select current directory     │
                        │ View volume information      │
                        │ Salvage deleted files        │
                        │ Purge deleted files          │
                        │ Set default filer options    │
                        └──────────────────────────────┘


View or set file and directory information; copy or move files and
subdirectories.
Enter=Select    Esc=Exit                                        F1=Help
```

Figure 24-3.   *The FILER Available options menu*

FILER is an excellent utility to use for managing the file system. Although NetWare Administrator also has file management features, FILER is often more convenient to use when you want to make quick changes, especially if you are at a workstation that doesn't run Windows or OS/2. You can perform the following tasks by using FILER:

■ View a list of the directories on a volume

■ View a list of the subdirectories and files within directories

■ Create new directories

■ Copy and move directories and files

■ View the names of the trustees of directories and files

■ Change the attributes of directories and files

■ Salvage deleted files

■ Purge deleted files from the system

NOTE: An even quicker way to view and manage the file system is to use the command-line utilities covered in Chapter 25. However, the commands require parameters that can sometimes become confusing. That's why FILER and NetWare Administrator exist.

Before getting started with these tasks, there is some preliminary information you need to know about FILER's operating features, such as how to set options and how to change your context in the directory tree.

Setting FILER's Default Options

You can choose the "Set default filer options" option on the FILER menu to make changes to the way FILER works. The menu shown in Figure 24-4 appears. Each option on the menu is described here:

- *Confirm deletions*   If this option is set to Yes, you must confirm every file deletion, which can be time consuming when deleting large groups of files or directories. You might want to set this option to No when you are sure you want to delete a group of files, and then set it back to Yes to protect against accidental deletions.

```
                           Filer settings
 Confirm deletions: No

 Confirm file copies: No
 Confirm file overwrites: Yes

 Preserve file attributes: Yes
 Notify if extended attributes (long names) are lost: No

 Copy files sparse: No
 Copy files compressed: No
 Force files to be copied compressed: No
```

Figure 24-4.   *The Filer settings menu*

- *Confirm file copies*   When set to Yes, you must confirm that you want to copy files.

- *Confirm file overwrites*   Set this option to Yes to prevent files from being overwritten without a warning. Set this option to No only temporarily when you are sure you want to copy over files.

- *Preserve file attributes*   Choose Yes to preserve extended attributes when copying files. These attributes are set to Normal when this option is set to No.

- *Notify if extended attributes (long names) are lost*   Set this option to Yes if you want to be warned when files that have extended attributes and long names are copied. Normally, when you copy these files, their extended attributes and long names are lost.

Changing Your Context in the Directory Tree

The current context, volume, and directory path are listed at the top of the FILER screen. You can choose other directories, volumes, and servers to work on by choosing the Select current directory option from the Available options menu. A dialog box appears that displays your current directory path, as shown here:

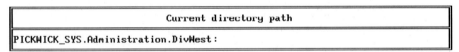

You can type a new directory in this box, or you can press the INS key to choose a new directory from a list, as shown here:

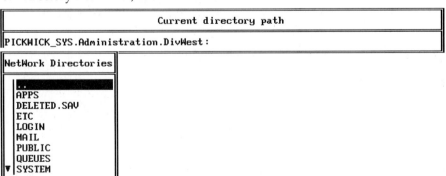

Select one of the directories and press ENTER to display the directory's subdirectories, if it has any. You can keep moving around the directory structure by selecting other directories from the list. The directory path in the Current directory path box changes to show the name of each directory you select. When you are done, press ESC to close the NetWork Directories list, and then press ENTER to accept the path in the Current directory path box.

To work with another volume, highlight the double-dot (parent directory) entry in the NetWork Directories list and press ENTER. This displays the Volumes dialog box:

```
┌─────────────────────────────────────────────────────────────────┐
│                             Volumes                              │
├──────────────────────────────────────────┬──────────────────────┤
│ [Additional Volume Objects]               │                      │
│ [Additional Servers]                      │                      │
│                                           │                      │
│                                           │                      │
│                                           │                      │
│                                           │                      │
└──────────────────────────────────────────┴──────────────────────┘
```

You have two choices in the Volumes dialog box. Choose [Additional Volume Objects] to work with another volume on your current server, or choose [Additional Servers] so that you can choose a volume on another server.

■ If you choose [Additional Volume Objects], the Object, Class dialog box shown in Figure 24-5 appears.

■ If you choose [Additional Servers], a menu of servers appears. After choosing a server from the menu, the Object, Class dialog box shown in Figure 24-5 appears.

In the Object, Class dialog box, you can move up and down the directory tree to locate volume objects. Click a container object to list any leaf objects and container objects it holds. When the new volume appears, highlight it and press ENTER. A list of directories on the volume then appears. Highlight the directory you want to work with and press ENTER.

When the correct directory path appears in the Current directory path box, press ESC to back out of the dialog boxes and return to the Available options menu. The new context, volume, and path appear at the top of the screen.

NOTE: You can change your context in the filing system at any time while managing files and directories.

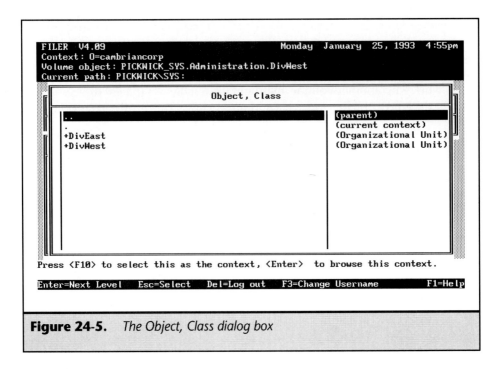

Figure 24-5.   *The Object, Class dialog box*

Viewing Volume Information

You can view information about the current volume by choosing the View volume information option from FILER's main menu. The following selection box appears:

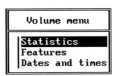

Each option is discussed in the following sections.

STATISTICS   Choose the Statistics option to view available space and file settings. The space on the volume used by compressed and uncompressed files is listed, along with information about how much space is saved by compressing files.

FEATURES   Choose the Features option to view the volume settings that were made during the volume's installation, such as its block size, name spaces, and whether compression and block suballocation are in use.

DATES AND TIMES   Choose the Dates and times option to view the creation date and time of the volume, the last time it was modified, and the last time it was archived.

Using File and Directory Management Options

You can choose either of the first two options from the FILER main menu to manage directories and files. The first option, Manage files and directories, lets you work with a complete listing of all directories and files. The second option, Manage according to search pattern, lets you specify a search pattern to display only certain directory names and filenames. After you set the pattern, you can begin managing files just as if you had picked the first option. If you don't want to set a search pattern, choose the Manage files and directories option from the FILER main menu and then jump to the section "Managing Files and Directories" later in this chapter.

Setting a Search Pattern

Before you start working with directories and files, you might want to set a search pattern so that you see only certain types of objects and files. Choose the Manage according to search pattern option from the Available options menu to display the dialog box shown in Figure 24-6. Use the fields in this dialog box as described in the following list. Use the arrow keys to move among fields, and press ENTER to edit fields. In the Exclude file patterns and Include file patterns fields, press ENTER to add new patterns, and then press INS. All the patterns make up a list of directories or files that will be excluded or included. To remove a pattern, highlight it in the list and press DEL.

- ■ *Pattern*   Use wildcard characters to specify the types of files you want to list. For example, to list all document files, type ***.DOC** or ***.TXT**.

- ■ *Exclude directory patterns*   Type a wildcard pattern that specifies directories you don't want to see in listings.

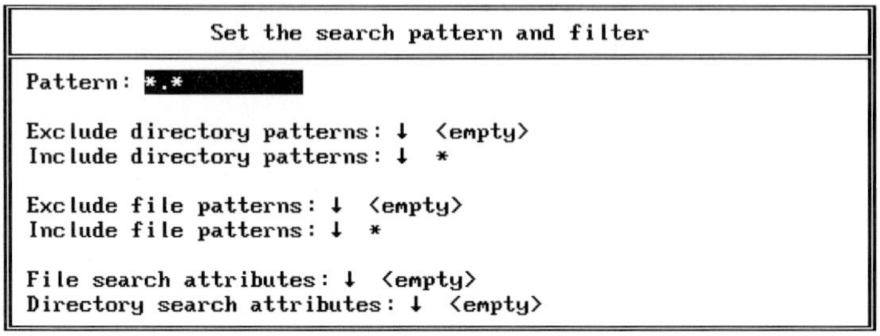

```
┌─────────────────────────────────────────────────────────────┐
│     ┌───────────────────────────────────────────────┐         │
│     │        Set the search pattern and filter      │         │
│     │  ┌─────────────────────────────────────────┐  │         │
│     │  Pattern: ███*.*████████████               │  │         │
│     │                                              │         │
│     │  Exclude directory patterns: ↓  <empty>     │         │
│     │  Include directory patterns: ↓  *           │         │
│     │                                              │         │
│     │  Exclude file patterns: ↓  <empty>          │         │
│     │  Include file patterns: ↓  *                │         │
│     │                                              │         │
│     │  File search attributes: ↓  <empty>         │         │
│     │  Directory search attributes: ↓  <empty>    │         │
│     │  └─────────────────────────────────────────┘  │         │
│     └───────────────────────────────────────────────┘         │
└─────────────────────────────────────────────────────────────┘
```

Figure 24-6.   *The Set the search pattern and filter dialog box*

- *Include directory patterns* Type a wildcard pattern that specifies directory names you want to see in a list.

- *Exclude file patterns* Specify a pattern for files you want to exclude from listings.

- *Include file patterns* Specify a pattern for files you want to include in listings.

- *File search attributes* Specify whether files that have the Hidden or System attribute should be included in listings. Press ENTER, and then press INS to choose attributes from a list.

- *Directory search attributes* Specify whether directories that have the Hidden or System attribute should be included in listings. Press ENTER, and then press INS to choose attributes from a list.

Once you've set a search pattern, don't press ESC to jump back to the main menu. Press F10 to begin managing files by using the search pattern you have selected.

Managing Files and Directories

When you choose the Manage files and directories option from the FILER Available options menu, or after you set a search pattern as discussed in the previous section, a list similar to that shown in Figure 24-7 appears. The list shows the subdirectories and files in the current directory. If you didn't set a new

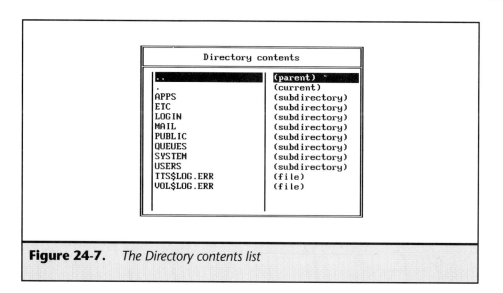

Figure 24-7. *The Directory contents list*

context by using the Select current directory option on the main menu, the subdirectories and files in the root directory of the current volume are listed.

From this list, you can move up and down the directory tree or choose to work on a different volume on a different server. You have the following options:

■ Highlight the parent (..) entry and press ENTER to move back up the directory tree. If you are at the root of a volume, choosing this option displays the Volumes menu so that you can choose another volume. You can choose another server from the Volumes menu by selecting [Additional Server], and then you can choose a volume on that server.

■ Highlight any directory and press ENTER to display the contents of that directory.

■ Highlight any directory or file and press F10 to view information about it.

■ Mark groups of directories and files for an operation such as moving or deleting them. Highlight each file and press the F5 key to mark it. Then press F10 to see a list of options you can perform on the group.

■ Highlight any directory or file and press F3 to rename it.

When you have located the area of the file system you want to work in, refer to one of the next few sections, depending on whether you want to work with single files and directories or groups of files and directories.

Working with a Single Directory

From the Directory contents list, highlight the directory you want to work with and press F10. The Subdirectory options menu appears:

```
┌──────────────────────────────────────────┐
│        Subdirectory options              │
├──────────────────────────────────────────┤
│ Copy subdirectory's files                │
│ Copy subdirectory's structure            │
│ Make this your current directory         │
│ Move subdirectory's structure            │
│ Rights list                              │
│ View/Set directory information           │
└──────────────────────────────────────────┘
```

Highlighting a directory and pressing ENTER moves you into the directory, so if you want to view options, be sure to press F10. From the Subdirectory options menu, you can choose any of the options described next.

NOTE: To delete a directory, highlight it and press the DEL key.

COPY SUBDIRECTORY'S FILES   Select this option to copy the files in the directory to another location in the filing system. A menu appears so that you can specify the destination. Press the INS key to choose from the list, using the techniques for moving around the directory tree that were discussed earlier. Remember, you can select the parent (..) entry to move up the tree; when you reach the root, you can choose another server and volume. After you have highlighted the destination directory, press ESC. The path to the directory appears in the Copy subdirectory to field. Press ENTER to execute the Copy command, or press ESC to cancel it.

NOTE: To copy directories, you'll need Read and File Scan rights in the source directories and Create, Write, and Modify rights in the destination directory.

COPY SUBDIRECTORY'S STRUCTURE   Select this option to copy (as opposed to move) an entire branch of the directory tree to another location. The directory becomes a subdirectory of the destination directory or volume you select unless it is moved to the root of a volume. When you select this option, you can choose a destination from a list of directories, or you can move back up the directory tree to select other branches, other volumes, or volumes on other servers.

MAKE THIS YOUR CURRENT DIRECTORY   Choose this option to open the directory and file list for the current directory. You can then perform operations on the contents of that listing.

MOVE SUBDIRECTORY'S STRUCTURE   Select this option to move (as opposed to copy) an entire branch of the directory tree to another location. The directory becomes a subdirectory of the destination directory or volume you select. When you select this option, you can choose a destination from a list of directories, or you can move back up the directory tree to select other branches, other volumes, or volumes on other servers.

RIGHTS LIST   Select this option to view the trustees of this directory and the rights they have to it. You cannot change rights from this list. To assign trustee rights, refer to the next option.

VIEW/SET DIRECTORY INFORMATION   Choose this option to view and change information about the directory, such as its owner, attributes, and trustees. When you select the option, a dialog box similar to that shown in Figure 24-8 appears.

```
                         Directory information for APPS
 Owner: CN=Admin.O=cambriancorp

 Creation date: 1-21-1993
 Creation time: 4:00pm

 Directory attributes: ↓  <empty>
 Current effective rights: [SRWCEMFA]

 Inherited rights filter:[SRWCEMFA]
 Trustees: ↓ CN=RBonati.OU=Administration.OU=DivWest.O=cambr

 Limit space: Yes
 Directory space limit:       1024 Kilobytes
```

Figure 24-8.   *The Directory information dialog box*

You can change the information in several fields of the dialog box, such as the owner, creation date and time, rights, and attributes. To change the information in a field, highlight it and press ENTER. You then typically press INS to select from a list.

- To assign directory attributes, refer to the section "Managing Directory Attributes."

- To change the Inherited Rights Filter, refer to the section "Managing Inherited Rights Filters."

- To change trustee rights, refer to the section "Managing Trustee Rights."

If you want to limit the amount of space that this directory can use, jump to the Limit space field, type **Y**, for *Yes*, and press ENTER. In the Directory space limit field, type the limit in kilobytes. This setting applies to all users. When you are done changing this menu, press F10 or ESC.

Working with a Single File

When you select a file from a directory listing and press F10 or ENTER, the File options menu appears:

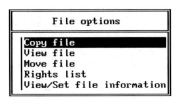

```
┌──────────────────────────────┐
│         File options          │
├──────────────────────────────┤
│ Copy file                     │
│ View file                     │
│ Move file                     │
│ Rights list                   │
│ View/Set file information     │
└──────────────────────────────┘
```

From this menu you can copy, move, or view the contents of the file.

NOTE: To delete the file, highlight it and press the DEL key.

To copy the file, choose the Copy file option from the menu. The Destination directory box appears:

```
┌──────────────────────────────────────────────────────┐
│              Destination directory                     │
├──────────────────────────────────────────────────────┤
│ PICKWICK_SYS.Administration.DivWest:                   │
└──────────────────────────────────────────────────────┘
```

Press the INS key to choose from a list of directories. Remember, you can choose another branch of the directory tree, or another volume, by highlighting the parent (..) option and pressing ENTER. As you progress up or down the directory tree, the Network Directories list displays directories at different levels. After selecting a directory, press ESC. You are returned to the Destination directory, where you can press ENTER to copy the file.

You can view the contents of text files by choosing the View file option from the File options menu, and you can view which users have rights to the file by choosing the Rights list option (you cannot set rights from this menu).

You use the View/Set file information option to view and change the attributes, Inherited Rights Filter, trustees, and date information for the file. Choosing this option displays a dialog box similar to that shown in Figure 24-9. Refer to the section "Managing File Attributes" later in this chapter for more information. The dialog box contains fields for the creation date, last accessed date, and last modified date for the file. You might change these dates to ensure that a file is included in a backup set or another date-specific set.

Working with a Directory Group

A directory group is a set of directories you mark by using the F5 key. You can then copy or move the directories to another location, and you can set inherited rights.

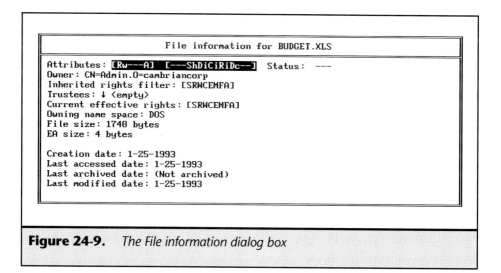

```
                    File information for BUDGET.XLS

 Attributes: [Rw---A] [---ShDiCiRiDc--]  Status:  ---
 Owner: CN=Admin.O=cambriancorp
 Inherited rights filter: [SRWCEMFA]
 Trustees: ↓ <empty>
 Current effective rights: [SRWCEMFA]
 Owning name space: DOS
 File size: 1748 bytes
 EA size: 4 bytes

 Creation date: 1-25-1993
 Last accessed date: 1-25-1993
 Last archived date: (Not archived)
 Last modified date: 1-25-1993
```

Figure 24-9. *The File information dialog box*

To select a directory, you highlight it and press the F5 key to mark it. Continue adding directories to the group in this way, and then press F10 to display a menu of options for working with the group, as shown here:

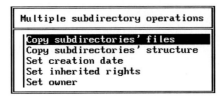

```
╔══════════════════════════════════════╗
║ Multiple subdirectory operations     ║
╠══════════════════════════════════════╣
║ Copy subdirectories' files           ║
║ Copy subdirectories' structure       ║
║ Set creation date                    ║
║ Set inherited rights                 ║
║ Set owner                            ║
╚══════════════════════════════════════╝
```

NOTE: To delete the group of directories, press the DEL key.

The first option copies the files in the directories, along with the directories themselves, to another location. The second option copies the entire structure of the directories, including their subdirectories and files.

NOTE: To copy directories, you'll need Read and File Scan rights in the source directories and Create, Write, and Modify rights in the destination.

The Set creation date option lets you change the creation dates associated with the directories. If you want to change the Inherited Rights Filters for the directories, choose the Set inherited rights option, and refer to the section "Managing Inherited Rights Filters" later in this chapter. Finally, choose the Set owner option to change the name of the person who owns this directory. You cannot change directory attributes when a group of directories is selected. You must change them for each directory individually.

Working with a File Group

It is common to mark a group of files in a directory (rather than work with one file at a time) so that you can copy them to another location, delete them, or change their attributes, trustees, and inherited rights. Highlight a file and press the F5 key to mark it. Continue selecting in this way until the group is complete. Then press the F10 key. You'll see the following menu:

```
┌─────────────────────────────┐
│ Multiple file operations    │
│ ┌─────────────────────────┐ │
│ │ Copy marked files       │ │
│ │ Set attributes          │ │
│ │ Set creation date       │ │
│ │ Set inherited rights    │ │
│ │ Set last accessed date  │ │
│ │ Set last modified date  │ │
│ │ Set owner               │ │
│ └─────────────────────────┘ │
└─────────────────────────────┘
```

If you choose the first option, the Copy files to menu appears. You can press INS to select a destination from a list of directories, as discussed previously.

You use the second option, Set attributes, to set the file attributes for the group of files. Refer to the section "Managing File Attributes" later in this chapter. The fourth option, Set inherited rights, is covered later in the section "Managing Inherited Rights Filters."

The Set creation date, Set last accessed date, Set last modified date, and Set owner options are all used to change the properties of the selected files. You highlight the option, press ENTER, and then specify the new value.

Managing Directory Attributes

To manage directory attributes, select a directory and then press the F10 key. The Subdirectory options menu appears. Choose the View/Set directory information option from this menu to display the dialog box shown in Figure 24-8.

NOTE: You cannot set attributes for a group of directories, only for a single directory.

Scroll down to the Directory attributes field and press ENTER. You see the Current attributes box, which might be empty. To add directory attributes, press the INS key. Your screen should now look similar to this:

```
┌──────────────────────────────────────────────────────────────────┐
│                 Directory information for QUEUES                   │
│  ┌────────────────┬─────────────────────────────────────┬───────┐ │
│  │Owner: CN=PICKWICK│          Current attributes         │corp   │ │
│  ├──────────────┐ │ │                                     │       │ │
│  │Creation date: 1-2│ │                                   │       │ │
│  │Creation time: 2:2│ │                                   │       │ │
│  │              │ │ │             <empty>                 │       │ │
│  │Directory     │ │ │                                     │       │ │
│  │Current e ┌────┴────────────────────────┐              │       │ │
│  │          │       Other attributes       │              │       │ │
│  │Inherited │├────────────────────────────┤│              │       │ │
│  │Trustees: ││Delete inhibit              ││West.O=cambr   │       │ │
│  │          ││Don't compress              ││              │       │ │
│  │          ││Hidden directory            ││              │       │ │
│  │Limit spa ▼│Immediate compression        ││              │       │ │
│  │Directory └────────────────────────────┘│              │       │ │
│  └────────────────────────────────────────┴──────────────┘       │ │
└──────────────────────────────────────────────────────────────────┘
```

To assign attributes, highlight an attribute and press the F5 key to mark it.
Continue selecting attributes in this way until all the attributes you want to assign
are selected, and then press the ENTER key. The attributes appear in the Current
attributes box. You can press ESC to back out to the main menu when you're done. A
description of directory and file attributes is provided in Table 24-1. Note that not all
of the attributes apply to directories. Some apply only to files.

Attribute	Full Name	Description
A	Archive Needed	When set, this attribute indicates that a file has been modified and needs backing up. It has no effect on directories.
Cc	Can't Compress	A status attribute that indicates a file cannot be compressed due to lack of disk space. It is not used for directories, and you cannot assign this attribute.
C	Compressed	A status attribute that indicates a file has been compressed. It is not used for directories, and you can't assign this attribute.
CI	Copy Inhibit	When set, prevents Macintosh users from copying the file. Not used for directories.
DI	Delete Inhibit	When set, prevents users from deleting a file or directory.

Table 24-1.   *File and Directory Attributes (Note: "Status" Attributes are
informational only)*

Attribute	Full Name	Description
DC	Don't Compress	When applied to a file, prevents the file from being compressed. When applied to a directory, prevents files in the directory from being compressed.
DM	Don't Migrate	When applied to a file, prevents the file from being migrated to a secondary storage device such as an optical disk jukebox. When applied to a directory, prevents files in the directory from being migrated.
X	Execute Only	Prevents users from copying a file, thus preventing software piracy. Not applicable to directories. Once set, it cannot be removed, even by the ADMIN user. The file can, however, be deleted, then restored from a backup or the original.
H	Hidden	Hides a file or directory in DIR listings and prevents the file or directory from being copied or deleted.
IM	Immediate Compress	When applied to a file, the file is compressed as soon as possible. When applied to a directory, the files in the directory are compressed as soon as possible.
M	Migrated	A status attribute that indicates that a file has been migrated to a secondary storage device such as an optical disk jukebox.
P	Purge	When applied to a file, the file is immediately purged from the system when deleted. When applied to a directory, the directory and any files it holds are purged when deleted. Purged files and directories cannot be recovered by using NetWare Administrator or FILER.

Table 24-1. *File and Directory Attributes* (continued)

Attribute	Full Name	Description
RO	Read Only	When set, prevents users from changing, deleting, or renaming a file. The D and R attributes are also assigned when RO is applied. Has no effect on directories.
RI	Rename Inhibit	When set, prevents users from renaming a file or directory.
S	Shareable	When set, allows multiple users to access the file at one time. Usually set on record-locking database files. Has no effect on directories.
SY	System	When set, prevents users from seeing the file or directory in a DIR listing.
T	Transactional	When applied to a file, the transaction tracking system will protect the file. Has no effect on directories.

Table 24-1.   *File and Directory Attributes* (continued)

Managing File Attributes

To change file attributes, you follow a procedure similar to that for changing directory attributes. Highlight the file, or use the F5 key to mark a group of files, and then press the F10 key.

- If you selected a single file, choose the View/Set file information option from the File options menu. A dialog box similar that shown in Figure 24-9 appears. Highlight the Attributes field and press ENTER.

- If you selected multiple files, choose the Set attributes option from the Multiple file operations menu.

The File attributes menu or the Current attributes menu appears, depending on whether the file currently has any attribute assignments. Press the INS key to add assignments, and then use the F5 key to mark the attributes you want to add; press ENTER when you're done. The new attributes appear in the list, and you can press ESC to return to the main menu. File and directory attributes are listed in Table 24-1.

NOTE: To remove attributes, follow the preceding steps, but use the F5 key to mark the attributes you want to remove, and then press the DEL key.

Managing Inherited Rights Filters

An Inherited Rights Filter lets you block the rights inherited from parent directories. You can block these rights at both the directory level and the file level.

■ If you select a single directory or file, choose the View/Set directory information option or the View/Set file information option from the Subdirectory options menu or the File options menu. Scroll down to the Current effective rights field, and press ENTER.

■ If you select multiple directories or files, choose the Set inherited rights option from the Multiple subdirectory operations menu or the Multiple file operations menu, and press ENTER.

The Inherited rights menu appears. The rights displayed in this menu are the rights that are allowed to be inherited.

■ To block rights from being inherited, remove them from the list. Highlight each right or mark multiple rights by using the F5 key, and then press the DEL key.

■ To add rights that are currently unavailable, press the INS key, and then mark rights on the list by using the F5 key. Press ENTER to add the rights.

When you are done changing the Inherited Rights Filter for the directories or files, press ESC to back out to the main menu. You are asked to confirm your changes.

Managing Trustee Rights

You make users trustees of directories and files so that they can access and change files. If a user has trustee rights to a directory, he or she also has trustee rights to the files in that directory, but you can change the trustee rights for individual files. For example, you could grant a user rights to change all files in a directory except those owned by managers.

NOTE: You can assign trustee rights to multiple directories or files at once.

To assign trustee rights, highlight the directory or file you want to assign rights to, and press the F10 key. Choose the View/Set directory information option or the View/Set file information option from the Subdirectory options menu or the File options menu. A dialog box opens, similar to that shown in Figure 24-8. Scroll down to the Trustees field and press ENTER. A list similar to that shown in Figure 24-10 appears.

Recall that both user objects and other NetWare Directory Services objects can be trustees of a directory or file. If you grant a container trustee rights to a directory, all the users that belong to that container also become trustees of the directory. There are three trustees in Figure 24-10, two of which are user objects. However, there are other potential trustees, such as users who belong to the OU=Sales object and users who inherit rights to the directory. They are not listed in this dialog box.

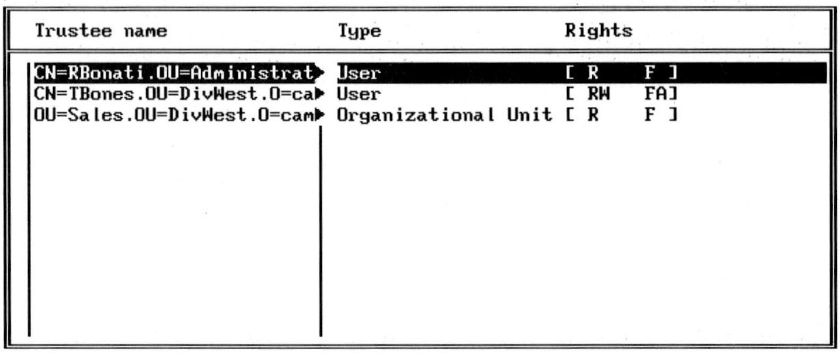

```
Trustee name              Type                  Rights

CN=RBonati.OU=Administrat▶ User              [ R      F ]
CN=TBones.OU=DivWest.O=ca▶ User              [ RW     FA]
OU=Sales.OU=DivWest.O=cam▶ Organizational Unit [ R    F ]
```

Figure 24-10.   *Assigning trustee rights*

Rights are listed in the Rights column. Each right is abbreviated by using the first letter of its name. The rights are briefly reiterated in Table 24-2.

Adding a Trustee

To add a trustee, simply press the INS key. An Object, Class dialog box similar to that shown in Figure 24-5 appears so that you can browse through the directory tree for the object that will be the trustee. Be sure to watch the Context field at the top of the screen so that you know which branch of the directory tree you are searching.

When you find the object that will be the trustee, highlight it and press ENTER. The object appears in the trustee list with the Read and File Scan rights. These rights allow users to list and view files in the directory but not to change them.

Right	Description
Supervisor	All rights to a directory, its files, and its subdirectories
Read	The right to open files
Create	The right to create new files and subdirectories in the directory
Write	The right to open and change files
Erase	The right to delete directories or files
Modify	The right to change the attributes or names of directories and files
File Scan	The right to see a directory listing
Access Control	The right to change the trustee assignments and Inherited Rights Filters of directories and files

Table 24-2. *Directory and File Rights*

Changing a Trustee's Rights

You can grant rights to a trustee or revoke a trustee's rights by selecting the trustee and then pressing ENTER. The Trustee rights box appears, to which you can add new rights or take away any rights that are listed.

To add new rights, press the INS key and then choose from the list. Use the F5 key to mark multiple rights. Press ENTER after you've selected the rights you want to add.

To revoke rights, select the rights in the Trustee list and press the DEL key. Use the F5 key to mark multiple rights.

NOTE: Remember that trustee assignments at the file level are not necessary if a user has appropriate rights to the directory where the file is located. However, you can grant or revoke these directory rights for individual files.

Salvaging and Purging Files

When a user deletes a file, NetWare keeps a copy of the file around for a while in case it needs to be recovered. The file does not appear in directory listings and is not available for use. The file is kept in a *salvageable* state until it is restored or it is purged from the system. Deleted files are kept in the directory where they were deleted. If a directory is deleted, its files are saved in a file called DELETED.SAV, which is located in the root directory of the volume.

NetWare Administrator and FILER both let you view a list of deleted files and recover files from that list. You can also permanently remove deleted files by purging them from the volume. Keep in mind that when the volume becomes full, NetWare purges recoverable files from it on a first-deleted, first-purged basis. Also, if you assigned the Purge attribute to a file or directory, the file or the directory's files will be purged immediately when deleted, and these files are not recoverable by using NetWare Administrator or FILER.

Salvaging and Purging Files with NetWare Administrator

To salvage deleted files by using NetWare Administrator, select the directory where the salvageable files are located and then choose Salvage from the Object menu. The dialog box shown in Figure 24-11 appears. At the top, you can change the following options:

■ *Include* Type a wildcard parameter in this field to specify the search pattern for the files you want to display.

■ *Sort Options* Click the down-arrow button and choose one of the sorting options on the drop-down list box.

■ *Source* Click the down-arrow button and choose to get the files from the current directory or from a deleted directory.

After you set the options, click the List button. A list of salvageable files appears. Click the files you want to salvage, and click the Salvage button to recover the files. Note the following:

■ You can select multiple files for salvaging.

■ Click the Purge button to permanently remove files.

■ You must have the Create right for a file to salvage it.

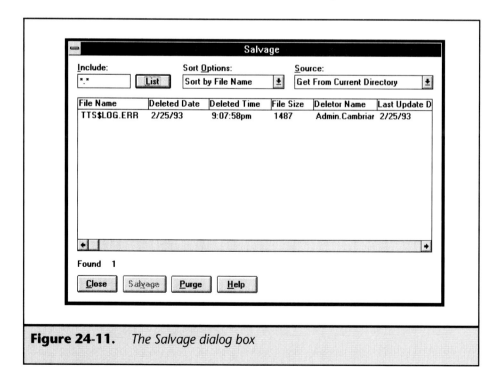

Figure 24-11. *The Salvage dialog box*

Salvaging and Purging Files with FILER

To salvage deleted files by using the FILER utility, choose the Salvage deleted files option from its main menu. The following menu appears:

```
            Salvage menu
┌─────────────────────────────────┐
│View/recover deleted files.      │
│Salvage from deleted directories.│
│Set salvage options.             │
└─────────────────────────────────┘
```

■ Choose the View/recover deleted files option to list the salvageable files on the current volume and salvage the files.

■ Choose the Salvage from deleted directories option if the files are in a DELETED.SAV file in the root directory.

■ Choose the Set salvage options option to pick from a list of sort order options.

When you choose the View/recover deleted files option, you are asked to specify a search pattern for the listing. If you press ENTER, all salvageable files are listed. Use wildcard characters to list specific files. Note the following:

■ Highlight the files you want to recover, and use the F5 key to mark them.

■ To change the sort order, press F3.

■ Press F6 to specify a wildcard pattern for marking files.

■ Press F8 to unmark files.

■ Press ENTER to recover a selected file or group of files.

■ If you select only a single file for salvaging, statistics for the file appear when you are asked if you want to recover it.

■ You can purge files from this list by pressing the DEL key after selecting the files you want to delete.

Disabling the Salvage Feature

You might decide you don't need the salvage feature. Perhaps salvageable files are taking up too much room on your volume and you have adequate backup of important files. Also, there is a slight increase in performance when the salvage feature is disabled. You can make NetWare immediately purge single files, groups of files, or all files in a directory by assigning the files or directory the Purge attribute.

To set the system default so that deleted files are immediately purged, set the Immediate Purge of Deleted Files option at the server to on. You can change this setting by starting SERVMAN and selecting the Console Set Commands option. Then choose the file system options and locate the option in the list.

CAUTION: If you set the Immediate Purge of Deleted Files option to on, all deleted files are immediately purged on the entire server and its volumes. You might wish to be more selective by marking directories with the P attribute flag instead.

CHAPTER 25

The commands listed in this chapter are executed at the command prompt. They provide useful information for system administrators, supervisors, and regular users. The commands include a number of options used to display network information or to change the settings of drive mappings, directory and file rights, and user objects. Whether or not users will have the ability to use any command that changes settings depends on their access rights to objects, directories, and files.

Other Directory and File Commands

The MAP Command

The MAP command lets you create *directory pointers* (often referred to as *drive mappings*), which are letters that define the location of a directory on a volume. You type the letter, as you do any drive letter, to switch to that directory. The MAP command is essential in the network environment. To simplify a complicated string, you can define a single drive letter that refers to a server, volume, and directory.

The MAP command is also used to create *search drive mappings*. A search drive is like the DOS path. It lets you specify the location of directories where program files are stored so you can run those programs when located in other directories. The operating system searches the drive mappings in order to locate commands you execute. Novell uses search drives in addition to the DOS path because the DOS PATH command does not accommodate the server and volume names necessary when referring to network directories.

Some guidelines for creating drive mappings or search drive mappings are as follows:

- The letters F through Z can be mapped to network drives. Local drives are the floppy disks and hard disks at a user's workstation usually assigned drive letters A through E and sometimes F, G, H, and so on. The first network drive is then assigned the next drive letter after the local drives.

- On OS/2 workstations, map drive P to the SYS:PUBLIC directory.

- For Windows workstations, map a search drive to the directory that holds Windows files, as discussed in Chapter 18.

- The first search drive mapping is assigned the letter Z, the second, letter Y, and so on, working backwards up the alphabet. Search drive mappings also have numbers (S1, S2, and so on) that specify the order they are searched. Only letters K through Z can be mapped as search drives.

- The order of search drives typically starts with the NetWare PUBLIC directory as S1, then a DOS directory as S2, the most commonly used application directory as S3, and so on. Users running Windows from the network need to have a search drive mapped to the Windows directory on the network drive.

- Use search drive mappings on DOS systems only. Search functionality is provided in OS/2 by the LIBPATH and DPATH commands.

- Drive and search mappings can be created at any time during a login session, but are only active during that session. Use the MAP command or

NETUSER utility to create drive maps. Windows users can use the NWTOOLS utility as well.

■ Place MAP commands in login scripts if you need the drive and search mappings for every login session. Supervisors can place commonly used MAP commands in container objects, and regular users can place MAP commands in their personal login script using NETADMIN or the NetWare Administrator.

■ If a drive map must be included in many different login scripts, and if there is a possibility that the directory it points to may change, create Directory Map objects and include them in the login scripts. To change a map, you then change the object rather than every login script.

■ Local drive mappings are those created by the PATH command on workstations. These mappings can be preserved by using the INS (Insert) option when creating NetWare search drive mappings.

The MAP command takes the following form,

MAP *option path*

where *option* is one of the options described next, and *path* is the directory you want to map. You may need to specify the Directory Services context, server name, and/or volume name in the command.

INS Insert a search drive.

DEL Delete a drive mapping.

N Map the next available drive.

R Make the drive a root directory.

P Map a drive to a physical volume name on a server rather than the Directory Services name for the volume.

C Change a regular drive to a search drive or a search drive to a regular drive.

MAP is best explained by example. The following discussions cover regular drive mappings, then search drive mappings.

Drive Mapping Examples

First of all, you can type **MAP** by itself to display the current drive mappings and search drives. Or, to display MAP help, type **MAP /?**.

To map a directory called FAX, in a volume called COMTOOLS, on a server called GATEWAY, you would type

```
MAP H:=GATEWAY/COMTOOLS:FAX
```

This command maps a specific drive letter to a directory. If you just wanted to map the next available drive letter—whatever that may be—to the directory, you would type

```
MAP N GATEWAY/COMTOOLS:FAX
```

NOTE: NetWare does not differentiate between the forward slash and backslash in MAP commands. You may use either, but it is generally accepted that the forward slash separates the server name from the volume name. The colon in the volume name is required and helps NetWare establish the syntax of the entire string when it includes server names. Otherwise, NetWare might think the server name was a directory name. Do not put a backslash after the colon to indicate the root level as you would in DOS. Use the colon only.

To map this volume and directory if it were in a context other than your current context, type a command similar to the following, which specifies the COMTOOLS volume and the FAX directory. Note how the directory name is appended to the end of the context string.

```
MAP H:=.COMTOOLS.SALES.CAMBRIACORP:FAX
```

To delete a drive mapping, type a command similar to this:

```
MAP DEL H:
```

A root drive mapping, or *fake root*, is seen as the root directory of a drive. Users assigned a fake root cannot move up the directory tree structure using the DOS CD command. To them, the directory is essentially the root directory of the network drive, even though it may physically be mapped to a subdirectory on the drive. You use fake roots for security reasons and when running some older applications that only operate if they can read and write files at the root level. For example, to map a directory called VOL1:\DOCS\BUDGETS to drive K as a fake root, you would type

```
MAP R K:=VOL1:\DOCS\BUDGETS
```

Users of this drive see BUDGETS as the root directory.

The C option lets you convert an existing drive mapping to a search mapping. For example, if you have drive letter I mapped as a drive, and you want to convert it to a search drive so you can run programs in it from another directory, you would type

```
MAP C I:
```

NetWare assigns I as the next available search drive, but retains the drive letter for the new search drive.

Search Drive Mappings

To map a search drive, you specify the number of the search drive. You can determine this number by typing **MAP** and viewing the current mappings. However, an easier way is just to specify the last possible search drive (S16), as shown here:

```
MAP S16:=VOL1:APPS\LOTUS
```

NetWare automatically assigns the directory the next available search drive number. So if you already had the following search maps:

```
S1:=Z:. PICKWICK/SYS:PUBLIC
S2:=Y:. PICKWICK/SYS:EMAIL
```

NetWare would create S3:=X:. VOL1:APPS\LOTUS. In this way, the order of the search drives is retained. NetWare simply adds the new search drive to the end of the list. If you wanted to make the directory the first search drive, you could type

```
MAP S1:=VOL1:APPS\LOTUS
```

However, this is not a good idea. It overwrites the existing S1 search drive, which is usually mapped to the \PUBLIC directory. You'll lose your search path to the directory, and you won't be able to execute NetWare commands like MAP. (To recover, switch to the directory using the DOS CD command, and remap S1 to the PUBLIC directory.) In addition, the original search drive mapping is "bumped" to a regular drive mapping, thus using up another drive letter. To preserve existing search drives, use the INS (Insert) option, as shown here:

```
MAP INS S1:=VOL1:
```

This shifts existing search drive mappings down in order and inserts your new mapping.

The NDIR Command

The NDIR command is used to view information about files, such as the size, creation date, owner (user who created the file), and attributes. You can also view information about directories, such as the inherited rights mask and your effective rights in the directory. Sorting options are available, as well as extraction options, so you can view only those files that relate to a specific query. For example, you could list all files created by a user before a certain date that have not been backed up.

NDIR is a powerful command with many options, but the number of options makes it difficult to use. You can display help screens, but it is recommended that you create batch files for those commands you use often. You can also use DOS redirection options to save NDIR listings in files or send the listings directly to printers. For example, you could type **NDIR > LPT1** to send a listing to a file.

The NDIR command has this general syntax:

NDIR *path options*

The options and specific syntax are described in the following sections.

HELP INFORMATION OPTIONS Help options for NDIR are shown here. Type the commands as shown to get specific help, or type the last option to see all help.

NDIR /? ALL   Display all help information.

NDIR /? SYN   Display syntax help.

NDIR /? AT   Display attribute filters.

NDIR /? FOR   Display format options.

NDIR /? RES   Display search filters.

NDIR /? SORT   Display sorting options.

NDIR /? OPT   Display miscellaneous options.

SPECIFIC INFORMATION OPTIONS   To display the specific type of information listed here, add the options provided.

/CO   Compressed file information

/D   Detailed file information

/DA   File date information

/MAC   Apple Macintosh files

/L   Long filename

/R   Filters and rights, file attributes

For example, to display a listing of files in the current directory and the rights you have to them, type the command:

```
NDIR *.* /R
```

To list document (DOC) files in a directory along with date information, you would type

```
NDIR *.DOC /DA
```

To list detailed information about a file called BUDGET.XLS, type

```
NDIR BUDGET.XLS /D
```

LISTING FILES BY ATTRIBUTES   The file attribute options let you list files according to the attributes they have. Use the /NOT option to display files according to attributes they don't have. The syntax is

NDIR *path* /*attributes*

or

NDIR *path* /NOT *attributes*

Here, *path* is the path to the directory where the files reside and/or a wildcard specifier, and *attributes* is one of the following:

A   Archive needed

Cc   Can't compress (status only, can't be assigned)

Ci   Copy-inhibit

Co   File compressed (status only, can't be assigned)

Dc   Don't compress

Di   Delete-inhibit

Dm   Don't migrate

Hi   Hidden

Ic   Immediate compress

M   File migrated (status only, can't be assigned)

N   Normal (read-write)

P Purge

Ri Rename-inhibit

Ro Read-only

Rw Read-write

Sh Shareable

Sy System

T Transactional

X Execute only

NOTE: Execute only protects executable files from virus attack in some cases. Once a file is flagged x, you can't remove the flag unless you copy over the file. Some programs will not run if their executable files are flagged x.

For example, to list all files in a directory that are flagged read-only, type the command:

```
NDIR *.* /RO
```

You can combine these options with the /NOT option. For example, to see which files are not marked indexed, type

```
NDIR *.* /NOT I
```

You can combine options. In the following example, file attributes are listed (/R) for DOC files. Files with the delete-inhibit attribute are excluded.

```
NDIR *.DOC /R /NOT DI
```

SORTING NDIR LISTINGS   The sorting options provide a way to list files according to date, owner, and size. You can use the /REV option to reverse the sort order in the listing. The syntax of the command is

NDIR *path* /SORT *option*

or

NDIR *path* /REV SORT *option*

Here, *path* is the path to the directory where the files reside and/or a wildcard specifier, and *option* is one of the following:

AC Last accessed date

AR Last archived date

CR Date last created or copied

OW Owner

SI Size

UP Last updated date

UN Unsorted (no specific sort order)

For example, to sort files according to the creator of the files, type

```
NDIR *.* /SORT OW
```

To reverse the listing, specify the /REV option as follows:

```
NDIR *.* /REV SORT OW
```

SPECIAL RESTRICTIONS   The options listed here are used to restrict the type of file that is displayed in listings, either by date, owner, or size. Date formats must be mm-dd-yy or mm/dd/yy. The command takes the form,

NDIR *path* /*options operator value*

or

NDIR *path /options* NOT *operator value*

Here, *path* is the path to the directory where the files reside and/or a wildcard specifier, and *option* is one of the following:

AC Last accessed date

AR Last archived date

CR Created/copied date

OW Owner

SI Size

UP Last updated date

The *operator* variable is one of the following, and *value* is a value you supply, such as a date or owner name.

LE Less than

EQ Equal to

GR Greater than

BEF Before

AFT After

The NOT option can also be used to list files not matching the specification. For example, you can execute commands that list file date information by replacing *option* in the following commands with AC, UP, AR, or CR, and specifying a date.

NDIR *path /option* NOT *mm-dd-yy*

NDIR *path /option* BEF *mm-dd-yy*

NDIR *path /option* NOT BEF *mm-dd-yy*

NDIR *path* /*option* AFT *mm-dd-yy*

NDIR *path* /*option* NOT AFT *mm-dd-yy*

Here are formats for specifying owner names:

NDIR *path* /OW EQ *name*

NDIR *path* /OW NOT EQ *name*

And here are formats for using the size option to list files according to their file size:

NDIR *path* /SI EQ *size*

NDIR *path* /SI NOT EQ *size*

NDIR *path* /SI LE *size*

NDIR *path* /SI NOT LE *size*

NDIR *path* /SI GR *size*

NDIR *path* /SI NOT GR *size*

You can combine options. The next example shows how you might list files by size and creation date. All files greater than 1000 bytes and created after 12/25/92 will be listed.

```
NDIR *.* /SI GR 1000 /CR AFT 12/25/92
```

VIEW OPTIONS   The remaining options are useful for listing a particular type of file that belongs to a set not covered by the previous options. The command takes the form:

NDIR *path option*

Here, *path* is the path to the directory where the files reside and/or a wildcard specifier, and *option* is one of the following:

/**DO** View directories only.

/**FI** View search drives where a file is found.

/**FO** View files only.

/**S** List information in all subdirectories.

/**SPA** View directory space information.

/**VER** View version information about files.

/**VOL** View volume information.

Finally, to scroll continuously through a screen of information, use the /C option.

NDIR Directory Listing Examples

This section gives some examples of how you would list directory information using the NDIR command. To list directories on other servers, specify the server name and volume name in the command:

```
NDIR GATEWAY\COMTOOLS:APPS
```

To view directory information for all subdirectories branching from the SYS: root directory, type the command:

```
NDIR SYS: /S /DO
```

To list directories on the SYS: volume owned by user DBoone, type a command similar to this one:

```
NDIR SYS: /OW EQ DBOONE /S /DO
```

The /S option searches all subdirectories.

To list all directories on the SYS: volume created after 12/25/92, type the command:

```
NDIR SYS: /CR AFT 12/25/92 /S /DO
```

NDIR File Listing Examples

You can combine NDIR options to list specific types of files. A small sampling is provided here. If you use long commands like those listed here on a regular basis, place them in a batch file, or add them to a menu, as covered in Chapter 29. You can also direct the file listing to a file with a command similar to the following:

NDIR *.* > *filename*

The listing is sent to the file represented by *filename*. You can then save the file for later use or print it.

The following example lists files on drive K that include *.DOC in their filename and are owned by John:

```
NDIR K:*.DOC /OW EQ JOHN
```

The next example lists files on drive K that include *.DOC in their filenames and have a size greater than 3000 bytes:

```
NDIR K:*.DOC /SI GR 3000
```

The following command lists files on drive K that include *.DOC in their filenames and are owned by John. The list is then sorted by size.

```
NDIR K:*.DOC /OW EQ JOHN /SORT SIZE
```

The next example lists files on drive K that include *.DOC in their filename, are owned by John, and were created after 12-25-92:

```
NDIR K:*.DOC /OW EQ JOHN /CR AFT 12-25-92
```

The following command lists all files in the SYS: volume owned by John. All subdirectory files are listed as well.

```
NDIR SYS: /OW EQ JOHN /S
```

The next command lists all files in the SYS: volume owned by John, in all subdirectories with a size greater than 3000 bytes:

```
NDIR SYS: /OW EQ JOHN /S /SI GR 3000
```

The next command lists all files owned by John, in all subdirectories of SYS: that have a size greater than 3000. The /FO option produces a list of files only.

```
NDIR SYS: /OW EQ JOHN /S /SI GR 3000 /FO
```

Finally, this last command lists all files on the SYS: volume that have the shareable and read-only attributes and that were accessed after 12-25-92:

```
NDIR SYS: S RO /AC AFT 12-25-92
```

The NCOPY Command

NCOPY is the NetWare COPY command. Its use is similar to the DOS COPY command. You specify a source directory and files and a destination directory and files. The command takes the following form:

NCOPY *source-files destination-files options*

Replace *source-files* with the directory and/or files you want to copy, and replace *destination-files* with the location of the directory where you want to copy files to. To change the name of files during a copy, specify the new names as part of *destination-files*. Use wildcard characters when working with multiple files. Replace *options* with one of the following:

/? Display help information.

/A Copy files that have their archive bit set. When an archive bit is set, it indicates that the file has changed or is new and needs to be backed up. In this way, you can use NCOPY for backup purposes, if necessary. This does not copy hidden and system files, which can be a potential problem for some program and database files.

/C Copy only DOS information. Extended attributes and name space information is not saved.

/F Copy sparse files.

/I Specify this option when you want to be informed if any files copied have lost non-DOS information, such as extended attributes or name space information.

/M Copy files with archive bit set, then clear the bit to indicate that the file has been backed up.

/R Specify this option to retain compression, but only if you are copying to a device that supports compression.

/R/U Specify this option to retain compression, even if copying to a device that doesn't support it. You can only uncompress the information if it resides on a NetWare volume.

/S Specify this option to include subdirectories when copying.

/S/E Specify this option to include subdirectories in the NCOPY command, even if they are empty.

/V Verify the file for accuracy after writing it (DOS only).

The NCOPY command supports wildcard characters, so you can specify groups of files. For example, to copy all the DOC files on mapped drive H to mapped drive J, type the command:

```
NCOPY H:*.DOC J:
```

To copy an entire directory branch called APPS to the root of the VOL1 volume and include subdirectories and any empty subdirectories, use a command similar to the following:

```
NCOPY SYS:APPS VOL1: /S/E
```

If the directories might contain non-DOS attributes or name spaces, type a command similar to the following to be warned of any problems:

```
NCOPY SYS:APPS /S/E /I
```

The FLAG Command

The FLAG command is used to view and change the attributes of files and directories. Recall that attributes determine what users can do with files, or how they are handled during backups, migrations, and file listings. In its simplest form, FLAG shows the attributes of all directories. Simply type **FLAG** at the command prompt to view attributes of files or specific files. You can use wildcard characters. For example, type the following to see the current attributes of all DOC files in the current directory:

```
FLAG *.DOC
```

To view help information for the FLAG command, use one of the following commands, depending on the type of help you want to see.

FLAG /? ALL View all help information.

FLAG /? FO View help on the file attributes that you can assign to files using the FLAG command.

FLAG /? DO View help on the directory attributes that you can assign to directories using the FLAG command.

FLAG /? MODES View help on assigning search modes.

FLAG /? SYNTAX View help on FLAG's syntax.

FLAG /? OPTIONS View a list of miscellaneous options.

Directory Attributes

Directory attribute options let you assign attributes to directories. The syntax is

FLAG *path attributes* (creates a new set of attributes)

or

FLAG *path + attributes* (add attributes to current set)

or

FLAG *path – attributes* (remove attributes from current set)

Here, *path* is the path to the directory, and *attributes* is one of the following:

N Normal

Dc Don't compress

Di Delete-inhibit

Dm Don't migrate

Hi Hidden

Ic Immediate compress

P Purge

Ri Rename-inhibit

Sy System

For example, to flag a directory for immediate purging of deleted files, type the command:

```
FLAG SYS:APPS\TEMPDOCS P
```

File Attribute Options

The file attribute options let you assign attributes to files. The syntax is

>FLAG *path attributes* (creates a new set of attributes)

or

>FLAG *path + attributes* (add attributes to current set)

or

>FLAG *path – attributes* (remove attributes from current set)

Here, *path* is the path to the directory where the files reside and/or a wildcard specifier, and *attributes* is one of the following:

A   Archive needed

Ci   Copy-inhibit

Dc   Don't compress

Di   Delete-inhibit

Dm   Don't migrate

Hi   Hidden

Ic   Immediate compress

P   Purge

Ri   Rename-inhibit

Ro   Read-only

Rw   Read-write

Sh   Shareable

Sy System

T Transactional

X Execute only

 NOTE: Execute only protects executable files from virus attack in some cases. Once a file is flagged x, you can't remove the flag unless you copy over the file. Some programs will not run when their executable files are flagged x.

For example, to flag all files in a directory as read-only, type the command:

```
FLAG *.* RO
```

Search Mode Options

The search mode options let you specify search modes for executable files. The command takes the form,

FLAG path /M=*mode*

where *mode* is a number defined as follows:

0 The default search mode in which executable files look for instructions in NET.CFG.

1 Search the path in the file, and if unavailable, search the default directory, then the search drive.

2 Search the path in the file first, then only the default directory.

3 Search the path in the file first, then the default directory, and finally, search drives, but only if the request is read-only.

4 Reserved.

5 Search a specified path first, then search drives. Or if there is no specified path, search the default directory, then the search drives.

6 Reserved.

7 Search a specified path first, if the open request is read-only.

The following command sets the search mode to 1 for all executable files in the current directory:

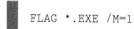
```
FLAG *.EXE /M=1
```

Other Options

The following are some other options you can use with the FLAG command.

ALL Set all attributes for the specified files or directories.

/C Use this option to scroll the listing continuously.

/S Include subdirectories.

/D List detailed information.

/NAME=*name* Change who owns the file or directory by replacing *name* with the new owner's name.

The RIGHTS Command

Use the RIGHTS command at the command prompt to view or change the rights that users and groups have to files, directories, and volumes. The basic command takes the form:

RIGHTS

You can type this in any directory to see what your current rights are. You'll see a list and description of the rights. To get help information for the RIGHTS command, type one of the following commands at the command prompt:

RIGHTS /? A View all help information.

RIGHTS /? S List the syntax of the RIGHTS command.

RIGHTS /? T List the options you can use to view and change trustee rights.

RIGHTS /? F   List the options for setting inherited rights filters.

RIGHTS /? I   List the options for viewing inherited rights.

RIGHTS /? O   View miscellaneous options.

Assigning Rights

To assign rights with the RIGHTS command, use the following form,

RIGHTS *path rightslist* /NAME= *user,user...*

or

RIGHTS *path* + *rightslist* /NAME= *user,user...*

or

RIGHTS *path* – *rightslist* /NAME= *user,user...*

Here, *path* is the path to a directory or file and *rightslist* is one or more of the rights listed next. Use the plus sign to assign additional rights to those already available and the minus sign to take away specific existing rights. If you don't use + or –, the rights you specify override any existing rights. Replace *user* with one or more users, separated by a comma, that you want to assign the rights to.

ALL   Assign all rights except supervisor rights

A   Access control

C   Create

E   Erase

F   File scan

M   Modify

N   No rights

R Read

S Supervisor

W Write

For example, to give users Hank and Frank the rights to read, file scan, create, and write in the current directory, type

```
RIGHTS . RFCW /NAME=HANK,FRANK
```

To add the erase right to the rights that Hank and Frank now have, type

```
RIGHTS . + E /NAME=HANK,FRANK
```

To remove all rights that Frank has, type

```
RIGHTS . N /NAME=FRANK
```

To give Sally all rights in the SYS:APPS directory (except the supervisor right), type the command:

```
RIGHTS SYS:APPS ALL /NAME=SALLY
```

Derived Rights

The following options are used to view a specific trustee's rights, to remove a trustee, or to view where the rights were assigned and inherited. The last option provides an important way to find out how a user inherited rights in a directory. The general syntax of the command is

RIGHTS *path option*

Here, *path* is a directory and/or filename, and *option* is one of the following:

/T View trustees.

/I View where the rights were assigned and inherited.

To scroll continuously and to search subdirectories when executing RIGHTS commands, add the following:

/C Scroll continuously.

/S Search subdirectories.

For example, to view trustees of the current directory, type

```
RIGHTS /T
```

To list how the user DBoone obtained rights in the current directory, type

```
RIGHTS . /NAME=DBOONE /I
```

The REM option removes a trustee from the directory or file specified in *path*. In the following command, replace *user* with a user's name.

RIGHTS *path* REM /NAME=*user option*

To remove trustee JJones from the SYS:APPS directory, type

```
RIGHTS SYS:APPS REM /NAME=JJONES
```

Inheritance Filter

Use the /F option to specify the rights in the inherited rights filter for a directory. The command takes the following form,

RIGHTS *path rightslist* /F

or

RIGHTS *path* + *rightslist* /F

or

RIGHTS *path – rightslist* /F

Here, *path* is the directory where you want to control inherited rights, and *rightslist* is one or more of the rights listed next. Use the plus sign to add rights (rights are not blocked) and the minus sign to block rights. If you don't use + or –, the rights you specify become the new inherited rights filter.

ALL   All rights filter through

A   Access control

C   Create

E   Erase

F   File scan

M   Modify

N   No rights

R   Read

S   Supervisor

W   Write

For example, to view the inheritance filter of the current directory, type

```
RIGHTS . /F
```

To set the inheritance filter so users do not have rights to create, erase, and write in the current directory, you would type

```
RIGHTS . -CEW /F
```

The RENDIR Command

Use the RENDIR command to rename a directory on a volume. The command takes the form:

RENDIR *path newname*

Here, *path* is the directory you want to rename, and *newname* is the new name you want to assign to the directory. For example, to rename the current directory WINDOCS, you would type

```
RENDIR . WINDOCS
```

You can also rename a mapped drive. For example, to rename the directory mapped to drive K with the new name WINDOCS, you would type

```
RENDIR K: WINDOCS
```

NOTE: *Renamed directories are tracked by NetWare for trustee rights assignments and IRF assignments, but login scripts, batch files, and menus must all be modified to reflect the new directory name.*

CHAPTER 26

Utilities and Commands for Users

NetWare users can load the NETUSER utility to access network resources, configure their current session, or change their personal login scripts. NETUSER is a text-based utility that runs from the DOS command line. For Windows or OS/2, NetWare provides the NetWare Tools dialog box, which contains a set of options for controlling drive maps, printers, queues, messaging, and other options. These utilities are covered in this chapter.

The NETUSER Utility

The NETUSER utility is designed for all network users. Type **NETUSER** at the DOS prompt to start the utility. You can perform any of the following tasks with NETUSER:

Access network resources
Create drive mappings
Change passwords and login scripts
Work with printers
Send messages to other users

The NETUSER main menu is shown in Figure 26-1. The current context of the user is displayed at the top, along with the printer assignments for each printer port. A description of each menu option is provided in the following sections.

NETUSER Printing Options

DOS reserves the printer port names LPT1, LPT2, and LPT3 for the attachment of local printers. Even though a physical printer port may not be available for attaching printers, the names are reserved. The NetWare operating system lets you assign a network printer at a remote location to one of these ports. Then when you print to the port from within an application, Microsoft Word or Lotus 1-2-3 for instance, the print job is diverted from the local physical port (if it even exists) to the network printer.

Of course, if you have a printer actually attached to your workstation, it is usually attached to the first physical LPT1 port. Most PCs only have one physical

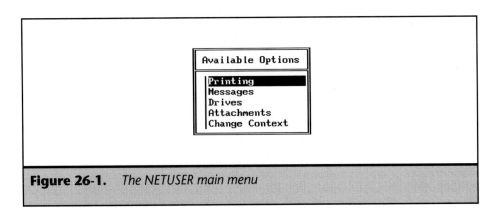

Figure 26-1. *The NETUSER main menu*

LPT port, so that leaves the other reserved printer names available for assignment to network printers.

Assigning Printers and Queues to Ports

Follow the steps listed here to add or change the network printer assigned to an LPT port on your computer.

1. Choose the Printing option on the Available Options menu. The following menu appears:

```
╔══════════════════════════════════════╗
║          Available Ports             ║
╠══════════════════════════════════════╣
║ LPT1: Local Printer                  ║
║ LPT2: Local Printer                  ║
║ LPT3: Local Printer                  ║
╚══════════════════════════════════════╝
```

The three LPT port names are listed. Normally, you reserve the LPT1 port for your local printer and assign network printers to LPT2 and LPT3. However, if you don't have a local printer, you can assign network printers to that port as well.

NOTE: If you need more ports, use the NETWORK PRINTERS option in the NET.CFG file as discussed in Appendix B.

2. Highlight the port you want to assign to a network printer and press ENTER. The following menu appears:

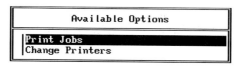

```
╔══════════════════════════════════════╗
║          Available Options           ║
╠══════════════════════════════════════╣
║ Print Jobs                           ║
║ Change Printers                      ║
╚══════════════════════════════════════╝
```

NOTE: You may need to change your context to locate the printer or print queues you want to send the print jobs to. Choose Change Context from the NETUSER main menu. By moving up and down the directory tree, you can choose printers in other departments or even other divisions and remote locations. Refer to the section, "NETUSER Context Options," later in the chapter.

3. Highlight the Change Printers option and press ENTER. You now see a list of available network printers and queues that have been set up by the network supervisor or print operator that looks similar to this:

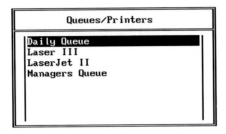

4. Choose the printer or a print queue you want to send your print jobs to. For more information about these options, see "About Printers and Print Queues." Press ENTER to select the printer or queue, and the Available Options menu reappears. If you choose a printer, its default queue appears for the port.

About Printers and Print Queues

On NetWare networks, you can send your print jobs directly to a printer, or to a print queue. If you choose a printer, the default queue used by the printer is automatically selected as the destination for print jobs. All print jobs go into queues so that network printers can accommodate more than one printer user. If a printer is busy, your print job waits in a queue until its turn comes for printing.

Queues can be designated for specific users. For example, you can create a queue and then give only managers access rights to use it. You then assign the queue to a printer with a high priority, so any jobs sent to that queue are printed before jobs that don't have access to the queue. A *print job configuration* is a special set of printing options you can assign to a print job. You could specify that all print jobs using the configuration print after 5:00 p.m., for example.

Print queues are actually located in directories on a volume, and they hold print jobs until they are ready to print. On a busy network, it is not unusual to have many print jobs waiting in a queue. If a queue is used often, several printers may service it. On the other hand, several queues may send print jobs to a single printer. For example, a high-speed laser printer might service a high-priority manager's queue, a lower-priority queue for other users, and an after-hours queue.

Working with Print Jobs

A print job is created when you send a file to a network printer or network queue for printing. The files you send to the network printer can be ASCII text files or print files. A *print file* has special significance. It is a file that contains all the printer formatting codes required to print a file, without actually running the application that created the file. In other words, you create a document and print it, but you specify a file as the destination rather than a printer. All the formatting codes are saved in the file so you can actually print the file at another time, or send the file to another user. One big advantage of print files is that you can schedule the printing of a block of files at a later time. Most popular applications support the creation of print files. However, when you create the file, you must be using the printer driver for the printer you intend to send the print file to.

To send print jobs to a printer, or just to view the status of print jobs you've already sent to a printer, choose the Print Jobs options from the Available Options menu. You see a list of existing jobs. The following options are available:

- Highlight a job and press ENTER to see information about that job.

- Highlight a job and press DEL to delete a print job from the list. Use the F5 key to mark multiple jobs for deletion. (Press F7 to unmark all jobs.)

- Press INS to add new print jobs, as described next.

Follow these steps to send a new job to a network printer:

1. Press INS. You see a menu similar to the following:

```
┌─────────────────────────────────────────────────────────────┐
│           Select Directory To Print From                     │
├─────────────────────────────────────────────────────────────┤
│PICKWICK\SYS:                                                 │
└─────────────────────────────────────────────────────────────┘
```

2. Type the name of the directory where your print files are located, or better, press INS to choose from a list.

3. When the list of directories appears, highlight a directory and press ENTER. If this is the directory that contains the files you want to print, press ESC. If not, select a subdirectory and press ENTER. Continue in this way until you find the subdirectory that contains the print files; then press ESC.

4. Pressing ESC in the previous step returns you to the Select Directory To Print From menu, with the name of the directory in its field. Press ENTER to see a list of files in that directory.

5. Highlight a file from the Available Files menu, or use the F5 mark key to highlight several files.

6. Press ENTER to choose the files for printing. The Print Job Configuration menu then appears.

Print job configurations are often created by supervisors or print operators to specify options for a print job, such as the number of copies and whether the job should be held and printed at a specific time or date. See your network supervisor for a list and description of available configurations. If you choose (Defaults) from the Print Job Configuration menu, the New Print Job to be Submitted menu appears, as pictured in Figure 26-2. From this menu, you can define your own configuration. Keep in mind that these settings are optional. For a description of each setting, press the F1 help key.

NOTE: There are some interesting options on the New Print Job to be Submitted menu. The "User hold" option lets you put the print job on hold until you release it. "Service sequence" is set by print queue operators to move a job in the queue. "Defer printing" lets you print a job at a later date.

7. Once you've defined the print job configuration, press the F10 key to save it.

The print job appears in the print job list with information about its sequence number, status, and job ID. At this point, you could insert other print jobs or

```
┌─────────────────────────────────────────────────────────────┐
│              New Print Job to be Submitted                   │
├─────────────────────────────────────────────────────────────┤
│Print job:                        File size:                  │
│Client:          admin[2]                                     │
│Description:     CHAP1.DOC                                    │
│Status:                                                       │
│                                                              │
│User hold:       No               Entry date:                 │
│Operator hold:   No               Entry time:                 │
│Service sequence:                                             │
│                                  Form:          0            │
│Number of copies: 1               Print banner:  Yes          │
│                                  Name:          admin        │
│File contents:   Byte stream      Banner name:   CHAP1.DOC    │
│Tab size:                                                     │
│                                  Defer printing: No          │
│Form feed:       Yes              Target date:                │
│Notify when done: No              Target time:                │
└─────────────────────────────────────────────────────────────┘
```

Figure 26-2.   *Print job configuration settings*

even delete a job by highlighting it and pressing DEL. Press ESC to return to the NETUSER main menu.

NETUSER Messaging Options

You can choose the Messages option on the NETUSER main menu to send messages to a single user or a group of users. You can also prevent incoming messages from appearing on your screen. Blocking messages is important if you are running an application that shouldn't be interrupted. For example, if you start a process, and then go to lunch with the expectation that it will be complete when you return, you'll be in for a surprise when you find that a message from another user has paused your system.

NOTE: You can also prevent an incoming message from completely stalling your system with the MESSAGE TIMEOUT option in NET.CFG. See Appendix B.

Choose Messages to display the following menu:

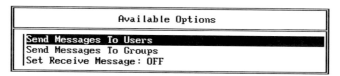

```
                    Available Options
  Send Messages To Users
  Send Messages To Groups
  Set Receive Message: OFF
```

■ To send a message to a single user or a select group of users, choose Send Messages To Users. A list of current users appears. Highlight a single user, or use the F5 key to mark a group of users.

■ To send a message to a group of users, choose Send Messages To Groups. A list of groups in your current context appears. To see a list of groups in other contexts, press INS twice to browse the directory tree.

■ To receive or block messages on your workstation, view the status of the Set Receive Message option. To change the status, highlight the option and press ENTER.

NOTE: Messages cannot exceed 45 characters in length. They appear on the recipient's screen immediately (and halt all processing at the workstation). Recipients must press CTRL-ENTER after reading the message to clear their screen and resume their program. Users who don't want a process to stop should inhibit messages while the process is running.

NETUSER Drive Mapping Options

To create new drive mappings and search drive mappings, select the Drives option on the NETUSER Available Options menu. The following menu appears:

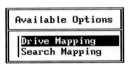

```
Available Options
Drive Mapping
Search Mapping
```

Choose the Drive Mapping option to associate a directory on the file server with a drive letter. Choose Search Mapping to create a search path to a directory that contains programs you need to run from another directory. Follow these steps to create a new drive map or search drive map:

1. With the Current Drive Mappings or Current Search Mappings menu visible on the screen, press INS.

2. NETUSER recommends the next available drive letter or search drive number. Press ENTER to accept the recommended letter, or press DEL and type a new letter if necessary.

3. The Select Directory menu appears. Press INS to browse the Directory Services tree and/or the directory structure of a volume. A menu similar to the following appears:

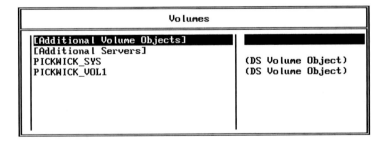

```
                        Volumes
[Additional Volume Objects]
[Additional Servers]
PICKWICK_SYS                      (DS Volume Object)
PICKWICK_VOL1                     (DS Volume Object)
```

4. From this menu, you can do one of the following:

■ If your current context displays a list of volumes, you can choose one of the volumes directly by highlighting it and pressing ENTER; then go to step 5.

- Choose [Additional Volume Objects] to see the Object, Class menu from which you can browse the Directory Services tree. Choose *parent* to move up the tree or an *organizational unit* to browse a branch of the tree. When you locate a volume, highlight it and press ENTER.

- Choose [Additional Servers] to see a list of other servers on the network. Choose a server; then choose a volume on it.

5. After selecting a volume, a list of directories appears. Choose a directory to see a list of its subdirectories; then continue choosing subdirectories, or press ESC to accept the current directory. Its name appears in the Select Directory window. Press ENTER to accept it.

6. NETUSER asks if you want to *map root* this drive. When map rooted, it appears as a root directory with no parents of its own. In other words, you can't move any farther up the directory structure. Some applications only run on map root drive mappings. Choose Yes or No and press ENTER.

The new drive map or search drive appears in the Current Drive Mappings menu. You can exit NETUSER and begin using the new drive maps. Remember that this drive mapping is only for the current session. To permanently map a drive, add a MAP command to your personal login script, as described in the next section.

NETUSER Attachment Options

When you choose the Attachments option on the NETUSER main menu, you can view server information, change your password, or change your login script. You are first asked to choose a server to work with; then the Available Options menu appears with the options described here.

Login Scripts   Select this option to edit your login script. You might want to add new drive mappings or search drive mappings. Refer to Chapter 28 for a discussion of login scripts.

Password   When you choose this option, you are asked to enter your old password, enter a new password, and to retype your password for verification.

Server Information   Choose this option to display information about the server.

NETUSER Context Options

Choose the Change Context option to change your current position in the Directory Services tree. You may need to do this so you can see printers, queues, users, and volumes when working with the other NETUSER menu options. Note that you can also change context from within these options, as described in the previous sections.

To change context, choose the Change Context option; then follow these steps:

1. Press INS to view the Object, Class menu.

   ■ Highlight the *parent* option to move up the tree.

   ■ Highlight an organizational unit container object to browse its branch of the directory tree.

2. Continue selecting in this way until you locate the objects you are searching for.

3. Press ESC; then choose Yes to accept the new context.

The Windows NetWare User Utility

If you use Microsoft Windows, you can access a set of NetWare utilities in three ways. In all cases, the NetWare Tools dialog box in Figure 26-3 appears.

■ Double-click the NWUser icon in the NetWare Tools group.

■ Press F6 to display the utilities.

■ From the File Manager, choose Network Connections from the Disk menu.

The NetWare Tools dialog box consists of a row of buttons at the top that you click to access or change different NetWare services. When you click one of the buttons, a different set of display options appears in the menu. The lower portion is split into two viewing windows, the right side of which displays the Directory Services tree.

Note the split bar on the dialog box. You point to it with the mouse. When the mouse pointer turns to a double-headed arrow, you click and slide the bar to the left or right to expand the left or right window.

The Resources field displays the NetWare Directory Services tree. You browse up through the tree by double-clicking the up arrow icons, which represent

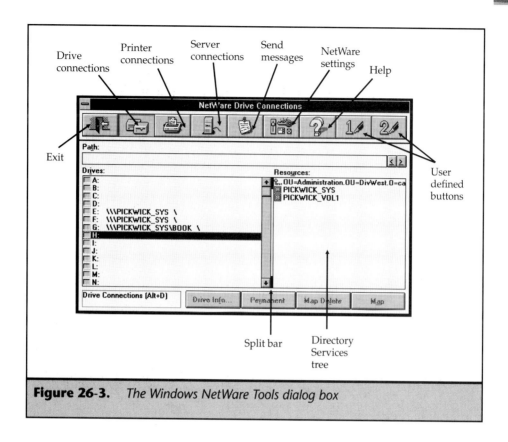

Figure 26-3. *The Windows NetWare Tools dialog box*

branches in the directory tree. Double-click the organizational unit icons to move down through the directory tree. As you move into container units, objects in those containers appear, depending on the tool you selected. For example, if you click the Send Messages button, you see user objects listed in the Resources field as you browse.

Drive Mappings

Click the Drive Connections button to map directories to drive letters. You can create drive mappings for your current session and make them permanent for future sessions.

To create a drive map, browse the directory tree in the Resources field until you find the appropriate volume object. Double-click the volume object to display a list of its directories. Double-click one of these directories if it has a subdirectory you want to map. When you find the appropriate directory or subdirectory, click it once with the mouse. The complete path appears in the Path field. Now click one of the drive icons on the left and click the Map button at the lower right.

The new drive mapping appears in the Drives window. If you start the File Manager, you'll see the new drive listed on its drive icon bar, and if you start a Windows application, you'll be able to access the drive like any other drive. Note the following:

- If you want to have the mapping every time you start Windows, click the Permanent button.

- To delete a drive map, highlight the drive letter on the left and click the Map Delete button.

- To view your effective rights in the directory, click the Drive Info button.

Printer Connections

When you click the Printer Connections button, a list of print queues in the current context appears. You can browse the directory tree to locate other network printers you might want to use. Once you've located the correct network printer queue, click it; then click the port on the left that you want to assign the network printer to and click the Capture button. The name of the print queue appears next to the printer port device name.

As mentioned in the first section of this chapter, printer ports LPT1, LPT2, and LPT3 are DOS-reserved device names that may or may not specify physical printer ports on your workstation. Most systems have at least one parallel printer port designated as LPT1. You can assign network printers to LPT2 and LPT3, if you want. Any print jobs you send to these ports from inside your application are redirected over the network to the network printers you select.

Note the following:

- If you want this printer capture setting every time you start Windows, click the Permanent button.

- To set special parameters for a printer, click it, and then click the LPT Settings button. The Printer Options dialog box appears, with various fields you can set to specify how print jobs are printed on the network printer. Click the Help button for a description of these fields.

- To remove the capture setting, click the port that is being captured and click the End Capture button.

Server Connections

Click the Server Connections button to log in or out of a server, change your password on that server, and view information about the server.

Send Messages

Click the Send Messages button to send a message to a single user, a select group of users, or user groups. Browse the directory tree in the Resources field to locate the container object holding the users and groups you want to send messages to. Note that there are two toggle buttons at the bottom of the dialog box. They are either Hide Groups and Hide Users, or Show Groups and Show Users, depending on their current toggled state. You can click these buttons to show only users, only groups, or both.

NetWare Settings

Click the NetWare Settings button to display a menu similar to Figure 26-4. You set options on this dialog box to customize the Windows/NetWare connection. Each option is discussed here.

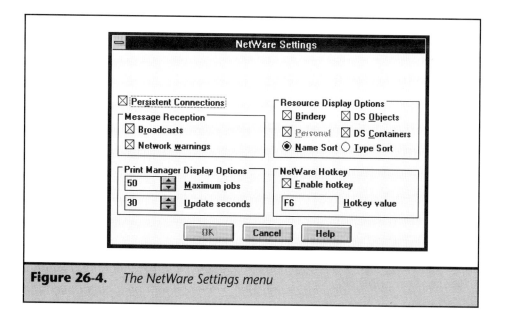

Figure 26-4. *The NetWare Settings menu*

Persistent Connections Reestablish settings in future sessions.

Message Reception The Broadcasts box determines whether your workstation receives messages from other users. You may want to disable this option if you don't want an incoming message to halt any active process. Network warnings are messages from the network operating system or DOS requester software.

Print Manager Display Options In the Maximum jobs box, set the number of print jobs that are listed in the Print Manager queue. The default is 50. In the Update seconds box, set the time interval in seconds for the Print Manager to update the Print Manager queue.

Resource Display Options In this field, select the type of objects you want to see in the Resources field on the NetWare Tools dialog box. Leave these boxes enabled in most cases unless there are too many objects showing in the box. Click Name Sort (sort by name of object) or Type Sort (sort by type of object), depending on the order you want the object listed.

NetWare Hotkey Set the hot key you want to use to display the NetWare Tools dialog box, or turn the hot key off.

The Help and User-defined Buttons

Click the Help button to display help about the NetWare Tools dialog box. The two User-defined buttons are used to set a path that is automatically inserted in the path or context field of the NetWare Tools dialog box when clicked.

NetWare Administrator

The name of the NetWare Administrator implies that it is designed for managers. However, regular users can start the NetWare Administrator and view information about their accounts, look at information about other users and objects, or search for network resources that they want to use.

   The type of access regular users have in NetWare Administrator is limited. The following defaults are assigned when a new user object is created:

■ Can change the login script

■ Can browse (view) all other fields, but not change them

■ Can view information about other user objects and resource objects

Of course, supervisors can change these defaults at any time. For example, the supervisor can block a user from seeing any information about any other user, such as an address and phone number.

OS/2 NetWare Tools Utility

OS/2 workstations can view and change network options with the NetWare Tools utility located in the NetWare group. The Tools menu contains the following options.

NOTE: Extensive help is available for each option. For more information, click the Help button after you select an option.

DRIVE MAPPINGS   When the NetWare Tools dialog box first appears, the Disk Drives list is open. You can map a directory to an available drive letter by double-clicking the drive letter. A search window opens so you can specify the volume and directory of the new drive map.

PRINTER PORTS   When you choose the Printer Ports option on the Tools menu, you see the list of available printer ports. Double-click a port name to display the Capture menu; then specify the printer or queue and the print job configuration for the print jobs you send to the designated port.

SERVERS OPTION   This option displays a list of currently attached servers along with the associated user name and connection number ID. If you double-click a listed server, you can log out of it.

USER LIST   Select this option to view the user list for a selected server. You will need to log into any servers you are not attached to.

VIEW PRINT QUEUE   Choose this option to view the print queues on the server in the current context. You can view queue information by double-clicking on the queue.

Command-Line Utilities

There are a number of command-line utilities available for users. These utilities were covered in previous chapters, but a brief description is included here for reference.

CX   Change the current context in the NetWare directory service tree.

NDIR   List files on NetWare volumes. A number of command-line parameters are available for sorting files and displaying specific information about files.

NCOPY   The NetWare copy command. It is similar to the DOS copy command, but automatically verifies writes to the disk for accuracy.

RIGHTS   View your current rights in a directory, or change the rights in the directory if you have the Access Control or Supervisor right.

SEND   Send messages to other users from the command-line prompt.

SETPASS   Change your password. The command prompts you for your old password; then asks for the new password and asks you to verify it.

WHOAMI   Display your current login status and context.

CHAPTER 27

NetWare Printing Services

NetWare v.4 includes enhanced printing services. The changes will make a network manager's job easier but will not waste any of his or her training in previous versions of NetWare. The most important change in NetWare printing is that you can use NetWare Directory Services to add, change, delete, and configure your network's printing services. Another change is that you can no longer configure a workstation as a dedicated print server; only NetWare v.4 file servers can run the print server process.

With NetWare v.4, you can perform all necessary print management tasks from within the Windows environment.

Printing services have been integrated with NetWare Administrator to make day-to-day management easier and more convenient. You can assign access rights, for example, by dragging and dropping a user object onto a printer object. In addition, Windows clients can access network printers via the Windows-based NetWare User utility.

You can also manage printing services by using text-based utilities, including PRINTCON, PRINTDEF, and PCONSOLE, which will be familiar to you if you've used previous versions of NetWare. The new Quick Setup option in PCONSOLE sets up a default print server, printer, and print queue and then configures the relationship among them. Another change is that you can choose a printer on the network by indicating the name of the printer; you do not have to know the queue name.

To set up printing services in NetWare, you can use text-based utilities or NetWare Administrator. Currently, some of the work must be done by using text-based utilities, but future versions of NetWare will provide all-inclusive Windows printer setup.

How NetWare Printing Services Work

Several NetWare Loadable Modules, menu-driven utilities, and command-line utilities make up the NetWare v.4 printing services. Even though the basic printing options remain the same as in previous versions of NetWare, NetWare Directory Services and Windows-based utilities offer new methods for print management.

As shown in Figure 27-1, NetWare printing services uses a central print server that runs on a file server. The print server manages shared printers throughout the network, including printers attached to the print server itself, printers attached to other file servers, and printers attached to workstations on the network. Basically, the print server takes advantage of all the printer ports on the network, whether they are on the print server, file servers, or workstations. Printers with direct network connections (i.e. their own Ethernet port) are also supported.

Here is a list of the tools and programs you can use to configure and use the NetWare v.4 printing features:

- *PCONSOLE.EXE*   A DOS-based program that network managers and users use to configure and control print servers, print queues, and printers

- *PSERVER.NLM*   This is the all important module that loads the print services management software at the designated file server. You load the module after configuring queues, printers, and the print server.

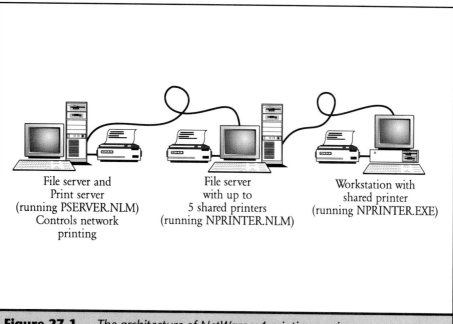

File server and
Print server
(running PSERVER.NLM)
Controls network
printing

File server
with up to
5 shared printers
(running NPRINTER.NLM)

Workstation with
shared printer
(running NPRINTER.EXE)

Figure 27-1. *The architecture of NetWare v.4 printing services*

- *NPRINTER.NLM* This NetWare Loadable Module lets you use the printer ports on the back of a file server other than the file server that is running the print server software. Another file server must be running PSERVER .NLM

- *NPRINTER.EXE* You run NPRINTER on a workstation to share printers attached to that workstation with other network users. NPRINTER cannot be used to dedicate a workstation as a print server

- *PUPGRADE.NLM* You load this module at the file server to upgrade printers defined in a NetWare v.3.11 bindery to NetWare v.4 NDS objects. It also upgrades print job configurations

- *NETADMIN.EXE* A DOS-based menu utility used to manage network objects. It is similar in function to the Windows-based NetWare Administrator. You can also use NETADMIN to set up essential printing services

- *PSC.EXE* A utility that provides the functions of PCONSOLE in a command-line format. Managers and users can use PSC to make quick changes to print services set-up

- *PRINTCON.EXE*   A menu utility that network managers and users use to define standard print configurations for letterhead, continuous-feed paper, and so on

- *PRINTDEF.EXE*   A menu utility that network managers and users use to define printers and special control codes. It is used mostly when the applications on the network are not network aware

- *CAPTURE.EXE*   A command-line utility used at workstations or in login scripts. It dedicates one or more of the parallel or serial ports on a workstation for network printing

- *NPRINT.EXE*   A command-line utility used at workstations to print ASCII text files to network printers

- *NETUSER.EXE*   A DOS-based menu utility that has options for setting up the printing environment.

- *NetWare Administrator*   A Windows-based or OS/2-based administrative console that managers use to control all types of network objects, such as printer objects, print queue objects, and user objects. You can use NetWare Administrator to manage essential network printing tasks, such as assigning rights to printers and print queues

- *NetWare User*   A Windows-based or OS/2-based utility that users use to capture printer ports to network printers, view available resources, map network drives, and so on

Print Queues

A print queue is a sort of buffer that holds a group of print jobs from network users until they can be printed. NetWare v.4 print queues reside on file servers, in the QUEUES directory of the SYS volume. If you do not use PCONSOLE's Quick Setup option to set up NetWare printing services, you will want to create the network print queues before you create printer objects and print server objects.

As in previous versions of NetWare, print queues exist in network directories and serve as receptacles for print jobs until the print server can send the jobs to a printer. In NetWare v.4, however, users do not need to be familiar with print queues to use network printers. NetWare Directory Services makes it possible for users to identify a printer solely by its name. When users send a print job to a printer, NetWare sends the job to a queue appropriate for that printer. NetWare Directory Services also allows users to search for printers in portions of the directory that they can view.

When you create a print queue, Netware generates a directory for it. The directory name is the same as the randomly generated ID number assigned to that queue. NetWare attaches the extension .QDR to every named queue. Within each new print queue directory, NetWare places two hidden system files whose names begin with Q_ and contain a derivation of the directory name. The two files have the extensions .SYS and .SRV, and only users with Supervisor-level access rights can view them.

Network Printers

You must define a printer object for each printer you want to share on the network. You can use the PCONSOLE utility or the NetWare Administrator utility to define these objects. As usual, you should make sure you are in the appropriate NDS tree context before creating the objects.

You can attach printers to the print server itself and to individual workstations on the network. A print server manages the flow of print jobs through print queues and to printers. Several queues might send their print jobs to a single printer, or several printers might service a single queue. First you create a printer object for each printer you want to share on the network, and then you assign it to a print server and assign queues to it.

Print Servers

The PSERVER.NLM module links queues and printers to print servers. It runs as a continuous process in the server; if you unload it, printer sharing is unavailable. Unlike previous versions of NetWare, version 4 allows the installation of print servers only at NetWare v.4 file servers. You cannot install a print server on a dedicated workstation. The PSERVER.EXE utility for workstation setup is no longer available.

A single print server can handle up to 256 network printers, including 5 local printers (3 parallel and 2 serial). Novell recommends one print queue per printer for ease of management. Each print queue can contain up to 1000 print jobs at a time; however, the queue administrator sees only the first 255 print jobs. When the first job is finished, it disappears from the screen and another print job scrolls onto the screen at the end of the list. Although NetWare's improved printing services can theoretically handle this many print jobs, it would be inefficient to run dozens of printers through one print server, and you will probably never need to test for these limitations.

Using a separate queue for each printer might seem like overkill, but it provides flexibility for configuring printers on the network. NetWare users can now identify network printers by name, no matter where they are geographically in the organization. So if a printer is configured correctly, users who have the appropriate rights can print to a printer simply by choosing the printer's name from the directory. They do not have to know where the printer is located or which printer queue stores its print jobs.

In most organizations printing is a mission-critical operation. If you also have heavy database or imaging applications running on the file server, you might consider running separate print servers on two or more file servers. This spreads out the printing management load.

An architectural change made to the NetWare v.4 printing services is the addition of NPRINTER functionality for printers attached directly to the network. A new breed of printers is being manufactured by Compaq, Hewlett-Packard, and other companies. These printers have their own network interface cards so that they can become a node on the network without being attached to a workstation or server. By taking advantage of the new APIs available for developers, third-party printer manufacturers can load NPRINTER.EXE into the printer's memory to service print jobs directly, bypassing a print server. After you define the printer object in the directory, the printer can begin servicing print jobs directly from an assigned queue. Consult the printer manufacturer's instructions for connecting a printer directly to a NetWare network.

Configuring Printing Services

The steps for configuring printing services are listed next. You can use either the text-based PCONSOLE.EXE utility or NetWare Administrator for steps 2 through 4. The fifth step is executed at the file server that will run the print server module.

1. If necessary, create special print forms and print job configurations by using the PRINTDEF and PRINTCON utilities, as discussed at the end of this chapter.

2. Create one or more print queue objects to which users will send print jobs. Queues can have different priorities. For example, you could give a manager's queue a higher priority than a clerk's queue so that its print jobs always print first.

3. Create printer objects that define printers attached to NetWare file servers and workstations. If a printer is not attached to a print server, you must specify that the printer is remotely attached.

4. Create a print server, and then define which printers it will service. When assigning printers to the print server, you can also define which queues the printers will handle.

5. Load PSERVER.NLM at the file server. PSERVER installs the print server defined in step 4 and services the printers and queues defined in steps 2 and 3.

6. To share printers attached to file servers that aren't print servers, load NPRINTER.NLM at the file servers. To share printers at workstations, run NPRINTER.EXE at the workstations.

Backward Compatibility of Printing Services

Because NetWare v.3.*x* volumes and servers appear in NetWare v.4 directories, users can access the print queues that reside on those servers while logged into the network as NetWare v.4 clients. However, you must use PCONSOLE to create a new entry in the NetWare Directory Services tree that serves as a logical representative of the v.3.*x* queue. From the PCONSOLE Available Options menu, choose Print Queues. Press F6 to select the file server containing the print queue. After you highlight the name of the queue and press ENTER, the queue name appears in the directory tree. NetWare will access the name of the queue in the directory tree and then send the print jobs to the bindery queue on the NetWare 3.*x* server. Be sure to add all applicable access rights to the new queue name in the directory tree.

The PUPGRADE Utility

The PUPGRADE utility provides the following options that let you upgrade previous NetWare printing configurations:

■ *Upgrade PRINTCON Database*   Allows you to convert NetWare v.3.1*x* print job configurations for use in NetWare Directory Services.

■ *Upgrade PRINTDEF Database*   Allows you to convert NetWare v.3.1*x* printer definitions and forms for use in NetWare Directory Services.

■ *Upgrade Print Server and Printers* Allows you to convert NetWare v.3.1*x* print servers and printers to NetWare Directory Services objects. Print queues are normally upgraded with the operating system.

You can refer to the NetWare v.4 printing services documentation for more information on using PUPGRADE to upgrade printing configurations.

Configuring Printing Services by Using PCONSOLE

This section explains how to install shared printers and printing services for NetWare by using the text-based PCONSOLE utility. Log into the network with Supervisor-level rights and then type **PCONSOLE** at the prompt to start the utility. The PCONSOLE main menu appears, as shown in Figure 27-2.

NOTE: *You can also set up printing services by using the NetWare Administrator. Refer to the section "Configuring Printing Services by Using NetWare Administrator" later in this chapter for more information.*

PCONSOLE provides a Quick Setup utility that simplifies the configuration process if you have only a few printers. This utility creates a print queue object, creates a printer object, and assigns the queue and printer to a print server. Alternatively, you can perform each of these steps individually to have more control over the options you can set for queues, printers, and print servers. The Quick Setup method is covered first.

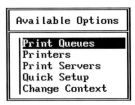

Figure 27-2. *The PCONSOLE main menu*

Using Quick Setup

You can use the Quick Setup option on the main PCONSOLE menu to configure a print server, network printer, print queue, and all the relationships among them. From the PCONSOLE menu, choose the Quick Setup option. The Print Services Quick Setup screen appears, as shown in Figure 27-3. This screen lists default settings that reflect your current context and printer configuration. Note that Quick Setup recommends a print server name that reflects the container name of your current context.

Be aware of your current context in the NetWare Directory Services tree. The objects for the printer and queue are placed at your current context if you accept the default settings. You can change contexts by selecting the Change Context option on the PCONSOLE main menu.

On the Quick Setup screen, you can accept the names assigned by PCONSOLE or you can customize them. If the printers and queues have a special purpose (such as after-hours printing only or manager-use only), give them names users will recognize.

The rest of the Quick Setup screen displays the name of the volume where NetWare will create the print queue, the printing mode when the banner is printed (a *banner* is a page that separates one print job from the next), and information about the printer. The Location field has the following options:

■ *Auto Load*   Choose this option if you have printers attached to the print server.

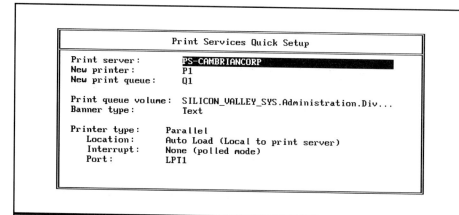

Figure 27-3.   *The Print Services Quick Setup screen*

■ *Manual Load* Choose this option if the printer you are configuring is not attached to the print server but is instead attached to a workstation or another file server. You must manually load NPRINTER.NLM at the remote file server or NPRINTER.EXE at the workstation.

Once the "plumbing" is in place, you can activate the print server by loading PSERVER.NLM. Refer to the section "Loading the Print Server (PSERVER.NLM)" later in this chapter. If you want to create print queue objects, printer objects, and print server objects manually by using PCONSOLE, refer to the next few sections.

Creating Print Queue Objects by Using PCONSOLE

To create a new print queue by using PCONSOLE, choose the Print Queues option from the PCONSOLE main menu. You see a list of existing print queues. Follow these steps to create a new queue:

1. Press INS, and then type the name for the queue. Remember to use a descriptive name if possible so that network users will know which features the queue has, or the location of the printer or type of printer the queue services.

2. PCONSOLE asks for the print queue's volume name. Specify the volume location for the print queue directory by typing it or by pressing INS and choosing a volume by using the Object, Class dialog box. After you've located and selected a volume, the new print queue name appears in the Print Queues list.

3. Highlight the queue you just created and press ENTER to view and change print queue information. The Print Queue Information menu appears:

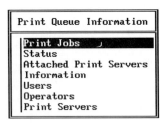

Most of the options on the Print Queue Information menu are used to view information about a queue. You can do one of the following when configuring a new queue:

- Choose Print Servers to specify the print server for the queue (assuming one has been created). This is an optional step. You can also do this later when defining print servers.

- Choose Users or Operators to specify who can use the queue and who is in charge of the queue.

- Choose Status to change the operating status of the queue.

You can use the Print Jobs option to submit jobs for printing to the queue (once everything is set up), and you use the remaining options to display information about the queue.

Defining Printers by Using PCONSOLE

To add a new printer definition, choose Printers from the PCONSOLE main menu, and then follow these steps:

1. When the Printers menu appears, any existing printers are listed. Press INS to add a new printer to the list.

2. Type the new printer name, making it as descriptive as possible, and press ENTER.

3. When the new printer name appears in the list, highlight it and press ENTER. A Printer Configuration screen similar to the following appears:

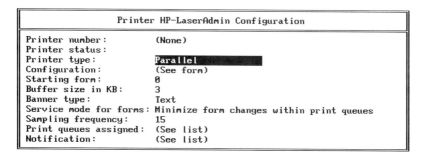

4. Define the printer by filling out the fields on this screen. When you highlight a field, a description of that field appears at the bottom of the screen. You can also press F1 for help. When you're done, press F10 to save the changes.

NOTE: *If the printer is attached to a workstation or to a server on the network other than the print server, choose "Remote, OTHER" in the "Printer type" field.*

Creating a Print Server Object by Using PCONSOLE

To create a print server object by using PCONSOLE, choose Print Servers from the PCONSOLE main menu. When the Print Servers menu appears, you will see a list of existing print servers, if there are any. To add a new print server, press INS, type its name, and press ENTER.

After the new print server name appears in the Print Server menu, you can highlight it and press ENTER to display the Print Server Information menu:

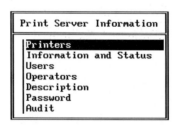

This is an important step because you use this menu to define which printers and queues the print server will service. If you don't complete this step, the printers and queues won't be available to network users. Each of the options on this menu is discussed here:

- *Printers* Choose this option and then press INS to add one of the printers you created in the previous section. You can browse the directory tree to locate the printer.

- *Information and Status* This option displays status information and lets you change the print server name used when advertising the server. You can change this name for troubleshooting purposes.

- *Users* You use this option to add or remove names of users or groups who can access this print server.

- *Operators* You use this option to add or remove names of users who help manage the print server.

- *Description* This option creates a description for the print server that will appear in some message boxes.

- *Password* You use this option to create or change a password that must be used to start the print server.

- *Audit* This option enables auditing for the print server.

After you create a print server, your primary task is to define the printers that it will service. In addition, you can define the queues that each printer will service (although you can also assign queues when defining printers). To assign printers, follow these steps:

1. Choose Print Servers from the PCONSOLE main menu, and then highlight the print server and press ENTER.

2. Choose the Printers option, and then press INS to add other printers.

3. Browse the NetWare Directory Services tree for the printer objects you want to assign to the print server. You must have created these printer objects, as discussed earlier in this chapter.

4. After you've added printers, you can define the queues they will handle. Highlight a printer and press ENTER, and then choose "Print queues assigned" from the Printer Configuration menu and browse the NetWare Directory Services tree to locate the queues you want to assign to the printer.

Configuring Printing Services by Using NetWare Administrator

You can create and configure print queue objects, printer objects, and print server objects by using NetWare Administrator if you have a workstation that runs Windows.

Creating Print Queue Objects by Using NetWare Administrator

To create a print queue by using NetWare Administrator, first change your context in the directory tree, if necessary, and highlight the container you want to hold the print queue object. Then choose Create from the Object menu. When the list of objects appears, double-click the Print Queue object.

At the Create Print Queue dialog box, do the following:

1. Type a name for the queue in the Print Queue Name field.

2. Choose the volume object that will hold the queue in the Print Queue Volume field.

3. Click the Define Additional Properties box, and then click Create.

A Details dialog box similar to that shown in Figure 27-4 appears. From this dialog box, you can change fields on the following pages:

■ *Identification* This page shows the logical description and physical location of the department where the print queue resides. You can change these fields as appropriate; they are mostly informational.

■ *Assignments* This page shows the printer and print server attachments for the queue. You view these assignments in the Details dialog box for the print queue, but you actually make the assignments in the Details dialog box for the printer.

■ *Operators* This page lists the objects that have a right to manage the queue and print jobs in the queue.

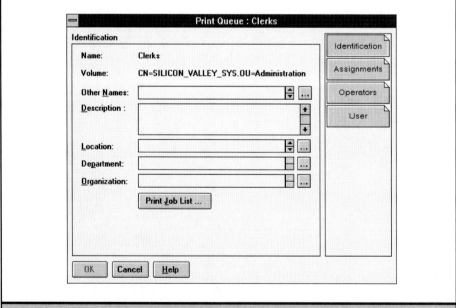

Figure 27-4. *The Details dialog box for a print queue object*

- *Users* This page lists the users who can access the queue. You must make the queue accessible by listing users or groups of users on this page in order for users to be able to use the queue. Click the Add button to add a user or group.

Defining Printers by Using NetWare Administrator

To define a printer by using NetWare Administrator, first change your context in the directory tree, if necessary, and highlight the container you want to hold the printer object. Then do the following:

1. Choose Create from the Object menu. When the list of objects appears, double-click the Printer object.

2. When the Create Printer dialog box appears, type a name for the printer in the Printer Name field, click the Define Additional Properties box, and click the Create button. A Details dialog box similar to that shown in Figure 27-5 appears.

At the right side of the dialog box are four buttons you click to define additional properties. The Identification page appears first so that you can specify the description, location, and other identification properties used for informational purposes. The Printer Status button at the bottom of the window lets you see if the printer is responding and accepting print jobs.

The Assignments Page

The Assignments page, which is shown in Figure 27-6, lists the active print server, the network print queues serviced by the printer, and the default print queue. You can click the Add button to assign additional queues to this printer. As you add queues to the lists, they appear in the Print Queues list.

- In Figure 27-6, the print server is PS-CAMBRIANCORP. You must create a print server and assign printers to it, as discussed shortly, before you will see a name in this field.

- The Print Queues field shows the queues that have been assigned to the printer. The priority of a queue is important when more than one queue is

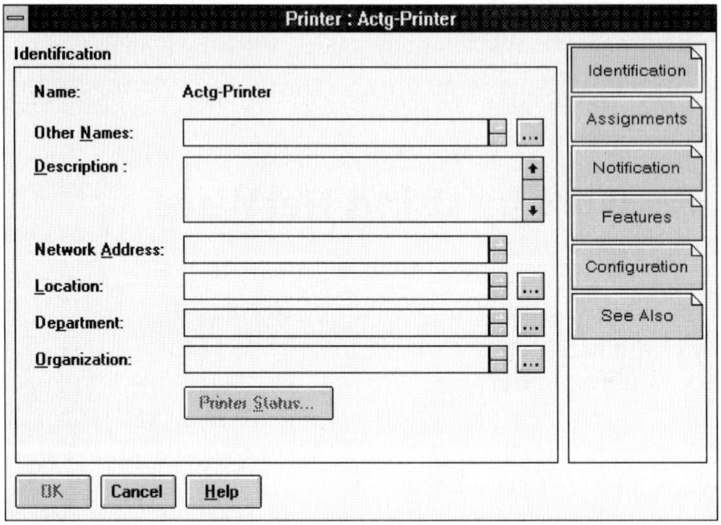

Figure 27-5. The Details dialog box for a printer object

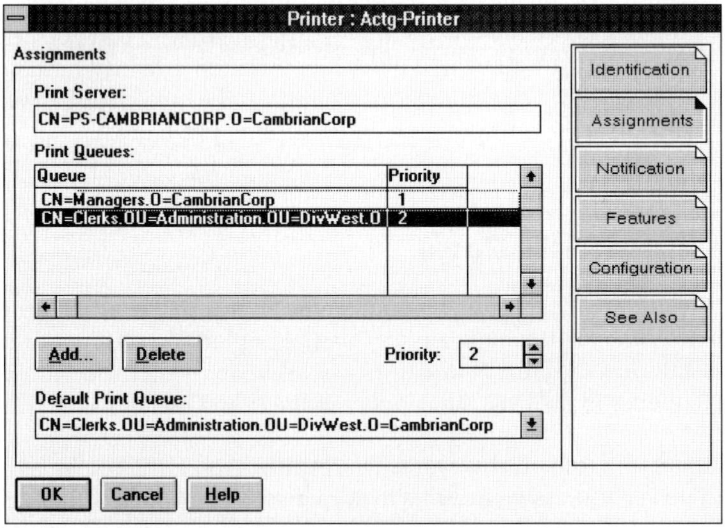

Figure 27-6. The Assignments page of the Details dialog box for a printer object

assigned to a single printer. Queues with high priority are serviced before queues with lower priority; so, for example, you might want to create a Managers queue that has a priority of 1 and a Clerks queue that has a priority of 2. To change the priority of a queue, highlight the queue and change the Priority field value.

■ The Default Print Queue field displays the name of the queue that is used by default if users choose to print to this printer object rather than to a queue object.

REMEMBER: *When you switch default queues, make sure users have access rights to the new queue.*

Other Printer Object Properties

The remaining pages of the Details dialog box for printer objects are discussed in this section. You use these pages to specify who should be notified when the printer has problems and to specify various features and configuration options.

NOTIFICATION   On the Notification page, you can specify a network object from the directory that should receive notification of print job completion or print job errors. You can also set the frequency with which the printer will notify you of the print job status messages.

FEATURES   Every printer has features that you need to know about when configuring applications or custom print jobs. The Features page includes fields where you can fill in important information about the printer. The typefaces supported, amount of memory in the printer (important for building custom fonts and storing large print jobs), and the printer's page description language are often useful information for users who need to print. Large companies that do a lot of in-house development might find a need to add new fields in the list of printer features. Refer to Novell's Server Application Program Development Kit for NetWare v.4 or call Novell.

CONFIGURATION   Use the Configuration page to choose the type of printer attached to the network: parallel, serial, AIO, UNIX, or AppleTalk. You can also specify the banner type (text or PostScript), the service interval (timeout delay between jobs), the buffer size, and the network printing form created by using PCONSOLE. To specify a remote printer (a printer that isn't attached to the print server) or to change communications parameters, click the Communications button. A dialog box similar to that shown in Figure 27-7 appears. Click the Help button for information on changing these options.

NOTE: Enable the Remote from Print Server button on the Communication dialog box if the printer is not directly connected to the print server.

SEE ALSO   On the See Also page, you can create a list of objects that might have related configuration information. For example, you could create a list of alternate printers with similar features and configurations that users might want to refer to if the printer is busy.

Creating a Print Server Object by Using NetWare Administrator

To create a print server object by using NetWare Administrator, first locate the appropriate context in the NetWare Directory Services tree. Click the container object in which you want to locate the print server, and then follow this step:

1. Choose Create from the Object menu to see the list of objects you can create in the container, and double-click the Print Server option. Type in a print server name, click the Define Additional Properties box, and click the Create button. The Details dialog box for print servers appears, as shown in Figure 27-8.

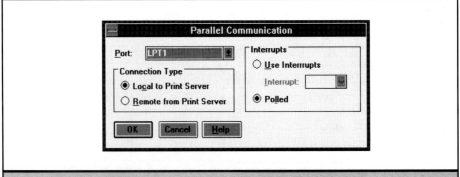

Figure 27-7.   *The Communication dialog box for printer setup*

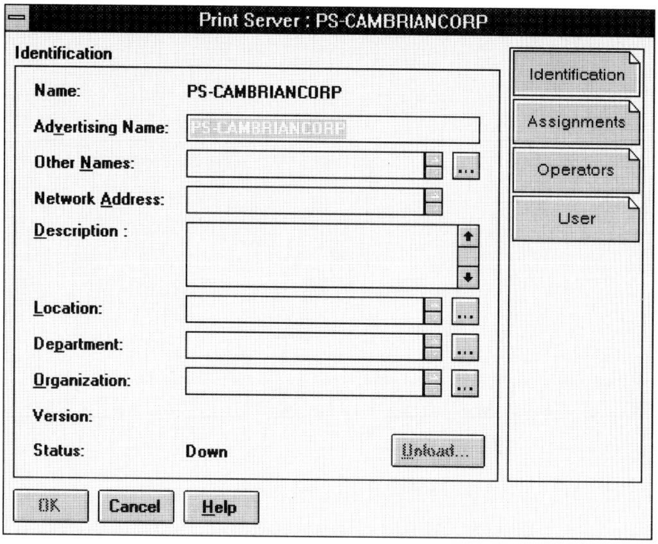

Figure 27-8. *The Details dialog box for a print server*

The Details dialog box for a print server is made up of four pages, which are discussed in this section.

IDENTIFICATION   Enter all the print server's physical configuration details on the Identification page. Note the Unload button at the bottom of the window, which lets you unload PSERVER.NLM from the system console remotely. (You cannot load the software remotely.) After you define the print server by using NetWare Administrator, you must load PSERVER.NLM at the server's system console. If that server is at a remote location you will need a local operator to perform the steps.

ASSIGNMENTS   On the Assignments page, you can view, add, or delete printers assigned to the print server. Assigning printers is an important step because the print server will not load properly unless one or more printers have been assigned to it. Click the Add button to assign new printers to the print server. You can then browse the directory tree to locate printer objects you created previously and assign them to the print server. After printers are added, the printer will receive print jobs in its queue.

NOTE: *If the printer is attached to a workstation, make sure to load NPRINTER.EXE at the workstation.*

OPERATORS   You define the users responsible for the print server on the Operators page.

USER   On the User page, you define users or groups who have access to the print server.

Loading the Print Server (PSERVER.NLM)

After you define a print server and assign queues and printers to it by using either PCONSOLE or NetWare Administrator, you can load PSERVER.NLM at a file server's system console by typing the following command:

```
LOAD PSERVER
```

The "Enter print server name" box appears with your current context in the NetWare Directory Services tree listed. To change the context, press ENTER. The "Contents of current context" box appears, in which you can browse the directory tree until you find the context that holds the print server object you created previously. Highlight the object and press ENTER. In a moment, the PSERVER main menu appears. From the main menu, you can select Printer Status or Print Server Information.

Printer Status

Highlight the Printer Status option and press ENTER to see a list of network printers that have been assigned to the current print server. You will not be able to see printers that have been assigned to another print server. Select a printer and press ENTER to view printer status information, as shown in Figure 27-9. The fields on this screen are discussed here:

■ *Printer* Shows the full NetWare Directory Services name of the printer

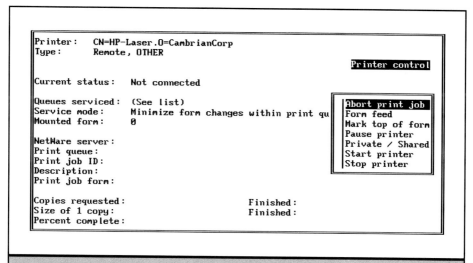

Figure 27-9. *The printer status screen for a print server*

■ *Type* Displays the type of connection, either locally attached to the print server, or attached to a workstation (Remote) or another file server (OTHER)

■ *Current status* Tells whether the printer is connected to the network. If the printer is remote, this field will say "Not connected" until you load the NPRINTER.EXE file on the workstation (or the NPRINTER.NLM file on the file server)

■ *Queues serviced* Select this field and press ENTER to see a list of queues. Press ENTER again to change the priority of a queue. As mentioned previously, queue priority provides a way to make sure some print jobs are printed before others

■ *Mounted form* Refers to a custom form created by using the PRINTCON utility. This field can be left as 0 if no special form is used

■ *Printer control* Selecting this field brings up a secondary menu (shown under the Printer control field in Figure 27-9) that contains several options you can select to manipulate the printer from the console. You can abort a print job, form feed a sheet of paper, mark the top of the current form, and pause, stop, and start the printer

All of the remaining fields are blank until a print job is sent to a queue and printer.

Print Server Information

When you choose the Print Server Information option from the PSERVER main menu, a Print Server Information and Status dialog box appears:

```
┌─────────────────────────────────────────────────────┐
│         Print Server Information and Status          │
├─────────────────────────────────────────────────────┤
│  Version:            4.0.0                            │
│  Type:               Netware Loadable Module         │
│  Advertising name:   PS-CAMBRIANCORP                 │
│  Number of printers: 2                               │
│  Queue service modes: 4                              │
│  Current status:     Running                         │
└─────────────────────────────────────────────────────┘
```

This dialog box lists the general characteristics of the print server, including its software version number, its program type, the official name by which it is known to the network, the number of printers it supports, the number of queue service modes, and its current status. Select "Current status" to see a menu that allows you to unload the print server.

Setting Up Remote Printers

Because a single NetWare print server can service up to 256 printers, you might want to create only one print server to handle all the printers on your network, assuming you have fewer than 256 printers. Five of those printers can attach to the back of the server itself. The remaining shared printers are configured at workstations or at other file servers.

The basic steps for defining a remote printer you want to share with other network users are listed here:

1. Attach the printer to an LPT port or COM port on a workstation or on a file server.

2. Use PCONSOLE or NetWare Administrator to create one or more queue objects for the printer, or determine which existing queue will service the printer.

3. Use PCONSOLE or NetWare Administrator to create a printer object for the printer. Be sure to specify that the printer is remote from the print server:

- If you're using PCONSOLE Quick Setup, choose Manual Load in the Location field.

- If you are configuring a printer by using PCONSOLE but you're not using Quick Setup, choose "Remote, OTHER" in the Printer type field of the printer configuration menu.

- If you are configuring a printer by using NetWare Administrator, click the Communication button on the Configuration page when setting up a printer, and then enable the Remote from Print Server option on the dialog box that appears (see Figure 27-7).

4. Use NetWare Administrator or PCONSOLE to follow the steps described earlier in this chapter for assigning queues to the new printer object.

5. Assign the new printer to a print server object by using NetWare Administrator or PCONSOLE. These steps are also described earlier in this chapter.

6. If PSERVER.NLM is already running at a file server, type **UNLOAD PSERVER** at the server's console and then bring the server back up. It should recognize the name of the new printer you entered in the directory.

After installing PSERVER, remote printers are still not available until you load INPRINTER.EXE at the workstation or a server. You can look at a remote printer's status by choosing Printer Status and selecting the printer. It will be listed as

Type: Remote OTHER
Status: Not connected

Perform step 7a if you are installing a workstation printer and 7b if you are installing a server printer.

7a. If you are installing a remote printer attached to a workstation, make sure you are logged into the network and have a search drive mapped to the SYS:PUBLIC directory. Then type **NPRINTER** to load the NPRINTER.EXE program. A list of current print servers appears. Choose a print server, and then choose a printer and specify whether it is attached to a local parallel or serial port. When everything is set, press F10 to complete the installation.

7b. If you are installing a remote printer attached to a file server, type **LOAD NPRINTER**, followed by the name of the print server you want to connect to and the number assigned to the network printer. (Look at the

Printer Status option of the PSERVER console at the file server to determine which printer number NetWare assigned to the new printer.)

After NPRINTER loads support for the printer attached to the workstation or file server, other users can access the printer from network-aware applications or with NetWare printing commands like those discussed in the remainder of the chapter.

Other Printing Utilities

There are five text-based utilities—PRINTDEF, PRINTCON, PSC, CAPTURE, and NPRINT—that are associated with printing. The PRINTDEF and PRINTCON menu utilities are used to define special printing options when you're using applications that are not network aware or need special settings beyond what you can define in the applications you print from. Many applications are network aware and let you print directly to shared network printers and queues. Others require the special settings discussed here.

It is important to understand the difference between print forms and print job configurations. A *print form* basically defines a paper size and gives it a name and number to which you can refer when specifying print jobs. You create a *print job configuration* by using the PRINTCON utility to define the parameters for a printing job. There can be many different print job configurations that users can choose from when sending jobs to a printer. Keep in mind, however, that these options are not important with most modern applications that define the parameters internally.

Each of these five utilities is briefly described in the following sections. Refer to each utility's help options for more information, or type a command similar to the following to display a description of the utility:

```
CAPTURE /?
```

PRINTDEF

You use PRINTDEF to define print forms and printer definition files (PDFs). To define a PDF, choose Print Devices from the PRINTDEF main menu, as described next. To create a new form, choose Forms.

A PDF defines the settings and parameters of a printing device, such as a Hewlett-Packard laser printer or an IBM line printer. NetWare has a large set of preconfigured PDFs in the SYS:PUBLIC directory for the most popular printers. You can list these files, which have the filename extension .PDF. You can use PRINTDEF to create a print device that you can refer to when printing from applications on the network or from NetWare printing utilities. The definitions you create with PRINTDEF can use existing PDF files, or you can specify your own parameters if a PDF is not available for your printer. Creating your own PDFs can be tedious, so you might want to contact the printer manufacturer for a PDF. Keep in mind that most applications don't need NetWare's PDF since they have their own printer definition files.

The PRINTDEF menu consists of an Edit and an Import option. You use Edit to create your own print device, and you use the Import option to call up one of the existing PDFs in the SYS:PUBLIC directory. Either way, you create a device that has a name and number you can refer to when running applications or using NetWare printing utilities. For example, you can use PRINTCON to create a default print form used by network queues. This print form can specify a particular PDF, such as the file for a Hewlett-Packard LaserJet printer.

PRINTCON

You can use the PRINTCON utility to create print job configurations. A print job configuration defines a set of parameters used to print a job, such as the printer definition file, the printer or print queue to use, the number of copies to print, and banner information. You can define any number of print job configurations and then let users choose the one they want to use when sending a print job to a printer. An example of the screen used to configure print jobs is shown in Figure 27-10.

At the top of the screen, you can specify the number of copies for the job and whether it should have a banner. At the bottom, you can specify the print device to use and the mode, which defines a special font. Note that jobs you define by using PRINTCON are sent to the printer specified in the Device field. This provides a way for you to define in advance the printers users will use when printing.

PSC

The PSC utility provides a way to control print servers and printers from the command line. You can use it in place of the PCONSOLE and NetWare

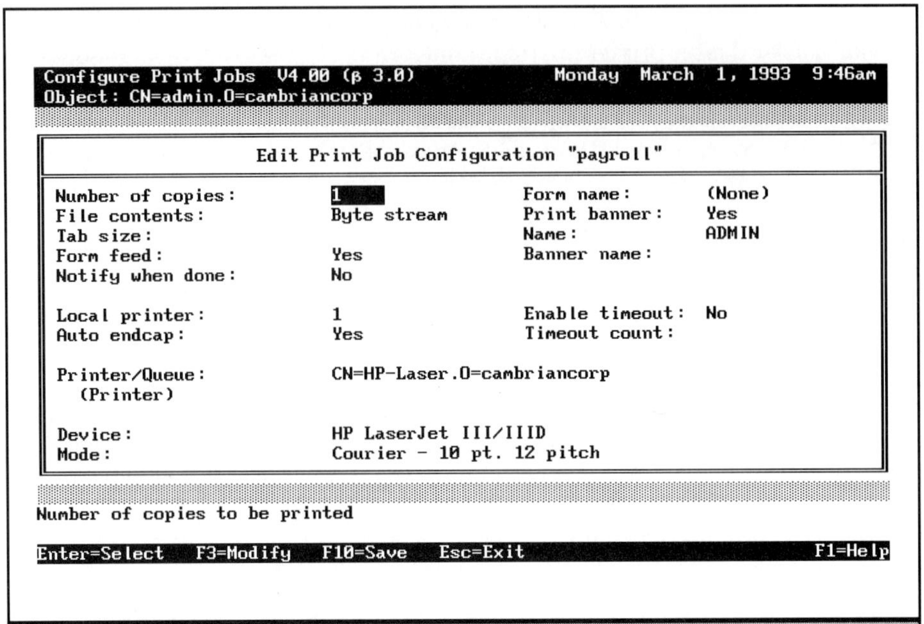

```
Configure Print Jobs  V4.00 (β 3.0)          Monday  March  1, 1993  9:46am
Object: CN=admin.O=cambriancorp

        ┌──────────────────────────────────────────────────────────────┐
        │              Edit Print Job Configuration "payroll"            │
        │                                                                │
        │ Number of copies:      1          Form name:      (None)       │
        │ File contents:         Byte stream  Print banner:  Yes         │
        │ Tab size:                         Name:           ADMIN        │
        │ Form feed:             Yes        Banner name:                 │
        │ Notify when done:      No                                      │
        │                                                                │
        │ Local printer:         1          Enable timeout:  No          │
        │ Auto endcap:           Yes        Timeout count:               │
        │                                                                │
        │ Printer/Queue:         CN=HP-Laser.O=cambriancorp              │
        │   (Printer)                                                    │
        │                                                                │
        │ Device:                HP LaserJet III/IIID                    │
        │ Mode:                  Courier - 10 pt. 12 pitch               │
        └──────────────────────────────────────────────────────────────┘

Number of copies to be printed

Enter=Select   F3=Modify   F10=Save   Esc=Exit                    F1=Help
```

Figure 27-10.   *The print job configuration screen*

Administrator utilities when you need to make a quick change to printing services. The command takes the following form:

PSC PS=*server* P=*printernum options*

where *server* is the name of the print server, *printernum* is the name of the printer, and *options* is one of the following options:

Option	Meaning	Description
CD	Cancel/Down	Cancels or downs a print server
FF	Form Feed	Forces a form feed on a printer
PAU	Pause	Pauses a printer
STAR	Start	Starts a printer
STO	Stop	Stops a printer
AB	Abort	Aborts a printer
STAT	Status	Displays the status of a printer

Option	Meaning	Description
M *char*	Mark	Marks the top of the form on the printer. You use this option to type a mark so that you can determine where printing will start on a form. Replace *char* with the character you want to type
MO F=*Name*	Mount Form	Mounts a form on a printer. Replace *Name* with the filename of the form
PRI	Private	Makes a remote printer private. The printer is no longer shared by other network users
SHA	Shared	Makes a remote printer shared. Undoes the PRI option

For example, you might type the following command to force a form feed on a printer called HP-Laser that is attached to a print server called ACCTG after you sent a job to it that didn't eject:

```
PSC PS=ACCTG P=HP-LASER FF
```

CAPTURE

Applications that are network aware, such as Microsoft Word and WordPerfect, let you specify and print directly to printers on the network. These applications display the printer names within their user interface. When printing from applications that are not network aware, you need a way to divert printing from local DOS printers to NetWare printers. You can use the CAPTURE utility to do this. It lets you divert print jobs sent to a local device name such as LPT1 or LPT2 to a network printer. Then, in your applications, you can simply send print jobs to the diverted port when you want to print to network devices.

For example, you could use the CAPTURE command in the following form to divert all print jobs sent to LPT2 to the print queue called Managers:

```
CAPTURE L=2 Q=MANAGERS
```

This command diverts print jobs sent to LPT2 to a printer called HP-LASER:

```
CAPTURE L=2 P=HP-LASER
```

To end the capturing of LPT2 as set up by one of the two previous examples, you would type the EC (End Capture) option as follows:

```
CAPTURE L=2 EC
```

The list of CAPTURE options and parameters is quite extensive. You can print them by typing the following command, which assumes that a local printer is attached to LPT1:

```
CAPTURE /? ALL > LPT1
```

NOTE: By default, only the device names LPT1, LPT2, and LPT3 are available on DOS workstations. You can increase the port names up to LPT9 by including the following command in the NET.CFG file, where x is the number of ports you need.

NETWORK PRINTERS = x

NPRINT

You can use the NPRINT utility to send a specific print job to a network printer without actually having to divert a printer port by using the CAPTURE utility. You add options to the NPRINT command to specify which network queue or printer you want to print to. The command takes the form:

NPRINT *filename options*

where *filename* is the path and name of the file you want to print, and *options* is an option that specifies various parameters, such as the queue, printer, and print server to use. You can also specify a banner to separate the print job from others, and you can specify a specific form or print job configuration. You can type the following command to print a complete description of the NPRINT command:

```
NPRINT /? ALL > LPT1
```

CHAPTER 28

Login Scripts

Login scripts are critical for setting up the environments of network users. A *login script* is a series of commands that execute when a user logs in. The commands placed in login scripts can map network drives for users, switch them to specific drives, display menus, and start applications.

Types of Login Scripts

There are three types of login scripts, all of which may execute when a user logs in.

System login script   The first type is the system login script, which is located in the container object that the user belongs to. (Note that there can be only one system login script for each user who logs in.) If the user belongs to the Sales department, for example, the login script for the Sales container object executes.

Profile login script   Next, there is the profile login script, which can belong to a group of users who don't necessarily belong to the same container. For example, you could create a profile login script for managers; then assign the script to managers in different containers. Profile scripts have no container boundaries, unlike default login scripts.

Personal login script   Users also have their personal login scripts, which supervisors can create, or users can create and modify on their own. Users can place commands in their personal login scripts that map the directories they have created in their own user subdirectories. They can also insert commands that execute personal menu systems (see Chapter 29) or start up programs they use on a regular basis. Users can modify their personal login scripts by accessing their user object in the NetWare Administrator or NETADMIN utility. By default, this is the only property of their user object that they can change unless the supervisor has revoked the right to do so or given them access to other properties.

NOTE: *The default login script runs if a personal login script has not been created. This is true even when system and profile login scripts execute.*

How and When Login Scripts Execute

When a user logs in, the system login script executes first, then any profile login scripts, and finally the personal login script. The order is important. It's usually necessary to map drives before running a menu or executing a program. While any login script can contain every essential command the user needs, be careful not to overwrite drive mappings or change environment settings that might have been set in other login scripts. Be aware of which letters are mapped to which drives. If you map drive G for all users in a container to a document directory, don't overwrite that drive mapping in a profile or user login script unless you really want to.

Assigning a System Login Script to a User

A system login script doesn't automatically execute for a user. You need to make the user a trustee of the container that holds the user object. In the NetWare Administrator, this is done by "dragging and dropping" the user object over the container object. The Object Trustees dialog box appears, with the Browse right selected and the name of the user object in the Trustees list box. Click OK to accept the settings.

To make a user a trustee of a container in NETADMIN, first select the container, then press F10. Choose "View or edit the trustee assignments to this object" from the Actions for Organizational Unit menu, then choose Trustees. Choose [All Properties Rights] and press ENTER. Type in the user object's name, or press INS to choose it from a list.

NOTE: You can simplify the procedure for assigning a system login script to several users by adding them to a group and "dragging and dropping" the group on to the container.

Creating and Assigning a Profile Login Script

Profile login scripts are established by first creating a profile object in the NetWare Administrator or NETADMIN. You then open the Details dialog box for the profile object and type the login script.

To assign a profile login script to a user object in NetWare Administrator, double-click the user object, then click the Login script button on the dialog box that appears. Type the name of the profile login script in the Default Profile field. You can also click the search button to browse the directory tree and choose the profile object.

To do the same in NETADMIN, select the user object you want to assign the profile to and press F10. Choose the "View or edit properties of this object" option, then choose "Groups/Security Equals/Profile." Highlight the Profile option, then press INS twice to choose a profile object from a list.

Directory Services Context and Login Scripts

In previous versions of NetWare, each server had a login script. Under NetWare v.4, users log into a specific context of the directory tree. The login script in the container of that context then runs (assuming users have been granted rights to it).

The INCLUDE login script command has a more important role in NetWare v.4 login scripts. INCLUDE commands call login script commands stored in separate text files. Typically, these files contain a set of routines you need in several different login scripts. The INCLUDE command lets you create one file with the routines, and then call it from many different login scripts. This way, you don't need to type the commands over. (See the later section, "INCLUDE" for a more detailed discussion of this command.)

Directory Services provides a unique opportunity to let managers in different departments contribute messages and commands to login scripts. For example, assume that the Personnel department has messages it wants users to read when they log in. Personnel can create these messages in a script file. INCLUDE statements in the login scripts can then call these script files to display their messages, or even run commands.

The important point is that parts of the login script are controlled by supervisors and managers outside the normal context of users (that is, their departments).

NOTE: Users must have Read rights to execute scripts called by the INCLUDE command.

The Default Login Script

On a new NetWare v.4 network, a simple default login script exists. Most administrators will quickly override this default script by creating new login scripts. It is listed and defined here for your convenience and as an example to help you get started with login scripts. Note that most commands in the script are MAP commands, which is typical. The numbers at the beginning of each line are not part of the script; they are identifiers for the explanation that follows.

```
1.   WRITE "Good %GREETING_TIME, %LOGIN_NAME."
2.   MAP DISPLAY OFF
3.   MAP ERRORS OFF
```

```
 4.   MAP *1:SYS:
 5.   MAP *1:=SYS:%LOGIN_NAME
 6.   IF "%1"="ADMIN" THEN MAP *1:=SYS:SYSTEM
 7.   MAP *2:=SYS:PUBLIC\OS2
 8.   MAP INS S1:=SYS:PUBLIC;
          INS S2:=SYS:PUBLIC\%MACHINE\%OS\%OS_VERSION
 9.   MAP DISPLAY ON
10.   MAP
```

The parameters with percent signs are login script identifiers that represent variables in the user's environment, such as the name supplied when logging in, or the version of DOS running on the system. These are described later under "Login Script Identifier Variables." An explanation of each line of the script follows.

1. This line displays a greeting message such as "Good morning, JJONES." The value of the identifier variable %GREETING_TIME depends on the current time, and %LOGIN_NAME is the name the user typed with the LOGIN command.

2. This line prevents MAP commands from displaying messages. It is used for esthetic reasons.

3. Line 3 prevents errors from displaying.

4. Line 4 maps the first drive to the SYS: volume. This mapping is only used if the user does not have a home directory, otherwise the next command overrides it.

5. This line maps the first drive to the user's home directory. If it doesn't exist, the mapping in line 4 is preserved.

6. If the user logging in is ADMIN, the command in line 6 maps the first drive to the SYS:SYSTEM directory.

7. The command in line 7 is only included in the script if the user logs in from an OS/2 workstation. It maps the second drive to the OS/2 utilities directory that branched from the PUBLIC directory on the SYS: volume.

8. Line 8 is a multiple command line—the semicolon separates two distinct mapping commands. It executes if users are working at a DOS or Windows workstation. The first part maps a search drive to the SYS:PUBLIC directory, and the second part maps to an appropriate DOS directory that matches the version of DOS they are running.

9. Line 9 restores the display of mapping information.

10. This line displays a list of mapped drives.

After the last command executes, the user sees a command prompt, along with the list of mapped drives.

Login Choices

Users logging into a NetWare network have some choices about the login scripts that run. When executing the LOGIN command, you can use any of the following parameters to bypass login scripts or specify a different login script.

/NS Specify this option to bypass all login scripts when you are trying to troubleshoot or set up new environments. No search drives are mapped, and your default directory is the LOGIN directory. You'll need to switch to the PUBLIC directory and manually execute MAP commands to set up search drives so you can work in other directories with NetWare commands. For example, to log in as the ADMIN user to the CambrianCorp organization and bypass the default or other login script, type

```
LOGIN .ADMIN.CAMBRIANCORP /NS
```

/S *filename* A better way to bypass your login script is to use this option to specify an alternate login script. Create a text file with login script commands such as MAP on a DOS drive, then execute the LOGIN command with this parameter, replacing *filename* with the path and name of the file you created. Include a command to map a search drive to the PUBLIC directory in the text file. For example, to log in as the ADMIN user to the CambrianCorp organization and run the commands in a text file called LOGIN.TXT on local drive C, type

```
LOGIN .ADMIN.CAMBRIANCORP /S C:\LOGIN.TXT
```

/PR=*object* You can direct LOGIN to run a login script that belongs to a particular object using this option. Replace *object* with the name of the object.

This way, you can specify a profile object or even another user object. The login script within that object executes when you log in. For example, to log in and execute the commands in a profile object called MANAGERS in the ADMIN container of the CambrianCorp organization, type

```
LOGIN .ADMIN.CAMBRIANCORP /PR=.MANAGERS.ADMIN.CAMBRIANCORP
```

Note the following regarding the /PR= option:

- You must specify the complete directory services path (context) of the object unless you are already in the same context as the object. If the context is a long name and you log in this way often, create a batch file.

- You can only use one /PR= option per logon. In other words, you can't run one profile login script, then another immediately after it.

- You cannot use /PR= in the same LOGIN command as the other options. In other words, you can't specify /S to run the commands in a file you've created and also specify /PR= to run a login script in an object.

Creating and Changing Login Scripts

To create new login scripts or change login scripts, first determine which type of login script you want to work with—system, profile, or personal. Then decide whether you want to use NetWare Administrator or NETADMIN to edit the login scripts. The steps for accessing the editing screens of each type of login script in NetWare Administrator are described here.

System login script Double-click the container where you want to create or edit the login script, then click the Login Script button.

Profile login script Create a profile object if it doesn't yet exist. Double-click the object and then edit the login script.

Personal login script In the NetWare Administrator, Double-click a user object, then click the Login Script button to open the login script editing window.

Editing Login Scripts

You can use editing keys like HOME, END, DEL, and the arrow keys to make changes to login scripts. In NETADMIN, the F5 (Mark) key is useful for highlighting a block of text you want to copy or delete. Press F5, then use the arrow keys to highlight the block of text you want to move or delete. Text removed with the DEL key is held in a buffer and can be inserted elsewhere by pressing the INS key.

There are a few rules for login scripts:

- Only users with the Supervisor right can edit the system login script. Users can edit their own personal login scripts unless that right has been revoked. Supervisors can grant any user the rights to change a profile login script.

- To run a DOS program from the login script, precede the executable program name with a pound sign (#). To run a DOS command in the login script, use the following form, replacing *filename* with the command to run:

    # COMMAND *filename* /C

- Text in a command line cannot exceed 150 characters. For clarity, try to use only 78 characters, which is the width of the edit window.

- Only one type of command per line is allowed, but you can place multiple drive maps on the same line, as in line 8 of the default login script listed earlier in this chapter. It is OK for the line to wrap to another line.

- Always make the login script command itself the first word on the command line.

Login Script Identifier Variables

Use variables in login scripts to customize login script commands for the type of machine used to log in, or the time and day of the login. Each variable is described briefly in Table 28-1. For example, you can assign a *long machine type* variable in the NET.CFG file, such as COMPAQ or IBMPS2. The login script can then use this variable to set up custom paths or execute special commands for computers assigned that name.

Some variables are automatically set by NetWare, such as the date and time. For example, the following WRITE command displays the message "Good Morning", "Good Afternoon", or "Good Evening". The variable

Variable	Description
Time and Date	
SECOND	Holds the current second (00-59)
MINUTE	Holds the current minute (00-59)
HOUR	Holds the current hour (1-12)
HOUR24	Holds the current hour in 24-hour time (00-23)
AM_PM	Holds the day or night specifier (a.m. or p.m.)
GREETING_TIME	This variable is either morning, afternoon, or evening, depending on the time of day
DAY	Holds the current day as a number (01-31)
NDAY_OF_WEEK	Holds the current weekday number (1-7, Sunday is 1)
DAY_OF_WEEK	Holds the day of the week in full format (Sunday, Monday, and so on)
MONTH	Holds the current month as a number (01-12)
MONTH_NAME	Holds the current month's name in full (January, February, and so on)
YEAR	Holds the year in full format (for example, 1993)
SHORT_YEAR	Holds the short format of the year (for example, 93)
User Information	
LOGIN_NAME	Holds the current user's login name
FULL_NAME	Holds the current user's full name
USER_ID	Number assigned to the current user
PASSWORD_EXPIRES	Number of days before password expires
LAST_NAME	The user's last name
Workstation Information	
STATION	Holds the number of the workstation

Table 28-1.   *Login Script Identifier Variables*

Variable	Description
Workstation Information	
P_STATION	Holds the 12-digit hex number of the physical workstation
MACHINE	The long machine name given to a workstation in the NET.CFG file with the command LONG MACHINE TYPE =
SMACHINE	The short machine name given to a machine by the NET.CFG file with the command SHORT MACHINE TYPE =
SHELL_TYPE	Version number of the shell or requester software
NETWARE_ REQUESTER	Holds the version number of the OS/2 requester
Network Information	
NETWORK_ADDRESS	The number of the network segment the workstation is attached to
FILE_SERVER	Name of the file server
Operating System Information	
OS	Holds the workstation's operating system (PCDOS, MSDOS)
OS_VERSION	Holds the version of the workstation's operating system (for example, v3.3, v5.0)
Conditional Commands	
ACCESS_SERVER	Returns True if access server is functional, otherwise returns False

Table 28-1. *Login Script Identifier Variables (continued)*

Variable	Description
Conditional Commands	
ERROR_LEVEL	A value indicating errors that have occurred; the error 0 indicates no errors
MEMBER OF "group"	Returns True if user is member of group, otherwise returns False
NOT MEMBER OF "group"	Returns True if a user is not a member of a group
Other	
%*n*	Pulls a variable from the LOGIN command line. Each word following "LOGIN" is numbered from 0 through 9. For example, in the login command LOGIN JJONES NEWS, JJONES is variable %0 and NEWS is variable %1. The login script might test for "NEWS" as variable %1 and display recent news within the company

Table 28-1.   *Login Script Identifier Variables* (continued)

%GREETING_TIME inserts "Morning", "Afternoon", or "Evening" based on the current time of day.

```
WRITE "Good %GREETING_TIME"
```

Most of the variables are used with the WRITE command. WRITE displays any text between quotation marks as messages. When used in this way, variables must be typed in uppercase and preceded with a percent sign, as shown in the previous example.

Variables in login scripts can cause the scripts to execute differently for every user, depending on the values the user's environment supplies. For example, the login script can execute a set of commands if a user belongs to a group, such as managers or clerks. The names of groups a user belongs to are pulled from the user's object during the login process.

NOTE: To include a variable in a WRITE command text string, type it in uppercase, as shown in line 1 of the default login script listed earlier. For clarity, and to make your login script easier to examine at a later time, type all variables in uppercase.

Some information comes from the environment of the user's workstation, such as the DOS type and version number. The NET.CFG file can include parameters that specify what variables should be. A good example is the LONG MACHINE TYPE= option, which names the machine type. By default, all machines have the name IBM_PC, but you can specify other names such as COMPAQ or IBMPS2. The following command, inserted in the NET.CFG file, gives a computer the name AST:

```
LONG MACHINE TYPE=AST
```

The login script identifier variable MACHINE now holds this value. Typically, you use the value to set a path to a directory that holds the DOS version used by the machine. For example, you map a drive in login scripts with a command similar to the following:

```
MAP INS S2:=SYS:PUBLIC\%MACHINE\%OS\%OS_VERSION
```

If, for example, the user is at a workstation with the name COMPAQ and using MS-DOS 5.0, this command would map the second search drive to SYS:PUBLIC\COMPAQ\MSDOS\5.0.

Login Script Commands

The following sections explain each of the login script commands and options. Some command-specific examples are given. See the section "Login Script Examples" at the end of the chapter for examples of how you can use the commands in the context of a complete login script.

- External Program Execution

You can execute external commands from a login script if you place the pound sign (#) in front of the command. The command takes the following form,

 # path/command parameters...

where *path* is the mapped drive letter or full path name where the command file is located. Replace *command* with the name of the executable file, and replace *parameters* with any parameters required to execute the program. Map all necessary search drives before executing external program execution commands. Use the option to execute NetWare commands like CAPTURE.

NOTE: *Starting major programs like word processors or spreadsheets from the login script can cause "out of memory" errors. Use the EXIT command and/or create a menu as discussed in Chapter 29.*

External command execution is different from command execution performed by the EXIT command. The login script is held in memory while the external program is running, and the remainder of the script resumes execution when the external program ends or is exited. The EXIT command ends the login script.

Examples

In the following example, a program called INSET is executed during a user's login script. Note that a search drive is first mapped to the directory where the program is located.

```
MAP S16:=SYS:INSET
# INSET
```

In the next example, the PCONSOLE program is started when a print queue operator with the login name PRINT-OP logs in. The IF...THEN...ELSE BEGIN login script command executes the PCONSOLE command only if the user has the login name "PRINT-OP".

```
IF LOGIN_NAME = "PRINT-OP" THEN BEGIN
    # PCONSOLE
END
```

An important command to include in login scripts is WSUPDATE. You typically use it to update workstation driver and shell files like IPXODI.COM or any other file that you need to update on a large number of NetWare client machines. The following command updates IPXODI.COM from the first search drive, which is usually PUBLIC:

```
#WSUPDATE S1:IPXODI.COM /LOCAL
```

Another command to execute is CAPTURE. The following example executes a CAPTURE command that sends files through LPT1 to printer HP-LASER.

```
#CAPTURE L=1 P=HP-LASER
```

ATTACH

Use the ATTACH command to attach to a bindery-based file server that is running NetWare v.2.x or NetWare v.3.x. The command is not necessary with NetWare v.4 servers. The command takes the following form,

ATTACH *servername/username;password*

where *servername* is the name of the server to attach to, *username* is the login name of the current user on the server, and *password* is the password required to gain access to the system.

ATTACH can be used in system login scripts to attach all users in the context to a bindery-based server, but do not include the *password* variable in the command. In this way each user is prompted for a password and security is not compromised. Users who need to attach to other servers on a regular basis should place the command in their personal login scripts.

Examples

The following command is placed in a JColgan personal login script to attach him to the server ACCTG:

```
ATTACH ACCTG/JColgan
```

BREAK

When the BREAK ON command is included in a login script, users logging in can stop the script by pressing CTRL-BREAK or CTRL-C. The BREAK OFF command is used to prevent a break in the login script.

This command is typically included when testing login scripts, or to provide a way to stop the execution of certain commands when you don't want to execute them for the current session. Place PAUSE and WAIT commands before the point you want to break so the script pauses. Then you can press CTRL-BREAK or CTRL-C to stop the login script, or any other key to continue with commands. All commands after the break do not execute.

The command takes the following forms:

BREAK ON

BREAK OFF

NOTE: When BREAK ON is specified, type-ahead keyboard input is not saved in the buffer.

Note that BREAK can be turned on for small segments of a login script, and then turned off again to prevent break-out.

CLS

CLS is the clear screen command for login scripts. Use it to clear off any screen information for displaying messages. The cursor jumps to the top left of the screen. Simply include CLS as a line in the login script.

COMSPEC

Use the COMSPEC command to specify the directory where the DOS COMMAND.COM file exists. Do not use this command on OS/2 workstations. When you enter an application, some of the DOS code in memory is discarded to create room for the application. When you exit the application, this DOS code must be replaced by executing COMMAND.COM again. COMSPEC specifies where COMMAND.COM is located. COMMAND.COM can be on a local DOS drive or on the server's hard drives.

The COMSPEC command takes the following forms:

COMSPEC=*drive*:COMMAND.COM

Here, *drive* is a local drive or the letter of a mapped directory where COMMAND.COM exists. You also can enter the command in the following form:

COMSPEC=S*n*:COMMAND.COM

Here, S*n* is the number of a previously mapped search drive.
Another form of the command is

COMSPEC=**n*:COMMAND.COM

Here, *n* is the directory where the *n*th network drive maps. Refer to the MAP command description in Chapter 25.

Examples

The following examples show how you can use the MAP command to map a search drive before you execute the COMSPEC command. In this way the COMSPEC command can include the letter of the search drive. Note that the %MACHINE variable holds the name of the directory specified in the workstation's SHELL.CFG file with the LONG MACHINE TYPE command.

```
MAP S3:=SYS:PUBLIC\%MACHINE\%OS\%OS_VERSION
COMSPEC=S3:COMMAND.COM
```

In the next example, the third network drive is mapped to a subdirectory of PUBLIC that matches the name specified in the identifier variable %MACHINE.

```
MAP *3:=SYS:PUBLIC\%MACHINE
COMSPEC=*3:COMMAND.COM
```

In this example, COMSPEC is specified on the local A drive:

```
COMSPEC=A:COMMAND.COM
```

CONTEXT

The CONTEXT command displays the current context and can be used to change the user's context in the Directory Services tree. You can use this command to change the context for the specific user logging in. The command takes the form,

> CONTEXT *context*

where *context* is the location in the directory tree where the user should be placed. Once a user is set in a particular context, he or she will see objects and containers at that level of the tree when using commands like NLIST, NETUSER, NETADMIN, and the NetWare Administrator.

You can use IF THEN statements to specify the context, based on the groups a user belongs to or a variable pulled from the command line (see % *n* in Table 28-1).

NOTE: CONTEXT in login scripts is different from specifying NAME CONTEXT in the workstation's NET.CFG file. The NET.CFG settings would change the context for any user logging in at that workstation. The CONTEXT command in a user login script sets the context for the specific user. Use NAME CONTEXT in the NET.CFG file to set the context so users can simply type their login names without typing a lot of additional context information.

Examples

The following command demonstrates how you would switch a user to the DivWest department in the CambrianCorp organization:

```
CONTEXT OU=DivWest.O=CambrianCorp
```

DISPLAY and FDISPLAY

The DISPLAY and FDISPLAY commands display the contents of text files. These text files can hold important login information, messages from managers, or messages from the network supervisor. For example, a message could inform users when a network server is down for maintenance. Use a text editor or word processor to create the text files displayed by DISPLAY or FDISPLAY. Note the following:

■ DISPLAY shows the entire contents of a file, including codes used for formatting. Only use DISPLAY with "pure" ASCII text files. FDISPLAY filters out formatting codes present in some word processed files.

■ For best results, save all messages you intend to display with DISPLAY or FDISPLAY as text-only, nonformatted files.

■ Use the DISPLAY and FDISPLAY commands when you need to display large blocks of text. The WRITE command, covered later, is best for one or two lines of text.

The commands take the following forms:

DISPLAY *path/filename*

FDISPLAY *path/filename*

Here, *path* is the full path to the file (or a mapped drive letter), and *filename* is the name of the text file created by an editor or word processing program.

Examples

In the following example, a text file called DAILY.DOC that contains important daily messages is displayed for users:

```
DISPLAY DAILY.DOC
```

Use the IF...THEN...ELSE to display messages only under certain conditions; for example, if the user is the member of a group or if the day is Friday. The next example assumes a text file exists in a directory called SYS:NEWS for each day of the week. The %DAY_OF_WEEK identifier variable is replaced with the name of the current day, which then matches a text file of the same name, such as MONDAY.DOC or TUESDAY.DOC. Of course, you can update the daily files as necessary. Note the use of the percent sign to specify the identifier variable in the command.

```
DISPLAY SYS:NEWS\%DAY_OF_WEEK.DOC
```

The following example uses the IF...THEN...ELSE statement in another form to display a message if the day is Monday:

```
IF DAY_OF_WEEK = "MONDAY" THEN DISPLAY SYS:NEWS\MEETINGS.DOC
```

The next example displays the message file COMPAQ.DOC in the SYS:NEWS directory if the workstations logging in have the machine name COMPAQ:

```
IF MACHINE = "COMPAQ" THEN DISPLAY SYS:NEWS\COMPAQ.DOC
```

DOS BREAK

Use the DOS BREAK command to specify that you can interrupt DOS commands with CTRL-BREAK or CTRL-C. This command is not the same as the BREAK ON command, which is used to interrupt a login script. The command takes the forms:

DOS BREAK ON

DOS BREAK OFF

The default is DOS BREAK OFF. See your DOS manual for more information.

DRIVE

Use the DRIVE command in a login script to switch users to a mapped drive. Normally, the first drive mapped becomes the default drive for the user after the login script completes. Typically, this is drive F and it is mapped to the user's home directory (although this is not mandatory). To switch to another mapped drive, you use the DRIVE command. It is sometimes necessary to do this when you are running commands that execute only if users are in the directory where the commands are located. After executing such commands, include another DRIVE command to place the users back in their personal directories.

The DRIVE command takes the form,

DRIVE *n*:

where *n* is a drive letter or,

DRIVE **n*:

where *n* is a drive number. In the first form the command switches to a drive that was mapped earlier in the login script. In the second form, the user is switched to the *n*th drive, which is a drive that may have been reordered due to the deletion of a previously mapped drive.

Examples

The following command switches a user to drive R, which was mapped by a previous command in the login script:

```
DRIVE R:
```

EXIT

The EXIT command stops the execution of the remaining commands in a login script. Usually you use the command with an IF...THEN...ELSE statement after a condition is evaluated as True or False. For example, an EXIT command may stop the login script for a user if that user is a member of a group, such as a group called TEMPORARY that includes the temporary personnel for a company. Any commands that follow the EXIT command are not executed. Do not use this command at OS/2 workstations.

NOTE: If you have changed the long machine name to a name other than the default, which is IBM_PC, include the PCCOMPATIBLE command before the EXIT command.

The EXIT command can take this form:

EXIT

Or the command can take this form,

EXIT "*filename*"

where *filename* in the second form is the name of an executable file with the extension COM, EXE, or BAT. For example, you can run a menu program after exiting the login script, as covered in the next chapter.

Here are some rules for using EXIT:

■ The PCCOMPATIBLE command must be placed before the EXIT command for non-IBM DOS systems.

■ The command specified with EXIT must be located in the current directory or in a mapped search drive.

■ The path to a command can be specified with EXIT, but the complete path and command cannot exceed 14 characters. The next rule also applies in this case.

■ If backslashes are used with commands, they must be typed twice to differentiate them from backslashes used in other NetWare commands. A double backslash counts as a single character.

Examples

Use EXIT by itself while writing and testing login scripts to exit the script and prevent subsequent commands from actually executing.

In the following example, a batch file called MENU.BAT is executed when exiting the login script:

```
EXIT "MENU"
```

The most common way to use the EXIT command is after evaluating a certain condition with the IF...THEN...ELSE command. In the following example, if a user belongs to the group TEMPORARY, the login script stops and executes a batch file called TEMPS.BAT. This batch file might switch temporary personnel to a special data directory and start the application program that they are assigned to work with, such as a database entry program.

```
IF MEMBER OF "TEMPORARY" THEN EXIT "TEMPS"
```

FIRE PHASERS

Use the FIRE PHASERS command to generate sounds that alert users to messages on the screen. The command takes the following form,

FIRE PHASERS *n* TIMES

where *n* is the number of times you want to fire the phasers.

Examples

The phasers are fired five times in the following example:

```
FIRE PHASERS 5 TIMES
```

Fire phasers only under certain conditions by using the IF THEN BEGIN command. In the following example, a WRITE command displays a message, phasers are fired, and the PAUSE command pauses execution of the login script so the user can read the message.

```
IF DAY_OF_WEEK = "Monday" THEN BEGIN
    WRITE "Meetings are every Monday at 3:00"
    FIRE PHASERS 2 TIMES
    PAUSE
END
```

GOTO

The GOTO command lets you branch to a different part of the login script, usually when a condition evaluated by the IF...THEN command is met. For example, you could include the following command to branch to a label called MANAGER: if the user belongs to a group called managers:

```
IF MEMBER OF "MANAGERS" THEN GOTO MANAGERS
```

The label that the command branches to must include a colon, as shown here:

```
MANAGERS:
```

NOTE: Do not use GOTO within multi-line IF...THEN commands.

IF...THEN

The IF...THEN command is one of the most useful commands for login scripts. You can use it to execute commands only when a specific condition is met. An IF...THEN command evaluates the truth or equality of a condition, then executes commands if true. For example, in the FIRE PHASERS example, a WRITE command and FIRE PHASERS are executed if the day of the week is Monday.

The IF...THEN command takes the form:

IF *conditional(s)* [AND;OR;NOR] THEN *command*

The ELSE Option

In the next example, the optional ELSE is used on a separate line, followed by an END command to close the IF...THEN.

IF *conditional(s)* [AND;OR;NOR] THEN
   (*commands to execute*)
   ELSE
   (*commands to execute*)
END

The *conditional* argument is evaluated, and if true, the *commands* following the THEN statement are executed. If false, the *commands* following the optional ELSE statement are executed. You can include another IF statement after ELSE to evaluate a true condition for executing commands under ELSE. If not true, then the entire IF...THEN...ELSE command sequence is bypassed. You must place an END statement at the end of the sequence for each IF...THEN command.

The BEGIN option

In this next example, if the condition is true, a series of commands are executed on one or more lines following a BEGIN statement until the END statement is encountered. If the condition is false, the commands are skipped, and processing of the login script continues with commands following the END statement.

IF *conditional(s)* THEN BEGIN
    (*commands to execute if true*)
END

Examples

The IF...THEN command typically evaluates the condition of identifier variables. Here are three examples:

```
IF DAY_OF_WEEK="Monday" THEN ...

IF MEMBER OF "TEMPS" THEN ...

IF NOT MEMBER OF "TEMPS" THEN ...
```

The first example is similar to the statements previously described under the FIRE PHASERS command. The commands following THEN are executed if the day of the week is Monday. In the second example, commands are executed if the user is a member of the group TEMPS. The last example is just the opposite—commands are executed only if the user is *not* a member of the group TEMPS.
    Note the following:

■ Values of conditionals must be enclosed in quotation marks.

■ A WRITE command must be on a separate line.

■ You can nest up to ten IF...THEN statements.

■ END must be included when the IF...THEN statements have a BEGIN and use more than one line.

You can place the IF...THEN command anywhere in a login script, and you can use it more than once. As mentioned, the command takes two forms. In the first form, the entire statement takes up one line, as shown here:

```
IF DAY_OF_WEEK = "Monday" THEN WRITE "Wake up, you!"
```

The second form of the command encompasses two or more lines between BEGIN and END statements. All commands between BEGIN and END are executed if the condition is true. Each command must be typed on a separate line. In the following example, MAP commands are executed if a user is a member of the group MANAGERS. Note that indenting sets off the commands between IF and END for clarity.

```
IF MEMBER OF "MANAGERS" THEN BEGIN
    MAP H:=SYS:MGR-DATA
    MAP I:=SYS:ACCTDATA
    MAP INS S3:=SYS:MGR-PROG
END
```

Since the mapped drives and search drives are only meant for managers, users who belong to the group MANAGERS will get the drive mappings. You can write similar statements for other groups.

Conditional Relationships

Six relationships can be evaluated with the IF...THEN command. These are listed in Table 28-2. In addition, you can use AND, OR, and NOR to form compound conditionals in which commands execute only if all the conditions are true together. In the following example, the manager's news file is displayed if the user belongs to the manager group and if the day is Monday:

```
IF MEMBER OF "MANAGERS" AND DAY_OF_WEEK = "Monday" THEN
DISPLAY SYS:NEWS\MGRNEWS
```

NOTE: The preceding command should be typed on one line.

Symbol	Relationship
=	Equal to
<>	Not equal to
>	Greater than
<	Less than
>=	Greater than or equal to
<=	Less than or equal to

Table 28-2.   *Relationships Evaluated by IF...THEN...ELSE*

Evaluating Command-Line Parameters

Parameters from the command line, such as the server name and user login name, are variables you can capture and use in login scripts. Each parameter has a parameter number. The command itself (LOGIN) is parameter %0. The second parameter is parameter %1, and so on. For example, in the following command, the server name EMAIL is parameter %1 and JJONES is parameter %2:

```
LOGIN EMAIL/JJONES
```

To use a parameter in a login script, simply insert its identifier variable in a command. For example, if JJONES types the following to log in:

```
LOGIN STARSHIP/JJONES ACCTG
```

Parameter %3 (ACCTG) can be used in the login script with a command like the one shown next to attach the user to the server.

```
IF %3="ACCTG" ATTACH ACCTG
```

This command would be interpreted as "If parameter %3 is equal to ACCTG, attach to the ACCTG server." You can simplify this to "ATTACH %3."

Evaluating Group Membership Conditions

You can evaluate whether a user is or is not a member of a group using the MEMBER OF or NOT MEMBER OF options with your IF...THEN commands. The commands take the following forms:

IF MEMBER OF "*groupname*" THEN *command*

IF NOT MEMBER OF "*groupname*" THEN *command*

Here, *groupname* is the name of the group the user belongs to, and *command* is the command to execute if the user is a member (or is not a member). The two examples below demonstrate how to use these commands on a single command line. They can also be used with block commands that use BEGIN and END.

```
IF MEMBER OF "SALES" THEN MAP T:=SYS:SALES

IF NOT MEMBER OF "TEMPS" THEN MAP J:=SYS:USERNEWS
```

INCLUDE

The INCLUDE command causes the login script to execute a set of commands in an external login script file. You can create this file with any text editor. For example, if you have a long set of commands to execute for a group of managers, you could place those commands in a text file called MANAGERS.LOG, then call that file from within a system login script. The command takes the form,

INCLUDE *path\filename*

where *path* is the path to the directory where the text file exists, and *filename* is the name of the file. This path must include the context name and Directory Services tree path if the file is stored on a volume outside of the current user's context. You can also run the login script of another object by using INCLUDE in the following form:

INCLUDE *objectname*

Replace *objectname* with the name of the user object or container object that contains the login script you want to run. If that object is outside the current context, include the path to the context and make sure any users who run the login script have Read and Open rights to it.

Some tips and techniques for using INCLUDE are listed here.

- If your login scripts are small, you probably won't need INCLUDE. But if they grow in size, you might want to break up the login script for clarity.

- Use INCLUDE to specify group login commands. For example, you could include the following command to run an external file for members of the Sales department. If you need to change the login commands for members of Sales, you edit SALES.LOG, not the main login script.

```
IF MEMBER OF "SALES" THEN INCLUDE SALES.LOG
```

- Since files called by INCLUDE are external text files, you can designate a user to make changes to the file. For instance, in the preceding example, the file might include WRITE commands that display messages about upcoming meetings or events. You can designate an administrative assistant to make those changes with a text editor, and he or she won't need to start NetWare Administrator or NETADMIN to make changes.

- If you are testing login scripts, you might want to place untested commands in an external file to simplify editing. It's often easier to change the external login files with a text editor than it is to load NetWare Administrator or NETADMIN for editing.

- Under NetWare Directory Services, potentially every container object can have its own login script. Chances are good that many of these scripts will have some commands in common, so you can add those common commands to a text file that you call from a container login script.

- You can nest INCLUDE statements up to ten levels deep.

- Users must have File Scan and Read rights to the file called by the INCLUDE command.

Examples

In the following example the file MANAGERS.LOG in the SYS:PUBLIC directory is included in the login script:

```
INCLUDE SYS:PUBLIC\MANAGERS.DAT
```

This next example calls a set of commands in a file called COMMON.LOG. Assume for this example that the file is created by the network administrator, and it contains commands that the administrator wants departmental supervisors to include in their container login scripts. The file is located in the administrator's context, which supervisors don't have access to. Therefore, only the administrator can alter the file, thus providing a network-wide set of commands that only the administrator controls. Of course, the administrator must make sure that departmental supervisors add the appropriate INCLUDE command to their departmental login scripts. Anyone needing access to this file from there login script will need File Scan and Read rights in the directory where the file exists. You can create a group called EVERYONE that includes all users on the network, then grant the EVERYONE group rights to the file.

```
MAP T:=.SYS.CAMBRIANCORP:LOGFILES
INCLUDE T:COMMON.LOG
```

To include a login script in another container, add an INCLUDE command similar to the following. In this example, the login script commands are in a file called MANAGERS.TXT in a directory called SCRIPTS.

```
INCLUDE SYS.SALES.DIVWEST.CAMBRIANCORP:SCRIPTS\MANAGERS.TXT
```

LASTLOGINTIME

Include the LASTLOGINTIME command in a login script to display the last time the user logged into the system.

MACHINE

Use the MACHINE command to specify the name of the machine where the user is logging in. The name may contain up to 15 characters. The command takes the form,

MACHINE = *name*

where *name* is the name you want to assign to the machine. The MACHINE command is often necessary for some programs written to run under PC DOS and does not apply to OS/2. The name can include identifier variables, as described earlier under "Login Script Identifier Variables."

MAP

The MAP command, as discussed in Chapter 16, is used extensively in login scripts to establish the mappings for all users and selected users. Recall that the IF...THEN...ELSE command can be used to map drives based on the groups a user belongs to and other identifier variables. For more information on MAP, see Chapter 25, or refer to the examples at the end of this chapter. There are two additional MAP options you can use in login scripts, MAP DISPLAY ON/OFF and MAP ERRORS ON/OFF.

MAP DISPLAY ON/OFF   As drives are mapped in a login script, they are displayed on the screen. Use this option to turn this display off to avoid screen clutter. If you want to display a user's drive mappings, include the MAP command on the last line of the login script.

MAP ERRORS ON/OFF   When errors are encountered during a login script, the error messages are not displayed if this command is used. In some cases you might use the IF...THEN...ELSE commands in a way that produces errors for some users even though the errors are not serious, since processing would continue with the next statement. You can use the MAP ERRORS OFF command to suppress the error messages. It is recommended that you not use this command until the login script has been completely tested and debugged.

These commands can be used anywhere within a login script; however, the OFF command must be used before the ON commands.

Mapping the "Next" Drive

It's not always a good idea to map a specific letter in the alphabet to a directory. For example, mapping drive F to a user's personal directory may work if the user logs in at a machine that has a last drive of D or E. But if the workstation has local drives called F, there will be a drive letter conflict. Use the nth drive option to overcome these problems when you're not sure of the drive lettering where a user is logging in.

An nth drive mapping takes the following form,

MAP *n:=path

where n is a number that specifies network drive 1, 2, and so on. In other words, the command MAP *1:=SYS:APPS is like saying "map the first network drive, whatever it may be, to the SYS:APPS directory." On some systems, that drive letter may be F, while on others it might be G or H. Remember that local drives can include hard disks, optical disks, and RAM disks, so the drive letters for local drives can get high.

Mapping Directory Map Objects

Recall that one of the objects available in NetWare Directory Services is the directory map object. The map object contains a drive mapping that you can change at any time. If you include the map object in login scripts, then you can easily change the mappings for all login scripts at the same time by changing the directory map object. It is usually necessary to change directory maps if you decide to move programs or files in directories that are mapped by many different login scripts. In the following example, the directory map object LOTUS in the Administration organizational object is mapped to search drive S3:

```
MAP S3:=CN=LOTUS.OU=Administration.OU=DivWest.O=CambrianCorp
```

Mapping to Another Context

Directories on volumes within a user's current context can be mapped by simply specifying the volume name and directory path. If you need to map a directory on another volume that is not in the same context as the user, you must specify that context. For example, the following command maps a directory called CUSTDATA on a volume and server in the Sales department to a user in the Administration department, assuming the Administration container is the user's current context.

```
MAP R:=CN=SYS.OU=Sales.OU=DivEast.O=CambrianCorp:CUSTDATA
```

NO_DEFAULT

Include this command in a system login script or a profile login script to prevent the default user login script from executing. A user's personal login script will still execute. Insert the command as shown here:

```
NO_DEFAULT
```

NOSWAP

Include the NOSWAP commmand to prevent LOGIN from being moved from conventional memory to high memory or onto disk when a workstation is low on memory. This causes a # command to fail, but the login script continues to execute.

PAUSE

You can use the PAUSE command to temporarily stop the login script from running, usually after displaying a message on the screen. Simply type **PAUSE** on a separate line. Processing continues when a key is pressed, or if the BREAK ON command was executed before PAUSE, users can break out of the login script by press CTRL-BREAK or CTRL-C.

Examples

In the following example the PAUSE command is placed after the WRITE command, which displays an extended message on the screen:

```
WRITE "Software licensing rules are enforced by the company."
PAUSE
```

PCCOMPATIBLE

Use the PCCOMPATIBLE command if the EXIT command does not work properly. The command designates non-IBM systems as compatible machines. If your machine is an IBM PC compatible but you have changed the long machine type in the NET.CFG file to another name in order to access a different version of DOS, you must use PCCOMPATIBLE in the login script.

Type the command in the login script before any EXIT commands as follows:

```
PCCOMPATIBLE
```

REMARK

You can use the REMARK command in a login script to include comments for your own use or for other users who may need to edit the scripts later. The command takes the following forms:

REMARK *text*

REM *text*

* *text*

; *text*

Here, *text* is the text to include in the remark. The REMARK command must be on its own line. REM in the following example is used to document the purpose of a series of MAP commands:

```
REM The following MAP commands are for managers only
```

SET

The DOS SET command creates variables that can be used in batch files after the login script has completed. You can use these variables in many of the same ways that you use identifier variables. The command takes the forms,

SET *name* = "*value*"

or

TEMP SET *name* = "*value*"

Here, *name* is the name of the variable, and *value* is the string that the variable is equal to. The value must be enclosed in quotation marks. Use the TEMP version of the command if you only want the variable to apply while the login script runs. For OS/2 workstations, the SET variables only apply while the login script runs.

While NetWare has an extensive set of its own identifier variables, DOS SET is often used to configure individual workstations for different programs. You can assign the NetWare identifier variable to DOS SET variables and use them later in batch files. In the following example, the NetWare identifier variable LOGIN_NAME is made equal to the DOS variable USER. The USER variable can then be used in batch files.

```
DOS SET USER=%LOGIN_NAME
```

SET_TIME

Include the SET_TIME command to set the time on the workstation to the same time as the server to which the user logged into. The command takes the form shown next, with the default setting of ON so that the workstation's time is always reset to the server's time.

SET_TIME ON/OFF

SWAP

Include this commmand to move LOGIN to high memory and free conventional memory so # commands can execute. If you specify a path, LOGIN is moved to disk.

WRITE

The WRITE command displays messages and other text. It can also be used with the identifier variables in a number of ways. The command takes the following forms:

WRITE "*text*"; *variable*

WRITE "*text %VARIABLE*"

In the first form the text to display is in quotation marks. An identifier variable can then be added to display one of the system variables. A semicolon separates text and variable. In the second form the same results are achieved, but all options are included within the quotation marks. Use semicolons to join several WRITE commands so they appear as a continuous block of text.

NOTE: When an identifier variable is used within quotation marks, it must be capitalized and preceded by a percent sign.

You can also use the following strings in WRITE commands:

\r Carriage return

\n New line

\" An embedded quotation mark

\7 A beep

The identifier variables that can be used with the WRITE command are listed in Table 28-1, earlier in this chapter. Enter each variable as shown, including the underscore characters if listed. WRITE replaces the identifier variable with the text or value identified by the variable.

Examples

The following example creates four blank lines, displays a greeting message for a user, and then creates four more blank lines:

```
WRITE "\n\n\n\nGood %GREETING_TIME, %LOGIN_NAME\n\n\n\n"
```

In the next command, identifier variables are used to display month, day, and year. Note that percent signs and uppercase letters are used because the identifier variable is within quotes. Also notice the use of the comma, which appears when the text is displayed.

```
WRITE "Today is %MONTH_NAME %DAY, %YEAR"
```

Login Script Examples

This section provides examples of login scripts that you can refer to when creating your own login scripts. The first script is the most basic. You might want to include it in a container object so it runs as a system login script for all users logging into the container. You can then let users customize their personal login scripts using NETADMIN or the NetWare Administrator. The lines are numbered only for convenient reference; they are not part of the commands.

```
 1.  MAP DISPLAY OFF
 2.  SET PROMPT = "$P$G"
 3.  MAP *1:=SYS:USERS\%LOGIN_NAME
 4.  IF OS2 THEN
 5.      MAP *2:=SYS:PUBLIC\OS2
 6.      ELSE MAP INS S1:=SYS:PUBLIC
 7.      MAP INS S2:=SYS:PUBLIC\%MACHINE\%OS\%OS_VERSION
 8.  END
 9.  COMSPEC=S2:COMMAND.COM
10.  MAP DISPLAY ON
11.  MAP
```

As mentioned, this is a basic login script, but you can build on it depending on your own needs. Each command is outlined here.

1. MAP DISPLAY OFF disables messages displayed by commands as they execute.

2. The SET PROMPT command sets the command prompt to display the current directory path.

3. This first command maps the user's personal directory to the first network drive letter. The *1 designates the first drive letter.

4. This command starts the IF...THEN command for lines 4 through 8. If the user is logging in from an OS/2 workstation, the 5th line executes, otherwise the 6th and 7th lines execute.

5. This command maps the second network drive to the \PUBLIC\OS2 directory for OS/2 users. Lines 6 and 7 are not executed for OS/2 users.

6. This command executes if the workstation is not an OS/2 workstation. It maps the PUBLIC directory to the first search drive (Z:).

7. This command maps the second search drive to a directory that holds the DOS version matching the DOS running on the user's workstation.

   For example, if the user logged in from an IBM PC workstation running DOS version 5.0, this command would map the second search drive to \PUBLIC\IBM_PC\MSDOS\5.0.

8. This ends the IF...THEN...ELSE command in line 4.

9. This sets the path to the COMMAND.COM file for DOS workstations. The search drive specified in line 7 is used.

10. This turns the display of messages back on.

11. This displays the current maps for the user.

The next example is more elaborate. It includes commands to display greeting messages and maps drives and search drives according to the groups users belong to. This login script is designed for container or profile objects.

```
 1.   MAP DISPLAY OFF
 2.   SET PROMPT = "$P$G"
 3.   MAP *1:=SYS:USERS\%LOGIN_NAME
 4.   IF OS2 THEN
 5.       MAP *2:=SYS:PUBLIC\OS2
 6.       ELSE MAP INS S1:=SYS:PUBLIC
 7.       MAP INS S2:=SYS:PUBLIC\%MACHINE\%OS\%OS_VERSION
 8.   END
 9.   COMSPEC=S2:COMMAND.COM
10.   PCCOMPATIBLE
11.   MAP *3:=SYS:PUB-DATA
12.   MAP INS S16:=SYS:APPS\LOTUS
13.   MAP INS S16:=SYS:APPS\WORD
14.   IF MEMBER OF "TEMPS" THEN BEGIN
15.       MAP F:=VOL1:ACCTDATA
16.       MAP INS S1:=VOL1:ACCTPROG
17.       DRIVE F:
18.       EXIT "START"
19.   END
20.   IF MEMBER OF "MANAGERS" THEN BEGIN
21.       MAP *4:=SYS:MGR-DATA
22.       MAP INS S6:=SYS:MGR-PROG
23.   END
24.   WRITE "\n\n\n\nGood %GREETING_TIME, %LOGIN_NAME\n\n\n\n"
```

```
25.   DISPLAY SYS:NEWS\%DAY_OF_WEEK.DOC
26.   PAUSE
27.   IF DAY_OF_WEEK="MONDAY" THEN DISPLAY
SYS:NEWS\MEETINGS.DOC
28.   PAUSE
29.   MAP DISPLAY ON
30.   EXIT "MENU MAIN"
```

This login script makes effective use of group names to assign drive and search mappings to users according to the groups they belong to. The lines are described here.

Lines 1 through 9   These are the same commands used in the previous example to set up a typical environment.

Line 10   The PCCOMPATIBLE enables the EXIT command in line 30 to execute on workstations that don't have the name IBM_PC.

Lines 11 through 13   These commands map data directories and program directories accessed by all user objects in the container.

Lines 14 through 19   These commands map an accounting data directory and its program directory for a group of temporary clerks (called TEMPS) with limited rights. Line 17 switches the TEMPS user to drive F; then line 18 exits the login script and runs START.BAT, which starts the accounting program.

Lines 20 through 23   These commands execute special drive mappings for users who belong to the MANAGERS group.

NOTE: You could use an INCLUDE statement to call an external file that has a set of commands for managers or other groups.

Line 24   A greeting message is displayed with the user's name included.

Lines 25 through 28   A greeting message is displayed that matches the day of the week, with a pause after each message.

Line 29   This command sets map display back on.

Line 30 This command exits the login script and starts the menu program called Main.

Displaying Login and Station Information

You can place the following commands in the system login script to display information about a system and the user who logs in. This information may be useful to the supervisor or technician who is attempting to resolve problems or assist a user. Insert the commands at the end of the login script so the information they display is not overwritten by other commands and include a PAUSE if necessary so you can read the screen.

```
WRITE "Login name = %LOGIN_NAME"
WRITE "User ID = %USER_ID"
WRITE "Workstation = %STATION"
WRITE "Workstation address = %P_STATION"
WRITE "Machine name = %MACHINE"
WRITE "Network address = %NETWORK_ADDRESS"
WRITE "File server name = %FILE_SERVER"
WRITE "OS Type = %OS"
WRITE "OS version = %OS_VERSION"
```

CHAPTER 29

T he NetWare menu system (hereafter called NMENU) helps you create menus to start programs or execute commands. You're already familiar with the types of menus NMENU can create if you've used any of the text-based utilities, such as NETADMIN, PARTMGR, FILER, and others. Basically, a menu consists of a main set of options that either execute commands directly or display a submenu with more options.

The NetWare Menu System

NOTE: NMENU is a product of Saber Software Corporation. An advanced version of this product is available by calling 800-338-8754 or 214-361-8086.

The basic steps for creating a menu are, first, to create a text file with commands that specify the following:

- The options on the main menu

- Commands that execute when a user selects an option

- Options on submenus, if they are called by a main menu command

The file must be an ASCII text file saved with the extension SRC. After creating the file, you compile it using the MENUMAKE command, then run the menu by typing **NMENU** followed by the menu's name. You can run menus from users' login scripts with the EXIT command.

A Sample Menu to Get You Started

In this section, you'll see how to create a simple menu just to become familiar with the steps. Details about the commands and options you can use in menu files are covered later under "NMENU Command Details." The menu you'll create in this example is pictured in Figure 29-1.

- When you select A on the USER OPTIONS menu, your current rights to directories are listed. The option executes an NDIR command in the background.

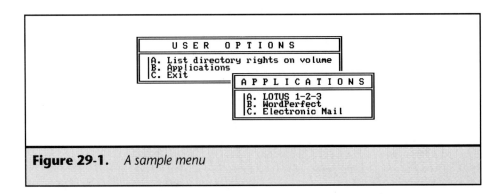

Figure 29-1.   *A sample menu*

- Item B on the USER OPTIONS menu displays the APPLICATIONS submenu, as shown in Figure 29-1, with three program options.
- Item C on the USER OPTIONS menu exits to DOS.

NOTE: You don't need to include an Exit option on menus. Without it, users can't exit to DOS, which is often beneficial for security reasons. Alternatively, you can include an Exit option that immediately logs the user off, as you'll see later. When testing menus, be sure to include an Exit option, at least temporarily so you can get out of the menu.

Step 1: Create a Directory for Temporary Files

Start by creating a directory where you want to store all the menu files. A good location for the menus is in a subdirectory of the PUBLIC directory called MENUS. All users who run menus in this directory must be trustees with Read, File Scan, Write, and Create rights.

Step 2: Create Temporary Directory Pointers

Next, modify your login script and the login script of any user who will use the menu by adding the following commands. The first command establishes the location where the menu program can store temporary files. The second command ensures that each user's temporary files are unique, which is important if all users will store temporary files in the same directory. If you want to store files somewhere else, specify the directory name.

```
SET S_FILEDIR="Z:\\PUBLIC\\MENUS\\"
SET S_FILE = "%STATION"
```

NOTE: Drive Z is used in this example because it is usually mapped as the first search drive and points to the PUBLIC directory.

After changing the login script, you can log in again to activate the new settings, or you can just type them at the command prompt without rebooting. If you type them at the command prompt, don't type the quotes and type only one backslash instead of two in the first command above.

Step 3: Create the Menu Text File

The commands that execute the menu must be placed in a standard ASCII text file. You can use the DOS EDIT command or other similar text editors to create the file. It must have the extension SRC. For this example, type in the commands shown next, but first switch to the SYS:PUBLIC\MENUS directory or the directory where you've decided to store the menu.

NOTE: Lines in the sample commands are indented for clarity. If a line is indented under another, it typically executes the option specified in the line above it.

```
MENU 1, U S E R   O P T I O N S
   ITEM List directory rights on volume {PAUSE}
      EXEC NDIR \*.* /R /DO /S
   ITEM Applications
      SHOW 2
   ITEM Exit
      EXEC EXIT
MENU 2, A P P L I C A T I O N S
   ITEM LOTUS 1-2-3
      EXEC LOTUS
   ITEM WordPerfect
      EXEC WP
   ITEM Electronic Mail
      EXEC Email
```

The first line sets up the main menu, or MENU 1, and gives it the name "USER OPTIONS." The name is character-spaced for esthetic reasons only. The next six lines under the MENU 1 header are the item lines that appear on the main menu, and under each of these item lines are the commands that execute when you choose the option on the menu. The EXEC and SHOW lines are the actual executable command lines in the menu file. Note the following:

- MENU and ITEM lines are *organizational.* They set the content and organization of menus.

- EXEC, SHOW, and other commands (described later in the chapter) are *control commands* that perform actions.

- The first ITEM line executes the NDIR command under it if selected from the menu.

- "ITEM Applications" executes the command SHOW 2, which jumps to line 8 and executes the MENU 2 line.

- "ITEM Exit" causes the EXEC EXIT command to execute, which returns the user to the command prompt.

- "MENU 2" and the lines under it display the APPLICATIONS menu you see in Figure 29-1. The EXEC commands under each ITEM line execute the commands that start the programs. Other information and commands may be necessary here, such as the path and commands that switch to mapped program or data directories.

NOTE: The commands under MENU 2 are examples only. You can substitute commands that work on your system, depending on the applications you use.

After you type in the commands, save the file with the name USER.SRC.

Step 4: Compile the Menu

Now you are ready to compile the menu. At the DOS prompt, type the following, assuming you are still in the same directory as the USER.SRC file:

```
MENUMAKE USER
```

MENUMAKE converts the SRC file to a DAT file. In a moment, you'll see a message that USER.DAT has been written. This indicates the menu was created successfully. If error messages are displayed, check the text file for spelling mistakes or incorrect lines, then try recompiling it.

NOTE: If MENUMAKE encounters a problem in your SRC file, it won't create the DAT file. Instead, it displays an error message with the line number where the error occurred in parentheses. Edit the file again and check the syntax of the line.

Step 5: Run and Test the Menu

To run the new menu, type the following command:

```
NMENU USER
```

Test the options on the menu to see how they work. Of course, the options on the APPLICATIONS menu will not work if you don't have the applications listed in Figure 29-1. If you specified your own applications, the options should execute. To execute menus from other directories, you can do one of the following:

- Move the DAT file to a directory that is already mapped to a search drive, such as SYS:PUBLIC. This doesn't waste search drive letters but moves the file out of the MENUS directory.

- Create a search drive mapping for the MENUS directory, which requires the use of a search drive letter.

- Map a drive to the current directory, then specify that drive letter when running the menu. For example, type the following to map drive H to the MENUS directory:

```
MAP H:=SYS:PUBLIC\MENUS
```

To run the menu, you then type the following:

```
NMENU H:USER
```

Step 6: Start the Menu from Login Scripts

Once your menu is created and working, add a command similar to the following at the end of users' login scripts to load the menu when they log on:

```
EXIT "NMENU USER"
```

Converting Menus Created Before NetWare v.4

If you have menus created with the menu utility in NetWare versions before version 4, follow this procedure to convert those menus to run under the new NMENU utility:

1. Create a directory for the menu files in which you and other users have the Read, File Scan, Write, and Create rights in the directory.

2. Execute the following command to convert the old MNU source files to the newer SRC format. Replace *name* with the name of the MNU file.

   MENUCNVT *name*

3. The file is converted to an SRC file. You can edit this file as necessary, then use the MENUMAKE command to compile it as discussed previously.

NMENU Command Details

Now we're ready to look at the menu commands in more detail. The rules for creating menus are listed here.

- The maximum number of menu levels is 11.
- The maximum number of menu screens is 255.
- The maximum number of characters in a menu name is 40.
- MENU 1 (the main menu) must be at the beginning, and all submenus it calls follow.
- Items on menus can be up to 60 characters in length.
- The maximum width of any line is 80 characters. If you approach the right edge, press ENTER and type a plus sign (+) to continue the same line.

The complete list of available menu commands follows. Remember that MENU and ITEM are organizational commands, and the rest are control commands that perform actions.

MENU Specifies a new menu

ITEM Specifies line items on menus

EXEC Executes a DOS command

SHOW Displays a submenu within the same menu program

LOAD Displays a menu in a different menu program

GETO   Requests optional information from users

GETP   Requests information and assigns it a variable so it can be used elsewhere

GETR   Requests required information from users

The MENU Command

The MENU command displays a new menu or submenu. The command takes the form,

MENU *number,name*

where *number* is the number of a submenu that you want to run, and *name* is any name you want to give it. You can call up to 255 submenus. The first menu is always number 1. Use the SHOW command to call a submenu.

The example menu text file shown earlier in "Step 3: Create the Menu Text File" shows two MENU commands. The first (MENU 1) displays the main menu with the heading USER OPTIONS. The second displays a submenu if "Applications" is chosen from the menu. A SHOW command under the ITEM line calls the menu.

The ITEM Command

Use the ITEM command to specify options on the menus created by the MENU command. ITEM takes the following form,

ITEM *name {options}*

where *name* is the name that appears as a line item in the menu, and *options* are one or more of the options listed next. Note that *name* can be up to 40 characters.

BATCH   Unloads the menu from memory to ensure the called program has enough memory to run

CHDIR   Returns user to original directory

NOECHO   Prevents operating system messages from displaying when the menu option is executed

PAUSE   Pauses output so user can read the display

SHOW   Displays the name of the command being executed

NOTE: if you include two or more options, you still only need one set of brackets; for example, {BATCH PAUSE}.

Note in Figure 29-1 that each item is assigned an alphabetic character to give users an easy way to select menu items. If you want to use different letters, type a caret (^) and the new letter immediately in front of the menu name. If the following changes are made to the USER.SRC menu file and the menu is recompiled, you see the menus with the new selection letters shown in Figure 29-2.

```
MENU 1, U S E R   O P T I O N S
  ITEM ^1List directory rights on volume {PAUSE}
    EXEC NDIR \*.* /R /DO /S
  ITEM ^aApplications
    SHOW 2
  ITEM ^xExit
    EXEC EXIT
MENU 2, A P P L I C A T I O N S
  ITEM ^1LOTUS 1-2-3
    EXEC LOTUS
  ITEM ^wWordPerfect
    EXEC WP
  ITEM ^eElectronic Mail
    EXEC Email
```

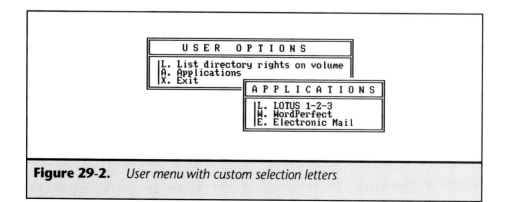

Figure 29-2.   *User menu with custom selection letters*

Using BATCH Options

Use the BATCH option to reduce the memory requirements of the menu system when running executable programs. If you don't specify the option, the menu system stays in memory while the application runs and can take up as much as 32KB of that memory. If you set the BATCH option, CHDIR (discussed next) is automatically set.

The options under MENU 2 are changed in the following example so that the menu system is removed from memory whenever a user runs one of the programs.

```
MENU 2, A P P L I C A T I O N S
   ITEM ^1LOTUS 1-2-3 {BATCH}
     EXEC LOTUS
   ITEM ^wWordPerfect {BATCH}
     EXEC WP
   ITEM ^eElectronic Mail {BATCH}
     EXEC Email
```

 CAUTION: Do not use this command with the EXEC DOS command discussed later. Use EXEC COMMAND to open a DOS session in which to run the command.

MEMORY TEST   Here's a menu example you can create that tests how much memory NMENU uses with and without the BATCH options. This is presented only as an example of a menu and a way to see how much memory the BATCH options save. Create the file, calling it MEMTEST, then compile it by typing **MENUMAKE MEMTEST**. Check the "Conventional memory" field of the display produced by each option for a memory comparison.

```
MENU 1, Memory Tests
ITEM MEM test with BATCH option {BATCH PAUSE}
EXEC MEM
ITEM MEM test without BATCH option {PAUSE}
EXEC MEM
ITEM Exit
EXEC EXIT
```

The CHDIR Option

Include the CHDIR option to ensure that the user is returned to the directory that is in effect before the EXEC commands under the ITEM line are executed. If you don't specify this option, the drive and directory switched to by the application remain in effect. You usually need this command to switch back to an original directory after using applications that change the directory.

The NOECHO Option

Include the NOECHO option to prevent messages from displaying. It works in the same way as the ECHO OFF command in DOS batch files. Use it when including DOS commands in menu options that display messages you don't want users to see.

The PAUSE Option

The PAUSE option is essential when running DOS commands from menu options. If you don't include it, users won't be able to see the last page of a screen display. For example, if a menu option executes a command to list files, those files will scroll off the screen, and the menu will be displayed before users can read the list. With the PAUSE command, the screen scrolling pauses, and the user sees the message "Press any key to continue."

The SHOW Option

The SHOW option simply displays the name of any DOS command that is being executed when a user selects a menu option with DOS commands. You might want to set this option when testing new menus so you can watch the progress of the commands. Otherwise, the default is not to show the commands.

The EXEC Command

The EXEC command performs actions when the ITEM option above it is selected. All EXEC commands between one ITEM line and another ITEM line are considered a set and executed when the ITEM is selected on the menu. For example, you might add the following lines to a menu to create an option that switches a user to a data directory that has been mapped to drive J and then starts the Microsoft Word program. Notice that the two commands are listed between ITEM lines. The indentation is for clarity only. Note that this example assumes Word and Lotus are on the search path.

```
ITEM Microsoft Word
   EXEC J:
   EXEC WORD
ITEM LOTUS 1-2-3
   EXEC K:
   EXEC LOTUS
```

The EXEC command takes the following form, where *command* is any command that runs a DOS program or utility:

EXEC *command*

You can also use EXEC in one of the following forms:

EXEC EXIT   You've already seen this command used in the previous examples. It provides an option so the user can exit the menu to DOS. Place it under an ITEM line called "ITEM Exit." You'll also need this command when creating and testing menus so you can get back to DOS yourself. When the menu is completely tested, you can remove this command if you don't want regular users to exit.

NOTE: If you don't include the EXEC EXIT command, you can't get out of a running menu, and consequently, you'll need to reboot the system. When security is required, use this command to prevent users from exiting the menu and working with DOS commands. Place the command that starts the menu in user's login scripts so the only environment they see is the menu and the commands it executes.

EXEC DOS   Use this command when you want to let users temporarily exit to DOS so they can use DOS commands. It starts a secondary processor, so users must type **EXIT** to return to the menu. Place this command under a menu option called "ITEM Use DOS Commands," or something similar.

EXEC LOGOUT   This command provides a graceful way to put an EXIT command in your menu, but prevent users from executing DOS commands in the network environment. Place this command under a menu line called "ITEM Exit and Log Out."

EXEC COMMAND   This command executes the DOS command processor and opens a DOS session for the execution of batch files or commands.

The SHOW Command

The SHOW command displays a submenu. You insert the command in a menu file in the form shown here, replacing *number* with the menu number you want to display.

SHOW *number*

For example, SHOW 5 displays the menu specified by the line MENU 5. In the example menu text file shown earlier under "Step 3: Create the Menu Text File," notice how the command SHOW 2 under the line "ITEM Applications" references the MENU 2 line, which displays the APPLICATIONS menu.

The LOAD Command

The LOAD command lets you call another menu program (one that has another filename). The command takes the form,

LOAD *filename*

where *filename* is the drive, path, and name of the menu program you want to run. For example, to load a menu program called APPS that displays a complete list of available applications, you would include the following commands:

```
ITEM Applications Menu
LOAD APPS
```

After another menu program is loaded, users can return to the original program by pressing ESC. This is the only time that users can actually escape out of a menu (but it still doesn't return them to DOS). If the loaded menu program contains an EXEC EXIT option, they are returned to DOS, not to the calling menu program.

The GETO, GETP, and GETR Commands

The GET options are used to request input from users. The input is used as parameters on the DOS command line. For example, you could request the parameters for NDIR, NLIST, and other NetWare commands. You can also request information that programs use when loading. For example, most word processors let you type in the name of a file to load along with the program. If you wanted to load the file REPORT.DOC in Microsoft Word, you would type **REPORT.DOC**. The filename in this case occupies a position on the command line known as parameter %1. The command itself is parameter %0. Each option on the command line is numbered sequentially. Any parameters you request with GETO, GETP, or GETR are placed in these parameter positions.

- The GETO option requests an optional response that users can bypass with their own response.

- The GETP option assigns a variable to user input such as %1, %2, and so on. It can then be used elsewhere in the menu file.

- The GETR option requires a response that the user can't bypass.

The commands take the following form:

GET*x prompt {prepend} length,prefill {append}*

- Replace *x* with either O, P, or R, depending on the command you use.

- Replace *prompt* with a text string that asks the user for input. For example, you could replace it with "Please type the file to load."

- Replace the optional *prepend* with a value that gets added to the beginning of the user response. For example, you could prepend the drive and directory path when asking users for the name of a file to load. If you don't want to prepend a value, type an open and close bracket { } in its place. If you want a blank space, enter the blank space between the brackets.

- Replace *length* with the maximum number of characters the user can type in the prompt. You must supply this value. However, replace it with 0 if this is an optional response (GETO) and the user only needs to press ENTER or ESC.

- Replace the optional *prefill* with a default response. The user can accept the default by pressing ENTER or change the response by editing the line. If you don't want to include a prefill, type a comma in its place.

■ Replace *append* with a value for the end of the user's response. If you don't want to append a value, type an open and close bracket { } in its place. If you want a blank space, enter the blank space between the brackets.

When a GETO, GETP, or GETR command runs, a dialog box appears in which users type the requested information. They can accept the default values you specify or press ENTER on a field to edit the contents of that field. Pressing F10 executes the options on the menu.

Examples

The first example creates a menu option that lists volume information. It requests the name of the server and the name of the volume to list. The commands to accomplish this are as follows:

```
ITEM List Volume Information {PAUSE}
   GETO Enter Server name: { } 20,PICKWICK,{\}
   GETO Enter Volume name: {} 20,SYS:,{ /VOL}
   EXEC NDIR
```

■ The first line simply adds the option to the menu with the title "List Volume Information." When users select this option, the following menu appears:

```
┌─────────────────────────────────────────────┐
│              User Input Requested             │
├─────────────────────────────────────────────┤
│ Enter Server name:              PICKWICK      │
│ Enter Volume name:                   SYS:     │
└─────────────────────────────────────────────┘
```

■ The next two commands request user input, and the last command appends the user input to the NDIR command, which lists information about the server and volume specified by the user.

■ The first GETO command displays the "Enter Server name:" option, and the first set of brackets in the command inserts a space. This space separates the user input from the NDIR command when it is appended. The value 20 is the length of the field.

■ PICKWICK is a suggested value for the server name. It appears in the menu as shown, but users can type over it with another server name.

■ Finally, the backslash is appended to the server name typed by users. This is required in order to separate the server name from the volume name requested by the next GETO line.

■ The second GETO line displays the field name "Enter Volume name:" with a 20-character field. It suggests SYS: as the volume name, then appends /VOL to the string. Note the space in front of this parameter, which separates it from the volume name.

■ The strings captured by both GETO commands are appended to the NDIR command in the fourth line and executed. The complete NDIR command is displayed as shown here, if the default values are used:

```
NDIR PICKWICK\SYS: /VOL
```

NOTE: Don't forget to include spacing where required in prepend and append information. Also, if you don't use one of the options, you still need to include the brackets or commas.

The GETP command saves input from users so you can use it in later commands. The first user input is parameter %1, the second is parameter %2, and so on. Do not recall %0, as your machine may lock up.

The following represents changes to the first example when GETP is used. Note that prepend and append information is not saved with user input parameters, so the following example has no prepend or append information in the GETP lines. However, you include this information in the command itself, as shown in the last line.

```
ITEM List Volume Information {Pause}
   GETP Enter Server name: {} 20,SILICON_VALLEY,{}
   GETP Enter Volume name: {} 20,SYS:,{}
   EXEC ECHO Listing volume %2 on server %1
   EXEC NDIR %1\%2 /VOL
```

Note the EXEC ECHO line. Here, both parameters entered by the user are appended to a message that is displayed on the screen. The last command then uses the parameters again to execute the NDIR command. Backslashes, spaces, and parameters are built into this command line.

The next example asks the user for the name of a file to load when starting Microsoft Word:

```
ITEM Microsoft Word
GETO Enter path to file: { } 30,SYS:PUBLIC\WORDDOCS\,{}
GETO Enter file to edit: {} 12,,{}
EXEC WORD
```

The first GETO command inserts a space, sets up a 30-character field, and prefills the field with SYS:PUBLIC\WORDDOCS\. Note that the last backslash on the prefill is important. It is needed to separate the path from the filename requested by the second GETO command, which asks for a filename in a 12-character field. In this example, users can type another path if necessary, or they can just use the existing path.

Changing Menu Colors

You can change the color configuration of the menus you create in the \PUBLIC\MENUS directory (or other directories where menus are stored) by running the COLORPAL utility. Follow these steps to edit menu colors:

1. Copy the IBM_RUN.OVL file in the SYS:PUBLIC directory to your menu directory with a command similar to the following, replacing the destination with the location of your menus directory.

```
NCOPY SYS:PUBLIC\IBM_RUN.OVL SYS:PUBLIC\MENUS
```

2. Type the following to start the utility for changing colors.

```
COLORPAL
```

3. Each option on the menu is for changing the color of a different portion of the menu. Press the F1 help key for more information. Select an option and press ENTER to change colors. On the color selection menu, press F5 to toggle between normal and blinking colors.

4. When you are done selecting colors, press ESC. Any menus you start from within the directory use the new color scheme.

Novell's Storage Management System (SMS) is a set of specifications for backing up information on networks that Novell hopes will become an industry standard. Its most important feature, support for multiple operating systems, may make this possible. Many major system manufacturers are already supporting the standard, and backup device vendors are including SMS support within their packages.

Backup Systems on the Network

Novell had many goals for the SMS during its development:

- Centralize and simplify the backup of NetWare data, no matter where it is on the network.

- Support the backup of many different file types (other operating systems).

- Make it easy for vendors to integrate their hardware or applications into the SMS, even as NetWare versions change.

- Continue to support old hardware devices as the SMS changes, and provide access to old backups way into the future. For example, you could access a 10-year-old backup even if the SMS software has changed over time.

Backup on networks is much more complex than backup on a single computer using one operating system. Networks consist of a diversity of operating systems and file types. In addition, files have special attributes (compression, migration, and so on) and rights information. Novell's SMS is designed to handle this diversity.

The volume of information to back up on a network is also an issue. The SMS will eventually work with a whole range of archiving devices, from single tape backup systems to optical jukeboxes that hold gigabytes of information. In this way, users can back up without worrying about backup device limitations. Because the SMS is modular, hardware vendors simply write drivers and modules so their equipment fits into the system.

How the SMS Is Implemented

A basic SMS configuration consists of an archive server that provides backup services and one or more target service agents (TSAs) that provide backup services for specific operating systems. TSAs are usually executable programs that run in DOS, UNIX, or Macintosh systems.

The arrangement is typically client-server based, in which the TSAs are clients and the archiving device is a NetWare Loadable Module running in a server, as shown in Figure 30-1. However, archiving devices can also be located on other systems, such as DOS workstations, Macintosh systems, or UNIX systems. Novell's SMS runs as a server process, but other vendors' systems may run in workstations.

The archive server consists of the Storage Device Interface (SDI). Think of SDI as a plug-and-play interface. Backup device vendors create modules that plug

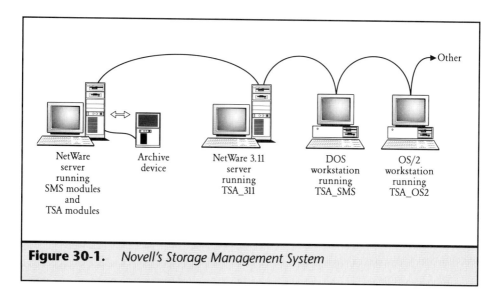

Figure 30-1.   *Novell's Storage Management System*

into the interface and allow the SMS to work with their hardware. The SMS itself doesn't really care about the type of hardware attached. That is all handled by the vendor's interface module, which is attached to the SDI. The SMS simply sends streams of data from TSAs to the device through the SDI interface. This modular design is what makes the SMS so viable for future growth.

All data in the SMS is stored using a special System-Independent Data Format (SIDF). Workstations running TSA software provide the data in SIDF, which the SMS sends to the SDI for storage on whatever archive device is attached. Because SIDF is standardized, it's possible to restore data to other devices and operating systems, as long as they accept SIDF data. The TSA software is responsible for providing the SIDF data. In this way, each TSA is designed to work with the idiosyncrasies—such as the file formats, attributes, resource forks (Macintosh), and other information—specific to the operating system it runs on.

Because TSAs simply provide SIDF data to SMS backup devices, they can change over time as the operating systems or platforms they run on change. This strategy is similar to Novell's workstation shell technology, in which each new shell version supports change in the operating system.

NetWare 4 SMS

The SMS under NetWare 4 consists of TSA modules you run to support the backup of external workstations or the backup of the server itself. Executable files are also included for DOS and OS/2 workstations so you can back up their data on the archive server. The SBACKUP module runs as a process in the NetWare server where the archive devices are located.

Note the following:

■ The server where you load SBACKUP requires 3MB of memory over the normal memory requirements of the server.

■ The current version of SBACKUP only supports 1/4-inch, 4mm, and 8mm tape. It does not support stacker and magazine devices.

■ The initial release provides backup support for NetWare 4 servers, NetWare 3.11 servers, DOS workstations, and OS/2 workstations.

■ SBACKUP will eventually support the backup of FTAM, Macintosh, and NFS name spaces.

The initial release of NetWare 4 provides the following loadable modules and device support. Other modules should be available from manufacturers on or shortly after the release date.

TAPEDAI.DSK   A generic tape driver that supports ASPI-compatible SCSI controllers

MNS16S.NLM and MNSDAT.DSK   These provide SBACKUP support for Mountain Network Solutions' SCSI controllers and tape systems

PS2SCSI.DSK   This provides SBACKUP support for IBM 2.2GB, 8mm tape devices that use PS2 SCSI controllers

AHA1540.DSK, AHA1640.DSK, AHA1740.DSK, and ASPITRAN.DSK   These provide SBACKUP support for Adaptec controllers

About Compression

The SBACKUP utility does not compress files, but you can back up files that are already compressed, such as those stored on NetWare 4 volumes (compression is on by default on NetWare volumes). Note the following:

■ During the backup, you can specify whether you want to back up compressed files in a compressed or uncompressed state. Uncompress the files if you intend to restore them to a non-NetWare 4 device, such as a NetWare 3.11 server.

■ Backup takes less time when the files are compressed.

The SBACKUP Utility

You run the SBACKUP utility at the SMS archive server. During the backup, data is sent to the archive device from the selected target device. Each backup session has a name and creates a "Backup Session Log" and a "Backup Error Log," which are stored in a continuously updated "Backup and Restore Log" file on the archive server. These files are also stored on the backup media, in case the originals are lost. They are re-created during a restore.

With SBACKUP, you can perform the following types of backups:

Full backup   Backup of all files

Incremental backup   Backup of files modified since the last full or incremental backup

Differential backup   Backup of files modified since the last full backup

Custom backup   Backup of files you specify

The "archive needed" attribute for files is cleared in the full and incremental backup, but not for the differential backup. In a custom backup, you can specify how SBACKUP should handle the attribute.

For more information on how files are handled during a backup, and the strategies you should use to create a backup schedule, refer to the NetWare manual *Supervising the Network*.

Starting and Using SBACKUP

Use the following steps to run the SBACKUP utility. It is assumed that the server in these steps has an archiving device installed.

1. First load the device drivers for the backup device. For example, at the server, type **LOAD MNS16S** to install support for a Mountain tape backup device.

2. Next, do one of the following, depending on the type of backup you want to do. Note that "host" server refers to the server to which the archive device is attached.

   Back up NetWare 4 servers To back up files on the host server, or another server, type **LOAD TSA_400** at the console, then go to step 3.

   Back up NetWare v3.11 servers At the host server, type **LOAD TSA_311** to load TSA support for the NetWare 3.11 server, then go to step 3.

   Back up DOS workstations At the host server, type **LOAD TSA_DOS**. Then at the DOS workstation, switch to the NWCLIENT directory, type **TSA_SMS**, and press ENTER. Go to step 3.

   Back up OS/2 workstations At the host server, type **LOAD TSA_OS2**. Then at the OS/2 workstation, execute the TSA_OS2 file. This file is located in the NETWARE directory with other workstation files. Go to step 3.

   Back up NetWare Directory Services database At the host server, type **LOAD TSA_NDS**. Go to step 3.

3. At the host server, type **LOAD SBACKUP** to load the SBACKUP utility. You are asked for some parameters, then you see the SBACKUP Main Menu, as shown here:

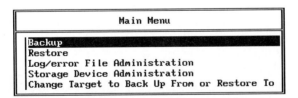

There are a number of parameters you can specify when loading workstation modules. Refer to the NetWare documentation for more information, or type the command followed by the /? help option. For example, to see options for the TSA_SMS DOS utility, type **TSA_SMS /?**. You can use these options to specify drives, directories, passwords, and other information when including the TSA commands in startup files or batch files.

From the SBACKUP Main Menu, you can choose any of the following options.

BACKUP   Choose this option to select the target server or workstation you want to back up. You also specify

- Location of session log and error files
- Backup device and media to use
- Type of backup, either full, incremental, differential, or custom

RESTORE   With this option you choose a target to restore to and what you want to restore. The log files contain backup sessions, and you can choose to restore one of these sessions. You can also restore from the tape if a log file is missing.

LOG/ERROR FILE ADMINISTRATION   Backup sessions create log files that you can view to see if any errors occurred or to get a list of backup sessions and their names.

STORAGE DEVICE ADMINISTRATION   Select this option to choose a storage device to back up to or restore from. This option also lets you check the status of a device or its media.

CHANGE TARGET TO BACK UP FROM OR RESTORE TO   This option lets you view and change the target to which you are attached.

NOTE: If you are backing up a server, you can load multiple TSAs for different operating systems, then back up files in any of those environments.

More About Log Files

If you choose Log/error File Administration from the SBACKUP Main Menu, you can choose to view a session log file or an error file. The contents of these files are covered next.

Session Log File Contents

A session log file contains information about the backup of a specific group of files. It holds the following information:

- Date and time of the backup
- Any descriptions specified for the backup
- Target from which the data was backed up
- Identification information for the media set
- Volume name, directory structure, and filenames that were backed up
- Index of data on the backup media

Error Log File Contents

The error log holds information you may need to consult about a particular backup session. The error log contains the same date, time, description, identification, and file information as the session log file, and also includes the following:

- Total number of parents and children that were successfully backed up
- Names of files that were not backed up and any errors that were generated

A Typical Backup Session

The following presents a typical backup session of files on the host server. The steps are briefly outlined here for reference only. You should run the utility yourself and refer to the NetWare manuals for more information.

1. Load SBACKUP at the host server as described under "Starting and Using SBACKUP."

2. Choose Backup from the Main Menu and choose a target from the list. If the target is quite a distance from your location, you may not see it at first. Press ESC, then do this step again.

3. If more than one TSA is loaded, choose one of the TSAs to back up the files within its environment. You'll be asked for a password.

4. Next, choose a device to back up to, if your archive system has more than one backup device.

5. You can next change the location of the session and error log files, or use the defaults.

6. Choose the type of backup you want to perform, either full, incremental, differential, or custom.

7. Type a description for the backup session.

8. Specify when you want the backup to start.

You can schedule the backup for after-hours or weekends, if necessary, to avoid excess network traffic and conflicts with files that are in use. Don't mount or dismount volumes or drivers during a backup session and don't attempt to compress files.

If you choose custom backup in step 6, you get a chance to select the files you want to back up. You can mark individual files or include or exclude files in a set. You can also choose whether you want to clear the archive attribute.

A Typical Restore Session

The following presents a typical restore session. The steps are briefly outlined here for reference only. You should run the utility yourself and refer to the NetWare manuals for more information. It's always a good idea to test a restore session with real backup data so you know how it works in case of emergency.

1. Load SBACKUP at the host server as described under "Starting and Using SBACKUP."

2. Choose Restore from the Main Menu, then choose a target to which you want to restore data.

3. Choose to restore using the session log files, or to restore without using the session log files.

   - If you choose to restore with session files, you select the session to restore.

   - If you choose to restore without session files, you specify the device where the backup media resides.

4. You can now choose files to include or exclude in the restore and how you want to handle files that might be overwritten.

The remaining steps in the restore procedure are to choose where you want the data restored to and to actually confirm that you want to begin the restore session.

CHAPTER 31

NetWare's Accounting System

etWare's accounting system lets you track the activities of users on specific servers so you can evaluate their use of resources and charge them, if necessary. For example, departments might need to charge other departments for the use of resources, such as disk storage, for budgeting purposes. Or a department might need to track the distribution of payments on a contract. Educational institutions and time-sharing services often track the use of system resources and then charge users for the time. In NetWare 4, accounting is set up on individual servers, much as it was under previous versions of NetWare.

Accounting System Overview

You install the accounting system separately at each server on the network. If you don't need accounting at a server, don't install it, since it takes up disk space and processing time.

While accounting is typically associated with billing users for the time and resources they use on the system, NetWare's accounting system also provides useful information about user logins and logouts. Supervisors can monitor usage logs to determine exactly how resources are being used and by what users. This information is useful when you need to determine whether additional equipment and storage systems are necessary and when you need to justify their purchase.

The accounting system charges users for their time or the resources they use with a point system. Points can have monetary value, or they can be thought of as "tokens" or "credits" that users can spend. A supervisor may allocate a certain number of points to a temporary user. When the user depletes those points, he or she may ask for more, which alerts the supervisor to the usage patterns and resource needs of that user. Points can be limited or unlimited, depending on how the supervisor needs to manage the system.

At an educational site, students can be given a certain amount of resources and charged for the resources they use. A report, produced at regular intervals, can help you establish charge rates based on usage. Conversely, students may buy a block of time and space at the beginning of the school term. When the block runs out, they can buy more. Students who are aware of their limits will not waste system resources.

Determining exactly what to charge for account usage is the first step. The best strategy is to establish a test period by installing the accounting feature and then tracking the system usage with users who have unlimited credit. At the end of the test period, you should have enough information to determine rates.

The ATOTAL utility is used to view accounting information. The utility compiles the accounting information and provides a list of connect times, service requests, block reads and writes, and disk storage requirements.

Types of Accounting

When you install the accounting feature at a server, user login and logout tracking is automatically tracked. Each user has an account of charges for the system resources he or she uses. Each file server designated as a chargeable system makes entries into user accounts.

Charges incurred by users fall into two main groups:

- Charges for the server's disk file space

- Charges for work performed by the server

If you charge for disk space, you'll need to come up with a rate and determine how often and at what times the file server should measure the disk space accessed by the user. The types of charges associated with a server are listed next. You can use one or all of these methods for charging.

- The amount of resources consumed not only from file servers but also gateways, print servers, and database servers

- The amount of time a user is logged on the file server

- The amount of information read from the file server disk

- The amount of information written to the file server disk

- The number of requests made to the file server for services

Installing the Accounting System

The accounting feature must be installed before it can begin tracking logins and logouts, and before you can use it to charge users for resources. You can use the NetWare Administrator or the NETADMIN utility to install the system.

Installing Accounting with NetWare Administrator

To install accounting on a server with the NetWare Administrator, locate the server in the directory tree and click it with the right mouse button. Choose the Details option to display the information dialog box for the server, then click the Accounting button. You are asked if you want to install accounting for this server, as shown in Figure 31-1. Click Yes to install accounting.

Once accounting is installed, the buttons shown next appear on the server's information dialog box. You click any of these buttons to set charge rates for the types of services listed on the buttons.

NOTE: *If you ever want to remove accounting from the server, click the Accounting button. You are asked if you want to remove accounting. All tracking services and file updates are suspended.*

Installing Accounting with NETADMIN

To install and use accounting features with the NETADMIN utility, choose Manage objects from the NETADMIN main menu. Browse the directory and select the server on which you want to install accounting. Choose Yes when asked if you want to install the accounting options. The dialog box in Figure 31-2 appears with options for setting charge rates. Choose the first option, Accounting servers, to select a server to work with.

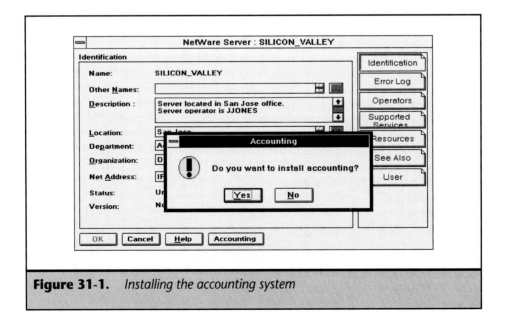

Figure 31-1.   *Installing the accounting system*

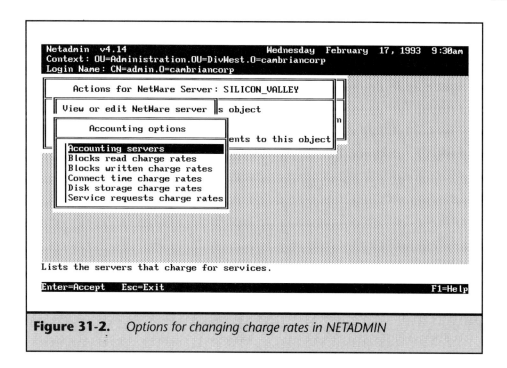

Figure 31-2. *Options for changing charge rates in NETADMIN*

Types of Charge Rates

There are several categories of rates you can charge users for services provided by a network server. Each option is described in the following sections.

Blocks Read Charge Rates

The Blocks Read option sets the charge rates for the amount of information read from the server drive. This is not the same as the charge for storing blocks on the disk, which is covered later under "Disk Storage Charge Rates." Charges are specified in half-hour increments and are assigned per blocks read, with one block being equal to 4096 bytes or 4KB.

NOTE: The Blocks Read amounts can be misleading, because every time a database is opened and read, charges are compiled, even if no work is done.

Each read from the drive is charged to the user's account. The Blocks Read option is important for servers that supply information to other users; for example, online services or database systems. Keep in mind that this option may inhibit users from using the system accurately or productively if they fear they may run out of credits.

Blocks Written Charge Rates

The Blocks Written option is similar to the Blocks Read option, except that users are charged for the amount of information written to the disk rather than read from the disk. Charges for blocks written to disk are not the same as charges for blocks of disk storage (covered under "Disk Storage Charge Rates"). Charges are specified in half-hour increments and are assigned per block written, with one block being equal to 4096 bytes or 4KB.

Each write to the drive is charged to the user's account. Be careful when using this option since some programs write to the disk continuously, and you would be unfairly charging users of the program. For example, when Windows is installed on the file server, it writes temporary files to the server and updates those files regularly. In addition, users may be less productive if they know they are being charged every time they write to the disk.

Connect Time Charge Rates

The Connect Time option charges users for each half hour of time they are logged into the server. It is important to consider the type of user and the resources available on the system before establishing this rate, however. If network usage is high, you may want to charge a higher rate to encourage users to perform their tasks on the system efficiently and not tie up the system for too long. This may not be appropriate for some systems, however, especially if the system is new and there are many first-time users.

Disk Storage Charge Rates

The Disk Storage option allows you to set up charge rates for each block of disk storage. A block is 4096 bytes or 4KB. A charge rate is established for every half-hour increment of disk storage use and is assigned on a block-day basis, which measures the number of blocks stored in a day. If the network has limited disk storage, charges can be established to encourage users to be more efficient in the way they store files and to keep their storage area clear of unnecessary files.

Service Requests Charge Rates

The Service Requests option establishes charge rates for general use of the server. Every time a request is made to the server for any operation, the user is charged. Charge rates are specified in half-hour increments, and the user is charged per request received. Users are charged for services from the moment they log in to the moment they log out.

NOTE: This charge rate will add numerous entries to the accounting file, since any activity makes Service Requests calls. Watch the size of the accounting file when using this option.

Setting the Accounting Charge Rates

You must determine the types of charges and the rates you want to charge users for services provided by a network server. In addition, you must set up an initial account balance and view the existing accounting information, either to help establish the initial rates or to bill users for usage.

Charge rates are established by specifying a multiplier and a divisor. The multiplier is the rate you want to charge, usually in cents, and the divisor is the number of units you want to charge for, usually 1. In addition, there can be up to 20 charge rates. In that way, you can charge different rates for different times of the day. For example, you might want to charge a higher rate for connect time charges during the day than at night.

Setting charge rates is a two-step process:

1. Create one or more charge rates.

2. Select a block of time, and then specify the charge rate that will be in effect during that time.

Setting Up Initial Account Balances

You set up the initial account balances for users by accessing their Account Balance dialog box. In the NetWare Administrator, double-click a user object, then click the Account Balance button on the dialog box. In NETADMIN, choose a user object, then from the resulting menu choose "View or edit properties of this object." Choose "Account restrictions" from the View or Edit user menu, and then choose "Account balance."

You can then do one of the following:

■ Specify a limited balance amount in the Account Balance field.

■ Select Allow Unlimited Credit.

■ Disable Allow Unlimited Credit and specify a low balance at which the user is denied access to network resources.

To monitor the use of the system for each user, set unlimited account balances. Keep in mind that users will be logged out when they reach their account balance limits. This may cause a lot of extra work on your part if you need to assign new balances.

Specify account balances in units. You can assign a specified amount of credit by entering No in the Allow Unlimited Credit field and then entering a balance in the Low Balance Limit field. If a negative number is entered in the Low Balance Limit field, users receive services until the charges have been used up. If you enter a positive number in the field, the user must maintain some value in the field. Users can always go to the supervisor and request additional services.

NOTE: *Account balances can also be assigned to the default user account in each container.*

Using NetWare Administrator's Charge Rate Dialog Boxes

The basic NetWare Administrator charge rate dialog box is pictured in Figure 31-3. This box is for Blocks Read charge rates, but it has the same features as the Blocks Written, Connect Time, Disk Storage, and Service Requests dialog boxes.

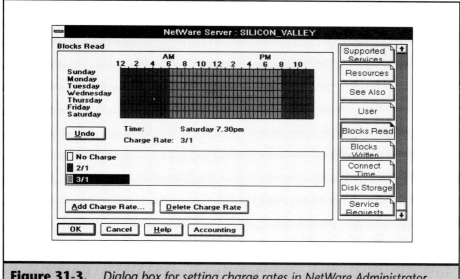

Figure 31-3. *Dialog box for setting charge rates in NetWare Administrator*

Setting Charge Rates

To set a new charge rate, click the Add Charge Rate button. The Add Charge Rate dialog box appears, as shown in the following illustration. You type the multiplier and the divisor in the dialog box fields and press ENTER. Methods for determining these values are discussed under "How to Calculate Charge Rates," later in this chapter.

If you want to change a charge rate, you delete the rate and re-create it. This poses a little problem since you cannot delete a rate if blocks of time are marked to use that rate. First undo any time blocks that use that rate, then highlight the rate and click the Delete Charge Rate button. Create the new rate following the procedure just given.

Specify a Rate for a Block of Time

Click on one of the charge rates you created. Then, in the upper part of the dialog box, click and drag through the time block you want to assign this charge rate to. A hollow box outlines the time blocks as you drag. When you let up on the mouse button, the block of time takes on the color assigned to the charge rate.

Using the NETADMIN Charge Rate Screens

The basic NETADMIN charge rate screen is shown in Figure 31-4. This screen is for setting Blocks Read charge rates, but it has the same features as the Blocks Written, Connect Time, Disk Storage, and Service Requests dialog boxes.

Setting Charge Rates

On the left of the screen are the 20 possible charge rates. The first charge rate is always 1. On the right are the time blocks, all of which are initially set to the 1 charge rate.

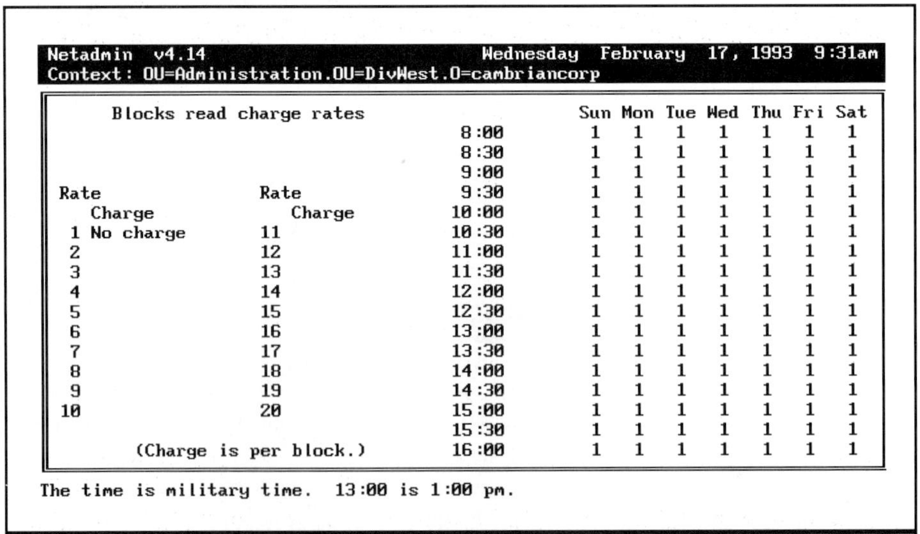

```
Netadmin  v4.14                    Wednesday  February  17, 1993  9:31am
Context: OU=Administration.OU=DivWest.O=cambriancorp

     Blocks read charge rates            Sun Mon Tue Wed Thu Fri Sat
                                    8:00   1   1   1   1   1   1   1
                                    8:30   1   1   1   1   1   1   1
                                    9:00   1   1   1   1   1   1   1
  Rate              Rate            9:30   1   1   1   1   1   1   1
     Charge            Charge      10:00   1   1   1   1   1   1   1
  1 No charge       11             10:30   1   1   1   1   1   1   1
  2                 12             11:00   1   1   1   1   1   1   1
  3                 13             11:30   1   1   1   1   1   1   1
  4                 14             12:00   1   1   1   1   1   1   1
  5                 15             12:30   1   1   1   1   1   1   1
  6                 16             13:00   1   1   1   1   1   1   1
  7                 17             13:30   1   1   1   1   1   1   1
  8                 18             14:00   1   1   1   1   1   1   1
  9                 19             14:30   1   1   1   1   1   1   1
 10                 20             15:00   1   1   1   1   1   1   1
                                  15:30   1   1   1   1   1   1   1
         (Charge is per block.)   16:00   1   1   1   1   1   1   1

 The time is military time.  13:00 is 1:00 pm.
```

Figure 31-4. *The basic NETADMIN dialog box*

To assign charge rates to a specific time of the day or week, press F5 (Mark) and use the arrow keys to highlight the exact area that will be given a specific time charge. When the total area is highlighted, press ENTER. A Select Charge Rate screen appears.

You can select an existing charge rate by highlighting one of the options, or you can define a new charge rate by selecting Other Charge Rate from this screen. Use the arrow keys to highlight either Multiplier or Divisor and enter the ratio established for a particular service. It is applied to the highlighted block of time.

How to Calculate Charge Rates

Charge rates can be established differently for each server on the network, although the network administrator should ensure that each system uses the same basic formula to establish rates. That ensures fairness when one department charges another for the use of its resources.

Initially, it's a good idea to set the accounting system on and track server usage. This will give you an idea of how to charge for services. After running the test for a week or two, use the server console-based ATOTAL utility to view the usage information and establish charge rates.

Accounting information is stored in the NET$ACCT.DAT file, which can get quite large. You should view a printout of its contents periodically or compile it with the appropriate accounting application (available from third-party developers), and then delete it from the system. A new file is then created by the accounting system as soon as a new user logs in.

Charge ratios are calculated with the following formula:

Charge rate multiplier/Charge rate divisor

The multiplier is the amount of money you want to charge for a service, such as Blocks Read. The divisor is usually 1, which specifies 1 unit of that service. This ratio is then assigned to specific times of the day, and up to 20 different ratios can be applied. In this way charges can be higher during the day than in the evening, for example. Charges are shown for each half hour during a weekly period and are applied in the following ways:

Blocks Read charge rates	Charge is per block
Blocks Written charge rates	Charge is per block
Connect Time charge rates	Charge is per minute

Disk Storage charge rates   Charge is per block-day

Service Requests charge rates   Charge is per request received

Assume you want to charge 2 cents for every unit of services requested or used. The multiplier is then 2 and the divisor is 1, or 2/1. For this charge rate, you type **2** in the Multiplier field and **1** in the Divisor field.

Charging fractional amounts requires a few more steps. Assume you want to charge $1.50 for 1 unit of service. You need to get rid of the decimal, so you multiply it by 100 to come up with 150. Likewise, you need to multiply the divisor by 100 to come up with 100. The charge rate is 150/100, so type **150** in the Multiplier field and **100** in the Divisor field.

Another way to decide how to charge for services is by how much money you want to make on the service. For example, assume you have determined with AUDITCON that 500,000 blocks of space are normally in use, and you want to receive a $1000 fee for that use. Also assume that each charge point is equal to 1 cent. The $1000 weekly charge is converted to 100,000 and becomes the multiplier. The 500,000 block of disk space becomes the unit value, and thus the divisor, as follows:

$$100,000/500,000 = 1/5$$

NOTE: If you just want to track usage, you must set up a rate for each category you want to view information on, even if it's just a 1 to 1 rate. Also, make sure there are no restrictions on the account balances.

Compiling Accounting Totals

You use the ATOTAL utility to compile the accounting information into a list that you can display on the screen or send to a printer or file. Switch to the SYS:SYSTEM directory or map a search drive to it, then type the following command to run the utility:

ATOTAL

To direct the listing to a file, type the following command, replacing *filename* with an appropriate filename:

ATOTAL > *filename*

CHAPTER 32

NetWare's Auditing System

The NetWare auditing system provides a way for a specially designated network user known as the *auditor* to track events on the network. The events fall into two categories: volume tracking and container tracking. Each auditing group can have a distinct password, so, for example, the auditor who tracks volume events cannot track container events. However, one auditor can track all of this if you choose to set it up that way.

Volume Events Auditors Can Track

The auditor first selects a volume to track, then enables the tracking of the events listed here. Alternatively, the auditor can track the activities of individual users, files, or directories. The following events can be tracked for a selected volume:

■ Creating and deleting directories

■ Creating, opening, closing, deleting, renaming, writing, and salvaging files

■ Modifying directory entries

■ Queue activities

■ Server events, such as changing the date and time, downing the server, and mounting or dismounting volumes

■ User events, such as login, logout, connection termination, space restrictions, granting of trustee rights, and disabling of accounts

Directory Service Events Auditors Can Track

Directory Service events are tracked for individual containers. The auditor first selects a container, then enables the tracking of the following events in that container.

■ Directory Services events; for example, when passwords change, when security changes, when restrictions change, and when entries are moved, removed, or renamed

■ Activities of a specific user, such as the supervisor

Overview of the Auditing Procedure

The network administrator makes a user an auditor, gives the user a password, then relinquishes control of audit tracking to the auditor, who immediately changes the password. From that point on, only the auditor can set up auditing features, view audit logs, and work in the designated audit directory. Auditing is set up at container levels and at volume levels. If container level auditing is enabled, it only applies to the current container, not subordinate containers.

The auditing system keeps a record of each activity designated for tracking. Auditors can view these text files in AUDITCON and apply filters to produce reports that show specific activities. The following types of filters are available for producing reports of auditing events:

- Report within a specific date and time range

- Report only specified events

- Include or exclude specific file and/or directory events

- Include or exclude specific user events

Once a filter is created, the auditor can send the report to a specific file, then open the file in a word processor, edit it if necessary, and print it. The auditor can also view the report directly onscreen while working in AUDITCON. The auditor also needs to manage the disposition of the auditing log files, which can grow quite large.

Installing the Auditing System

The procedures in this section are for the supervisor who creates the auditing user. Once the auditor is created, the supervisor starts AUDITCON, creates an initial password, and then gives the password to the new auditor. The new auditor then immediately changes the password to prevent the supervisor from accessing the auditing system.

The procedure for setting up an auditor is similar to setting up a user. You create a user object and make sure to specify a personal directory for that user to access. The directory is used to store the files the auditor creates. Make sure to map a search path to the SYS:PUBLIC directory as well, and grant the auditor rights to the directory if his or her user object was created in the directory tree above the volume object.

To set up the initial auditor password, log in as a supervisor and start the AUDITCON utility by typing **AUDITCON** at a workstation. The AUDITCON menu appears as shown here:

```
┌─────────────────────────────┐
│ Available Audit Options     │
├─────────────────────────────┤
│┌───────────────────────────┐│
││Audit Directory Services   ││
││Change Current Server      ││
││Change Current Volume      ││
││Display Audit Status       ││
││Enable Volume Auditing     ││
│└───────────────────────────┘│
└─────────────────────────────┘
```

You can change the current server or change the volume with the options on this menu. The top and bottom options are of interest here.

Enable Auditing for a Container   You can assign an auditing password for each container in the Directory Services tree. Choose Audit Directory Services from the AUDITCON menu, then choose Audit Directory Tree. You can then browse the directory tree for a container and press F10 to select it. Choose Enable Container Auditing on the menu that appears, then specify a password. The menu now displays Auditor Container Login. The auditor would select this option to view and change the auditing features of the container.

Enable Volume Auditing   Choose this option to enable auditing for the current volume. Look at the top of your screen for this information. You are asked to enter and reenter a password. The AUDITCON menu now appears, as shown in Figure 32-1.

You should now give the container or volume passwords to the designated auditors and refer them to the "Activities for Volume Auditors" or "Activities for Container Auditors" section in this chapter.

Figure 32-1.   *AUDITCON menu after enabling volume auditing*

Activities for Volume Auditors

This section is for auditors assigned to track volumes. Type **AUDITCON** to start the auditing utility. You see the menu pictured in Figure 32-1. Choose Audit Volume Login, then type the password you were given by the supervisor. The following menu appears:

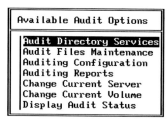

 NOTE: *Change the password you use to access the volume auditing options. To do this, choose Auditing Configuration, then choose Change Audit Password.*

Enabling Volume Auditing Events

To audit events on the volume, you must first specify which events you want to audit. Choose Auditing Configuration from the main menu, then choose one of the following options. Press F1 if you need help setting these options.

Audit By Event Choose this option to display the following menu, then choose each option from this menu to see a list of events you can track. To enable an event, highlight it and press F10.

NOTE: Event options are either "Global," "and," or "or." "Global" records all the designated events throughout the volume; "and" records events only for users being audited; "or" records events for all users.

Audit by File/Directory   Choose this option to select a file or directory you want to track activities in. Browse the directory tree to highlight a directory or file, then press F10 to enable tracking.

Audit By User   Choose this option to track a user's activity. Highlight the user and press F10 to enable tracking.

The remaining options on the Auditing Configuration menu are used to change the configuration or status of auditing. Press F1 to view help for the options on the menu.

NOTE: The Audit Options Configuration menu has important settings that determine what to do if the auditing file becomes full. The volume can be dismounted or audit tracking can stop, depending on your selection.

Activities for Container Auditors

This section is for auditors assigned to track volumes. Type **AUDITCON** to start the auditing utility. You see the menu pictured previously, in Figure 32-1. Choose Audit Directory Services, then choose Audit Directory Tree. Browse the directory tree to locate the container you want to audit and press F10, then choose Auditor Container Login. Type the password you were given by the supervisor. The menu in Figure 32-2 now appears.

```
          Available Audit Options
         ┌─────────────────────────┐
         │ Audit Files Maintenance │
         │ Auditing Configuration  │
         │ Auditing Reports        │
         │ Display Audit Status    │
         └─────────────────────────┘
```

Figure 32-2.   *Auditing options for containers*

The first option is used to manage the auditing files once they become full or need to be removed. The second option is used to enable auditing events. The third option is used to view and report on the auditing events, and the last option displays the current status of auditing in this container.

NOTE: To change your password, choose Auditing Configuration, then choose Change Audit Password.

Enabling Container Auditing Events

Choose Auditing Configuration from the Available Audit Options menu to enable auditing events. You can choose one of the following options:

Audit By DS Events Choose this option to select the Directory Services events possible in the container you want to track. Highlight an event and press F10 to enable it.

Audit By User Choose this option to select a user from a list. The user's activities in the container are tracked. Auditors will probably want to track the supervisor's activities.

The remaining options on the menu are used to change the auditing configuration for the container and the password, or to view the current status. You can also disable auditing for the container.

NOTE: The Audit Options Configuration menu has important settings that determine what to do if the auditing file becomes full. The volume can be dismounted or audit tracking can stop, depending on your selection.

Viewing and Reporting Auditing Information

You can create and view auditing information for volumes and containers and create reports for the events once the auditing system has had an appropriate amount of time to track the auditing events you selected. To do this, choose

Auditing Reports from the Available Audit Options menu (shown in Figure 32-2). The following menu appears:

```
┌─────────────────────────┐
│   Auditing Reports      │
├─────────────────────────┤
│ Display Audit Status    │
│ Edit Report Filters     │
│ Report Audit File       │
│ Report Audit History    │
│ Report Old Audit File   │
│ View Audit File         │
│ View Audit History      │
│ View Old Audit File     │
└─────────────────────────┘
```

Choose the first option, Display Audit Status, to check the current status of the auditing files. You should do this periodically to ensure they don't overrun their specified sizes. You can send auditing information to a report file, then start over with a new auditing file if necessary.

The remaining options on the Auditing Reports menu are as follows:

Edit Report Filters   Choose this option to specify filters for the display and reporting of auditing information. Initially, you see "no filter." Press INS to create a new filter and display the following menu. Press F1 to get a description of the options on the menu. To add an option, press ENTER, then choose an existing setting, or press INS to create a new setting.

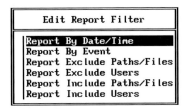

```
┌──────────────────────────────┐
│      Edit Report Filter      │
├──────────────────────────────┤
│ Report By Date/Time          │
│ Report By Event              │
│ Report Exclude Paths/Files   │
│ Report Exclude Users         │
│ Report Include Paths/Files   │
│ Report Include Users         │
└──────────────────────────────┘
```

Report options   Choose one of the Report options to send the current or old audit data file, or audit history file, to a standard text file for editing and printing.

NOTE: Audit File and Old Audit File contain auditing information. The Audit History file contains information about the auditor's activities.

View options Choose one of the View options to immediately view the information specified by the Report option filter.

Managing the Auditing Files

From the main AUDITCON menu, choose Audit Files Maintenance to close, copy, delete, or display information about the auditing files. If you are working in a container object, choose this option from the Available Audit Options menu for the container object.

THE
COMPLETE

REFERENCE

PART SIX

Monitoring and Maintenance

CHAPTER 33

This chapter discusses three utilities that are included with NetWare to help network administrators and supervisors monitor and maintain their networks: Remote Console, SERVMAN, and MONITOR. You use these utilities to monitor servers and networks. SERVMAN and MONITOR are basically local monitoring utilities. You use them to view the statistics of servers and the networks attached directly to them.

Network Management Tools and Techniques

Remote Console

NetWare's Remote Console utility allows authorized users to execute console commands from a location other than the server's console, such as a workstation or a remote terminal connected by a modem. Remote Console simplifies the management of servers that are scattered throughout an organization.

To manage a console remotely, you must first install the REMOTE.NLM module at each server you want to manage from your workstation. From your workstation, you then execute RCONSOLE.EXE, which is located in the SYS:SYSTEM directory of the server you are logged into. All servers that have Remote Console installed appear in an Available Servers list. You choose a server and enter its password access code. At that point, you see a screen that looks just like the console at the server. In fact, the console screen at the server duplicates your workstation screen as you issue commands and display information.

There are two possible Remote Console setups:

■ Load remote support so that you can operate from a workstation on the network

■ Load remote support so you can operate from a workstation attached via asynchronous communications lines

The asynchronous connection method has several advantages for network supervisors. It provides an alternate path to a remote server should the network cabling go down or suffer from traffic problems that limit communications over it. You can access the server by using its serial port. This method also gives you the freedom to travel, assuming that you carry a portable computer that has a modem and all the necessary Remote Console software. You can connect to your server and monitor its activities any time and anywhere.

You can place the commands that load remote console support in the server's AUTOEXEC.NCF file. You encode the required password and store it in this file so that the server will start and load remote support without asking for the password. When the password is encoded, you will get a keyword to use to access the console.

Loading Remote Console for Use at a Local Workstation

As previously mentioned, before you can run Remote Console from a workstation on the network, you must load the support modules at the servers. Perform the following steps on each server you want to manage remotely:

1. Type the following command to load the REMOTE module:

   LOAD *path*\REMOTE *password*

   where *path* is the drive or directory where REMOTE.NLM can be found if it is not in the SYS:SYSTEM directory, and *password* is the keyword that lets you access the console from a workstation. You will be asked for a password if you do not specify it in this command.

2. Type the following command to load the RSPX remote SPX support module, replacing *path* with the drive or directory where RSPX.NLM can be found if it is not in the SYS:SYSTEM directory:

   LOAD *path*\RSPX

Now you are ready to set up a remote console session at a workstation. You must have Read, Write, File Scan, and Create rights in the SYS:SYSTEM directory to run the RCONSOLE.EXE file located there.

3. At the workstation, map a drive to the SYS:SYSTEM directory. The following example maps drive J:

   MAP J:=SYS:SYSTEM

4. Switch to the drive you just mapped, and type the following command:

   RCONSOLE

5. If you installed REMOTE on more than one file server, you'll see a list of available servers.

6. RCONSOLE asks for the remote console password. Type it and press ENTER.

You are now working in the remote console. Refer to the section "Using Remote Console" later in this chapter for instructions on working in a remote session. If you want to include these commands in your AUTOEXEC.NCF file, refer to the section "Starting Remote Console from AUTOEXEC.NCF" later in this chapter.

Loading Remote Console for Use at a Remote Workstation

You can remotely manage NetWare servers from a workstation that is attached to a server via asynchronous communications. This attachment can be made by using a null-modem cable, or it can be made over the phone lines by using a modem. To connect over the phone lines, follow the steps listed next to set up call-in support at the server, and then connect to the server by using the RCONSOLE command.

1. Type the following command to load the REMOTE module:

   LOAD *path*\REMOTE *password*

   where *path* is the drive or directory where REMOTE.NLM can be found if it is not in the SYS:SYSTEM directory, and *password* is the keyword that lets you access the console from a workstation. You will be asked for a password if you do not specify it in this command.

2. Load the NetWare Communications Port Interface:

   LOAD AIO

3. Load a communications board driver by typing a LOAD command followed by one of the drivers listed in Table 33-1. The driver you use depends on the type of asynchronous interface cards you have installed. Table 33-1 lists several drivers that are supplied with NetWare. You might need to copy drivers that are supplied with your board to the SYS:SYSTEM directory of the server.

Driver	Description
AIOCOMX.NLM	The Novell communications driver. Type **LOAD AIOCOMX ?** for a description of the command and its options
AIOACI.NLM	The communications driver for Newport Systems Solutions asynchronous boards
AIODGCX.NLM	The Digiboard C/X driver
AIODGXI.NLM	The intelligent driver for a Digiboard communications card
AIOCXCFDG.NLM	The Digiboard configuration manager driver
AIODGMEM.NLM	The Digiboard memory manager
AIOESP.NLM	The communications driver for Hayes ESP communications cards. An I/O port, interrupt, and direct memory access (DMA) channel are required
AIOWNIM.NLM	The communications driver for Gateway Communications WNIM boards. An I/O port and DMA channel are required

Table 33-1. *Communications Board Drivers*

4. After loading a communications driver, load the asynchronous communications NLM by typing the following command:

    LOAD RS232 *port speed* n c

Replace *port* with the number of the communications port, and replace *speed* with the baud rate. If you don't specify this information, you will be asked for it. Use the "n" parameter if you are using a null-modem cable, and use the "c" parameter to enable the call-back feature.

The call-back feature ensures that the user calling in is at a site that is authorized to access the network. It checks the caller's ID against a list of phone numbers and then calls the user back at that site. Intruders calling from an unauthorized site will not be able to access the network. You need to create a call-back file that contains a list of phone numbers authorized to call into the network. Use a text editor such as EDIT.NLM to create the file. Name it CALLBACK.LST and store it in the SYS:SYSTEM directory. Type a phone number on each line of the file.

Connecting via a Modem

To use Remote Console from a workstation connected via a modem, you'll need the following files from the server. Using the NCOPY command, copy these files to a floppy disk and take them to the remote site. If you already have a network connection to the server, simply copy them from the server to your remote workstation.

```
SYS:SYSTEM\RCONSOLE.EXE
SYS:PUBLIC\IBM_RUN.OVL
SYS:SYSTEM\NLS\ENGLISH\RCONSOLE.MSG
SYS:SYSTEM\NLS\ENGLISH\TEXTUTIL.MSG
SYS:SYSTEM\NLS\ENGLISH\TEXTUTIL.IDX
SYS:SYSTEM\NLS\ENGLISH\TEXTUTIL.HEP
SYS:SYSTEM\NLS\ENGLISH\RCONSOLE.HEP
SYS:SYSTEM\_AIO.OVL
SYS:SYSTEM\IBM_AIO.OVL
SYS:SYSTEM\CMPQ_AIO.OVL
SYS:SYSTEM\_RUN.OVL
```

Now follow these steps:

1. Type **RCONSOLE** at the remote site to start the utility. At the Remote Console menu, choose Asynchronous to make the modem connection.

2. If this is the first connection, choose Configuration from the next menu.

Specify the modem, port, baud rate, and other settings from the Modem Configuration menu. Be sure to specify a connection ID, which is the name or number that the server uses to identify your workstation.

3. When the configuration is complete, press ESC, save the changes, and choose Connect to Remote Location to dial out.

4. A list of server sites appears, but this list might initially be blank. Press the INS key to specify a new location name and phone number, and then press ESC to add it to the list.

5. Choose a phone number and then press ENTER to make the connection.

Once you connect to the server, the call-back feature, if enabled, hangs up your connection and calls you back. When you are connected, you see the console prompt and can access the server as you normally would. Refer to the section "Using Remote Console" later in this chapter for details on working in a remote console session.

Starting Remote Console from AUTOEXEC.NCF

You can place any of the commands listed in previous sections in the AUTOEXEC.NCF file, but you must first encrypt the password for security reasons. The password is replaced by an encrypted keyword in the file. Follow the procedure listed next. These procedures assume you have already loaded REMOTE.NLM at the server.

1. Type the following command to encrypt the password:

    REMOTE ENCRYPT

2. Type in the password you want to use to start the remote console session.

3. An encrypted keyword appears at the console. Write down this keyword.

4. Edit the AUTOEXEC.NCF file by using EDIT.NLM. Add the following line to the file to load REMOTE.NLM, replacing *key* with the keyword you wrote down in the previous step.

    LOAD REMOTE -E *key*

Using Remote Console

After you access the server console by using Remote Console, you can access the server console utilities as if you were sitting at the console itself.

Remember that all activities performed at the remote console are mirrored on the screen of the file server. If you lock the file server's console, the remote console locks as well, so you'll need to physically lock the server's keyboard or secure the server system in a safe place to prevent users from accessing the console or viewing your activities.

The following keys are available in the remote console session:

■ ALT-F1 Access the Remote Console Available Options menu (see Figure 33-1)

■ ALT-F2 Exit Remote Console

■ ALT-F3 Cycle backward through the Remote Console screens

■ ALT-F4 Cycle forward through the Remote Console screens

■ ALT-F5 Show the current workstation address

The Remote Console Available Options Menu

You access the Remote Console Available Options menu, which is shown in Figure 33-1, by pressing ALT-F1. The options on the menu are described in the following sections.

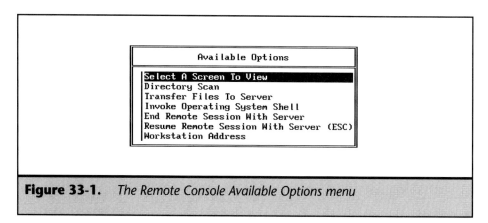

```
                    Available Options
 ┌──────────────────────────────────────────────┐
 │Select A Screen To View                         │
 │Directory Scan                                  │
 │Transfer Files To Server                        │
 │Invoke Operating System Shell                   │
 │End Remote Session With Server                  │
 │Resume Remote Session With Server (ESC)         │
 │Workstation Address                             │
 └──────────────────────────────────────────────┘
```

Figure 33-1.   *The Remote Console Available Options menu*

SELECT A SCREEN TO VIEW   When you choose the Select A Screen To View option, a list of available screens appears. If you loaded MONITOR at the console, MONITOR SCREEN and SYSTEM CONSOLE appear in the Available Screens menu. To enter console commands, select SYSTEM CONSOLE. The console colon (:) prompt appears so that you can execute any console command as you normally would at the file server. Of course, you wouldn't want to dismount volumes, down the server, or make other changes that would affect network operations unless they are vital and you have warned the network users.

DIRECTORY SCAN   Select the Directory Scan option to view directories and files on the file server. Type the drive letter and/or path of the directory you want to view. You can use wildcard characters to list specific files, the same way you would use them with the DOS DIR command. Press the PGUP and PGDN keys to scan long lists.

TRANSFER FILES TO SERVER   Select the Transfer Files To Server option to transfer files from a workstation drive to any drive on the server. Two menus appear. The first asks for the source files, and the second asks for the destination directory on the server. As with the DOS COPY command, you can use wildcard characters to specify groups of files. Make sure your remote session is secure. Unauthorized users could transfer viruses or cause damage to the file system by using the file transfer feature.

INVOKE OPERATING SYSTEM SHELL   Select the Invoke Operating System Shell option to temporarily return to the operating system prompt. You can then execute DOS commands on local drives or network drives. Because of the amount of conventional memory used by Remote Console and the secondary environment it invokes, you might not be able to run some utilities and programs.

END REMOTE SESSION WITH SERVER   Select End Remote Session With Server to end a remote console session. You are returned to the Available Servers menu, where you can select another file server or press the ESC key to return to DOS.

RESUME REMOTE SESSION WITH SERVER   The Resume Remote Session With Server option simply removes the Remote Console menu and returns you to the console prompt.

WORKSTATION ADDRESS   Select the Workstation Address option to display the network address of your current workstation.

SERVMAN

The SERVMAN utility displays general information about the server and detailed information about network communications, the storage system, and the network. The information is statistical in nature and can be only viewed in most cases. SERVMAN also provides a convenient way to use the SET command, which sets various server options and startup parameters. SERVMAN provides a list of those options along with a description and a suggested setting. If you change a SET parameter, SERVMAN makes any required changes to the startup files for you.

NOTE: Keep in mind that much of the information displayed by SERVMAN is the same information you see when running MONITOR. SERVMAN typically displays current settings and feature summaries, such as the size of a volume. MONITOR provides statistical information about the performance and operating characteristics of a server during the time it has been running.

To start SERVMAN, type the following command at the server console or from a remote console session:

LOAD SERVMAN

You see two menus. The top menu (called GENERAL INFORMATION) displays the following statistics about the server:

- *Processor Utilization* The percentage of the server's CPU that is in use. This number changes as users log in and out and as they work with applications and files. This value should remain below 80 percent; otherwise you might need to upgrade the microprocessor or move some processes, applications, or heavy users to another server

- *Server Up Time* The amount of time the server has been up is significant. NetWare adjusts its settings over time to match the load placed on it by workstations and internal processes. The longer the server is up, the more likely the settings will match those required for everyday use. If a server has been up only a few hours or a few days, the operating information displayed by SERVMAN (and MONITOR) is not likely to be representative of your system's normal operating environment

NOTE: Once NetWare has established workable settings, write them down. You can then change Set options to match them so the server can immediately reestablish the optimized settings if it is downed and restarted.

■ *Processor Speed*   The speed rating of the microprocessor in your system. It is determined by the CPU clock speed (25 MHz, 33 MHz, 66 MHz, and so on), the CPU type (80386, 80486, Pentium, and so on), and the number of memory wait states. For comparison, a 16 MHz 80386 microprocessor is rated at 120, and a 33 MHz 80486 microprocessor might have a rating of 260. Unusually low values might indicate that the microprocessor has been set to a slower clock speed. Check the computer's front panel or run diagnostics on the system to make sure it is running at its fastest clock speed

The Available Options menu provides a list of the information you can view or change:

```
Available Options

Console Set Commands
IPX/SPX Configuration
Storage Information
Volume Information
Network Information
Exit Server Manager
```

Options that are important for newly installed servers are discussed next.

The Console Set Commands option displays the following menu, which lets you change operating system parameters for the items listed:

```
Categories

1. Communications
2. Memory
3. File Caching
4. Directory Caching
5. File System
6. Locks
7. Transaction Tracking
8. Disk
9. Time
10.NCP
11.Miscellaneous
```

These options can also be set by using the SET command at the server console or by typing the commands into the AUTOEXEC.NCF or STARTUP.NCF file. SERVMAN simply provides a quick way to browse through the commands and insert them in the startup files. Some commands take effect only after restarting the server; others can be set on or off during the current session for testing and benchmarking purposes. If you make changes to console SET commands from within SERVMAN, you are asked if you want to save those changes to the AUTOEXEC.NCF or STARTUP.NCF file if the commands are normally placed in those files.

SERVMAN options are discussed in the next few chapters:

- For server settings, refer to Chapter 34.

- For disk storage system settings, refer to Chapter 35.

- For network communications settings, refer to Chapter 36.

Altering Server SET Parameters

As mentioned earlier, you can use the SERVMAN utility to view and change the operating parameters of the server. The default settings should be adequate in most cases, but you might need to change settings depending on your hardware configuration and the NLMs you are running at the server. It's usually best to set options after a period of running and analyzing the server, unless you are specifically instructed to change settings by a software or hardware vendor.

Saving Changes to the Startup Files

After you make changes to SET options and are ready to back out to the Available Options menu, the following menu appears:

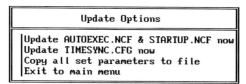

```
                    Update Options

Update AUTOEXEC.NCF & STARTUP.NCF now
Update TIMESYNC.CFG now
Copy all set parameters to file
Exit to main menu
```

- Choose the Update AUTOEXEC.NCF & STARTUP.NCF now option to add the changes to the startup files.

- Choose the Update TIMESYNC.CFG now option only if you have made changes to the Time options.

■ Choose the Copy all set parameters to file option if you want to copy the changes to a file and edit them separately.

■ Choose the Exit to main menu option to return to the Available Options menu without making changes to the startup files.

NOTE: For more information on SET options in SERVMAN, refer to Chapters 34, 35, and 36.

MONITOR

You can use the MONITOR NetWare Loadable Module to view information about server and network activities, such as the following:

■ Overall activity and utilization

■ Cache memory status

■ Connections and their status

■ Disk drives

■ Mounted volumes

■ LAN drivers

■ Loaded modules

■ File lock status

■ Memory usage

The main MONITOR screen displays statistics about several important network functions. After one minute of nonactivity, a moving snake appears to prevent screen burn. As network usage increases, the snake moves faster and its tail gets longer. Press any key to restore MONITOR's display.

Loading MONITOR

To load the MONITOR module at the file server console or at a workstation that is running as a remote console, type the following command:

LOAD *path*\MONITOR *parameters*

where *path* is the path to the MONITOR.NLM file if it is located outside the
SYS:SYSTEM directory. *Parameters* can be one or both of the following:

Parameter	Description
ns (no saver)	Turns off the screen saver option
nh (no help)	Saves memory if you do not need the help functions

The Main MONITOR Screen

The main MONITOR screen, shown in Figure 33-2, displays the following
information about network functions:

- *Server Up Time* The amount of time the server has been running

- *Utilization* The percentage of time the processor is busy. A high
  percentage indicates an overworked server. If this value is above 80
  percent, upgrade the server or move some processes off of it to another
  server. You should also check to make sure the server has enough memory
  to operate efficiently

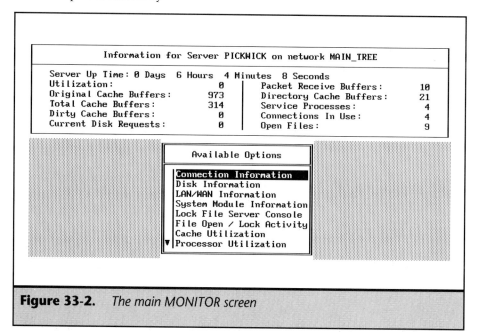

Figure 33-2. *The main MONITOR screen*

■ *Original Cache Buffers*   The number of cache buffers (in blocks) available when the server was first booted. Compare this number to the total number of cache buffers

■ *Total Cache Buffers*   The number of blocks currently available for file caching. Check this number after loading NLMs to ensure adequate memory is available for caching

■ *Dirty Cache Buffers*   The number of file blocks waiting to be written to disk. This value should be well below the Total Cache Buffers value. It will shoot up under peak loads when users save a lot of files, but it should trickle back down to an acceptable level. As an example, if only one user saves a file, the value shoots up and then returns to 0 after a few seconds as the cache buffers are written to disk. On large networks that have many users saving files, this value might never reach 0. You can change how fast this number builds by adjusting the Maximum Concurrent Disk Cache Writes option, as discussed in Chapter 35

■ *Current Disk Requests*   The number of disk requests waiting for service. To gauge disk requests, compare the value during slow (evening) hours to the value during peak time

■ *Packet Receive Buffers*   The number of buffers available to receive incoming packets from workstations. The default is 10, but the server dynamically allocates more buffers as necessary, which uses up RAM that might be required for other processes. You can set an upper and a lower limit in the SERVMAN utility, as discussed in Chapter 36

■ *Directory Cache Buffers*   The number of buffers allocated to handle directory caching

■ *Service Processes*   The number of "task handlers" allocated for station requests. The server might allocate additional processes when station requests run abnormally high, and these processes are not released until the server is downed

■ *Connections In Use*   The number of stations currently attached to the file server. The maximum number available depends on the level of NetWare you purchased from Novell

■ *Open Files*   The number of files currently accessed

Below the status information is the Available Options menu. Choose any option on the menu to see more detailed information about that topic. The following sections describe these options.

Connection Information

Select Connection Information from the MONITOR Available Options menu. When the Active Connections menu appears, select a workstation connection from the list. You can clear a connection by selecting it and pressing the DEL key. After a connection is selected, a Connection Information screen appears, as shown in Figure 33-3. Any files that the user currently has open are displayed at the bottom of the screen. You can highlight any file to view its record lock information, which is described later in this section.

The Connection Information screen displays the following information:

■ *Connection Time*   The amount of time the user has been connected

■ *Network Address*   The network address, station address, and socket address of the user's workstation. Sockets represent the addresses of processes running in multitasking operating systems like OS/2

■ *Requests*   The number of requests the connection has made since it was booted

■ *Kilobytes Read*   The number of kilobytes the connection has read from the disk

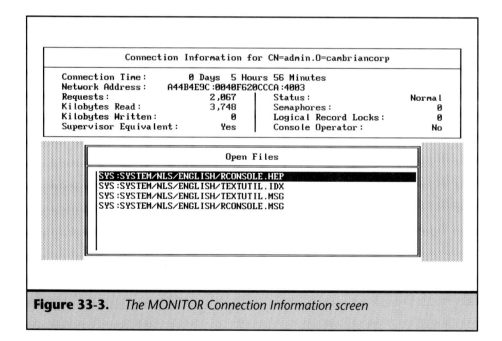

Figure 33-3.   *The MONITOR Connection Information screen*

■ *Kilobytes Written*   The number of kilobytes the workstation has written to the disk

■ *Supervisor Equivalent*   Whether the user at the workstation has supervisor equivalence

■ *Status*   The status can be Normal (logged in and functioning), Waiting (waiting for a file to be unlocked), or Not-logged-in (attached but not logged in)

■ *Semaphores*   The number of semaphores the connection has open. *Semaphores* are used to request the use of a resource and help limit how many tasks can use or change a resource at the same time

■ *Logical Record Locks*   The number of locked records the connection is using. Records are locked to prevent other users from accessing them at the same time as the user

■ *Console Operator*   Whether the user logged into the workstation has server console operator status

Listing a Connection's Physical Record Locks

Users can lock the records of a database so that other users cannot access the records simultaneously. It might be necessary to see which workstation has which records. Highlight the database in use by the workstation in the Open Files window and then press ENTER. The Record Lock screen appears, which lists the following information:

■ *Start*   The offset in the file where the lock begins

■ *End*   The offset in the file where the lock ends

■ *Record Lock*   One of the following:

  Locked Exclusive   Locked so that no one else can access the records or range of bytes

  Locked Shareable   Other stations can read but not write to the records or range of bytes

  Locked   Logged for future locking; specified when the lock is completed

  TTS Holding Lock   Unlocked by the application but locked by the transaction tracking system because of incomplete transactions

■ *Status*   One of the following:

Logged   A set of records is being prepared for locking to prevent deadlock

Not Logged   A normal condition in which there are no pending requests for a set of locks

Disk Information

Select Disk Information from the MONITOR Available Options menu to display information about hard disks. If more than one disk exists, you are asked to pick from a list. The Drive Status screen appears, as shown in Figure 33-4, with the options described here:

■ *Volume Segments On Drive*   Select this option to view a list of volumes on the drive.

■ *Read After Write Verify*   Select this option if you want to change the way the operating system handles disk write verifications. You can select one of the following:

Software Level   This is the default setting in which NetWare ensures that data written to disk is the same as data in memory. If the data is not the

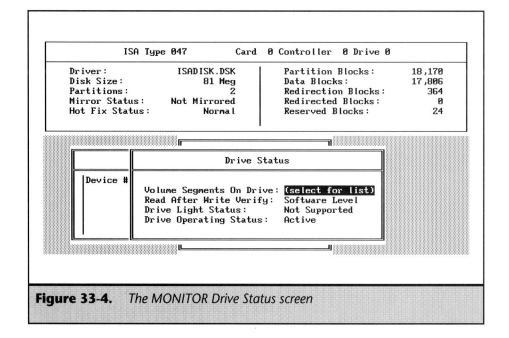

Figure 33-4.   *The MONITOR Drive Status screen*

same, NetWare assumes a bad block, redirects the data to the Hot Fix redirection area, and marks the block as unusable.

Hardware Level   You should choose this option if the disk performs its own verification.

Disable   Select this option with caution. NetWare's performance might improve if you turn the verification process off, but files written to disk will not be checked and they might be written to a corrupt block on the disk.

■ *Drive Light Status*   Select this option to flash the light on a disk drive for testing purposes and to identify the physical disk.

■ *Drive Operating Status*   Select this option to deactivate or activate a drive. Use this option with care! If you deactivate a drive, users might be disconnected and open files might be lost.

Highlight the Volume Segments on Drive field of the Drive Status menu and press ENTER to view the following information at the top of the screen:

■ *Driver*   The name of the driver for the disk

■ *Disk Size*   The size of the disk in megabytes

■ *Partitions*   The number of partitions on the disk

■ *Mirror Status*   The disk may be labeled Mirrored, Not Mirrored, or Remirroring (an indication that a disk has been installed and data is being transferred from the primary to the mirrored disk)

■ *Hot Fix Status*   The disk can be Normal (Hot Fix is functioning) or Not-hot-fixed (Hot Fix has failed or been disabled). If the latter message appears, a serious problem has occurred that requires your immediate attention. You should make sure all users are logged out of the drive, dismount it, and check it for problems

■ *Partition Blocks*   The total space on the partition, in blocks

■ *Data Blocks*   The space (in blocks) available for the storage of data

■ *Redirection Blocks*   The block size of the Hot Fix redirection area

■ *Redirected Blocks*   The number of blocks redirected to the Hot Fix redirection area. Check this value periodically to ensure you aren't running out of Hot Fix space. It may also indicate drive problems.

■ *Reserved Blocks*   The number of blocks reserved for Hot Fix tables

To view the volume segments on the drive, select Volume Segments On Drive from the Drive Status screen.

LAN/WAN Information

Select LAN/WAN Information from the MONITOR Available Options menu to view information about LAN drivers. If multiple adapters exist, they are listed on the LAN Driver Information screen. Select an adapter from the list and press ENTER to display information about the adapter, as shown in Figure 33-5. Use the arrow keys to view additional information. LAN driver information can help in determining if a LAN is overloaded (when compared to another LAN attached to the server) or not working properly. The screen displays the following information about the selected driver:

■ The name of the driver and its parameters

■ The current driver version

■ The address of the network board in the file server

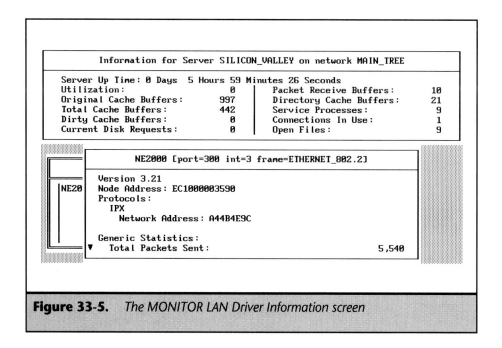

Figure 33-5. *The MONITOR LAN Driver Information screen*

■ The communications protocol bound to the driver with BIND

■ The network address assigned to the network card. This appears only if IPX is bound to the board

Following are descriptions of the more important fields under the heading Generic Statistics. The existence of some fields depends on the type of network card driver loaded.

■ *Total Packets Sent* The number of packets sent from the file server through the LAN card. Compare this number to the same number for other network cards in the server. If one card has more traffic than another, you might want to distribute the load more evenly or add another network card to take up the extra load

■ *Total Packets Received* The number of packets received by the file server since it was last booted. You should compare this information to that of other cards to ensure that one card is not handling more traffic than another

■ *No ECB Available Count* This field is a counter that increments each time a packet could not be received because a receive buffer was not available. The file server allocates more buffers after such incidents until a maximum limit is reached. If this value becomes high, you can increase the maximum limit by using the SERVMAN utility, as discussed in Chapter 36. Doing so affects memory used by other processes, but this won't be a problem on a system with plenty of memory

■ *Send Packet Too Big Count* The number of packets that could not be sent because they were too big for the board to handle. This indicates a discrepancy in the maximum packet size values used on the network

■ *Receive Packet Overflow Count* The number of packets received that were too big to store in a cache buffer. A high number might indicate a discrepancy in the packet size values used on the network, or it might indicate a need to update a software package that does not work well on the network

■ *Receive Packet Too Big Count* The number of packets received that were too large. May indicate a failing network card

■ *Receive Packet Too Small Count* The number of packets received that were too small. May indicate a failing network card

■ *Send Packet Miscellaneous Errors* The number of general errors that occurred when packets were sent. A high value might indicate hardware problems

■ *Receive Packet Miscellaneous Errors* The number of general errors that occurred when packets were received. A high value might indicate hardware problems

■ *Send Packet Retry Count* The number of errors that occurred when the server tried to send packets but could not because of hardware errors. Errors of this sort might indicate a faulty cabling system or faulty network hardware at the workstation. They might also reflect natural delays over WAN links

■ *Checksum Errors* The number of data errors indicated by a mismatch in the checksum byte. A high value indicates faulty hardware, or cable problems such as interference

■ *Hardware Receive Mismatch Count* The number of errors that occurred because specified packet lengths did not match. A high value indicates faulty hardware, or cable problems such as interference

System Module Information

Select the System Module Information option on the Available Options menu to view information about each of the NetWare Loadable Modules currently running in the server.

Select a module from the System Modules list and press ENTER. A list of the resource tags that are being used by the module appears. Press ENTER to view the following information about the tag:

■ *Tag* The name of the tag that the NetWare Loadable Module gave to a resource. Resource tags are used by the operating system to track system resources

■ *Module* The name of the module using the tag

■ *Resource* The type of resource the tag is using

■ *In Use* The amount of the resource that has been allocated by using this resource tag

File Open/Lock Activity

Select the File Open/Lock Activity option on the Available Options menu to display information about the activities of a file, such as which connections are using the file, how the file is being used, and whether it is locked.

When you select this option, a list of directories appears. You might need to select the parent (..) entry to return to a parent directory. When the correct directory is reached, you can select the file to view. A double menu appears that has the following options:

- *Use Count* The number of connections that have the file open, logged, or locked

- *Open Count* The number of connections that have the file open

- *Open for Read* The number of connections reading the file

- *Open for Write* The number of connections writing to the file

- *Deny Read* The number of connections that have opened the file for exclusive use

- *Deny Write* The number of connections that have the file and will not let other stations write to it

- *Status* A file can have a status of Locked or Not Locked. Other users cannot access locked files

- *Conn.* A list of the connections that are using the file

- *Task* A number assigned by the shell to an application program

- *Lock Status* One of the following regarding the records of a file in use:

    Exclusive No one else can read or write to the record

    Shareable Others can read but not write to the record

    TTS Holding Lock The transaction tracking system has locked the file because transactions are not complete

    Logged A set of records is being prepared for locking to prevent deadlocks

    Not Logged The normal condition, which indicates that no requests have been made for the file

Cache Utilization

The Cache Utilization option on the Available Options menu displays a menu of statistics that you can monitor and track over a period of time to determine whether you need to change cache settings. The following information is displayed on the Cache Utilization screen (as shown in Figure 33-6):

■ *Allocate Block Count* The number of block requests made in the disk cache since booting the server. Use this number as a general reference

■ *Allocated from AVAIL* The cache might have blocks that are not in use. This is the number of cache blocks that were made available from the "not in use" list

■ *Allocated from LRU* Cache blocks with information that has not recently been accessed are available for other uses. This value indicates the number of block requests made from the Least Recently Used (LRU) list of blocks

■ *Allocate Wait* The number of cache block requests that had to wait for available cache blocks. A high number indicates a need for more memory

■ *Allocate Still Waiting* The number of times a cache block request had to wait behind another request that was waiting. Like Allocate Wait, a high value indicates a need for more memory

■ *LRU Sitting Time* Information waits in the cache until it is needed again. The oldest block of information is the Least Recently Used (LRU) and is the first to be discarded if blocks are needed for new information. This value indicates the amount of time information has been sitting in the LRU block since the last reference to the information

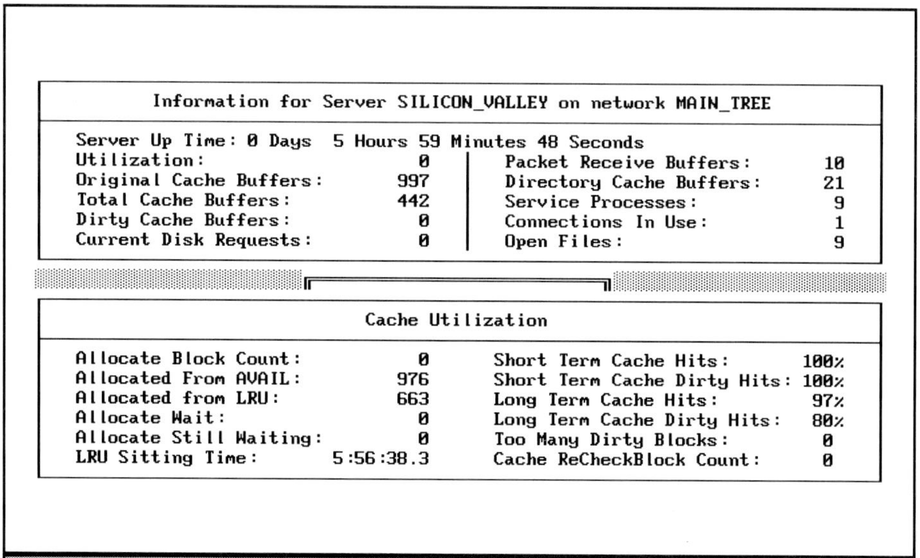

```
          Information for Server SILICON_VALLEY on network MAIN_TREE

     Server Up Time: 0 Days  5 Hours 59 Minutes 48 Seconds
     Utilization:                    0     Packet Receive Buffers:      10
     Original Cache Buffers:        997     Directory Cache Buffers:     21
     Total Cache Buffers:           442     Service Processes:            9
     Dirty Cache Buffers:             0     Connections In Use:           1
     Current Disk Requests:           0     Open Files:                   9


                              Cache Utilization

     Allocate Block Count:            0     Short Term Cache Hits:      100%
     Allocated From AVAIL:          976     Short Term Cache Dirty Hits: 100%
     Allocated from LRU:            663     Long Term Cache Hits:        97%
     Allocate Wait:                   0     Long Term Cache Dirty Hits:  80%
     Allocate Still Waiting:          0     Too Many Dirty Blocks:        0
     LRU Sitting Time:        5:56:38.3     Cache ReCheckBlock Count:     0
```

Figure 33-6. *The MONITOR Cache Utilization screen*

- *Short Term Cache Hits* The percentage of disk cache requests that could be obtained from the cache within the last second

- *Short Term Cache Dirty Hits* A percentage value that indicates the number of disk cache requests over the last second that were already in the cache and already dirty

- *Long Term Cache Hits* This percentage value indicates the amount of information that could be obtained directly from the cache

- *Long Term Cache Dirty Hits* A percentage value that indicates the number of disk cache requests that were already in the cache, and the block was dirty

Processor Utilization

The Processor Utilization option on the Available Options menu displays information about server processes (threads) and hardware interrupts. The list is large. You can scan through it and then select an item and press the F1 key to get more information about the item.

The information screen that appears for each item shows current statistics about the item, along with the overhead required to gather the information. The sampling rate is once every second. The overhead is generated only while the screen is open.

Resource Statistics

All processes have a resource tag that the server uses to track the use of resources. Select Resource Statistics from the Available Options menu and then choose a process for which you want to view resource tag information from the Tracked Resources list. The Resource Tags list appears, and you can highlight a tag and press ENTER to view the following information about it:

- *Tag* The tag name

- *Module* The name of the module that allocated the resource tag

- *Resource* The type of resource that is being tracked

- *In Use* The amount of the resource that has been allocated by using the resource tag

Memory Statistics

Select the Memory Statistics option from the Available Options menu to view detailed information about how NetWare and NetWare Loadable Modules are using the server's memory. A screen similar to that shown in Figure 33-7 appears. The top of the screen shows the currently allocated memory information for all modules:

■ *4K Cache Pages*   The number of cache pages in the allocated memory pool

■ *Cache Page Blocks*   The number of cache pages that have been requested and placed in the allocated memory pool

■ *Percent In Use*   The percentage of memory in use in the allocated memory pool

■ *Percent Free*   The percentage of allocated memory that is not in use

■ *Memory Blocks In Use*   The amount of memory (in blocks) that has been allocated and is in use

■ *Memory Bytes In Use*   The amount of memory (in bytes) that is in use

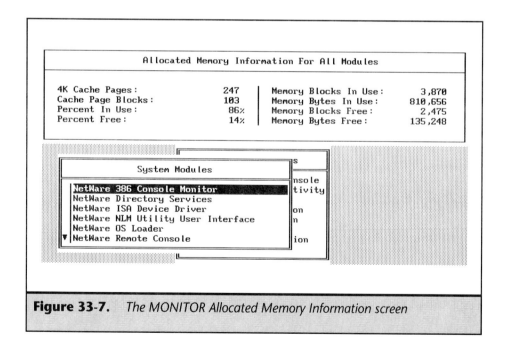

Figure 33-7.   *The MONITOR Allocated Memory Information screen*

■ *Memory Blocks Free*   The amount of memory (in blocks) that has been allocated and is available for use

■ *Memory Bytes Free*   The amount of memory (in bytes) that is available for use

The System Modules menu displays a list of the currently loaded modules. Select a module and press ENTER to display detailed information about that module's memory usage. The information displayed is the same as that described in the previous list, but for the individual module.

Scheduling Information

Select the Scheduling Information option from the Available Options menu to show the current processes running on the server, along with statistics about the processes. The information is gathered every two seconds and displayed on the screen. The overhead required to gather and display this information is also displayed. The columns of the display are described here:

■ *Name*   The name of the process

■ *Sch Delay*   The scheduling delay value for the highlighted process. Press the plus (+) or minus (-) key to increase or decrease the value

■ *Time*   The time the CPU spent executing code for a process or servicing an interrupt routine

■ *Count*   The amount of time a process ran during a sample period or the number of interrupts serviced during a sample period

■ *Load*   The percentage of time the CPU spent in the process or interrupt

CHAPTER 34

T his chapter presents an overview of the commands you can execute at a server console or a remote server console to monitor and change the settings of a server. File system options are covered in Chapter 35, and network communications options are covered in Chapter 36.

Server Commands and Performance Options

Viewing Server Information

You type the commands discussed in the following paragraphs at the file server console or remote console command line to display information about the file server and its networks.

THE VERSION COMMAND   The VERSION command displays the file server's version information and copyright notice. The following information is listed:

> NetWare version number
> Licensing information
> OEM identification number
> Serial number
> Number of licensed connections

THE NAME COMMAND   The NAME command displays the name of the file server.

THE VOLUMES COMMAND   The VOLUMES command displays a list of currently mounted volumes. The names spaces and flags for those volumes are also listed.

THE TIME COMMAND   The TIME command displays the server's current time and date settings. Time zone information is also displayed, along with network time synchronization status.

THE CONFIG COMMAND   The CONFIG command displays the following information:

- The name of the file server

- The internal network number of the file server

- The loaded LAN drivers

- The settings on the network boards, which you need to know when installing additional boards

- The node addresses of the network boards

- The protocol bound to each board (IPX or another protocol)

- The network numbers of the network boards

- The frame types assigned to the network boards

■ The names assigned to the network boards

THE MEMORY COMMAND   The MEMORY command displays the total amount of installed memory that the operating system can address. On EISA systems, NetWare will address memory above 16MB if you use the REGISTER MEMORY command. Make sure you properly configure the server by using the utilities that come with it.

THE MODULES COMMAND   The MODULES command displays information about the modules currently loaded in the file server. The short name used to load each module is displayed, along with a descriptive string or long name for each module. A version number might also be displayed.

THE DISPLAY NETWORKS COMMAND   The DISPLAY NETWORKS command displays the following information about the currently available networks:

■ Their network numbers. Both the internal and external network numbers are displayed

■ The number of networks that must be crossed (the number of hops) to reach the network from the current network is displayed in front of the slash. A 0 indicates the current network

■ The estimated time in ticks (1/18 of a second) for a packet to reach the network from the current network is displayed after the slash

■ The number of known networks is displayed at the bottom of the screen

THE DISPLAY SERVERS COMMAND   The DISPLAY SERVERS command displays a list of the currently available servers and the number of networks that must be crossed to reach each server from the current server.

THE SPEED COMMAND   The SPEED command displays the speed of the server's microprocessor. Speed ratings are determined by the CPU clock speed, the type of microprocessor, and the number of memory wait states. Here are some examples for comparison:

CPU	Speed Rating
Intel 80386SX at 16 MHz	95
Intel 80386 at 16 MHz	120
Intel 80386 at 20 MHz	136
Intel 80486 at 33 MHz	265

If the SPEED command displays a lower speed rating for a system, check to make sure the CPU speed has not been reduced by using an on-board switch or the microprocessor's configuration program.

THE TRACK ON COMMAND   The TRACK ON command displays the type of network traffic received by and sent by the server. You can use the command to locate problems with network communications or simply to monitor the type of traffic at the server. TRACK ON is discussed in Chapter 36.

THE CLS COMMAND   The CLS (clear screen) command clears any text from the console screen. You can also type OFF to execute this command.

Changing Server Settings

This section discusses changing a server's settings and parameters.

The Server Startup Files

There are two server startup files. STARTUP.NCF is stored in the DOS directory and typically contains the disk driver information that is required to boot the server. AUTOEXEC.NCF is stored in the SYS:SYSTEM directory of the server. It executes after the operating system loads. AUTOEXEC.NCF typically contains commands to do the following:

- Set the time zone and other time settings
- Set the time synchronization server type (single reference time server, primary time server, reference time server, or secondary time server)
- Set the bindery context used by NetWare Directory Services when it does bindery emulation
- Set the file server name
- Set the file server IPX internal network number
- Load LAN drivers
- Bind LAN drivers to IPX, TCP/IP, and other protocols
- Mount volumes

There are several ways you can change settings in or add settings to the startup files:

- Type the following command to load the NetWare console editor and edit the AUTOEXEC.NCF file:

    LOAD EDIT SYS:SYSTEM\AUTOEXEC.NCF

- Load the INSTALL utility and then choose Maintenance/Selective Install. From the Installation Options menu, choose NCF Files Options and then choose either Edit AUTOEXEC.NCF file or Edit STARTUP.NCF file.

- Load the SERVMAN utility and choose Console Set Commands. Make the changes to the appropriate settings and specify that you want the changes added to the startup files.

The first two methods place you directly in the console editor so that you can make changes. The third method is the easiest way to configure options because it displays a list of the options and their descriptions and then makes the changes for you.

When working in the editor, you can move around by using the normal cursor movement keys, such as the arrows keys, PGUP, PGDN, HOME, and END. You can use the BACKSPACE and DEL keys to delete text. Some of the other keys you can use are listed here:

F5	Mark text to copy or delete
F6	Copy marked text to a buffer
INS	Insert the text that's in the buffer at the new location
ESC	End editing; you are prompted to save the file

Server Settings

You can change the name of the file server, its network numbers, and its IPX internal number by altering the AUTOEXEC.NCF file and then rebooting the server.

- To change the name of the file server, change the setting of the FILE SERVER NAME line in the AUTOEXEC.NCF file.

- To change a LAN card network number, change the setting of the BIND statement for the LAN card driver. At the console, you can also unbind the

LAN driver for the network and bind it again, specifying a new network number in the process.

■ To alter the IPX internal network number, change the setting of the IPX INTERNAL NET line by typing a new number for the network.

Be sure to down the server and reboot it after making changes to the AUTOEXEC.NCF file unless you can also make the changes from the console (BIND, for example).

Setting the Time and Date

To view the server's current time and date, type the following:

TIME

To set a new time at the console, type the following, replacing the date and time placeholders with the appropriate information:

TIME *month/day/year hour:minute:second*

Enabling and Disabling the Transaction Tracking System (TTS)

The transaction tracking system (TTS) is enabled when you boot a NetWare server. Some application developers might want to disable it to test transactional applications. You might also need to disable it to run some applications, but do this only if you're instructed to do so by the vendor and be aware of the implications of doing so. To disable TTS, type **DISABLE TTS** at the console command line. To enable TTS, type **ENABLE TTS** at the console command line.

Implementing Streams

The Streams environment allows multiple transport communications protocols to be integrated. To implement the environment, add the commands described in the following sections to the AUTOEXEC.NCF file so that they are loaded every time the file server boots. You should load the Streams modules in the following order:

STREAMS
CLIB
TLI
IPXS
Other Streams modules as required

THE STREAMS MODULE   STREAMS is used if a NetWare Loadable Module requires the CLIB module or uses Streams-based protocol services. You must load STREAMS before you load CLIB. Use the following command to load STREAMS:

LOAD *path*\STREAMS

where *path* is the path to the directory where CLIB.NLM is stored if it is in a directory other than SYS:SYSTEM.

THE C LIBRARY (CLIB) MODULE   You load the C Library (CLIB) module if you have a NetWare Loadable Module such as PSERVER or BTRIEVE that requires it. CLIB is a library of routines and functions that NLMs can use. You must load CLIB before you load the module that requires it, and you must load the STREAMS module before you load CLIB.
To load the CLIB module, type the following command:

LOAD *path*\CLIB

where *path* is the path to the directory where CLIB.NLM is stored if it is in a directory other than SYS:SYSTEM.

THE TRANSPORT LEVEL INTERFACE (TLI) MODULE   Load the Transport Level Interface (TLI) module if an NLM requires TLI communication services. You must load STREAMS and CLIB before you load TLI. You might also need to load one of the Streams-based NLMs listed in the following sections.
To load the TLI module, type

LOAD *path*\TLI

where *path* is the path to the directory where TLI.NLM is stored if it is in a directory other than SYS:SYSTEM.

THE STREAMS-BASED IPX (IPXS) MODULE   Use the IPXS NLM if Streams-based IPX protocol services are required. Load the module after the STREAMS module by typing

LOAD *path*\IPXS

where *path* is the path to the module if it is in a directory other than SYS:SYSTEM.

THE MATH LIBRARY (MATHLIB) MODULE   Use the MATHLIB module if the server has a math coprocessor. You must load CLIB before loading MATHLIB. To load MATHLIB, type

LOAD *path*\MATHLIB

where *path* is the path to the module if it is in a directory other than SYS:SYSTEM.

THE MATH LIBRARY C (MATHLIBC) MODULE   Use the MATHLIBC module if the server is an 80386 system that does not have a math coprocessor. You must load CLIB before you load MATHLIBC. To load MATHLIBC, type

LOAD *path*\MATHLIBC

where *path* is the path to the module if it is in a directory other than SYS:SYSTEM.

Freeing Memory by Using REMOVE DOS

Use the REMOVE DOS command to remove DOS from the server's memory. The memory that DOS used is made available for file caching. Use this command if memory is low or to increase security at the file server. When DOS is removed, NLMs cannot be loaded from the file server's DOS drives. To remove DOS, type

REMOVE DOS

When you use REMOVE DOS, the file server reboots when the EXIT command is executed.

Registering Memory Above 16MB

Use the REGISTER MEMORY command to register memory above 16MB. You specify the starting address and the length of the memory above 16MB in the command. Typical addresses are listed in Table 34-1. The command takes the following form:

REGISTER MEMORY *start length*

where *start* is the starting address of the memory and *length* is the memory length, as shown in Table 34-1. When the memory is successfully added, the message "Memory successfully added" appears. If the memory is not added, make sure you are specifying the parameters correctly.

NOTE: *Use REGISTER MEMORY only with actual memory that is installed in the file server. Do not use it with shadow RAM, because shadow RAM might be mapped to lower memory.*

Users and Connection Information

This section discusses how to manage users and workstation connections. It covers how to find out the workstation number of a user, disconnect a user's connection, and broadcast messages to specific users. Before disconnecting any users, be sure to send a message to their workstations so that they can save their work and log out properly. In some cases, you might need to disconnect a workstation because it has locked up and you need to free the files or database information it is holding. The first option discussed in this section helps you determine the number of a workstation in use by a user.

Total Memory	Starting Address	Memory Length
16MB to 20MB	1000000	250000
16MB to 24MB	1000000	500000
16MB to 28MB	1000000	750000
16MB to 32MB	1000000	1000000
16MB to 36MB	1000000	1250000
16MB to 40MB	1000000	1500000

Table 34-1. *Starting addresses and lengths for registering memory above 16MB*

Determining a User's Workstation Number

The following procedure can help you determine a user's workstation address and other information about a user's connection.

1. Type the following command to load the MONITOR module:

   LOAD *path*\MONITOR

   Replace *path* with the drive or directory where MONITOR.NLM can be found if it is not in the SYS:SYSTEM directory.

2. Select Connection Information from the MONITOR Available Options menu.

3. When the Active Users list appears, use the arrow keys to scan the list, and press ENTER to see information about a workstation connection.

Your screen will look similar to that shown in Figure 34-1. The user's network address appears in the upper window, along with other information about the user's connection. Below that is a list of the files that the user has open. If any of the files are database files, you can select a database file and press ENTER to view the record range in use by the user.

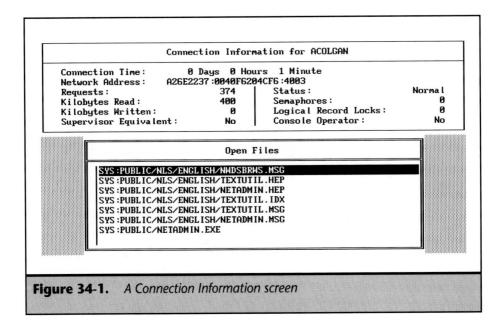

Figure 34-1.   *A Connection Information screen*

NOTE: You can disconnect a user by highlighting the user's name in the Active Users list and pressing DEL. *Answer Yes to the "Clear Connection?" prompt.*

Disabling and Enabling User Logins

You use the DISABLE LOGIN console command to prevent users from logging into the file server. Issue this command when the server needs maintenance. To allow users to log into the server after the DISABLE LOGIN command has been executed, type ENABLE LOGIN.

Broadcasting and Sending Messages

You use the BROADCAST and SEND commands to send a message (55 characters maximum) to all users or to specific users. Use the commands to inform users when a server is undergoing maintenance or other service and will be down for a while.

The commands take the following forms:

SEND "*message*" TO *user* (or *station number*)

BROADCAST "*message*" TO *user* (or *station number*)

Replace *message* with your message, between the quotation marks, and replace *user* with the user's name. If you don't specify a user, the message is sent to all the users who are currently logged in. You can specify a user's workstation number instead of his or her name. Separate multiple user names and station numbers with commas. For example, to send a message to the user JOHN and to workstations 4 and 6, you would type the following command:

SEND "Please log off the system soon" TO JOHN, 4, 6

The message appears at the top of each user's screen. They can clear it by pressing CTRL-ENTER.

NOTE: To determine a user's workstation number, follow the instructions in the section "Determining a User's Workstation Number" earlier in this chapter.

You can use the NETUSER command to block SEND messages at a workstation so that a running process is not paused. You can also set the MESSAGE TIMEOUT option in the NET.CEG file so a workstation continues processing after a set time if a user doesn't clear a broadcast message.

Clearing Connections

You use the CLEAR STATION command to disconnect a workstation from the file server. You would use this command for one of two reasons: to disconnect a workstation at a distant location that was left on by a user or to disconnect a crashed station that left files open on the server. Use the CLEAR STATION command with caution, however. It removes all file server resources allocated to a station, closes all open files, and erases the internal tables used by the file server to track the station. If the workstation is in the middle of a transaction when you execute the CLEAR STATION command, data that is being written to a file might be corrupted.

The command takes the form

CLEAR STATION *n*

where *n* is the number of the workstation. For example, to clear workstation 10, you would type the following command at the console:

CLEAR STATION 10

Securing and Locking the File Server Console

You can secure and lock the file server console to prevent unauthorized users from accessing the server. If the server is locked, a password is required to regain access.

Securing the Console

You secure the console by typing SECURE CONSOLE at the console prompt. When you have secured a console, the following security measures are implemented:

- NetWare Loadable Modules cannot be loaded from any directory except SYS:SYSTEM. This prevents intruders from introducing "Trojan horse" modules that might access or alter important information.

- Keyboard entry into the OS debugger is prevented.

- The date and time cannot be changed, which is important for accounting and auditing purposes and for preventing users whose accounts have time restrictions from accessing the system.

The SECURE CONSOLE command also removes DOS from the server's memory so that the server reboots when the EXIT command is executed from the file server console. To further secure the system, lock the keyboard or place the server in a secure location.

Locking the Console by using MONITOR

To lock the console by using MONITOR, start the MONITOR NetWare Loadable Module by using the following command, replacing *path* with the path to the directory where MONITOR.NLM is located if it is not in the SYS:SYSTEM directory:

LOAD *path*\MONITOR

When the Available Options menu appears, select Lock File Server Console. Type a password that can be used to regain access to the console. To regain access to a locked console, press a key to clear the screen saver and then type the password.

The Server Error Log

Server error messages are stored in a file called SYS$LOG.ERR, which is stored in the SYS:SYSTEM directory. You can view this error log with a text editor. To view this file by using EDIT.NLM, type the following command:

LOAD EDIT SYS:SYSTEM\SYS$LOG.ERR

The date and time of each entry are listed, along with a code that provides a look-up reference in the Novell Error Message manuals. You should consult the error log when the server or network is having problems, and you should periodically delete the file as it grows and takes up disk space. Copy the file to backup media or print it before deleting it.

Downing the Server

NetWare provides a number of ways to shut down the server. You can use the RCONSOLE command at a workstation, the file server console, or a remote console. It is important that you shut down the file server properly to ensure data integrity. Write all cache buffers to disk, close files, and update the directory and file allocation tables properly.

If files are open, you are asked if you still want to down the server. Always close files by using the appropriate applications, unless you are sure the files will not be corrupted when the server is downed.

NOTE: Use the SEND console command to warn users when a server will be brought down. You can also use the workstation SEND command.

Type DOWN at the file server console or a remote console to down the server. You can then invoke the EXIT command to return to DOS. If have used the REMOVE DOS command, the server is rebooted since DOS is no longer loaded in memory.

NetWare Operating System SET Values

The SERVMAN utility provides a convenient way to change the server's startup parameters and other settings. You start the utility by typing LOAD SERVMAN. Then choose Console Set Commands from the Available Options menu. This section discusses server settings, which are found in the Miscellaneous section. The next few chapters discuss settings for the file system and network communications.

NOTE: *This section covers only options that are important to the normal operation of the server. Some options should always be left on, and so they are not mentioned. Other options not mentioned are those used by programmers for writing and testing NLMs.*

ALLOW UNENCRYPTED PASSWORDS   NetWare versions 3.0 and later encrypt passwords for security reasons. However, encryption can cause problems if you have servers running versions of NetWare previous to v.3.0. By default, the Allow Unencrypted Passwords parameter is set to Off. Set it to On to allow users to use both unencrypted and encrypted passwords.

AUTOMATICALLY REPAIR BAD VOLUMES   This option's default setting is On, which causes NetWare to run VRepair when a volume fails. If you prefer to run VRepair on your own, set this option to Off. VRepair is discussed in Chapter 35.

DISPLAY SPURIOUS INTERRUPT ALERTS   An interface card in the server might create spurious interrupts, which indicates a malfunctioning card. The Display Spurious Interrupt Alerts option is set to On by default. If a spurious interrupt message occurs, remove all cards from the server and then remount them one by one until the message appears again. Report the problem to the card's vendor for additional assistance. A new driver or updated card might be available. This option should be left set to On, but it is mentioned here so that you'll know what to do if an alert occurs.

DISPLAY LOST INTERRUPT ALERTS   In some cases a card might request a service from the server by issuing an interrupt and then lose track of the interrupt before the server can respond. These lost interrupts indicate a hardware driver problem or a defective board. If the Display Lost Interrupt Alerts parameter is set to On, NetWare displays messages when lost interrupts are detected. To test drivers and hardware, set the option to On and then monitor lost interrupt messages. To determine which driver or board is defective, unload all the drivers and then reload them one at a time until the problem resurfaces. This option should be left set to On, but it is mentioned here so that you'll know what to do if an alert occurs.

DISPLAY DISK DEVICE ALERTS   Set this parameter to On if you want to display informational messages about hard disks when a disk driver is loaded or unloaded, when the file server is booted or downed, and when attempting to isolate disk driver or hardware problems. The default setting is Off.

HALT SYSTEM ON INVALID PARAMETERS   Set this option to On if you want the server to halt when an invalid process or condition occurs. The default setting is Off, which causes the server to display a system alert and continue operating.

NEW SERVICE PROCESS WAIT TIME=*time*   You set *time* to the amount of time the operating system should wait after receiving a request for another service process before making the allocation. The default setting is 2.2 seconds, and the range is 0.3 seconds to 20 seconds.

MAXIMUM SERVICE PROCESSES=*number*   Set *number* to the maximum number of service processes that the operating system can create. The current number can be viewed by using MONITOR, as described in Chapter 33. If the server is low on memory, decrease this number until you add more memory. Increase the number if the service process number in MONITOR is at its maximum. Increasing the number helps only if more than 20 requests are waiting for disk I/O to complete. The default is 20, and the range is 5 to 40.

REPLACE CONSOLE PROMPT WITH SERVER NAME   The default is On, which displays the server name in the console's colon (:) prompt.

SOUND BELL FOR ALERTS   This option is set to On, which causes NetWare to sound an alarm when alerts are displayed. Set this option to Off if the alarms are frequent and annoying and you are aware of the problem.

UPGRADE LOW PRIORITY THREADS   Some threads that have a low priority, such as file compression, might fail to execute when certain NLMs are running. If this occurs, set the Upgrade Low Priority Threads option to On to upgrade the priority of the threads. The default setting is Off.

CHAPTER 35

T his chapter discusses file system management on NetWare servers. Techniques for installing, removing, testing, partitioning, and formatting hard drives are discussed. Some of this material was covered in Chapter 15 to prepare you for NetWare installation, but remember that INSTALL provides a menu-driven procedure for setting up hard disk partitions and volumes. This chapter discusses console commands for disk management and procedures for dismounting, unmirroring, testing, and replacing drives.

Managing Disk Storage

This chapter also covers the VREPAIR utility. VREPAIR is used to repair structural damage to a volume's file allocation table (FAT) and directory entry table (DET) and restore access to its files.

Disks, Partitions, and Volumes Under NetWare

NetWare servers support a number of different disk configurations. All of these configurations support some form of fault tolerance in which the data is written in two places simultaneously. Any discussion of NetWare disk storage systems must include fault tolerance, since running without it in a business environment would be ludicrous. The disk configurations are as follows:

- *Disk mirroring*   A primary drive and a backup mirroring drive share the same disk controller.

- *Disk duplexing*   The primary drive and the backup mirroring drive are both attached to their own controller.

- *RAID systems*   RAID systems are typically external subsystems that attach to a controller card installed in the server. Refer to the operator's manual for specific instructions on installing and managing RAID systems.

Note that some disk controllers handle mirroring on their own, and they do so more efficiently than the mirroring provided by the NetWare operating system. You set up this mirroring when installing the disk controller.

NOTE: Do not install NetWare's software mirroring on controllers that perform their own mirroring in hardware. Duplexing, however, is provided in software only by NetWare and should be configured using the INSTALL utility, as discussed under "Procedures for Installing and Managing Disks." Do not set up hardware mirroring if you plan to duplex drives.

You use the INSTALL utility to load a driver for each disk controller or SCSI host bus adapter installed in the server, not for each drive attached to the controllers or adapters. Always try to load disk drivers in the same order so that disk device numbering remains the same.

Device Numbering

All drives have a specific number that identifies them to the operating system. The numbering scheme consists of a five-digit number, as defined here:

- The first two digits are assigned by the operating system when you select a driver for a disk controller. They identify which driver is used.

- The third digit is the number of the controller board or host adapter in the server, but not its channel number. The first driver you load becomes the first board in the numbering scheme, so make sure you always use the same driver load order.

- The fourth digit represents the controller number. On SCSI systems, more than one controller may be attached to the host bus adapter.

- The fifth digit represents the actual disk attached to the controller.

You use these disk ID numbers when configuring (mirroring and duplexing) and maintaining the drives in the server. NetWare may display the number when a disk error occurs. For example, you might see the following device information associated with an error message:

Device #3 (20101)

The number in parentheses is the device number, whereas #3 is a logical number that relates to the order in which the disk drivers were loaded. If you change the load order, the logical number and the third digit of the device number change, so be aware of these changes when identifying drives.

Chapter 14 provides several illustrations of device numbering on different disk systems. A duplexed system is shown in Figure 14-1. Figure 14-2 illustrates device numbering for embedded SCSI drives when two host adapters are mounted in a server that has an existing controller (ST506, ESDI, or IDE). Figure 14-3 illustrates device numbering for SCSI systems that use nonembedded controllers. In this case, each controller supports multiple drives, all of which are attached to a single host adapter.

Logical Device Numbering

The logical device number defines the sequential order in which disk drivers are loaded. When the first driver is loaded, the first disk attached to the controller for that driver becomes device number 0. The second disk attached to that controller becomes device number 1. When the next disk driver is loaded, the first disk attached to its corresponding controller becomes device number 2. This sequential numbering continues up to the last drive.

As mentioned, the logical device number changes if you change the load order of drivers. For example, if you load the driver for the second controller before the first controller, the disks attached to it become device 0 and 1 instead of device 2 and 3. Another potential problem occurs if you unload a disk driver, then reload it. For example, assume one driver supports logical device number 0 and 1 and another supports device 2 and 3. If you then unload the first driver and reload it, its disks become logical device 4 and 5, since the operating system does not reorder device numbers. Note that this is only a problem if you are not aware of the new logical device numbers. Be sure to keep track of which disk you are referring to.

NOTE: To reset logical device numbers, make sure disk drivers are specified in their proper load order in the CONFIG.NCF file, then down the server and reboot it.

Partitions

Partitions are divisions of disks. Typically, the first disk in a server contains a small DOS partition, and the remainder of the disk forms the first NetWare partition. All other disks in the partition are identified by a physical partition number and a logical partition number. The physical partition number is a sequential number that identifies each partition, one after another. The logical partition number identifies mirrored or duplexed pairs.

Each partition is assigned a Hot Fix redirection area that is two percent of the partition's space. When blocks are found to be failing or defective, the NetWare operating system moves data in the blocks to the Hot Fix redirection area. If you are using an older drive, you might want to increase the redirection area size, since the disk might be more susceptible to block failure than a newer drive.

Figure 35-1 shows a system with two controllers and two drives attached to each controller. The first controller and its two drives form the primary data storage area. Note that a small DOS partition exists on the first drive. The second controller and its drives form the duplexing system. Each drive has its own partition numbers. The DOS partition is physical partition 0, and the remaining partitions are numbered from 1 to 4. However, NetWare assigns logical partition numbers to mirrored drives, so partitions 1 and 3 are viewed as logical partition 1, and physical partitions 2 and 4 are viewed as logical partition 2.

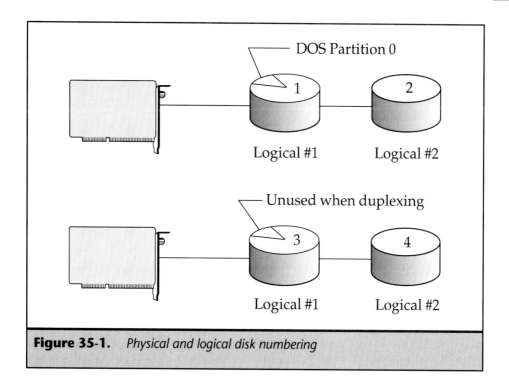

Figure 35-1. *Physical and logical disk numbering*

These logical partition numbers are important when viewing information about mirrored disks. Logical mirrored partitions are listed in the INSTALL and MONITOR server utilities as follows:

    Mirrored: Logical Partition #1
    Mirrored: Logical Partition #2

However, the physical partitions that make up a mirrored set are listed as shown next. Note the device number at the end of each line that identifies the driver, controller, and disk attached to it.

    In Sync - NetWare partition 1 on Device #0 (20000)
    In Sync - NetWare partition 3 on Device #1 (20100)

Each NetWare physical partition contains its own Hot Fix redirection area. Any messages you see relating to Hot Fix redirection use physical partition numbers.

As with logical device numbers, logical partition numbers are dynamic. If you remove mirroring and duplexing, then reset it without downing and rebooting the server, the logical numbers will change. Be aware that numbers have changed or reboot the server.

Volumes

Above the partition level are volumes. A volume is part of a partition. It may take up all of the partition or only part of it. A volume may *span* from one partition to part or all of another partition. The space in a volume is divided into equal blocks that can range from 4KB to 64KB in size. A volume used entirely for one or a few large database files benefits from large block sizes, while volumes with many small files benefit from volumes with small block sizes.

Volume Segments

Volumes can extend over physical partitions. A single disk can contain up to 8 volume segments that belong to one or more volumes. Each volume can consist of up to 32 volume segments. The first segment of a volume on a disk is segment 0, the second is segment 1, and so on.

Since segments can span drives, expanding a volume is a simple matter of adding a new segment to it. But spanned volumes should be duplexed to guard against disk failure. A failure of one disk in the spanned volume prevents access to all segments in the volume.

Volume FATs and DETs

Volumes consist of the file allocation table (FAT) and the directory entry table (DET). The FAT simply identifies every block in which a file is located. Files might be broken up into several parts and placed in noncontiguous blocks. The FAT tracks the blocks for the file. Each entry in the FAT indicates a block of the file's information and points to the next FAT entry, which indicates the next block and next FAT entry. NetWare maintains two copies of the FAT, in case one becomes corrupted.

The DET contains directory information for the volume. Blocks that are part of the DET are designated as either directory types or file types. Directory-type entries contain subdirectory information, and file-type entries contain information such as filename, attributes, time and date stamps, and size. There are two DETs per volume to guard against corruption.

NetWare places copies of the FAT and part of the DET in cache memory to improve performance. Only the portions of the DET that correspond to recently requested files remain in cache memory. NetWare compares copies of the FAT and DET when mounting a drive to ensure that everything matches. If they don't match, the volume must be repaired with the VREPAIR utility, covered later in this chapter under "Repairing Volumes with VREPAIR." A volume also doesn't mount if the server doesn't have enough memory to cache the entire FAT and the part of the DET needed to mount the volume. You'll then need to increase memory and take steps to optimize the available memory.

Name Space Support

Name space support in NetWare supports non-DOS files, such as files created on Macintosh, OS/2, UNIX, or FTAM systems. When name space support is added to a volume, *every* DOS file-type and directory-type entry on the volume gets an additional directory entry. Each additional name space support installed adds another directory entry to the file and directory entries. Because of this, you should place name space support on separate volumes from DOS files.

An entry in the DOS file entry holds the name of the name space that contains additional information about a file. If the file is a Macintosh file, the name space entry contains resource fork and Finder information. If additional name space support is loaded after Macintosh support, a name space link in the Macintosh name space entry points to the new name space entry in a daisy-chain fashion. The DOS name is the ultimate reference, however. When a non-DOS file is requested, both the DOS directory entry and the name space entry are cached. The DOS directory entry points to the actual location of the file on disk, and the name space entry contains non-DOS information about the file.

Note that there are some performance benefits to creating a name space when creating a volume. That is because the system creates the DOS directory entry and the name space entry at the same time, guaranteeing that both entries are in the same directory entry block and cached together. Thus, the system only needs to cache one block. However, if name space support is added to an existing volume, file fragmentation virtually guarantees that corresponding DOS/name space entries will be created in the same directory entry block. Such files require two block reads from disk—one for the DOS block and one for the name space block at its separate location.

As mentioned, it's a good idea to create separate volumes for name space support. The most important benefit is that DOS files not needing name space support don't use extra disk space.

File Compression

By default, the File Compression field is set on. Files that have not been accessed for a certain period of time are automatically compressed. However, when a compressed file is accessed it must first be decompressed, but the time it takes to do so is usually negligible. Once a volume is created with file compression set on, you cannot change it without deleting and re-creating the volume. In most cases, you should use file compression, but check with your application vendors to ensure that compression is compatible. You may need to store some applications on volumes where compression is not used. Note that this option allows the volume to support file compression, but you must still flag files you want to compress using SET commands. Plan on placing all files you need to compress in a single volume.

Block Suballocation

With the Block Suballocation field set on, the volume stores files more efficiently by storing files in smaller increments than the value set in the Volume Block Size field. For example, assuming block suballocation is off and a volume block size of 4KB exists, a 6.5KB file would still require 8KB of disk space. With block suballocation on, that file requires only 6.5KB of disk space. Any "leftover" free blocks are used in the future to store fragments from other files.

The combination of file compression and block suballocation maximizes the disk space on a volume.

The NetWare File Caching System

NetWare's performance is attributable in large part to its caching of data and file tables. Besides buffers for caching files and directory entry tables, NetWare's turbo indexing feature improves access to the file allocation table. You can change the SET options (discussed at the end of this chapter) to gain performance improvements on systems that don't have enough memory to handle the majority of disk reads from cache memory (assuming information requested could be in cache memory if it were available). The default settings are often adequate, but you may need to change them to match your network environment.

Workstations request disk I/O from the server. When the server receives the request, it determines whether the request can be satisfied from the information in the cache, or whether it needs to schedule a disk read. Likewise, disk writes are first placed in the cache, then scheduled for writing to disk. Because all disk reads and writes go through the cache, it is important to ensure that there is adequate cache memory available. You can use the MONITOR utility to check cache memory statistics.

There are two SET parameters that are useful for balancing read/write operations. In some environments, many small write operations to disk can cause a loss of performance for clients reading from the disk. In that case, it is often beneficial to increase the time the system waits before it writes information in the cache to disk.

NOTE: Information in the cache that has not been written to disk is referred to as "dirty."

You can increase the time the system waits before writing information to disk with the Dirty Disk Cache Delay Time parameter discussed at the end of this chapter. The default setting is 3.3 seconds. In other words, after 3.3 seconds, the information in the cache is old enough (aged) to be written to disk. All read operations stop so the system can write the dirty cache buffers to disk. You can increase this wait time to as high as 10 seconds. Be careful about setting this value too high. If the system should hang up, as much as 10 seconds of disk write information could be lost. Make sure your system has adequate backup power, and if writing database information, make sure the TTS (transaction tracking system) is active (the default settings).

Another setting that improves performance in an environment where there are a lot of disk writes is Maximum Concurrent Disk Cache Writes. When the system is ready to write information in the cache to disk, by default, only 50 writes occur. This prevents the write operation from taking too much time and lets users' requests for disk reads be serviced promptly. However, if there are more writes than reads (perhaps most reads are satisfied from cache memory), then you can increase the number of disk writes. The maximum value is 4000. As always, the more memory your system has for caching, the less it will need to access the disk for reads. You can therefore increase this value to improve performance.

The MONITOR utility displays the number of dirty cache buffers. If this value is high and remains high, there is a problem with the disk/cache system. You'll probably need to increase memory and then increase the number of writes to disk using the Maximum Concurrent Disk Cache Writes setting to improve the situation. If 75 percent of the cache buffers are dirty, you should take these steps immediately.

Viewing File System Information

You can view file system information using the MONITOR or SERVMAN utility. The MONITOR utility provides short-term and long-term disk statistics, while SERVMAN displays file system information and features. As always, the longer the server is up and running, the more accurate its statistical information will be. In other words, the effects of peaks in usage tend to be balanced out over time.

MONITOR Disk Information Menu

MONITOR provides information on its Disk Information menu. For a discussion of this information refer to the "Disk Information" section in Chapter 33.

MONITOR Cache Utilization Menu

Cache statistics can be viewed by choosing Cache Utilization from MONITOR's Available Options menu. These options are covered in Chapter 33 under "Cache Utilization."

SERVMAN Storage Options

To view storage information, choose Storage Information from the SERVMAN Available Options menu. A screen similar to Figure 35-2 appears. This screen initially displays information about adapters installed in the server. Scroll through the list of adapters in the Storage objects window if there are multiple adapters. To view device information, scroll to one of the indented objects and press ENTER in the Storage objects window. To view partition information, scroll to one of the twice-indented objects and press ENTER.

SERVMAN Volume Information

To view volume information, choose Volume Information from the SERVMAN Available Options menu. A screen similar to Figure 35-3 appears. In the lower window, scroll to the volume you want to see. Its features, statistics, and current settings appear in the upper window.

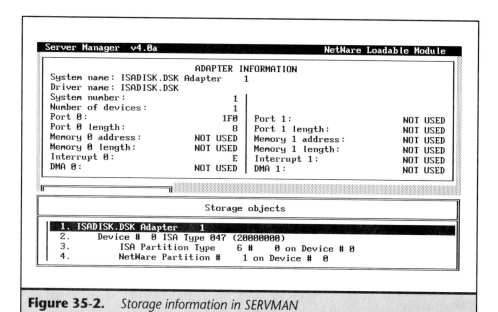

```
Server Manager  v4.0a                          NetWare Loadable Module
┌──────────────────────────────────────────────────────────────────────┐
│                        ADAPTER INFORMATION                             │
│ System name: ISADISK.DSK Adapter    1                                  │
│ Driver name: ISADISK.DSK                                               │
│ System number:              1                                          │
│ Number of devices:          1                                          │
│ Port 0:                   1F0    Port 1:                   NOT USED     │
│ Port 0 length:              8    Port 1 length:           NOT USED     │
│ Memory 0 address:    NOT USED    Memory 1 address:        NOT USED     │
│ Memory 0 length:     NOT USED    Memory 1 length:         NOT USED     │
│ Interrupt 0:                E    Interrupt 1:             NOT USED      │
│ DMA 0:               NOT USED    DMA 1:                    NOT USED     │
├──────────────────────────────────────────────────────────────────────┤
│                        Storage objects                                 │
├──────────────────────────────────────────────────────────────────────┤
│ 1. ISADISK.DSK Adapter     1                                           │
│ 2.      Device #   0 ISA Type 047 (20000000)                           │
│ 3.          ISA Partition Type    6 #    0 on Device #  0               │
│ 4.          NetWare Partition #     1 on Device #  0                    │
└──────────────────────────────────────────────────────────────────────┘
```

Figure 35-2.   *Storage information in SERVMAN*

```
                        VOLUME INFORMATION
 File system name: NetWare v4.0 File System
 Names spaces loaded:DOS
 Compression:                ON  │ Sub allocation:              ON
 Migration:                 OFF  │ Read only:                  OFF
 Block size:               8192  │ Sub allocation unit size:  3584
 Sectors per block:          16  │ Fat blocks:                  16
 Total blocks:             7680  │ Free blocks:               2875
 Freeable limbo blocks:     872  │ Non freeable limbo blocks:    0
 Directory size (blocks):   160  │ Migrated files:               0
 Directory slots:          5120  │ Used directory slots:      2333
 Extended directory space in 0  │
─────────────────────────────────
  Available Options
  Console Set Commands
─────────────────────────────────
                  Mounted volumes
─────────────────────────────────
 SYS          62,914,560 bytes capacity 63 % full
 VOL1          4,194,304 bytes capacity 2 % full
```

Figure 35-3.   *Volume information in SERVMAN*

Procedures for Installing and Managing Disks

Disk drivers are loadable modules that provide links between the operating system and disk controller boards. NetWare comes with a set of drivers, and others are available from drive manufacturers. There are two ways to install or modify the file system configuration:

- Load the INSTALL utility and use its menu-driven options to choose and load disk drivers.

- Use console commands to manually load or unload drivers.

The advantage of using the INSTALL utility is that it describes available drivers and presents brief help information. However, if you know the name of the driver, you can load it just as easily with the LOAD command, which takes the following form:

LOAD *path/driver parameter*

Here, *path* is the path to the directory containing the loadable module, if it is not in the SYS:SYSTEM directory. The *driver* is the name of the driver, and *parameter* is one or more of those from the following list. Note that parameters are specified to configure each driver to match the settings of the disk adapter.

DMA=#   Replace # with a DMA channel to reserve for the driver.

INT=#   Replace # with the hardware interrupt set on the board. The operating system uses hexadecimal values for the interrupts, so 10=A, 11=B, 12=C, 13=D, 14=E and 15=F.

MEM=#   Replace # with the memory address to reserve for the driver.

PORT=#   Replace # with the I/O port to reserve for the driver.

SLOT=#   On Micro Channel machines and EISA systems with BusMASTER slots, replace # with the number of the slot in which the board is installed. The interrupts, memory addresses, and I/O ports are set with the reference or configuration disk supplied with the board.

For example, the following command loads the ISADISK driver at interrupt F and port 170:

```
LOAD ISADISK INT=F PORT=170
```

If you do not specify parameters, NetWare prompts you for those it needs (some are read directly from the board).

You can add the LOAD command to the CONFIG.NCF file in the DOS directory where the SERVER.EXE file is located. All disk LOAD commands must be in this file rather than AUTOEXEC.NCF, because the disk must be initialized before NetWare can load. Be sure to specify the disk driver parameters when adding the LOAD command to the file, otherwise you'll need to enter them every time you start the server. Remember that no two cards can share the same interrupts and I/O ports. You can load a driver multiple times if more than one card exists, but the board setting and drive parameters for each must be different.

NOTE: The PS/2 drivers PS2ESDI and PS2MFM do not need parameters because they are self-configured.

Server systems using the AT class of disk controllers must be installed using the ISADISK.DSK loadable driver module. Type **LOAD ISADISK** to load the disk driver. The default interrupt is E, but you can change it to B, C, or F using the INT= option. The default I/O port is 1F0, but you can change it to 170 using the PORT= option. Make sure the board settings are set appropriately if you make the optional settings.

NOTE: The ISADISK driver module can be loaded twice if two disk controllers are present. The first controller uses I/O port 1F0 and interrupt E. The second controller uses I/O port 170 and interrupt F.

Unloading Disk Drivers

If you need to upgrade a disk driver or remove it so a disk can be replaced or removed, use the following procedure. First, dismount all volumes that use the disk with this command:

DISMOUNT *volume*

Here, *volume* is the name of the volume. Repeat this command for each volume. Next, type the following command to unload the disk driver, where *driver* is the name of the disk driver to unload:

UNLOAD *driver*

Overview for Adding Internal Hard Disks

The basic steps for installing an internal disk are outlined below, then covered in detail later. To install a new drive in a server, the server must be downed because the drive and its controller must be mounted internally.

1. Down the server and install the drive.

2. Reboot the server and load the INSTALL module by typing **LOAD INSTALL**.

3. Install new disk drivers if necessary.

4. Partition the disk.

5. Run a disk surface test (optional).

6. Format the disk (optional).

7. Establish disk mirroring (optional).

8. Create and mount volumes.

Overview for Adding External Hard Disks

External hard disks run under their own power and connect to a host bus adapter that is presumably already installed in your server. You can usually add new drives without having users log out of the server. You will need to dismount any volumes that have segments on the external disks, however. Here are the steps for adding external hard disks:

1. Type the following command, where *volume* is the name of the volume you want to add an external disk segment to:

DISMOUNT *volume*

2. Unload the disk drivers associated with the disk system by typing the following command, replacing *driver* with the name of the driver to unload:

    UNLOAD *driver*

3. Power down the external disk system and install the new driver.

4. Power up the external disk system, then reload and remount the driver and volume with the following commands:

    LOAD *driver*
    MOUNT *volume*

5. If necessary, load DISKSET or other utilities supplied with the drive to place identification information about the external disk on the EEPROM chip of the host bus adapter. Refer to the manual supplied with the external disk system for more information.

6. Type the following command at the console prompt, then create a partition and designate it as a segment for volumes.

    LOAD INSTALL

Load and Configure Disk Drivers

After installing a drive, you need to restart NetWare and install drivers for it. You can use the LOAD *driver* command at the console prompt, or you can start the INSTALL program. INSTALL is covered here.

1. Type the following at the server console to load the INSTALL utility:

    LOAD INSTALL

2. At the Installation Options menu, choose Disk Driver Option. The Select a Disk Driver menu appears.

3. Choose a driver from the list, or if you don't see the driver you need, load it from disk by pressing INS.

4. Specify the interrupt number, port value, and other information for the driver and press F10 to continue. If the driver doesn't load, you have conflicting interrupt and port values. Try different settings or reconfigure the board.

5. After the driver successfully loads, you can add other disk drivers if necessary by repeating these steps.

You can install the same driver more than once to support multiple boards, as long as each board has different interrupt and port settings.

Partitioning Disks

Partitions are divisions of hard drives set aside for a particular operating system. Use the INSTALL loadable module at the console to create or change a disk partition, as discussed here.

Creating Partitions

To create a disk partition, follow these steps:

1. At the Installation Options menu, select Maintenance/Selective Install.

2. Choose Disk Options.

3. Choose Modify Disk Partitions and Hot Fix from the Available Disk Options menu.

4. Choose Create NetWare Disk Partition from the Disk Partition Options menu. If multiple disks exist, first select the disk to partition from the Available Disk Drives menu.

NOTE: If you want to repartition an existing disk, refer to the next section, "Deleting Partitions."

5. Change the size of the data area and the Hot Fix redirection size if necessary. If this is an older drive, you might want to increase the redirection area above the default value listed.

6. When done, press ESC and select Yes to create the partition.

To create other partitions, repeat the preceding steps. If you want to mirror or duplex the partitions, refer to "Mirroring and Unmirroring Disks" later in this chapter.

Deleting Partitions

You delete partitions if you want to reconfigure a disk used for another operating system into a NetWare partition. NetWare allows only one NetWare partition per disk. You might also reconfigure a partition because the Hot Fix redirection area has been used completely. Before deleting any partition, make sure you have good backups of the data.

Load the INSTALL module at the console and follow these steps to remove a partition:

1. Unmirror the drive if necessary, as described in the next section. If the unmirrored disk is labeled "Not Mirrored," delete the volumes on the partition, as discussed in the section, "Managing Volumes."

2. Choose Disk Options from the Installation Options menu, then choose Modify Disk Partitions and Hot Fix from the Available Disk Options menu.

3. Choose Delete any Disk Partition from the Disk Partition Options menu.

4. Choose the partition to delete from the Available Disk Partitions menu and press ENTER.

5. When done, press ESC to exit the menu. Refer back to the previous section to repartition the disk if necessary.

Mirroring and Unmirroring Disks

Mirroring duplicates information on one partition to another partition. Duplexing performs mirroring when two disk controllers are present. For simplicity, the term *mirroring* is used for both here.

Mirroring Hard Drives

To initially establish a mirrored pair or group of NetWare partitions, use the following steps. You must have established the partitions on the physical disks before proceeding.

1. Load the INSTALL module by typing **LOAD INSTALL** at the console prompt.

2. Select Disk Options from the main menu.

3. Select Mirroring from the Available Disk Options menu.

The status window appears showing a window similar to this:

```
╔═══════════════════════════════════════╗
║       Available Disk Partition        ║
╟───────────────────────────────────────╢
║Not Mirrored: Logical Partition #1     ║
║Not Mirrored: Logical Partition #2     ║
║Not Mirrored: Logical Partition #3     ║
║Not Mirrored: Logical Partition #4     ║
╚═══════════════════════════════════════╝
```

The status of the partitions is one of the following:

Not Mirrored   The partition is not currently mirrored to another partition.

Mirrored   The partition is currently mirrored to another partition.

Out of Sync   The partition was mirrored to another partition, but is currently unmirrored from that partition.

4. Highlight one of the partitions to be the primary partition in the mirrored pair and press ENTER. The following menu appears, indicating that the partition is "In Sync" with itself and has no data problems:

```
╔═══════════════════════════════════════════════════╗
║          Mirrored NetWare Partitions              ║
╟───────────────────────────────────────────────────╢
║ In Sync -    NetWare partition 1 on Device #0 (21000)║
╚═══════════════════════════════════════════════════╝
```

5. Press INS to select a partition for mirroring to the device you selected in step 4.

A window appears with a listing of available partitions. Only those partitions that are the same size or larger than the partition you selected in step 4 appear.

6. Choose a partition attached to a different controller than the first to ensure fault tolerance.

NetWare proceeds to synchronize the partitions. Any current mirror tables are flushed, and the operating system is alerted of the new components that make up the mirrored set. The operating system then checks the selected partitions for matching sync bits, time stamps, and blocks. Be patient during this phase. It may take a while to synchronize disks with a lot of directory and file information. However, users can continue using the server while disks synchronize in the background.

When the mirroring process is complete, the status of both disks should appear as "In Sync."

Unmirroring Hard Disks

You unmirror disks when you need to upgrade a disk, add a new disk, or swap a good disk for a failed disk. Note that NetWare usually unmirrors a failed disk automatically, so all you need to do is replace it and remirror the disks. You can unmirror disks if you need to delete a partition, conduct a surface test, or change the Hot Fix redirection area. Follow this procedure to unmirror disks:

1. Ensure that all users are logged off the server if the disk you need to replace is an internal disk. If the disk is external, you can often replace it without shutting down the server, but you will need to dismount any volumes attached to it.

2. Dismount all the volumes that have segments on the disk by using the DISMOUNT *volume* command at the server console.

3. Load INSTALL, then choose Disk Options to display the Available Disk Options menu. Choose Mirror/Unmirror Disk Partitions from this menu.

4. Highlight the partition to unmirror and press the DEL key. The unmirroring process begins.

Once the unmirror process is complete, you can remount the volume to allow users access to it, but it runs without mirroring protection. The available partition is listed as "Not Mirrored," and the disabled drive is listed as "Out of Sync." Volume information on the "Out of Sync" drive is unavailable.

Remirroring Partitions

After replacing the faulty disk in the former mirrored pair, follow the procedure in the previous section, "Mirroring Hard Drives," to resynchronize mirroring for the new pair. You'll need to dismount the volume before remirroring, so make sure users are logged out or not using the volume. Remirroring takes place in the background, so users can log back in and access other volumes while the drives synchronize.

Managing Volumes

As disks become full, you increase the size of volumes. Since volumes can have multiple segments, expanding a volume is a simple matter of adding a new drive and creating a segment on the drive that you make a part of an existing volume. Placing segments of volumes on multiple hard disks increases performance, but it is essential that you duplex the volumes.

When the server is booted, volumes are mounted, making the files on the volume visible to the operating system and its users. The FAT and parts of the DET are loaded into memory. If there is not enough memory to hold the FAT and part of the DET, the volume does not mount.

Creating Volumes

Volumes are created within the partitions of hard drives. If you haven't loaded disk drivers and partitioned the drives, you cannot create volumes. Refer to the previous sections on loading drivers and partitioning disks if you need to.

To create a new volume, follow these steps:

1. Load INSTALL and choose Maintenance/Selective Install.

2. Choose Volume Options from the Installation Options menu.

3. Press INS to add a new volume. The New Volume Information screen appears. Free space on existing volumes is listed. If space is not available, you'll need to add a new disk or modify existing volumes.

4. To name the new volume, highlight the Volume Name field and type a name.

5. Press ESC to use the available disk space for the volume, or select the volume and press ENTER to type in a preferred volume size in blocks and then press ESC.

6. Press F10 to save your changes.

7. Select Mount All Volumes or Mount Volumes Selectively to mount all or selected volumes, respectively.

Mounting and Dismounting Volumes

The DISMOUNT console command makes volumes unavailable to users so you can perform maintenance and upgrades. Be sure to use the SEND command to warn users before dismounting a volume. To dismount a volume, issue the following command, where *volume* is the name of the volume to dismount:

DISMOUNT *volume*

NOTE: *You can also dismount a volume from INSTALL.*

Expanding a Volume

You can increase the size of a volume by adding a new volume segment. The volume segment can be any available part of an existing or new drive. Follow these steps to increase the size of a volume:

1. Load INSTALL and choose Maintenance/Selective Install.

2. Choose Volume Options from the Installation Options menu.

3. When the Volumes list appears, press INS.

4. A list of segments appears if any are available. Select a segment from this list and press ENTER.

5. A list of volumes appears. Select a volume and press ENTER, then press ESC and F10 to save your changes.

Deleting Volumes

To delete a volume, first make sure no one has files open on the volume and back up any data to be saved. Then follow these steps:

1. Load INSTALL and choose Maintenance/Selective Install.

2. Choose Volume Options from the Installation Options menu.

3. Select the volume to delete and press DEL.

4. You are asked to confirm the deletion. Choose Yes to delete the volume.

Supporting Non-DOS Files (Name Space)

To support non-DOS files, a name space loadable module must be linked with the operating system. Name space modules have the extension NAM and are loaded at the server with the LOAD command. Once you load the module, use the ADD NAME SPACE command to configure the volume(s) so you can store the files. Note that NetWare v.4 supports OS/2 files without the need to load name space support. If possible, don't add name space to the SYS volume.

Loading Name Space Support

Use the LOAD command at the server to load the name space module. The command takes the following form:

LOAD *namespace*

Here, *namespace* is the name of the name space module, which is assumed to be stored in the SYS:SYSTEM directory. If the module is in another directory, specify the path before *namespace*. The name space module for Macintosh support is MAC.NAM, so you would type **LOAD MAC** to install Macintosh support. Be sure to place the LOAD command for name space support in the CONFIG.NCF file so it loads every time you restart the server.

Adding Name Space to a Volume

After loading a name space with the LOAD command, use the ADD NAME SPACE command at the console to specify the volume that will support non-DOS files. The command takes the following form:

ADD NAME SPACE *name* TO *volume*

Here, *name* is the name of the variable for the name space module loaded at the server (MAC, for example), and *volume* is the name of the server volume.

> NOTE: *You only type the ADD NAME SPACE command once, when installing the name space.*

Upgrading Name Space

It may be necessary to upgrade a name space module if the manufacturer produces a new version. You can update the module without downing the server. However, if the SYS volume is using the name space, or if SECURE CONSOLE or REMOVE DOS commands have been used, you must down the file server, copy the updated module to the file server boot directory, and then reboot the file server.

To update the name space module without downing the server, follow these steps:

1. Back up the data on all volumes that use the name space module.

2. Dismount all volumes that use the name space module.

3. Type the following command to unload the name space module, replacing *namespace* with the name of the module:

   UNLOAD *namespace*

4. Copy the new module from its floppy disk to the directory that holds the existing module.

5. Load the new module by typing the following command, replacing *namespace* with the name of the module:

   LOAD *namespace*

6. Remount the volumes by typing

   MOUNT ALL

Disk Options Available in MONITOR

Disk options can be accessed by loading the MONITOR utility at the file server console or remote console. When the Available Options menu appears, choose Disk Information, then choose a disk drive. The Drive Status screen appears, as shown previously in Figure 35-2. The following sections describe how to make changes in the options listed.

Changing the "Read After Write Verify" Status of a Disk

The Read After Write Verify option ensures that data written to disk matches the information in memory. Most disk drives support this feature. You can change the status to one of the following options to improve performance or temporarily test the drive. Select Read After Write Verify from the Drive Status screen to change the settings.

Software Level Verify   The driver performs the read after write verification.

Hardware Level Verify   The controller performs the read after write verification.

Disable Verify   Read after write verification is not used. While this may speed performance, it should not be used on a regular basis since data may be corrupted.

Flashing the Hard Disk Light

The Drive Light Status option is used to physically identify a hard disk and correlate it to the drive listed in the System Disk Drives window. Some drives do not support this option and will display a "Not Supported" message in the field.

Activating or Deactivating a Hard Disk

You can set drives to active or inactive status by selecting Drive Operating Status from the Drive Status screen. When the Operating Status screen appears, select one of the following options:

Activate Drive This option sets the drive to active and displays information in the information window about the drive when it is selected.

Deactivate Drive This option sets the drive to inactive and removes information about the drive from the status window.

CAUTION: *Make sure no users are accessing a drive you plan to deactivate.*

Mounting and Dismounting Removable Media

Removable media must be mounted before being used and dismounted before being removed from the drive. The driver for the disk must support removable media. Choose Removable Drive Mount Status from the Drive Status window and then select one of these options:

Mount Drive Mounts the media

Dismount Drive Dismounts the media

Locking or Unlocking a Removable Media Device

The Removable Drive Lock Status option is used either to prevent media from being physically removed or to allow it to be removed. The driver must support this option. Select the Removable Drive Lock Status option from the Drive Status screen and choose one of the following options:

Lock Drive Locks the device so media cannot be removed

Unlock Drive Unlocks the device so media can be removed

Working with File Compression

File compression stores disk files in less disk space by dynamically compressing the files before they are stored. The files are decompressed when opened. You enable file compression at the volume level, but you can control which directories or files on the volume are compressed.

Compression and decompression do add some overhead. Don't set the feature on files or directories that require quick access—a customer database, for example. Compress files that are not accessed often. You might want to place compressed files on a separate volume, so access to other volumes is not affected.

When installing a volume, you choose whether you want to enable file compression or not. Once you set it on, you can't turn it off, but you can prevent any files on the volume from being compressed by using SET parameters or by controlling compression at the directory or file level. Since file compression can be controlled at the directory and file level, it's a good idea to enable file compression for all volumes. Refer to the next section, "Enabling File Compression for an Existing Volume," to set compression on if you've already created a volume without file compression.

Use the FLAG command or FILER to set the following compression attributes for files and directories:

Ic (Immediate Compress)   This attribute marks a directory so that all the files in it are compressed as soon as the operating system is able to do so. When applied to a file, the file is compressed on disk as soon as possible.

Dc (Don't Compress)   This attribute marks directories so the files in it are never compressed. This can be applied to individual files so they are never compressed.

You can mark a directory with the Immediate Compress attribute and then mark specific files in it with the Don't Compress attribute.

Enabling File Compression for an Existing Volume

If you want to set file compression on for a volume that you've already created, follow these steps:

1. Load INSTALL and choose Maintenance/Selective Install.

2. Choose Volume Options from the Installation Options menu.

3. Select the volume and press ENTER.

4. The Volume Information menu appears. Jump to the File Compression field and set it on.

SET Parameters for File Compression

The following SET parameters control the settings of the file compression system. You can use the SERVMAN utility to change any of these settings.

ENABLE FILE COMPRESSION   Setting this option off prevents any files from being compressed, even if the compression is set on for the volume.

DAYS UNTOUCHED BEFORE COMPRESSION   This option sets the number of days the system waits before compressing a file that has not been opened. The default value is 7.

COMPRESSION DAILY CHECK STARTING HOUR   Set this option for the hour when the file compressor starts scanning each enabled volume for files to compress. Midnight is 0 and 11:00 p.m. is 23. You typically set this value for an hour that is outside of regular work hours.

COMPRESSION DAILY CHECK STOP HOUR   This is the hour that the file compressor stops scanning for and compressing files. Midnight is 0 and 11:00 p.m. is 23. Set this value so file compression stops before peak hours on a busy server. If this value is the same as Compression Daily Check Starting Hour, compression runs all the time.

MINIMUM COMPRESSION PERCENTAGE GAIN   This option sets the minimum percentage amount that a file must compress before the file compressor actually compresses it. The default value is 2 percent. You might want to raise this percentage to prevent the system from spending time compressing files that don't benefit much from compression.

DECOMPRESS PERCENT DISK SPACE FREE TO ALLOW COMMIT   This option sets the percentage of disk space that must be free before a compressed file is committed to an uncompressed state. It prevents files that are uncompressed from taking up all the disk space. The default setting is 10 percent, but you might want to raise this value if your hard disk space fluctuates to low values.

DELETED FILES COMPRESSION ON   This setting determines whether to compress deleted files (files that can be recovered or purged). A 0 setting means don't compress, 1 means compress the next day, and 2 means compress immediately.

Repairing Volumes with VREPAIR

The VREPAIR utility corrects minor hard disk problems at the volume level, which means that the utility affects only the volumes you specify. If the primary file allocation table or directory table becomes corrupted, VREPAIR compares the primary tables with their mirrored counterparts and makes corrections. VREPAIR may be required in the following situations:

- Disk read and write errors are occurring.

- A power failure has corrupted a volume. This occurs if the power goes out while files are being written to disk. FAT and directory mismatches prevent the volume from mounting.

- A mirroring error occurs when the server boots.

If a name space is loaded and there is not enough memory for the name space, VREPAIR can return volume tables to the size they were before the name space support was added. (See the next section for more information on name spaces.)

 NOTE: *Novell has suggested that you run VREPAIR as many times as necessary until you don't see any more errors. If the same error occurs twice, you may have a hardware problem.*

Setting Up VREPAIR

If the SYS volume won't load, you won't be able to run VREPAIR unless you keep a copy of the program on the DOS partition of the server's drive, or you can copy the files to a diskette that you carry in your tool kit. The files you need are listed here:

VREPAIR.NLM   Loadable module

V_MAC.NLM   Macintosh name space support module

V_OS2.NLM   OS/2 name space support module

Copy files for other name spaces as well, such as V_FTAM.NLM. To run the version of VREPAIR on the DOS partition, you load SERVER.EXE to get to the console prompt, then load the VREPAIR NLM.

Loading VREPAIR

In most cases you cannot mount a volume that requires VREPAIR, but if the server is up, type the following command to remove the volume that is having problems. Replace *volume* with the name of the volume.

DISMOUNT *volume*

If the SYS volume is dismounted, you must run VREPAIR from the DOS partition or floppy disk where you stored the VREPAIR files. Start the server by typing **SERVER**, then type the following command at the console prompt to set up a search path to VREPAIR. Replace C:\DOS with A: if the files are on floppy disk.

SEARCH ADD C:\DOS

NOTE: Unmirror any mirrored volumes before running VREPAIR.

Next, type the VREPAIR command at the console, as shown here:

LOAD VREPAIR

Setting VREPAIR Options

To set VREPAIR options, select the second option from the VREPAIR menu. The current settings are listed at the top of the screen, and other possible settings are listed at the bottom. If you type a numbered entry, the current setting changes. The default settings are described next.

Name Space Problems

If you just added name space support and a volume won't load, there is not enough memory to mount the volume. Choose the alternate option only if files have not been stored in the name space yet. Doing so removes the name space and all extended file information with it. DOS information is retained, however.

> *Default option*   Quit if a required VREPAIR name space support NLM is not loaded.

> *Alternate option*   Remove name space support from the volume.

Forced Update Option

The alternate option for this entry should not be selected if the server crashed when you were updating important files. Use the default option only, unless the first attempt at repairing the volume fails and the volume resides on a mirrored disk.

> *Default option*   Write only *changed* directory and FAT entries out to disk.

> *Alternate option*   Write all directory and FAT entries out to disk.

Save in Memory Option

VREPAIR runs faster if it can save changes in memory and then write to disk when it is done. If there are few changes, use the default option. If there are many changes and VREPAIR might run out of memory, choose the alternate option.

> *Default option*   Keep changes in memory for later update.

> *Alternate option*   Write changes immediately to disk.

Deleted File Handling

You can choose whether you want VREPAIR to purge deleted files (files that are recoverable). Keep the default option if you want to retain the files. Choose the alternate option to delete the files and improve VREPAIR's performance.

Default option   Retain deleted files.

Alternate option   Purge all deleted files.

Starting the Repair Process

After selecting one of the options, return to the main menu and choose option 1, Repair a Volume, from the Options menu. If more than one volume has been mounted, select the volume to be repaired.

At any time, you can press F1 to change the current VREPAIR settings listed here:

1   This option pauses VREPAIR after each error to let you view a screen that describes the error. To speed through VREPAIR, press F1 and change this option so it doesn't pause. You can log errors in a file (option 2) and view the file later.

2   This option logs all errors in a text file. Any errors found are written to a file you specify.

3   This option stops volume repair.

Tracking VREPAIR

VREPAIR makes several passes over a volume in an attempt to repair it. Each pass builds on the information accumulated in the previous passes. VREPAIR first checks the FAT blocks, then counts the directory blocks, and finally, checks the directory FAT entries. VREPAIR stops if it can't validate the FAT and DET entries, in which case you'll need to restore the volume from backup. Each step is described next.

FAT BLOCKS CHECK   Recall that there are two copies of the FAT. VREPAIR compares the two copies for discrepancies. VREPAIR uses information from the secondary FAT if it has no errors or fewer errors than the primary FAT. If VREPAIR can't repair the corrupted FAT from the secondary FAT, it displays an error message indicating that it can't repair the volume. You'll need to restore it from backup. If the comparison was successful, VREPAIR checks the DET, as discussed next.

MIRROR MISMATCH CHECK   When "Mirror Mismatches>" appears, VREPAIR is checking to ensure that the primary and secondary directory tables are the same. If there is a mismatch, the entry that is the most valid is used to repair the DET. In some cases, information in a name space support module is used by VREPAIR to determine which DET entry is most valid for rebuilding the table. When this step completes, the tables match for the most part. However, the process is not perfect. There may be some entries that are impossible to rebuild, and so some files may be lost. You'll need to restore those files from backup.

DIRECTORIES CHECK   During this step, "Directories>" appears on the screen. VREPAIR is checking the validity of DET entries defined as "directory-type." These are the directory and subdirectory entries for the volume. The name, starting block, attributes, and other information are checked. Invalid entries are fixed if possible, but any entries that can't be fixed are freed up so they can be used later. Any name space support modules are called during this process to check the validity of directory entries in the name space. It is important that the name space NLM be on the disk where VREPAIR.NLM is located.

FILES CHECK   During this phase, "Files>" appears on the screen. VREPAIR checks the DET entries defined as "file-type." The chain of FAT entries for files is checked, along with the name and attributes for the files. Mismatches are corrected if possible. The links in the chain are verified with the secondary copy of the FAT. In some cases, files are truncated if VREPAIR can't find the next file link in either the primary or secondary file entry. You'll see a message that the file was truncated, and you'll need to restore the file from backup. Name space support modules are called during this phase to validate file entries in name space areas. If a name space was removed, a number of "invalid name space" messages appear.

TRUSTEES CHECK   During this phase, "Trustees>" appears on the screen. The NetWare operating system stores the first eight trustee assignments in the file entry itself, then stores additional entries in special *tnode* tables. VREPAIR ensures that the *tnode* structure is valid. In a valid structure, the file points to a *tnode* table, which itself points to another *tnode* table (if it exists), and so on. The last *tnode* must point back to the file.

DELETED FILES CHECK   During this phase "Deleted Files>" appears on the screen. Recall that deleted files are not actually removed from disk until you purge the files. The NetWare operating system creates special deleted file lists that contain information about the location of the files, how long they have been deleted, and other information it needs to recover the files if necessary. During this phase, VREPAIR simply checks to ensure that deleted files are in the same deleted entry block and that they have valid filenames, name space, and trustee entries. If there is a problem with a file, its space is freed up and the file can't be recovered.

INVALID ENTRIES CHECK   During this phase, "Invalid Entries>" appears on the screen. When non-DOS files are stored on a NetWare volume, they contain an entry in the DOS name space which points to an entry in another name space. These links can become invalid, and it is during this phase that VREPAIR attempts to restore invalid name space links. If VREPAIR can't fix invalid links, it makes the entry valid only to the DOS name space so the entry doesn't lose its DOS entry-naming characteristics and attributes. The links to other name space entries are lost, however. If you've saved VREPAIR information to a file, you'll have a list you can work with to restore these files from backup.

FREE BLOCKS CHECK   During this phase, "Free Blocks>" appears on the screen. VREPAIR simply finds blocks claimed by the FAT or DET that are currently empty and makes those blocks available for other files to use.

VREPAIR Completion

When VREPAIR is done, a screen displays the number of FAT and directory repairs. Select Yes to write the repairs to disk, and press any key to return to the Options menu. Type **0** to exit VREPAIR. If the volume cannot be mounted, you can run VREPAIR again, choosing different setup options, as discussed earlier. If VREPAIR can't fix the volume, you must delete it, re-create it using INSTALL, and restore data to it from backup.

Removing Name Space Support with VREPAIR

The only way to remove name space support from a volume is with VREPAIR. If you've added name space support to a volume and it fails to come up because the volume is too full, you'll need to remove the name space.

To remove the name space support, follow these steps:

1. Start VREPAIR, then go into the Options menu and type **1** so that it changes to "Remove name space support from the volume."

2. Type **3** to choose the third option, so it reads "Write changes immediately to disk."

3. Run VREPAIR by choosing the first option from the main menu.

4. A warning screen appears to verify which name space you want to remove. Choose the name space to start the process.

SET Options for the Filing System

The options listed in this section change the startup parameters or settings for the file system. You can change these parameters by loading SERVMAN and choosing Console Set Commands from the Available Options menu. File system settings can be found under the following menu headings:

■ File Caching

■ Directory Caching

■ File System

■ Locks

■ Transaction Tracking

■ Disk

File Caching

The file caching system is one of the most important features of NetWare. It ensures that files are available on a timely basis by keeping them in memory. Most of the default settings are adequate, but you might want to make the following changes, depending on your configuration and network users.

■ Make sure your system has enough memory to handle caching efficiently. You can view cache utilization with MONITOR.

■ To speed up disk writes, you can change the Maximum Concurrent Disk Cache Writes to 100, but this will cause server utilization to increase. However, if the disk seems slow to respond to read requests, set the value of this setting lower, say around 10.

■ If you receive "Insufficient Memory" alerts when loading NLMs at the server, you can allocate more memory to server processes by increasing the Minimum File Cache Buffers setting.

- If users make frequent small writes to the disk, change the Dirty Disk Cache Delay Time to 7.

- You can have the server display a warning message when the cache buffers reach their minimum memory allocation by setting the Minimum File Cache Buffer Report Threshold to a setting of 100.

MINIMUM FILE CACHE BUFFERS   Most available memory is allocated to the file cache buffers, but loadable modules and other tasks may require some of this memory. Set this value to the minimum number of file cache buffers that must always be available to prevent the operating system from allocating the buffers to other tasks. The default is 20, and the range is 20 to 1000. Keep in mind that if the minimum is too high, other tasks may not be able to load due to insufficient memory.

MAXIMUM CONCURRENT DISK CACHE WRITES   This advanced parameter sets how many write requests for changed file data can be put in the elevator before the disk head begins a sweep across the disk. Set the number high to service write requests more efficiently, or low to service read requests more efficiently. To determine a setting, use MONITOR to monitor dirty cache buffers. If the number of dirty cache buffers is above 70 percent, increase this setting. The default setting is 50, and the range is 10 to 100.

DIRTY DISK CACHE DELAY TIME   This advanced parameter sets the time a write request stays in memory before being written to disk. Reduce the time to prevent data in buffers from being lost if the server should go down; however, this drastically reduces performance. The time can be increased to improve performance when many small write requests are handled, but the additional information in the cache is lost if the server crashes. The default value is 3.3 seconds, and the range is 0.1 to 10 seconds.

MINIMUM FILE CACHE BUFFER REPORT THRESHOLD   Use this parameter if you want to be warned when memory normally available to the file cache buffers is getting close to the minimum specified with the Minimum File Cache Buffers parameter. Set this to the number above the minimum setting at which the operating system warns you of low buffers. The default setting is 20, and the range is 0 to 1000.

Directory Caching

Directory caching ensures that files are easily located by keeping the directory tables in memory. Note that directory caching and file caching must be balanced.

If you provide too many directory caches, memory is taken away from file caches, and vice versa. You can check memory and cache statistics with MONITOR.

■ Change the Maximum Concurrent Directory Cache Writes setting to 25 and the Dirty Directory Cache Delay Time to 2, if users make frequent small writes to the disk. However, if disk read requests seem slow to respond, change the Maximum Concurrent Directory Cache Writes value to 5.

■ Another way to improve the response of disk read requests is to set the Directory Cache Buffer NonReferenced Delay setting to 60.

■ If directory searches seem slow, double the values of the following settings:

>   Maximum Directory Cache Buffers
>   Minimum Directory Cache Buffers
>   Directory Cache Allocation Wait Time

NOTE: If the server is low on memory, you may need to decrease the value of the Maximum Directory Cache Buffers setting.

DIRECTORY CACHE BUFFER NONREFERENCED DELAY   Set this delay to the amount of time a directory entry is allowed to be cached before being overwritten by another entry due to inactivity. The operating system allocates more directory cache buffers if the time is increased and file access improves. Performance decreases if time is reduced since directory entries are less likely to be in the cache, but the number of directory cache buffers is reduced. The default setting is 5.5 seconds, and the range is 1 second to 5 minutes.

MAXIMUM DIRECTORY CACHE BUFFERS   Once directory cache buffers are allocated, they are not returned to memory for file caching unless the server is rebooted. Because of this, it may be important to set a maximum number of directory cache buffers. The default setting is 500, and the range is 20 to 4000.

MINIMUM DIRECTORY CACHE BUFFERS   Set this number to the minimum number of directory cache buffers that must be available at all times, but do not set it so low that the performance of file access is reduced. Keep in mind that the minimum number could be more than the server needs on small networks. These unused buffers may be better off allocated to the file cache. If the file server responds slowly to directory searches when first booted, the Minimum

Directory Cache Buffers setting is too low. You can view this information with MONITOR. The default setting is 20, and the range is 10 to 2000.

DIRTY DIRECTORY CACHE DELAY TIME   This advanced parameter sets how long the operating system keeps a directory table write request in memory before writing it to disk. Increasing the delay improves performance but increases the possibility of directory table corruption. Decreasing the delay has the opposite effect. The default is 0.5 seconds, and the range is 0 to 10 seconds.

MAXIMUM CONCURRENT DIRECTORY CACHE WRITES   This advanced parameter sets how many write requests for directory cache buffers can be put in the elevator before the disk head begins a sweep across the disk. Set the number high to service write requests more efficiently, or low to service read requests more efficiently. The default setting is 10, and the range is 5 to 50.

DIRECTORY CACHE ALLOCATION WAIT TIME   This parameter sets the amount of time the operating system waits before allocating a new directory cache buffer after it has just allocated one. During the wait time, all requests for a new directory cache buffer are ignored. If the setting is low, a peak in usage could cause more directory cache buffers to be allocated than are normally needed. If the setting is high, the operating system allocates directory cache buffers more slowly than is required to serve normal requests. Decrease the time if directory searches seem slow after the server has been running 15 minutes. The default value is 2.2 seconds, and the range is 0.5 seconds to 2 minutes.

File System

File system parameters control warnings about full volumes, file system purging, and the reuse of turbo FATs. Use the option on the File System menu to set warnings for low volumes, to control what happens to purged files, and to set file compression parameters.

- ■ In Miscellaneous, set Display Disk Device Alerts on. This will display activity messages about disk drives, such as when they have been added, activated, deactivated, or downed. Such messages can help you isolate disk problems, but they are usually not necessary when the drive is operating normally.

- ■ If users frequently access large files (64 blocks or more in size), set Turbo FAT Re-Use Wait Time to about 10 minutes to improve disk reads.

■ You can have the operating system warn you when a volume is almost full. To change the threshold values for the warning, choose File System from the Categories menu and change the following values:

    Volume Low Warning Threshold=512
    Volume Low Warning Reset Threshold=512

NOTE: The file compression options were discussed previously, under "Working with File Compression."

IMMEDIATE PURGE OF DELETED FILES   Set this value on if you want to immediately purge deleted files without the possibility of salvaging them. The default setting is off. This can be used to free disk space and improve performance slightly, but accidentally erased files are permanently lost.

VOLUME LOW WARN ALL USERS   The default setting is to warn users when a volume is full. To turn the feature off, set its value to off.

VOLUME LOW WARNING THRESHOLD   Set this number to the amount of free disk space (in blocks) that must remain before the operating system issues a low disk space warning to users. The default value is 256 blocks, and the range is 0 to 100,000 blocks.

VOLUME LOW WARNING RESET THRESHOLD   When a volume is almost full, its available disk space may move up or down in the warning messages range as users create and delete files. To prevent the warning message every time the volume dips below the threshold, set this number to a minimum amount of space above the threshold before users are again warned of low space. This parameter can be set at the console when a volume becomes low on space. The default is 256 blocks, and the range is 1 to 100,000 blocks.

MINIMUM FILE DELETE WAIT TIME   Set this to the amount of time a deleted file stays in a salvageable state on the volume. During this time range, deleted files will not be purged automatically even if the volume is full and users are unable to create new files. The default is 1 minute, 5.9 seconds, and the range is from 0 seconds to 7 days.

FILE DELETE WAIT TIME   Set this to the amount of time the operating system waits before purging a file. When a file's delete wait time has been exceeded, it is marked as purgeable and is removed as soon as the volume needs additional space. The oldest purgeable file is removed first. Set this value high if there is a need to keep files in a salvageable state for long periods of time and if a volume is not limited on disk space. The default is 5 minutes, 29.6 seconds, and the range is 0 seconds to 7 days.

MAXIMUM SUBDIRECTORY TREE DEPTH   This advanced parameter sets the number of subdirectory levels supported by the operating system. Replace the number with the number of levels to support if it is over 25. When upgrading from a previous version of NetWare that has more than 25 levels, use this parameter to specify the number of subdirectories. The default is 25, and the range is 10 to 100.

TURBO FAT REUSE WAIT TIME   This advanced parameter determines how long a turbo FAT buffer remains in memory after an indexed file is closed. Once the time has been exceeded, the buffer is allocated to another indexed file. The operating system automatically builds turbo FAT entries for files that have more than 64 FAT entries. Because these indexes take time to build, they should not be immediately removed if there is a chance you will need to open the file again, as is often the case with some accounting packages. Increase the time to keep the index in memory longer, especially if plenty of memory is available. Decrease the time to release the memory for other indexes. The default is 5 minutes, 29.6 seconds, and the range is 0.3 seconds to 1 hour, 5 minutes, 54.6 seconds.

Locks

Lock parameters are used to control the number of open files and the number of record locks the operating system and workstations can handle. With a file lock, a workstation has exclusive use of the file. With a physical record lock, other users are prevented from accessing a particular record in a file. With a logical record lock, an application assigns a name to each section of data that needs to be locked and then locks the name when the data is accessed.

MAXIMUM RECORD LOCKS PER CONNECTION   Set this to the number of record locks a station can use at one time. Increase this number if error messages occur because a workstation cannot lock enough records. The default is 500, and the range is 10 to 10,000.

MAXIMUM FILE LOCKS PER CONNECTION   Set this to the number of open and locked files a station can use at one time. Increase this number when a station cannot open enough files. An OS/2 station may need a number higher than the default. It may also be necessary to increase the number of file handles in the NET.CFG file of the workstation. The default is 250, and the range is 10 to 1000.

MAXIMUM RECORD LOCKS   Set this to the maximum number of record locks the operating system should handle. Increase the number if users are having problems running applications because there are not enough record locks. Decrease the number if users are using too many file server resources. Use MONITOR to view record locks. The default is 20,000, and the range is 100 to 200,000.

MAXIMUM FILE LOCKS   Set this to control the number of open and locked files handled by the operating system. Use MONITOR to view the number of open files during a peak usage period. If the number of current open files is near the default, increase the number. Decrease this number to restrict file server resources. The default is 10,000, and the range is 100 to 100,000.

Transaction Tracking

The following parameters can be used to control the transaction tracking system (TTS).

AUTO TTS BACKOUT FLAG   This parameter determines if incomplete transactions are automatically backed out when a crashed server is rebooted. The default is off, which means that you are asked if you want to back them out. Set the value on to automatically back out the transactions upon rebooting.

TTS ABORT DUMP FLAG   Set this value on to create a TTS log file that contains the information that was backed out of a file. The file is called TTS$LOG.ERR and is stored in the SYS:SYSTEM directory. The default value is off.

MAXIMUM TRANSACTIONS   Set this to the number of transactions that can occur at the same time. The default value is 10,000, and the range is 100 to 10,000.

TTS UNWRITTEN CACHE WAIT TIME   This advanced parameter specifies how long transactional data is held in memory. Some blocks of transactional data wait for other transactional blocks to be written first. If one of these blocks reaches its maximum time limit, it is written to disk as soon as possible. The default time of 1 minute, 5.9 seconds is usually sufficient, but a range of 11 seconds to 10 minutes, 59.1 seconds can be specified.

TTS BACKOUT FILE TRUNCATION WAIT TIME   Set this to the amount of time allocated blocks remain available for the TTS backout file when the blocks are not currently being used. The default is 59 minutes, 19.2 seconds, and the range is 1 minute, 5.9 seconds to 1 day, 2 hours, 21 minutes, 51.3 seconds.

CHAPTER 36

Managing Network Communications

As you've learned in previous chapters, a NetWare LAN is composed of an operating system, servers, workstations, and a cabling system. The operating system handles workstations as clients, based on a client-server architecture. Clients access services from file servers and other service providers.

A NetWare requester within each workstation intercepts commands for remote services (as opposed to local DOS, OS/2, or Macintosh services) and sends them to NetWare servers. A typical example of the redirection provided by the NetWare shell is the client's ability to print on a network printer. From an application, the user selects what looks like a normal DOS printer port (say LPT2). This port is really redirected to a network printer by the shell so all data sent to it for printing is sent out to the designated network queue.

All network communications is handled by *packets,* or *frames.* If a client needs some service from the server, the request is placed in a packet and sent out over the network. Packets contain routing information that directs them to their destination. Think of an envelope with an address. Inside the envelope is the "payload," in this case, a request for service. In a simple file transfer, the payload might contain text, and if the file is large, many packets are required to transfer it.

The discussions in this chapter focus on packets. We'll talk about packet types, packet sizes, optimizing packet delivery, and packet analysis. Network communications is not possible without packets. The reason is simple: Many workstations and servers share the same cable system. By breaking their transmissions into packets, many workstations can access the cable at basically the same time without monopolizing it. Think of cars on a freeway, each getting on at some point and getting off at their destination. The analogy of "network traffic" is appropriate.

First, we cover commands you execute at the server console to load and unload LAN drivers and to bind and unbind protocols to and from those drivers, then we discuss ways to optimize communications.

Adding and Removing LAN Cards at the Server

You can install a number of LAN cards in a NetWare server as long as each card has different settings. The console LOAD and BIND commands are used to install LAN drivers and bind protocols to the drivers. The UNBIND and UNLOAD commands are used to remove LAN drivers. Of course, you can use the INSTALL utility to accomplish the same tasks. The commands are covered here as an alternative to INSTALL.

Loading LAN Drivers

NetWare includes a number of LAN drivers that support a variety of network cards. You can load these drivers with the LOAD command. In addition, the LOAD command can be inserted into the AUTOEXEC.NCF file so it executes every time the server starts. The INSTALL utility does this for you automatically.

When executing the LOAD command, you'll need to specify parameters for the driver, such as I/O ports and interrupts. Parameters are described in "LAN Driver Options."

The LOAD command takes the following form,

LOAD *path\driver parameters*

where *path* is the driver and/or directory where the driver is located, if it is not in the SYS:SYSTEM directory. Replace *driver* with the name of the LAN driver and replace *parameters* with one of the options described in the next section.

NOTE: *Token Ring adapters must be attached to the Multistation Access Unit (MAU) before the Token Ring driver will load.*

LAN Driver Options

If you include the LOAD command in the AUTOEXEC.NCF file, specify some or all of the following parameters, as necessary. Some parameters are read directly from the LAN boards, but you can specify an option to "force" a new setting in some cases.

DMA=#	Replace # with a DMA channel to reserve for the driver.
INT=#	Replace # with the hardware interrupt set on the board.
MEM=#	Replace # with the memory address to reserve for the driver. Some ISA drivers prompt for this parameter. For MCA and EISA boards, the parameters are set with the reference disk that comes with the computer.
PORT=#	Replace # with the I/O port to reserve for the driver. Some ISA drivers prompt for this parameter. For MCA and EISA boards, the parameters are set with the reference disk that comes with the computer.
SLOT=#	On Micro Channel and EISA machines, replace # with the number of the slot in which the board is installed, which then usually means you don't need a port number.
NAME=*boardname*	Assigns a unique name to a board's configuration so you can identify the board more easily when multiple boards of the same type are installed. The *boardname* can be as long as 17 characters.

FRAME=*string*	Replace *string* with the type of packet header to use with NetWare. The default for Ethernet is Ethernet_802.2, and the default for Token Ring is Token-Ring. Other standards are discussed later in this chapter.
NODE=#	Replace # with a node address that overrides the one set on the board, if the driver supports the change. Use this option only if you know the node address does not conflict with any other on the network.
RETRIES=#	Replace # with the number of retries to perform when a packet transmission fails. This optional parameter can be modified only at the command line when the driver is loaded.
LS=#	Sets the number of link stations for the Token Ring driver. This optional parameter can be modified only at the command line when the driver is loaded.
SAPS=#	Sets the service access point stations for Token Ring. This optional parameter can be modified only at the command line when the driver is loaded.
TBC=#	Sets the transmit buffer count for Token Ring. This optional parameter can be modified only at the command line when the driver is loaded.
TBZ=#	Sets the transmit buffer size for Token Ring. The default assigns the maximum packet size allowed by either the board or the operating system. This optional parameter can be modified only at the command line when the driver is loaded.

Examples

Type the following to load the LAN driver for the network interface cards in your system. Replace *driver-name* with the name of the driver. Specify a path if it is not in the SYS:SYSTEM directory.

LOAD *driver-name*

If you use this format at the console prompt, you are asked for interrupt, memory, I/O port settings, and other information as necessary.

To include the command in the AUTOEXEC.NCF file, specify the parameters described previously. For example, the following specifies an interrupt of 3 and a memory address of C0000 for the Novell TRXNET driver:

```
LOAD TRXNET INT=3 MEM=C0000
```

Binding and Unbinding Protocols to Drivers

The console BIND command links a protocol stack to a LAN driver. The command takes the following form,

BIND *protocol* TO *name parameters*

where *protocol* is the name of the protocol to bind, and *name* is either the name of the previously loaded driver or the board name you assigned when loading the driver.

If you have more than one network board of the same type in the file server, use the *name* option to differentiate between boards. Include the following parameters in the startup file so you are not prompted for the information every time the server starts. Not all parameters need to be specified.

DMA=#   Replace # with a DMA channel for the driver.

INT=#   Replace # with the hardware interrupt set on the board.

MEM=#   Replace # with the memory address for the driver.

PORT=#   Replace # with the I/O port for the driver.

SLOT=#   On Micro Channel machines, replace # with the number of the slot in which the board is installed.

FRAME=*string*   Replace *string* with the type of packet header to use. Refer to "Ethernet Frame Types" for a list of frame types.

NET=#   Replace # with a unique network number for the LAN segment attached to the board when using the IPX protocol. If multiple boards are installed, each must have a different number.

Use the UNBIND command in the same way as the BIND command to remove a communications protocol from the LAN driver of a network board. The command takes the form shown here, and you can specify the parameters just described.

UNBIND *protocol* FROM *name parameters*

For example, the following command binds IPX to the NE2000 board:

```
BIND IPX TO NE2000
```

To unbind the IPX protocol from the NE2000 board, you would type the following command:

```
UNBIND IPX FROM NE2000
```

The LOAD command allows boards to be assigned names as a way to differentiate one from the other. The next example assumes that the name ACCTG was assigned to a LAN card with the LOAD command (using the NAME parameter). IPX is bound to the ACCTG interface card.

```
BIND IPX TO ACCTG
```

Include the BIND command in the AUTOEXEC.NCF file so binding occurs every time the network starts. Specify parameters on the command lines so you or other operators do not have to type them when the server boots.

NOTE: For more information on all these commands, refer to the Novell manuals or the manuals that come with LAN adapters.

Communications on NetWare Networks

Everything you need to know about a particular type of packet is defined by the communications protocol in use. Recall from Chapter 6 that protocols define the rules of communications. They ensure that a sender sends information that a receiver can understand. They also provide error checking and guaranteed delivery of packets with acknowledgment in some cases. At the media access level, it is often more appropriate to refer to packets as frames, which consist of the following elements:

Destination address	Source address	Routing information	Data

The various media access methods such as Ethernet and Token Ring have more than one frame type because of "loose" standardizations. However, frames are "surrounded" by other information such as error checking codes, which together form a packet of information that is transmitted from one node to another on the network. The following sections describe communications processes and features. You'll need to be somewhat familiar with this material when using protocol analyzers that list packets along with information about the packets, such as their source, destination, purpose, and content. This information helps you determine which stations or what processes are causing problems on the LAN. For example, if the packets from a single station have a lot of CRC (Cyclic Redundancy Check) errors, the station probably has a bad card. If there are a large number of packets with CRC errors from many stations, there is probably a problem with the LAN segment itself.

Let's briefly take a closer look at the NetWare media access protocols and their frame types, then the client-server architecture of NetWare, to see how communications on NetWare networks can be monitored and evaluated to improve performance or detect problems.

Ethernet

On Ethernet networks, every packet sent over the media is visible to every station on the local segment. Stations look at packet addresses to determine if they are the intended destination of the packet. Since all the stations share the same cable, any station can send a packet, but a collision occurs when two stations access the cable at the same time. When a collision occurs, both stations "back off" for a random period of time and try again.

As you'll see later, collisions are the cause of performance loss on Ethernet networks. As more and more stations access the network, more collisions occur. In addition, stations need to transmit more often because they need to resend failed transmissions. The network bandwidth becomes saturated and performance drops noticeably. One solution is to divide the network by adding another network card in the server. Another is to use a protocol analyzer (discussed later in the chapter) to see if a station is producing an excess amount of traffic or is acting erratically.

Ethernet Frame Types

There are four Ethernet frame types used on NetWare networks. NetWare v.4 can support any of these frame types simultaneously. In previous versions of NetWare, problems occurred with stations using frame types different from the server's. Frame types are specified in the NET.CFG file at the workstation and within the AUTOEXEC.NCF file at the server. During NetWare v.4 server installation, you can choose to add any of these frame types. INSTALL adds a LOAD command to the AUTOEXEC.NCF for each type.

ETHERNET_802.3   This is the old default frame type for NetWare. It is prevalent on workstations configured for previous versions of NetWare. Configure this frame type at the server if you need it.

ETHERNET_802.2   This IEEE and OSI standard frame type is the new default frame type for NetWare v.4.

ETHERNET_II   This frame type assigns a unique packet header that is used on AppleTalk Phase I networks, networks connected to DEC systems, or to computers using the TCP/IP protocol.

ETHERNET_SNAP   Use this frame type on AppleTalk Phase II networks.

Token Ring

Token Ring is a ring topology that is physically configured as a star. In other words, cables branch from a central box or Multistation Access Unit (MAU), but cables contain two twisted pair so the signal goes from the box to the workstation, then back to the box and to the next workstation. The last station in the series forms a connection through the MAU to the first station, thus closing the ring.

In a Token Ring network, each adapter keeps track of where it is in the ring. Traffic flows in one direction, so each adapter has an upstream neighbor and a downstream neighbor. (When analyzing the network with protocol analyzers like LANalyzer, problems can often be isolated by looking at the traffic activity between an adapter and its upstream or downstream neighbors.) When a node with a Token Ring adapter connects with the network, the adapter must find a place in the traffic stream. It verifies that it has a unique address, then it determines its upstream neighbor (to which it will transmit network traffic) and its downstream neighbor (from which it will receive network traffic). In this way, each adapter is a repeater.

The adapter can only transmit its own packets when it controls a special *token* that grants it permission to transmit. The adapter adds its data to the token and sends it as a packet over the network.

There are a number of processes that take place on Token Ring networks, as listed here. Of particular interest in this chapter is the last, which describes Token Ring's process of error recovery.

Station Insertion process These are the processes a station goes through when it first connects with the network. It checks the adapter, checks the MAU, verifies its address on the network, polls for neighbor stations, and requests initialization.

Ring Poll process This process gets the address of the nearest active upstream neighbor every seven seconds.

Ring Purge process In case of token error, this process lets the network resume normal operations.

Monitor Contention process This process establishes a new Active Monitor, which is a single station that provides clock signals for the network.

Beacon process This process helps the network recover from hard errors. The ring does not function during this process. A special "beacon frame" is sent out from the first station to detect the error. The beacon eventually locates the station with a problem. That station disconnects itself and the ring is restored. A protocol analyzer can indicate the location of problem stations from the beacon frame information.

NetWare Client-Server Architecture

NetWare is a client-server network operating system. Workstations run special software that diverts requests for network services to NetWare servers. The servers respond to the workstations with the information or services they need.

There are a number of different protocols and services used by NetWare to transmit information over the network or perform diagnostic services. When you run protocol analyzers, you see packets related to the protocols and services listed below.

BCAST (Broadcast Message Notification)   Informs idle workstations that a message is pending. The message appears at the top of the workstation's screen.

DIAG (Diagnostic Support Protocol)   Tests connections and gathers information about the network. NetWare clients use the Diagnostic Responder to reply to diagnostic requests. Note that you can disable the diagnostics responder when loading IPXODI at workstations and save about 3KB of workstation memory by typing the following:

```
IPXODI /D
```

IPX (Internetwork Packet Exchange)   The built-in NetWare protocol for transferring data packets across the network. Each packet has an address that indicates its source, destination, and network number. The inclusion of the network address allows internetworking. Note that SPX adds to IPX by providing a mechanism to ensure packet delivery at the expense of adding traffic overhead.

NCP (NetWare Core Protocol)   Consists of procedures that the NetWare operating system follows to handle requests from clients. At the workstation, NCP requests are diverted by the NetWare shell software from the local operating system to the server. The NCP consists of every possible service that workstations might need from the server, such as directory and file services, network connection maintenance, printing, and others. This communication process takes place continuously throughout the network. Workstations form NCP requests, packetize them, and send them over the network. At the server, NCP requests are received, unpackaged, and interpreted. NCP is covered further in the next section.

NetBIOS (Network Basic Input Output System)   Provides support for IBM and Microsoft NetBIOS-compatible applications.

RIP (Routing Information Protocol)   Provides a mechanism that allows routers on an internetwork to send their routing table information to other routers. If a router should fail, other routers will know of alternate routes. RIP allows routers to broadcast changes in routes to other routers.

SAP (Service Advertising Protocol)   Provides a way for servers to let workstations and other servers know about the services they have to offer. Workstations can monitor SAP broadcasts to locate the services they need.

SPX (Sequenced Packet Exchange)   SPX provides a higher level of service than IPX and thus has more overhead. It provides a way to acknowledge that a packet has been received, in the same way you might request a "return receipt request" when mailing an important letter. If you don't need SPX at workstations, you can save about 9KB of memory by loading IPXODI with the /A option, as shown in the following example. This also removes the Diagnostic Responder.

```
IPXODI /A
```

Watchdog   Looks for idle workstations and logs them out.

NCP Communications

As mentioned earlier, NCP (NetWare Core Protocol) contains procedures that the NetWare operating system uses to handle requests from clients. This communication process takes place continuously throughout the network. Workstations form NCP requests, packetize them, and send them over the network. At the server, NCP requests are received, unpackaged, and interpreted. Understanding NCP messages and viewing them with protocol analyzers can help you determine which services are most often requested of the server. From this information, you can determine whether a particular server is overloaded or having problems.

You can also track what users are doing on the network. Each NCP packet contains a code that identifies the type of service requested or being serviced. These codes are easily identified by most protocol analyzers, and you can usually filter them to see a particular type of service or traffic from one workstation. A brief description of some of the calls is listed here.

- Login and logout requests

- Directory handling requests (such as create, list, rename, delete, and others)

- File handling requests (such as open, close, create, erase, and others)

- Server requests (clear connections, down the file server, get disk information, get file server information, send messages, and others)

- Messaging services (send or receive messages)
- Printer and queue services
- File locking and unlocking services

This list only describes the general category of service requests and responses. There are hundreds of calls, each with a specific purpose and code. For example, the request "Create Directory" has a specific request type number (2222), a function code (22), and a subfunction code (10). For the purposes of this discussion, these codes are not important. However, they do point out how workstations communicate with servers and how you can track the activities with a protocol analyzer.

For example, you might want to track a user's activities because you suspect the user might be engaging in unauthorized activities, or you might want to track the activities of a user for auditing purposes. Novell's LANalyzer can filter out the packets produced for a single user's workstation and produce a log of every service requested by the user.

By following the stream of NCP requests and responses between a server and its client, you can watch users log in and log out, start applications, access files on the server, communicate with other users, and perform a number of other activities. However, for the most part, you track packet flow to isolate problems or bottlenecks in communications.

Packet Size Negotiations

The larger the size of the packet used in client-server communications, the better the performance. When a client attaches to a server, a packet size is negotiated. The maximum size of the packet depends on settings at both the workstation and the server. For example, if the server can handle a 4KB packet and the workstation can handle a 1KB packet, they will negotiate a common packet size of 1KB.

Keep in mind that large packet sizes require more communications buffers at the file server, which reduce the amount of memory available to other processes. There is a trade-off between network performance and available memory. NetWare automatically allocates a buffer as necessary within a specific range.

At the workstation, you can increase the packet size with the following option in the NET.CFG file,

IPX Packet Size Limit = *value*

where *value* is the maximum packet size that the workstation adapter can handle. The default value is 4096 (or is driver-specified) and the range is 576 to 6500.

At the server, you can change the SET option, called "Maximum Physical Receive Packet Size," to increase the size of the packet. To access this option, load SERVMAN, then choose Console Set Commands from the Available Options menu. Choose the Communications option, then make the change to the setting. To avoid using excess memory for communications buffers, do not exceed the largest packet size used by a client on the network.

The following are default packet sizes for common network adapters:

Token Ring 4Mbs	2154
Token Ring 16Mbps	4202
Ethernet	1130
Arcnet	618

NOTE: Some routers may have a packet size limitation. Refer to "Large Internet Packet Support" later in the chapter.

More About Packet Receive Buffers

The more packet receive buffers there are, the better the server's performance. However, these buffers use system memory needed by processes, so you must balance buffer allocation against available memory.

Communications buffers are dynamically allocated by the server between a minimum and a maximum range. The minimum number of buffers is ten, or can be set by the "Minimum Packet Receive Buffers" setting in the file server. Over time, the server increases the number of buffers to handle its typical loads. Eventually, the server establishes an optimum setting that provides enough buffers for normal use, yet doesn't take up too much system memory. The longer the server is on, the more accurately its buffer settings will be balanced to lulls and peaks in traffic.

When you turn the server off, you lose the dynamically configured buffer settings. The server starts recalculating the buffers when it is restarted, but users may notice a slowdown in network performance until balanced settings are restored. However, if you do need to down the server, you can avoid this problem as follows:

1. Start MONITOR and note the number of receive buffers in use.

2. Start SERVMAN, then choose Console Set Commands from the Available Options menu.

3. Next, choose Communications and set the "Minimum Packet Receive Buffers" to a quantity close to what the server dynamically configured.

For example, if MONITOR shows that the server has dynamically allocated 75 buffers over time, set "Minimum Packet Receive Buffers" for 50 to 75. The lower amount lets the server configure lower amounts of buffers if necessary to save memory but at the same time provides a higher starting point for reallocating buffers.

In some cases, you may need to control dynamic buffer allocation during unusual peaks in the server's load. For example, a server that normally operates with 50 receive buffers may get a surge of activity and raise its buffers much higher. The "Maximum Packet Receive Buffers" setting ensures that the server never allocates more than the set number of buffers during a peak in activity. This prevents the server from allocating too much system memory for buffers. Be careful when setting this parameter. If the buffer allocation is already close to the maximum setting, you may need to raise the maximum buffer settings and install more memory to compensate for memory shortages.

One last setting controls how long the server waits before allocating new buffers. "New Packet Receive Buffer Wait Time" has a default setting of 0.1 seconds, but you can increase it to as high as 20 seconds. An increase causes the server to wait, and possibly avoid short peaks in activity, before allocating new buffers.

Burst Mode Techniques

Not all packets contain requests for services. Packets also contain data; for example, when they are transferring a file. When a user requests a file from the server, the server starts sending packets that contain the data of the file. In previous versions of NetWare, every packet sent required a response, and the NCP protocol specified that only one packet could be on the line at a time. The request/response mechanism is often referred to as a "Ping-Pong" communications scheme, and it is in large part responsible for excess traffic on the network, which slows performance.

In NetWare v.4, this has changed, with built-in support for burst mode packet transfer. *Burst mode* lets the workstation make one request for a file. The server then responds with a continuous stream of packets without the need for a reply, thus improving performance. A single response is sent after the burst of packets has been received to acknowledge the receipt.

Burst mode greatly reduces the amount of traffic on the network. Of course, it also works when a workstation sends files to a server, or over a WAN connection. When analyzing network traffic with protocol analyzers, you'll see burst mode streams listed as "Burst Packets." Burst mode improves performance in the following environments:

- LAN segments that typically transmit large files

- WANs with slower (9600-baud or less) asynchronous links

- Internetworks linked with bridges and routers

- WANs using X.25 packet switching or T1 and satellite links

The size of the burst mode packets is negotiated between the workstation and server. There is a NET.CFG parameter called PB BUFFERS that sets the number of packet burst buffers at the workstation. If PB BUFFERS is set to 0, packet burst mode is disabled for the workstation. Slow machines like older PCs and XTs don't benefit from burst mode because they cannot transfer information over their own bus fast enough to keep up with burst mode. You'll need to disable burst mode in these machines if the network has problems or the workstation loses packets.

The PB BUFFERS value can be from 0 to 10. On fast workstations, you can set the value as high as 10, but the machine may saturate the network's bandwidth. You should start with a low or medium setting and keep in mind that the higher the setting, the more of the workstation's memory is required.

Large Internet Packet Support

NetWare v.4 automatically supports large internet packets (LIPs). LIPs provide a way to route large packets across routers on an internetwork. While workstations directly connected to servers can negotiate large packet sizes, the presence of a router limited the size to 576 bytes in previous versions of NetWare. This was a precautionary measure since NetWare didn't always know the packet handling capability of routers on the network.

NOTE: Remember, larger packet sizes require larger communications buffers, and thus more memory.

By default, NetWare v.4 uses LIPs and allows workstations and servers to negotiate packet sizes larger than 576 bytes, even if a router is present. Basically, the setting causes NetWare to ignore its router check during packet size negotiation. However, you must ensure that routers can transfer larger packet sizes. If a router exists on the network that can't negotiate the larger packet size, you need to revert to the 576-byte packet size or replace the router.

To revert to the 576-byte packet size at the server, set the LIP setting off. It is located in the SERVMAN utility. Choose Console Set Commands from the Available Options menu, then choose NCP settings. Set the Allow LIP option to off.

Controlling SAP Traffic

The Service Advertising Protocol (SAP) is used by servers, print servers, gateways, and other service providers on a NetWare network to advertise their services. Workstations look at SAP messages to locate servers to attach to. A SAP broadcast normally occurs every 60 seconds and includes the name, network address, and type of service provided by a server. In some cases, SAP packets can become too numerous on a network and must be reduced by filtering. NetWare v.4 has options you can set in the SERVMAN utility to control SAP traffic.

SAP traffic is usually excessive on large networks. With SAP filtering, you can reduce the amount of network traffic generated by SAP, hide servers by filtering their SAP packets, and reduce or eliminate SAP traffic from rarely used servers. Network security can be improved by filtering SAP traffic, and you can prevent users from seeing servers they don't use, thus reducing network traffic. SAP filtering can also restrict traffic to local LAN segments and keep it off of remote segments that don't need to see the SAP packets.

To access SAP parameters and filtering options, load SERVMAN and choose the IPX/SPX Configuration option from the Available Options menu. Choose a LAN segment to work with. The SAP Parameters options and SAP Filtering options are then available as discussed next.

SAP PARAMETERS   The SAP Parameters options let you configure SAP parameters for a selected LAN segment. The options are shown in Figure 36-1. Most importantly, you can change the interval between SAP broadcasts, in 30-second intervals. The default is 60 seconds, but you can increase this value to reduce network traffic caused by SAP packets from this server. If you increase it, the user may need to wait a little longer when connecting to servers, but overall traffic performance improves. Other options are also listed. Refer to the Help option for a description.

SAP Filtering   SAP Filtering options let you control the services arriving from a network or departing from a network. You first select a LAN segment, then

```
                         SAP Parameters
   Periodic Broadcast (30 sec unit): 2
   Aging Out Interval:               4
   Get nearest server reply:         ON
   Number of SAP Entries per packet: 7
   SAP Changed Information only:     OFF
```

Figure 36-1. *SAP Parameters options*

select a filtering option (arriving or departing). A menu similar to Figure 36-2 appears, and you can choose one of the following:

Enable or Disable SAP Filtering If you choose Enable, you can then select the types of services you want to filter.

SAP Filtering Action This lets you specify whether to restrict or allow the services listed in the Service List, as described next.

Service List Press ENTER on this option, and a list of services, as shown in the following illustration, appears. Choose a service and press ENTER.

```
              Services Departing from Network=A44B4E9C
   SAP Filtering:          DISABLE
   SAP Filtering Action:   Restrict Services in list
   Service List:           (see list)
```

Figure 36-2. *SAP Filtering options*

```
┌──────────────────────────────────────────┐
│          Server type menu                │
├──────────────────────────────────────────┤
│▲│Btrieve server                          │
│ │█File server█                           │
│ │Job server                              │
│ │Named pipes server                      │
│ │NAS SNA gateway                         │
│ │Other type                              │
│ │Print server                            │
│ │Remote console server                   │
│ │SMS target agent server                 │
│ │Time synchronization server             │
└──────────────────────────────────────────┘
```

Routing Information Protocol (RIP)

All IPX packets contain both a network address and a node address. The network address is a LAN segment number, and the node address is the physical address of a node on a LAN segment. The physical address is hardwired to network adapters in most cases. The network address is used to route packets from one LAN segment to another.

Routing Information Protocol provides a way for routers (NetWare servers can be routers) to pass routing information among themselves. Routing information is stored in tables at each router. Workstations can locate the fastest route to a network number by broadcasting a route request. You see these route requests if you set TRACK ON at the server, as discussed in the next section. Routers perform the following tasks to keep themselves updated with the latest internetwork information:

■ Request routing information from other routers to update their internal tables

■ Respond to route requests from other routers

■ Periodically broadcast their presence to make sure other routers are aware of the internetwork configuration

■ Broadcast whenever a change in the internetwork configuration is detected

Note that RIP broadcasts are restricted to a single LAN segment only. However, routers attached to that LAN segment receive RIP broadcasts, update their own routing tables, and pass the new routing information on to the next router. Products like Novell's LANalyzer are useful for monitoring and testing routing efficiency. Delays in packet exchange may indicate faulty routers, inefficient routing paths, or servers which have improperly shut down.

You can change RIP parameters with the SERVMAN utility. Start SERVMAN at the server console or remote console and choose IPX/SPX Configuration from the Available Options menu. Then choose RIP Parameters from the next menu. You then select a network segment to work with, and the RIP configuration screen appears. This screen lets you change the interval between RIP broadcasts from the default of 60 seconds to higher values, thus reducing network traffic. You might want to do this if your network has only a few routes, little internetwork traffic, and/or the router information rarely changes. For information on changing the other parameters, press F1 to view the help screens.

Tracking RIP and SAP with TRACK ON

The TRACK ON console command displays the tracking screen, as shown in Figure 36-3. TRACK ON can display all network packets coming into or going out of the server. Type **TRACK ON** to initiate tracking and **TRACK OFF** to turn it off. Press ALT-ESC and CTRL-ESC to toggle between the TRACK screen and the normal console. Press any key to temporarily stop scrolling and another key to resume scrolling.

TRACK ON displays server, network, and connection requests. The packets are listed on the screen as either IN, which indicates incoming packets, or OUT, which indicates outgoing packets. The sending or receiving network number and node address are also displayed.

Route information is displayed as follows:

Direction [Net-address:Node-address] Time Net_num Hops/Ticks Net_num Hops/Ticks ...

A description of each of these options is described in the following paragraphs.

Direction   If the packet is being received, IN is displayed. If the packet is going out, OUT is displayed.

Net-address   The eight-digit hexadecimal network number assigned to the LAN board that received or transmitted the packet.

```
IN     [2B783CC6:000000000001]   7:10:06 am   SILICON_VALL   1
IN     [2B783CC6:000000000001]   7:10:07 am   SILICON_VALL   1
IN     [2B783CC6:000000000001]   7:10:11 am   MAIN_TREE___   0
OUT    [2B783CC6:FFFFFFFFFFFF]   7:10:22 am   A44B4E9C   1/2
OUT    [A44B4E9C:FFFFFFFFFFFF]   7:10:22 am   2B783CC6   1/2
IN     [2B783CC6:000000000001]   7:10:34 am   SILICON_VALL   1
IN     [A44B4E9C:0040F620CCCA]   7:10:41 am   Get Nearest Server
OUT    [A44B4E9C:0040F620CCCA]   7:10:42 am   Give Nearest Server SILICON_VALLEY
IN     [A44B4E9C:0040F620CCCA]   7:10:42 am   Route Request
OUT    [A44B4E9C:0040F620CCCA]   7:10:42 am   2B783CC6   1/2
IN     [A44B4E9C:0040F620CCCA]   7:10:42 am   Route Request
OUT    [A44B4E9C:0040F620CCCA]   7:10:42 am   2B783CC6   1/2
IN     [A44B4E9C:0040F620CCCA]   7:10:42 am   Route Request
OUT    [A44B4E9C:0040F620CCCA]   7:10:42 am   2B783CC6   1/2
IN     [A44B4E9C:0040F620CCCA]   7:10:44 am   Route Request
OUT    [A44B4E9C:0040F620CCCA]   7:10:44 am   2B783CC6   1/2
IN     [A44B4E9C:0040F620CCCA]   7:10:44 am   Route Request
OUT    [A44B4E9C:0040F620CCCA]   7:10:44 am   2B783CC6   1/2
OUT    [2B783CC6:FFFFFFFFFFFF]   7:10:52 am   SILICON_VALL   1   SILICON_VALL   1
            MAIN_TREE___   1   MAIN_TREE___   1
OUT    [A44B4E9C:FFFFFFFFFFFF]   7:10:52 am   SILICON_VALL   1   SILICON_VALL   1
            MAIN_TREE___   1   MAIN_TREE___   1
IN     [2B783CC6:000000000001]   7:11:01 am   SILICON_VALL   1
<Use ALT-ESC or CTRL-ESC to switch screens, or any other key to pause>
```

Figure 36-3.   *The TRACK ON screen*

Node_address The node address of the card in the server or router that received or transmitted the packet. In most OUT transmissions, the address is FFFFFFFFFFFF, indicating that the packet has been sent to all nodes.

Time Displays the time the information was transmitted.

Net_num The unique eight-digit hexadecimal number of a LAN segment.

Hops The number of routers a packet traversed to reach the destination network.

Ticks The time, in 1/18 second increments, that a packet takes to reach the specified network if a packet were transmitted from the machine displaying the TRACK ON. The tick value is used to differentiate between routes that have different transmission values, such as asynchronous communications links. The router will send packets along the fastest route, if possible.

TRACK ON will also display SAP information. The *Net_num* field is replaced by the server name. This is the name of the server or device that is advertising its services.

A third type of information displayed on the TRACK ON screen is the "Get Nearest Server" and "Give Nearest Server" requests and responses. If the packet is IN, it represents a workstation request for a server connection. If the packet is OUT, it represents the server's response.

Diagnosing with TRACK ON

TRACK ON can provide information about two types of problems on the network that can help you isolate the location of the problem.

A FILE SERVER COULD NOT BE FOUND   When this error occurs, a workstation is having problems communicating with a server.

- If you see "Get Nearest Server" and "Give Nearest Server" packet transmissions to the workstation, communications between the client and server is operating correctly.

- If none of these lines appears for any workstation, the problem is in the cable, a hub or concentrator, or caused by an improper connection or termination.

- If only "Get Nearest Server" appears, the workstation is sending requests, but the server is not responding. Check the file server from another workstation. If it still doesn't respond, a network card is faulty or the cable has a problem.

UNKNOWN FILE SERVER   When this message occurs, activate TRACK ON on all file servers and check server send and receive packets. Look for improperly configured network numbers on servers or routers that can cause this failure.

Using MONITOR to View and Analyze LAN/WAN Information

The MONITOR utility provides some vital information and statistics about network communications processes. While you can't look at packet information and do protocol analysis like you can with optional products such as Novell's LANalyzer, you can view communication activities to get a feel for how your network is operating and any changes you may need to make.

You can start MONITOR at a server console, or by starting a remote console session. Type **LOAD MONITOR** to start the program. When the main menu appears, choose LAN/WAN Information from the Available Options menu. Then select a LAN driver, if more than one is installed in the server, and press ENTER. A screen similar to Figure 36-4 appears.

For this discussion, we are interested in the Generic Statistics listed in the lower window. Almost all drivers you install in a NetWare server provide information for the Generic Statistics options. If you scroll down this list, you'll reach a Custom Statistics listing, which provides information specific to the LAN driver you selected. The manufacturer of the board can supply you with information on how to decipher custom statistics.

Total Packets Sent and Received

The Total Packets Sent and Total Packets Received statistics indicate how many packets have been sent or received on the specific LAN driver you selected. This

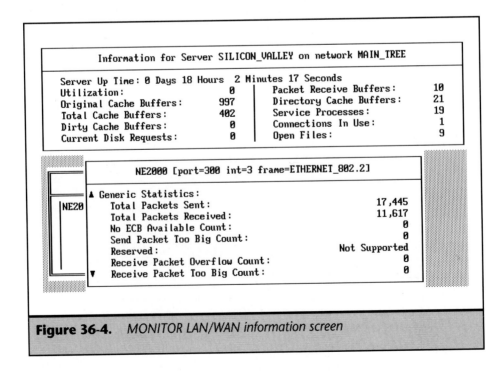

Figure 36-4. *MONITOR LAN/WAN information screen*

information should be periodically compared with any other LAN drivers installed in the server. If one LAN driver is supporting more traffic than another, you might want to take steps to balance out the load. For example, you could determine which stations are producing excessive traffic and move some of them to the other LAN segments. Keep in mind that some network cards can support more traffic on their segments than others, and high-speed backbones are usually meant to handle large amounts of internetwork traffic.

The server may be routing some packets to other LAN segments. In that case, both LAN segments will send or receive the packets. If a large number of packets from a workstation are routed through one server to another server, move that workstation to a LAN segment that is directly attached to the server the workstation primarily communicates with. You can determine this by querying the user about which server he or she connects with most often, or by using a protocol analyzer.

No ECB Count Available

An ECB is an Event Control Block. The number of ECBs controls the number of requests the server can receive. The No ECB Available Count value is closely associated with the number of packet receive buffers available on the server. Packet receive buffers hold requests from workstations until the server has an available process to handle the request. The maximum packet receive buffers is 1000, and the minimum is 10 (you can change these values in SERVMAN).

NetWare starts with 10 packet receive buffers and starts increasing the number of buffers if no new buffers are freed up for use after a set period of time. In some cases, NetWare may need more buffers, but hasn't reached the threshold for actually increasing those buffers. That's when the No ECB Count Available value increments. To resolve the problem (if it occurs on a regular basis), increase the value of the Minimum Packet Receive Buffers setting in SERVMAN. Choose Console Set Commands from the SERVMAN Available Options menu, then choose Communications from the Categories menu. You'll then see the option and can change its value. A change is made to the CONFIG.NCF file, and the new setting takes effect only after rebooting the server.

Send and Receive Packets Too Big

The Send Packet Too Big Count and Receive Packet Too Big Count typically indicate a problem with a network card or cabling. If send packets are too big, the problem is with a network card in the server. If receive packets are too big, you'll need to locate a faulty card in one of the workstations on the LAN segment. A protocol analyzer is useful in this situation.

Send and Receive Packets Too Small

The Send Packet Too Small Count and Receive Packet Too Small Count typically indicate a problem with a network card or cabling, similar to the previous paragraphs. If send packets are too small, check the network card in the server. If receive packets are too small, check for faulty cards in workstations on the LAN segment. As before, a protocol analyzer is useful in this situation.

Other Errors

Most of the remaining options show errors related to hardware or software. You might want to look at any of the following:

- Driver is old or incompatible. Update the driver.

- A software application is using the wrong packet sizes. Check with the vendor for an update.

- Packets have been corrupted during transmission. Check routers, hubs, and cables.

- A network interface card is faulty.

REMEMBER: For send errors, check the server. For receive errors, check workstations on the LAN segment.

Using SERVMAN to Track and Change Communications Settings

The SERVMAN utility displays network information if you choose the Network Information option from the Available Options menu, as shown in Figure 36-5.

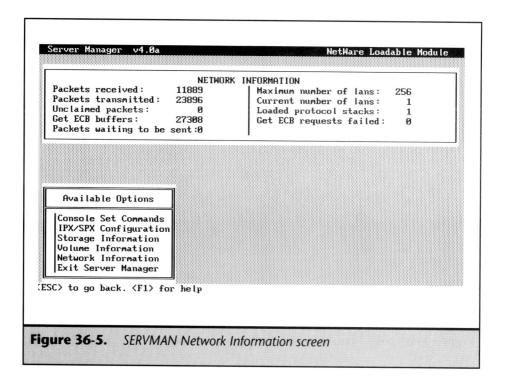

Figure 36-5.   *SERVMAN Network Information screen*

You can also view and change IPX/SPX, RIP, and SAP settings by choosing the IPX/SPX Configuration option on the Available Options menu. The SAP settings on this menu are the most important for improving network performance and were covered previously in this chapter.

Finally, you can choose the Console Set Commands option to change the SET commands for network communications. When the Categories menu appears, choose Communications to change the options pictured in Figure 36-6. Note that each option includes a help window that describes its purpose and settings.

Analyzing Networks

One thing about networks you can't avoid is that as they grow in size, their performance drops. Of course, you can spend more money and upgrade the entire network to 100 Mb/sec hardware, but in most cases, you'll need to tweak settings and look for bottlenecks in the system.

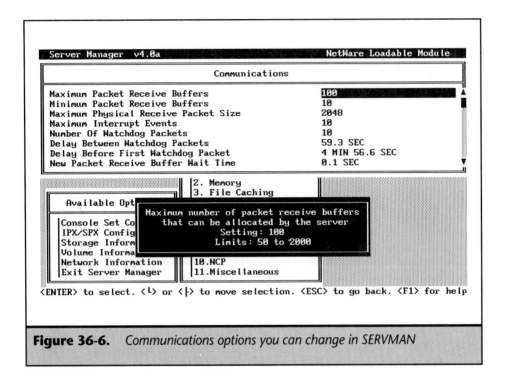

Figure 36-6. Communications options you can change in SERVMAN

You need to be on the lookout for improperly configured devices or overworked servers. You should also watch for excess WAN traffic. Cable testers and LAN analysis products can help you determine the source of problems. If you have a LAN with over 50 nodes, such products are easily justified, especially if the nodes are scattered over a large area. They let you analyze the network from your office and locate potential problem areas.

Novell LANalyzer for Windows is an optional management application used to monitor network operations and analyze packet traffic on Ethernet and Token Ring networks that use IPX, TCP/IP, and AppleTalk protocols. LANalyzer is available as a separate product from Novell.

You use LANalyzer for daily or periodic monitoring of the network. Periodic monitoring can produce long-term trends that help you observe changes in network traffic. These trends might point out potential problems or identify users who are requesting more and more of the network's services. With LANalyzer, you can correct or adjust the hardware and settings of a network before problems occur. You can also pinpoint the source of problems causing slow network response, failed connections, and excess network traffic.

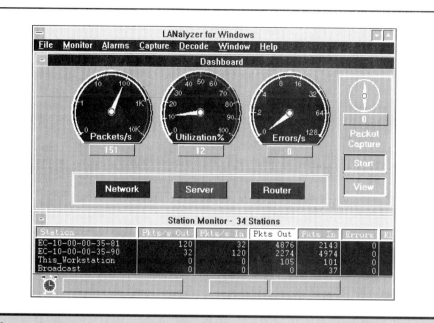

Figure 36-7. *The LANalyzer main window*

NOTE: LANalyzer can only analyze one network segment at a time

The LANalyzer Window

The LANalyzer window is shown in Figure 36-7. It consists of a Dashboard and several fields that display current and long-term statistics about the network.

■ The Dashboard shows real-time information about the network, such as the number of packets sent per second, the utilization of the network, and the number of errors per second. Two needles appear if you specify that you want to filter out certain types of packets.

NOTE: Utilization in this case is the bandwidth, or packet-carrying capacity, of the network.

- The Station Monitor window shows a table of active stations and their current statistics.

- The lower portion of the window shows an alarm and a message window, which alerts you to unusual events on the network.

- The Packet Capture field is used to capture a series of packets for analysis.

Figure 36-8 shows a typical packet capture window. In this case, a word-processed document file is transferred to the server. The summary window shows a list of packets transmitted. You can click on any packet to view detailed information about it, which appears in the middle decode window. At the bottom is a hexadecimal window that shows the contents of the packet. LANalyzer has a filtering feature that lets you specify a particular workstation for analysis, and/or the types of packets you want to view. You can also filter on a specific protocol, such as NetWare IPX, AppleTalk, or TCP/IP.

LANalyzer also has graphing capabilities. A graph can show real-time events or display historical data for trend analysis. You can also print station monitor data, packet capture data, and graphs, or import the data into a spreadsheet for custom analysis.

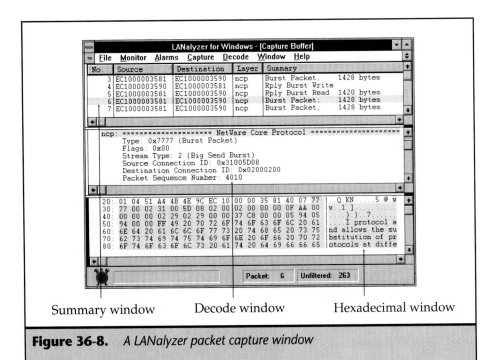

Summary window   Decode window   Hexadecimal window

Figure 36-8. *A LANalyzer packet capture window*

What You Can Do with a Protocol Analyzer

Many of the tasks you can do with a protocol analyzer have already been mentioned. Here is a list of these tasks:

- Determine which network stations are the most active on the network. If a workstation is using too much of a LAN segment's bandwidth, you might want to move it to another LAN segment.

- Locate workstations that are generating errors. If you notice in MONITOR that there is an increase in the number of packets received that are too large or too small, use a protocol analyzer to determine which network workstation is generating the most errors. You'll probably need to replace the network adapter in this station.

- Filter and view specific types of packets, such as SAP or RIP packets. You can use this information to adjust the broadcast frequency of SAP and RIP and reduce network traffic.

- Filter packets by their protocol type (IPX, TCP/IP, AppleTalk, and so forth) to determine the type of network traffic crossing a LAN segment.

- Get short-term and long-term trends about the network's performance. If you know what your network's peaks are, you can more accurately change settings, such as Minimum Packet Receive Buffers, as discussed earlier.

- Set alarms that alert you when unusual network events occur, such as a surge in a particular type of packet or an increase in errors.

- Load test the network by sending out diagnostic packets. Tests can help you check the network cabling, monitor transmission delays, or test node adapters.

Of course, this is only a small sampling of protocol analyzer activities. Products differ in their capabilities, so you should check with the manufacturer and read product evaluations in trade journals.

THE
COMPLETE
REFERENCE

PART SEVEN

Appendixes

APPENDIX A

Upgrading to NetWare v.4

All the methods available to upgrade a server to NetWare v.4 take advantage of your existing network. If you are performing an across-the-wire or same-server upgrade (which are described in Chapter 15), station yourself at a workstation, and then copy the files on the Migration disk to a directory called MIGRATE. You'll run the migration from this directory. If you are performing an in-place upgrade (which is also described in Chapter 15), you'll boot the server with the In-Place Upgrade disk. Refer to the section in this appendix that relates to your upgrade method.

NOTE: *Before you follow the steps in this appendix, ensure that you have reliable backups of existing data, just in case something goes wrong.*

Across-the-Wire and Same-Server Upgrades

The steps to follow when performing an across-the-wire upgrade or a same-server upgrade are listed in this section. Refer to Chapter 15 for prerequisite information.

1. Switch to the MIGRATE directory on the workstation, and type **MIGRATE**.

2. Choose Standard Migration or Custom Migration from the Select a migration option menu.

    2a. If you chose Custom Migration from the menu, choose Across-The-Wire migration or Same-Server migration from the next menu.

3. On the next menus, choose the source server type and then the destination server type.

4. Type the name of the working directory.

5. In the Define the NetWare source server block, highlight Server and press ENTER to choose the source server to migrate.

6. If you chose the custom migration option, highlight the Information to be migrated field, and select from the following menu. Refer to Help for more information about choosing these options.

```
Select information to migrate to NetWare
All information
Trustee assignments
Users
User restrictions
Groups
Default account restrictions
Accounting charge rates
Print queues and print servers
```

7. To select specific volumes to migrate, highlight the Source volumes to migrate field, and then select the volumes you want to migrate from the list.

8. To specify the destinations of specifically selected volumes, highlight the Volumes destinations field, and match new volume names to the source volumes.

9. Highlight the Passwords field, and then press ENTER to choose an option. If you choose "Assign random passwords", view the NEW.PWD file in the SYSTEM directory of the new server for a list of new user passwords. If you choose "Assign no passwords", you can use default account restrictions to force users to enter new passwords the first time they log in.

10. Press F10 to display the Select a migration action menu.

   ■ If this is an across-the-wire migration, choose the Start migration option from the menu to begin the migration.

   ■ If this is a same-server migration, choose Migrate to the working directory, from the menu, to copy the selected information to the workstation hard drive.

11. When the migration is completed, you can view the migration log by choosing View Migration Reports.

12. Choose Exit to quit the migration utility.

NOTE: Follow the remaining steps only if you are performing a same-server upgrade.

13. Install NetWare v.4 on the server as discussed in Chapters 15 and 16.

14. Restore the data files from your backup set.

15. Restart the migration utility as per step 1 in this list.

16. Choose the Custom Migration option.

17. Make sure the working directory is the same one you specified in step 4.

18. Move the highlight to the step 3 fields on the configuration form, and enter the destination information so that you can move the bindery information in the working directory to the new destination server. Don't change the source server information.

19. Make sure the Password field is filled out as per step 6.

20. Press F10 to continue the migration after filling out the configuration form.

21. Choose the Migrate from the working directory option from the menu.

22. When the migration is complete, you can view the migration report and exit as per steps 8 and 9.

After exiting, you should view the user login scripts to ensure that their commands match the new system and its directory and user structure. You should also check print queues and printer servers, user accounts, and the security system. Also try running any applications that were migrated from the old server. Print the NEW.PWD file in the SYSTEM directory, if you chose to assign random passwords, so that you can give users their new passwords.

In-Place Upgrade: NetWare v.2.1x to NetWare v.3.11

This section outlines the upgrade of a NetWare v.2.1x server to a NetWare v.3.11 server. These steps prepare the server so that you can upgrade to NetWare v.4, which is outlined in the next section. You'll use the In-Place Upgrade disk to accomplish these steps. Chapter 15 describes the upgrade process.

Before you start the upgrade, be aware of the following:

- You should have reliable backups of the data that is stored on the server. This upgrade changes the server's disk format.

- The server must be an 80386 or better system with at least 8MB of memory.

- You'll need about 10 percent more disk space to accommodate the NetWare v.3.11 files.

- A 5MB DOS partition is recommended to hold the server startup files.

- Passwords are not retained, but you can choose to have new passwords created. They are stored in a file called NEW.PWD in the SYS:SYSTEM directory.

- VAPs, core printing services, and user volume/disk restrictions are not upgraded.

Four steps take place during the upgrade. First, the existing system is analyzed to ensure there is enough memory and disk space to complete the upgrade. Second, the disks are analyzed to determine how they must be changed to conform to NetWare v.3.11. This step analyzes the Hot Fix redirection area, disk blocks, directory and file tables, and directory and file attributes. Third, the disks are modified (blocks are moved and v.3.11 tables are created). Finally, the v.2.1*x* bindery is upgraded to v.3.11.

Follow these steps to upgrade the server:

1. Start the v.2.1*x* server, and type **CONFIG** at the server console. Record the settings for future reference.

2. Run the BINDFIX command to delete the mail subdirectories and rights of nonexistent users. This step also fixes the bindery.

3. Down the server.

4. Place the Upgrade disk in the server's floppy drive and restart the server. DR DOS is loaded when the server reboots.

5. Type **A:SERVER** to start the upgrade.

6. Type the new file server name.

7. Type the IPX internal network number, which is explained in Chapter 15.

8. Test the compatibility of existing drivers as follows. If a driver doesn't load, you might need to replace it.

   8a. Load the disk drivers by using the following command, replacing *disk_driver* with the name of a driver. (Disk drivers are listed in Chapter 15.) Load the drivers in the order listed with the CONFIG command in step 1. You'll need to specify interrupts and I/O settings for each card.

   LOAD A:*disk_driver*

   8b. Load LAN drivers by using the following command, replacing *lan_driver* with the name of the driver for your LAN card. Refer to Chapter 15 for a list of LAN drivers.

   LOAD A:*lan_driver*

   8c. If the LAN drivers loaded successfully, unload them, to conserve memory, by using the following command:

   UNLOAD *lan_driver*

9. Load Macintosh file support by using the following command:

   LOAD A:MAC

10. You are ready to start the upgrade utility. At the console prompt, type the following command, replacing *parameters* with appropriate options in the list after the command. If you do not specify these options, you are

prompted for information during the upgrade. Those who prefer an automatic upgrade should specify appropriate parameters in the 2XUPGRDE command.

LOAD A:2XUPGRDE /*parameters*

- /B   This option runs the upgrade in batch mode. This is an automatic mode for experienced users that displays only error and status messages.

- /P0   Specify this option if you don't want to create a DOS partition.

- /Px Specify this option to create a DOS partition. Replace x with the size of the partition, in megabytes. The default is 5MB.

- /R+   Specify this option to assign random passwords. The passwords are placed in the NEW.PWD file.

- /R   Specify this option to not assign random passwords. This is the default option.

For example, to run the upgrade in interactive mode (the default) and create random passwords, specify a 5MB partition, and type the following command:

LOAD A:2XUPGRDE /P5 /R+

CAUTION: This is a point of no return. Should the system fail, no data on the drive will be recoverable. You must have reliable backups before continuing.

11. If you did not specify the /Px option when starting the upgrade, you are asked to enter a size for the DOS partition. Enter a size of 5MB or greater.

Upgrade now proceeds through its steps of analyzing, modifying, and translating the NetWare v.2.1x information to NetWare v.3.11. You'll see a number of messages on the screen that inform you of the upgrade process.

12. If you did not enter the /R+ parameter, you are asked if you want to create random passwords for users. Enter your choice.

When the upgrade is complete, you'll see a screen that lists the upgraded status of each disk. Press any key to return to the console prompt. You're now ready to upgrade to NetWare v.4.

In-Place Upgrade: NetWare v.3.x to NetWare v.4

The steps to upgrade from Netware v.3.x to NetWare v.4 are listed in this section. If you just performed the NetWare v.2.x to NetWare v.3.11 upgrade, you should continue with the steps in this section to upgrade to NetWare v.4. To prepare for the upgrade, do the following:

- Ensure you have reliable backups of the existing system.

- If you have any deleted files on the NetWare v.3.x server that you want to salvage, do so now by running the SALVAGE utility.

- Make sure all users are logged out.

- Make sure there are no user name conflicts between this server and other servers that are part of or will be part of the NetWare v.4 NetWare Directory Services tree.

- If you used the Ethernet 802.3 frame type in NetWare v.3.1x, be sure to install support for this frame type on the new server, or change your workstations to Ethernet 802.2.

The steps in this upgrade and the menus that appear are similar to those in the normal NetWare v.4 installation, which is covered in Chapter 16. You can refer there for more information. During the upgrade, the bindery objects are placed in the same context as the server. You should have this context information ready. For example, an upgraded server that belongs to the Sales department of XYZ Corporation might have the context OU=Sales.O=XYZCorp. All bindery objects from the existing server are made part of this context.

Here are the steps for the upgrade:

1. Down the server if necessary, and type **EXIT** to return to DOS. Make a backup of any existing NetWare boot files and drivers in the DOS partition.

2. Place the Install disk in a floppy drive; then switch to the drive, and type **INSTALL**.

3. Choose Upgrade NetWare v.3.1x to v.4.0. This starts the file copy process. You can specify another directory for the files, but the default is usually sufficient.

4. The installation program will copy the v.3.*x* STARTUP.NCF file into the specified boot directory and start the server by using these commands.

5. The disk driver specified in the file is used. If you didn't copy the file, or it didn't exist, you see the disk driver selection menu. Choose a disk driver as outlined in the section "Step 6: Select and Load a Disk Driver" in Chapter 16.

6. After loading disk drivers, a screen appears that lets you unmark files you don't want to copy during the installation. To unmark a file, highlight it and press ENTER. Press F10 to accept the marked files and continue with the installation. You might be asked to insert various disks as you proceed.

7. Install examines the LAN drivers in your AUTOEXEC.NCF file and gives you a chance to modify the file. Follow the instructions on the screen during this step. You'll also get a chance to select a new LAN driver and bind a protocol to it. These steps are outlined in Chapter 16 in the section "Step 10: Load the LAN Drivers."

8. You're ready to configure NetWare Directory Services. Refer to steps 11 through 13 in Chapter 16 for more information on specifying the context of the server.

NOTE: If any bindery objects conflict with NetWare Directory Services objects, you can rename the bindery object or merge its contents into the conflicting objects.

9. The AUTOEXEC.NCF and STARTUP.NCF files appear for viewing and editing. You can make changes now or later. Press F10 to save the files and complete the upgrade.

This completes the upgrade. You can refer to Chapter 17 for post-installation information. When upgrading from a bindery-based system to NetWare v.4, you should review the object, property, and file system rights of the upgraded objects. You can also delete any old files on the upgraded server, such as v.2.1*x* system files and VAPs.

B

APPENDIX

T he NET.CFG file contains commands that set configuration parameters for NetWare workstations. Each workstation can have its own NET.CFG file that contains entries to change the environment for that workstation; however, many workstations will have settings in common, so you can simply copy the file from one workstation to the next. NET.CFG is similar to the SHELL.CFG file used in previous versions of NetWare.

NET.CFG Workstation Configuration Commands

NET.CFG is a standard ASCII text file that you can change by using most text editors. The file contains headers that separate different types of commands. For example, you specify the startup parameters for the network interface card driver in the link driver section. The header names for each section are

Link driver *driver name*
Link support
NetBIOS
Protocol IPXODI
NetWare DOS Requester
NetWare shell
TBMI2

All of these sections might not exist in your file, but there will be at least one link driver section that includes the interrupt settings and other board settings you specified when installing the workstation software. If you add lines to the file, you need to add the appropriate header names.

The NET.CFG commands are too extensive to describe completely in this book, and they are listed here for quick reference only. You can refer to the *NetWare Workstation for DOS* manual and the NetWare help database for more details about these commands.

NOTE: *You can execute many of the commands discussed here at the command line. Refer to the NetWare workstation manuals for more information.*

Link Driver Commands

This section discusses the commands included in the link driver section of the NET.CFG file. The NET.CFG file will contain a link driver section for each network driver you installed, and each section header will have the appropriate driver name. For example, the link driver header name for a Novell NE2000 compatible card would be

```
LINK DRIVER NE2000
```

The six hardware commands you can specify in a link driver section are listed next. Some commands are appropriate for only certain types of cards. For example, DMA is required only on NE2100 cards, and FRAME and PROTOCOL are used for all Ethernet and Token Ring cards. Refer to the Novell documentation for a detailed configuration table.

- *DMA* Configures the DMA channel number used by the card
- *INT* Specifies which interrupt the network adapter uses
- *MEM* Specifies the memory range used by the card
- *NODE ADDRESS* Specifies a hexadecimal node address that overrides the adapter
- *PORT* Specifies the port address range for the adapter
- *SLOT* Specifies the slot number that the adapter is installed in

The remainder of the link driver commands are software related. They specify the frame type, protocols, and other settings required by the adapter card, depending on its network type. If you are using the LANSUP driver, most of these commands are of interest.

- *ALTERNATE* Specifies a nonprimary board for LANSUP, Token Ring, NTR2000, and PCN2L drivers
- *FRAME* Specifies the frame type used by the board
- *LINK STATION* Specifies the number of link stations needed for the LANSUP driver
- *MAX FRAME SIZE* Specifies the maximum frame size
- *PROTOCOL* Specifes additional protocol stacks for LAN drivers
- *SAPS* Specifies the number of Service Access Points needed for the LANSUP driver

Link Support Commands

There are four commands in the link support section. You use them to specify communications settings and protocol stack options for the Link Support Layer.

- *BUFFERS* Specifies the number and size of receive buffers maintained by the Link Support Layer

- *MAX BOARDS* Specifies the maximum number of logical boards available to the Link Support Layer

- *MAX STACKS* Specifies the maximum number of logical protocol stacks available to the Link Support Layer

- *MEMPOOLS* Configures the memory pool size used by the Link Support Layer

NetBIOS Commands

You can use the following commands to alter the NetBIOS environment, if it is being used. These commands are in the NetBIOS section.

- *NETBIOS ABORT TIMEOUT* Specifies the amount of time NetBIOS waits for a response before terminating a session

- *NETBIOS BROADCAST COUNT* Sets the total time needed to broadcast a name resolution packet. Multiply this value by the NetBIOS broadcast delay value

- *NETBIOS BROADCAST DELAY* Determines the time, in ticks, needed to broadcast a name resolution packet across the network. Multiply this value by the NetBIOS broadcast count value

- *NETBIOS COMMANDS* Increase this value if NetBIOS command error 22 occurs

- *NETBIOS INTERNET* Set this value to Off if your network has only one LAN segment. Set it to On (the default) when LAN segments communicate by using bridges and routers

- *NETBIOS LISTEN TIMEOUT* Sets the amount of time NetBIOS waits for a session packet before it requests a session packet

- *NETBIOS RECEIVE BUFFERS* Sets the number of receive buffers used by NetBIOS

- *NETBIOS RETRY COUNT* Determines the number of times NetBIOS sends a packet to establish a session with a remote partner

- *NETBIOS RETRY DELAY* Sets the packet send delay, in ticks, for session reestablishment

- *NETBIOS SEND BUFFERS* Sets the number of send buffers
- *NETBIOS SESSION* Sets the number of supported NetBIOS sessions
- *NETBIOS VERIFY TIMEOUT* Sets the time interval at which NetBIOS sends packets to determine if a session is still active
- *NPATCH* Used to patch a value into the NETBIOS.EXE data segment

Protocol IPXODI Commands

The following commands are used to change the IPXODI protocol settings.

- *BIND* Use this command to force a protocol binding to a specifically named board rather than to the first board found
- *INT64* Sets interrupt 64h compatibility for applications that need it
- *INT7A* Sets interrupt 7Ah compatibility for applications that need it
- *IPATCH* Used to patch locations in the IPXODI.COM file
- *IPX PACKET SIZE LIMIT* Sets the packet size limit used by a driver
- *IPX RETRY COUNT* Sets the number of times a packet should be resent if packets are lost
- *IPX SOCKETS* Specifies the maximum number of sockets, or subaddresses, that IPX can have open at the workstation
- *MINIMUM SPX RETRIES* Sets the number of retries before a disconnected session is assumed
- *SPX ABORT TIMEOUT* Specifies the time to wait before aborting a session that is not responding
- *SPX CONNECTIONS* Specifies the maximum number of simultaneous SPX connections
- *SPX LISTEN TIMEOUT* Sets the amount of time SPX waits for a session packet before requesting a session packet
- *SPX VERIFY TIMEOUT* Sets the interval at which SPX sends packets to determine if a session is still active

NetWare DOS Requester Commands

You use the following commands to configure the DOS requester and its VLMs (Virtual Loadable Modules).

- *AUTO RECONNECT* Reconnects a client after a disconnection. If set to Off, users must reconnect manually

- *AVERAGE NAME LENGTH* Specifies the space of the server name table

- *CACHE BUFFERS* Sets the number of cache buffers used for nonshared, nontransaction-tracked files. Used by FIO.VLM

- *CACHE BUFFER SIZE* Sets the buffer size used by the FIO.VLM cache buffers

- *CACHE WRITES* Sets cache writes on or off for the FIO.VLM module. When set to Off, integrity increases but performance decreases

- *CHECKSUM* Specifies the level of NCP (NetWare Core Protocol) packet validation. Higher levels improve integrity but decrease performance

- *CONNECTIONS* Specifies the maximum number of connections. Higher values require more memory

- *DOS NAME* Specifies a five-character operating system name that you can access by using the %OS variable in login scripts

- *FIRST NETWORK DRIVE* Specifies a network drive letter other than the default for the workstation

- *HANDLE NET ERRORS* Sets error handling methods

- *LARGE INTERNET PACKETS* Specifies the maximum packet size across bridges and routers. Set to Off if a bridge or router can't handle packets that contain more than 576 bytes

- *LOAD LOW CONN* When set to On (the default), CONN.VLM is loaded in conventional memory. Loading in upper memory (when set to Off) reduces performance but saves memory

- *LOAD LOW IPXNCP* When set to On (the default), IPXNCP.VLM is loaded in conventional memory. Loading in upper memory (when set to Off) reduces performance but saves memory

- *LOCAL PRINTERS* Overrides local printer port limitations set by the BIOS (which looks at physical ports)

- *LONG MACHINE TYPE* Specifies a six-character name for the machine that you can access by using the %MACHINE variable in login scripts

- *MAX TASKS* Specifies the maximum number of active tasks for DESQview and Windows

- *MESSAGE LEVEL* Sets how boot messages are displayed

- *MESSAGE TIMEOUT* Sets the amount of time (from 0 to 6 hours) before messages are cleared and the machine can continue processing if a user does not intervene

- *NAME CONTEXT* Sets a startup context in the NetWare Directory Services tree. Set to the user's container on a single-user system

- *NETWORK PRINTERS* Sets the number of LPT ports (up to nine) that the DOS Requester can capture

- *PB BUFFERS* Sets the Packet Burst protocol on or off. The default setting is On

- *PREFERRED SERVER* Specifies the server to attach to first when logging in

- *PREFERRED TREE* Specifies the tree to set a context in if more than one exists

- *PRINT BUFFER SIZE* Sets the print buffer size

- *PRINT HEADER* Sets the buffer size used for printer initialization information

- *PRINT TAIL* Sets the buffer size used to hold post-print-job initialization information

- *READ ONLY COMPATIBILITY* When set to On, allows NetWare v.2.1 read/write calls to open a file

- *SEARCH MODE* Sets the method used to locate a file if it is not in the current directory

- *SET STATION TIME* Sets the time synchronization method

- *SHOW DOTS* Set to On to have the DOS . and .. directory entries appear in directory listings

- *SHORT MACHINE TYPE* Specifies a four-character machine name you can access as the %SMACHINE parameter in login scripts

- *SIGNATURE LEVEL* Sets enhanced security support levels. Setting higher levels improves security but decreases performance

- *TRUE COMMIT* Specifies data integrity over performance or vice versa
- *USE DEFAULTS* Sets how VLMs should be loaded by VLM.EXE
- *VLM* Use this option to specify other VLMs to load

NetWare Shell (NETX) Commands

The following options go under a heading called "NetWare shell," and provide support for the old NETX shell file if it exists.

- *ALL SERVERS* Sets how End of Task messaging is sent to servers
- *ENTRY STACK SIZE* An expanded memory setting that ensures code is visible in the memory page frame
- *ENVIRONMENT PAD* A value that can be increased to ensure programs can update the environment
- *EOJ* Specifies that files, locks, and semaphores will be closed at the end of a job
- *FILE HANDLES* Specifies the number of files that can be open simultaneously
- *HOLD* Sets whether access files should be held open. Some older programs might need this set to On
- *LOCK DELAY* Sets the wait time for trying to get a file lock. Set the value higher on busy networks if associated errors occur
- *LOCK RETRIES* Specifies the number of times the shell attempts to get a lock
- *MAX CUR DIR LENGTH* Specifies path size handling above the DOS default 64 bytes
- *MAX PATH LENGTH* Specifies the maximum path length, up to 255 characters
- *PATCH* Used to path an address in the shell
- *SHARE* Specifies whether a child process can inherit the resources of its parent. The default setting is On
- *SIGN 386 MODE* Sets how NCP packet signatures are handled in Windows 386 enhanced mode

- *SPECIAL UPPERCASE* Enables the shell to call DOS and translate uppercase ASCII characters above 128. The default setting is Off
- *TASK MODE* Sets the way multitasking programs are handled

TBMI2 Commands

You use the following commands with TBMI to change the task-switching environment.

- *DATA ECB COUNT* Specifies the number of data event control blocks (ECBs)
- *ECB COUNT* Specifies the number of nondata event control blocks (ECBs)
- *INT64* Sets interrupt 64h handling for applications that require it
- *INT7A* Sets interrupt 7A handling for applications that require it
- *USING WINDOWS 3.0* Provides task handling for Windows version 3.0

APPENDIX C

Directory Services Partition Management

NetWare Directory Services (NDS) uses a distributed database called the NetWare Directory Database (NDB) to track Directory Services objects (not directories and files). The database resides on a network of servers, not just one server, to ensure its survival in the event a server crashes. This is accomplished by segmenting the database into partitions and storing each partition on appropriate servers on the network. You can copy (replicate) partitions to other servers to provide backups and improve performance. The Windows-based Partition Management utility or the text-based PARTMGR utility are used to create, remove, join, divide, synchronize, and rebuild partitions. Partitions are only created at container objects in the NDS directory tree.

Partition replicas are copies of a partition stored on the server where the partition was created, and stored on other servers where the replica is copied to provide fault tolerance. There are three types of replicas:

- *Master*   The master replica is the only replica in which the structure of the directory for a partition can be changed. You can create a new partition by changing only the master replica, but objects can be created, modified, and deleted in the master and the read-write replicas. When a new NetWare server is installed, a master replica is created and stored on the server on which the new partition was created. If the master replica is lost or corrupted, another replica must be made from the backup master replica.

- *Read-Write*   This replica is changeable. It synchronizes with other replicas when a change has been made. Partition information can be read from and written to this replica.

- *Read-Only*   Partition information can be read from this partition, but only the read-write or master replica can write to it.

The reason for replicating partitions to other servers is to protect the information in them should a server go down. It also improves performance since object information is obtained by workstations or servers from the nearest partition, an important consideration if users are at remote locations and connected by relatively slow WAN links. If information about objects at remote sites is stored locally, users can query the local read-write version of a replica, rather than use the WAN links to query the remote master replica. Administrators can also change read-write replicas, rather than change master replicas. Updates to read-write replicas are then made to other replicas in the background by NetWare.

Of course, the replicas must be continuously synchronized. As changes are made to partitions, all replicas of the partition on other servers are automatically updated. These updates are made as soon as possible but not immediately since constant synchronization would introduce too much internetwork traffic and reduce network performance. The time synchronization services ensure that all servers have the latest information as soon as possible. The delay in synchronizing replicas is not critical. Delays of a few seconds in supplying information to replicas about new user objects or resources does not usually cause any problems.

Timestamps help avoid problems that might occur if an object in the database is changed at two different locations. When the two replicas are synchronized, the timestamps are compared and only the most current information is used. Timestamps are part of the Time Synchronization Services.

A partition is automatically created when you install the first NetWare v.4 server. This first default partition includes the root of the directory tree down to the container you specify for the first server. In the following illustration, the default partition includes all the containers and servers listed. Note that two servers were installed in the Administration container, but they still belong to the default partition because no new branch was specified when the second server was installed.

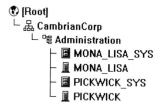

The next illustration shows a new partition. It was formed automatically when the new container, called Sales, was created to hold the server object, called MARANTZ.

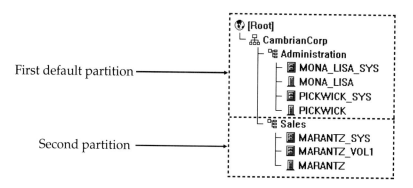

Note that partitions always form at container objects in the directory tree. All objects that branch from that container are part of the partition. However, the partition does not introduce any barriers to the access of its object by users in other partitions. Partitions simply provide fault tolerance and quicker access to Directory Services information.

Partition Management Utilities

You may wonder why you need to manage partitions if they are automatically defined during server installation. First of all, you can create, delete, rebuild, and synchronize partitions. But most important, you can define replicas on other servers that duplicate Directory Services information.

There are two utilities used by administrators or supervisors to manage partitions: Windows Partition Manager and PARTMGR. You access Windows Partition Manager, the Windows NetWare Administration's built-in partition management utility, from the Tools menu. Or you can use the text-based utility, PARTMGR. The basic interface of both utilities is discussed first, followed by a description of partitioning activities.

The Windows Partition Manager

You access the Windows Partition Manager from the NetWare Administrator. Choose Partition Manager from the Tools menu to display the Partitions dialog box pictured in Figure C-1. Initially, you see the root directory of the tree in the Partitions field.

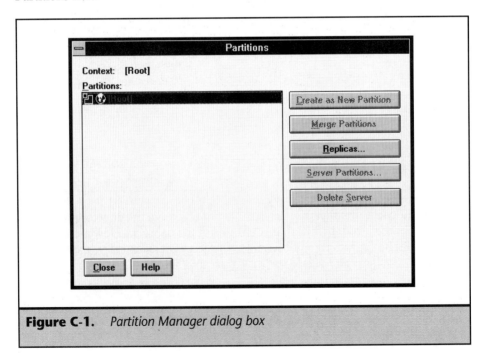

Figure C-1.   *Partition Manager dialog box*

You can browse the tree starting at the root by double-clicking the root icon. Browsing the tree in Partition Manager is the same as browsing the normal NetWare Administrator tree, except that you only see containers and servers. As you scan through the tree, notice the following:

■ The following icon appears in front of containers that have been partitioned:

■ If you click a partitioned container, the Merge Partitions and Replicas buttons are available. Merge Partitions is used to remove a partition by merging it with the next upper partition. Click the Replicas button to view the Partition Replicas dialog box, as shown in Figure C-2. On this dialog box, you can create other replicas, delete a replica, change a replica's type, or update corrupted replicas.

■ If you click an unpartitioned container, only the Create as New Partition button is available, which you click to create a new partition starting at that container.

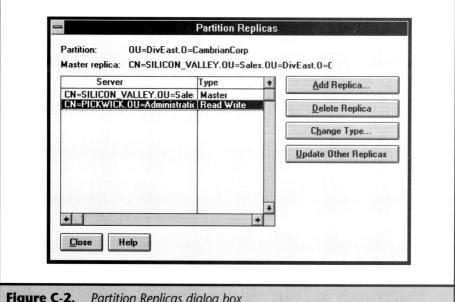

Figure C-2.   *Partition Replicas dialog box*

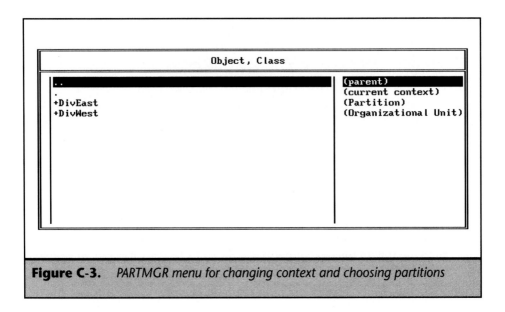

Figure C-3.   *PARTMGR menu for changing context and choosing partitions*

Refer to the later section, "Partition Management Tasks," for instructions on using Partition Manager to accomplish various partition management tasks.

The PARTMGR Utility

PARTMGR is a text-based utility you start at the DOS command prompt. The following menu appears when you start the utility:

Choose Manage partitions in most cases because the second option, Change context, can be done anywhere in the Manage partitions menus. The Object, Class menu appears, as shown in Figure C-3. You browse through the directory tree on the left in the normal way, choosing (parent) to move up the tree and containers to move down the tree. Note that the right side of the menu lists which containers are partitioned.

On the Object, Class menu, you can choose any nonpartitioned container and press F10 to make it a new partition. If you highlight a container that is already partitioned and press F10, you see the following menu, on which you can make selections to manage the partition:

```
┌─────────────────────────────────────────────┐
│ Partition Management for: OU=DivEast         │
│╔═══════════════════════════════════════════╗│
│║View/Edit replicas                         ║│
│║Repair replica time stamp                  ║│
│║Merge with the parent partition            ║│
│╚═══════════════════════════════════════════╝│
└─────────────────────────────────────────────┘
```

Partition Management Tasks

The following sections describe the tasks you can perform in the Windows Partition Manager or the PARTMGR utility. Note that you must have supervisor rights in the container object you plan to partition.

NOTE: Do not delete server objects that contain NDS partitions or replicas. Contact Novell's technical support for information on this procedure.

Creating a Partition

Partitions are created at container objects in the directory tree. You browse the directory tree to locate the container where you want to create a new partition. A master replica is created and stored on the server where the partition resides.

Splitting an existing partition follows the same procedure as creating new partitions. You split a partition when it becomes too large and when some of the information in it is not needed at the locations where replicas of the partition are located. Partitions use server memory, so you can reduce memory requirements in those servers by splitting the partitions.

NOTE: If you split a partition to reduce the size of its replicas, you can remove the part of the replica you don't need to reduce memory requirements. However, you may want to keep the replica on the server for backup purposes.

Using Partition Manager to Create a Partition

To create the partition with the Partition Manager, first locate the container object where you want to create the new partition. Highlight the container, then click the Create as New Partition button. The new partition is automatically created, and the master replica is automatically stored on the server. A partition icon appears in front of the container name.

You can view information about the master replica by selecting the container you partitioned and clicking the Replicas button. The server and its partition type appear on the list.

Using PARTMGR to Create a Partition

Start the text-based partition manager by typing **PARTMGR**, then choose Manage partitions from the Partition Administration menu. Browse the directory to locate the container where you want to create a new partition. Select it and press F10, then answer Yes to create the new partition. The (Partition) label appears to the right of the container name. Now you can make additional replicas on other servers by following the instructions in the later section, "Creating Replicas."

Merging Partitions

You merge a partition into a partition at a higher level in the directory tree if the information in both partitions is accessed by the same users and is required in replicas on other servers. Merge only small partitions that have information needed by the same users. Do not merge large partitions that end up holding a lot of information users don't need. Memory requirements of large partitions can reduce the amount of memory available in the server for other processes.

REMEMBER: The partitions can only be merged up into parent partitions.

Merging Partitions with Partition Manager

Browse in the Partitions field to locate the container you want to merge. Click the container, then click the Merge Partitions button. The partition is merged into the partition above it, and the replicas of the partitions are merged.

Merging Partitions with PARTMGR

Browse the directory tree to locate the container you want to merge. Highlight the container name and press the F10 key to select it. From the menu, choose "Merge with the parent partition." The partition and its replicas are merged into the upper parent partition.

Creating Replicas

You create a replica of a partition on another server to provide a backup copy in case the server where the partition is located should go down. Use the following instructions to create a replica, depending on whether you are using Partition Manager or PARTMGR.

Creating a Replica with Partition Manager

To create a replica with Partition Manager, browse the directory tree to locate the container of the partition you want to create a replica of on another server. Select the container object, then click the Replicas button. Click the Add Replica button, then browse for the server where you want to place the replica. You must highlight a server icon to complete the operation. When the server appears, click it. Then choose a replica type, either read-write or read-only, and click OK.

Creating a Replica with PARTMGR

Choose Manage partitions from the Partition Administration menu, then browse the directory tree to locate the container you want to make a replica of on another server. Highlight the container object, then press F10. Choose View/Edit replicas from the Partition Management menu, then press INS to display the following menu:

```
┌──────────────────────────────────────────────────────────┐
│                      Add replica                         │
├──────────────────────────────────────────────────────────┤
│                                                          │
│  Replica type:                    Read Write             │
│                                                          │
│  Store on server:                                        │
│                                                          │
└──────────────────────────────────────────────────────────┘
```

Press ENTER in the Replica type field to choose a different replica type from a list. Then press ENTER in the Store on server field to select the server where you want to store the replica. Press INS to browse the Object, Class menu for the server. When you locate the server, press ENTER, and its name appears in the Replica to be stored on server box. Press ENTER again to accept the name.

Changing a Replica's Type

You may need to change a replica to a different type. For example, you could change a read-write replica to a read-only or master replica. If you change a replica to master, the old master replica converts to read-write. If the master replica becomes corrupted, you may need to convert an existing read-write replica to a master replica, and then delete the old master replica.

Changing a Replica's Type with Partition Manager

Browse the directory tree to locate the container that holds the replica you want to change. Click the Replicas button, select the replica you want to change, and click the Change Type button. The Change Replica Type dialog box appears, as shown in the following illustration. Choose a replica type and click the OK button. If you choose Master, the current master replica changes to read-write.

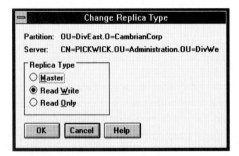

Changing a Replica's Type with PARTMGR

Select Manage partitions from the Partition Administration menu, then locate the container that holds the replica you want to change. Press F10 and choose View/Edit replicas from the Partition Management menu. Select a replica to change, then press F10. Choose a new replica type and press F10 again. If you choose Master, the current master replica changes to read-write.

Deleting Replicas

If for some reason you need to delete a master replica (because it is corrupted), first make a read-write or read-only replica (of the master replica) on another server, by changing its replica type. Then delete the old master replica, which will have changed to a read-write replica.

Deleting a Replica with Partition Manager

Browse the directory tree and highlight the container of the partition to delete. Click the Replicas button. In the Server list, highlight the replica to delete and click Delete Replica.

Deleting a Replica with PARTMGR

Choose Manage partitions from the Partition Administration menu. Browse the directory tree to locate the partition to delete, then highlight the container of the partition and press F10. Choose the View/Edit replica option, then highlight the replica to delete, and press DEL to remove the replica.

Repairing a Replica

You may need to repair a master partition from a replica if it becomes corrupted. You must have a replica of the master partition on another server that is not itself corrupted. Follow the steps here to repair the master replica.

Repairing a Replica with Partition Manager

Browse the directory tree to locate the replica you want to use for the rebuild. Select the partition, then click the Replicas button. When the Partition Replicas dialog box appears, choose the replica in the Server list and click the Update Other Replicas button. You are asked to confirm your actions.

Repairing a Replica with PARTMGR

Choose Manage partitions from the Partition Administration menu. Browse the directory tree to locate the partition you want to repair, then press F10 and choose "Repair replica time stamp" from the menu. A list of replicas appears. Select a replica and press ENTER to repair its timestamps.

Repairing the NetWare Directory Services Database with DSREPAIR

DSREPAIR is a console utility you load at a server to check and repair Directory Services partitions, replicas, and file system problems. If the NetWare Directory Database becomes corrupted, it will not open. You will see error messages at the server indicating that there is a problem. The DSREPAIR utility can often fix such problems, but you may need to reinstall the NDB. To fix problems over the entire directory tree, run DSREPAIR at each server.

To use DSREPAIR, go to the server that is having problems and follow these steps:

1. Load DSREPAIR.

2. Choose option number 1 to make changes to the DSREPAIR settings.

3. On the settings menu, press 2 to send any messages that appear on the screen to a file, so you can check them later.

4. Leave the other options as they are, and press 7 to return to the main menu.

5. Press 2 to begin the DSREPAIR test.

DSREPAIR locates problems and tracks them in a database. When the test is complete, you can choose to make the repairs that DSREPAIR has determined you need. Once you are finished, be sure to exit the DSREPAIR utility, since it locks the Directory Services database when running.

If DSREPAIR does not fix a partition problem on the server, you may need to restore a partition from one of its replicas, as discussed previously, or you may need to reinstall Directory Services. Call Novell technical support at 1-800-LAN-KIND before proceeding.

APPENDIX D

NetWare's High Capacity Storage System

The High Capacity Storage System (HCSS) in NetWare 4 provides a way to *migrate* files from fast magnetic storage systems to slower, higher-capacity optical storage systems, as shown in Figure D-1. When the files are needed again, they are de-migrated. Files that are accessed rarely or only on a weekly or monthly basis are candidates for migration. Moving them to optical storage frees space on the server.

HCSS optical devices are commonly referred to as *jukeboxes*. They read and write to rewritable optical disks and use an autochanger mechanism that mounts and dismounts disks as requested. A typical jukebox may contain up

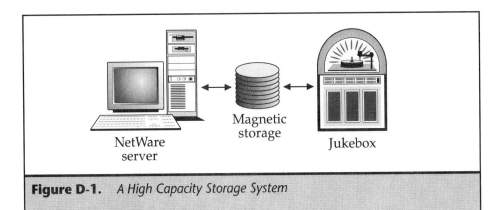

Figure D-1.   *A High Capacity Storage System*

to four optical drives and a device that picks disks from a bay and inserts them in the drives as needed. You can remove and lock up disks for safekeeping, or move them to other optical devices.

HCSS provides an alternative to archiving, in which files are copied to tape or other backup media and then stored. Because HCSS files are essentially always online, HCSS eliminates the hassles associated with retrieving files from conventional data archives. For example, a user doesn't need to contact the archive operator who then locates the tape (or other) archive, mounts it, and restores the data. Users who need migrated files access them by searching a familiar NetWare directory structure. Access to migrated files may take a little longer, but not as long as it takes to retrieve files on conventional archives.

HCSS is designed for law firms, hospitals, insurance companies, and other organizations with documents that are rarely accessed. The benefits HCSS provides to large, geographically diverse organizations are also important. For example, an insurance agent could call up an insurance company's central archives and access old client records without an operator's intervention (assuming the agent has access rights to do so).

Structure of HCSS

The hardware of HCSS consists of the optical jukebox and the server to which it is attached. The server must have free space on its magnetic disks to cache the HCSS data. Caching is an important aspect of HCSS.

Basically, users never access files directly from optical disks. They request a file, and it is moved to the designated HCSS volume on the server's magnetic disk. The size of the HCSS volume determines the number of de-migrated files that are available to users at any one time. As new files are requested, they are de-migrated to the HCSS volume, and the least recently used files are migrated to optical disks, as shown in Figure D-2. In this respect, de-migrated files are cached on the HCSS volume in the same way that magnetic disk reads and writes are cached in memory.

The size of the HCSS volume must be at least large enough to hold the largest de-migrated file. If the volume size is small, there may not be enough room to hold all the files users request for de-migration, or the HCSS system will need to take extra time to migrate files in the volume to make room for new files. The larger the volume size the better. You need to consider whether users' requests can be satisfied by files that have already been de-migrated, or whether users will always request files that must be de-migrated. In other words, what are the chances that a file needed by one user will have already been de-migrated by another user? If this is unlikely, all file requests will need to be de-migrated and there will always be an access delay. You must ensure that the HCSS volume is large enough to hold all the files that may be requested at one time.

Files stored on HCSS devices exist in directory structures that look similar to NetWare directory structures. The typical arrangement is to set up a volume on the NetWare server and in that volume store only files you need to migrate.

Note the following:

■ Only one NetWare volume per server can support HCSS. You should create a specific volume for HCSS and store only HCSS files on it.

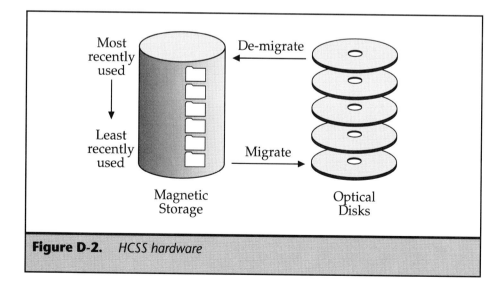

Figure D-2. *HCSS hardware*

- The volume can contain any number of HCSS directories at the root level.

- You control files in the HCSS volume by setting thresholds. When an upper threshold is met (the volume is getting full), files begin migrating to optical disk until a lower threshold is met.

- You can specify the time of day for migration in order to avoid peak hours.

- If the HCSS volume becomes full due to user requests for files, the least recently used files are moved to optical disk.

- Access rights to HCSS directories and files is controlled in the same way they are controlled for other NetWare directories.

A typical HCSS directory structure starts with a root directory called HCSS. From this directory branch subdirectories that relate to the sides of an optical disk. For example, a law firm might have subdirectories such as CASES392, CASES492, CASES592, and so on. Users see files in these directory structures as if they were on local magnetic disk. If they request a file, it is de-migrated into the HCSS volume. Except for a slight delay in access time, users may be unaware that the file was de-migrated from optical disk.

Installing an HCSS

This section is meant to provide a quick overview of the installation process for those considering the use of an HCSS. Consult your hardware documentation and the NetWare manuals for more detailed information. The first release of NetWare 4 supports the following SCSI adapters and jukeboxes from Adaptec and Hewlett-Packard:

- Hewlett-Packard C17*xx* series jukeboxes

- Adaptec AHA1x40 series SCSI adapters

Install these devices as outlined in the owner's manuals. At the NetWare server, you need to first configure a volume for HCSS. This volume is used to hold files migrating or de-migrating from the HCSS device. Use an existing volume that has the following settings, or create a new volume with these settings using the INSTALL utility.

- Set file compression off

- Set block suballocations off

■ Set data migration on

Now you can load the driver files for the optical disk systems by including the following command in the STARTUP.NCF file. This example loads an Adaptec AHA1740 board.

LOAD AHA1740 DEV_ENBLE=00 PORT=*address*

Add the next two commands to the AUTOEXEC.NCF file. The first command loads the Hewlett-Packard jukebox module, and the second command loads the HCSS module.

```
LOAD HPCHGR
LOAD HCSS
```

After adding these two commands, down the server and reboot it to make the new commands effective. Note that you can also enter these commands at the console prompt and avoid downing the server. If you do type the commands at the console, type the following command as well:

```
SCAN FOR NEW DEVICES
```

NOTE: Media is ejected until the HCSS directory structure is installed. Type **MEDIA REMOVED** *at the console for each disk that is ejected.*

One last change is to add the following lines to the Windows NWADMIN.INI file under the heading [Snapin Object DLLs]. The NWADMIN.INI file is in the Windows directory.

```
Vis HCSSDecider=hdecsnap.dll
Vis HCSSObject=hobjsnap.dll
Vis HCSSMedia=hmedsnap.dll
```

Configuring the HCSS File System

Once the hardware is installed and the drivers are loaded, you can start Windows and create the HCSS file system. A brief description of the procedure is outlined in the following list. Refer to the NetWare manuals for detailed information.

1. Choose a volume for the HCSS root directory and make sure the volume has the "migration" attribute.

2. Create the HCSS root directory. You can call it HCSS or any other name, and you can create multiple root directories if necessary.

3. Create subdirectories within the HCSS root directory that correspond to sides of the optical disks. Each disk side is assigned a media label with the same name as the subdirectories.

4. Prepare the optical disks by loading them in the jukebox, formatting and labeling the disks, and assigning them to a specific HCSS root directory.

You load optical media using the NetWare Administrator. The option HCSS Media appears on the Object menu (assuming you added the lines to the NWADMIN.INI file discussed earlier). From the HCSS Media menu, you choose HCSS Load Media, then insert the optical disk. A dialog box appears that shows the state of the media and whether it needs formatting. All the procedures for step 4 can be handled from this dialog box.

5. After optical disks are loaded, you set thresholds for the HCSS volume. Using NetWare Administrator, click the HCSS volume, then choose HCSS Threshold from the Options menu.

   There are three threshold values:

   Migrate when　The default value is 90%, which means that files are automatically migrated when the volume is 90% full.

   Migrate until　The default value is 60%, which means that file migration stops when 40% of the volume's space has been cleared.

   Migration time　Set the time of day when files should begin migrating. The default is 1:00 a.m.

There are a number of other options on the NetWare Administrator menu you can choose to manage the HCSS file system. For example, you can unload, reload, and reformat optical disks, or you can modify the HCSS root directory structure.

When an optical disk is unloaded, all files that were cached in the HCSS volume are first migrated back to the disk, and its HCSS subdirectory is removed. Be aware of the file attribute "don't migrate." If this attribute is set and a disk is unloaded, the unload will fail. You'll need to remove this attribute so the file can migrate and the disk can unload.

Index

D

M

U